# What others are saying about Wade Gilbert's *Coaching Better Every Season*

"I first heard Wade speak about quality coaching at the Hockey Hall of Fame. The message he shared that day, summarized in this impressive book, is a proven approach to building better athletes and programs. I highly recommend coaches at all levels of sport read this book and apply Wade's strategies in their coaching."

Greg Schell, Coordinator of Hockey Development, Toronto Maple Leafs Hockey Club

"Dr. Gilbert's research on coaching is the best coaching science we've got. He has studied, learned from, and collaborated with successful coaches around the world, including national, Olympic, and world championship coaches—and John Wooden himself. I highly recommend the book, which most certainly will have you *Coaching Better Every Season.*"

Ronald Gallimore, PhD, Distinguished Professor Emeritus, UCLA

"*Coaching Better Every Season* is for all coaches truly committed to being better at their craft. Wade's approach and strategies have real-world, practical application for coaches around the world at all levels, from youth sport to those at the Olympic and national team level."

Cameron Kiosoglous, PhD, US Rowing National Team Coach

"*Coaching Better Every Season* is a must read for any coach at any level seeking to build a championship program, positive team culture, and lasting tradition. It is a book you will want to continually refer to as a coach's guide throughout each season."

Jeffrey Huber, PhD, Big Ten, NCAA, USA, USOC Coach of the Year, 13-time USA Diving National Coach of the Year

"*Coaching Better Every Season* is the most comprehensive coaching book I have read. Dr. Gilbert has a knack for speaking and writing about the heart of coaching and leadership. It is a must read for any coach who wants to be successful and continually stay ahead of the game."

Guy Krueger, Education and Training Manager, USA Archery

"Dr. Wade Gilbert has provided me with a wealth of invaluable knowledge that I share regularly in my interactions with coaches and athletic directors. His acute insights on what it takes to become a better coach, and a better person, and to build a legacy through a better program are exactly why every coach should read this book."

Pat Riddlesprigger, Athletic Manager, Fresno Unified School District, California

"Dr. Gilbert is widely recognized as a leader in coach education. His guidance for coaches—not just coaching theory but also applied practical advice—allows us to be more effective in what we do."

Ken Martel, Technical Director, USA Hockey

"If you are like my former coach John Wooden, who improved his coaching every year until his retirement, *Coaching Better Every Season* will be most valuable, as it will provide a roadmap for your passionate pursuit of perfection."

Swen Nater, Author, Former UCLA, NBA, and ABA basketball player

"Wade brings to this book a marvelous blend of research, insights, and strategies about coaching that provide a master blueprint for building successful sport programs."

Jean Côté, PhD, Professor and Director, School of Kinesiology and Health Studies, Queen's University

"Over the last five years, Wade has been an integral part of rebuilding the athletics program at Fresno High School. The results have been both dramatic and measurable. Simply put, Wade provided us with the tools that changed the culture of our entire athletics program. With *Coaching Better Every Season*, you can too."

David Barton, Athletic Director, Fresno High School

"In *Coaching Better Every Season*, Wade Gilbert masterfully incorporates the art and science of coaching into a system that promotes greatness. His book provides a clear and compelling road map for developing the people who are producing the results."

Ralph Pim, EdD, Sport Adviser and Team Consultant
Director of Competitive Sports (retired), United States Military Academy

"*Coaching Better Every Season* should be a mandatory read for all coaches."

Chuck Kyle, 2-time *USA Today* High School Coach of the Year, Saint Ignatius High School, Cleveland, Ohio
Youth Football Advisor, Cleveland Browns

"*Coaching Better Every Season* articulates the role of coaches in building teams as centers of learning. Dr. Gilbert's book is the perfect resource for those who desire sustainable programmatic success; it is a must read for coaches at every level."

Jon LeCrone, Commissioner, Horizon League

"Working with Wade and applying the strategies he shares in *Coaching Better Every Season* has helped me set the vision and standards for our wrestling program."

Troy Steiner, Head Coach, Fresno State University Wrestling

"Internationally known coaching expert Wade Gilbert has the rare ability to link science and practice in creative ways for coaches, as shown in this book."

Robin S. Vealey, PhD, Professor and Graduate Director, Department of Kinesiology and Health, Miami University

"The concepts and strategies Dr. Wade Gilbert shares in *Coaching Better Every Season* have bolstered my ability to build and sustain a successful program, with success defined by so much more than wins and losses. I truly believe that the knowledge and tools provided in *Coaching Better Every Season* have been paramount to my development as a coach."

Breanne Nasti, Head Coach Women's Softball/Assistant Athletic Director, Adelphi University

"This book will help us all be better coaches to our athletes."

Jeanne Fleck, Head Coach, Fresno State University Women's Swimming and Diving

"Dr. Wade Gilbert provides a perfect blend of research-based information, front-line coaching applications, and compelling examples throughout his book. *Coaching Better Every Season* is a major contribution to the education and practice of coaches."

John Bales, President, International Council for Coaching Excellence

# Coaching Better Every Season

## A Year-Round System for Athlete Development and Program Success

Wade Gilbert, PhD
California State University, Fresno

HUMAN KINETICS

**Library of Congress Cataloging-in-Publication Data**

Names: Gilbert, Wade, author.
Title: Coaching better every season : a year-round system for athlete development and program success / Wade Gilbert.
Description: Champaign, IL : Human Kinetics, [2017] | Includes bibliographical references and index.
Identifiers: LCCN 2016016581 (print) | LCCN 2016018567 (ebook) | ISBN 9781492507666 (print) | ISBN 9781492544104 (ebook)
Subjects: LCSH: Coaching (Athletics)
Classification: LCC GV711 .G55 2017 (print) | LCC GV711 (ebook) | DDC 796.07/7--dc23
LC record available at https://lccn.loc.gov/2016016581

ISBN: 978-1-4925-0766-6 (print)



The web addresses cited in this text were current as of August 2016, unless otherwise noted.

**Developmental Editor:** Kevin Matz; **Managing Editor:** Caitlin Husted; **Copyeditor:** Bob Replinger; **Indexer:** Katy Balcer; **Permissions Manager:** Martha Gullo; **Graphic Designer:** Kathleen Boudreau-Fuoss; **Cover Designer:** Keith Blomberg; **Photographs (cover):** © Human Kinetics; **Photo Asset Manager:** Laura Fitch; **Photo Production Manager:** Jason Allen; **Senior Art Manager:** Kelly Hendren; **Illustrations:** © Human Kinetics, unless otherwise noted; **Printer:** Versa Press

Human Kinetics books are available at special discounts for bulk purchase. Special editions or book excerpts can also be created to specification. For details, contact the Special Sales Manager at Human Kinetics.

Printed in the United States of America 10

The paper in this book is certified under a sustainable forestry program.

**Human Kinetics**
1607 N. Market St.
Champaign, IL 61820
Website: www.HumanKinetics.com

In the United States, email info@hkusa.com or call 800-747-4457.
In Canada, email info@hkcanada.com.
In the United Kingdom/Europe, email hk@hkeurope.com.

For information about Human Kinetics' coverage in other areas of the world, please visit our website: **www.HumanKinetics.com**

E6528

**Tell us what you think!**
Human Kinetics would love to hear what we can do to improve the customer experience. Use this QR code to take our brief survey.

**To my loving partner and wife, Jenelle,
and the inspirational team
we've been blessed to coach:
Jazmyn, Madelyn, and Kyler.**

**To my parents, who continue to coach me
with endless patience and compassion:
Barb, Rick, Jackie, and Bren.**

# Contents

# Acknowledgments

I have always been passionate about sport, teaching, and learning. I am forever grateful to my parents who planted that seed very early in life. I recall a photo of my father teaching me how to swing a golf club at age two. The golf experiment was short-lived but it provided the foundation for a lifetime of sport involvement.

At that point I had a firsthand glimpse into the world of coaching. Like anyone who has played sport long enough, I have vivid memories of both outstanding and harmful coaches. Somehow I think this disparity greatly influenced my career path and has compelled me to learn all that I can about high-quality coaching.

I knew I found my calling when studying physical education at the University of Ottawa. Several professors invited me to work with them. Dr. Normand Chouinard gave me a rare opportunity to learn from a master coach while I worked alongside him during ice hockey courses and camps. Norm's passion for coaching greatly influenced my own approach to coaching.

During my formative years at the University of Ottawa, I learned from master scientist and teacher Dr. Pierre Trudel. Like all good coaches, Pierre provided just the right mix of support, challenge, and inspiration. My life and career have been enriched immeasurably by the time spent with Pierre and the ongoing collaboration we have to this day 25 years later.

It is during that time when I forged lifelong partnerships with fellow graduate students whose research has greatly influenced the ideas shared in this book: Drs. Jean Côté, Gordon Bloom, and Diane Culver. This is where I met my co-coach in life, Dr. Jenelle Gilbert. Her love, support, and patience are incomparable. She deserves special recognition for living with the moodiness and disrupted sleep schedule that come with writing a book.

It is also at the University of Ottawa where I connected with Dr. John Salmela, another pioneer in the world of coaching science. Among the many things I am grateful to John for is introducing me to Dr. Tara Scanlan at the University of California at Los Angeles.

One of the defining moments of my career was when Tara entrusted me with driving John Wooden to and from a teaching session at UCLA. Little did I know it at the time, but that was the beginning of a long journey connected to coach Wooden and those who knew him well. The messages in this book are greatly influenced by what I learned from my partners in the Coach Wooden–inspired BeLikeCoach team: Dr. Ronald Gallimore, Swen Nater, and Mark Siwik.

I have now spent more time at California State University at Fresno than I have in any other place along the journey—17 years and counting. Fresno State has proven to be a rich and rewarding learning experience. Fellow sport science faculty members Tim Hamel, Mike Coles, John McMillen, and Scott Sailor have taught me much about high-quality teaching, leadership, and work–life balance, key themes throughout this book. I am extremely grateful to Jody Hironaka-Juteau, dean of the College of Health and Human Services, for supporting the sabbatical request that allowed me to complete much of the first draft of the book.

While at Fresno State I drew great inspiration from the dozens of coaches who have so generously given of their time to visit my classes and share their wisdom. I have learned the most from the thousands of students I have taught at Fresno State, particularly graduate students who have worked closely with me such as Nicole Kulikov-Hagobian, Rachael Bertram, Mark Lasota, Matt Emmett, Bree Nasti, and Nadine Dubina.

Special recognition goes to one of my very first graduate students, David Barton. Many of the ideas presented in this book are directly informed by my collaboration with Dave. Our partnership started in 2001 and continues to this day in our current work at Fresno High School where Dave is the athletics director. Whether we're sitting in a coaching seminar at Fresno High or meeting over a run or mountain hike, Dave's joyful spirit and tireless commitment to helping coaches get better have been a great source of inspiration.

The insights shared in this book have also been significantly shaped by the many experiences I've had working on special projects. These include editing the *Journal of Coaching Education* and the *International Sport Coaching Journal* alongside Dr. Mike Sheridan, participating in USOC coach education seminars with Christine Bolger and Chris Snyder, and speaking at coaching events around the world. Through these opportunities precious relationships have been formed with championship coaches such as Guy Krueger, Mark Smith, and Vern Gambetta and renowned coaching scientists such as Dr. Cliff Mallett, Dr. Tania Cassidy, and Dr. Rui Resende.

Just as it takes a village to raise a child, it takes a village to complete a book. The quality of this book is a direct result of the support and guidance provided by the world-class team at Human Kinetics Publishers. Members of this team include Mark Allemand, Caitlin Husted, Martha Gullo, Kevin Matz, and reviewers of the book.

Over the past few years the most influential coach in my life has been Ted Miller, vice president of Human Kinetics. The time and effort Ted has invested in me and this book are immeasurable. This book is as much his accomplishment as it is mine.

Coach Wooden believed that *love* was the most important word in the English language. To all those who have coached me through the journey, thank you for the love you have shown. I hope this book meets your expectations and the high standards you have inspired me to reach.

# Introduction

Thank you for taking time out of your busy professional schedule and personal time to read this special coaching book. I say special because it is unlike any coaching book you have read before and will forever change at least some aspects of how you coach. By implementing the principles and strategies advanced in the following pages, you will definitely be *Coaching Better Every Season.*

This book is written for coaches who seek to build and sustain successful programs. It's also for coaches who want to improve at their craft, are open to change, and respect what quality research and former and current stellar members of their profession have to offer.

Great coaches separate themselves from the pack because they "have high expectations for their athletes but even higher expectations for themselves."[1 (p. 23)] But simply expecting excellence in no way ensures it. Anyone who has coached knows that the job isn't easy. The challenges are real. Coaching can be complicated. Messy. Frustrating.

Despite what some claim, there are no secrets to success. Nor does one morph into a great coach by merely copying the best. Becoming and being even a competent coach is a journey that has no shortcuts. *Coaching Better Every Season* is a carefully drafted map that will help coaches successfully navigate the remainder of their coaching careers. Those willing to invest in learning and then applying the best practices of distinguished coaches and the science of quality coaching presented in this book will come out ahead.

Successful coaching requires knowledge of both effective coaching methods and the principles that underpin them. That knowledge is then used to create a system for long-term coaching success, for sustainable and meaningful success across every season. No secrets, no shortcuts, no magic formulas—just time-tested strategies grounded in enduring principles of effective coaching.

The insights shared in this book represent the lessons I have learned from over 25 years of studying, teaching, and working alongside thousands of coaches across all types and levels of sport. Many of the most valuable points made come from my daily work with local youth sport, high school, and college coaches.

I'm also a scientist who collaborates with leading researchers on a wide range of coaching projects such as writing major reviews of coaching science,[2–5] serving as editor-in-chief of the *International Sport Coaching Journal,* and being a featured speaker at coaching seminars and conferences around the world. This part of the journey has provided me with opportunities to teach and collaborate with some of the world's most successful coaches, including Olympic and world championship coaches and Coach of the 20th Century, John Wooden.[6] His timeless wisdom has greatly shaped my views on quality coaching, as it has many others who had the good fortune to learn directly from him.[7, 8]

Much of this book is organized according to the four seasons of an annual coaching cycle: preseason, in-season, end of season, and off-season. Each season in the coaching cycle requires a different coaching focus, referred to as the four Es (see figure I.1). And the cycle recurs every year.

The preseason is a time to envision and build team culture. During this phase successful coaches review the core values and coaching philosophy that guides their work and, together with their athletes, set realistic but challenging goals. The preseason is also the time when successful coaches invest heavily in team-building activities to promote team trust and quality coach-athlete relationships.

The in-season phase of coaching is used to enact the season plan. In-season, for the purposes of this book, includes the entire competitive schedule, spanning from early exhibition games through end-of-season tournaments. In this phase successful coaches spend many hours preparing detailed practice plans and competition strategies. Running effective practices requires an awareness of teaching and learning principles and a long-term view of athlete development. Quality coaching during competitions depends on a coach's ability to notice the performance trends and make the right tactical adjustments at the right time. Efficient practices and quality in-competition adjustments are surefire ways to guide athletes to peak performance.

At the end of season, successful coaches evaluate program performance. A comprehensive program evaluation requires a review of coach, athlete, and program performance information. Besides evaluating objective performance statistics, successful coaches seek feedback from other coaches, athletes, and athletics administrators. The end-of-season phase is also the time to recognize athlete and team accomplishments formally and build on program strengths.

The off-season is the phase when successful coaches work diligently to enhance their coaching and their programs. Although the off-season is a time to recharge, the most successful coaches balance rest and recovery with deliberate learning designed to close high-impact performance gaps. Coaching skills are enhanced

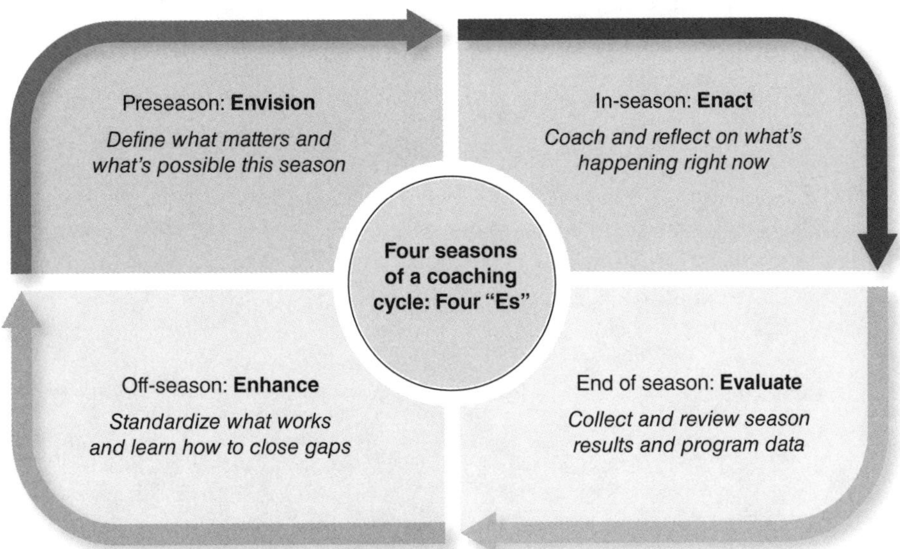


**Figure I.1** Four seasons of an annual coaching cycle: the four Es.

when coaches use the off-season to strengthen their learning network and build learning groups to tackle specific coaching needs and performance issues.

By separating a coach's work into these four phases, I have provided a clear and manageable method for coaches to develop their athletes, their programs, and themselves in efficient and meaningful ways. If applied each year, the favorable results compound, just as interest does in a good investment.

Championship football coach Tom Coughlin, who built successful programs at the college and professional level and led the New York Giants to two Super Bowl wins, once said, "The foundation of winning is the structure you build, the culture you instill, and the people you work with every day."[9 (p. 59)] Although winning a championship is a rare accomplishment, every coach can experience a winning season when we broaden the definition of winning to encompass individual athlete development and strengthening of the team as a whole.

Effective coaches don't just build athletes; they develop people and build programs, and their influence can last a lifetime. Legendary high school cross country coach Joe Newton, whose teams have won 28 state titles in his more than 60 years of coaching, might be well into his 80s, but his age in no way diminishes his enthusiasm to coach every day. Maybe that's why roughly 200 young men want to be part of York High School's (Elmhurst, Illinois) Long Green Line each year. They aren't running all those miles each week just to cross a finish line first. Rather, they're drawn to the sport because of the experience their coach offers them to challenge and improve themselves and to be a part of something bigger than themselves. Indeed, the Joe Newtons of our coaching community don't just win titles; they shape and forever positively affect the lives of thousands of young men and women.[10]

I have no doubt that by applying the strategies and principles shared in this book you will have a more rewarding and long-lasting coaching experience. Moreover, your athletes and program benefit in countless ways when you are *Coaching Better Every Season*.

# Part I

# PRESEASON

## Envision

Chapter 1

# Define Purpose and Core Values

**Key Concepts**

- Coaching purpose
- Problem setting versus problem solving
- Core values
- Sustained excellence
- Coaching core ideology
- Building team culture
- Coaching Golden Circle
- Coach as people builder

On September 4, 2004, one of the most remarkable win streaks in sport finally ended. The De La Salle High School football team lost its first game in over 12 years. The team had compiled a record 151 consecutive wins by an average score of 47–9, all led by head coach Bob Ladouceur. To put the streak in perspective, the previous record for most consecutive wins by an American high school football team was 72 games, a streak that had stood for 22 years.

When asked about how they would handle the defeat, Coach Ladouceur calmly explained that his coaching approach was not driven by wins and records. One loss, no matter how dramatic, did not change any of that.

> We were never fighting for wins. We were fighting for a belief in what we stood for, the way we believe life should be lived and people should be treated. Winning is a by-product of how you approach life and relationships.[1 (pp. xi–xii)]

Coach Ladouceur, like all successful coaches, understood that the first step to becoming a successful coach is to identify the purpose and core values that define you and your program. The next step is to work relentlessly on creating an environment for your athletes that teaches and reinforces the purpose and core values.

Bob Larson/Zuma Press/Icon Sportswire

Record-setting coach Bob Ladouceur shaping and monitoring team climate at De La Salle High School in Concord, California.

To achieve competitive greatness, coaches must be aggressive and disciplined in instilling their purpose and core values throughout their sport program. As renowned seven-time national collegiate volleyball championship coach Russ Rose explained,

> Any athlete that wears the Penn State uniform must have the dedicated work ethic and commitment to carry on the tradition and core values that guide the success of our program: working hard every day in practice, going hard and competing with the heart of a champion every point, every game, every match.[2 (pp. 51–52)]

Coaching purpose and core values drives how you will approach coaching and what goals you will set with your athletes each season. The most successful coaches know that purpose and core values are the foundation for creating a winning team culture. The purpose of this opening chapter is to explain how to identify and communicate these fundamental beliefs—your coaching purpose and core values.

## REFLECTING ON WHY YOU COACH

Most coaching books start with a discussion of the importance of creating a coaching philosophy and follow up with a section on creating goals. But to define a coaching philosophy and set goals, you must first understand and express why you coach and what principles will guide how you coach.

A coaching purpose defines why you do what you do; it is your fundamental reason for being (a coach). Your purpose also represents your motivations for coaching. Coaches by nature are competitive and driven to succeed. This attribute combined with outside pressure from others to win can easily cause coaches to lose sight of their true purpose. A traumatic life moment is often the trigger that causes a coach to pause and reflect on the why. For three-time national college football champion coach Urban Meyer, a combination of dealing with serious health issues and listening to his daughter speak at a public ceremony caused him to realize how absent he had become from her life.[3] For renowned high school football coach Joe Erhmann, the moment came while attending his brother's funeral. In his deeply personal account of how he discovered his coaching purpose, Coach Erhmann explains how he came to identify his true purpose as a coach: "'My Why': I coach to help boys become men of empathy and integrity who will lead, be responsible, and change the world for good."[4 (p. 110)]

Whereas clarity of coaching purpose serves as a beacon for navigating the choppy waters of coaching, core values are the expectations and standards that coaches and their athletes use to hold each other accountable and build a culture of excellence. Some coaches such as Hall of Fame professional basketball coach Pat Riley describe a team's core values as a covenant or agreement that holds teams together.[5] Successful coaches ensure that the program core values are clearly aligned with their coaching purpose.

One of the most successful coaches of the 21st century is professional football coach Bill Belichick. His coaching purpose was formed early in life, perhaps even as young as 6 years old when he eagerly helped his father, a college football coach at the time, analyze game film. His coaching purpose is rooted deeply in the pursuit of excellence and a love of football. The single core value that has long served as the guiding principle for all the teams he has coached is summed up in the simple mantra "Do your job!"[6, 7] Unwavering commitment to this core value is demonstrated through relentless preparation, incredible attention to details, a team-first attitude, and an intense work ethic.

You will know you have found your coaching purpose when your purpose is inseparable from who you are as a person. For example, all-time winningest college baseball coach Augie Garrido once said, "I coach baseball to its core because it is in my core."[8 (p. 12)] Your purpose and core values, then, serve as a window into your coaching soul—the essence or embodiment of who you are as a coach and why you coach.

The most effective coaches are acutely sensitive to this basic concept. In fact, 11-time professional basketball championship coach Phil Jackson includes the word *soul* in the title of his best-selling book about how to coach championship teams.[9] Coach Jackson explains that his purpose and core values are grounded in his deeply held concern for connecting with athletes and creating what might be considered an enlightened basketball environment—one in which he helps athletes find personal meaning in the sport experience.

A coaching purpose and core values do not need to be validated by others. A purpose and values are right if they are personally meaningful and inspirational. Together, your purpose and core values make up what is sometimes referred to as your core ideology—your enduring character and identity as a coach.[10, 11] Your core ideology as a coach matters because it gives meaning to your work and has the power to ignite passion and sustain the long-term commitment required to become an effective coach.

## COACHING WITH CARE

The importance of starting with your why as a coach can be better understood by referring to what Simon Sinek calls the Golden Circle.[12, 13] Based on a mathematical principle referred to as the golden ratio and his review of successful leaders and companies, Sinek explains that the Golden Circle is a series of three successively larger circles.

The first circle represents why you do what you do; the second circle embodies how you do what you do; the third circle illustrates what you do. In other words, the why is your coaching purpose, the how is the daily actions—guided by your core values, taken to bring the purpose to life—and the what is the result of these actions (successful athletes and sport programs).

An example of a coaching Golden Circle for successful high school coaching can be created using the examples of Bob Ladouceur[1, 14] and Charles Kyle,[15] both recipients of multiple National Coach of the Year awards. The three levels of a coaching Golden Circle that fits the purpose and values of championship coaches are presented in figure 1.1.

Both coaches describe their coaching purpose as a sort of calling—a deeply held view that they were meant to coach and lead young men through the sport of

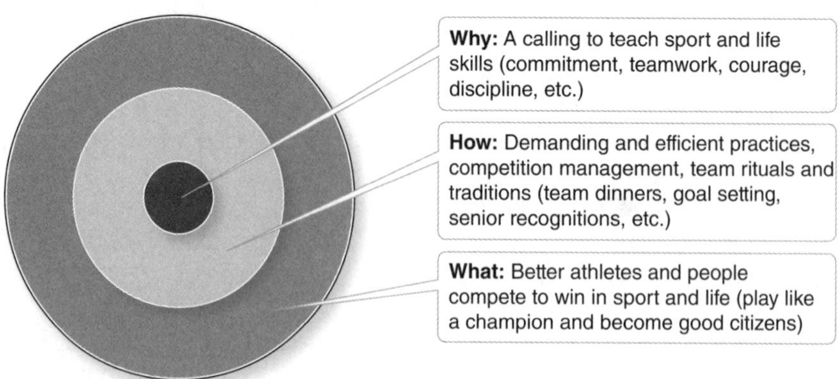


**Figure 1.1** Championship coaching Golden Circle.

football. Teaching in carefully planned practices that are physically and mentally demanding for their athletes, coaching their athletes to success in competitions, and creating a wide range of team traditions and rituals is how they accomplish their coaching why. The results of their relentless and disciplined commitment to becoming better while honoring their purpose and core values are winning programs and athletes who succeed in sport and life.

One of the most dominant college sport programs of all time is the women's soccer team at the University of North Carolina. Under the direction of head coach Anson Dorrance, the program has won 22 national championships in women's Division I soccer. Coach Dorrance, a rare coach who has been inducted into his sport's Hall of Fame while still actively coaching, has coached for nearly 40 years and is quick to recognize that having clearly articulated core values is a cornerstone to building a durable culture of success.

Coach Dorrance describes the team's core values as part of the fabric of the team. The team has 12 core values (see figure 1.2). Each core value has a corresponding statement that captures its essence. The statements, some several paragraphs long, include passages from philosophers and poets and a note from a former player.[16, 17] Each season athletes are expected to memorize the core values and the core value statements. Examples of statements for the core values of "We don't whine" and "We work hard" follow.[16 (p. 91)]

- **We don't whine:** The true joy in life is to be a force of fortune instead of a feverish, selfish little clod of ailments and grievances complaining that the world will not devote itself to making you happy. (George Bernard Shaw, playwright)
- **We work hard:** The difference between one person and another, between the weak and the powerful, the great and the insignificant, is energy—invisible

## Figure 1.2 Core Values for Anson Dorrance and University of North Carolina Women's Soccer Program

- We don't whine.
- The truly extraordinary do something every day.
- We want these four years of college to be rich, valuable, and deep.
- We work hard.
- We don't freak out over ridiculous issues or create crises where none should exist.
- We choose to be positive.
- We treat everyone with respect.
- We care about each other as teammates and as human beings.
- When we don't play as much as we would like, we are noble and still support the team and its mission.
- We play for each other.
- We are well led.
- We want our lives to be never-ending ascensions.

determination. . . . This quality will do anything that has to be done in the world, and no talents, no circumstances, no opportunities will make you a great person without it. (Thomas Buxton, philanthropist)

In a seminar Coach Dorrance shared that the core value that resonates most strongly with him is the final one: "We want our lives (and not just in soccer) to be never-ending ascensions, but for that to happen properly our fundamental attitude about life and our appreciation for it is critical." In fact, Dorrance keeps a comic strip from Calvin and Hobbes (his favorite) on the outside of his office door as a constant visual reminder, for himself and others who visit him in his office, of this core value.[18] In the comic strip the main character shouts out, "I want my life to be one of never-ending ascension," as he streaks down a hill on a wagon.

For coaches who are serious about learning more about how core purpose and core values set the foundation for sustained excellence, the business research conducted by Jim Collins and Jerry Porras is a must read.[10, 11] Collins and Porras conducted exhaustive research in an effort to learn what separates the leading durable companies from their competitors. They focused on companies that consistently outperform their market competitors and survive much longer, such as Boeing, Hewlett-Packard, 3M, Sony, and Proctor & Gamble.

The key finding from their research is that these world-class companies clearly understand, and follow, their purpose and core values. The purpose and core values remain fixed, whereas the markets, company leaders, and business

Andy Mead/YCJ/Icon Sportswire

Setting high standards while treating others with respect is an important core value for coach Anson Dorrance and his teams.

strategies are in constant flux. The founders of great companies understood that their greatest contribution to the business was not their technical, business, or leadership skills but their ability to instill an enduring character as the basis for all activity within the organization. Long after the founders leave the company, the purpose and core values serve as a continued source of inspiration and guidance.

The New Zealand All Blacks men's rugby team is routinely used around the world as a model for how to create and instill purpose and core values for sustained excellence in sport. The All Blacks are the most successful sport team in history, having won 75 percent of their matches across their 100-plus-year history. Although other professional sport teams are renowned for their championship streaks, no other sport organization has a record of relentless success comparable with the All Blacks.

Three core values serve as guiding principles for the team from year to year and are critical to sustaining their level of success: (1) pride in winning, (2) pride in the All Blacks legacy, and (3) willingness to evolve.[19–21] I can personally attest to the accuracy and power of these core values based on my first-hand experience learning from All Blacks coaches when I was invited to speak at the New Zealand national coaching conference in 2015.[22]

Pride in being selected to the team is evident in the players' ability to recite matches played by previous teams and identify with athletes who previously wore the same jersey number. One athlete stated that this identification with predecessors connects current players all the way back to the very first All Blacks who put on a jersey in 1884, James Allen. This deep connection to the past creates a great sense of honor and privilege to play for the All Blacks.

The winning spirit is sustained by a relentless quest to find a competitive edge. Doing this requires coaches and athletes to be brutally honest in their self-assessments and view failures as simply feedback for winning. For example, former head coach Graham Henry explained how his willingness to evolve as a coach—an All Blacks core value—was critical to helping the team regain the world championship title in 2011.

> I've been coaching for 37 years. . . . [When I started] I was very directive as a coach . . . pretty authoritarian. But now it's . . . a group of people trying to do something together. . . . I think that's evolved naturally. . . . If you didn't change [as a coach], you were history.[21 (p. 65)]

The core values that serve as guiding principles for the All Blacks are observed in everyday symbols, rituals, and rites—collectively referred to as artifacts. Three of the most visible artifacts are the black jersey, the *Haka*, and player-driven leadership.

The All Blacks' jersey, which is black with a silver fern, has remained virtually unchanged since it was adopted in the 1880s. For the All Blacks the original design of the jersey is a sacred symbol of their purpose and core values and therefore is not something to be tampered with.

Even if you have never watched an All Blacks rugby match, you likely have seen or at least heard of the *Haka*, the pregame dance ritual performed by every

All Blacks team since the team was founded. The *Haka*, of which there are various forms, is a traditional and historical rite of the native Maori people of New Zealand. Although the *Haka* has remained a constant ritual for the All Blacks, its meaning and relevance has evolved over time.

Consistent with the core values of pride and the need for constant evolution, an athlete-driven leadership ritual was created in the 1950s that still shapes current leadership practices for the All Blacks. The ritual, referred to as the "back seat of the bus," was created as a way to sustain the core values while also providing a sense of ownership and autonomy. The back seat of the bus was always reserved for the senior leaders of the team. Athletes who occupied the back seat of the bus held council on team discipline, protocols, and team tactics. The core value of athlete-driven leadership lives on today with the creation of an athlete leadership group.

Collectively, research on the world's greatest companies and most successful sport team of all time shows how critical it is to identify and nurture your purpose and core values.

## GUIDING YOUR COACHING DECISIONS

Coaching purpose and core values should be used to inform everyday coaching decisions. Coaches gain credibility and build a culture of collective accountability when they demonstrate to their athletes that they will not sacrifice core values for short-term wins. Championship college basketball coach Chantal Valleé describes a decision early in her coaching career to suspend five of her starting athletes as a defining moment in her quest to build a winning culture.[23] After learning that several key players had behaved in a way that was inconsistent with the team's core values right before an international trip to play against a national team, she decided to leave the players at home. She knew that this decision would severely hurt the team's chances of winning the game, but she also realized that showing the team that the core values are more important than the outcome of a single basketball game was critical for building the right team culture and long-term success. The team lost the game by 50 points, but it was a defining moment in establishing a culture of excellence, one that would see her teams go on to win five consecutive national championships.

I share here two approaches to identifying and committing to purpose and core values that I used in my collaborations with college and high school coaches. The first example comes from a three-year collaboration with a collegiate golf coach. Although the coach initially came to me seeking an answer to a specific problem, I suggested we take a different approach by focusing first on problem setting instead of problem solving.

This process of first making sense of a situation before trying to solve it is referred to as problem setting. We set problems based on our personal experiences and values. Problem setting provides us with a frame of reference against which to identify, and test, potential solutions. When faced with difficult situations successful leaders pause to set the problem first (reflect on how the situation is similar to, and different from, previous situations encountered and how the situation fits with their core ideology). Only after they have carefully set the problem do they move to the process of problem solving (identifying and testing potential strategies for resolving the problem).[24, 25]

I then asked the coach a series of questions designed to stimulate a discussion on the problem itself, namely, why this situation was viewed as a problem that warranted the expenditure of precious time and energy. Through this process we were able to uncover the coach's why—not only for the coach personally but also for the golf program (why do I coach, and why do we have a golf program?). This process naturally reveals whether the original coaching issue is in fact a problem that needs to be solved. If the coaching situation does not detract from your ability as a coach to achieve your why, then it does not merit spending your time and effort; it is a nonissue.

This lesson is critical for coaches because there simply isn't enough time to chase and try to resolve every situation that arises. Clearly defining your purpose and core values gives you focus and direction and allows you to identify those situations that you can and should ignore.

Learning what and whom to ignore is a defining characteristic of successful leaders. I vividly recall listening to a member of the world-renowned Blue Angels U.S. Navy flight demonstration team speak in one of my coaching classes about the importance of quickly learning how to focus on the things that matter most—in his case, returning from a flight alive.

This skill of learning what to ignore has sometimes been referred to as a triage approach to decision making (and coaching).[26] A clearly defined coaching purpose and core values set boundaries for helping you make decisions by providing thresholds of engagement. Every coach can ignore some situations—those that lie outside the boundaries of what truly matters as defined by the purpose and core values.

With the golf coach we ultimately settled on the following three core values:

- Passion: Nurture love for the game of golf and competing.
- Achievement: Strive to achieve our competitive and personal goals.
- Respect: Demonstrate genuine regard for self, others, and the game of golf.

Only after we completed this exercise, over the course of several meetings, did we notice that the acronym—PAR—was a perfect fit for the sport of golf. The PAR concepts were reinforced constantly across all coaching decisions and program events. For example, the PAR core values were prominently displayed on recruiting materials and at the team banquet. The coach, and the program, now had boundaries of relevance.

PAR was used as the compass to guide decision making from that point forward. The coach found this process of identifying purpose and core values to set and solve coaching problems helpful. In the coach's view, it directly contributed to the team's success, including their first win of the season, which followed several weeks later.

The second example comes from five years of ongoing work with the athletics department at a large public high school. Several years ago, the athletics director reached out to me about creating a vision for athletics at the school—a common purpose and core values that would serve to give focus to coaches' work and build a culture of sustained excellence.

Over the course of the entire first year we worked at learning the history, values, and cultural norms of the school and the athletics department. Our focus was on identifying the why for the coaches and the program. Purpose and core values cannot be forced on people; they must come from within those who will be expected to live and work in accordance with them. Purpose and related core values must be deeply meaningful on a personal level; otherwise they are simply empty statements—things important to someone else.

After a year of observing, listening, and reflecting on what we were learning, we developed our first draft of the purpose and core values. Over the next two years we used the purpose and core values to guide our effort to change team culture, and we continued to update and adjust the purpose and core values. The purpose for the high school sport program is "to inspire and build youth through competitive sport." The core values are the following:

- Participate: We create sport programs that are accessible and inclusive to all.
- Retain: We create sport programs that inspire participants to continue their sport participation.
- Engage: We create sport programs that are enjoyable and result in skill development.
- Compete: We develop consistently competitive sport programs and student-athletes.

Years of testing have demonstrated that these ideals have deep meaning and relevance for the coaches and administrators in this setting. Taking the time to define and communicate your purpose and core values is well worth the effort. As with the golf example shared earlier, athletes and teams at the high school are experiencing more success, and coaches report that they are much more focused in their work. Even more impressive is the 15 percent increase in sport participation in the four-year period because we committed to defining, teaching, and using a clear purpose and core values to guide our coaching. Although at first glance the exercise may seem to be purely academic, the evidence is undeniable: Knowing your purpose and core values as a coach is critical for building successful sport programs.

One of the most valuable activities for identifying your purpose and core values is to engage in critical reflection on who you are and want to be as a person and to identify others who exemplify a similar purpose and values. Simply thinking about it is not enough. You must take the time to write down your thoughts about purpose and core values. When you write about your purpose and core values, you reconnect to the larger purpose that inspired you to become a coach.[27] Preseason is a perfect time for this exercise because the big-picture perspective can easily disappear during the long grind of the season when you are likely to develop a narrow focus on immediate issues that demand attention.

The values worksheet created by Dan Zadra is a simple tool that will help coaches bring clarity to their purpose and core values.[28] The worksheet is one of

## Figure 1.3 Coach Values Worksheet

What are the three things I like most and least about myself as a coach?

Who is the happiest coach I know?

Who are the two coaches I like and respect the most, and why?

Who am I as a coach?

From W. Gilbert, 2017, *Coaching better every season: A year-round system for athlete development and program success* (Champaign, IL: Human Kinetics).

the first activities in a workbook about deciding how you will live your life over the next five years. This workbook was given to me by a successful coach who used it with his teams, and I have since "paid it forward" with other coaches. I have adapted the values worksheet for coaches (see figure 1.3). I believe that the activity will get you thinking about how you will define and share your coaching purpose and core values.

After completing the coach values worksheet, you will be ready to write out your coaching purpose and core values. Think of the coach values worksheet as a mental warm-up for the real work needed to identify and describe your purpose and core values. Next, you will move to completing the coaching purpose and core values worksheet to help you articulate your why (see figure 1.4). This process will help ensure alignment between your purpose, core values, and coaching behaviors.

Start by writing out your coaching why by completing the prompt "As a coach, I exist to . . . ." Try to be succinct; keep your why to a few lines and one sentence. This account is not the place for an elaborate statement about your coaching philosophy. Your coaching philosophy is an outgrowth of your purpose and core values, and it will be addressed in chapter 2 of this book. Reflect deeply on what compels you to coach. What is the driving force that motivates you to make all the personal sacrifices and investments to have the privilege of coaching?

There is no one model or best response to this question. But there is a right answer—an honest reflection of your reason for coaching. Only a genuine purpose will keep you grounded and focused on the things that truly matter, particularly when you encounter the inevitable ethical and moral dilemmas that all coaches face.

Over the years I have coached various youth sport teams. Using my own situation as an example, I would state my coaching purpose as follows: "As a youth sport coach, I exist to instill a lifelong love of play, physical activity, and sport in young people." This statement accurately captures what drives me to coach kids. For me, youth sport, particularly recreational youth sport, should always be playful,

## Figure 1.4 Coaching Purpose and Core Values Worksheet

**Coaching purpose (why do you coach?): As a coach, I exist to . . .**

______________________________________________

______________________________________________

| Core value | Core value action statement |
|---|---|
| | |
| | |
| | |
| | |
| | |
| | |

fun, and physically engaging. I believe the best I can do as a coach in this setting is to create an experience for kids that will not only make them want to return the following season but also nurture in them a lifelong passion for movement and play.

This coaching purpose fits for me; it is true to who I am and my views on youth sport. You have to find your coaching purpose—the one that is true to who you are and your views on sport (and the level of competition and age of the athletes you coach). How will you know if you got it right? You will know it when you share your coaching purpose with others and it just feels right. It's not rehearsed; it's from the heart. It speaks directly to who you are and the type of contribution you want to make to the world as a sport coach.

The next step in defining your coaching purpose is to identify the core values (three to five are typically sufficient) that best represent how you will enact your purpose. When describing how to write core values, Simon Sinek advises to write the values as verbs. For example, he differentiates the core value *integrity*, which is vague and nondirective, from the statement "Always do the right thing," which is action-oriented and more specific. Another example is the difference between the core value *innovation* and the directive "Look at the problem from a different angle"; one is simply an ideal, whereas the other provides specific guidance for living the core value on a daily basis.

In the coaching purpose and core values worksheet, you will notice a two-column table for completing the core values part of the exercise. The first column is used to identify the core values. The second column is used to write an action statement related to the core value that describes, in a general sense, how you will enact the core values. Without clearly defined examples of what the core values look like in action, athletes will not have a clear understanding of how to behave on a daily basis in ways that are consistent with the standards. This point was reinforced for me through conversations with Dr. Ralph Pim, longtime director for competitive sport at West Point Military Academy, who explained that core values "have to become actions. Describe what you think 'right' looks like for each core value. Also describe what you think 'right' does not look like."[5 (p. 79)]

For example, in my coaching I would add the core value *athlete centered* and the corresponding core value action statement "Always make time to learn about each athlete's unique personality, learning style, and needs." Without the action statement, the core value itself is undefined and left open to interpretation. This deficiency is particularly problematic if you are creating core values for a team or sport organization.

In my work with high school athletic departments with dozens of sport coaches and frequent turnover, we provided not only a core value concept but also the associated core value actions. The action statements provide real and specific guidance on how we should behave as coaches to ensure alignment with our core values and purpose.

Jim Collins provides a core value evaluation checklist for companies to use when determining whether a core value is credible and warrants inclusion in your list.[29] Using his checklist as a guide, I adapted the questions to fit a sport-coaching context. As you work to identify core values for potential inclusion in

## Figure 1.5 Core Value Evaluation Checklist

| Core value question | Yes | No |
|---|---|---|
| 1. If you were to start a new team or club, would you build it around this core value regardless of the setting? | | |
| 2. Would you want to hold this core value, even if at some point in time it became a competitive disadvantage? | | |
| 3. Do you believe that those who do not share this core value do not belong on your coaching staff? | | |
| 4. Would you personally continue to hold this core value even if you were not rewarded for holding it? | | |
| 5. Would you change coaching jobs before giving up this core value? | | |

From W. Gilbert, 2017, *Coaching better every season: A year-round system for athlete development and program success* (Champaign, IL: Human Kinetics).

your own list, test each core value against the following questions (see figure 1.5). This step is the final one in creating your coaching purpose and core values. A core value is considered authentic and worthy of inclusion if you answer yes to each of the questions.

For a coaching purpose and core values to be most effective, they must then be clearly articulated with your athletes and other members of your team. In the words of Louis Van Gaal, head coach of 2014 World Cup medalists, the Netherlands, and one of the world's most famous soccer teams, Manchester United, "The boys in my squad knew from day one what the vision of Van Gaal stood for. That was very important. I was clear to them. I made sure there was transparency."[30]

One way to check the transparency of your purpose and core values, after you have clearly defined them yourself, is to ask your athletes whether they can identify them. First, start by writing a response, in one page or less, to the following prompt: "I know I will have succeeded as a coach if . . . ." Your answer to this prompt will reveal your coaching purpose and core values.

Then, ask your athletes to write a response, in one page or less, to a similar prompt: "I know I will have succeeded as an athlete if . . . or we will have succeeded as a team if . . . ." Compare the athletes' responses to your response. The main elements of your purpose and values should be clear to see across the athletes' responses. This simple exercise will quickly reveal potential gaps in your ability to model your coaching purpose and teach the core values.

One of the most common strategies used by successful coaches to ensure that core values are transparent is to post them throughout the athletics facility and give each athlete a written copy of the core values.[31, 32] Although posters are a simple and inexpensive way to display team core values, some teams even paint them onto the walls in locker rooms or where athletes train. One of the most famous examples of this is the "Play Like a Champion Today" sign that hangs on the wall leading out of the locker room onto the playing field for the Notre Dame college football team. In 1986 legendary coach Lou Holtz had the sign painted and displayed there permanently. He instructed the players to touch the sign as they exited the locker room before games—a core value tradition that is still enacted by players today:

> Every time you hit this sign, I want you to remember all the great people that played here before you, all the sacrifices that your teammates have made for you, all the people, your coaches, your parents, who are responsible for you being here.[33]

## GETTING ATHLETES' INPUT

How much ownership, or input, should athletes be given in setting core values? Core values, which typically are derived from your coaching purpose, should be open to discussion and may even be slightly altered each year to fit the particular group of athletes you are coaching. Successful coaches testify that athletes' buy-in to the core values is much greater when they are given an opportunity to collaborate on defining core values.

When establishing core values in the preseason, some coaches like to give athletes a list of 20 to 30 sample core values as a starting point.[5, 31] Athletes are then instructed to review the list and select the ones they believe are most important to team success and add any new ones to the list they think are missing. The coach can then guide the team in a discussion about their selections and help the team narrow their list down to a few shared core values that are most meaningful to that particular team for the upcoming season. Two examples from successful coaches are used to illustrate this type of preseason core values exercise in action.

One of the coaches in Dr. Lynn Kidman's research on athlete-centered coaching shared the story of how he successfully established core values with a boys' high school volleyball team.[34] He initially provided the team with a list of 30 values to use as a guide or starting point. He then asked them to pick the top six and create definitions of the values. Although athletes were asked to help identify and define the core values for the team that season, the coach set boundaries and facilitated the process to ensure that the core values were aligned with his coaching purpose.

After the volleyball team agreed on the core values, they collaboratively wrote value statements to serve as behavioral guidelines—specific strategies that each team member would be expected to follow to demonstrate his commitment to the team's core values (see figure 1.6).

The coach took the exercise one step further, understanding that a single, concise statement was needed to serve as a constant reminder of the collective core values. The team decided that "Binding together to be better" was the statement that best captured their core values, and it became their rallying cry for the season. This example illustrates how coaches can provide athletes with a sense of ownership in creating core values for a team while also ensuring that the values ultimately are aligned with their personal coaching purpose.

## Figure 1.6 Core Values for High School Volleyball Team

**Core value summary statement: Binding together to be better.**

Talk constructively at appropriate times.

Take care of things outside volleyball so that we can enjoy the game and our season.

Respect each other at all times.

Attend all trainings—physically, mentally, and socially.

Remain positive no matter what.

Always demonstrate positive winning posture.

Always be there for my teammates.

The second example of seeking athlete input when identifying and defining core values comes from Hall of Fame basketball coach Mike Krzyzewski. In 2005 Coach Krzyzewski accepted an invitation to take over a team that went 4-3 at the 2004 Olympics and settled for a bronze medal. According to Krzyzewski, a defining moment in the team's preparation for the 2008 Olympics was the meeting held to define their core values.[35]

Before the team meeting he met separately with four of the team leaders, including Kobe Bryant and LeBron James. Coach Krzyzewski understood that for the athletes to adopt the core values, they had to believe that the values were relevant to them and not imposed on them by the coaching staff. He used the individual meetings to explain to the leaders the purpose of the team meeting, suggest some potential core values such as communication and trust, and ask them to be ready to share their core values in front of the team.

At the end of the emotional team meeting, 15 core values, referred to as their gold standards, were identified (see figure 1.7). These core values were used to guide all coaching and athlete behavior throughout their Olympic preparation and the tournament, which they won while going undefeated.

# CREATING A WINNING TEAM CULTURE

One of the biggest challenges for coaches is to figure out how to share their coaching purpose and teach core values to a different group of athletes every season. Although some athletes will likely return, rarely will a team have exactly the same group of athletes from one season to the next. Furthermore, at some point in your career you may find yourself in the position of taking over an existing team from another coach.

When taking over a team, coaches frequently talk about changing the culture as the first step toward instilling their coaching purpose and core values. Team culture has been defined as a pattern of shared assumptions that guides behavior. Culture comprises both the obvious artifacts of the team, such as team documents, basic operating procedures, and the physical arrangement of team facilities, and the less obvious norms and rituals.

## Figure 1.7 2008 Olympic Basketball Team Core Values

1. No excuses: We have what it takes to win.
2. Great defense: This is the key to winning the gold; we do the dirty work.
3. Communication: We look each other in the eye, and we tell each other the truth.
4. Trust: We believe in each other.
5. Collective responsibility: We are committed to each other, and we win together.
6. Care: We have each other's backs, and we give aid to a teammate.
7. Respect: We respect each other and our opponents, we're always on time, and we're always prepared.
8. Intelligence: We take good shots, we're aware of team fouls, and we know the scouting report.
9. Poise: We show no weaknesses.
10. Flexibility: We can handle any situation; we don't complain.
11. Unselfishness: We're connected, we make the extra pass, and our value is not measured in playing time.
12. Aggressiveness: We play hard every possession.
13. Enthusiasm: This is fun.
14. Performance: We're hungry; we have no bad practices.
15. Pride: We are the best team in the world, and we represent the best country.

Three-time national college football championship coach Urban Meyer shares a compelling example of how he built a winning team culture founded on three core values in the preseason of the year that the Ohio State Buckeyes won the first College Football Playoff championship in 2014. They started the preseason by creating a blueprint for communicating the core values with absolute clarity.

The core values were described as "what we believe," and the core value action statements were described as "how we behave." Besides listing the core value and an associated core value behavior, Coach Meyer and his staff also listed the expected outcome that would result from living the core value and core value behaviors on a daily basis. Collectively, these components become known as the Ohio State University Football Culture Blueprint (see figure 1.8).[3]

You will notice in Coach Meyer's example that the core value behavior for relentless effort is "Go as hard as you can, four to six seconds, point A to point B." This guideline is in reference to the duration of a typical play in football (four to six seconds) and the fact that athletes need to be ready to push themselves with maximum effort in whatever direction required (forward, backward, sideways—A to B). This example shows how a core value can be translated into a meaningful and observable behavior guideline for athletes in practice and in competition.

One of the more remarkable team culture turnarounds orchestrated by a coach is the transformation of the British cycling team by Sir Dave Brailsford. When Coach Brailsford inherited the team, they were ranked 17th in the world and had won just

## Figure 1.8 OSU Football Culture Blueprint

| What we believe | How we behave | Outcome we achieve |
|---|---|---|
| Relentless effort | Go as hard as you can, four to six seconds, point A to point B. | We are tougher than any situation or opponent we face. |
| Competitive excellence | Constant focus on mental reps and game reps. | You are prepared to make the play when your number is called. |
| Power of the unit | Uncommon commitment to each other and to the work necessary to achieve our purpose. | Brotherhood of trust. Combat motivation. |

Reprinted from U. Meyer and W. Coffey, 2015, *Above the line: Lessons in leadership and life from a championship* season (New York: Penguin), 67.

two bronze medals at the 1996 Olympics. Coach Brailsford immediately began by creating a wide range of strategies for teaching athletes the core values that aligned with his coaching purpose.[36]

The core values were summarized in the CORE acronym—commitment + ownership + responsibility = excellence. A team charter representing the core values was printed on all gear and on every bike (see figure 1.9). Coach Brailsford and cycling observers cite the British cycling team's rise all the way to number one in the world and 12 medals at the 2012 Olympics as clear evidence that investing time and energy into coaching purpose and core values activities is well worth the effort.

Experienced coaches with decades of success are a great source of wisdom for learning how to use your coaching purpose and core values to build team culture. When asked about the keys to his success, J.T. Curtis Jr., American high school football coaching legend and 2012 National Coach of the Year, alluded to complete adoption across the program of a common purpose and shared values.[37] Although coaching strategies, rules of the game, and athletes have regularly changed across his 40-year coaching career, he attributes his national-record 26 state titles largely to his timeless coaching purpose and core values. His coaching purpose is grounded in a deep concern for developing his players not only into great athletes but also into great people. Nonnegotiable core values include work ethic, positive attitude, and commitment to team.

Pioneering American swim coach James "Doc" Counsilman, also with more than 40 years of coaching experience, is another prime example of a coach who was extremely successful at building team culture every season. Renowned for his ability to coach athletes to championships and records—at one point his swimmers held the world record in every single swimming event—he is perhaps equally well known for his scientific approach to coaching. He repeatedly described his why for coaching as existing to help athletes meet their basic, individual psychological needs.[38] He listed the need for love and affection, recognition, and a sense of belonging as common needs for athletes at any age and competitive level. Much like other championship coaches, he viewed his coaching purpose as a people builder.

## Figure 1.9 Team Charter Representing Core Values for the British Cycling Team

This is the line.
The line between winning and losing.
Between failure and success.
Between good and great.
Between dreaming and believing.
Between convention and innovation.
Between head and heart.
It is a fine line.
It challenges everything we do.
And we ride it every day.

Although few formal studies exist on how coaches instill their purpose and core values to build team culture, two examples can shed light on this difficult process. In the first example, researchers examined 10 American collegiate coaches who had all been hired to lead unsuccessful teams and who then coached those same teams to championships within five years.[39] All 10 were quick to attribute their rapid success to the instillation of a team culture clearly aligned with a purpose and core values.

Coaches referred to the team culture as a mind-set and "the way we do things around here." Instilling a team culture began with clearly communicating a small set of core values specific to their team and their environment. Although specific core values varied among the coaches, they could be regrouped into three types of core values: relationships (building trust), behavioral (daily actions), and strategic (skills and tactics fundamental to achieving success). Adoption of the new team culture typically took up to three years.

Coaches used four tactics to instill the core values that served as the foundation for the desired culture.

1. **Defining and repeatedly articulating the desired values:** This goal was accomplished through improving regular and formal communication channels, such as an increase in the number of meetings with individual athletes and sharing of a wide range of performance statistics.

2. **Creating teaching tools to help athletes understand the core values:** Role modeling behaviors by all members of the coaching staff that exemplify the core values was considered the most effective teaching tool. Other effective teaching tools included regular assignments that distributed leadership across the team and inclusion of lectures, guest speakers, and sharing of anecdotes and stories.

3. **Designing specific recruiting and scouting techniques to secure players who held the same core values:** This approach starts with defining the

desirable attributes sought in potential team members (e.g., passionate, mature, coachable). Coaches were unwilling to let talent override personal attributes when selecting a recruit. The best way to determine whether a recruit possesses the desirable attributes is to observe the athlete in challenging or crisis situations in competition. Recruits must also be vetted by the current team members to determine potential fit with the team culture. Finally, coaches were extremely patient recruiters, always willing to wait if needed to find the recruit with the profile that matched the desired core values and culture.

4. **Implementing reward and punishment systems to reinforce the core values:** Common rewards and punishments were used, such as playing time and symbolic rewards (e.g., helmet stickers, special shirts).[40] Regardless of the exact reward or punishment, to be effective it must clearly reinforce the core values. For example, if core values are responsibility and respect and a coach notices that the team left a locker room full of litter, then the coach may require them to complete a trash collection activity the following day.

The second example comes from a study of college coaches in Canada who were renowned for their ability to rebuild losing programs into conference and national champions.[41] Four common themes were found: (1) a focus on individual athlete growth, (2) strong coach organizational skills, (3) a lifelong commitment to learning, and (4) a strong vision for where and how they wanted to build their programs. Their coaching purpose could be summed up as holistic development of athletes. Their coaching was driven by their vision of themselves as builders—builders of athletes, builders of people, builders of programs.

To lend further credence to this builder purpose for coaching, the lead author of the study, Chantal Valleé, adopted the coaching purpose and values she learned through her research after she became a college head coach. The results of her coaching journey are truly remarkable. She has transformed the culture of a college basketball program from worst in the country to an unprecedented five consecutive national championships.[23]

Creating a team culture that represents and reinforces your coaching purpose and core values takes years and requires an aggressive, disciplined, and systematic approach. Constant repetition of multiple coaching strategies that recognize behaviors consistent with the desired team culture, combined with recruitment of athletes who embody the core values, are effective strategies for building and sustaining your team culture.

A common theme among the most revered coaches is a core purpose grounded in the view that quality coaches are people builders. It should come as no surprise then that Graham Henry and Wayne Smith, coaches of the world's most successful sport team, the New Zealand All Blacks, created the mantra "Better people make better All Blacks" to serve as a constant reminder of this core purpose.[20] Similarly, championship college soccer and lacrosse coach Jay Martin, whose teams never had a losing season in his 38 years of coaching at Ohio Wesleyan University, used the following creed as his guide: "Great people . . . Great teams . . . Great results."[42] Quality coaches know that adopting people building as the foundation of their core purpose directly contributes to improved performance

The Canadian Press/Jacques Boissinof

**Chantal Valleé built a championship team culture with a strong vision and focus on athlete development.**

on the field because development of people skills, such as communication and decision making, makes for better athletes.

Championship collegiate basketball coach Dawn Staley, who is renowned for building team culture, summed it up well when she explained, "This isn't just about the four years they spend with me. This is about their whole lives."[43] Coach Staley models this people-builder purpose by coaching with discipline and passion and by providing her athletes with opportunities to learn life skills by being mentored by successful women in other fields.

## Wrap-Up

The world's most successful coaches always start by asking themselves why they coach. A clear understanding of your purpose and core values serves as the compass that provides the stable guidance needed to navigate your coaching journey each season. Everything else in your coaching world will be in a constant state of change. You will have to adapt your coaching strategies constantly to keep pace with these changes, but the rituals, traditions, and symbols you and your athletes create to embody your purpose and core values should remain relatively fixed. Although all coaches will need to find the purpose and core values that fit best with their style and the profile of their athletes, the vision of a sport coach as a people builder is a common theme found among the most successful coaches. In the words of distinguished championship basketball coach Don Meyer, "Your program must have an overriding purpose which is clearly visible and which teaches lessons beyond winning."[44]

Chapter 2

# Connect Values to Philosophy

**Key Concepts**

Coaching philosophy
Coaching effectiveness
International Sport Coaching Framework
Functional and task-related competence
Athlete-centered coaching
Pyramid of Teaching Success in Sport
Cross-generational relationships
Critical incidents and storytelling

Now that you have articulated your coaching purpose and core values, you can use them to define a coaching philosophy. Recall that your coaching purpose and core values represent your why. Your coaching philosophy describes how you will approach your role as a coach and how you will ensure that you are staying true to your purpose and core values. Your coaching philosophy guides your everyday coaching decisions and actions.

Although your coaching purpose and core values will remain relatively stable across your coaching career, successful coaches understand that they may need to adjust their philosophy every season. The way you shape the learning environment and coach each season should match the needs and profile of the athletes you are coaching.

For example, Sean Foley, who has coached some of the world's top-ranked golfers such as Tiger Woods, Justin Rose, and Lee Westwood, explains that he needs to adjust his coaching philosophy slightly for each athlete he coaches: "I'm not coaching golfers; I'm coaching human beings who deal with love and hate and fear and all those different aspects in the emotional arena. If you look at them as just a golfer, you're missing out."[1]

The story of two-time Super Bowl championship coach Tom Coughlin provides a vivid case for the importance of having a stable coaching purpose and values while being open to adjusting a coaching philosophy. Renowned for his rigid and authoritarian style of coaching, Coach Coughlin was challenged late in his career by his athletes on the New York Giants professional football team to adjust his coaching philosophy. Feedback from key leaders on the team and trusted colleagues made it clear that his coaching philosophy was destroying team culture. He realized that his coaching philosophy, although effective with athletes earlier in his career, was not effective anymore and he was in danger of being fired.

> I was a dinosaur, and if I was going to survive I had to adapt. . . . You have to establish your principles and stick to them while also finding a way of making what you do relevant to the people you're working with. You can't expect to succeed by doing the same things the same way when the world around you is changing. I had to learn that.[2 (pp. 116–117)]

At the start of the 2007 season he made important changes to his coaching philosophy, namely by showing his athletes that he genuinely cared for them while still maintaining his core values of discipline and structure. Coach Coughlin and his players believe that his willingness to evolve his coaching philosophy was a key turning point for the team. Adjusting his coaching philosophy in an effort to make stronger emotional connections with his players launched a season that culminated with what is considered one of the greatest Super Bowl victories of all time. In the championship game his New York Giants defeated the New England Patriots, who came into the game as heavy favorites and with the best record in NFL history (18 wins and 0 losses).

Your coaching philosophy is best viewed as a flexible set of principles based on your coaching purpose and core values, typically expressed as a list of statements that guide how you will coach. The purpose of this chapter is to describe recommendations for writing the guiding statements that will become your coaching philosophy and share examples of coaching philosophies created by wise coaches. The preseason is an ideal time to review your coaching philosophy. As Jon Hammermeister wrote in *Cornerstones of Coaching*, "It's safe to say the wise coach is the one who takes the time to think through and formalize his or her personal coaching philosophy."[3 (p. 25)]

## ESTABLISHING A PHILOSOPHY

A commonly recommended approach to developing your coaching philosophy starts with understanding who you are as a coach and as a person (i.e., your coaching purpose) and learning about your athletes. Championship diving coach Jeff Huber provides a list of questions that coaches should ask themselves when creating their coaching philosophy.[4 (pp. 375–376)]

There is no one right answer to these questions. Answering these questions will help you become a better coach because you will have a greater sense of what matters most to you as a coach. The following are some of the coaching philosophy questions suggested by Coach Huber:

1. Why do I coach?
2. What are my values?
3. What types of experiences do I want my athletes to have?
4. What is the definition of athletic success?
5. What is the purpose of sport?
6. What are my responsibilities to my athletes?
7. How should I discipline my athletes?
8. What are my ethical standards?

Besides knowing yourself and your athletes, to achieve full development of your coaching philosophy, you must acquire deep knowledge of your sport—namely, the customs, rules, traditions, values, strategies, and ethics unique to the sport you are coaching. These three types of knowledge—knowledge of yourself, knowledge of your athletes, and knowledge of your sport—provide the foundation for the integrated definition of coaching effectiveness.[5–7]

Coaching effectiveness has been defined as the ability to guide athletes and teams to improvements in four areas: (1) competence as a sport competitor, (2) self-confidence to meet the demands of sport and life, (3) ability to build and sustain positive connections with others, and (4) ethical behaviors such as empathy and respect, globally referred to as character. Collectively, these four outcomes of quality coaching are referred to as the four Cs (competence, confidence, connection, and character).

Effective coaches learn to use knowledge of themselves, their athletes, and their sport to optimize athlete development appropriate to the setting in which they are coaching. Self-knowledge requires introspection—a willingness to subject your views and assumptions to scrutiny from yourself and others. The genuine awareness that results from regular introspection is sometimes referred to as intrapersonal knowledge.

Knowledge of your athletes requires sensitivity to individual and changing athlete needs and profiles. People who are skilled at communicating with and understanding others are sometimes described as having good people skills, also referred to as high emotional intelligence. Emotional intelligence is generally viewed as an ability to identify, use, understand, and manage emotions.[8]

Finally, knowledge of your sport is most evident in the decisions you make as a coach. Effective decision making, sometimes referred to as strategic knowledge, requires the ability to anticipate the potential outcomes of your coaching decisions.[9] A simplified overview of how these three types of coaching knowledge underpin coaching philosophy and directly affect coaching effectiveness is provided in figure 2.1.

Knowledge of yourself, your athletes, and your sport—the three components of the integrated definition of coaching effectiveness—provides you with the right foundation for developing your coaching philosophy. This approach to developing your coaching philosophy, and the role it plays in your ability to become an effective coach, is clearly identified as one of the keys to successful coaching in *International Sport Coaching Framework*.[7]

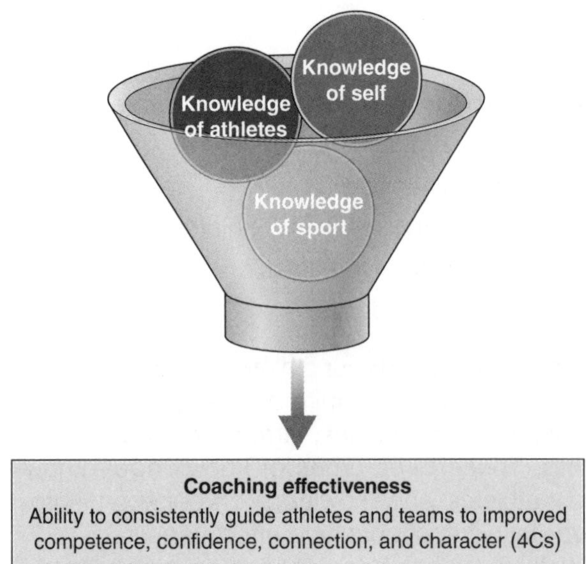


**Figure 2.1** Coaching philosophy.

This framework provides a global blueprint for sport coaching, and sport organizations around the world have adopted it as a guide. Coaching philosophy is situated within *International Sport Coaching Framework* as an example of your functional competence as a coach. Coaching philosophy is described as functional competence because it serves as the map for how you function as a coach. Much as you use a road map to navigate a new city, you use a coaching philosophy to help your athletes reach their destination.

Just as a road map with missing pieces can result in your getting lost, a coaching philosophy without a full appreciation of all the tasks a coach must perform will lead to subpar performance. *International Sport Coaching Framework* refers to the primary tasks of a sport coach as task-related competence. The six primary tasks of a coach are to (1) set vision and strategy, (2) shape the environment, (3) build relationships, (4) conduct practices and prepare for competitions, (5) read and react to the field, and (6) learn and reflect.

In sum, a well-developed coaching philosophy guides how you should function while performing the many challenging tasks of a coach. In this sense, a strong coaching philosophy drives your ability to coach effectively. The relationship between functional competence (coaching philosophy), task-related competence, and coaching effectiveness is illustrated in figure 2.2.

## EXAMINING COACHING PHILOSOPHIES OF EFFECTIVE COACHES

Urban Meyer, three-time national championship college football coach, is a vivid example of a coach who has used a well-developed coaching philosophy to

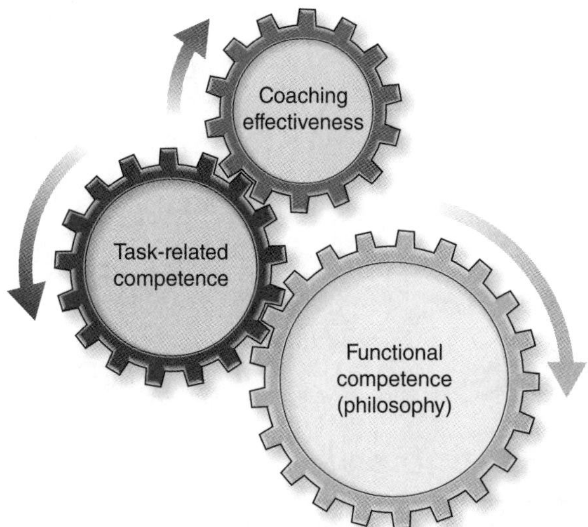


**Figure 2.2** The relationship between functional competence (coaching philosophy), task-related competence, and coaching effectiveness.

create a culture of sustained excellence. One of the core values that underpin his coaching philosophy is that sport, football in his case, is a vehicle for helping young people become mature and productive adults.

Meyer has created a three-tiered (blue, red, gold) incentive-based reward system for connecting his core values to the leadership philosophy he uses to coach his athletes.[10] The blue-red-gold system works like this.

All athletes enter the team at the blue level, which is the lowest status and has the fewest earned privileges (because the player, regardless of his character or potential, has yet to demonstrate the behavior standards with the team). For example, blue-level athletes have eight hours of mandatory academic tutoring each week and are not allowed any unexcused absences from classes.

To graduate to red-level status, athletes must show a record of good academic performance and adherence to team behavior standards. By earning red-level status, athletes are granted more freedom and trust and have fewer conditions imposed on them. Those athletes who most consistently demonstrate the behavior standards are rewarded with the gold-level designation. In coach Meyer's words, these athletes have shown they deserve to be treated like grown men. Coaches meet weekly to review and nominate athletes for movement up and down levels. When an athlete is promoted to a higher level, he is formally recognized for the achievement in front of the entire team, much like a graduation.

Much can be learned by reviewing the coaching philosophies of effective coaches such as Urban Meyer. I have selected five examples to share, two specific to high school coaching and three in high-performance coaching, that provide valuable guides for creating your own coaching philosophy.

Rich Graessle/Icon Sportswire

Ohio State Buckeyes' head coach Urban Meyer teaches and encourages athletes to become leaders.

## Successful High School Coaching Philosophies

Forty-eight outstanding high school coaches in the United States were asked to share their views on their coaching philosophies.[11] The coaches represented the sports of football, volleyball, and basketball, and they had collectively won 175 state championships.

The core of their coaching philosophy was an emphasis on building people, not just athletes. The coaches believed that they gained credibility, respect, and trust by embracing a deep concern for building positive relationships with their athletes. For example, athletes were given opportunities to participate in important decision making as a way to foster independence and commitment.

The coaches also shared a philosophy that included setting and communicating high expectations and standards of conduct. Instead of viewing discipline as a problem requiring a stringent set of rules and policies for punishment, coaches viewed discipline issues as simply another opportunity to teach and reinforce their coaching philosophy. An emphasis on earned, equitable treatment as opposed to equal treatment for all was also a core component of their coaching philosophy. Communication of their coaching philosophy through postgame rituals and frequent one-on-one communications was a regular and continuous part of their coaching.

Another look into high school coaching philosophies involved nine coaches from the sports of basketball, ice hockey, soccer, volleyball, and wrestling. Each was identified as a model high school coach, and each was interviewed along with 16 of her or his student-athletes.[12]

All nine coaches subscribed to an athlete-centered coaching philosophy—one in which they viewed their primary role as helping to develop good people, not just good athletes. These model coaches viewed sport as a tool to prepare their athletes for life outside of sport. They adjusted their coaching philosophy slightly each season, depending on the profile of their athletes. The coaches recognized that they had to develop an awareness of their athletes so that they could modify their coaching philosophies to meet athlete needs and develop transferable life skills. For example, one coach shared how he emphasized inclusion and participation because the region where he coached provided few organized sport opportunities.

The coaches used a range of innovative strategies to teach and reinforce their coaching philosophy. One coach required all athletes to complete a midseason anonymous peer evaluation in which they identified one strength and one weakness for each teammate. The coach then summarized and shared the findings with each athlete as a way to promote continuous improvement and openness to feedback—both important life skills.

## Successful High-Performance Coaching Philosophies

Typically, every biography and autobiography of high-performance sport coaches includes an overview of their coaching philosophy. With this in mind, an analysis was completed of the biographies and autobiographies of five coaches who had coached teams to multiple championships and who were recognized as among the all-time best coaches in their sports.[13] At the time of the study, the coaches had collectively won 29 championships: Scotty Bowman (9 ice hockey championships), Van Chancellor (4 women's basketball championships), Joe Gibbs (3 football championships), Phil Jackson (9 men's basketball championships), and Joe Torre (4 baseball championships). Six characteristics were common across the coaching philosophies of all the coaches:

1. Genuine care for players and consideration of their individual needs
2. Creating team togetherness and working coach-athlete relationships
3. Setting clear and defined roles for every player on the team
4. Deep passion and drive for winning
5. Adoption of a leadership approach that fits their personality and values
6. Perspective on their sport as just a game, not the sole purpose in their life

These common features of a championship coaching philosophy are also evident in today's successful coaches. For example, coaches like Steve Kerr (basketball), Jill Ellis (soccer), and Joel Quenville (ice hockey) all emphasize building quality relationships with their athletes while also adopting unique leadership styles that best fit their personalities.[14] Such recurring themes in coaching philosophies may represent timeless principles of championship coaches in high-performance sport settings.

Another study examined the life stories of eight legendary coaches in the sports of soccer, track and field, rugby, swimming, and netball.[15] An analysis of the coaches' accounts revealed several common themes in their coaching philosophies.

First, they all emphasized an athlete-centered coaching approach—one that required a constant effort to learn about each athlete's particular learning styles and development needs. Second, the team always came first. The best way for teaching and reinforcing this aspect of their philosophy was to identify and articulate everyone's role and function on the team. Third, team success is dependent on creating a positive working relationship with each athlete. Empathy and genuine care for each player, as both an athlete and a person, were core components of their coaching philosophies. Finally, the coaches viewed themselves as teachers and emphasized technical skill development. Coaches frequently spoke about efforts to create optimal learning environments in which athletes felt confident and comfortable with risking failure.

A final example of a successful coaching philosophy in high-performance sport comes from a close look at the approach of American football coach Pete Carroll. In 2014 Carroll became one of only three coaches ever to win both a Super Bowl at the professional level and a national championship at the collegiate level.

Coach Carroll attributes his success to a philosophy that encompasses a deep and genuine personal concern for every athlete on his teams.[16] He noted the challenge of modeling this part of his philosophy when coaching a large football team, but in his mind this element is nonnegotiable. Showing players that he cares about them not only as athletes but also as people, with each requiring an approach unique to the player's personal needs and situations, is what he refers to as the love component of his coaching philosophy.

Although he believes that developing knowledge of each athlete is critical, the pursuit of individual glory can never supersede a commitment to the team. His philosophy of team first drives his focus on helping every player on the team find a sense of purpose and value in his unique role on the team. This approach allows Carroll both to meet individual athlete needs (for self-worth, purpose, and skill development) and to protect the team-first spirit.

## TAKING AN ATHLETE-CENTERED APPROACH

The preceding discussion has shown that the consensus across successful coaches and leading scientists and sport organizations is that the best coaches always place athlete development at the core of their coaching philosophy. Athlete-centered coaches view the coach-athlete relationship as a partnership. For example, Aimee Boorman, long-time coach of gymnastics sensation Simone Biles, emphasizes the importance of listening to athletes and supporting them based on their needs. When asked about the keys to their successful partnership that resulted in Biles winning four gold medals at the 2016 Olympics, Coach Boorman explained that "It's her gymnastics. I'm just her guide."[17] This approach is most commonly referred to as an athlete-centered coaching philosophy. For example, both *International Sports Coaching Framework* and *National Standards for Sport Coaches*[18] in the United States list an athlete-centered coaching approach as the number one characteristic of quality coaching.

To help you better understand what an athlete-centered coaching philosophy looks like in action, this chapter presents a framework for effective coaching and examples from championship coaches.

## Pyramid of Teaching Success in Sport

The Pyramid of Teaching Success in Sport[19] is a popular athlete-centered coaching philosophy framework. Legendary American college basketball coach John Wooden is often identified as a primary source for creating an athlete-centered coaching philosophy. My interactions with and study of Coach Wooden made it clear that athlete learning was the core of his coaching philosophy.[20] Coach Wooden credited his unparalleled success to a relentless quest to improve his ability to teach athletes how to reach their potential in sport and life—what he referred to as competitive greatness.

His athlete-centered coaching philosophy has endured long after his life and career ended, in large part because of his willingness to share his coaching philosophy through the creation of his Pyramid of Success.[21] His Pyramid of Success includes 15 blocks, each representing a desirable outcome for his learners,

AP Photo

Coach Wooden, who had an athlete-centered coaching philosophy, doing what he valued most—teaching.

ranging from industriousness and enthusiasm on the corners to poise, confidence, and competitive greatness at the apex.

Although Coach Wooden's original Pyramid of Success provides an overview of athlete characteristics that informed his coaching philosophy, it does not identify the characteristics that coaches should embody if they want to model an athlete-centered coaching philosophy. After a comprehensive review of the literature and reflections on our experiences with Coach Wooden, a group of us created the Pyramid of Teaching Success in Sport (PoTSS). The PoTSS is best viewed as a coach's version of Coach Wooden's original Pyramid of Success for athletes.

The PoTSS includes 15 athlete-centered coaching characteristics organized into five tiers (see figure 2.3). The foundational tier reinforces that an athlete-centered coaching philosophy starts with a deep concern for connecting to and building quality relationships with athletes. This first tier includes love, friendship, loyalty, cooperation, and balance. Love and balance were selected as the cornerstones of the PoTSS because they are considered timeless and universal principles of athlete-centered coaching. Love is defined as the selfless

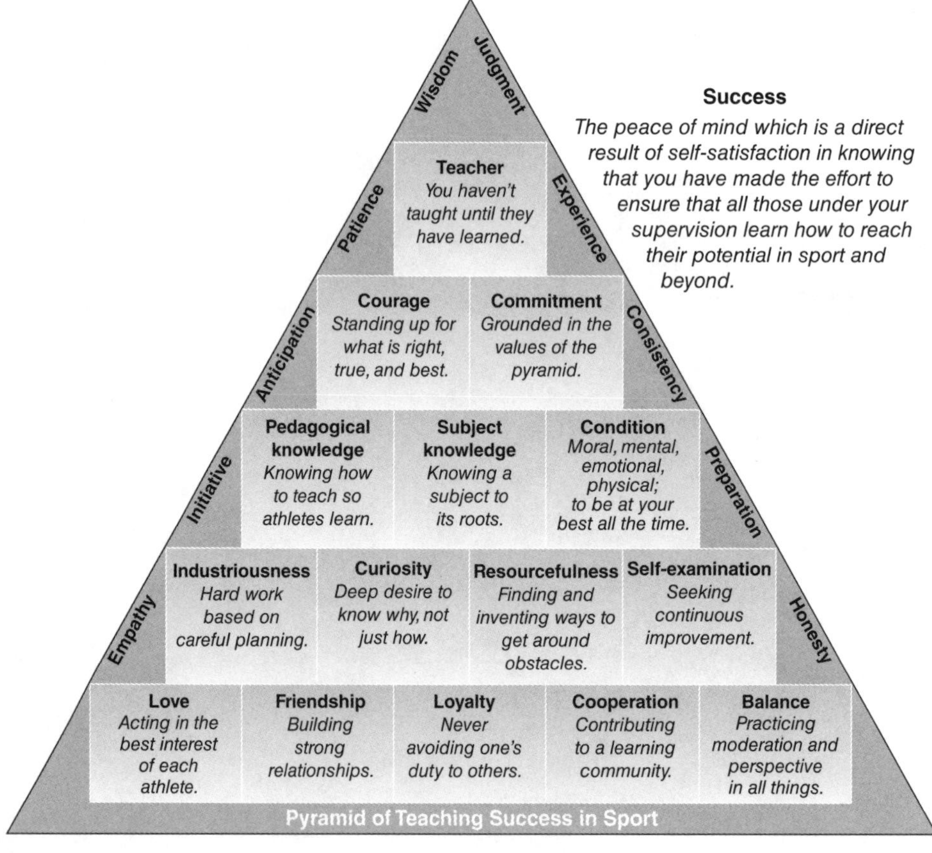


**Figure 2.3** Pyramid of Teaching Success in Sport.

Courtesy of BeLikeCoach (www.belikecoach.com). 

altruistic and unconditional dedication to athlete improvement and success. A coach exhibits balance when his or her actions are aligned with the athlete-centered coaching philosophy. A genuine concern (love) for athletes means that perspective is needed to inform coach decision making, ensuring that a balanced decision can be made.

The second tier includes industriousness, curiosity, resourcefulness, and self-examination. Whereas the first tier focuses externally on connection to the athletes, the second tier focuses internally on self-awareness and self-growth. An athlete-centered coaching philosophy requires coaches to embrace continuous improvement of their ability to help their athletes meet their learning needs.

The third tier, considered the heart of the PoTSS, captures the essence of teaching: pedagogical knowledge, subject knowledge, and condition. Being knowledgeable about your particular sport (subject knowledge) is not enough. Adoption of an athlete-centered coaching philosophy requires teaching skill, that is, the ability to translate what you know into meaningful learning experiences for your athletes (referred to as pedagogical knowledge, or knowledge of teaching). Just as athletes require fortitude, coaches require physical, mental, and moral conditioning to model an athlete-centered coaching philosophy.

Because of the public and interpersonal nature of coaching, coaches face countless moral and ethical challenges. Courage and commitment, the two characteristics represented in the fourth tier of the PoTSS, are needed to stay on course and ensure that coaching actions are consistent with an athlete-centered coaching philosophy. The apex of the PoTSS is the teacher. Great coaches think of themselves first as teachers—teachers of sport and teachers of life. The ultimate characteristic of a coach who embodies an athlete-centered coaching philosophy is teaching, evident in one of Coach Wooden's favorite maxims, "You haven't taught until they have learned."[22]

Adoption of an athlete-centered coaching philosophy results in reimaging how we define success in sport. Contrary to the popular definition of success that depends on defeating others, in the PoTSS success is defined from a self-referenced perspective: "Peace of mind which is a direct result of self-satisfaction in knowing that you have made the effort to ensure that all those under your supervision learn how to reach their potential in sport and beyond."[19 (p. 89)]

## Athlete-Centered Coaching Examples

Each year the National Football League Foundation recognizes outstanding high school football coaches in America. One year, 10 of the finalists for this prestigious award were asked to describe their coaching philosophies as part of a study of successful coaches.[23] All identified athlete development as the core of their coaching philosophy.

Although they each held some unique philosophical beliefs, seven components appeared across all of their athlete-centered coaching philosophies. These essential seven components for creating an athlete-centered coaching philosophy would apply equally well for all high school coaches and across all sports.

1. Create a positive and fun sport environment.
2. Every player is valued, regardless of skill level or role on the team.
3. Rules are few, but expectations are clear and demanding.
4. Open, honest, and clear communication is essential.
5. Care about the players and work to understand each of them.
6. Develop player self-esteem and love of the game.
7. Self-discipline and responsibility are essential for success.

The 10 coaches in the study employed a range of strategies to reinforce their athlete-development coaching philosophies, including having team meetings, forming player advisory groups, modeling behaviors consistent with the philosophy, and creating positive reinforcement reward systems.

Positive reinforcement reward systems can be helpful when coaching young athletes, a strategy sometimes referred to as positive charting.[24] One such system that coaches can easily adapt to their own setting is built around the acronym PRIDE:

**P** = positive
**R** = respect
**I** = initiative
**D** = determination
**E** = enthusiasm

PRIDE serves as an excellent touchstone of an athlete-oriented philosophy because for athletes to maximize their potential in sport and achieve success in life, they must take pride in what they do (how they train, how they compete, how they treat themselves and their teammates). The acronym is a simple way to represent and remember the core components of the philosophy.

During each practice and competition, coaches take note of players who demonstrate any of the PRIDE behaviors. Coaches can then quickly state their observations at the end of the event and select a few players who best exemplified one or more of the PRIDE behaviors that day. These players can then be formally recognized in front of the team and earn a PRIDE reward. Examples of rewards could be a helmet sticker, a badge, or points that go toward a drawing for team apparel or a gift card at the end-of-season banquet. Coaches can watch a short video produced by the Positive Coaching Alliance that shows how a high school football coach uses positive charting during a practice. Coaches can then reflect on how they might use this type of proven coaching strategy with their own athletes.[24]

The next example of an athlete-centered approach comes from Marc Trestman, a long-time professional football coach in the United States and Canada who is considered one of the great teachers of the game. Coach Trestman believes that coaches are in the people business. Building quality relationships founded on trust and respect and investing time to understand each player's individual learning styles and needs are the foundation of his coaching. Coach Trestman refers to his athlete-centered coaching approach as his coaching mantra, which includes six guiding principles:[25 (p. 262)]

1. Be hard working, humble, and disciplined, with a common respect for everyone in the organization, our opponents, and the game of football.
2. Be a resource to every player in developing his football skills and character to the highest level possible, and at the same time have him internalize that everyone associated with the team and organization is entirely interconnected with one another.
3. Communicate to all players that they have to be accountable and that the success of the team is directly related to their individual commitment and effort.
4. Clearly define the standard of performance in all areas as well as the role and responsibility of every member of the organization.
5. Put into place a system of football that is flexible to the existing talent and personnel.
6. Produce highly efficient play at every position in order to win games on a weekly basis.

A final example of an athlete-centered coaching philosophy in action comes from Beth Anders, a pioneering American field hockey coach. In a coaching career spanning 30 years, Coach Anders coached teams to nine national championships, became the first coach to pass the 500-win mark, and retired at the end of the 2012 season as the all-time winningest Division I collegiate field hockey coach. Coach Anders also served as the U.S. national team coach for field hockey three times.

Whereas Coach Trestman uses six principles to describe his athlete-centered coaching philosophy, Coach Anders created a simple formula, supplemented with a list of eight athlete behaviors and four coaching actions.[26] Coach Anders sums up her coaching philosophy in the following formula: How + Why = Journey or process. *How* refers to actions and strategies, whereas *why* refers to the values that shape the *how*. In this sense, Coach Anders combines philosophy (*how*) with purpose and core values (*why*). Her commitment to continuous improvement and learning how best to meet the development needs of her athletes is evident in the outcome of the formula—helping players become better athletes and better people.

As a way to help athletes learn and internalize her coaching philosophy, Coach Anders created a list of eight athlete actions that demonstrate adherence to her athlete-centered coaching philosophy:

1. Accept responsibility and be accountable for your actions and learning.
2. Respect other players and expect respect in return.
3. Demonstrate trust, honesty, and loyalty. These three characteristics require unconditional giving.
4. Contribute to an atmosphere with shared purpose.
5. Engage in healthy competition. Go hard and challenge every situation you encounter.

6. Keep things in perspective. People are the most important factor. Therefore, enjoying what you do and with whom you chose to accomplish your goals is most important.
7. Control only those things you can control. Play within your abilities and be yourself.
8. Take care of yourself, both mentally and physically.

The Pyramid of Teaching Success in Sport, together with examples of how championship coaches define and model their coaching philosophies, reinforces the wisdom of adopting an athlete-centered coaching philosophy. Not surprisingly, when coaches make an effort to learn about their athletes' lives outside sport, athletes' enjoyment, commitment, and perceptions of their ability all increase.[27] As you learn about more examples of athlete-centered coaching philosophies, you will become better equipped to create and communicate your own athlete-centered coaching philosophy.

## CREATING YOUR OWN ATHLETE-CENTERED COACHING PHILOSOPHY

An athlete-centered coaching philosophy requires constant attention because the profile of athletes changes every year, if not every season. Although athletes may enter and leave a program frequently, keeping athlete profile cards allows a coach to notice tendencies and coaching strategies that are effective for working with various types of athletes.

Coach Wooden kept index cards with personality traits and effective coaching strategies for each player he coached. This strategy helped him quickly identify athlete tendencies and needs. Even though the athlete may have been new to this program, he could review notes on previous athletes who shared a similar profile.

A sample athlete profile card that will provide coaches with valuable and current information about their athletes is provided in figure 2.4. This type of card provides a place for coaches to record basic information such as date of birth and family profile (e.g., names and ages of close family members), as well as space to note coaching strategies that are most and least effective when working with this athlete. For example, for an athlete who requires extra time to process emotions, beside "Responds best when" a coach might write "given a few extra minutes and more personal space to think through behaviors before I intervene."

Most recently, high-performance coaches are increasingly using cutting-edge tools such as DISC profiling to create detailed athlete profiles. DISC profiling provides coaches with an in-depth awareness of an athlete's behavioral tendencies and communication styles (D = dominance: direct and guarded, I = influence: direct and open, S = steadiness: indirect and open, C = conscientious: indirect and guarded).[28] As part of my work with the U.S. Olympic and national team coach education program, I have seen firsthand the power of comprehensive DISC profiling for high-performance coaches. DISC profiling requires considerable time and guidance from trained facilitators, but several consulting groups work extensively with coaches and athletes who are interested in using this tool.[28, 29]

## Figure 2.4 Athlete Profile Card

Name: ______________________ Date of birth: ______________

Family profile: ______________________

Other athletes on the team connects most with: ______________________

Previous athletes reminds me of: ______________________

Responds best when: ______________________

Responds worst when: ______________________

From W. Gilbert, 2017, *Coaching better every season: A year-round system for athlete development and program success* (Champaign, IL: Human Kinetics).

Maintaining up-to-date knowledge of athletes includes following cultural and demographic trends that shape the views and actions of your athletes. Typically, the age gap between coach and athlete is at least one generation, meaning that different political, social, and cultural histories will have shaped your athletes. Successful coaches understand that they can't rely on the pop culture and sporting examples that shaped their development to convey their coaching philosophy to current athletes.

I recall a high school girls' tennis coach who was frustrated at the team's lack of intensity. The program had suffered from a long history of poor performance, so in his mind the prevailing culture accepted mediocrity. The coach then excitedly told me that he just left a team meeting where he used some examples from legendary winners in sport to try to instill his coaching philosophy and a winner's attitude. I asked him what examples he used, and he told me that he primarily used American professional football coach Vince Lombardi.

Vince Lombardi, one of the most successful coaches in American sport history, was renowned for his fiery and intense character, particularly as it related to making the effort to win. Young high school tennis players, however, aren't likely to be inspired by stories of a coach not from their sport and from an era long ago. To the coach, Lombardi was relevant and meaningful; he represented all the qualities of a winner that resonated with the coach and the generation in which he was raised. The same could not be said for the 15-year-old female tennis players he was coaching in 2015.

The tennis coach would have been much better served by using current examples from women's tennis or other popular athletes to whom the girls would relate. He would have to do some homework, but successful coaches make this type of effort.

Dawn Staley, championship college and Olympic women's basketball coach, is a prime example of a coach who knows how to relate to her athletes. Coach Staley, a superb player herself who transitioned immediately from playing to coaching, found it easy to connect with her athletes in the first few years of her coaching career. But as the age gap widened between her and her players, she found making the connection more challenging. After accepting a new head-coaching position at a high-profile college, the first thing she committed to doing was to update her coaching philosophy to reflect the views and needs of the current generation of athletes she would be coaching.

> I was further from the game since retiring a couple of years earlier, and, to be honest, the gap between my age and the players' ages had widened. It gets more and more difficult to reach the players as quickly as before. Fifteen years ago, it was instant—I could make an immediate connection with a player in no time at all. Five years go by, and it gets harder. Now, 15 years later . . . it's a good thing I like challenges. My goal is always to decrease the amount of time it takes for us to make a connection, because that's where it all starts.[30]

Bryan Lynn/Icon Sportswire

South Carolina Gamecocks head coach Dawn Staley understands the importance of being able to relate to and connect with athletes.

By working diligently to close the coach-athlete generation gap, Coach Staley has become one of the rising stars of coaching. She led her team to a number one national ranking for the first time in school history in 2014.

One way to stay current and close the generation gap between coach and athlete is to review generation profile reports produced by groups such as the Pew Research Center (www.pewresearch.org/millennials/) and Generations at Work.

For example, people born between 1980 and the mid-1990s are commonly referred to as the Millennial generation, also known as Generation Y. Millennials born after 1990 have subsequently been called Generation iY because they are the first generation in history to grow up with social media as a regular part of their everyday lives.[31, 32] Most recently, those born after 1996 have been classified as Generation Z. They have learned from watching their older siblings to be a bit more cautious, private, and sensible with social media than the previous generation.[33] Adopting an athlete-centered coaching philosophy means that coaches must be willing to adapt how they coach to meet the evolving needs and learning styles of athletes from different generations. This approach is essential for building meaningful connections with your athletes, sometimes referred to as cross-generational relationships.

Former professional football coach Jim Tomsula provides a vivid example of how a coach can use knowledge of athlete generational differences to meet athletes where they are, instead of trying to make them adapt to how you were coached or what may have worked for you with previous athletes.

After being hired as the new coach of the San Francisco 49ers, Coach Tomsula, at age 47, acknowledged that he didn't like, or know much about, social media. This attitude was problematic because he inherited a team of athletes with an average age of 25, a Generation iY team. Coach Tomsula realized he would have to adapt his coaching philosophy (his how), not his coaching purpose or core values (his why), to be a more effective coach.

By attending a weekly meeting to learn about new apps and technology being used by his athletes, coach Tomsula and his coaching staff changed how they communicate and teach.[34, 35] The standard 2-hour team meetings were replaced with 30-minute meetings interspersed with 10-minute social media breaks to keep athletes focused and allow them to get their social media fix. Training schedules were sent electronically to athletes instead of being distributed on paper copies as was done in the past. All members of the coaching staff adjusted their coaching philosophy to embrace the new ways that their athletes learn and communicate. As Kevin Clark wrote in the *Wall Street Journal*, "Instead of the coaches making Millennials change, the coaches are changing to better work with the Millennials."[34]

These examples illustrate that coaches need to keep a flexible coaching philosophy that evolves with their athletes, and the only way to do this is to stay current with learning about the profile of your athletes. Regularly updating athlete profile cards and learning about the technological and cultural changes that affect how your athletes learn and communicate are effective ways to build knowledge of your athletes. This knowledge is critical for ensuring that your coaching philosophy stays fresh and relevant.

# USING KEY EVENTS TO SHAPE A COACHING PHILOSOPHY

Critical incidents experienced as a coach can contribute significantly to the development and refinement of a coaching philosophy.[36] And because a coaching philosophy is fluid, evolving as the coach develops as a coach and person, coaches need to reflect frequently on key experiences and ways in which they may alter their approach.

John Wooden's Pyramid of Success was the result of decades of personal reflection stimulated by recurring critical incidents he experienced as a coach and teacher. Coach Wooden acknowledged that it took many years of coaching practice and personal introspection before his coaching behaviors were consistently aligned with his coaching philosophy.[37]

Therefore, you should set aside time each preseason to contemplate how you have dealt with important events in the past and how you will handle them in the future. You may find it particularly beneficial to supplement this type of self-reflection with open and genuine discussions with your trusted coaching peers about how you handle critical incidents. The purpose of group reflection is not to arrive at consensus. Instead, the goal of group discussions on critical incidents is to stretch and test your assumptions about effective coaching and use new insights to refine and update your coaching philosophy.

Critical incidents provide a natural and logical gateway into deeply personal and reflective discussions about coaching philosophies. Some of the more common events and issues that coaches find significant relate to athlete discipline, intensity, focus, commitment, and relationships (between coach and athlete, athlete and athlete, and coach and team). When engaging in critical incident reviews, the events should not be thought of as problems to be solved. Rather, the incidents should be considered simply as points for reflection on fundamental questions about your coaching philosophy.

Human Kinetics Coach Education[38] provides several examples in one of its course workbooks of critical incidents that coaches encounter, particularly in high school settings. In reading and reflecting on each of these coaching scenarios, consider what you would do.

## Playing-Time Scenario

Fall camp is ending, and John, your senior quarterback, comes into your office after practice with a problem. John is a great kid and has become the leader of your team. He's been your starting quarterback for the past two seasons and has been selected as a team captain for the second straight year by his teammates. Over the summer, a transfer quarterback moved into your district, and he's winning the position. John is obviously disappointed. He knows that the backup quarterback gets little playing time over the course of a season, and he wants to quit the team.

## Disrespectful Athlete Behavior Scenario

Kandace, one of your starters, has a problem with authority. She's a good player but constantly complains about calls made by the officials, even when they're obviously correct. In overtime against your league rival, Tamika drives for the basket and is stripped of the ball by an opposing player. The official does not call a foul, and Kandace instantly begins complaining. The official on the other side of the court runs into the play and calls a foul on the defender. Kandace mouths off to the first official and begins beating her chest. She is immediately hit with a technical foul.

## Problem Parent Scenario

Fred is a former baseball player who played in the minor leagues for a few years and is now living in your district. His daughter Sue is a member of your softball team. Fred is continually complaining about your game tactics and the way you're teaching Sue how to hit. He is vocal in the stands at your games and has started attending your practices. He's becoming a real nuisance, and his actions are having a negative effect on Sue's attitude and performance. Sue's teammates are beginning to make fun of her because of her dad. You think you need to do something before Fred's actions wreck the entire season.

## Different Cultural Background Scenario

Mike shows up for your first preseason workout and wants to try out for your wrestling team. After watching him for just a few minutes, you can see that he is a talented athlete who could be a starter. He is a junior and has just moved from another country. At the end of the practice as you work your way through the locker room, you notice that no one is making an effort to speak with Mike. You have always talked to your team about the importance of respecting each other as teammates, but this group has never had a teammate from another country.

Reprinted, by permission, from American Sport Education Program, 2012. *Coaching principles workbook,* 4th ed. (Champaign, IL: Human Kinetics), 15, 16, 60.

What do the responses you envisioned making to each of these four incidents tell you about your coaching philosophy? Is this philosophy aligned with your coaching purpose and core values? Is this philosophy consistent with the values of your current generation of athletes? Reflecting on such circumstances and your reaction to them, and perhaps discussing them with other coaches, will help you further form and refine your coaching philosophy.

Another valuable resource for this type of exercise is the book about coaching dilemmas published by Timothy Baghurst and Anthony Parish,[39] which includes a wide range of detailed coaching scenarios such as coaching girls versus coaching boys, running up the score, stretching the rules, and athlete injuries.

I vividly recall a critical incident discussion I had with one of my former students who had secured a position as a head coach of a collegiate team. The coach called me seeking guidance near the end of the season. Although the team had experienced tremendous early season success, they were in the midst of a prolonged late-season losing streak. We spent the first hour of our conversation in problem-setting mode. I asked questions such as the following in an attempt to stimulate coach reflection on the critical incident, particularly as it related to the coach's philosophy: Why do you think the team is struggling? How are the athletes coping with this issue? What do you think they need at this moment?

This coach's philosophy was certainly athlete-centered; the coach believed in providing athletes with choice and input into team decisions. I challenged the coach to connect potential strategies for resolving the critical incident back to this athlete-centered coaching philosophy. The coach, in a hurried attempt to solve the problem, lost sight of the coaching philosophy that had guided early season coaching decisions. The coach had shifted into a coach-centered approach—coach as sole leader, director, and problem solver for the team.

After much discussion and agreement that no significant technical or tactical issues were plaguing the team, we decided to give complete ownership of the final practice before the playoffs to the team. With only one practice remaining the primary goal would be to enact and reinforce the core values and coaching philosophy (shared leadership and athlete autonomy). Regardless of the playoff outcome, we could then be assured that the critical incident would be used as a teachable moment, particularly for those athletes who would be returning the following season.

The team, although somewhat baffled at first because they were expecting the coach to lead them out of their dismal situation (i.e., solve the problem), responded beautifully to the opportunity. The coach remained to observe the practice from a distance and noted that the team embraced the challenge and completed the practice with joy and enthusiasm. In essence, this one moment was a reminder for them to take ownership of their situation and play with purpose and passion. The team proceeded to set a school record for wins and advanced further into the playoffs than any team in school history. The moral of this critical incident story is that as a coach you must pause and reflect on a regular basis and use your coaching philosophy as a guide to pose questions about how you coach.

## COMMUNICATING YOUR COACHING PHILOSOPHY

Effective coaches often employ storytelling to help convey the principles of their coaching philosophy, not only to their athletes but also to members of their coaching staff, the sport organization, and the media. Leaders across history and disciplines have used stories because they are powerful tools that connect with both our logic and our emotion.

Renowned psychologist and leadership guru Howard Gardner identified three types of stories used by effective leaders: (*a*) stories about the self, (*b*) stories about the group, and (*c*) stories about values and meanings.[40]

Self-disclosure, or stories about yourself, provides a genuine and intimate opportunity to teach your athletes not only about the principles of your coaching philosophy but also about how you formed your philosophy. The key is making that journey and its outcome meaningful to the athletes. Championship football coach Pete Carroll made sharing personal stories a feature of training camp heading into the 2016 NFL season. Athletes believed that hearing details about Coach Carroll's personal history and life decisions that shaped his coaching philosophy was very helpful, with one high-profile player noting that "it helped us to reconnect with him, to relate with him."[41]

Sharing stories about the group, a tactic of the New Zealand All Blacks rugby team coaching staff who tell tales of battles encountered and won by past teams (see chapter 1), both instill a sense of pride and reinforce a philosophy.

Stories about values and meaning can be a bit more complex, but they can be effective when handled adroitly. For example, 11-time championship professional basketball coach Phil Jackson used a passage from Rudyard Kipling's *The Second Jungle Book* to teach his 1990–1991 Chicago Bulls team, including Michael Jordan, about the importance of developing group intelligence and harmonious play.[42 (p. 91)] He explained how he was looking for a story that summed up the principle of group dynamics that he thought that particular team needed to integrate into their philosophy. The passage, reprinted here, was eventually adopted as the team motto and helped propel the team to their first championship:

> Now this is the Law of the Jungle—as old and true as the sky;
>
> And the Wolf that shall keep it may prosper, but the Wolf that shall break must die.
>
> As the creeper that girdles the tree-trunk, the Law runneth forward and back—
>
> For the strength of the Pack is the Wolf, and the strength of the Wolf is the Pack.

Great coaches also know that they alone cannot be the sole storytellers on the team if they want their athletes to embrace their coaching philosophy. For example, Hall of Fame championship American college coach Sharon Pfluger created a pregame storytelling tradition called the Psych.[43] Every member of the team is paired with a teammate and is responsible for a pregame message, or story, that could be in the form of a poem, a personal thought, or even a gift that represents the message. Coach Pfluger believes that this long-standing storytelling tradition is one of the keys to her unprecedented success, having coached teams to 19 collegiate championships in two sports (11 in lacrosse and 8 in field hockey).

With the advent of social media platforms, storytelling options have greatly increased for coaches. As a coach you can quickly and easily share inspirational quotations, media reports, and your own creations to reinforce your coaching philosophy.

Although many successful coaches use storytelling as a way to express and model their coaching philosophy, storytelling is also a valuable way for coaches to refine and improve their philosophy.[44] Coaches may find it easier and more practical to write a story about times when they believe they modeled an athlete-centered philosophy than to write a philosophy statement. Taking time when out of season to write short stories about coaching situations that vividly represent the underlying ideals of their athlete-centered philosophy will force coaches to examine how well their behaviors align with the philosophy. Ultimately, as influential coaching author Rainer Martens noted, "A philosophy is not really expressed by what you say, but by what you do!"[45 (p. 13)]

If you work with athletes of high school age or younger, scheduling time in the preseason to share your coaching philosophy with parents is critical. Many coaches cite dealing with parent issues as the greatest source of stress, and coaches often jest that the best place to coach is at an orphanage.

The most widely recommended strategy for communicating your coaching philosophy with parents is to hold a preseason parent orientation meeting.[46, 47] Ideally, this meeting will be scheduled a during or after a team practice session to minimize scheduling conflicts and time demands. For example, the meeting can be held at the end of a practice when most parents typically are returning home from work. During the meeting the athletes can scrimmage under the supervision of another member of the coaching staff.

You should plan to set aside at least 45 minutes for your preseason parent meeting. A sample agenda for a parent preseason orientation meeting is provided in figure 2.5. Although the primary purpose of the meeting will be to share your coaching philosophy, in the meeting you should also address expectations, logistics, and common questions and parent concerns.

## Figure 2.5 Agenda for Preseason Parent Orientation Meeting

**Coach introductions** (3 minutes)

Thank parents for attending and recognize their contribution to the sport experience, share your coaching history and qualifications, offer other personal information deemed relevant to your role (occupation).

**Philosophy** (5 minutes)

Overview of the key points that guide and shape your coaching philosophy (role and purpose of competitive sport, teaching style, role of the coach, views on athlete development), and sources that have informed your philosophy (influential coaches, coaching and athletic experiences, clinics, research or literature), goals for the season.

**Expectations** (7 minutes)

Standards, expectations, and rules for coach, athlete, and parent behavior (communication guidelines, codes of conduct).

**Logistics** (10 minutes)

Overview of practice and competition schedule and sites, practice length, time athletes are expected to arrive before events, tournament and postseason schedules, use of social media or team apps to communicate and share updates, team functions (banquets, team-building, or social events).

**Common questions** (8 minutes)

Assignment of athlete roles and playing time, nutrition and supplements, rules and equipment, insurance or medical examinations, safety (concussion or injury protocols, heat and hydration guidelines), relevant online videos and other resources for parents to learn more information and view demonstrations.

**Open discussion** (12 minutes)

Encourage parents to share their insights (not just questions) about how to work together to make this a positive sport experience.

Many coaches also find it helpful to send a letter to parents before the meeting in which they describe their coaching philosophy. This information gives parents time to reflect on how your coaching philosophy aligns with their views and expectations for the sport experience, leading to a more productive discussion at the meeting. An example of a parent letter written by a high school varsity basketball coach is provided in figure 2.6.[46]

## Figure 2.6 Sample Preseason Letter to Parents—High School Basketball

Dear Parents,

I would like to take this time to explain my philosophy of coaching and describe how your daughter will be involved with our basketball program.

I strongly believe that the foundation of a successful program is discipline. The discipline that I am referring to is explained in our guide booklet under our team commitments. I expect our basketball players to abide by all school rules and regulations as well as our team commitments.

Because your daughter has elected to try out for our team, I want to address the question of participation. Basketball is an extracurricular activity. It is completely voluntary, but after your daughter makes the decision to try it, I hope you will encourage her to be committed and participate fully until the end of the season. If a player makes the decision to leave the team, I would want to discuss that decision with the player and her parents to make sure that all sides involved have the opportunity to express their ideas and concerns. After the decision is made, we need to stand by the decision.

I also need to say that no player is guaranteed any playing time whatsoever. Playing time is earned with quality practice time. The coaching staff makes that determination.

A common question that arises concerns who will play JV basketball. JV basketball is reserved for all sophomores and juniors. Any freshman choosing not to play freshman basketball for reasons other than participation in a different fall sport must get permission of the coaching staff, administration, and parents, before the freshman season, to try out for JV or varsity basketball. Those players choosing to participate in a different fall sport will be given the opportunity to try out for JV or varsity basketball.

A major part of our program centers on academics. We are governed by the PIAA, which requires a student athlete to be passing a minimum of four credits. This is monitored through biweekly and triweekly grade checks.

To improve our chances of accomplishing our goals for this program, we need several things to happen. First, we need to avoid injuries. Second, we need to show our athletes that education is first and athletics are second. If an athlete is not eligible, she cannot participate. Finally, we need to accept our roles in the game. The coaching staff realizes that we can't please everyone all the time. My job is to operate a program that will provide a sound educational experience for our players. Remember that your role is to provide encouragement and support for your daughter. I'm sure she will experience both success and disappointment at some time in life. I hope she will learn how to deal with both and discuss both situations with you and me alike. It will be helpful when discussing basketball to do it in a positive, encouraging manner for the betterment of our team.

Looking forward to seeing you in the stands.

— *Varsity Head Basketball Coach*

Perhaps the most famous example of a coach philosophy letter to parents is the one written by professional baseball coach Mike Matheny when he was coaching his son's youth baseball team. The letter, commonly referred to as the Matheny Manifesto, can be downloaded free at his website (http://mikematheny.com/#manifesto). A review of his letter may provide you with some ideas on how to write your own letter to parents.

## Wrap-Up

Your ability to reach your potential as a coach, and in turn help your athletes become their best, in sport and in life, hinges on a commitment to identifying and living your coaching philosophy. A coaching philosophy guides how you will coach, also referred to as your functional competence. Building and refining a coaching philosophy requires knowledge of yourself, knowledge of your athletes, and knowledge of your sport—the same three characteristics that define effective coaching. The most effective coaches use this knowledge to navigate the many challenging tasks of a coach, referred to as your task-related competence.

Although you will need to model a coaching philosophy that is true to your personality, purpose, and core values, compelling evidence shows that the world's most successful coaches adopt an athlete-centered coaching philosophy. Examples such as *International Sport Coaching Framework* and the Pyramid of Teaching Success in Sport, together with models from championship coaches, provide ideal starting points for sharpening your coaching philosophy. Keep your coaching philosophy current and relevant by staying abreast of the needs and profiles of your current generation of athletes, and use tools such as storytelling to teach them about the underlying values that shape your approach to coaching.

# Chapter 3

# Set Target Outcomes

**Key Concepts**

Target outcomes
Target conditions
Sharing a vision
Pillars of success
Goal setting
SMART goals
Goal-setting paradox
Performance gap charting
Monitoring goal progress
High-impact performance targets

When was the last time you got in your car with your family or a group of friends and just started driving aimlessly? If you've never done this, try it sometime. You can be sure that almost immediately someone in the car will ask, "Where are we going?" Entering a season without a clear sense of what you and your athletes aspire to achieve is like driving around without a destination. Eventually, you will arrive somewhere, but as legendary Hall of Fame baseball coach and player Yogi Berra famously quipped, "If you don't know where you are going, you might not get there."[1 (p. 53)]

The exceptional persistence and discipline needed to maintain difficult training schedules over many months, or in some cases years, that make up a competition cycle requires a compelling and inspirational target. All coaches set goals; that is certain. Much can be learned, however, about how to set, monitor, and adjust goals.

Renowned American swim coach James "Doc" Counsilman, considered one of the great innovators in the history of coaching, concluded, "A good coach sets goals with his athletes, but realizes that they aren't ground in stone. You have to be flexible and realistic and avoid setting goals that are incompatible with your athletes' ability."[2 (p. 354)] Coach Counsilman's observations about goal setting are rich with insights. Notice he emphasized setting goals *with* his athletes, not *for* his athletes. Also, observe his advice about setting realistic goals that fit each athlete and the importance of using goals as a guide instead of a fixed point.

In the past few years I have shifted from exclusively using terms such as *goals* and *goal setting* to more of an emphasis on the terms *target outcomes* and *target conditions*. By definition, goals and targets are nearly synonymous. The word *target*, however, immediately brings to mind an image of something you aim to hit from a distance. This image also reinforces that a gap separates you from the target. In coaching, however, where the gap is represented as time (i.e., preseason to postseason), that gap is filled with countless unforeseeable events. Just as when you physically try to hit a target, you use feedback from each attempt to adjust the next shot. These small incremental adjustments are the only way to close the gap between your current performance and your target outcome.

Closing gaps between "what is" and "what is possible" will keep your focus on the process and the next best step—referred to as the target conditions.[3] Constant monitoring of your athletes' ability to take the next best step provides you with insight for fine-tuning coaching strategies needed to move across the gap. In sum, the best way to increase your chances of hitting the target is to work diligently and efficiently to close performance gaps.

Perhaps the most valuable aspect of setting performance targets and identifying the required target conditions is that it provides you with a simple tool for aligning your coaching purpose, core values, and everyday coaching actions. The most successful coaches use a variety of strategies to set and evaluate target outcomes and target conditions. This chapter will help you identify the strategies that will work best for you to chart the most direct path to your target destination.

## SHARING A CLEAR VISION

Before setting goals with your athletes, you must set aside time to share a compelling vision for what is possible. Setting a goal to win a league championship provides the target, but unwavering commitment to doing all the little things needed to achieve the target will fade without a strong vision for why the goal is worth pursuing. Using the car analogy again, goals pinpoint the destination and vision provides the fuel needed to get there. Painting a clear vision gives purpose to the journey and answers the question "Why do we want to go there?"[4]

Championship coaches like Pete Carroll understand that vision must always come before goals. In his words, "You need the ability to illustrate the big picture—and then set the wheels in motion."[5 (p. 322)] Holding a preseason vision meeting with your athletes is a time-tested strategy for setting the wheels in motion. At the start of the meeting you should ask the athletes to identify their target outcomes for the season. To make the shift from targets to vision, you then need to ask the athletes to describe not just the target outcome but also the type of experience they would like to have and the way they will want to remember the season.

Sport psychologist and leadership consultant Jeff Janssen, who has helped many championship coaches use this approach, recommends posing the following three questions to athletes in the preseason vision meeting:[4 (p. 39)]

- What could we achieve if we really put our hearts and minds to it?
- How far could we go if everything came together by the end of the season?
- What kind of season would we like to have so that we look back on it with fondness and feel it was worth all the time and energy we put into it?

After these questions have been answered, athletes are asked to identify the 10 most important characteristics that all team members will need to have to reach their target outcome for the season. Janssen refers to these characteristics as the pillars of success. Much like pillars that support a structure, the characteristics have to remain tall and strong across a season for a team to achieve daring target outcomes.

Each player is required to print his or her 10 characteristics on a separate sheet of paper as an individual exercise in a group meeting. Time is then set aside for a group discussion on the characteristics until consensus is achieved. The pillars of success are the target conditions—the "ways of being" that members of the team must whole-heartedly adopt to increase the likelihood of achieving the target outcomes. Examples of the pillars of success, identified by successful teams Janssen has worked with, include the following:

- Swimming and diving: fun, dedication, respect, confidence, team pride, support, mental toughness, communication, consistent work ethic
- Basketball: accepting roles, communication between players, communication with coaches, confidence, hard work, discipline, desire, talent, unselfishness, responsibility, enthusiasm, unity
- Gymnastics: sacrifice, respect, positive, keep problems outside gym, motivated, accepting roles, daily goals, give 100 percent, communication, team pride

With the pillars of success firmly in place, Janssen recommends holding a formal ritual in which each athlete signs a contract that demonstrates her or his commitment to honor the vision and the pillars.

Some coaches, like championship rugby coach Nick Hill, prefer to have just the head coach and captain sign on behalf of the team at the end of the team vision meeting. Figure 3.1 is an example shared by Coach Hill with an under-18 boys' team that went undefeated, something the club had achieved just once in 45 years.

Completing this type of preseason vision meeting works because it ensures that athletes take an active role in setting the target outcomes, provides them with a compelling vision for why the targets matter, gives them guidance on how to get there, and results in a written display of the targets and the team's commitment to the journey.[6]

The relationship between target outcomes, vision, and target conditions is summarized in figure 3.2. This visual provides a simple reminder for coaches to keep in mind that target outcomes provide the destination, vision fuels the journey, and target conditions help athletes stay focused on the behaviors and mind-set needed to close the gap between where they are and where they want to go.

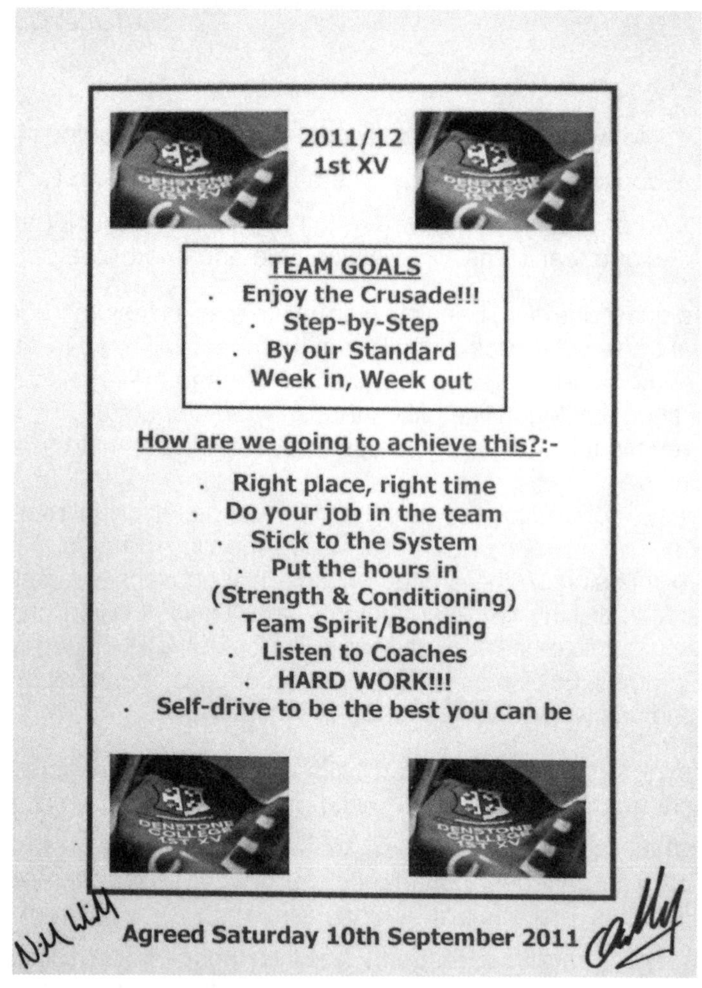

2011/12
1st XV

TEAM GOALS

- Enjoy the Crusade!!!
- Step-by-Step
- By our Standard
- Week in, Week out

How are we going to achieve this?:-

- Right place, right time
- Do your job in the team
- Stick to the System
- Put the hours in (Strength & Conditioning)
- Team Spirit/Bonding
- Listen to Coaches
- HARD WORK!!!
- Self-drive to be the best you can be

Agreed Saturday 10th September 2011

**Figure 3.1** Under-18 boys rugby team contract.

Courtesy of Coach Nick Hill (www.nickhillcoaching.com).

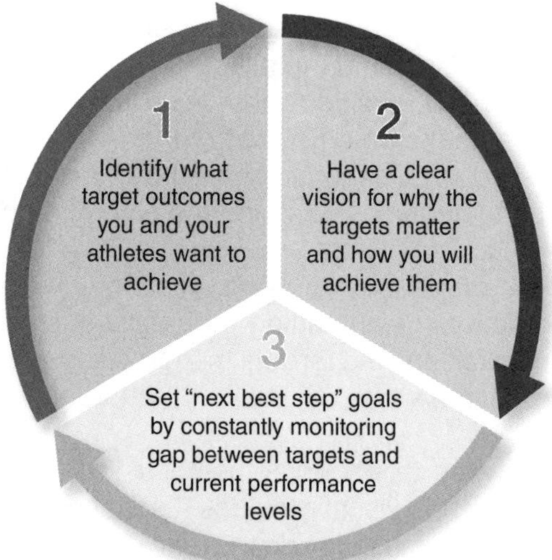


**Figure 3.2** The relationship between target outcomes, vision, and target conditions.

# SETTING EFFECTIVE GOALS

Hundreds of studies have been published on goal setting in sport.[6–8] The consensus is that goal setting is perhaps the most effective and important strategy that a coach can use to build a successful sport program. Evidence shows that goal setting is well worth the effort.[9] Goals direct attention to the behaviors and attitudes that affect performance. Setting goals raises excitement about the journey ahead, resulting in a more satisfying experience for coaches and athletes. Finally, goals lead to the higher levels of effort and persistence needed to complete the journey.

Most goal-setting approaches can be traced back to a simple framework proposed nearly 40 years ago, referred to as the SMART way to write goals.[10] Goals are SMART when they are **s**pecific (clearly written), **m**easurable (progress can be observed and tracked), **a**ttainable (appropriate training resources and coaching support are provided), **r**ealistic (within reach of the athlete's current level of performance), and **t**ime bound (have a due date).

Examples of SMART goals for various sports, written by Dr. Damon Burton and Dr. Thomas Raedeke, experts on goal setting and coaching, are listed here.[6] Keep in mind that although these goals are specific, measurable, and time bound, only you will know what is attainable and realistic with your particular athletes.

- To run the 1,500-meter race on Saturday in 3:57.
- To keep the player I'm guarding from having more than three open shots in the next game.
- To make solid contact with the ball 80 percent of the time in batting practice this week.
- To block the correct person every time in today's scrimmage.
- To score a 72 in the golf championship on Tuesday.
- To extend my concentration at practice today from five to six minutes.

The SMART approach to setting goals is appealing because of its simplicity. Decades of research shows that for goal setting to be effective, coaches need a deeper understanding of the goal-setting process.[11] The key findings for coaches from this goal-setting research are the following:

- Goals that are ambitious, but realistic, are most effective.
- To increase their commitment to the goals, athletes must be included in the goal-setting process.
- Goals should be set for both the individual athlete and the team as a whole.
- Although putting goals in writing is helpful, whatever method is used must ensure that the goals are clear to athletes and coaches alike.
- Goals should be stated in positive terms (what they will do) to encourage athletes to focus on what they want to achieve, as opposed to negative behaviors they should avoid.
- Short-term and long-term goals are needed; the short-term goals should represent the incremental steps needed to achieve the long-term goals.

- Besides stating the outcome, goals should be set for how the outcome will be achieved (referred to as process and performance goals).
- Process goals describe how a skill should be performed (e.g., follow through on a shot). Performance goals describe how well a skill should be performed (e.g., make 75 percent of your free throws in basketball).
- Goals must be regularly evaluated and adjusted to fit the current reality of the athletes and coaches (e.g., goals may need to be lowered because of injury or raised because of advances in techniques or equipment).

Although most athletes and coaches recognize the importance of goal setting, they do not consistently follow these goal-setting principles. Setting and regularly evaluating goals require a considerable time commitment from coaches. The time is well spent, however, because teams led by coaches who use these goal-setting principles have a higher sense of team cohesion, play better together, work harder for each other, and stay more focused on achieving their goals than teams led by coaches who neglect the principles.[12]

A series of studies with tennis athletes and their coaches highlights both the strength of these goal-setting principles and potential goal-setting challenges.[13] Athletes overwhelmingly preferred moderately difficult goals that were focused on specific tennis skills, physical conditioning, motivation, and general tennis strategies. Participating in setting their own goals, trusting their coach's expertise, and being rewarded for achieving their goals all increased commitment to the goals. On the other hand, factors cited as barriers to achieving goals included lack of time, too many goals, lack of confidence in ability to achieve the goals, and goals that were too vague.

Although coaches' perceptions on goal setting matched athlete responses fairly well, some important differences were identified. For example, coaches believed that setting team goals was more effective than reported by the athletes. Also, coaches believed that peer pressure and writing down goals were stronger influences on goal-setting effectiveness than did their athletes. Lastly, athletes tended to set more outcome goals than the coaches did.

Two follow-up studies were then completed by the same researchers with high school and college coaches from across a wide range of individual and team sports.[14, 15] The coaches were selected based on their reputation and self-identification as goal setters. Team goals were typically first dictated by the coaches but then adjusted with athlete feedback. Athletes were given much more ownership of their individual goals. Goal-setting practices were often nonsystematic and very loose. Many goals were not formally written down or even formally evaluated, but the coaches did acknowledge a conscious effort to identify goals and monitor progress toward goal achievement.

Both objective and subjective information was used to inform goal evaluation and adjustments. Objective information included practice and competition statistics, whereas subjective information included coach and athlete feedback. Coaches also tended to set goals a bit too high, creating undue pressure on both themselves and their athletes. Coaches must be careful to temper their preseason expectations with a realistic assessment of the current needs and abilities of their athletes. Lastly, regardless of the sport or goal-setting strategies used, common barriers to goal achievement included mental (lack of confidence, effort, motivation, or attitude; excessive pressure) and physical (injury, illness, lack of ability) challenges.

Avoiding goal-setting disagreements or confusion can be accomplished through regularly questioning, listening to, and observing the athlete over the course of a season.[16] This approach will reduce the likelihood of goal-setting missteps and create a shared understanding of athlete and coach goals, emotions, and perceptions of ability. The unique playing environment that shapes each athlete's experience (e.g., his or her role on the team, composition of the team, sport culture) must also be considered when evaluating goals. An overview of this approach to effective goal setting is provided in figure 3.3.

## Program Targets

Successful coaches understand that setting athlete and team goals is not enough to build a culture of sustained excellence. Athlete and team goals are important, but ultimately they must build toward the broader goals for the program. Setting program goals requires coaches to look far into the future and envision their dream for the program. Thinking about program goals is a legacy-building exercise. The best coaches are visionaries, and they see their programs for what they eventually can become, not just for what is possible this season.[27]

When Coach Geno Auriemma took over as head coach of the University of Connecticut women's basketball team in 1985, the program looked nothing like the 11-time national championship setting that it became. They didn't remotely resemble a championship program. In his words, they had "no history, no office, no fans, no real gym, and metal bleachers they only roll out for the really big games. The problem with that is, back then, there are no big games."[28 (p. 22)]

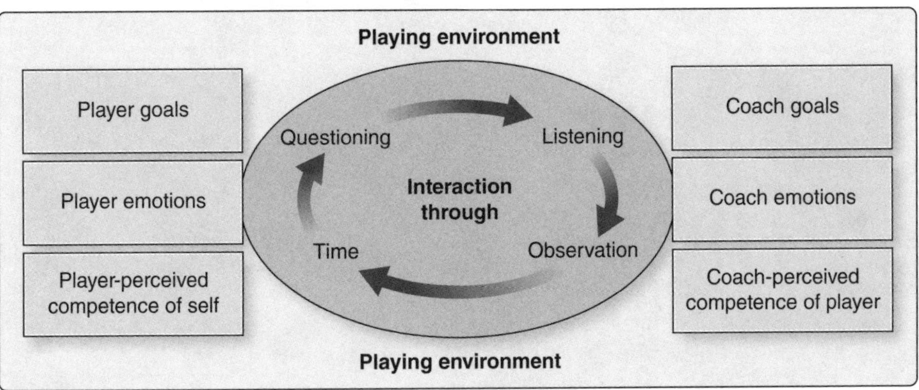


**Figure 3.3** Avoiding goal-setting disagreements or confusion can be accomplished through regularly questioning, listening to, and observing the athlete.

From A. Maitland and M. Gervis, 2010, "Goal-setting in youth football. Are coaches missing an opportunity?" *Physical Education and Sport Pedagogy* 15(4): 323-343. © Association for Physical Education. Reprinted by permission of Taylor & Francis Ltd, www.tandfonline.com, on behalf of Association for Physical Education.

The first thing Coach Auriemma did when he met with the team was set performance goals. The immediate goal was not to finish in the last two spots in their league, a place they had become accustomed to finishing, because those two teams had to play an elimination game to qualify for the year-end league tournament. This goal was certainly not the vision for excellence that Coach Auriemma had for the program, but it was a SMART goal for that season.

Coach Auriemma quickly realized that to build a national powerhouse in women's basketball, he needed to focus on goals for the program that far exceeded the goals of his current group of athletes. He and his coaching staff identified recruiting as their number one program goal. They understood that to achieve their BHAGs (big hairy audacious goals), they needed to recruit athletes who shared the same vision and were capable of making that type of commitment to excellence.

From that moment on, he committed himself to investing all his energy into creating the type of program that would appeal to the nation's best basketball athletes—one where the best athletes could realize their personal goals while competing against the best in the nation. Progress was slow, but steady, and the program is now considered the greatest of all time in women's college basketball.

The lesson to take from Coach Auriemma and other championship coaches is that momentary athlete and team goals must always be considered within a broader vision for the program. Program vision provides meaning and hope to a coach's work, gives purpose to his or her leadership, and acts as a shield

AP Photo/Alex Brandon

Head coach Geno Auriemma giving performance feedback to center Tina Charles during a game.

against burnout by helping the coach look beyond the ups and downs of any one particular season.

In the remainder of this section, I share an example from my work of how I helped high school coaches set annual program targets that build toward a culture of sustained excellence. The example is based on a five-year partnership with a large high school athletics department, working across 23 sports.

During the preseason each head coach participates in a 30 to 45-minute preseason target outcomes meeting with the athletics director. The coach and the athletics director jointly set target outcomes related to four core values that underpin the athletics program: participation (maximize sport participation at the school), retention (inspire student-athletes to return to the team each year), engagement (create positive sport experiences that optimize athlete learning), and competitiveness (develop athletes and teams who consistently demonstrate high levels of performance). The coaches have learned that a commitment to setting SMART targets related to each of these core values helps them realize their vision of becoming a program of excellence.

For participation, a target is set for ideal program size (e.g., How many student-athletes ideally should we have in our soccer program to ensure we have a healthy and competitive program?). Program size refers to all levels of participation at the school—freshman team, junior varsity team, and varsity team. The target outcome is set by careful analysis of multiple factors that affect participation in this setting, such as available resources to support the team, previous roster sizes, and history and tradition of the sport at the school. This step is important in setting a realistic and meaningful participation target outcome. The ideal roster size must be practical, but because participation is a core value, the target outcome should be somewhat challenging to achieve. In this sense the target outcome serves to motivate the coach to build an exciting sport program that will attract student-athletes to the team.

For retention, we always set the target outcome at 75 percent. Students who graduate from the school are not counted when setting the retention target. Although when we first started this project we aspired for a retention target of 100 percent, we quickly realized that even in the best situations expecting every student-athlete from the previous season to participate the following season is not practical. For example, in a large high school (more than 2,500 students) new students who regularly move into the school each year may displace existing members of a sport team. Also, although coaches typically can make room for all eligible and interested participants on freshman and junior varsity teams, rules limit the roster size of varsity teams. Based on the results we have seen, the best coaches in this setting are able to retain approximately 75 percent of their potential returning student-athletes each season. Maintaining a high retention rate for a high school sport program is critical for sustaining team culture and traditions.

Successful programs are led by coaches who create positive sport experiences that optimize athlete learning, something we refer to as engagement. We measure athlete engagement each season by asking athletes about their experience in the program. Based on a comprehensive review of the research on quality coaching and expected athlete learning outcomes,[29, 30] along with coaching behavior guidelines used in this particular school district, we created a brief questionnaire that each athlete completes at the end of the season.

Student-athletes are asked to rate their experience on a 7-point scale (1–3 negative, 4 neutral, 5–7 positive). We set the same engagement program target for every coach: to have all student-athlete responses in the 5 to 7 range (positive scores). The full questionnaire and a detailed account of how it is used in the postseason appear in part 3 (postseason) of this book. Sample questions include the following:

- My coach prepared me to meet the physical demands of my sport.
- My coach made sure I really understood the goals of the team for the season.
- My coach treated all players, parents, officials, fans, and fellow coaches with respect.
- I trust my coach.

The final core value for which we set target outcomes is competitiveness. This area requires much more discussion than the participation, retention, and engagement targets. Each coach is asked to identify 7 to 10 high-impact performance targets. Examples of sport-specific competitiveness indicators include runs scored (baseball and softball), yards rushing (football), first-serve percentage (tennis), shots on net (soccer), and pars per round (golf).

Each coach is challenged to think of performance targets that if achieved would put their athletes and teams in position to be consistently competitive. The focus is on identifying targets that are known, in this type of sport setting, to be linked to success. For example, the baseball coach, whose teams have won over 600 games in his coaching career, has learned that teams have the greatest chance of winning if they meet the following targets each game: allow fewer than three walks, commit fewer than three errors, put at least 10 runners on base, strike out less than the opponent does, and win the late innings (fifth through seventh). These standards are what we refer to as high-impact performance targets; they matter because they have been shown over time to be highly associated with team success.

Note that these high-impact performance targets are negotiated each season with each coach. The targets need to be realistic and may need slight adjustments each season because of factors such as strength of schedule and team composition. We view each coach as a content expert—they know their athletes and their sport—so they are in the strongest position to determine the right high-impact performance targets each season. Taking this approach also provides the coaches with ownership of the goal-setting experience, thereby increasing their commitment and motivation to help their teams achieve the goals. The role of the athletics director is to stretch the coach to set challenging yet realistic competitiveness targets each season.

A sample overview of program targets for the sport of football is provided in figure 3.4. The head football coach who helped identify these program targets is renowned for rebuilding losing high school football programs and has been recognized over his three-decade career with multiple Coach of the Year awards.

**Figure 3.4 Fresno High School Football Program Targets Example**

| Target outcome | Program targets | Evidence |
|---|---|---|
| Participation | 115 student-athletes (40 on freshman team, 30 on junior varsity team, 45 on varsity team) | Final rosters |
| Retention | 75 percent of potential returners (all student-athletes who are enrolled in the school from the previous season's teams) | Final rosters |
| Engagement | All student-athlete responses in the 5 to 7 range (positive scores on a 7-point scale) | Student-athlete questionnaire |
| Competitiveness | Season: win rivalry game, top three finish in league, playoff win, all-league recognition for at least two athletes<br>Per game: fewer than two turnovers, rush for 175 or more yards, pass for 150 or more yards, fewer than four offensive penalties, fewer than four defensive penalties, no kicks blocked, no returns allowed for touchdowns, hold opponent to less than 150 yards rushing and less than 70 yards passing | Season statistics |

This example shows how we set meaningful program targets that, if achieved each season, will lead to a sustained culture of program excellence.

## Athlete Targets

When setting goals with your athletes, your target outcomes must simultaneously be realistic and daring. Athletes are competitive by nature and will usually set daring long-term goals such as winning the league championship or becoming the best in the league (or the world). These targets are what leadership experts Jim Collins and Jerry Porras refer to as BHAGs, or big hairy audacious goals.[17]

Through their extensive research they discovered that the world's most successful companies all set BHAGs as a way to inspire and motivate their teams to sustain coordinated collective effort over long periods. In their words, BHAGs provide a catalyst for team spirit. Although BHAGs are inspiring, the chance is good they will not be achieved, at least in the short term. In fact, Collins and Porras conclude that BHAGs may be achieved only 50 to 70 percent of the time. This probability of success is fine as long as the group believes that achieving the BHAG is possible.

The target outcomes that you set with your athletes should stretch the group, including you, but they will be valued only if they are grounded in a realistic evaluation of your current conditions. Achievement of the BHAGs that you and your athletes set may not be possible for several years, but—and this is a key point—the team must believe that although the task is daunting, achieving the

BHAGs is possible if everyone commits to the intermediate target conditions, or process goals.

Jeff Janssen[4] likes to start the process of setting target outcomes by asking coaches and their athletes to answer two questions honestly: What can you achieve? and What do you want to achieve? When answering the first question you should consider things such as the athletes' current talent level, strength of schedule, and past performances. When answering the second question you should help your athletes align their wants with the purpose, core values, and coaching philosophy that define your program.

Dr. David Yukelson, long-time sport psychology consultant to championship coaches and teams at Penn State University, recommends using a three-step goal-setting activity with athletes in the preseason.[18] Each athlete is asked to respond, in writing, to three prompts:

1. List three goals for the upcoming season.
2. List potential barriers or challenges you foresee that will keep the team from achieving these goals.
3. List three things you personally will need to contribute to the team to increase the likelihood that the team will reach their goals.

This type of simple exercise has numerous benefits. First, it provides you with insight into your athletes' perceptions of what is possible this season. Second, it alerts you to potential issues to watch for that may already be infecting the team. Third, it provides athletes with a sense of ownership and personal investment into the goal-setting process.

From the athletes' perspective, goal setting is always driven by their deeply held desire for independence, perceived ability, and craving for feedback and approval from the coach.[15] These competing interests—freedom and support—represent a sort of goal-setting paradox for coaches.

On the one hand, athletes must be given freedom to set and shape their goals. On the other hand, these goals must align with coach and team goals and values. One of the greatest challenges that coaches face is learning how to balance what athletes want to, and think they can, achieve with what the coach believes is best for the team and the role that each athlete needs to play. In the words of one experienced high school coach, "There are things they want to do and things they need [to] do. My job is to make those two things the same."[19 (p. 68)]

Effective goal setting requires an ongoing open and honest discussion between coach and athlete to share their reasons for setting certain goals. A commitment to this goal-setting conversation, initiated in the preseason and continued throughout the season, will allow coaches to identify important ways for increasing and sustaining athlete motivation to counter goal achievement setbacks and challenges.

Building on the research evidence and suggestions from leading sport psychology consultants, I have created a tool that coaches can use to deal with the goal-setting paradox and bridge the potential gap between an athlete-set goal and a coach-set goal. I refer to this tool as the athlete and coach shared goal-setting worksheet (see figure 3.5).

## Figure 3.5 Athlete and Coach Shared Goal-Setting Worksheet

Athlete: ______________________ Coach: ______________________

Season (time frame for achieving the goals): ______________________

### Athlete goals

What do you believe is possible this season?

1.

2.

3.

4.

5.

### Coach goal feedback

What the coach believes is possible and what challenges might affect goal achievement.

1.

2.

3.

4.

5.

### Updated athlete goals

Based on the coach's feedback, write your updated goals.

1.

2.

3.

4.

5.

I agree that these goals are attainable and commit to doing whatever is necessary to overcome potential challenges to achieving these goals this season.

______________________ ______________________

Athlete signature Coach signature

From W. Gilbert, 2017, *Coaching better every season: A year-round system for athlete development and program success* (Champaign, IL: Human Kinetics).

Completion of this worksheet requires three steps. The first step is to have the athlete write her or his goals for the upcoming season. These can, and should, include a range of outcome, performance, and process goals. Space is set aside for five goals in the worksheet as a way to help the athlete get started.

The second step is for the coach to read the athlete's goals and reflect on how appropriate each goal is for that particular athlete. Coaches should refer back to the goal-setting principles presented earlier in this chapter as a guide for evaluating the athlete's written goals.

For example, the athlete's perception of what a SMART goal is may not match what the coach believes is appropriate. Athletes may set goals too high when they are not ready for the challenge. Coaches may set goals too low, believing that the athletes aren't yet capable, although they may be closer than the coach realizes. The only way to ensure that the right targets are set is for the coach and athlete to share their perceptions of what is possible.

The coach should think of potential challenges that could affect the athlete's ability to achieve the goals this season. Athletes may fail to consider potential challenges when writing their goals. Successful coaches are effective at balancing goal encouragement with a shrewd analysis of challenges to achieving the goals.

After the coach has taken some time to reflect and comment on the athlete's written goals, the worksheet is returned to the athlete. The athlete is then given an opportunity to adjust the original goals based on the coach's feedback. The final step is for the athlete and coach to meet briefly to discuss any remaining differences of opinion and then sign the worksheet to show their commitment to the goals.

An example with a high school soccer athlete shows how this process might work. In the preseason team meeting, the coach distributes the worksheet to each athlete and asks the athletes to write down their five most important goals for the season. When the athletes are done, they give their worksheets to the coach. After the meeting the coach carefully reviews each worksheet. The goals are evaluated based on the coach's knowledge of the athlete's history, current performance level, role on the team, the opponents that the team will be facing, and the coach's experience coaching similar athletes.

For example, a senior athlete who plays the striker position may set a target of scoring 15 goals in the season. Although the coach agrees that the athlete is talented enough to score that many goals, the coach suggests the athlete set the target at 10 to 12 goals. The coach believes that this target is more realistic and attainable because she plans to give some younger athletes playing time at the striker position to build their confidence at the position and prepare the team for when the senior athlete graduates at the end of the season. Also, the coach has scheduled several opponents that they have not played before. These teams are strong defensively and concede few goals. These factors, which may be overlooked or unknown to the athlete, will definitely affect her ability to achieve a target of scoring 15 goals this season.

The coach repeats this reflective process for each of the athlete's written goals and writes a summary of her feedback on the worksheet. The worksheet should be returned to the athlete within a few days of the when the athlete first completed it. The athlete is instructed to review the coach feedback, write her updated goals, and return it to the coach within two or three days. Ideally, depending on the size of the team and the coach's resources, the coach will meet with each athlete for 5 to 10 minutes to discuss the updated goals. The athlete and coach will both sign the worksheet showing their agreement and commitment to the goals. The coach then makes a copy of the worksheet so that both athlete and coach have a record of what they aim to achieve in the coming season. For teams with large rosters such as football or cross country, position or assistant coaches may complete this process and report to the head coach.

After the season target outcomes have been set, coaches should help athletes identify short-term goals that will help them close the gap between "what is" and "what is possible." These small intermediate steps will be used to make adjustments along the way. Using the target outcomes agreed on through the athlete and coach shared goal-setting activity (worksheet 3.5), coaches can help athletes identify some short-term goals for each target outcome. Besides identifying short-term goals, the athlete and coach will benefit from listing goal achievement strategies they will use to close the gap between the short-term goals and the target outcomes. A sample goal-setting and goal achievement strategies worksheet, based on one created by coaching experts Dr. Lynn Kidman and Dr. Stephanie Hanrahan,[20] is provided in figure 3.6 to help coaches and their athletes with this process.

Five-time national champion and all-time winningest American college baseball coach Augie Garrido likes to illustrate physically for his players how focusing on short-term goals will bring them closer to their target outcome of winning a championship. Coach Garrido shares how distinguished sport psychology consultant Ken Ravizza created a goal imagery exercise that he used in the preseason with each of his teams.[21]

The exercise involves setting out a long line of baseballs across the floor of a room. Each baseball indicates a different phase of the season, each requiring different short-term goals to ensure that the team is moving in the right direction and continually closing the gap between the first and final ball—making it to the national championship game. Coach Garrido believes that this simple exercise, which could be adapted to any sport, has helped his athletes see the importance of focusing on the daily and short-term goals that will lead to achievement of their desired target outcomes.

Another exercise designed with the same purpose in mind is the penny jar example created by Jeff Janssen.[4] The athletes are instructed to deposit a penny into a jar each day that they believe they have made wise choices that show commitment to the target conditions that have been agreed on by the team in the preseason. Each day that they make poor or undisciplined choices, they are instructed to remove a penny from the jar. Instead of having athletes keep individual jars, the coach might decide to have one team jar that is kept in the coach's office or the team locker room.

This type of exercise serves as a visual reminder of the importance of committing daily to making a deliberate investment in getting better. Each penny individually may not seem like much, but over time the investment, particularly when viewed collectively across all the players' jars or when using a team jar, clearly reinforces the cumulative effect of small, incremental steps.

## Figure 3.6 Goal-Setting and Goal Achievement Strategy Worksheet

| Target outcomes | Strategies for achieving |
|---|---|
| Season goal #1:<br>Short term: | |
| Season goal #2:<br>Short term: | |
| Season goal #3:<br>Short term: | |
| Season goal #4:<br>Short term: | |
| Season goal #5:<br>Short term: | |

From W. Gilbert, 2017, *Coaching better every season: A year-round system for athlete development and program success* (Champaign, IL: Human Kinetics).

The best coaches go to great lengths to identify not only the gap between "what is" and "what is possible" but also the specific performance and process goals that must be attained to close the gap. Three-time national champion and Hall of Fame American college football coach Tom Osborne set performance and process goals that were grounded in both his coaching philosophy and the conditions in which his teams had to play.[22]

Nebraska, the area of the country where Coach Osborne coached his entire college football career, was renowned for harsh and windy weather. Taking this condition into consideration, Coach Osborne set performance goals that emphasized a ground attack (running) as opposed to a passing game. He typically set 10 to 12 goals for his offense, such as averaging six yards per rush. He also set specific performance goals for every other aspect of the game, such as defense and kicking.

The performance goals were firmly grounded in Coach Osborne's comprehensive analysis of performance trends in college football. For example, a goal for his team on kickoff returns was to stop the opponent from advancing the ball past the 23-yard line. Why the 23-yard line? Coach Osborne learned that the odds of the opponent's scoring on a drive dramatically increased if they started beyond that point, almost tripling if the opponent reached the 35-yard line on a kickoff return.

Following the game the entire coaching staff would review how well they achieved their goals. Regardless of the outcome on the scoreboard, the game was viewed as a success (i.e., the team performed well) if they met 10 of their 12 performance goals, whereas the game was viewed as a poor effort if the team met fewer than 4 of their performance goals. This type of regular and systematic review of postgame performance and process goals is a hallmark of effective coaches.

For three years I worked closely with the head coach of Fresno State's women's golf team. We decided to conduct our own statistical analysis of the performance gaps between our team and the top teams in the country, using key performance indicators in golf such as number of pars and putts per round and the number of times an athlete hit the green on her approach shot.

We created a chart for each athlete on the team, showing her most recent statistics in direct comparison with the top-ranked players in the country and in the conference. The purpose of this activity was to inspire athletes to strive for excellence. This activity provided the athletes with objective and visible data that clearly illustrated the gap between their current performance and that of the best in the country. It also provided the coach with a clear view of what performance areas to emphasize in practices, specific to each athlete's performance gap needs.

After each tournament we updated each athlete's performance chart. Because of our renewed practice focus on closing gaps, the athletes noticed slow and steady progress in reducing the disparity between themselves and the best teams. One of the areas where we consistently noticed a performance gap across the entire team was putting. Finding creative ways to work on this skill on a daily basis became a focal point for us. As the team made incremental improvements in their total putts per round (fewer putts), they slowly began to move up the standings in each tournament, culminating with a tournament victory in which the team set a tournament scoring record.

I have also used this strategy with basketball teams, but besides charting team performance gaps, we also charted performance gaps specific to the various positions. In a sport like golf everyone plays the same position, but in a team sport an athlete's performance should be measured against other athletes who play the same position. For example, when working with a basketball team we charted the gap between the game performance statistics for the top guards, top forwards, and top centers in the conference and the country and the performance of our guards, forwards, and centers.

Mike Hebert, a member of the American Volleyball Coaches Association Hall of Fame, consistently invested time in charting performance gaps as a way to set goals with his teams throughout his coaching career. In the preseason Coach Hebert liked to prepare a chart comparing his team's performance on seven critical game statistics against the performance of the top four teams in the country from the previous season. He referred to this chart as his championship template.[23] (See figure 3.7.)

**Figure 3.7 Championship Template 2009**

| School | Kills (K) | Attack errors (E) | Total attack attempts (TA) | Kill efficiency (K – E/TA = KEff) | E% (E/TA) | K% (K/TA) | Kills per set (K/S) |
|---|---|---|---|---|---|---|---|
| PSU | 1734 | 428 | 3352 | .390 | .128 | .517 | 14.9 |
| Stanford | 1731 | 454 | 4069 | .314 | .112 | .425 | 14.7 |
| Nebraska | 1714 | 590 | 4166 | .270 | .142 | .411 | 14.5 |
| Texas | 1719 | 447 | 3795 | .335 | .118 | .453 | 14.6 |
| Average | 1725 | 480 | 3846 | .324 | .125 | .449 | 14.7 |
| Minnesota | 1680 | 626 | 4512 | .234 | .139 | .372 | 10.6 |

Reprinted, by permission, from M. Hebert, 2014, *Thinking volleyball* (Champaign, IL: Human Kinetics), 43.

Notice in Coach Hebert's performance chart example that he illustrated the gap between his team and each of the top four teams plus the average of the top four teams. Athletes may perceive the average as a more realistic target. Consistent with how the golf coach and I used our performance charts, Coach Hebert used his chart to set performance goals and identify training needs for his athletes.

The overriding goal of these types of activities is to identify and close performance gaps. My experiences, and those reported by legendary coaches across sport, show that performance gap charting is an effective coaching strategy for helping athletes and teams meet their target outcomes.

## MONITORING PROGRESS TOWARD TARGETS

Simply writing down goals for the season and then leaving them in a binder or posting them on a wall is not a recipe for effective goal setting. Progress toward achieving the goals must be constantly evaluated for several reasons. First, evaluation shows athletes that the coach cares about their development, regardless of their role or position on the team (starter or nonstarter, rookie or veteran). Second, frequent checks on goal achievement progress are crucial to ensuring that the goals remain relevant and appropriate. Over the course of a season many factors will influence an athlete's ability to achieve goals that are set in the preseason (injury, team makeup, role on the team, team strategy, and so on). Lastly, regularly monitoring progress toward goals exposes training needs so that coaches can make incremental adjustments to keep athletes on target.

The frequency with which goal progress is monitored depends on the type of goal, athlete needs, and the coaching context. For example, some coaches and athletes find it useful to chart their progress on a daily basis.[6] Although expecting to see physical performance gains on a daily basis is not realistic, when averaged across a week of training and competing, physical performance gains may be evident. Also, athletes may find it helpful to chart the degree to which they were able to meet training and mental (e.g., attitude, focus) goals each day. A sample goal progress logbook for a week of training and competing is provided in figure 3.8.

Daily monitoring of goals was key to the success of Hall of Fame college football coach Bill Snyder in rebuilding the losing program he inherited into one of the nation's elite teams.[24] In his first season with the team, after each practice, he would walk around the locker room and ask every single player the same question: "Did you get better today?" With time, every player answered yes and was able to tell him how he improved. This daily monitoring of goal progress helped build a culture of continuous improvement that kept athletes focused on setting and meeting daily goals.

A more formal example of daily goal monitoring, but specific to competitions, is the strategy adopted by highly successful ice hockey coach Dennis "Red" Gendron. Coach Gendron has the rare distinction of having coached teams to championships at the high school, college, and professional (National Hockey League) levels. Following each game he displayed the team's performance goals on a large chart on the wall.[25] The team would gather around the chart and review their performance statistics.

Coach Gendron believed that the teams took great pride in this exercise and found that achieving at least two-thirds of the performance goals always resulted in a win. This strategy provided immediate feedback to the athletes while reinforcing the connection between short-term and process goals and team success.

Coach Gendron supplemented the postgame review of team goals by requiring each athlete to complete a self-assessment of his goal progress. Target conditions were jointly set in a preseason meeting with each athlete. The target conditions

## Figure 3.8 Weekly Goal Progress Logbook Example

| **Goal setting** | **Week of:** | | | | | | | | | |
|---|---|---|---|---|---|---|---|---|---|---|
| Goals | Current level (%) | Goal level (%) | M | T | W | Th | F | Game | Performance average |
| 1. | | | | | | | | | |
| 2. | | | | | | | | | |
| 3. | | | | | | | | | |

Reprinted, by permission, from D. Burton and T.D. Raedeke, 2008, *Sport psychology for coaches* (Champaign, IL: Human Kinetics), 62.

identified how each athlete could make a positive, significant contribution to the team in every game, regardless of his role. These athlete-specific target conditions were then used to create a performance wheel for each athlete. Following each game the athlete completed a self-evaluation using the performance wheel, ranking his quality of performance on a scale of 1 to 5 for each target condition (see figure 3.9).

You will notice in Coach Gendron's performance wheel that the target conditions are not written as measurable goals. For example, standards are not established for shots on goal or passing the puck. That is OK because the purpose of the exercise is to remind athletes about how they should be contributing to the team and to stimulate reflection on how they are performing on a regular basis.

As a coach you may decide to meet with each athlete periodically across the season to review trends he or she is noticing in the performance wheel analysis. You may also decide to make a copy of the performance wheel for each athlete and complete your own evaluation of the players after each game. I have found that comparing athlete and coach evaluations of goal progress is a useful strategy for identifying misperceptions and stimulating open, honest, and constructive feedback about performance.

If frequent monitoring of goal progress isn't practical or appropriate for your coaching context, you may prefer to have athletes periodically complete goal assessments a few times across a season. Recall from earlier in this chapter how Jeff Janssen helped college teams identify the pillars of success that would lead to achievement of their target outcomes. Occasionally throughout the season the athletes were asked to rate the team's progress on achieving these target conditions.

Athlete perceptions on goal progress were then graphed and shared with the team, helping the athletes identify gaps between what they agreed to do in the preseason and what was actually happening. When this type of goal-monitoring exercise is done on a regular basis, coaches and their athletes can use the results

**Figure 3.9** The performance wheel.

Reprinted, by permission, from D. Gendron, 2003, *Coaching hockey successfully* (Champaign, IL: Human Kinetics), 22.

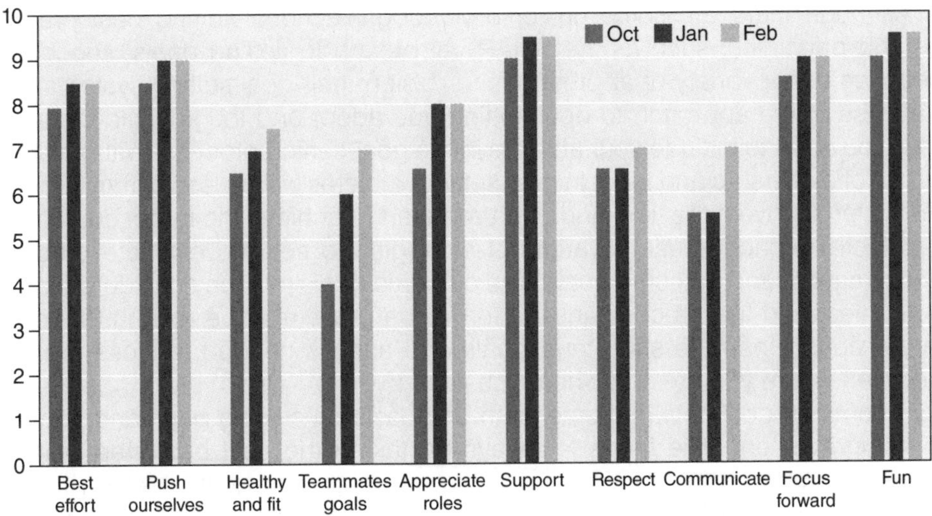


**Figure 3.10** College swim team goal progress monitoring results.

Reprinted, by permission, from J. Janssen, 1999, *Championship team building: What every coach needs to know to build a motivated, committed and cohesive team* (Tucson, AZ: Winning the Mental Game), 81. www.JanssenSportsLeadership.com

to recalibrate the team's direction and focus. An example of how the results from this type of exercise can be displayed, using a successful college swim team, is shown in figure 3.10.

Regardless of how often you think you and your athletes need to check progress toward achieving your target outcomes, effective coaches periodically set aside time for goal monitoring. The process may be informal, but it is reinforced nonetheless. For example, championship college football coach Bo Schembechler had his athletes write team and individual goals on 3-by-5-inch (7.5 by 12.5 cm) index cards.[26] These cards were then placed in a plastic sleeve with the team's logo and colors. Athletes were instructed to carry the cards with them at all times as a constant reminder of what they wanted to achieve and what they should be doing to reach individual and team goals. In this sense there was no formal or regular goal-monitoring strategy, but goal monitoring was still built into the program culture.

## Wrap-Up

Setting targets, commonly referred to as goal setting, represents a fundamental coaching responsibility. It is difficult to imagine coaching a sport without first identifying the desired result and charting the path to achieve it. Goals matter because they provide direction and focus for you and your athletes. However, an over-emphasis on achieving competitive goals can inadvertently lead to unethical behavior and actually lower athlete motivation.[31,32] Perhaps, then, the most valuable aspect of goals is that they provide daily reminders of the type of effort and focus required to become better.

Although there are some universally recognized goal-setting best practices and principles, such as the SMART approach to setting goals, successful coaches use a variety of approaches to design their goal-setting systems. Regardless of the approach to goal setting you adopt and the specific tools you use, you need to include your athletes in the goal-setting process. Without some sense of ownership and input in goal setting, athletes will be less committed and motivated to invest the time and effort required to achieve the target outcomes.

Effective coaches use a variety of strategies to set and evaluate process, performance, and outcome goals. The outcome goals may be considered target outcomes, and the process and performance goals may be thought of as the target conditions—the short-term goals and actions needed to close the gap between where you are and where you want to be.

A common goal-setting theme is an emphasis on closing gaps and continuous improvement. The focus is always on taking the next best step that will sustain forward momentum toward achieving long-term goals. Making time in the preseason to reflect on the program targets that will put your athletes in the best position to realize their goals while also moving you closer to realizing your vision for the program is a proven strategy for building a culture of sustained excellence.

# Chapter 4

# Build Trust and Cohesion

**Key Concepts**

Mutual trust
Role perceptions
Coach-athlete relationships
Group and team dynamics
Team building
Cohesion
Task cohesion
Social cohesion
Collective efficacy
Leadership
Transformational leadership
Servant leadership

Forging a group of individual athletes into a cohesive and high-performing team is one of the eternal coaching challenges. The dilemma constantly challenges all coaches, including the world's best, such as 11-time NBA champion coach Phil Jackson and all-time winningest college baseball coach Augie Garrido. Coach Jackson used to joke that sometimes he wrote "magician" on employment forms.[1] Coach Garrido, who coached teams to five national titles, referred to magic when describing how he built championship teams: "I don't have a secret recipe for pulling a team together. Sometimes it's a constant battle throughout a season. Then in other seasons, magic happens. The quality of the team depends on the strength of the player relationships."[2 (p. 176)]

How, then, do successful coaches manage to solve the cohesion puzzle more often than other coaches do? Whether coaching females or males, and regardless of differences in coaching styles, championship coaches all have one thing in common: They make building relationships with their athletes a top priority.

U.S. women's national soccer team coach Jill Ellis, who in 2015 led the American team to their first World Cup championship in 16 years, has been lauded by current and former players alike for her open and honest communication style. Moreover, she placed great emphasis on learning how to connect with players in ways that are uniquely meaningful and relevant to each one of them.[3]

Another recent example is Golden State Warriors coach Steve Kerr, who took advice given to him from championship football coach Pete Carroll.[4] In just his first year of coaching the team, Kerr built a culture of trust and engagement by making relationship building a regular part of his daily routine en route to the team's first basketball championship in 40 years. A quotation from Coach Kerr summarizes the emphasis that championship coaches place on relationship building with their athletes: "To me, the Xs and Os . . . they're an important part of coaching but a relatively small part. Eighty percent of it is just relationships and atmosphere."

This chapter reveals how the best coaches unlock the magic of high-performing teams by creating environments built on mutual trust and quality relationships. Although team building is a never-ending process, preseason is the ideal time to emphasize team-building activities that instill a strong sense of team cohesion.

AP Photo/Darren Abate

Golden State Warriors head coach Steve Kerr is renowned for building strong relationships with his players, such as All-Star forward Draymond Green.

## ESTABLISHING MUTUAL TRUST

Athletes will never reach their peak performance unless a deliberate and sustained effort to teach and build trusting relationships occurs between teammates and between athletes and coaches. At the beginning of a career, most coaches focus on building their knowledge of the game. But with experience, the best realize that more time should be spent on building relationships. Hall of Fame volleyball coach Mike Hebert summed it up well when he shared,

> As I entered the final years of my career, I realized that I was on the verge of identifying the most important element in building team success. Without it, there can be no journey to the top. No dynasties. No championships. But if you can harness its power, you will find your program on the way to levels of achievement that had been impossible before. The element I am speaking about is trust.[5 (p. 58)]

I vividly recall a conversation I had with a national team coach shortly after the team, which was expected to place high in the world championships, was prematurely eliminated from the tournament. We both noted how odd it was that athletes, including one who was recognized as the best in the world, did not perform well at the world championships but were now again dominating the game with their professional teams.

What changed in a few weeks for these athletes? They were still competing against the world's best, but now they appeared much more relaxed and confident. Why couldn't they compete like that with their national team? We realized that what plagued the national team was a culture of distrust. This circumstance commonly occurs when teams are put together quickly and coaches and athletes do not have enough time to build trusting relationships through shared experiences.

Mutual trust is defined as being comfortable with exposing vulnerabilities, fears, weaknesses, and needs with others. Trust allows athletes to focus their time and energy on the business of getting better and contributing to team goals by releasing unhealthy and energy-sucking worries about potential motives and consequences of the actions of coaches or teammates.

Trust rests on the assumption that the moral standards and intimate details of a relationship will not be violated. This concept is perhaps the most important one for coaches to grasp when planning how to build a cohesive team. Every single athlete and coach is vulnerable, all the way from young novices up to world champions. Achieving peak performance depends on the degree to which coaches and athletes feel comfortable exposing and sharing vulnerabilities, so that they can provide each other with the necessary emotional, physical, and technical support to overcome challenges and sustain positive momentum.

Dr. Brené Brown, whose TED talk on the power of vulnerability has been viewed nearly 25 million times, explains that being vulnerable requires the courage to allow others to see our imperfections.[6, 7] Through her extensive research she has found that showing vulnerability is a sign of authenticity that fosters trust. Furthermore, the ability to show empathy and experience things like love and belonging requires vulnerability. Many of the greatest coaches of all-time reference love as a cornerstone of their successful coaching philosophy, including John Wooden, who described love as acting in the best interest of each athlete.[8] Clearly, the willingness to embrace vulnerability is critical for building meaningful and trusting coach-athlete relationships.

Leadership scientist Kurt Dirks conducted a landmark study with 30 American collegiate basketball teams that showed beyond a doubt the power of trust and the way in which it directly influences team performance.[9] A series of trust surveys and interviews were matched with a wide range of potential factors that could influence team performance (e.g., prior team performance, coach and player experience, team talent level).

Athletes' trust in their coach had a significant effect on the team's winning percentage. In fact, teams that reported the highest levels of trust in their coaches performed the best. Conversely, teams that reported the lowest levels of trust in their coaches performed the worst; the least trusted coach was fired at the end of the season on a team that won only 10 percent of their games. Team performance measured over the four years before the study also had a significant positive effect on the athletes' trust in the coach. Collectively, these findings show that trust in the coach is partly based on the coach's prior record and in turn directly affects future team performance.

Other research corroborates this conclusion, showing that coaches will appear more trustworthy if they have a past record of modeling core values and respect (reputation), are currently modeling core values and respect (performance), and demonstrate self-confidence, professionalism, and dignity (appearance).[10]

One of the most common mistakes that coaches make is underestimating the amount of time and effort needed to build trusting relationships with athletes. Trust is perhaps the most valuable asset of high-performing teams, whether it is a team comprising a single coach and one athlete or a large team of dozens of athletes and coaches working together. Trust is the foundation and core of cohesion. Coach Urban Meyer summed it up well when reflecting on the keys to winning the inaugural College Football National Playoff Championship in 2015: "I am convinced that this unique bond was the fuel that energized our championship run. It would not have happened without the enormous investment we made in teaching and building trust among our coaches and players."[11 (p. 131)]

Trust can be thought of as confidence in someone else's character. Trust has sometimes been described as a bet that you make based on your assumptions about how others will react in relation to your own behaviors.[10] For example, an athlete demonstrates trust in her coach and teammates when she is willing to take a calculated risk during a competition. She is betting that her coach and teammates will not reprimand or belittle her if the risk results in failure.

We cannot expect our athletes to trust us, and each other, simply because we are the coach or because we play on the same team. Assuming the role of the coach is the launching point for building a bank of trust. Much as regular deposits must be made to a bank account to offset withdrawals, coaches and athletes must make frequent deposits to their trust account to build and sustain healthy relationships.[11] This approach is consistent with that used by championship high school coaches to build athlete character.[12]

Depending on your actions as a coach, you will be making either deposits or withdrawals from the trust bank. Your goal as a coach should be to make regular and systematic efforts to increase the balance in your coaching trust bank. Every time you don't follow through on a promise to an athlete or your team, fail to show empathy or make time to listen to an athlete's concerns, or act in a way that is inconsistent with the core values that you espouse, you are making a withdrawal from the trust bank. Without constant self-analysis and open communication with your athletes, you likely will not even be aware of the trust withdrawals until it is too late to recover.

This circumstance is exactly what happened with the national team example that I shared earlier in this chapter. The team fell into trust bankruptcy at the worst possible time, when the eyes of the sporting world were on them during the world championships. When a team reaches the trust bankruptcy point, recovery is difficult, if not impossible. Typically, the only option is to terminate the relationship and start over with a different group. Much as a business is forced to restructure and liquidate its assets when declaring bankruptcy, sport teams typically replace coaches and transfer or release athletes when they fall into trust bankruptcy. In the national team example the head coach was fired a few months after the world championships when it became evident that the team could not recover from their trust bankruptcy.

Nowhere is this situation more evident than in professional sport. At this level, coaches are regularly fired only to reappear soon afterward as the coach of a competing team. This coaching carousel is well documented in all professional sports.[13–16] The common practice of replacing the head coach in the middle of a season shows no consistent results. An immediate positive outcome may or may not occur; long-term improvement in performance may or may not happen.

These conflicting results only serve to reinforce that the opportunity to reset the trust ledger through a coaching change rests on the ability of the new coach to rebuild, and sustain, a positive balance in the trust bank. Just as a company that declares financial bankruptcy cannot expect a name change and a move into a new building to address the root cause of the problem, teams and coaches that fail to seize trust bankruptcy as an opportunity to begin rebuilding trust and cohesion will soon revert to a negative balance in the trust bank and continue to underperform.

Coaches must appreciate that despite their best efforts to make regular deposits into the team's trust bank, small withdrawals are constantly being made by others—athletes, other coaches, competitors, media, and the myriad of program stakeholders that surround and influence athletes. For that reason, coaches must develop and implement regular and systematic trust and cohesion-building activities that will ensure constant deposits to the trust bank over the course of a season.

An adapted version of the Trust in Leadership survey created by Kurt Dirks is a simple tool that coaches can use to regularly monitor athletes' and teams' trust balance. The higher the score is, the greater the trust in the coach is. In my work with coaches and teams, we focus on zones of achievement, so when using the Trust in Coach Leadership survey I would consider scores in the 5 to 7 range as acceptable target zones of trust. Questions for which the scores fall below 5 are

## Figure 4.1 Trust in Coach Leadership Survey

This questionnaire is designed to assess your relationship with your head coach. Circle the number that best corresponds to how you generally feel about your relationship with your head coach. For statements that you strongly agree with, circle a 7. For statements that you strongly disagree with, circle a 1.

| | **Strongly disagree** | | **Neither agree or disagree** | | | **Strongly agree** | |
|---|---|---|---|---|---|---|---|
| 1. I can talk freely to my coach. | 1 | 2 | 3 | 4 | 5 | 6 | 7 |
| 2. My coach will listen and care if I chose to share my ideas, feelings, or problems. | 1 | 2 | 3 | 4 | 5 | 6 | 7 |
| 3. My coach acts with professionalism and dedication. | 1 | 2 | 3 | 4 | 5 | 6 | 7 |
| 4. I can rely on my coach to help me improve my skills. | 1 | 2 | 3 | 4 | 5 | 6 | 7 |
| 5. Given my coach's past performance, I believe in my coach's ability. | 1 | 2 | 3 | 4 | 5 | 6 | 7 |
| 6. I would feel a sense of loss if my coach left. | 1 | 2 | 3 | 4 | 5 | 6 | 7 |
| 7. Other players and coaches trust and respect my coach. | 1 | 2 | 3 | 4 | 5 | 6 | 7 |

Adapted from K.T. Dirks, 2000, "Trust in leadership and team performance: Evidence from NCAA basketball," *Journal of Applied Psychology* 85(6): 1004-1012.

considered out of the zone and should be carefully examined by the coach in an effort to rebuild and sustain trust and team cohesion.

Ideally, this type of survey (figure 4.1) would be given to the athletes during the preseason and then periodically throughout the season. Athletes should not write their names on the surveys, and the coach should have someone else collect the surveys. This protocol will encourage the athletes to respond truthfully. Coaches can then use the survey as a way to spot check the team trust account and make adjustments as needed.

# Forming Coach-Athlete Relationships

Successful coaches have long known that the time and energy invested in building quality relationships with their players pay huge dividends. For example, Eddie Robinson, one of the winningest college football coaches of all time, proclaimed that showing genuine care for each of his players was the cornerstone of his coaching approach.[17] More recently, Cameron McCormick—longtime coach of the world's top golfer, Jordan Spieth—revealed that building quality relationships with athletes was at the top of his list for becoming a successful coach, based on his study of the world's best golf coaches.[18]

I suppose it is only fitting that one of the greatest determinants of sporting success is the quality of the relationship between coach and athlete, yet it is also one of the most unstable and complicated aspects of coaching. Part of the reason that coach-athlete relationships present so many challenges is that coaches must comprehend how an athlete's emotions, thoughts, and behaviors are interconnected.

The 3+1 Cs conceptual model of coach-athlete relationships provides an extremely valuable framework for making sense of coach-athlete relationships.[19] The first C refers to closeness, defined as mutual respect, trust, and emotional connection. Closeness is considered the emotional, or feeling, component of coach-athlete relationships. How close an athlete feels to coaches and teammates is highly personal and subjective, and it ebbs and flows within a relationship. Closeness will fade without continued effort to nurture the feeling and attachment needed to build mutual trust.

One of the simplest techniques a coach can use to nurture closeness with athletes is appropriate and positive touch. Positive touch is a fundamental basic human need that elicits physiological and emotional responses that build closeness and trust. Examples of positive touch in sport include high fives, fist and chest bumps, and pats on the back.

A few years ago a successful coach shared with me a study conducted with athletes who played in the National Basketball Association.[20] In the study all positive touches between teammates were recorded across one season. Athletes and teams that more frequently used positive touches during games won more often and demonstrated more cooperative behaviors (e.g., assists, setting screens, on-court communication, and so on). I later learned that at the time of the study, two-time league Most Valuable Player Steve Nash had the highest positive touch score.

The coach who shared the study with me was gracious enough to allow one of my graduate students to analyze her coaching staff's positive touch profile during games and practices. We learned that the athletes were aware of the coaches' positive touch efforts and believed that generally they increased their feelings of closeness to the coaches and overall team cohesion.[21] Note that during the time we made our observations, the team won two consecutive conference championships, lending further support to the effect of positive touch on team success.

The second C in the 3+1 Cs coach-athlete framework refers to commitment. Commitment is described as the cognitive (thinking) component of coach-athlete relationships because it represents intentions to continue a relationship. Whereas closeness is a feeling of connection, commitment is a conscious choice to invest time and energy into sustaining that connection over time.

The third C refers to complementarity, which captures the degree to which coach and athlete are willing to cooperate in shared efforts to achieve target outcomes. Cooperation requires empathy and compassion, because coaches and athletes alike must be willing to consider alternative views and engage in friendly and constructive dialogue.

The +1 in the 3+1 Cs coach-athlete relationship framework refers to coorientation, which is the degree to which relationship perspectives held by coaches and athletes are in agreement. For example, athletes may feel as if they are committed to their coach but at the same time believe that their coach is not committed to them. When coorientation is low, one person's views on the relationship do not match the perceptions of how the other person views the relationship (e.g., I feel close to you, but I don't think you feel close to me).

The ability to read the feelings, thoughts, and intentions of others correctly has been referred to as empathic accuracy.[22] In this sense, empathic accuracy is similar to what is commonly referred to as emotional intelligence. Successful coaches have high emotional intelligence because they are skilled at reading people and then using those intuitions and observations to make effective decisions.[23]

The surest way to show players that you care about them is to ask them about their lives and then give them your undivided attention. Feeling like their emotional needs are being met while being supported by their coach is a key difference between the world's best athletes and those who are less successful.[24] In 2015 when two-time national college basketball champion coach Billy Donovan accepted his first head coaching position in the NBA, he immediately scheduled face-to-face meetings with every player on the team. The purpose of the meetings was to make a personal connection with each player and show the player that he cared about him, not only as a professional basketball athlete but also as a person. The team quickly learned that Coach Donovan "was a guy who values that type of interaction"[25] and soon regained their position as one of the league's dominant teams.

Never forget that you are coaching people first and the sport second. Keep a file for each athlete to record notes about things and people that are meaningful to them. Regularly check in with each athlete and update her or his life file. Some head coaches like to give their athletes a survey to complete at the start of the season that includes questions about their dreams, passions, favorite subjects in school, and family.[26] Other coaches find that setting aside a few minutes before practices for social time allows them to speak with athletes about their lives while they are starting to warm up.

For relationship building to work, however, coaches must also be willing to share information about people and things that are meaningful to them. If you want your athletes to share with you, you must share with them. Ultimately, building relationships with athletes is an act of courage, for both the coach and the athlete. Each must have the courage to be vulnerable.

An effective strategy for building relationships and showing vulnerability is the Hero, Highlight, and Hardship exercise developed by Jon Gordon.[27, 28] In a team meeting each athlete and coach takes turns describing someone who has inspired him or her (hero), a positive uplifting experience (highlight), and adversity that the person has overcome in life (hardship). This type of exercise will work only if a trusting and emotionally safe team environment has been created where everyone is willing to be vulnerable.

The most widely recommended and most effective coaching strategy for building and sustaining quality coach-athlete relationships is communication. The simple approach taken by coaching scientist and former college coach Robin Vealey is one of my favorites. She uses the acronym PITCH to teach coaches how to create optimal communication with their athletes and within their teams:[29]

- Productive (emotions in control, positive, efficient)
- Informational (specific and relevant feedback)
- Timed (close to the behavior or event when possible)
- Consistent (alignment with core values, congruency between verbal and nonverbal language)
- Honest (no hidden messages or mind games)

Coaches can use this acronym as a simple cue for improving communication with their athletes by reminding themselves to PITCH it when they are about to relay a message.

A more comprehensive tool that coaches can use to improve and regularly check on their communication skills is the Guidelines for Sending Effective Messages survey prepared by Damon Burton and Thomas Raedeke.[30] As seen in figure 4.2, the survey includes a short description of 16 effective communication guidelines along with a coach self-assessment component for each of the guidelines. Following the description of the communication guideline, coaches are asked to self-rate themselves on a scale of 1 (weak) to 5 (strong) on their current ability to communicate in a way that is consistent with the guideline. Coaches can sum their scores to reveal an overall rating of their communication effectiveness.

I recommend that coaches complete this communication self-assessment in the preseason as a reminder of the guidelines and again two or three times during the season as a preventative check-up to ensure they are modeling the communication guidelines.

## Identifying Athletes' Best Roles

Creating a high-performing team starts with building trusting relationships. An effective way to build this trust is by sharing the leadership responsibilities with your athletes. A common way for coaches to distribute leadership across a team is to assign formal roles to athletes, such as team captain.

At the start of the 2014 season, the Montreal Canadiens, historically the most successful franchise in the National Hockey League, was faced with a dilemma because of the departure of their team captain. A typical response would have been simply to assign, or elect, another team captain. Instead, sensing the need to restore and nurture cohesion in a young team with a deficiency in veteran leadership, the coach took an unprecedented approach. He announced that for the 2014–2015 season, the team would have not just one captain but four cocaptains.[31]

Two veteran players would serve as permanent cocaptains throughout the season to provide stability and to recognize their senior leadership on the team. At the same time, two emerging leaders on the team would share another cocaptain role—one for home games and one for away games. This unusual decision is a prime example of how, with some creative thinking, coaches can promote shared leadership across a team to build team cohesion.

## Figure 4.2 Coach Communication Guidelines Self-Assessment

### 1. Messages should be direct.

Coaches who are weak on this quality avoid straightforward, direct communication. Their athletes may not know where they stand. These coaches assume others know what they expect, want, or feel. Rather than expressing their message directly, they hint at what they have in mind or they expect others to be mind readers. In other cases, they may tell someone else, hoping the message will get to the intended recipient indirectly. The problem is that indirect messages are often distorted and misperceived.

How strong are you in sending direct messages?

1 2 3 4 5

Weak Strong

### 2. Own your messages.

Use "I" and "my," not "the team," or "we" when referencing your messages. You disown your messages when you say, "The team feels . . .," or "Most people think you are . . .," when it is really what you believe. Using others to bolster what you have to say implies cowardice in expressing your own messages and failure to take ownership.

How strong are you in owning your messages?

1 2 3 4 5

Weak Strong

### 3. Messages should be complete and specific.

Tell the whole story without leaving out important information. Provide the person with whom you are speaking all the information he or she needs in order to fully understand your message. Watch for leaps in logic, unknown assumptions, and unstated intentions.

How strong are you in making your messages complete and specific?

1 2 3 4 5

Weak Strong

### 4. Messages should be clear and consistent. Avoid double messages.

Coaches who say one thing one day and then something else on another violate this principle as do coaches who send contradictory messages. "I really want to play you, but I don't think this is a good matchup for you." "I think you're a fine athlete, but you'll just have to be patient." This example of a double message (acceptance and rejection) leaves the athlete confused and probably hurt. Double messages have contradictory meanings, and usually are sent when you are afraid to tell the person directly something that may offend him or her.

How strong are you in sending clear and consistent messages?

1 2 3 4 5

Weak Strong

### 5. Messages should clearly state needs and feelings.

Because our society frowns on those who wear their emotions on their sleeves, we tend not to reveal our feelings and needs to others. Yet revealing our needs and feelings is a foundation for developing close relationships and opening the communication channels. Sharing needs and feelings opens the door for the other person to do the same. Unexpressed needs and hidden feelings result in unfilled expectations.

How strong are you in clearly stating your needs and feelings?

1 2 3 4 5

Weak Strong

### 6. Messages should separate fact from opinion.

State what you see, hear, and know, and then clearly identify any opinions or conclusions you have about these facts. You say to your son when he returns home late one night, "I see you've been out with the Williamson kid again." In the context in which it is spoken, your son receives the message, but he is not certain exactly what your concern is about the Williamson boy. A better way to send this message would be (a) "That was the Williamson kid, was it not?" (verifying a fact); and then (b) "I'm concerned that you spend so much time with him. I worry that he will get you into trouble" (stating your opinion). Although your son may not be pleased with your opinion, this message is far less ambiguous than the first one.

How strong are you in separating fact from opinion in your messages?

1 2 3 4 5

Weak Strong

### 7. Messages should be focused on one thing at a time.

Focus your message on one topic or issue at a time. Jumping from topic to topic only confuses the listener. Are your messages frequently disjointed thoughts because you don't take the time to organize your thinking?

How strong are you in focusing your messages on one thing at a time?

1 2 3 4 5

Weak Strong

### 8. Messages should be delivered immediately.

When you observe something that upsets you or that needs to be changed, don't delay sending a message. Sometimes holding back can result in you exploding later about a little thing. Responding immediately also is a sound principle for giving effective feedback. However, if your emotions are clouding your judgment, it is sometimes better to wait until a better time to deliver your message.

How strong are you in delivering messages immediately when you see the need to do so?

1 2 3 4 5

Weak Strong

### 9. Messages should not contain hidden agendas.

This principle means that the stated purpose of the message is identical with the real purpose. Hidden agendas and disguised intentions destroy relationships. Ask yourself these two questions to determine if your message contains hidden agendas: Why am I saying this? Is it because I want him or her to hear it or is there something else involved?

How strong are you in avoiding messages that contain hidden agendas?

1 2 3 4 5

Weak Strong

### 10. Messages should be supportive.

If you want the other person to listen to your messages over time, you cannot deliver them with threats, sarcasm, negative comparisons, or any type of judgment. Eventually the person will avoid communicating with you or will simply tune you out whenever you speak. Your cumulative messages need to demonstrate support for the person.

How strong are you in sending supportive messages?

1 2 3 4 5

Weak Strong

*(continued)*

**Figure 4.2** *(continued)*

**11. Verbal and nonverbal messages should be congruent.**

You tell your player it was OK to make the error, but your negative body gestures and facial expressions contradict your words. The two conflicting messages confuse your player and hurt your credibility in future communication.

How strong are you in making your verbal and nonverbal messages congruent?

1 2 3 4 5

Weak Strong

**12. Messages should be redundant. (That is, you should repeat the message. Get the point?)**

That's correct. Repeat the key points in a message to reinforce what you are saying. Preview what you are going to tell them, tell them, and then review what you just told them. However, be aware that too much repetition results in the other person not listening, so you must be discriminating in your redundancy. You can create redundancy by using additional channels of communication to bolster your message. For example, show a picture or video along with explaining the skill.

How strong are you in making your messages optimally redundant?

1 2 3 4 5

Weak Strong

**13. Messages should be at the receiver's level and frame of reference.**

Speak at the level of the receiver in a way that they can readily understand. Your messages can be much better understood if you tailor them to the experiences of the person with whom you are communicating. For example, it is inappropriate to use complex language when speaking to young athletes who do not have the vocabulary to understand what is being said. Make sure the message being sent is understandable given athletes' age, development, and experience.

How strong are you in sending messages that are appropriate for the receiver's level of readiness and understanding?

1 2 3 4 5

Weak Strong

**14. Messages should be checked for understanding.**

Look for verbal and nonverbal evidence that the person with whom you are speaking is receiving the message as you intended. If you are unsure of the person's understanding, ask him or her to summarize the main points of the message or ask questions to assess comprehension. Athletes may be hesitant to ask questions if they do not understand for fear of appearing stupid in front of others.

How strong are you in obtaining feedback to make certain the person understands your message?

1 2 3 4 5

Weak Strong

**15. Messages should be attention grabbing.**

You need to hook the person into listening. Grab their attention by using their name or by explaining why it is important for them to understand the information you are communicating.

How strong are you in sending attention grabbing messages?

1 2 3 4 5

Weak Strong

## 16. Messages should consider an athlete's learning style.

Some athletes are visual learners, others are auditory learners, while yet others learn through doing (i.e., kinesthetic learners). Messages will be more easily comprehended if they accommodate an athlete's learning style.

How strong are you in considering the listener's learning style in sending messages?

1 2 3 4 5

Weak Strong

**Total your ratings and see where you fall in the following subjective scale:**

| | |
|---|---|
| 61-70 | Excellent |
| 51-60 | Good |
| 41-50 | Average |
| 31-40 | Weak |
| 30 or less | Help! |

Reprinted, by permission, from D. Burton and T.D. Raedeke, 2008, *Sport psychology for coaches* (Champaign, IL: Human Kinetics), 18-21.

When athletes are asked to serve in a leadership role, coaches should be prepared to train them to lead. Skill as an athlete is commonly mistaken with leadership ability. For example, often the best player on the team is designated as the team captain, but that athlete may have poor leadership ability. To address this problem in high school sport, Dan Gould spearheaded a group that created the Captain's Leadership Training Program (CLTP).[32]

In this innovative program athletes learn how to become an effective team captain by attending a half-day clinic and completing activities described in a team captain handbook.[33] Activities cover topics such as role of the captain, team building, effective communication, team motivation, and handling tough situations. For example, leadership principles are shared from championship coaches, such as the six keys to leadership offered by Super Bowl–winning coach Mike Shanahan:

- Teams matter more than individuals.
- Every job (role) on the team is important.
- Treat everyone with respect.
- Share victories and defeats (win as a team, lose as a team).
- Accept criticism.
- Keep your coach well informed.

Perhaps one of the most valuable lessons you can teach your team leaders is how to resolve conflict constructively. Dysfunctional teams always look to others, namely the coach, to solve their problems when conflict arises (as it most surely will in any team). High-performing teams are taught strategies for taking ownership of their conflicts and learn an important life lesson. In his captain leadership handbook, Dan Gould recommends using the STAR approach to resolving team conflict: **S**top (ask what happened), **t**hink (about causes and consequences of what happened), **a**ct (gather facts and listen to all sides), and **r**eact (create a workable solution). An example of the STAR steps in action from Gould's athlete handbook is reproduced in figure 4.3.

Mutual trust is enhanced by a clear and agreed-on understanding of the role that each person on the team is expected to play. Sport teams typically have both formal (e.g., captain) and informal (e.g., team jester) roles. Whether a role is formal or informal, the key is to ensure that the coach and athlete have the same

## Figure 4.3 STAR Conflict Resolution Example

| | | | |
|---|---|---|---|
| **S** | Stop! | Ask yourself: What Happened?<br>What was the conflict about?<br>Who was involved? What events and emotions led up to the problem? | *Example:*<br>Jen, our goalie, let in a game-winning goal with ten seconds left in the third period. Mel, our defenseman, snapped at Jen after the game and made several negative comments about her playing ability both to her face and behind her back. |
| **T** | Think | What made you or your teammates angry and upset? What are the potential consequences if the conflict goes unresolved? | *Example:*<br>Mel is likely feeling angry because this was the last game of her high school career. As a senior, this game was really important to her and it has abruptly come to an end with one poor play by her teammate. Jen has likely lost confidence in her goaltending ability and may have some resentment towards Mel. This may affect not only their friendship, but also Jen's performance next season. |
| **A** | Act | Gather all the facts and hear all sides. Remember your decision-making pointers described above: Write down all possible options and solutions and rank order them based on which solutions will produce the best and worst case scenarios. | *Example:*<br>Ask other teammates who were present at the time of the incident what happened. Approach Jen and Mel individually and hear their stories as well. Ask each of them if and how they are willing to resolve the issue. Write down the options: 1. Suggest that they work this one out on their own. 2. Call a meeting and be present to mediate the situation. Rank order: Jen and Mel's personalities seem to clash enough as it is and Jen noted that she doesn't want to talk to Mel alone. Choose option 2. |
| **R** | React | Offer the most appropriate solution or compromise to the problem. | *Example:*<br>Suggest to Jen and Mel that all three of you meet to resolve the issue together. Set some rules for the discussion (speak calmly and avoid hurtful words). Explain the importance of apologies and forgiveness in this particular situation. |

perception of the athlete's role. Trust dwindles in circumstances of role ambiguity, role conflict, and role overload.[34]

The most effective way to counter these potential role perception issues is to create and monitor a formal communication system within the team. The communication strategies you put in place should adhere to what I refer to as the three Cs of effective communication for coaches—clarity, consistency, and commonplace. The only way to know whether an athlete truly understands, accepts, and values his or her role on a team and trusts the coach and teammates is to ensure that communication is clear, consistent with core values and coaching philosophy, and occurs on a frequent and regular basis (commonplace).

Depending on the type and level of sport you are coaching, you may need to assign other roles to your athletes, such as starter or backup. If not handled properly, role assignment can be the source of much conflict within a team and can severely detract from cohesion and trust. Athletes are much more receptive to accepting roles if a high level of trust has been established and if the coach clearly explains the rationale for the decision along with the importance of all roles to the overall success of the team. The coach should explain that a backup or reserve role is not a lesser role, but a role that is different from and as important as the role of a starter. Athletes normally express initial frustration with this decision. These feelings will subside if the athlete and the team continue to show skill improvement.

The story of John Wooden and Swen Nater is a great example of how a coach and athlete successfully handled athlete role assignment. I had the good fortune of working with Swen on numerous projects, and he shared this story with me on several occasions. When Swen was being recruited to play center for coach Wooden's basketball team, another center by the name of Bill Walton was set to assume the starting role. Coach Wooden asked Swen to commit to the team by agreeing to serve as Walton's backup for the duration of his college basketball career.

Coach explained to Swen that his role would be to make Bill Walton the best college center ever to play the game. If Swen could do that, the team would experience great success, and Swen would become a great center in his own right. Swen not only accepted the role but embraced it, partly to show Coach Wooden that he was as good as or better than Walton. With Swen in the backup role the team won two national championships, Walton became one of the greatest centers in collegiate basketball history, and Nater enjoyed a successful 10-year career as a professional basketball player.

## UNDERSTANDING TEAM DYNAMICS

When a group shares a collective goal and holds common perceptions about group structure, they have taken important steps toward becoming a team. The study of how groups and teams evolve and function is often referred to as group or team dynamics.[35] Decades of research on group and team dynamics provides coaches with a deep well of information about how to shape and guide their teams.

Much of what is known about team dynamics can be traced to a landmark paper written by Bruce Tuckman in 1965, in which he proposed his influential four-stage model of group development.[36] The four stages of team dynamics are popularly referred to as forming, storming, norming, and performing.

The forming stage typically occurs in the preseason when athletes are either returning to a team or joining it for the first time. In this stage, athletes will be testing the coach to learn the boundaries of acceptable, and expected, behavior. This period is when athletes are naturally most receptive to learning about the team's core values, the coach's philosophy, and team goals. Athletes will need guidance as they search for the ground rules and cultural norms that govern team behavior.

One of my favorite activities for helping groups complete the forming stage of group development is people bingo, adapted from Jeff Janssen.[37] Coaches can use this activity in several ways. One way is to gather little-known facts about the athletes in advance of one of the first team meetings, select one fact about each athlete, and print it on to a card that looks like a bingo card (each box on the card represents one of the athletes). At the team meeting the coach hands each athlete a bingo card and gives the athletes 10 or 15 minutes to complete their cards by finding the teammate who is paired with the fact in each box on the bingo card and writing the teammate's name in the box.

A second way to use people bingo is more effective with extremely large groups, such as might be encountered at a summer sport camp or program-wide social events when athletes from multiple teams gather. In this case, every box on the people bingo card is filled with a random fact, and athletes are instructed to find anyone else at the event who can be paired with one of the facts.

One of the high school athletics directors I work with likes to use this activity as an icebreaker at his annual preseason coaches' meeting. Although many coaches know each other, they seldom know the unusual facts about their coaching peers that the athletics director places on the bingo cards.

An example of a people bingo card that I have used is included in figure 4.4. Coaches can adapt the card to fit any group size by changing the number of rows and columns on the card.

The second stage of group development is storming, typically the most emotionally charged stage of group development. Emotions normally run high in this stage because athletes are trying to reconcile their personal needs, values, and orientations with the core values, philosophies, and goals of the team. In other words, in this stage athletes are trying to learn how to fit in with their teammates and with the team culture. Experienced coaches know it is inevitable that sub-groups will form on every team. It is normal to expect that athletes, particularly on large teams, will want to spend more time with other athletes who share similar backgrounds and personal interests. However, coaches must be vigilant in watching for the formation of sub-groups that pull apart a team, commonly referred to as cliques.[38] Cliques create fault lines within a team and cannot be tolerated.

Certainly, this type of conflict can be minimized by recruiting and selecting athletes and coaching staffs who already have the same values, philosophies, and goals as the head coach.[38] But some conflict and the storming stage are inevitable parts of team dynamics. Without strong leadership guidance from the coach, many teams never progress past the storming stage.

## Figure 4.4 People Bingo Card

Your name: ______________________________

*Instructions:* The first person to achieve bingo (any line) and the person with the most spots filled after 10 minutes each wins an award. You can use each person only once, and you can use yourself once. Print name of person in the grid.

Someone who…

| | | | | | | |
|---|---|---|---|---|---|---|
| has climbed Half Dome | has a surname that starts with H | owns a motorcycle | has a snake | is a coach | has attended the X Games | plays a musical instrument |
| has visited Canada | has attended the Olympic Games | has run a marathon | is married | has visited Asia | has the same eye color as you do | has a horse |
| is a referee | has a birthday in a month starting with J | has a daughter | is enrolled in a different major than you | has a cat | was on the high school track team | has visited Europe |
| played high school softball | has a dog | has visited Africa | has attended an MLS game | has a tattoo | has a son | is a first-generation college student |
| knows how to snowboard | knows how to ice skate | has done a triathlon | was born in a foreign country | has climbed Mt. Whitney | is a Fresno State athlete | has a brother |
| has visited Australia | can sing (well) | surfs | can juggle | has attended an MLB game | is bilingual | is an out-of-state student |
| has at least five siblings | played high school soccer | has a sister | has visited Mexico | has an iTunes account | played high school football | was born in Fresno county |

From W. Gilbert, 2017, *Coaching better every season: A year-round system for athlete development and program success* (Champaign, IL: Human Kinetics).

Coaches can use any activity that promotes shared understanding and communication to address conflict in the storming stage. The root of interpersonal conflict is miscommunication based on faulty assumptions and inaccurate or incomplete information. We arrive at conclusions about others or situations by making leaps from observations to assumptions. As with climbing a ladder, each assumption we make about what we see brings us closer to our final judgment about the person or the situation, a situation referred to as climbing the ladder of inference.[39, 40]

For example, an athlete is speaking at a team meeting and notices out of the corner of her eye that a teammate appears bored. The athlete immediately makes an assumption about what she sees. The athlete will interpret the behavior differently depending on the teammate. She may interpret the bored behavior as the person simply being tired, if the speaker perceives the teammate to be a hard worker and has an established relationship with her.

Or the speaker may interpret the bored behavior as disinterest and disrespect, if the teammate is new to the team or has a reputation for laziness. The point is, without asking about the behavior, we are destined to make incomplete assumptions and potentially arrive at faulty conclusions, which erodes trust and team cohesion.

Coaches can create an environment of accurate and informed communication within their teams by teaching athletes to check their assumptions regularly by asking, before inferring, about their teammates' behaviors. In the example used to illustrate this point, the athlete speaking at the team meeting, or the coach, could pause to check her assumptions about the bored athlete by posing a question to the athlete such as, "You appear distant today. Is everything OK?" This type of assumption check shows genuine interest and care and is a proactive strategy for avoiding unnecessary conflict.

One strategy that coaches can use to create this type of healthy team communication environment has been referred to as reflective listening by sport psychologist David Yukelson.[41] Reflective listening involves suspending assumptions by pausing to ask questions of teammates to learn their point of view. In the example of the bored teammate, it is possible that the teammate was up late consoling a friend or family member who was stressed. This emotionally draining experience resulted in her coming to the team meeting in a state of exhaustion. Without an assumption check, she could be perceived as lazy and bored.

If the coach is successful in navigating through the conflict inherent in the storming stage, teams are then ready for the norming stage. At this point in the development of a team, athletes show more acceptance of their role on the team, core values and goals, and the personalities of their teammates and coaches. In this stage, athletes move from a "me" attitude to a "we" attitude. This stage presents a window of opportunity for coaches to build on emerging harmony within the team by designing activities that nurture open communication and sharing of opinions.

Coach Tony DiCicco, who led the American women's national soccer team to Olympic and World Cup championships, and Colleen Hacker, the team's sport psychologist, share how they used the power of one to teach athletes to adopt a "we" attitude.[42] They used the acronym TRY to reinforce commitment to team: Take responsibility yourself. Athletes were also encouraged to ask themselves two simple questions repeatedly: What is your influence on the team? and What is your influence on the game? They believed that these types of simple cues contributed greatly to their unprecedented team success and adoption of a "we" attitude.

Another strategy that has proved effective for leading teams through the norming stage is the creation of a team reward system.[43] Instead of rewarding athletes for individual performance accomplishments, the coach can reward the entire team if they meet collective goals. Performance goals that can be met only through the collective efforts of each athlete fulfilling his or her responsibility to the team include maintaining a certain time of possession in soccer or lacrosse, or holding an opponent to a specified number of yards gained in football or shots in ice hockey.

The fourth and final stage of group development is performing. If a coach is successful at guiding a team through the three previous stages, team energy and focus can be fully invested in achieving team goals. This stage is sometimes referred to as the functional stage because athletes and coaches trust each other and are willing to share ideas openly and take risks while constructively trying to close performance gaps.

The focus during this stage is on problem solving and continuous improvement. This often-elusive stage is a hallmark of championship teams. Trust is high, and team members experience a certain freedom and peace of mind. Yogi Berra, who won 10 championships as a player and 3 more as a coach, believed that there were three keys to being a good teammate: "Never prejudge someone, never make excuses and hide from responsibility, and never try not to help a teammate."[44 (p. 9)]

Hall of Fame American volleyball coach Mike Hebert has created a checklist of athlete behaviors that differentiate performing teams from storming teams (figure 4.5).[5] This type of checklist should be shared with athletes and posted in the locker room or in the team handbook as a constant reminder of how to earn trust from teammates and coaches.

## BUILDING THE TEAM

Team building is the systematic and deliberate actions you take to promote closeness, connection, unified purpose, and shared commitment to team goals among your athletes. All-time winningest American college baseball coach Augie Garrido molds his players into championship teams by adhering to what he considers the five universal truths of effective team building:[2]

1. It's amazing what can be accomplished when no one cares who gets the credit.
2. Every role is important, but finding the right person for the right role is critical.
3. On a fully functioning team bonded by mutual respect, anyone can take the lead at any given time.
4. Constant and clear communication is essential to a team's welfare.
5. The greatest achievements are the result of united efforts, not individual performance, because you have someone to share success with.

Coaches commonly implement formal team-building activities early in the season as a way to bring a team together. The process of setting team goals, or target outcomes, is a highly effective team-building activity.[41] Teams that participate in preseason team goal-setting exercises are more cohesive if the initial goal-setting activity is followed up with regular checks on the team goals. For example, an effective strategy is for coaches to evaluate team goals and adjust

## Figure 4.5 Teammates Versus Complainers

| Teammates | Complainers |
|---|---|
| Are open to change. | Resist change. |
| Have "can do" orientation. | See reasons they cannot do things. |
| Build on successes and strengths. | Focus on finding problems to fix. |
| Look for the challenge in situations. | Are overwhelmed by problems. |
| Take responsibility for their actions. | Avoid blame or responsibility. |
| Think in terms of new possibilities. | Are limited by what worked in the past. |
| Are good listeners. | Are poor listeners. |
| Have a continuous supply of energy. | Run out of energy quickly. |
| Make decisions easily. | Wimp out in the face of tough decisions. |
| Feel in control of their environment. | Feel victimized by their environment. |
| Are driven to excel by challenge and risk. | Are afraid to take risks or face challenges. |
| Work hard all the time. | Work hard only when they feel like it. |
| Enjoy inner calmness. | Suffer excessive inner stress. |
| Are present- and future-oriented. | Cannot let go of the past. |
| Learn and grow from mistakes. | Are devastated by failure. |
| Have high self-esteem. | Have low self-esteem. |
| Pursue goals with discipline. | Have trouble managing a commitment to goals. |
| See past personal differences with teammates and offer support. | Are stuck on petty bickering. |

Reprinted, by permission, from M. Hebert, 2014, *Thinking volleyball* (Champaign, IL: Human Kinetics), 194.

them if needed with their athletes and teams at regular intervals across a season. Breaking the season into smaller blocks of time, such as blocks of three games, is one such approach that has proved effective in research with high school teams.[45]

A common example of a preseason team-building activity is a team camping trip. Coaches schedule and plan the trip, but when the team arrives at the campsite, athletes are responsible for setting up camp, preparing meals, and cleaning. This transfer of ownership and responsibility forces the athletes to work together and often removes them from their comfort zone. Many coaches who have used this strategy report that most of their athletes have never been camping, and even if they have, they weren't the ones responsible for setting up tents and cooking outdoors.

This simple cost-effective activity also has the added benefit of removing some of the noise from athletes' daily lives by putting them in a quiet, isolated environment in which they have no choice but to collaborate and learn about each other. This team-building activity is an excellent way to identify team leaders and the various roles that each athlete naturally feels comfortable playing on the team. For example, who gathers the team together and maps out a strategy for distributing the workload? Who immediately accepts her or his assigned role and quietly gets to work, and who reluctantly adheres and perhaps even challenges or confronts her or his teammates? A preseason camping trip will naturally create the conditions for a team to work through the forming, storming, norming, and performing stages of team building.

Although preseason team-building activities are common, the most effective coaches understand that team building is an ongoing everyday effort across a season. Successful coaches set aside regular time in their weekly schedules for team-building activities in an effort to improve communication and interpersonal relationships. Scheduling team-building meetings, or at least setting aside some time during other types of regular team meetings, is recommended.

Some coaches recommend starting these meetings by having athletes respond, either orally or in writing, to team-building reflection questions such as the following: What have you done today or this week to help or support a teammate? What have you done in the past week to improve team cohesion?[46]

Coaching scientist and team-building consultant Jon Hammermeister shares the example of team Tuesdays that he helped create with the United States ski team.[46] Time is set aside on Tuesdays for team-building activities, but athletes are responsible for leading the session. Some activities that athletes commonly devise include inspirational storytelling, showing motivational movies, creating team highlight presentations, and even writing team chants or songs.

Besides scheduling athlete-led team-building sessions, coaches can draw from a wide range of coach-led team-building activities. Some examples shared by Jon Hammermeister include the Trust Fall, Human Knot, Human Pedestal, Magic Carpet, E-File, and Performance Profile.[46 (pp.167–171)] Instructions for one of these activities, E-File, are reprinted in figure 4.6.

Another team-building strategy increasingly used by effective coaches is engaging in community service activities. Every community has needs that provide countless opportunities for volunteering and serving others. Volunteering a few hours each month at a hospital or assisted-living residence, tending a community garden, participating in community cleanups, or assisting with local food drives are all team-building activities that have the added benefit of making a positive contribution and building goodwill in the community.

Regardless of the specific team-building activities used, the full value of team-building exercises will not be realized unless the activity is followed by a formal debriefing. Immediately following a team-building activity, athletes will be in an emotionally vulnerable state that presents coaches with a golden teachable moment.

Team-building activities serve the same purpose as priming an engine. The activity creates an optimal state of athlete readiness to learn about team cohesion, team core values, and their own strengths and weaknesses as team builders.

## Figure 4.6 E-File Team-Building Activity Instructions

### Objective

The *E* in E-File stands for enthusiasm. The activity is designed to teach and reinforce the importance of being a good teammate by serving as a source of positive energy and support for each other. At the end of the activity each athlete on the team receives an enthusiasm file filled with statements of admiration from every other teammate. This activity can be done at any time during the season, but it may be most effective late in the preseason after the team has had some time to train and compete together so that the enthusiasm comments will be more authentic.

### Materials Required

Pencils, a pad of paper, and one file folder for each athlete

### Procedure

1. Give each athlete a pencil, a sheet of paper, and a file folder.
2. Ask each team member to write down their names on their file folder and place it in the center of the room.
3. Then ask them to write down 3 things that they admire about EACH other member of the team. They should use a separate sheet of paper for each team member. For example, if a soccer team has 12 team members, then each athlete will fill out 11 sheets of paper (everyone except him/herself) with 3 positive statements about each team member on each one.
4. Once they have completed all of the positive statements, have the athlete place the sheet of paper in the corresponding folder of each athlete.
5. When this process is complete, the coach should collect the folders, review them to insure all of the statements are POSITIVE, and then add his/her own statements to each athletes' file.
6. The following day, the coach passes back each athlete's "ENTHUSIASM" file and has the athletes review the statements enclosed. If done correctly, each athlete on our hypothetical soccer team would have 33 positive statements, plus 3 or more from the coach as a reminder of the important contributions they make to the team. This reminder is an excellent "feel good" exercise and can immediately help with team climate.
7. Reviewing the "E-File" from time to time can help athletes when they find their confidence or attitude waning.

### Discussion Questions

1. How did you feel when you reviewed your "E-File?"
2. Why is it important to feel "enthusiastic" when playing sports?
3. What does this exercise tell you about how important you are to the team?
4. What does this exercise tell you about how important your teammates are to the team?

Reprinted, by permission, from J.J. Hammermeister, 2010, *Cornerstones of coaching: The building blocks for sport coaches and teams* (Traverse City, MI: Cooper Publishing), 228.

Coaches should use the time immediately following a team-building activity to lead the team in an open discussion about the meaning and lessons that can be derived from the activity. The goal of the debriefing period is not to solve any team-building issues, but to stimulate self- and collective-reflection about team dynamics.

## STRENGTHENING TEAM COHESION

Cohesion is typically thought of as the degree to which a group feels connected and remains united while pursuing a common purpose or goal. Connection to one another is considered a form of social cohesion, whereas working toward a common goal is considered a form of task cohesion.[47]

One of the most compelling questions asked about cohesion is whether cohesion causes improved performance or whether improved performance increases cohesion. Thankfully, coaches don't have to comb through hundreds of research papers to learn the answer to these questions. Reviews of the research show that cohesion is both a cause and a result of improved athletic performance.[48, 49] Some other findings about cohesion and performance include the following:

- Both social and task cohesion are highly linked with improved team performance.
- Social cohesion is more strongly connected with improved team performance than task cohesion.
- Cohesion matters for both individual and team sports.
- The relationship between cohesion and improved performance is evident for both genders, but it is extremely high for female athletes.

An often-cited cohesion study by Paul Turman with college student-athletes, both males and females across a range of sports, sheds light on the types of coaching strategies that either contribute to or detract from team cohesion.[50] Turman found that abusive language and ridicule, particularly public ridicule, were coaching behaviors that greatly reduced team cohesion and trust. On the other hand, any coaching behavior that fostered trust and positive relationships had a strong positive influence on team cohesion. The coaching strategies that contributed most to team cohesion included frequent praise, coach enthusiasm, playful teasing and joking with players, motivational team-oriented speeches, setting team goals, creating team unity councils, and scheduling quality opponents.

Many successful coaches use the concept of a player unity council to build cohesion and trust among a team. In the Turman study football players reported that two senior athletes from each position on the team formed the unity council, which was responsible for bringing team issues to the coaching staff. Player councils are most effective when they hold meetings at frequent and regular intervals as way to be proactive in identifying and resolving team cohesion issues.

Conversely, athletes report a decline in team cohesion and trust when coaches show unequal treatment or favoritism among the team and when coaches embarrass or ridicule athletes in public.[50] Belittling or demeaning an athlete erodes confidence and respect, so this type of coaching behavior is clearly counterproductive.

Treating all athletes the same, however, is a more complicated issue. Legendary American championship college football coach Bo Schembechler's famous mantra was "The team, the team, the team."[51] He believed that coaches must apply one standard equally to all players on a team. This equal-treatment standard served his teams well, as he compiled a record of 234-65-8 across his 27 years as a head coach in college football.

Unlike Coach Schembechler, 10-time national collegiate champion basketball coach John Wooden believed that equal treatment is not equitable treatment. Coach Wooden used the standard of fairness to guide his coaching behaviors.[52] He believed that every player deserved to be treated fairly, meaning that each athlete was treated differently depending on how he behaved. Coach Wooden reported that this strategy enhanced team cohesion because athletes knew in advance that they would have to work hard to earn the type of respect, trust, and treatment they desired.

I asked one of Coach Wooden's former athletes, two-time national champion and former professional basketball player Swen Nater, about this apparent contrast between two legendary coaches. Swen, a championship coach in his own right, explained that treating everyone the same is in fact unfair. Swen shared the example of dealing with players who are late to practice. If the coach has one standard for dealing with this issue (e.g., if you are late, you won't start in the next game), that standard is not fair because it does not take into account the history, tendency, work habits, or contributions of the offending athlete.

For example, is it fair to apply the same punishment to two athletes who arrive late to practice if one is a model teammate and first-time offender and the other one has a poor work ethic and shows a general lack of respect for the coach and team rules? What is the correct approach? Which one contributes most to building team cohesion? I believe that the most effective approach is the one that fits with your personal coaching values and philosophy. Regardless of whether the athletes or other coaches agree or disagree with your approach, trust and team cohesion will be enhanced if you are authentic, transparent, and consistent in your coaching behaviors and your treatment of your athletes.

Team meals are a fun and effective way to build team cohesion. For example, high school football coach Bob Ladouceur made Thursday night team meals at his home a pregame ritual throughout his record-setting career.[53] Instead of the traditional approach of bringing athletes together for a prepared meal, coaches can have the athletes prepare the meal as a way to increase the effect of the activity on building team cohesion.

For example, athletes can be given the responsibility of planning the menu and preparing some or all of the team meal.[54] Athletes can be required to plan the meal, generate a grocery list, prepare the meal, and clean up afterward. This type of activity forces team members to assume leadership, designate roles, negotiate and come to consensus on a menu, and learn about each other (food allergies, food preferences, food preparation skills, and so on).

I collaborated on a study in which a version of this team-building strategy was tested with youth soccer and basketball coaches.[55] Coaches took their teams on a shopping trip to the grocery store, where athletes were allowed to select ingredients for the team meal. Before the shopping trip the coach debriefed the athletes about healthy food choices and athlete nutrition. All coaches reported that the team-prepared meal activity resulted in improved team cohesion, bonding, and communication, all with the added benefit of teaching athletes about healthy food choices and nutrition.

## INCREASING COLLECTIVE EFFICACY

Cohesion and trust are increased when athletes and coaches have confidence in each other's ability to meet the challenges of intense training and competition. The term that describes this type of group confidence is *collective efficacy*. Group confidence directly influences how team members interact with and trust each other to meet collective goals.[10, 35]

College Football Hall of Fame coach Bobby Bowden credits unwavering teammate belief in each other as the key ingredient in his two national championship teams. In the preseason he would often tell his team a story about holding the rope as a way to instill group confidence.[56 (p. 10)]

> What did our 1993 national championship team and 1999 championship team do that was in common? They held the rope!
>
> What does holding the rope mean? You are hanging from the edge of a cliff 500 yards in the air. The only thing between you and falling to the ground is a piece of rope with the person of your choice on the other end.
>
> Who do you know that you can trust enough? Who do you know who has enough guts to withstand rope burn, watch blood drip from his hands, and still not let go?
>
> Look around and ask, "Who can I trust to hold the rope?" Who will let his hands bleed for me? If you can look at every member of your team and say they will hold the rope, then your team will win!

Collective efficacy is both enhanced by and contributes to team cohesion. That is, teams that feel more connected to each other and team goals feel more confident in their ability to perform successfully. Teams with high levels of group confidence consistently outperform teams with low levels of group confidence. Moreover, teams with high collective efficacy are more committed to team goals, report higher levels of satisfaction and effort, and describe lower levels of anxiety and stress.

Coaches should be aware of at least five potential sources of collective efficacy: (1) past performances, (2) verbal persuasion, (3) vicarious experiences, (4) motivational climate, and (5) team size. For example, teams with a record or history of successful performance show greater confidence in their ability to perform successfully in the future. Teams with high collective efficacy take great pride in winning and always set extremely high performance standards, largely because they identify themselves as winners who can overcome any challenge.

Collective efficacy also appears to increase when coaches regularly share inspirational stories about leadership and teamwork, as a form of verbal persuasion. Note, however, that coaches should be careful to tailor motivational speeches to the needs of their athletes at particular times in a season and present them in a way that is consistent with the coaches' leadership style.

Coaches can also help their teams improve their group confidence by showing them examples of other athletes and teams like them, referred to as actor-observer similarity,[9] performing successfully. In this sense, the athletes and teams experience success vicariously by watching the successful performances of others.

When athletes see other performers like them (e.g., same gender, sport, and level of competition) succeeding, and the coach inspires them to believe that they too have the skills and work ethic needed to reach the same level of achievement, collective efficacy can increase and performance can improve. For that reason, among others, championships are common across multiple sports in some high schools and colleges. Positive vicarious experiences stimulate a "Why not us?" attitude that is contagious among fellow athletes and teams. Athletes routinely see other athletes and teams like them succeeding, which builds a culture of confidence. Perhaps the old saying "Success breeds success" should be amended to "Success breeds shared confidence, which breeds success."

In his book *Championship Team Building*,[37] sport psychologist Jeff Janssen shares many innovative activities that coaches can use or adapt to build collective efficacy on their teams, such as Secret Psych Pals, I Got Your Back, Confidence Circle, and Support Squad. For the Secret Psych Pals activity, each athlete on the team draws a name of a teammate from a hat. The athlete is then responsible for secretly supporting the teammate over a specified time, typically one week. Athletes can write anonymous notes, leave treats in the teammate's bag, or perform any other type of deed that makes the teammate feel good about him- or herself and know that he or she is a valued member of the team.

With the I Got Your Back and the Confidence Circle activities, the team is brought together in a team meeting. Each athlete is given a sheet of paper with the word "strengths" printed across the top.

In the I Got Your Back activity, the sheet of paper is taped to the back of each athlete's shirt. The athletes walk around the room writing the strengths they see in their teammates on the sheet. At the end of the activity, athletes remove the sheets of paper from their backs and read what their teammates wrote about them.

A variation of this exercise is the Confidence Circle. This time, instead of taping the strengths sheets to their backs, the athletes sit in a circle and pass their strengths sheets around the circle. Teammates write in a strength until their own sheets return to them.

The last example of a collective efficacy exercise is the Support Squad (see figure 4.7). Athletes are paired up at the beginning of a week. Each athlete then completes the Support Squad worksheet. Notice on the worksheet that each athlete writes down her or his goals for the week (Challenge me to . . .), potential barriers to achieving the goals (Support me if I struggle with . . .), and effective strategies for dealing with likely setbacks (If I get frustrated, remind me to . . .).

The final two sources of collective efficacy that coaches can directly address are motivational climate and team size. Coaches who provide frequent praise and encouragement and who focus on the process of improvement as opposed to

## Figure 4.7 Support Squad Worksheet

Date: ______________________________

Name: ______________________________

Challenge me to . . .

______________________________

______________________________

______________________________

Support me if I struggle with . . .

______________________________

______________________________

______________________________

If I get frustrated remind me to . . .

______________________________

______________________________

______________________________

Reprinted, by permission, from J. Janssen, 1999, *Championship team building: What every coach needs to know to build a motivated, committed and cohesive team* (Tucson, AZ: Winning the Mental Game), 146. www.JanssenSportsLeadership.com

winning at all costs create the type of motivational climate most associated with increased team confidence. In this type of environment athletes experience less anxiety because coaches put less pressure on the outcome and short-term wins and focus more on the process and long-term success.

Finally, some evidence suggests that as team size increases, collective efficacy decreases.[57] Certainly, with large teams such as in football, getting all members of a team to share the same passion and commitment to team goals and confidence in each other's abilities can be difficult. Coaches should therefore adopt a shared or distributed leadership approach. All members of a coaching staff and the athletes themselves, particularly those who are assigned formal leadership roles, must have the confidence and freedom to act as collective efficacy builders.

# COACHING WITH AN APPROPRIATE LEADERSHIP STYLE

Leadership is generally defined as a process of influence. A coach's leadership style, then, comprises the behavioral processes that a coach uses to influence his or her athletes. Two recommended leadership styles for effective sport coaching are transformational leadership and servant leadership.

Transformational leaders inspire others to become self-directed and motivated while de-emphasizing personal interests and goals in the pursuit of collective team needs and goals. Features of a transformational leadership style include ethical behavior, shared leadership, leading by example, and using frequent praise and encouragement.[58, 59] Giving frequent encouragement and helping athletes pull the lessons from performance failures creates an environment where athletes feel safe enough to risk failure.[60]

The transformational leadership style features four types of leadership behaviors, referred to as the four Is: idealized influence (modeling humility, modesty, and core values), inspirational motivation (serving as an eternal optimist, showing enthusiasm for shared goals), intellectual stimulation (inspiring creativity and risk taking), and individualized consideration (showing compassion and empathy for the unique needs of others).[61]

Transformational leadership is often contrasted with transactional leadership. Transactional leadership features an emphasis on leading through coercion and rewards. One way to think about the difference between transformational and transactional leadership styles is to consider transformational leadership as a style that emphasizes doing the right thing whereas transactional leadership is a style that emphasizes doing things the right way.[61]

Research with effective sport coaches shows support for adopting a transformational leadership style. Coaches who are transformational leaders are effective at clearly articulating and sharing an envisioned future for the team (inspirational motivation) while also providing multiple opportunities for shared leadership and athlete input on decision making (intellectual stimulation).[62]

Transformational leadership is considered a form of "we leadership." Jon Martin, who has never had a losing season in 38 years as a college soccer and lacrosse coach, is a prime example of a "we leadership" coach.[63] Coach Martin achieves transformational leadership by creating a sense of shared ownership: "We empower everybody. They all have a say in the decision-making process, our trainers, assistant coaches, players, everyone."[(p. 63)]

Athletes who play for coaches who adopt a transformational leadership style report greater enjoyment, collective efficacy, and cohesion.[64] Furthermore, when athletes play on a team with transformational peer leaders (fellow athletes on their team), they score higher on measures of task and social cohesion. In other words, playing on a team with a coach and fellow athletes who model transformational leadership behaviors inspires greater self-confidence, commitment to team goals, and positive relationships with the coach and teammates.

Finally, team cohesion has been found to be strongly influenced by four transformational leadership behaviors: (1) fostering acceptance of group goals, (2) promoting teamwork, (3) adopting high-performance expectations, and (4) considering personal feelings and needs. Transformational leadership behaviors modeled by team captains and coaches that separate high-performing teams from low-performing teams are high performance expectations, inspirational motivation, and appropriate role modeling.

One of the greatest professional athletes of all time, ice hockey player Wayne Gretzky, is an example of a peer leader who exemplified all the characteristics of a transformational leader. Many who worked and played alongside him consider his transformational leadership behaviors a key reason for the unprecedented success his teams experienced while he played for them.[65]

Another recommended leadership style is servant leadership. Servant leadership, like transformational leadership, is other-centered. The servant leadership style, however, places a greater premium on integrity, morals, and empathy—virtues that supersede any concern for sport-specific goals. Legendary award-winning and national championship college basketball coach Don Meyer is perhaps the most famous example of a coach who embodied the qualities of servant leadership.[66]

Servant leadership is sometimes considered an upside-down, or inverted, leadership style because the goal is to serve rather than lead. Characteristics, or virtues, of servant leaders are ethical and caring behavior, shared decision making, humility, altruism, and integrity—all of which directly contribute to trusting relationships. Coaches who adopt this leadership style view themselves as stewards whose primary role is to build and enable athletes by focusing on their strengths rather than their weaknesses.

Adopting elements of a servant leadership approach to coaching appears to offer many benefits.[67–70] Athletes who play for servant leadership coaches report higher scores on personal and team satisfaction, team cohesion, sport enjoyment and motivation, confidence and coping skills, and respect for the coach.

Furthermore, teams coached by servant leader coaches have been shown to outperform teams coached by nonservant leader coaches. Athletes not only prefer to play for servant leader coaches but also set higher achievement targets, believe that they are improving more, are more resilient, and indeed are more successful.

American college football coach Jim Tressel, who coached teams to five national championships, is an example of someone who coached with a servant leadership style. Consistent with servant leadership principles, Coach Tressel explained to me that success in coaching starts with compassion for those you are entrusted to lead. Compassion means showing care, respect, and concern for all your athletes, regardless of their ability or role on the team.[71]

Transformational and servant leadership styles have the same core purpose—an overriding concern for helping athletes meet their technical, physical, and emotional needs. In this sense, transformational and servant coach leadership styles might best be viewed as athlete-centered leadership styles.

For coaches who may think that this type of leadership style is a soft approach, think again. Successful coaches who adopt an athlete-centered leadership style are strong willed and sometimes autocratic, but they also regularly model trust, inclusion, and compassion. Successful coaches sometimes refer to this as a blended approach to coaching—a delicate balance between pushing athletes to their limits and showing compassion and support.

This approach is embodied by championship coaches across sports, and it applies equally well to coaching male and female athletes. Lori Dauphiny, two-time national Coach of the Year who has coached rowers for over 20 years, said, “I'm always supportive, but at the same time I have to push pretty hard. I have to be tough with them.”[72 (p. 188)] Love and high expectations are cornerstones to her successful coaching approach.[73] Similarly, Jack Del Rio, longtime coach in the National Football League, started his tenure as head coach of the Oakland Raiders by instilling a culture of positive reinforcement to counterbalance the tough and demanding standards to which he held the athletes.

> We're developing young men, loving them up with positive praise, not just a constant beat down. We're going to drive them and push them hard and point out mistakes, but don't just dwell on it. That goes back to more of the positive thinking and positive reinforcement and helping them (have) positive energy and seeing themselves doing it right.[74]

Hall of Fame college volleyball coach Hugh McCutcheon, who has coached both the U.S. men's and women's teams to Olympic medals using an athlete-centered coaching approach, is perhaps the best example to show that this approach works regardless of athlete gender.[75] Coaches such as Dauphiny, Del Rio, and McCutcheon are successful and revered by their athletes because they blend toughness with love and compassion to create a caring climate.

Athlete-centered leadership is a balanced approach in which coaches set clear roles and boundaries for athletes while also providing opportunities for distributed leadership and athlete input, sometimes referred to as control with benevolence.[76, 77] In the end, the label assigned to the leadership style is less important than the awareness that athletes prefer, and perform best, when coaches create learning environments built on trust, inclusion, and compassion.

## Wrap-Up

Whether a team comprises one coach and a single athlete, or several coaches and dozens of athletes, long-term, durable success hinges on a coach's ability to build quality relationships. Ultimately, coaches are in the people business. Effective coaches never lose sight of this fundamental insight.

Relationship building is challenging and never-ending work that requires commitment to open communication and a genuine desire to understand the views of others. Athletes who play for coaches who regularly model compassion, integrity, shared decision making, and ethical and caring behaviors consistently report high levels of trust and satisfaction with not only their coaches but also their teammates. High levels of mutual trust foster closeness, commitment, collective efficacy, and cohesion within teams and are directly linked to enhanced performance.

Coaches who fail to monitor their trust banks by making regular trust deposits to counter trust withdrawals that will surely occur across a sport season are in danger of having teams that fail to break through the storming stage of team building. Although time consuming and sometimes emotionally and physically draining, creating and scheduling a wide range of relationship-building and communication activities is well worth the investment.

When asked what they cherish most from their careers, all championship coaches say that it was the relationships they built with their athletes along the way. Take a page from the playbooks of the world's most successful coaches and set aside time in your daily routine to make a personal connection with each of your athletes. This simple strategy leads not only to better performance but also to a more enjoyable and enriching sport experience.

# Part II

# IN-SEASON

## Enact

## Chapter 5

# Develop Athletic Talent and Skill

### Key Concepts

Genetic influences on athletic skill
Deliberate practice
Long-term athlete development
Physical literacy
Developmental model of sport participation
Free play
Sport sampling
Multilateral development
American Development Model
Athlete development models in action

On January 11, 2015, 17-time Grand Slam tennis champion Roger Federer achieved the rare milestone of winning 1,000 professional matches. Following the match he said he was glad that the match was mentally and physically challenging.[1] Great athletes across sport relish playing against the best and in big moments in competition. How much influence does a coach have in developing this athletic talent and skill, and how much of this drive to succeed and willingness to risk failure and work ethic is inborn?

Considerable debate has occurred over how much of athletic talent is determined by genetics versus training and coaching. Genetics undeniably lays the foundation for an athlete's potential to succeed in any given sport. Nowhere is this point more evident than in the visually stunning photography project completed by Howard Schatz.[2,3] A quick look at the series of photographs comparing Olympic athletes across different sports illustrates that although training and quality coaching are critical to athlete development, body size and type play a significant role in an athlete's ability to succeed in specific sports.

The most decorated Olympic athlete of all-time, U.S. swimmer Michael Phelps, who won 28 medals (23 gold, 3 silver, 2 bronze), is perhaps the most vivid example in support of the influence of genetics on developing athletic talent. Often referred to as the flying fish, he was gifted with what many consider the perfect swimming body—above average wingspan compared with body height, joint hyperextension, size 14 feet (European size 48.5), disproportionately long upper body, and perhaps most unusual of all his ability to produce less than half the amount of lactic acid of rival swimmers, allowing him to recover much quicker.[4]

The constant advance of new technologies provides greater insight into how our genes influence and shape who we become. David Epstein, in his book *The Sports Gene*, draws on results of some of these techniques to show the various genetic advantages possessed by the world's greatest athletes.[5]

One compelling example is high jumper Donald Thomas, who won the world championships in only his second year of training. In 2007 Thomas defeated defending world and Olympic champion Stefan Holm of Sweden, who had devoted most of his life to developing his talent as a high jumper. It was later learned that Thomas was blessed with unusually long legs and more important, a much longer than average Achilles tendon relative to his height, both of which are significant competitive advantages in jumping. Showing further support for the role of genetics in developing athlete talent, despite six years of coaching following his entry into professional high jumping, Thomas did not improve even one centimeter.[5]

Although successful coaches acknowledge the indisputable role of genetics in developing athletic skill, they also recognize that the expression of genetic potential rests on a coach's ability to create an optimal setting for talent development. Although each athlete possesses unique characteristics, humans in general are much more alike than dissimilar, sharing over 99 percent of the genetic sequence.[6] This discovery has largely rendered the quest for a single sport gene obsolete and illustrates the critical role of the coach in helping athletes reach their potential.

Whether helping a young athlete make a high school team or preparing an experienced athlete to challenge for a spot on a professional or Olympic team, the actions of quality coaches are governed by a few common principles of athlete development. The purpose of this chapter is to describe principles of athlete talent development and ways in which successful coaches employ these principles in their everyday practice.

## CONDUCTING PRACTICES

No athlete masters a skill or reaches her or his potential without practicing for thousands of hours. A long-standing view in sport is that more is better when it comes to practice. Every sport and every generation has its own version of the star athlete who boasts about practicing just a little bit longer than the competition.

For example, former college Athlete of the Year and the first female basketball player to score 1,000 points in a single season Jackie Stiles was renowned for her self-imposed 1,000-shot practice routine.[7]In college she wouldn't allow herself to leave the gym until she made 1,000 baskets, taking shots from various spots around the court. Although this volume of practice undoubtedly contributed to the development of her basketball skill, it may have also caused her to require 13 surgeries and end her career after just two years of professional basketball.

Athletes like Stiles, as well as coaches, often wear practice volume like a badge of honor. In the lead-up to the 1992 Summer Olympics in Barcelona, T-shirts with the slogan "No Pain, No Gain, No Spain" were often seen, and this became a mantra for prospective U.S. Olympic athletes.[8, 9]

In recent years the popularity of a theory used to explain differences between expert and novice has inadvertently fueled this overemphasis on practice volume for developing athletic talent and skill. The theory, known as deliberate practice, was introduced to the world in a 1993 paper published by a group of scientists lead by K. Anders Ericsson.[10] Deliberate practice was widely debated and discussed in the scientific literature for 15 years before it exploded onto the coaching scene through the publication of best-selling books such as *Outliers*[11] and *The Talent Code.*[12]

The key for coaches to understanding deliberate practice is that it is the type and quality of practice, not the overall volume, that contribute most to the development of athletic talent and skill. Deliberate practice is a special type of practice that requires intense mental concentration and high physical effort. This kind of practice is designed specifically to close critical performance gaps at an appropriate level of difficulty with a focus on long-term improvement.[10, 13, 14]

A summary of the defining features of deliberate practice and suggestions for coaches to consider when developing athletic talent and skill is provided in table 5.1. Notice how the features of deliberate practice are different from the common focus of many athletes and coaches on the amount of practice. Practicing longer does not contribute to skill development if the practice is not focused and is not directly relevant to closing performance gaps.

Deliberate practice might be considered stretch practice because it stretches athletes to work outside their comfort zones. Some studies have found that when asked to reflect on their training histories, expert athletes report that deliberate practice was highly enjoyable, a direct contrast to findings from the original research with musicians.[15] But when asked to reflect on how enjoyable deliberate practice is while actually engaged in it, expert athletes rate it as highly unenjoyable.

Contemporaneous observation is a more accurate gauge of the physical and mental demands of deliberate practice. Despite rating deliberate practice activities as unenjoyable and difficult, the most successful athletes will select such activities over less demanding and perhaps more fun practice activities because they realize the long-term value of deliberate practice.[16] This commitment to deliberate practice appears to be a key difference between expert and less successful athletes.

When Ericsson first reported on his deliberate practice studies, he found that it took approximately 10 years and 10,000 hours of deliberate practice to become an expert. The 10-year, 10,000-hour finding soon incorrectly became known as a training rule, and many people assumed that they would achieve expert athlete status after they reached that magical deliberate practice milestone. Likely the most extreme example of this belief is the golfer who at age 30 famously launched the Dan Plan in his attempt to become a professional golfer despite having no competitive sport experience and having never played a full round of golf.[17]

## Table 5.1 Defining Features of Deliberate Practice and Considerations for Coaches

| Deliberate practice features | Coaching considerations |
|---|---|
| Demands full concentration and accurate mental images of the skill | Provide sufficient demonstration and verbal instruction before initiating athlete deliberate practice. Use video, teaching cues, and keywords to help athletes focus on critical components of the skill or tactic. Set aside time during practice for athletes to reflect on their performance and discuss with coaches and peers. |
| Requires near-maximal physical effort and sufficient recovery | Provide athletes with frequent rest periods both within and between practices. Keep deliberate practice sessions short and intense. Focus on quality of practice activities as opposed to amount of time spent in practice. |
| Involves well-defined and specific goals for practicing just beyond the comfort zone | Closely monitor and track athlete skill development as frequently as possible (during and after each practice and competition when possible). Combine objective performance data (statistics) with subjective information (coach observations) to identify critical performance gaps and to offer the correct level of difficulty for training activities. |
| Not perceived as enjoyable because of effort requirement | Avoid designing practice sessions that include only deliberate practice activities. Include some activities, particularly at the end of practice, that are less demanding and more enjoyable. Allow some time for athletes to practice or refine their strengths. |
| Focus on long-term improvement with coaching support | Expect many failures and setbacks because of the focus on closing performance gaps and the high demands of deliberate practice. Identify and immediately reinforce small improvements in any aspect of the skill or performance. Encourage and support risk taking and recognize effort and positive attitude toward practice. |

Since the original deliberate practice study was published, the 10-year, 10,000-hour rule has been found not to fit the talent development profile of elite athletes around the world. In his recent update on deliberate practice, Ericsson himself refutes the 10,000-hour rule.[15] He explains that it was author Malcolm Gladwell who coined the 10,000-hour rule based on a review of his expertise research. A review of the current deliberate practice research in sport shows wide variability in the number of deliberate practice hours needed to become an expert athlete. Some athletes need much more than 10,000 hours, whereas other athletes require less than 4,000 hours.[13]

A vivid example of this variability is elite rowing athlete Helen Glover, who took up rowing at age 22 and was never before a competitive athlete. With just two years of training (deliberate practice) she won a silver medal in the world championships, and within four years she became an Olympic champion.[18] As this example and the research clearly show, no rule applies to deliberate practice. Even elite athletes in the same sport often show great variability in the amount of deliberate practice needed to reach the pinnacle of their sport.

This conclusion illustrates a key lesson for coaches about deliberate practice. Athletes don't necessarily need more practice; they need better practice. Deliberate practice is better practice because as Dr. Ericsson explains, "If you never push yourself beyond your comfort zone, you will never improve."[14 (p. 18)]

Coaches must also keep in mind that by definition athletes will only be able to complete short bouts of deliberate practice because of the intense mental and physical demands of this type of practice. The potential benefits of deliberate practice for developing athlete talent and skill will be wasted unless coaches balance the need for deliberate practice with deliberate recovery.[13]

Coaches must carefully and constantly evaluate their athletes' readiness to handle increasing levels of deliberate practice. The appropriate amount and type of deliberate practice will vary for each athlete, and coaches should always remember to watch for signs of mental and physical fatigue. Knowing when to pause or reduce deliberate practice activities will greatly decrease the likelihood of injury during practices.

The gains achieved from deliberate practice training will quickly be lost unless practice activities are also included that allow athletes to recover and prepare for the next bout of deliberate practice. Championship coaches such as Bob Bowman, long-time coach of Michael Phelps, counter-balance deliberate practice with regular low-intensity and fun practice sessions.[19] For example, he has offered his athletes "Friends Friday," when swimmers were allowed to bring a friend to practice to workout with them.[20] The newcomers provided a regular and much needed spark, raising everyone's energy level while rekindling their excitement for swimming.

## PROMOTING LONG-TERM ATHLETE DEVELOPMENT

Successful coaches know that they must adjust how they coach to fit the level of the athletes they are coaching. Although a coach's core values and many elements of his or her coaching philosophy are relatively stable, helping athletes develop their talent requires coaches to situate their coaching in the long-term, multiyear chain of athlete development.[21] The most widely adopted athlete development framework in the world is the long-term athlete development model (LTAD).[22]

The LTAD model was created by a group of sport scientists to counter the prevailing "great by chance" approach to athlete development. Noticing that no standardized guide was available to help coaches and sport organizations design optimal athlete training and competition settings, the group proposed a multistage model that identifies unique athlete developmental profiles across the lifespan. The LTAD model comprises seven stages. Coaches may find it helpful to think of the seven stages of athlete development as three progressive phases of sport participation, each with unique considerations for coaches. The three phases are physical literacy, excellence through high-performance sport, and active for life (see figure 5.1).

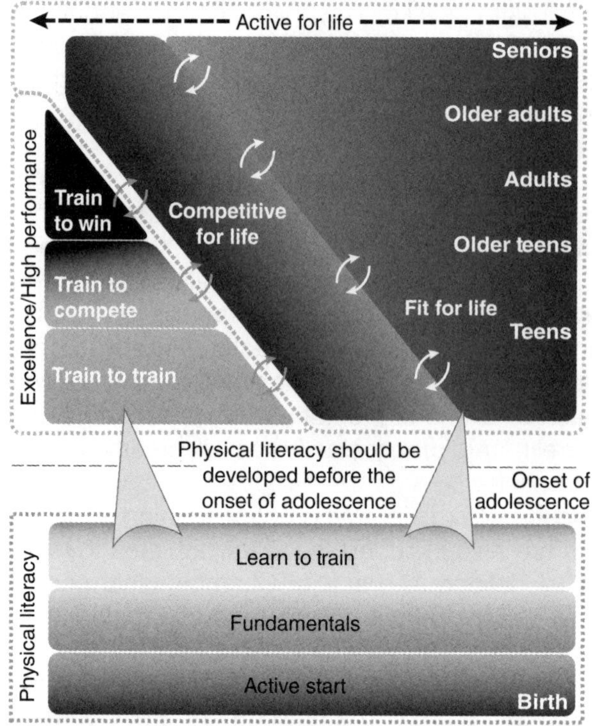


**Figure 5.1** Phases and stages of long-term athlete development.

Reprinted, by permission, from I. Balyi, R. Way, and C. Higgs, 2013, *Long-term athlete development* (Champaign, IL: Human Kinetics), 36.

The first phase includes LTAD stage 1 (active start), stage 2 (FUNdamentals), and stage 3 (learn to train). This phase represents initial entry into organized sport for young athletes, typically those under the age of 12. During this phase coaches should focus on teaching basic movement skills such as coordination, agility, and balance while creating a fun sport experience that will cause the young athlete to want to return the following season. The overarching term used to describe this phase is physical literacy. Physical literacy is defined as the ability and motivation to participate in physical activity, which includes organized sport experiences.

The second phase includes LTAD stage 4 (train to train), stage 5 (train to compete), and stage 6 (train to win). During this phase of participation athletes develop and refine their athletic talent and skill to their fullest potential. Most participants in this phase will have already had some exposure to organized sport and coaching. Although coaches should teach and reinforce fundamental movement skills across all phases, the coach's role during the second phase should shift more to teaching sport-specific skills and tactics.

By this point, athletes are generally thought to be more ready to respond physiologically to training. Coaches typically integrate aerobic and strength training during this phase. Coaching athletes in this phase requires coaches to have in-depth knowledge of their sport and know how to prepare athletes for high-performance competitive situations. Some athletes may never reach this phase, but others, depending on the sport and their level of physical and emotional readiness, may enter this phase quite early. Also, keep in mind that this phase really has no upper age limit; some professional and Olympic athletes compete in their 40s and 50s, and masters athletes compete well beyond that age.

Regardless of the phase at which an athlete leaves organized sport, the goal of the LTAD model is to increase the likelihood that all sport participants will reach the third phase, or stage 7 (active for life). Those who continue to play sport in this phase will likely do so without a coach (e.g., organized recreational adult sport). Additionally, many athletes in this phase will transition to the role of the coach, guiding other athletes through the LTAD stages.

A discussion of the LTAD model would be incomplete without acknowledging some of the critiques that have emerged since its introduction. Many have criticized LTAD because of the suggestion that distinct training windows correspond to specific stages of development and that these stages can be identified by the age of the athletes.[23, 24] The creators of LTAD, however, acknowledge that each athlete develops at a unique pace; therefore, the age ranges are offered simply as approximations.[22] Furthermore, athletes at any age will benefit from quality training if it is appropriately matched to their current level of growth and maturation, something referred to as "synergistic adaptation."[25]

Also, the LTAD creators explain that age can be measured in many ways, the most common— and the most problematic from an athlete development perspective—being chronological age. For example, two 12-year-old athletes may differ in developmental age (physical, mental, cognitive, and emotional maturation) by as much as 6 years (e.g., one may be more similar to a typical 9-year-old, whereas the other may be more similar to a typical 15-year-old).[26]

Coaches must also be sensitive to what is referred to as relative age when designing training for their athletes.[27] Many sport organizations group participants by arbitrary birthdate cutoffs (e.g., participant must be 8 years old or younger by December 31 of a specific year to be eligible to compete in a specific age division). A substantial amount of research shows the overrepresentation of athletes in professional sport who were born early in the selection year.[28] Using the example provided, the athlete who turns 8 years old on December 31 may be at a considerable disadvantage to the athlete who turns 8 on January 1 of the same year. The athlete with the early birthdate will likely be much stronger, bigger, and faster and therefore able to handle more advanced training.

Finally, coaches should be careful to avoid the conclusion that athlete development progresses in a tidy linear fashion, that early success in one stage of development predicts success in later stages of development.[29, 30, 31] Early signs of athletic talent and skill are extremely poor predictors of future success as an athlete. Based on findings from the talent development research, the growing trend to attempt to identify and recruit talented athletes at very young ages is futile at best and harmful at worst. Athletes who are labeled as talented at an early age may expect that they can rely on their talent and thus lower their commitment to effortful practice. This mind-set is harmful to long-term athlete development because it impedes an athlete's ability to handle the demands and setbacks associated with deliberate practice[32] (see detailed discussion on the importance of a growth mind-set to quality practice in chapter 7).

In sum, there does not appear to be any one right or best pathway for developing athletic talent and skill; studies show wide variation in the early sport experiences of professional and championship adult athletes. Furthermore, the overwhelming majority of high-performance adult athletes did not play on regional or national select teams in the early stages of their talent development.

Although debate has continued about the value and accuracy of the LTAD model, no one denies that it has had a profound influence on how coaches are advised to develop athletic talent and skill. LTAD should not be viewed as the recipe for developing athletic talent and skill, but it does provide coaches with many valuable ideas and suggestions to consider when designing training and competition environments. LTAD raises coaches' awareness of the need to consider each athlete's unique readiness (physical, mental, emotional, and cognitive) for progressive levels of training and competition.

## Developmental Model of Sport Participation

The developmental model of sport participation (DMSP)[33] provides a complement to the more well-known LTAD model. When viewed together, the two models give coaches a comprehensive and well-rounded understanding of athlete development.

Two features unique to the DMSP that have important implications for coaching are unstructured play and sport diversification. Although a high amount of focused, deliberate practice is clearly needed to become a skilled athlete, research also shows that expert athletes grow up in environments that allow frequent play.[34, 35]

Recall that a defining characteristic of deliberate practice is that it is challenging and requires intense focus. If deliberate practice is not counterbalanced with opportunities for uncoached practice, referred to as free play, then coaches place their athletes at increased risk of emotional and physical burnout and overuse injuries. A defining characteristic of free-play activities is that they are organized and led by the athletes themselves to maximize enjoyment and intrinsic motivation.[36] Spontaneous games of pickup basketball or soccer that are common to community parks and schoolyards are prime examples of free play. Left on their own, athletes typically modify the rules and the teams as the game progresses to ensure competitive balance, maximum participation, and fun.

Studies, including one with members of the 2014 World Cup German national soccer team,[37] comparing the world's best athletes with those who peak at lower levels of amateur sport show that the world's best spend more time in unstructured free play at early ages of sport participation than less successful athletes do. Vivid examples of the creative skills that athletes often develop through unstructured free play can be seen in popular skill demonstration videos of world-class athletes such as soccer star Ronaldinho and golfer Tiger Woods.[38]

Coaches can build free play into the athlete development experience in several ways. They can set aside some time for free play in each practice. For example, 8 to10 minutes can be set aside at the start of the practice for athletes to practice skills they select on their own. Depending on age and the ability of the athletes to work independently, this approach is valuable because it provides athletes with a few minutes to transition into structured practice and gives them a sense of ownership and input into their skill development.

Coaches may prefer to set aside time at the end of the practices for free play. When used this way, free play can be used as a reward for completing coach-directed practice activities and demonstrating respect and character throughout the practice session. Either way, when athlete-directed free play is built into the talent development process, athletes are still developing skills and, just as important, having fun.

Free play has also been found to be extremely valuable for nurturing creativity. For example, research has shown that adults with above-average creativity scores participated in roughly an equal amount of deliberate practice (organized sport) and free play (informal, unorganized sport) when they were children.[39] It has also been found that adults with the lowest creativity scores spent a much higher percentage of their time in organized sport as opposed to free play when growing up. Similarly, another study with high-performance athletes found that the most creative athletes accumulated roughly the same number of hours in deliberate practice as less creative athletes did, but they far exceeded less creative athletes in the number of hours spent in free play.[40]

Evidence is increasingly showing that providing athletes with a balance between formal structured deliberate practice and informal unstructured free play opportunities is extremely beneficial to athlete talent development (see figure 5.2). This balanced approach to developing athlete skill and talent works because athletes learn proper techniques and tactics during deliberate practice and use free play to experiment and take risks without interruptions or fear of failing to meet someone else's performance expectations.

The second key lesson for coaches from the DMSP addresses the issue of early sport specialization. The opposite of early specialization is sport diversification, or sampling. Contrary to popular belief, considerable evidence shows that high-performance athletes sample many sports rather than specialize in one sport at an early age.[33, 41, 25, 31] For example, 90 percent of all athletes selected in the first

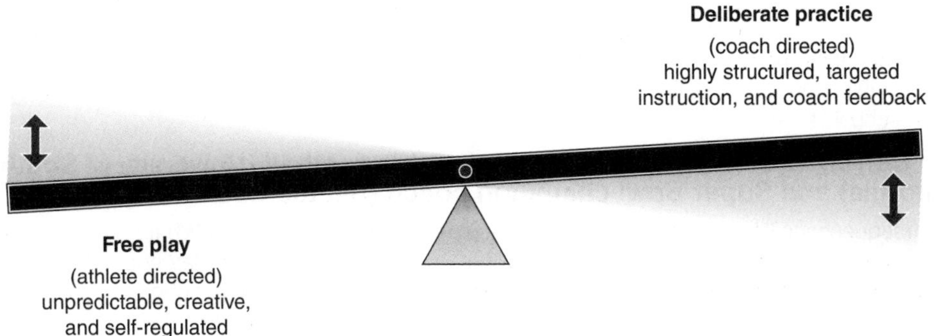


**Figure 5.2** Balanced approach to developing athletic skill and talent.

round of the 2016 National Football League (NFL) draft were multisport athletes in high school, continuing a trend that has been evident for many years now.[42–44] Furthermore, most college and Olympic athletes in the United States also played multiple sports up to high school, and college coaches typically prefer recruiting multisport athletes.[46–49] Successful coaches consistently seek out multisport athletes because they understand that sport sampling builds better athletes (see figure 5.3).

A prime example of the value of sport sampling is the U.S. women's national soccer team that won the 2015 World Cup. An informal survey of the athletes on that team found they collectively had played 14 different sports growing up and overwhelmingly recommended sport sampling.[49] Abby Wambach shared that she

## Figure 5.3 Successful Coaches' Views on Sport Sampling

### Nick Saban, multinational championship football coach, University of Alabama

"I see the mistake of tunnel vision especially in youth sports. Instead of letting kids play three or four sports all the way through high school, parents are encouraging or forcing their kids to pick one sport as young as seven or eight! Their rationale is that for them to be successful at that sport, they need to concentrate on it as early as possible. But if a young person plays various sports, he or she actually develops more skills and is exposed to more competitive situations, which later can affect development in a positive way."[48 (p. 65)]

### Tim Corbin, 2014 national championship baseball coach, Vanderbilt University

"I don't like it [early sport specialization]. When a young man or woman invests all of their time in one sport there is a feeling that they will develop more in that sport. I think there are both mental and physical issues with that. I think kids get stale. There are some overuse and injury issues. Developing athletic skills is paramount to no matter what [sport] you are doing. So I'm of the opinion of really, really branching out. I always tell parents, let your kids play other sports and they'll develop. I don't like the pressure we put on kids to specialize in one sport. I think it hinders their growth."[47]

### Dom Starsia, four-time national championship lacrosse coach, University of Virginia

"My trick question to young campers is always, 'How do you learn the concepts of team offense in lacrosse or team defense in lacrosse in the off-season, when you're not playing with your team?' The answer is by playing basketball, by playing hockey and by playing soccer and those other team games, because many of those principles are exactly the same. Probably 95 percent [of our players] are multisport athletes. It's always a bit strange to me if somebody is not playing other sports in high school."[46]

### Pete Carroll, two-time national championship football (University of Southern California) and Super Bowl champion coach (Seattle Seahawks)

"The first questions I'll ask about a kid are, 'What other sports does he play? What does he do? What are his positions? Is he a big hitter in baseball? Is he a pitcher? Does he play hoops?' All of those things are important to me. I hate that kids don't play three sports in high school. I think that they should play year-round and get every bit of it that they can through that experience. I really, really don't favor kids having to specialize in one sport."[46]

believed that the time she spent playing youth basketball was critical in helping her develop her world-class soccer skills, particularly her legendary ability to score goals by heading the ball into the net.

> **Playing basketball had a significant impact on the way I play the game of soccer. In basketball I was a power forward and I would go up and rebound the ball. So learning the timing of your jump, learning the trajectory of the ball coming off the rim, all those things play a massive role.**

Many coaches and parents fear that without early sport specialization, such as year-round baseball or swimming for young children, young athletes will fall behind and fail to realize their sport potential.[50] But early sport diversification, as opposed to early sport specialization, is linked with longer and more successful involvement in sport.[51] In fact, some research has shown that athletes who play three or more sports between the ages of 11-15 were more likely to play for a national team than those who specialized in just one sport.[52] Although early specialization may lead to quick improvement, the goal of a long-term approach to athlete development is to help athletes achieve their best performances later in their sport careers after they have reached physical and emotional maturity, typically around the age of 18 or older.

Athletes should play multiple sports each year to develop a strong foundation of general athletic skills, engaging in what is sometimes referred to as multilateral development.[51] The purpose of multilateral development is to build good athletes who have a broad foundation of athletic skills. This base will improve their resilience and ability to adapt to the increased training and competition demands when they decide to specialize in a single sport. Finally, sampling multiple sports helps young athletes avoid burnout and overuse injuries that occur from repeating the same movements without sufficient rest.

Figure 5.4 is a simple illustration for reinforcing the importance of promoting sport sampling and multilateral development for young athletes. Although the appropriate age for specializing in one sport will vary depending on the athlete's maturity and the particular sport, the general recommendation is for athletes to sample multiple sports through the end of their high school sport experience (up to age 18).

The principle of sampling is not limited to the type of sports that a young athlete plays. Young athletes benefit tremendously from sampling different roles and positions within the sports they play. Quality coaches understand that relegating young athletes to a single position or role on a team at an early age limits their long-term development. Ensuring that young athletes have opportunities to learn and play different positions within a sport allows them to develop a more comprehensive understanding of the game. Common practices such as assigning the biggest athlete to the goalkeeper position in soccer or to first base in baseball severely stunt their long-term growth and ability to play other positions.

The most successful coaches and sport clubs adopt a position-sampling approach to athlete development. For example, Spain's Sevilla Football Club, considered one of the world's top soccer clubs, doesn't assign athletes to a specific position until the ages of 16 or 17.[53] Their approach to teaching their athletes

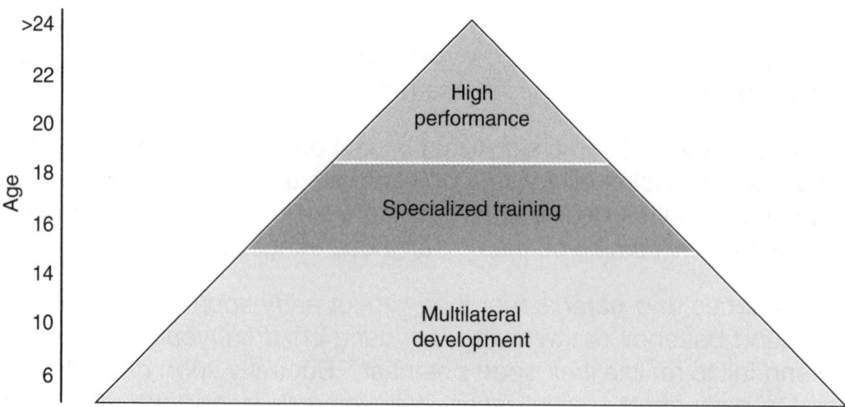


**Figure 5.4** Long-term and multilateral approach to athlete development.
Reprinted, by permission, from T.O. Bompa, 1999, *Periodization training for sports* (Champaign, IL: Human Kinetics), 39.

how to play all the positions in soccer has paid tremendous dividends. Many of their athletes are selected to play on a national team or on elite professional teams, and their club routinely produces some of the best soccer players in the world.

In sum, early diversification, or sampling, works because young athletes continue to develop transferable sport skills such as agility, balance, strength, and coordination and learn lessons from across sports that make them more versatile as athletes and improve their decision-making skills. For example, learning how to shield the ball from an opponent in soccer will help the athlete when playing other team sports such as basketball, lacrosse, and ice hockey in which similar possession skills are needed.

Sport sampling is one of the key recommendations of the recent International Olympic Committee consensus statement on athlete development, prepared by the world's leading sport scientists.[54] When working with athletes all the way through high school sport, coaches who work in the best interest of their athletes will not force them to play one sport year-round. Quality coaches understand the long-term value of having athletes participate in multiple sports each year. A considerable body of evidence now shows the multiple physical, social, and emotional benefits of early diversification (sampling) compared with the ill-advised and common push for early specialization.

An overview of these the two contrasting athlete talent development pathways, early specialization and sport sampling, is illustrated in the developmental model of sport participation (figure 5.5).[35]

## American Development Model

Inspired by the LTAD and DMSP models, in late 2014 the United States Olympic Committee (USOC) created an adapted version of these models to help guide athlete development and coaching in the United States. The USOC version,

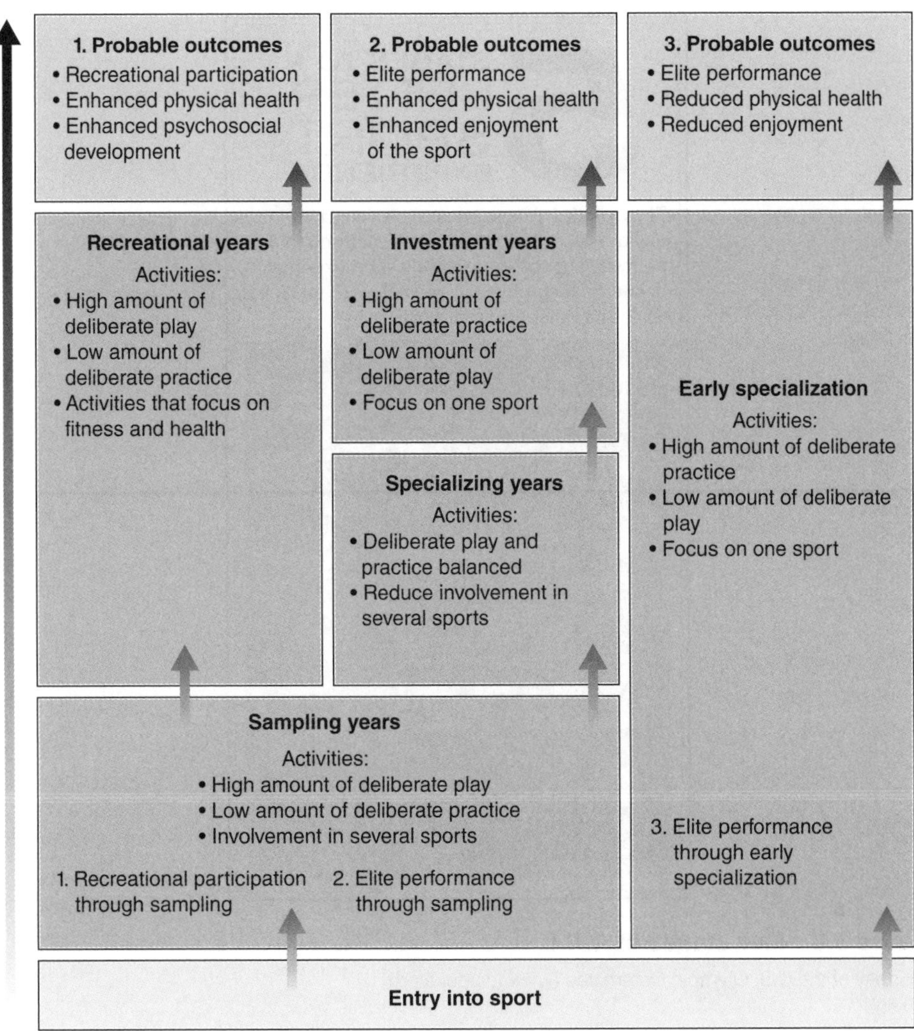


**Figure 5.5** Developmental model of sport participation.

From J. Côté, J. Murphy-Mills, and D. Abernethy, 2012, The development of skill in sport. In *Skill acquisition in sport: Research, theory and practice*, 2nd ed., edited by N.J. Hodges and A.M. Williams (Abington, Oxon, UK: Routledge), 269-286. Reproduced by permission of Taylor & Francis Books, UK.

referred to as the American Development Model (ADM), includes five stages of athlete development, illustrated in figure 5.6.[55]

Stage 1 is referred to as the discover, learn, and play phase for youth ages 0 through 12. When coaching in stage 1, coaches should focus first on creating safe and fun sport experiences that will motivate young athletes to return to sport year after year.

In stage 2 (develop and challenge), for athletes ages 10 through 16, athletes are ready to handle greater emphasis on sport-specific skill development, including individual and group tactics. When coaching athletes in stages 1 and 2, coaches should encourage multisport participation so that athletes can avoid

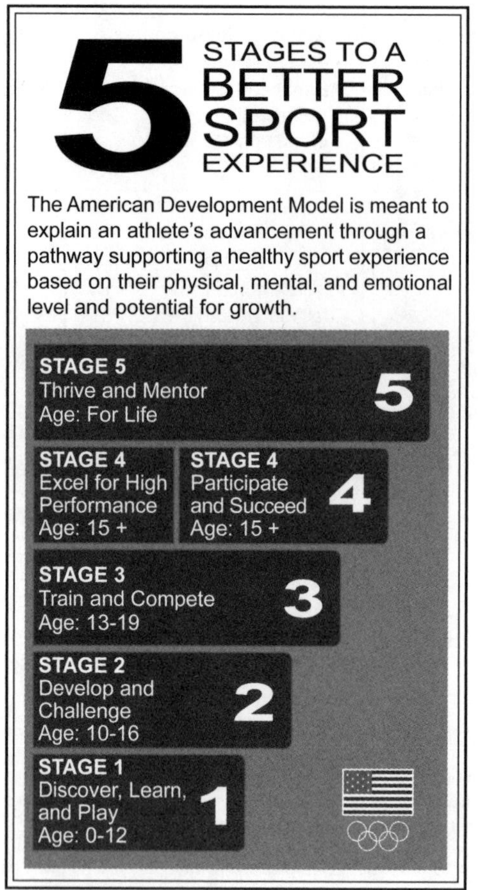


**Figure 5.6** Five stages of ADM.

Courtesy of the U.S. Olympic Committee (www.teamusa.org).

overuse injuries and burnout while continuing to develop foundational skills such as agility, coordination, strength, and balance.

Most high school sport coaches will be working with athletes in stage 3 (ages 13 through 19), the train and compete stage of athlete development. During this stage, competitive athletes will have to limit their sport involvement to one or two sports so that they can focus on more specialized and more intensive training and competition schedules.

Stage 4 of the ADM represents an important fork in the road for young athletes, typically those around the age of 15 for most sports, with the exception of early maturation sports such as gymnastics and figure skating for most female athletes. During this stage athletes will shift to an exclusive focus on either a high-performance pathway or a participation pathway. In this stage of development, coaches should be helping all athletes, regardless of the pathway that best fits their profile, find opportunities to continue reaping the many health and social benefits from continued participation in sport. For example, although a coach may be working as a high school varsity coach (high-performance pathway in most settings), she or he should be willing to serve in the local community to create ongoing sport opportunities for athletes who shift into the participation pathway.

The ADM includes a fifth stage, labeled thrive and mentor, that emphasizes the ultimate goal of any athlete development model—being active for life. Stage 5 represents another level of unlimited opportunities not only for athletes but also for coaches looking to extend their coaching careers. For example, although much of adult recreational sport is uncoached, the global expansion of competitive masters sport (ages 35 and older) provides coaches with opportunities to coach athletes across their lifespan. Coaching athletes in stage 5 is most effective when coaches are sensitive to athlete individual differences and needs because by the time athletes reach this stage of development, they are participating in sport because they want to improve their health and fitness but still enjoy the opportunity to test themselves and compete against others.[56]

Although several models of athlete talent development are recommended, coaches can use the common principles from these models to reflect on their athlete skill development practices. A summary of the principles of athlete development across the three models discussed in this chapter (LTAD, DMSP, ADM) is provided in table 5.2. The table includes a list of reflective questions for coaches to use as they design their own approaches to athlete development that aligns with their core values, coaching philosophy, and the context in which they coach.

## Development Models in Action

Examples of three highly regarded athlete-centered talent development models are shared to illustrate how coaches and sport organizations can put the principles of athlete development into action. The three examples are USA Hockey's American Development Model, U.S. Youth Soccer's player development model, and Baseball Canada's long-term athlete development system.

Sensing a need to save ice hockey in America from declining participation and failure to keep pace with other countries, in the mid-1990s USA Hockey embarked on a bold effort to reengineer ice hockey in America. The leadership of USA Hockey realized that their existing philosophy on coaching and athlete development was not sensitive to athlete needs at different stages of development. A one-size-fits-all coaching philosophy was the predominant approach to athlete development. The coaching and training practices of high-performance ice hockey were used as a guide to structure ice hockey training for young athletes.

After extensive consultation with other leading sport organizations and review of the athlete development literature, USA Hockey created what they now refer to as the USA Hockey American Development Model (ADM).[57] Their ADM provides an explicit age-appropriate coaching and athlete-training philosophy for all ice hockey clubs across the country. The core values driving this new philosophy are play, love, and excel. Play means keeping the game simple with a low priority on game outcome, love means nurturing a lifelong passion for the game, and excel refers to creating the right conditions for helping all athletes reach their potential as ice hockey players.

**Table 5.2 Coach Reflection Checklist for Using Principles of Athlete Development Models**

| Athlete development principle | Coach reflection checklist |
|---|---|
| Providing athletes with opportunities to sample a wide array of sports and positions builds a foundation of early sport participation. | ☐ Is a mandatory off-season period provided to prevent sport-specific burnout or injury?<br>☐ Do I encourage my athletes to participate in other sports during the off-season?<br>☐ Do I teach and allow my athletes to play multiple positions within a sport? |
| The sport environment should match the developmental level of the athletes. | ☐ Do dimensions of the playing surface maximize skill development and participation for athlete age and size?<br>☐ Is the playing equipment modified to match physical capabilities of the athletes (e.g., ball or goal size)?<br>☐ Do practices outnumber competitions, regardless of the age and level of athlete development? |
| Athlete chronological age may not match athlete biological age. | ☐ Do I hold the same high standards for all my athletes?<br>☐ Do I pay too much attention to physical maturity as opposed to skill and attitude?<br>☐ Does our sport organization provide participation opportunities for all athletes, regardless of skill level, to increase the likelihood of retaining late bloomers? |
| Athlete readiness for training and competition demands varies widely. | ☐ Do I regularly evaluate my athletes' ability to achieve training and performance targets?<br>☐ Do I adjust my training and performance goals throughout the season to ensure I am achieving the appropriate challenge-skill balance for each athlete?<br>☐ Do I regularly update my coaching knowledge to ensure I am current with the latest athlete development practices? |
| Shift to sport specialization still requires a balance of practice and play. | ☐ Even as my athletes progress to higher levels of development and competition, do I schedule regular time in practices for free play?<br>☐ Do I allow regular breaks in formal training to encourage athlete-initiated free-play sessions? |
| Alignment and appropriate sequencing should be evident across progressive levels of athlete development. | ☐ Do I regularly communicate with coaches in my sport who are developing athletes at the level below me (feeder programs) and at the level above me (next step for my athletes)?<br>☐ Do all the teams in our club or sport organization share and understand the same core values and athlete development philosophy? |
| A long-term view of athlete development is required, emphasizing enjoyment and love of the game. | ☐ Do I make training and strategic decisions that overemphasize immediate competitive success at the expense of long-term development?<br>☐ Do I allow athletes to have ownership and input into their development process as a way to nurture enjoyment and long-term commitment to the sport?<br>☐ Do I punish athletes for making mistakes, or do I keep my focus on the long-term goal and use mistakes as opportunities for enhanced teaching? |

From W. Gilbert, 2017, *Coaching better every season: A year-round system for athlete development and program success* (Champaign, IL: Human Kinetics).

The USA Hockey ADM philosophy, or how they implement their why, includes athlete-centered coaching strategies such as (*a*) practice environments that are fun and engaging, (*b*) a focus on foundational skills, (*c*) teaching through activity-based, skill-based, and role-based games, and (*d*) promoting peer teaching opportunities.

USA Hockey has experienced great success with the implementation of their athlete-centered ADM philosophy. In 2013–2014, after five years of full ADM philosophy implementation, USA Hockey reached an all-time record number of ice hockey participants, which was a significant increase from the number of participants before the ADM philosophy was implemented. USA Hockey's ADM provides compelling evidence for the effectiveness of adopting an athlete-centered coaching philosophy.

A second example of athlete development principles in action is U.S. Youth Soccer's player development model (PDM).[58] First released in 2012, the PDM provides guidance for coaches who serve over three million youth soccer players annually. The PDM includes three broad stages, or zones, of athlete development that fit the context of soccer: zone 1 (under 12 years old), zone 2 (13 through 17 years old), and zone 3 (18 years old and older).

In zone 1 the coaching focus should be on teaching players basic ball handling skills and general rules and principles of the game. In zone 2 the emphasis shifts to teaching tactical skills, team formations, and game strategies. Finally, in zone 3 coaches focus more on preparing athletes to compete at the highest levels of soccer, including college, professional, and national teams.

A key feature of both the USA Hockey and U.S. Youth Soccer athlete development models is the recognition that athletes in different stages, or zones, of development require different types of coaching. For athletes to develop their full athletic talent and skill, they must have the right type of coach and coaching at each stage of development.

This finding was one of the key conclusions from the landmark talent development study published by renowned scientist Benjamin Bloom in 1985.[59] In that study 125 experts across many fields, including elite athletes, were interviewed about their talent development process. The study revealed that the athletes rarely had the same coach throughout their sport development journey. Athletes commonly changed coaches when they outgrew the abilities or strengths of their current coaches. For example, the type of coach needed for an athlete in early stages of development (focus on fun, maximizing participation, and emphasizing position and sport sampling) is a different type of coach from the one needed for an athlete in later stages of development (deep knowledge of how to teach advanced technical and tactical skills, focus on strategy and competition readiness).

Both the coaching and the training and competition environments are changed at each stage to facilitate appropriate and quality coaching. For example, the field dimensions and ball size vary across age groups in soccer, and youth ice hockey teams often practice and play cross-ice or half-ice to maximize engagement and skill development for all players.

Coaches often neglect to consider how adult-sized sport environments are viewed from the perspective of a young athlete. All coaches should be required to watch the two brief videos prepared by ice hockey and soccer associations to illustrate what typical sport environments look like from the vantage point of a young athlete.[60, 61] After watching these videos coaches will have a much better appreciation for why and how they need to modify the design of training and competition environments to optimize long-term athlete development.

Much like USA Hockey and U.S. Youth Soccer, Baseball Canada was stimulated to adopt a long-term, athlete-centered coaching approach because of decreasing rates of participation in the sport. In 2003 Baseball Canada identified the prevailing coach-centered coaching approach, with its emphasis on short-term wins, as one of the primary reasons for the deteriorating status of the sport. A decision was made to reengineer baseball in Canada around a long-term, athlete-centered coaching approach, driven by three core values:[62]

1. To develop optimal training, competition, and recovery programs that meet athlete needs at each stage of their biological development and maturation
2. To provide equal opportunity for all players to participate and reach their full potential
3. To create a world-class program of excellence that will be athlete-centered and coach driven

These athlete-centered core values (why) were then translated into an athlete-centered coaching philosophy (how) specific to nine different stages of athlete development, one corresponding to each inning of a baseball game. For example, in the first inning of a baseball athlete's development (typically ages 6 and under), the coaching focus should be on fundamental movement skills and play. Although the recommended coaching focus varies across the nine innings of athlete development, all coaching strategies must be firmly grounded in the overarching long-term, athlete-centered coaching approach.

Baseball Canada is widely regarded as a world leader in the effort to integrate a long-term athlete-centered coaching approach across an entire sport. The full scale of this effort and the way on which the long-term, athlete-centered coaching approach drives all components of the system is illustrated in the *Covering All Bases* graphic prepared by Baseball Canada (see figure 5.7).

The first inning of athlete baseball development starts to the right of home plate, at the bottom of the image. Coaches use the long-term, athlete-centered coaching approach through each successive inning, moving counterclockwise around the bases. The ninth and final inning, active for life, is located on the pitcher's mound in the center of the figure. Even in this final stage of baseball participation, a long-term, athlete-centered coaching approach is advocated to sustain a lifelong passion for the game.

## Wrap-Up

The core responsibility of coaches across sports and at any level of competition is to help athletes develop their talent and skill. Although each athlete's unique genetic profile undoubtedly shapes the talent development process, successful

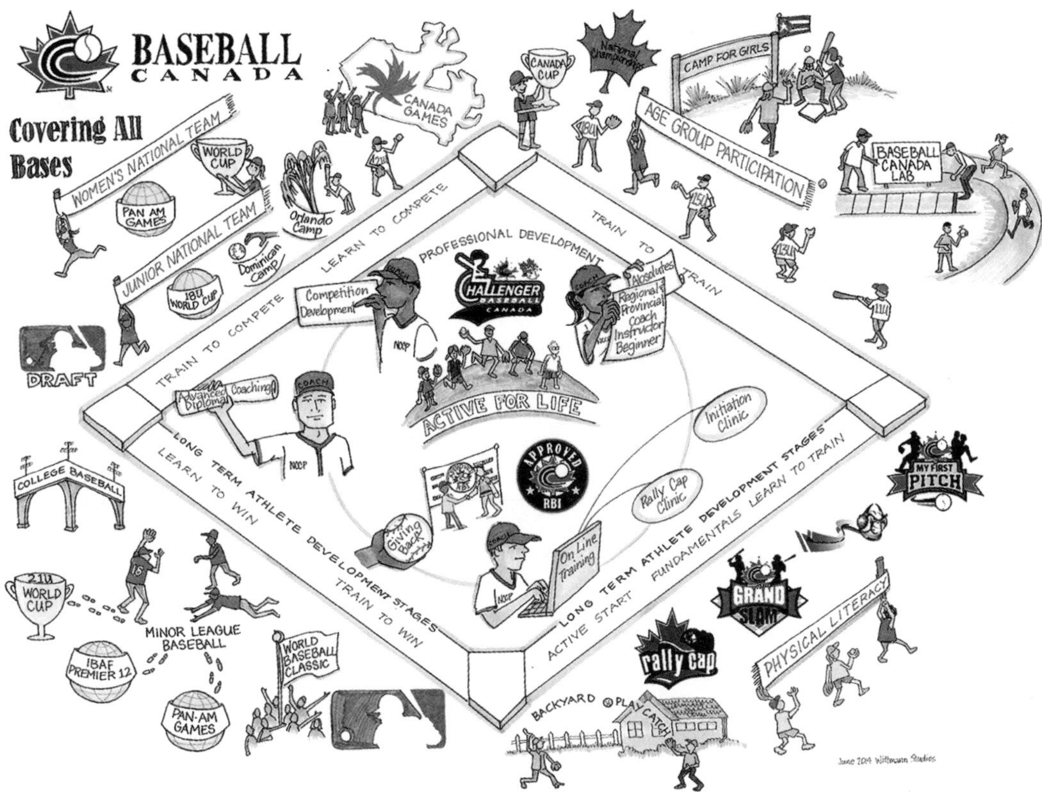


**Figure 5.7** Baseball Canada infographic.

Courtesy of Baseball Canada (www.baseball.ca).

coaches create environments that maximize opportunities for focused, deliberate practice. The best coaches regularly monitor athlete profiles so that they can design practice activities that provide just the right amount of challenge for each athlete's current skill level.

Because of the high levels of mental and physical effort required for deliberate practice, quality coaches also build time into athlete development schedules for deliberate recovery and free play. Many of the world's greatest athletes highlight the critical role of unstructured free play in their ability to achieve expert performance levels, while also stressing the importance of sport sampling in the early phases of talent development.

Careful reflection on popular athlete development models such as the long-term athlete development model and the developmental model of sport participation, and the way in which sport organizations around the world enact them, will help coaches create their own strategies for optimizing the development of athletic talent and skill.

# Chapter 6

# Optimize Athletes' Learning

**Key Concepts**

Individual learning needs
Athlete prior knowledge
Athlete learning values
Goal importance
Expectancies
Component skills
Expert blind spot
Instructional cues and feedback

The previous chapter provided a broad overview of the most effective way to develop talent across different stages of athlete development. The goal of the present chapter is to help coaches understand the learning process itself. Whereas chapter 5 gives coaches guidance on how they should adjust their coaching depending on where their athletes are in the long-term development process, chapter 6 shows coaches how to use the science of learning to become more effective teachers.

The coaches who are most highly regarded across sport are renowned for their ability to teach. One such example is legendary former Major League Baseball coach George Kissell, who was affectionately referred to as The Professor because of his passion for teaching the fundamentals of baseball. Many fellow coaches shared the view expressed by Hall of Famer Sparky Anderson, who considered coach Kissell "the greatest baseball fundamentalist I have ever known."[1]

Coach Kissell spent his entire 69-year baseball career in the St. Louis Cardinals' system, which is widely considered to have one of the best player development programs in professional sport. Much of the Cardinals' success—11 World Series championships and consistent playoff contenders—is attributed to their emphasis on teaching baseball fundamentals and developing coaches who are quality teachers.

Another legendary coach widely acknowledged as one of history's greatest sport teachers, John Wooden, was notorious for repeating the maxim "You haven't taught until they have learned."[2] This adage serves as a timeless reminder that coaching effectiveness rests first on a coach's ability to teach. Effective teaching, however, rests on a coach's awareness of how learning works.

Reflecting on five decades of experience coaching world-class athletes and doing research on athlete development and coaching, Dr. Alan Launder and fellow coach Wendy Piltz summarized their insights on athlete learning in a working model of instruction they called the 15 Ps of perfect pedagogy.[3] Pedagogy, the formal term used to describe teaching, is a good word for coaches to remember because all successful coaches view themselves first as teachers.[1] The 15 Ps of perfect pedagogy are the following:

1. Plan.
2. Prepare the learner.
3. Prepare a protected learning environment.
4. Present the task efficiently.
5. Pretest.
6. Provide opportunities for plenty of practice.
7. Practice should be pertinent.
8. Practice should be purposeful.
9. Practice should be playful.
10. Practice should be progressive.
11. Practice should be paced.
12. Practice should be personalized.
13. Provide feedback.
14. Praise performance.
15. Project poise, patience, and passion.

An awareness of learning principles, such as those identified in Coach Launder's 15 Ps of perfect pedagogy, provides coaches with the foundation for making wise decisions about how to design training sessions and how to use teachable moments effectively in competition settings. The purpose of this chapter is to illuminate what has been discovered about learning principles and how coaches can apply them.

## HOW ATHLETES LEARN

Learning is generally defined as having three components: process, change, and experience.[4] Although people commonly equate learning with an observable outcome, such as the ability to hit a golf ball successfully or run a pass route in football, this way of thinking about learning is flawed. Learning is better viewed as the process that leads to the desired outcome, or a change in knowledge, attitude, or behavior.

For example, on the path to developing the ability to hit the golf ball or run the pass route, much learning that is not readily observable is required to perform the skill. To hit the golf ball successfully, the athlete will need to learn how to select the appropriate club for the particular situation. The athlete will also need to learn how to assess the weather and course conditions. Finally, the athlete will need to learn how to identify and manage her or his emotions in preparing to execute the shot. These examples are just a few aspects of the process of change that occurs over time, whether within a single training session or across many months or years.

Furthermore, each person experiences the process of learning in a unique way. The role of the coach is to create the right conditions for a learning experience to occur, while appreciating that each athlete will experience every learning activity differently based on experience, knowledge, attitudes, skills, and learning profiles. An individualized approach to teaching athletes is one of the hallmarks of great coaches.[5, 6]

In the remainder of this chapter, four broad principles of athlete learning are described, along with sample coaching strategies. These principles are based on a comprehensive review of the research on teaching and learning.[4, 7, 8] The principles and sample coaching strategies are summarized in table 6.1.

## ASSESSING ATHLETES' PRIOR KNOWLEDGE

Athletes do not come to coaches as blank slates. All athletes bring diverse knowledge and views based on years of experience, whether through participating in sport, by observing sport, or, more likely, through some combination of both types of experience. These experiences shape how athletes approach learning and how they attempt to make sense of coaches' instruction.

Athletes' prior knowledge can accelerate learning if it is appropriate, accurate, sufficient, and activated in the learning process. Coaches must also recognize,

**Table 6.1 Principles of Athlete Learning and Sample Coaching Strategies**

| Learning principle | Sample coaching strategy |
|---|---|
| Prior knowledge can help or hinder athlete learning. | Have athletes explain or demonstrate a skill before attempting to teach it to gauge readiness to learn the skill. |
| Athlete motivation directly influences the learning process. | Ask athletes for feedback on the difficulty of learning activities to help find the right challenge-skill balance. |
| Skill mastery requires athletes to learn component skills. | Try describing and then walking through the steps needed to perform a skill before teaching it to your athletes. |
| Combine deliberate practice with targeted specific feedback. | Identify in advance feedback cues and feedback bandwidths to help athletes meet learning and performance standards. |

however, that prior knowledge can hinder athletes' learning if it is inappropriate, inaccurate, insufficient, or not activated during the learning process. For example, novice soccer players commonly believe that the most effective way to kick a soccer ball is with their toes, often referred to as a toe kick. Another example comes from a conversation I once had with an Olympic archery coach who revealed that novice archers incorrectly assume that accuracy is increased by closing one eye (both eyes should remain open and the head should be turned to face the target). These examples of inappropriate and inaccurate prior knowledge, referred to as misconceptions, need to be corrected before introducing new skills.

Learning occurs best when new knowledge is connected to existing and accurate knowledge. Novices tend to organize knowledge sequentially or in a random disconnected way. Experts, on the other hand, organize their knowledge into related clusters, referred to as chunking. It is believed that chunking is a primary reason why experts can analyze and perform skills more quickly and accurately than novices can.[4]

Before introducing a new skill or working with a new group of athletes, coaches need to set aside time to get a sense of what the athletes already know and think about the skill. One way to do this is to ask the athletes to describe what they know about a topic, such as bunting in baseball. This strategy will unveil what is referred to as the athletes' declarative knowledge.

Another approach is to have the athletes demonstrate the skill. Using the baseball bunting example, athletes could take turns showing the coach how they would execute a bunt while explaining game scenarios when bunting would be appropriate. This approach provides coaches with insight into the athletes' procedural knowledge—knowing how and when to execute a skill.

Coaches can help athletes trigger and access prior knowledge by following up athlete descriptions and demonstrations with why questions. For example, coaches could ask athletes to explain why they would bunt in specific situations or why they adjusted their body position at a specific moment. Why questions force athletes to access prior knowledge and make new connections to this knowledge, a technique called elaborative interrogation.[4]

Coaches can use numerous strategies to gauge athletes' prior knowledge. Speaking with the athlete's previous coach will likely shed light on the athlete's prior knowledge and the types of coaching strategies that seem to be most effective when working with that athlete. Having athletes complete a brief series of skill tests and even short written tests in the preseason can help coaches spot tendencies and prior knowledge that can be used as a leverage point for accelerated learning.

A fun team activity that will reveal much about athletes' prior knowledge is a group brainstorming session. For example, a coach might hold a team meeting to ask questions such as "What do you think of when you hear the term *mental toughness*?" and "What comes to mind when you think about character in sport?" This strategy combined with the use of follow-up why questions will quickly reveal the prior knowledge that coaches may need to correct and reshape before performance improvements can be realized.

Another strategy for determining athlete prior knowledge is to use periodic athlete written self-assessments. For example, before introducing a new skill or strategy, coaches could have athletes complete a brief self-assessment to gauge their familiarity with the skill or strategy and identify the appropriate starting point for practice activities. Although a natural time to do this would be in the preseason when the coach is mapping out practice schedules, athletes could complete short self-assessments at the end of practices for skills or strategies that the coach could introduce in upcoming practices. Two examples of sport-specific athlete self-assessment tools, one for swimming[9] and one for football,[10] are provided to help coaches prepare athlete self-assessment tools that fit their particular context (see figure 6.1).

This strategy serves a dual purpose. First, it provides the coach with a quick and easy way to get a sense of the athletes' readiness to learn the skill or strategy and the most effective entry point for teaching the skill or strategy. Second, it serves as an advanced primer for learning and performance by focusing the athletes' attention on relevant cues to prepare for quality practice.

## Figure 6.1 Sample Athlete Self-Assessments

### Self-Assessment for Swimming Technique

How familiar are you with the underwater butterfly kick?

- ☐ I have never heard of it.
- ☐ I have heard of it but don't know what it is.
- ☐ I have some idea of what it is but don't know how or when to use it.
- ☐ I have a clear idea of what it is but haven't used it.
- ☐ I can explain what it is, and I can demonstrate it.

### Self-Assessment for Football Strategies

*Instructions:* For each of the following defensive strategies, place a check mark in the cells that describe your experience.

| Defensive strategy | Have never used this | Have seen other athletes use it | Have used this in practice | Have used this in competition |
|---|---|---|---|---|
| 3-4 run defense | | | | |
| 4-3 run defense | | | | |
| 8-man-front run defense | | | | |
| Cover 2 zone pass defense | | | | |
| Cover 3 zone pass defense | | | | |
| Cover 1 free pass defense | | | | |
| Cover 1 free press pass defense | | | | |

From W. Gilbert, 2017, *Coaching better every season: A year-round system for athlete development and program success* (Champaign, IL: Human Kinetics).

Priming works because it stimulates perceptions, thoughts, emotions, and behaviors that are necessary for optimal learning and performance.[11] For example, studies show that athletes perform skills faster when they are told to think about animals that are fast such as cheetahs, as opposed to thinking about animals that are slow such as turtles. Both speed and accuracy of performance increase when athletes are given pre-performance activities that have them focus on words associated with fluency such as *flow* and *automatic*.

Legendary basketball coach John Wooden made a habit at the end of each practice of telling his players what they were going to work on in the next practice. He believed that this preview contributed directly to athlete readiness and focus for deliberate practice.[2] Contrary to Coach Wooden's experience, however, recent studies on priming have found that the priming effect may be short lived, sometimes as little as five minutes after the priming cues are introduced.[11]

Ideally, coaches will prime athletes the day before a new skill or strategy is introduced and again right before it is performed. Also, the effectiveness of priming will be enhanced if coaches have athletes envision how they will personally perform their role in a team tactic, not just visualize how the team will execute the strategy.

Lastly, coaches can facilitate athletes' efforts to build richer and stronger knowledge connections by providing them with similar examples of how to think about a skill. For example, when introducing a new offensive strategy, a coach could start by explaining to the athletes how the new strategy is like other strategies they have learned. This technique stimulates the athletes' recall of prior knowledge and serves as an advance organizer to help them make more accurate and stronger connections between new knowledge and existing knowledge.

## UNDERSTANDING MOTIVATION AND THE LEARNING PROCESS

Effective coaches devote considerable time to identifying and creating training activities for their athletes. But even the most creative and engaging learning activities will miss the mark if coaches do not also consider the influence of their athletes' motivation to engage in the learning experience. Athlete motivation determines the intensity, persistence, and quality of their learning efforts.

Two primary drivers create athlete motivation to learn. The first driver is the subjective value that athletes place on the goal of the learning activity, sometimes referred to as goal importance. Coaches should not assume that their athletes will automatically see the relevance of learning goals or training activities. Coaches need to offer a clear explanation of not only the what of learning goals and practice activities but also the why.

Research and feedback from athletes show the value of providing athletes with the rationale for selecting a particular approach to practicing a skill.[12, 13] For example, in the weeks leading up to the 2015 Super Bowl, athletes playing on the New England Patriots, the team that eventually won the championship, explained why they liked playing for renowned football coach Bill Belichick:

> He has always backed his arguments up. By arguments, I mean what he's trying to coach and teach you. I think anyone that's coaching, you shouldn't have to take them on their word. They should be able to point to you where it has actually worked, where it has been effective.[13]

The second driver of athlete motivation to learn is the beliefs, or expectancies, they hold about their ability to complete the learning activity. Coaches can help athletes see the value in their training activities and increase their expectancy of skill mastery by connecting training activities to one or more common value sources: attainment value, intrinsic value, and instrumental value.[4]

The first value source is attainment value, which refers to the personal satisfaction that an athlete feels when performing or learning a skill. The need to feel competent and learn how to navigate our environment successfully is a basic human need.[14] A simple way to help athletes fulfill their attainment value is to start each practice session with activities that have a high success rate.

For example, the coach can start each practice by repeating an activity that the athletes have successfully performed in the past. A good approach is to select a short activity that will ideally also serve as a dynamic physical and mental warm-up, thereby increasing the efficiency of time use and increasing athletes' readiness to learn new skills. Then, each practice session can end with a more challenging activity that is perhaps just beyond the reach of most of the athletes. This activity can be repeated at the end of each practice until all or most of the athletes can complete it successfully. This approach to starting and ending each practice session with challenging, yet possible, activities will promote athletes' sense of attainment.

The second value source is intrinsic value, sometimes also referred to as intrinsic motivation. Intrinsic value can be increased by creating practice activities that allow athletes to experience the joy of training and reconnect them with their love for the sport. Moments when athletes lose themselves in the activity because of the high intrinsic value attached to it are often described as being in the zone or flow experiences.[15, 16]

Although there are multiple components and sources of flow, challenge-skill balance has been identified as the golden rule of flow. Challenge-skill balance refers to the match between an athlete's current skill level and the difficulty of the task.

If athletes perceive the task to be too far beyond their current skill level, they will approach it with low intrinsic value. In their mind it is too hard and not worth trying to attain, which can lead to anxiety. On the other hand, if athletes perceive the task to be too far below what they are capable of doing, they will also approach it with low intrinsic value. In these situations the task is perceived as too easy and again not worth the time and effort, leading to boredom or apathy.

The goal for coaches is to create learning activities that are just beyond the athletes' current skill level but are perceived by the athletes to be at least within reach. These types of activities hit the sweet spot of athlete learning and offer the greatest chance of allowing athletes to experience moments of flow and nurture the intrinsic value they will attach to the training activity (see figure 6.2).

These learning sweet spots are also commonly referred to as zones of proximal development, a widely influential learning concept first coined by psychologist

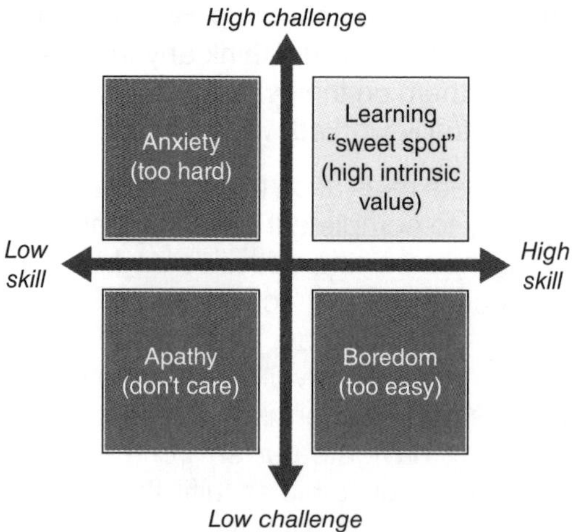


**Figure 6.2** Sweet spot of athlete learning.

Adapted, by permission, from S.A. Jackson and M. Csikszentmihalyi, 1999, *Flow in sports* (Champaign, IL: Human Kinetics), 37.

Lev Vygotsky in the early 20th century.[4] Skill improvement will be greatest when coaches can create learning activities that are between what the athletes can already do without assistance and what they cannot do on their own. In other words, the difficulty of the learning task is proximal (close) to the athletes' current ability and the task can be successfully completed with appropriate support from the coach. The purpose of these learning zones is to provide athletes with guided opportunities for purposeful struggle that increase the rate of learning.[17]

The analogy of a slide ruler may be a useful way for coaches to think about how the zone of proximal development can be used to find the sweet spot of athlete skill level, athlete motivation, and coach support when designing learning activities (see figure 6.3). Much as the center portion of a slide ruler is moved back and forth to identify the correct response to a problem, effective coaches move the zone of proximal development back and forth for each athlete to create optimal learning experiences. The zone will need to be moved forward as the athlete masters a specific skill. The zone may need to be moved backward as the athlete attempts to learn a different skill or when an athlete is returning from injury or the off-season.

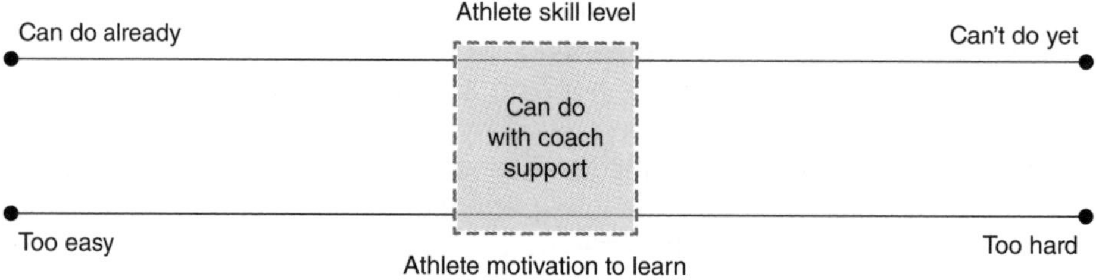


**Figure 6.3** Zone of proximal development for athlete learning.

Coaches can find the appropriate challenge-skill balance, which naturally will fluctuate across a season and will vary with each athlete, by providing athletes with time to reflect during or after practices. Much can be learned simply by asking the athletes for their feedback on the degree of challenge and their perceived readiness to complete learning activities successfully. Many coaches hold group feedback sessions while athletes are gathered for their cool-down or stretching at the end of practices. Coaches can ask questions such as these: "What was the most valuable part of practice today?" and "What do you think we need to spend more time on in our next practice?"

The third and final source of value for athlete learning is instrumental value, also referred to as extrinsic motivation. Athlete motivation to learn can be increased when coaches provide incentives, in the form of rewards, when athletes successfully complete learning activities. Some common types of extrinsic rewards used by coaches include recognition T-shirts, playing a game selected by the athletes, earning time off, or holding a team party.[18]

For example, Nell Fortner, Olympic championship women's basketball coach who also coached college and professional basketball, rewarded her professional athletes with a free pass from difficult conditioning drills if they could make 25 out of 25 free throws during a practice.[19] Although this type of reward may be common and appropriate for professional athletes, more appropriate extrinsic rewards for youth, high school, or college athletes could include special recognitions for hardest worker or best teammate.

For example, some coaches like to present athletes with a construction helmet for outstanding work ethic. Jon Gordon wrote a popular book on how a college lacrosse team used this strategy both to recognize athlete character and to honor a fallen teammate.[20]

The women's ice hockey team at Harvard also used the hard hat strategy to increase athlete extrinsic motivation.[21] They award three distinctions following each game—a plastic hard hat for the hardest worker, a rubber duck for the top defender, and a feather boa for the top performer. Particularly noteworthy in the Harvard example is that the hard hat winner is selected by the previous winner as a way to increase the value that athletes place on the award. In addition, a sticker with the winner's jersey number is placed on the helmet each time it is awarded.

I have witnessed this hard hat extrinsic motivation reward ritual in person in youth ice hockey settings as well. The effect of this simple strategy on athlete motivation was clear in the joy and pride expressed in the athletes' response after being selected to receive the hard hat.

Another example of a coaching strategy used to reward and recognize athlete performance and increase the instrumental value that athletes place on learning comes from my work with a college basketball team. Given the popularity of superhero movies such as *Avengers*, *Captain America*, and *Iron Man* at the time when we were working together, the coach decided to use a superhero shield as a tool for recognizing athlete learning and performance.

The coach purchased a replicable of the shield used by Captain America. At the end of each week of practices, the coaching staff formally recognized the one athlete who best modeled the team's core values that week. Each athlete was also provided with a Captain America shield key chain to clip to his backpack. The key chain served as a constant visual reminder of the instrumental value of hard work and commitment to the team.

For this type of instrumental value activity, coaches could also consider displaying their team's core values directly on the shield. Furthermore, each time an athlete is rewarded with the shield, a sticker with the athlete's jersey number could be added to the shield. At the end of the season the shield could then be prominently displayed in the team locker room to recognize that team's commitment to the core values and team work ethic.

## TEACHING COMPONENT SKILLS

All sport skills, regardless of the degree of complexity, from running an intricate passing route and catching a thrown ball in a football game to running a short distance in a straight line in a 100-meter track race, require the ability to perform multiple skills. These related skills, such as focus and emotional control and the ability to read and react to performance conditions including opponents, weather, and teammates, are referred to as component skills.

When selecting skills to teach, coaches first must clearly identify all component skills that will influence athletes' ability to perform the target skill successfully. This task often proves to be a difficult and overlooked step in designing effective learning activities. One reason that this aspect is often challenging for coaches is that they incorrectly assume that the athletes already possess the component skills. A simple way to check for athletes' readiness to perform the target skill is to present them with a scenario or introduce them to the target skill and ask them to identify all the other skills they will need to perform the target skill. Most certainly, novice athletes will miss many of the important component skills.

For example, when attempting to teach even a basic skill such as throwing in baseball or softball, athletes will need to know how to move their feet, rotate the torso, draw back the arm, grip the ball, stretch the throwing arm in front of the body during release, and develop a feel for the amount of force required to reach different distances. Using this example, coaches could demonstrate a throw or show a video of a throw and then ask the athletes to identify and describe the important steps. Many inexpensive coaching applications that include short demonstration videos are now available for mobile devices, such as the *Go Coach* series developed by Human Kinetics, which has apps for popular sports such as basketball, soccer, football, and baseball.[22]

The second and more common reason that many coaches neglect teaching component skills is because they are in a much different and more advanced stage of learning. Coaches can easily overlook component skills because they simply don't think about them anymore.

The vast majority of coaches, particularly coaches who work in high-performance contexts such as high school varsity, college, Olympic, and professional sport settings, accumulate thousands of hours as athletes themselves.[23-25] Studies of successful American high school and college coaches in sports such as basketball, football, softball, volleyball, and track and field show that coaches averaged more than 3,000 hours of participation as athletes before they became coaches.

Those years spent practicing the skills they now are attempting to coach often result in what is referred to as an expert blind spot.[26] People with a lot of experience and knowledge in an area tend to overlook basic steps when trying to teach skills to others that they now perceive as easy. Expert or experienced coaches are highly susceptible to forgetting what it was like to try to learn basic sport skills.

A description of skill development stages helps illustrate why coaches often work with an expert blind spot. On the path toward mastering a skill (expertise), learners progress through several stages. In the common three-stage model of skill mastery[27, 28] athletes start in the mental stage (thinking about how to perform the skill). In the second stage athletes focus on using what they learned in the mental stage to refine and improve their skill. This stage is referred to as the practice stage. Finally, with increased and appropriate practice, athletes may reach the automatic stage of skill mastery, in which they can perform the skill more reliably and with less conscious effort.

A more recent extension of this basic three-stage model is the four-stage model of skill mastery that illustrates how learners move from not knowing what they don't know to not thinking about what they know how to do.[4] In the first stage, unconscious incompetence, novice athletes are unaware of what they need to know to perform and master the skill. In other words, they don't know what they don't know.

In the second stage, conscious incompetence, athletes have developed awareness of what they are supposed to do and the component skills needed, but they have yet to master the ability to perform the skill. They have now progressed to knowing what they don't know. When athletes have learned to perform the skill using their knowledge of how to perform it, they have shifted into the third stage of mastery, conscious competence. Although they can now perform the skill, they still have to think about many of the steps needed to perform the skill successfully. Finally, with many hours, and often years, of focused practice, athletes may become highly proficient in performing the skill and achieve the fourth stage of skill mastery, unconscious competence.

The stage models of skill mastery and the fact that coaches typically spend thousands of hours learning sport skills as an athlete explain why coaches can easily fall victim to the expert blind spot when designing learning activities (see figure 6.4). Most coaches will have achieved some level of automaticity in the sport

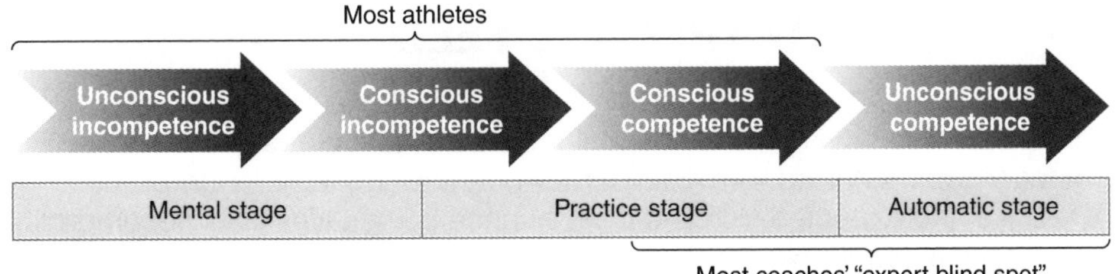


**Figure 6.4** Stages of skill mastery and the expert blind spot in coaching.

skills they are trying to teach, whereas most of their athletes will be attempting to learn the skills from a starting point that requires considerable mental processing.

Perhaps for those reasons, many great athletes fail to make the transition to being a successful coach. Expert performers struggle with trying to explain how they do what they do; they don't think about the component skills or the steps needed to execute the skill successfully.[29] Many successful coaches were only average athletes, and some never even competed in the sport in which they achieved their success as a coach.[30]

Fortunately, coaches can use many strategies to overcome their expert blind spot. First, when designing learning activities, coaches should try to list all component skills needed to perform the practice activity. Coaches should ask themselves the question, "What would athletes need to know, or know how to do, to be able to complete what I am asking them to do in this activity?"

To ensure that important component skills are not overlooked, coaches should then try a walk-through of the practice activity on their own. Moving from trying to describe it to trying to implement it will surely reveal minor, but important, component skills that should be added to the skill description and practice activity.

Second, coaches should discuss and test their description of the practice activity and component skills with another coach, ideally a less experienced or less skilled coach who may still be in the conscious competence stage of skill mastery. For this reason, among others, coaches should bring less experienced or early career assistant coaches into their program when possible.

Third, an extremely valuable strategy for identifying overlooked component skills is to try explaining how to perform the target skill to someone outside coaching or a coach of a different sport. These people will not have the coach's sport-specific expert blind spot and therefore can likely help identify important steps and component skills that have been inadvertently skipped.

Lastly, a great way for coaches to improve their ability to teach and eliminate their blind spots is to record themselves in the act of coaching. A simple way for coaches to do this is to wear a GoPro camera during a practice and then watch the video to see and hear what it is like to be coached by them. Super Bowl champion coach Jon Gruden is an advocate of this strategy. He has prepared an insightful short video to illustrate this strategy in action, while also explaining why it is valuable for improving your ability to help athletes learn.[31]

## COMBINING DELIBERATE PRACTICE AND SPECIFIC FEEDBACK

Recall from chapter 5 that a hallmark of great athletes and successful coaches is commitment to thousands of hours of focused practice designed to close performance gaps, referred to as deliberate practice. But deliberate practice will not result in the expected skill and performance gains unless it is accompanied by appropriate feedback.

There are two general types of feedback.[8, 32] An observation made by the coach is referred to as augmented feedback. Insights that athletes generate from their own observations are referred to as task-intrinsic feedback. For example, a coach telling a runner to shorten his or her stride is providing augmented feedback, whereas a baseball pitcher making small adjustments between pitches based on the result of the pitch is using task-intrinsic feedback.

As a rule, coaches should encourage athletes to learn how to use their own task-intrinsic feedback as much as possible. Coaches should limit their use of augmented feedback to situations when it will help direct the athlete's attention to the critical sources of task-intrinsic feedback.[32] During competitions athletes typically have limited or no access to coach-augmented feedback, so coaches need to teach their athletes how to make adjustments based on intrinsic feedback.

Coaches should consider three questions when deciding how best to provide targeted specific feedback: What type of feedback should I give? How should I give the feedback? When should I give the feedback?

Feedback historically has been described as either positive or negative. Telling an athlete, "Good job—way to follow through on that swing" is an example of positive feedback, whereas telling an athlete, "You started your swing too late" would be considered negative feedback. But this way of describing feedback has been criticized because it oversimplifies the important role of corrective feedback in the learning process; corrective feedback should not be viewed as negative. Recently, sport scientists have replaced positive and negative feedback with the terms *promotion-oriented feedback* (recognizing desirable or correct behaviors) and *change-oriented feedback* (identifying errors or undesirable behavior).[33]

The appropriate use of change-oriented feedback is critical for athlete learning and improved performance. For example, four characteristics define quality change-oriented feedback:[33]

- It is given in a considerate tone of voice.
- It is focused on the behavior, not the person.
- It is coupled with solution options from which the athlete can select.
- It is based on clear and realistic learning goals familiar to the athlete.

Another common way to think about feedback type is to distinguish between outcome and performance feedback. Outcome feedback focuses on what the athlete did—the result of the skill attempt. Performance feedback focuses on how the athlete did what she or he did—the way in which the skill was executed.

The most successful coaches resist the temptation to provide outcome feedback because athletes typically see the outcome for themselves (e.g., they hit the target or they didn't). But athletes can benefit from the coach's summary outcome feedback, which athletes are not likely to notice on their own. For example, at the end of a series of tennis serves the coach might provide the athlete with a summary of ball placement feedback. After a few minutes of serving practice the coach could tell the athlete how many times the ball was served to the corner of the service area.

Providing athletes with feedback about how they performed the skill is more valuable than outcome feedback. Performance feedback is valuable because it directs athletes' attention to aspects of the skill that are critical for successful performance. For example, a basketball coach might tell an athlete to keep the shoulders square when shooting. In tennis the coach might remind the athlete to "push, point, and hit" when serving (push the ball up gently on the release, point the release hand at the ball, and hit to focus the eyes on the ball at the moment of contact), or "sweep the dishes off the table" to get a feel for the proper way to hit a forehand shot.[34]

Performance feedback serves as a valuable learning cue because it directs the athlete's attention to the most important aspects of proper skill execution. The examples of learning cues prepared by skill instruction expert Dr. Craig Wrisberg[8] provides a valuable guide for coaches when preparing relevant learning cues (see figure 6.5).

Performance feedback also has the benefit of helping athletes learn how to self-identify performance errors and rely more on intrinsic feedback. Coaches can teach athletes how to tap into their intrinsic performance feedback more effectively by having them practice technical skills with their eyes closed, when it is safe to do so.[8] This approach will help athletes learn to focus on how the movement feels as opposed to focusing too much, or even exclusively, on the observable outcome.

For athletes with moderate or advanced skills, coaches should consider occasionally distracting them, or screening off their vision, for part of a skill attempt.[35] For example, in a basketball jump shot activity, coaches could have a defender place a hand in front of the shooter's face, or a coach could even hold up a piece of paper or cardboard taped to the end of a broom handle near the end of the

## Figure 6.5 Using Learning Cues to Focus Athletes' Attention

Effective coaching often involves saying the right thing at the right time. Timely and relevant learning cues direct athletes' attention to the thoughts and feelings that contribute to successful performance. Here are some examples from several sports:

- **Baseball:** Look for the seams, keep the hands inside the ball, stride and hit (for batters), hit the catcher's glove, follow through, just this pitch (for pitchers)
- **Basketball:** Make sharp cuts (on offense), keep the shoulders square (when shooting), quick slide steps (on defense)
- **Football:** Run to daylight (for ball carriers), keep your head on a swivel (for special-teams players running downfield), finish the kick (for placekickers)
- **Swimming:** Keep the legs tucked (on the flip turn), explode (off the blocks), relax and maintain rhythm (throughout each length during a distance event)
- **Tennis:** Hit the ball on the rise (for ground strokes), firm grip at contact (for volleys), lift and release (for the ball toss on the serve)

Keep in mind that athletes need to be given some time to try out new strategies and evaluate feedback on their own. More instructions are not always better. Therefore, it's important to resist the temptation to "overcoach," and one way to do this is through the timely use of learning cues.

Reprinted, by permission, from C.A. Wrisberg, 2007, *Sport skill instruction for coaches* (Champaign, IL: Human Kinetics), 99.

shot. This method forces athletes to learn how to identify and use visual cues and then focus on the shooting process as opposed to the outcome.

Two-time world soccer Player of the Year Cristiano Ronaldo provides a vivid example of how a world-class athlete can learn to perform successfully with only limited visual and outcome information. As part of a televised sport science project, Ronaldo was challenged to head a passed soccer ball into a net with the lights turned off, first partway through the kick and then just as the ball was kicked.[36] In both conditions he successfully made adjustments in the dark to head the ball into the net because of his learned ability to identify relevant visual cues quickly.

When considering how to give feedback, coaches have several options. The most common option is oral feedback. When giving oral feedback coaches must be careful not to overload the athlete with too much information. As a rule, coaches should give feedback on only one or two aspects of a skill when providing oral feedback.[8]

Of course, the value of oral feedback depends on the athlete's ability to receive the feedback. Coaches should consider teaching their athletes how to receive oral feedback by having them practice the HEAR principle: *Head* up, *Eyes* front, *Attend* fully, and *Remain* silent.[37] Once the coach has finished giving the oral feedback then the athlete should be given an opportunity to ask questions or share her or his observations. A valuable way for coaches to know whether the oral feedback was received as intended is to ask the athlete to repeat or paraphrase the feedback before attempting the skill again.

Coaches increasingly use video replay to give feedback to their athletes. When giving visual feedback coaches need to consider the viewing angle to ensure that the athlete can see the performance from the desired perspective. For example, when deciding where to stand while videotaping a softball pitcher, the coach should consider whether the athlete should see herself performing from a side view, front view, or rear view. No one perspective is more effective than another; they all can provide valuable visual feedback, but the feedback perspective should match the coach's goals for the learning activity.

Coaches have many options available to them for visual feedback aids. Popular and sophisticated examples include Dartfish and Coach Logic, which provide coaches with many options for analyzing and viewing athletes' movement patterns.[38, 39] Many professional athletes and their coaches use such video analysis programs, particularly for sports in which even minor technical adjustments can result in large performance gains.

With the advent of smartphones and other handheld devices that can be used to produce high-quality video recording, coaches can also access express versions of video analysis programs that can be downloaded as mobile applications. Finally, sport-specific visual feedback programs are becoming more common. For example, soccer coaches increasingly use programs such as Prozone[40] to show athletes feedback on aspects such as passing and receiving accuracy.

Although the use of visual feedback is becoming more commonplace for coaches at all levels of competition, coaches must carefully weigh the pros and cons of showing visual feedback to one athlete at a time or to groups of athletes as a whole. Athletes generally find great value in well-prepared and efficient video feedback sessions.[41, 42] But athletes also report a drop in confidence if they are the focus of repeated skill errors during team feedback sessions. Coaches should use visual feedback with athletes one-on-one when possible and be careful to avoid overusing examples of skill errors from the same athletes during team visual feedback sessions.

Deciding when to give feedback is the third key decision that coaches must make when teaching. When in doubt coaches should remain silent and avoid giving excessive, unnecessary, or distracting feedback. In fact, in some studies athletes report they want augmented feedback from the coach as little as 10 percent of the time.[8] Most important, coaches should avoid telling athletes what they can clearly see or feel themselves, such as the observation that a shot or pass was unsuccessful. When coaches provide feedback too frequently, athletes are less likely to retain what they learn and often struggle to transfer the learning to performance situations.

The key to feedback frequency is timeliness and skill complexity. As a rule, coaches should provide the minimum amount of relevant feedback when it is most needed.[4, 8, 32] A low rate of feedback from the coach appears to be more effective when the skill to be learned has low complexity. On the other hand, athlete learning and performance does benefit from high feedback frequency, perhaps even as much as after each skill attempt, when the skill to be learned is highly complex in relation to the athlete's ability to perform the skill.[43]

For example, heading a crossed ball in soccer is generally considered a highly complex skill, in contrast to a less complex skill such as passing back and forth with a teammate without defensive pressure. When athletes are first learning how to head a crossed ball in soccer, they are likely to benefit from frequent feedback from the coach, whereas much less frequent feedback would be needed for the passing activity.

The frequency of coach feedback can also be determined by setting feedback zones, commonly referred to as bandwidth feedback.[8] Taking the unique profile of the athlete or team and the goal of the practice into account, coaches can establish zones of acceptable performance. Coaches give feedback only when athlete performance falls outside the performance zone.

For example, the feedback bandwidth for a novice volleyball athlete learning how to serve might be quite large so that the athlete can develop a feel for the movement and learn to pay attention to intrinsic feedback. The coach might step in to provide feedback only if the athlete is repeatedly using incorrect movement patterns, indicating that the athlete is not noticing intrinsic feedback cues. As the athlete's skill level improves, the feedback bandwidth should be narrowed so that the athlete can make increasingly smaller refinements.

To avoid creating athlete dependency on augmented feedback, before giving feedback coaches should consider asking athletes to share what they are noticing about their performance. This form of delayed feedback, sometimes referred to as subjective error estimation, has repeatedly been shown to lead to greater and quicker skill improvements than reliance on coach-augmented feedback.[31, 44]

For example, a coach might see that a soccer athlete is consistently kicking shots over the net during a shooting activity. The coach notices that the athlete is leaning too far back in the shooting stance, causing the ball to sail high in the air. After allowing the athlete several attempts to self-correct the error without augmented feedback, the coach could pull the athlete aside and make the following type of statement: "I noticed many of your shots are too high. What do you think might be causing that?" This approach encourages athletes to draw on their own task-intrinsic feedback, gives them some ownership of the learning experience, and teaches them how to self-correct performance errors—a critical skill in competitions when the coach is unable to provide immediate feedback.

Finally, although coaches will naturally look to provide feedback on athlete errors, they should make a conscious effort to provide feedback on successful performances. Athletes report greater intrinsic motivation and feelings of competence when they are given feedback after successful skill attempts as opposed to when they make mistakes.[45] For example, visual feedback should be used to show athletes examples of successful skill performance, not just errors. Using visual feedback in this way counterbalances time spent reviewing skill errors and helps build enthusiasm for video feedback sessions.

The key lesson here for coaches is that they should make a conscious effort to spread the feedback they give to their athletes between successful and unsuccessful skill attempts. Tom Osborne, one of the most successful and revered American college football coaches of all time, is a prime example of a great coach who understood the importance of providing athletes with feedback on their strengths as a way to enhance learning long before the science proved him right. "When we have conferences with our Nebraska players," he said, "we always start out by discussing what their strengths are. Everyone needs to hear this."[46 (p. 43)]

## Wrap-Up

Successful coaches view themselves as master teachers. Becoming an effective teacher-coach requires an understanding of basic learning principles and the way in which they can be adapted to fit the learning needs of specific athletes. Learning is best regarded as an ongoing process of change, not a fixed point or outcome. The learning process is enhanced when coaches help athletes connect prior knowledge to new learning experiences. Knowledge connection is further strengthened when coaches prime athletes with advance organizers before they introduce new learning activities.

Athlete motivation plays a central role in learning. Coaches need to show athletes how the learning activities will help them reach their performance goals. When athletes believe that a learning activity will have a direct effect on their ability to achieve their goals, they will attach greater value to the experience and be more motivated.

Before introducing new skills or tactics, coaches must take the time to identify all the component skills that athletes will need to complete the activity successfully.

Although this step will extend the amount of time needed to prepare practice sessions, it will help coaches counterbalance their own expert blind spot. When coaches miss important component skills, athlete learning will be compromised.

Finally, deciding on the amount, type, and frequency of feedback should also be considered when designing athlete learning experiences. Each athlete's unique learning profile will determine how coaches balance their feedback approach and set appropriate feedback bandwidths.

Chapter 7

# Design Effective Practice Environments

**Key Concepts**

Mastery practice goals
Growth mind-set
Learning scorecards
Eight principles of practice design
General motor programs
Random versus blocked practice
Autonomy-supportive coaching
Functional variability
Gamelike approach
Maximum individual participation

Designing quality practice sessions is the most basic of all coaching activities. According to five-time national collegiate baseball championship coach Augie Garrido, "Games and championships are won in practice first."[1 (p. 139)] How a coach designs practices determines how much athletes will learn because practice design directly influences athlete commitment to practice.

Great athletes naturally see the value in practice and will not only eagerly attend coach-led practice sessions but also train on their own. Muhammed Ali, one of the greatest athletes of all time, summed it up well in his often quoted statement: "The fight is won or lost far away from witnesses—behind the lines, in the gym, and out there on the road, long before I dance under those lights."[2]

But anyone who has coached knows that not all athletes automatically see the value in practice or commit to giving full effort in every practice session. The most motivated athletes appreciate that they get to practice, whereas less motivated athletes complain of having to practice. Nothing is more frustrating for a coach than watching athletes give poor effort or complaining about having to practice.

Perhaps the most renowned example of this is the "We talkin' 'bout practice" press conference held by former league Most Valuable Player and 11-time NBA

All-Star Allen Iverson.[3, 4] Although much has been written about his state of mind (and sobriety) while giving the press conference, his famous rant has come to symbolize a lack of motivation to give 100 percent in practice sessions.

Some athletes mistakenly believe they should save their energy for competitions, when it really matters. Yet the most successful coaches and athletes know that competition success comes only through focused and effortful practice. Two-time Super Bowl championship football coach Tom Coughlin said it best:

> The three words that I absolutely guarantee have never been said at one of my practices are "It's only practice.". . . A quality performance is the natural extension of practice. The harder you work in practice, the easier the performance will be.[5 (p. 173)]

One of the primary causes of athletes' devaluing practice is their experience with poorly designed practice sessions. Well-intentioned but ill-designed practices not only hurt player development but also erode team culture and confidence in the coach. Research on coaching, along with my own observations and discussions with coaches and athletes around the world, shows that coaches are rarely taught how to design quality practice sessions.

Although great coaches have always made time to watch how other successful coaches run their practices, the science of quality practice design is relatively new. In 2000 renowned sport expertise researcher Janet Starkes coined the term

AP Photo/Bill Kostroun

New York Giants' coach Tom Coughlin was notorious for planning detailed and efficient practice sessions.

*practice microstructures* to describe what expert athletes do in practice and how their practice differs from those of less skilled athletes.[6] The results of her research on practice sessions across sport with coaches from high school to Olympic level were consistent and sobering; quality practices are the exception, not the norm.

In general, her research showed that athletes were inactive nearly half of every practice and spent much of their time practicing skills they had already mastered. This profile of a typical practice leads to boredom, off-task behavior, and discipline issues. It stunts athlete development because most time is spent on proving what they can already do as opposed to the more difficult task of improving weaknesses.

A quality practice nurtures athlete motivation and maximizes athlete skill development. Coaches must keep this in mind when selecting each activity to include in a practice session. Learning how to design quality practices is the surest way to increase coaching effectiveness and athlete success.

The purpose of this chapter is to describe the common design features of quality practices. Quality practice design includes four features:

- Feature 1: Set challenging and specific practice goals.
- Feature 2: Keep athletes physically and mentally active throughout the practice.
- Feature 3: Give athletes choices and ask them for input on practice design.
- Feature 4: Create competitive gamelike practice activities.

## SETTING CHALLENGING AND SPECIFIC PRACTICE GOALS

Coaches and athletes typically have no problem setting long-term goals for the season, such as winning a championship. But coaches less commonly set clear and specific goals for each practice session. To maximize athlete learning through efficient use of time, coaches must also set goals for every practice. Championship coaches, like seven-time national collegiate champion volleyball coach Russ Rose, meticulously plan their practice sessions to ensure that "every practice has a goal and every drill has a specific purpose."[7 (p. 47)]

Athlete learning will be optimized when the practice goals stretch the athletes just outside their comfort zone. In *The Little Book of Talent*, author Daniel Coyle refers to this talent development principle as reachfulness.[8] Practice goals that challenge athletes but are realistically attainable create practice environments of high engagement and maximize learning by inspiring athletes to reach forward to achieve the goals.[9, 10] Creating reach or stretch practice goals has the added benefit of keeping athletes focused on practice by creating the right conditions for optimal, or flow, experiences (see discussion on flow and optimal experiences in chapter 6).

Athletes are competitive by nature and respond enthusiastically to practice activities that are just beyond their current abilities yet possible to accomplish with full focus, concentration, and appropriate support from the coach. For example, outstanding high school coaches report that communicating high expectations for athletes is one of the best ways to avoid wasting precious practice time dealing with discipline issues.[11]

World champion volleyball coach Karch Kiraly shared that he sets challenging practice goals by designing what he refers to as ugly practices. When practice activities force athletes to stretch just beyond their current skill level, they make many mistakes, resulting in what will look to an outsider like an ugly practice. The mistakes, when appropriately framed as learning opportunities, are simply stepping-stones to higher levels of performance.

Besides being set at the right level of challenge, practice goals should be worded in a way that emphasizes that effort and success are within the athlete's control.[12] These types of goals are referred to as mastery goals. Athletes rate coaches who adopt a mastery approach to coaching as better teachers, are more satisfied with their sport experience, and are less anxious.[13, 14] Mastery goals are contrasted with ego goals, in which the emphasis is on not making mistakes and judging success as defeating someone else (or being the best at a practice activity).[15]

When setting mastery practice goals, coaches can benefit from using the CARS goal-setting acronym: challenging, attainable, realistic, and specific.[16] By regularly reviewing athlete progress, coaches will be able to determine what is challenging, attainable, and realistic for their particular athletes. In terms of being specific, coaches should write practice goals that clearly specify the behaviors and conditions that must be met if the performance is to be considered successful.

Examples of mastery practice goals for common technical skills in basketball are provided in table 7.1. The mastery goals in this case are based on the recommended cues and steps for learning how to perform the technical skills successfully.[17]

When coaches set mastery practice goals and design their practices from a mastery approach, they are also helping athletes develop a growth mind-set.[18] Renowned psychologist Carol Dweck has shown through decades of research that people with a growth mind-set approach learning and challenges with more enthusiasm and view mistakes as opportunities to get better. Failures are fertilizer for deeper learning and improved performance. People with a growth mind-set

**Table 7.1 Sample Mastery Practice Goals for Basketball Technical Skills**

| Practice activity | Mastery goal |
|---|---|
| Speed dribbling | Complete each run through the activity in less than 10 seconds while keeping the ball under control and the eyes up. |
| Layup | Improve the number of layups made from the last practice from both sides of the basket by focusing on driving up off one leg with both hands up, gently releasing the ball with one hand, and banking the ball off the backboard. |
| Jump shot | Make at least 50 percent of uncontested shots taken from specific spots on the floor, remembering to start from a balanced position, jump with both feet, straighten the arm, and wave good-bye to the ball. |
| Chest pass | Place each chest pass in such a way that it is easily retrievable by a moving teammate by keeping two hands on the ball, stepping forward, and pushing the ball out at chest level. |

view their ability as something that can be improved and controlled through effortful and deliberate practice.

A simple cue that coaches can use to help athletes develop a growth mind-set is the acronym FAIL, which means first attempt in learning.[19] Coaches can help athletes understand that mistakes are a normal and needed part of the learning process. To help build a growth mind-set, coaches can teach athletes to add the word *yet* to the end of self-critical statements that are commonly used when learning new skills.[20] For example, when an athlete who is struggling to learn how to play defense states in frustration, "I'm no good at defense," he or she should be reminded to restate it as, "I'm no good at defense . . . yet." This simple strategy, when used consistently and combined with quality practices, will increase athlete persistence and willingness to learn from failures.

When coaches set mastery goals for their athletes, they are teaching them to focus more on improving their ability as opposed to proving their ability. This subtle but critical difference will have a long-lasting and profound effect on how athletes approach practice and performance setbacks.

A prime example of an athlete who embodies a growth mind-set is tennis great Rafael Nadal. During his career he suffered what most athletes would consider a crippling defeat. At the 2012 Australian Open tennis tournament he lost in the final in the longest match in history for a major tennis tournament—5 hours and 53 minutes.[21] When asked about his emotions after the match, he stated that it was a special match he would remember forever, not because of the loss but because of how hard each athlete played right until the end. Nadal did not let the loss define or deter him even though it was the seventh straight championship final he had lost to the same opponent. Nadal continued to take a mastery approach to his practice, and he beat his rival late that same year and six of the next seven times they met.

The challenge practice goals and an associated rationale should always be communicated before the practice. Athlete motivation, from youth to Olympic levels, increases when coaches explain why practice activities are important and specifically how they will improve specific aspects of their performance.[12] For example, a soccer coach might tell her or his athletes that the reason they are going to play a 3v3 small-sided possession game is because it will help them improve their spacing and passing during matches.

I also use this strategy when coaching. One of the most popular practice activities I designed for my youth baseball team is a game that requires athletes to field and throw a ball to a pyramid of targets at home plate. We use two upside-down buckets for the first level (1 point), a water jug for the second level (2 points), and a stuffed toy for the third level (3 points). I make a point of explaining the rationale of the activity every time we play it. I tell the athletes that we do this activity because it will help us improve our throwing accuracy to our catcher when an opponent is trying to steal home. Without providing the rationale the coach is assuming that the athletes will make the connection between a fun practice game and actual game situations.

Telling athletes the why behind what they will do is an effective coaching strategy for several reasons.[22] First, athletes value the activities more if the rationale is clear, and they therefore invest more effort into the activities. Second, when coaches share the rationale for practice activities, they are building trust and strengthening the coach-athlete relationship.

Ideally, coaches will share the practice goals with athletes even before the athletes arrive at practice. For example, coaches can share goals for the next practice at the end of the previous practice, much as Coach John Wooden did during his tenure as basketball coach at UCLA. Sharing the practice goals in advance serves multiple purposes. First, it gives athletes time to mentally prepare for the practice challenge. Second, it connects the practices and the practice goals to one another across a season.

With the availability of multiple electronic communication options, some coaches may prefer to share practice goals with the athletes between practice sessions. The practice goals can then be reinforced at the start of the practice, and athletes can be given an opportunity to ask questions about the goals before starting the practice.

However, setting challenging practice goals is not enough. Quality coaches design goal evaluation systems to track each athlete's progress toward the goals.[9] For example, five-time national college football championship coach Jim Tressel attributed much of his success to the daily goal evaluation system he used with his athletes. For each day of training Coach Tressel and his staff graded each athlete's practice performance on a scale of 1 to 5. The results were posted after every practice, and players were encouraged to discuss their grades with the coaches. A summary of the goal evaluation grading scale that Coach Tressel shared with me is provided in table 7.2.

These types of grading systems, sometimes referred to as scorecards for learning, serve as reminders that we are what we count.[8] Perhaps one of the most detailed and well-known examples of tracking practice goals in coaching is the competitive cauldron system developed by University of North Carolina women's soccer coach Anson Dorrance, who has lead his teams to 22 national championships. Coach Dorrance, who also coached the U.S. national team to the inaugural women's World Cup championship, has learned that "players do what you inspect, not what you expect."[23]

With the competitive cauldron, every aspect of an athlete's performance in a practice is graded, from effort to fitness to small-sided game outcomes to techni-

**Table 7.2 Sample Practice Goal Evaluation Grading Scale**

| Grade | Description |
|---|---|
| 1 | Performed like a national champion today. |
| 2 | Performed like a conference champion today. |
| 3 | Performed average today. You were present but didn't perform to your potential. |
| 4 | Performed below average today. If you perform like this in a game, you likely will lose. |
| 5 | Performed poorly today. If you perform like this in a game, you will be helping the competition defeat us. |

cal and tactical skill attempts.[24, 25] Coach Dorrance shared with me that the first version of his competitive cauldron included 9 practice performance metrics, but it has evolved over decades of coaching to include 19 performance indicators. At the end of practice the athletes' grades are reported to the team, and athletes earn rewards or punishments based on their scores. The system works well for Coach Dorrance's teams because he has found that it motivates athletes to compete and focus at the highest levels in every practice activity.

Because of the considerable time and resources needed to adopt a competitive cauldron practice goal-tracking system, this approach has received mixed reviews and is not recommended for all coaches.[26] It is presented here because it is a well-known system, and it reinforces the need for coaches to create some type of practice goal feedback system. Just as Coach Dorrance adapted what he learned from observing legendary basketball coach Dean Smith run his practices, other coaches should create their own practice goal feedback systems that are meaningful and practical for their particular settings.

Although the value of setting challenging practice goals is clear, one cautionary note should not be overlooked. High expectations without the appropriate support and guidance from the coach can severely demoralize an athlete.[9] For example, if coaches set challenging practice goals and fail to help the athletes when they struggle or punish them with extra running or other penalties if they don't achieve the goals, then coaches are sending a mixed message. The high expectations communicate that the coach believes in the athlete, but the lack of guidance and fear of being punished erode trust and harm the coach-athlete relationship.

## KEEPING ATHLETES MENTALLY AND PHYSICALLY ACTIVE

One of the most common errors that coaches make is scheduling practice sessions that are too long. When asked about practice design, legendary professional soccer coach Sir Alex Ferguson responded, "Every training session was about quality. We didn't allow a lack of focus. It was about intensity, concentration, speed—a high level of performance."[27 (p. 6)] When coaches overextend practices, athletes inevitably lose focus and are more likely to get injured.

In the United States nearly 500,000 injuries are estimated to occur annually in high school sport practices.[28] Nearly 70 percent of those injuries occur in the second (60 percent) or third (9 percent) hour of practice. Furthermore, over 70 percent of the injuries incurred in practice cause athletes to miss three or more days of valuable training. The prevailing overemphasis on excessively long practices has surely contributed to these high injury rates in practice. Well-organized and efficient practices should be designed to maximize skill development in a safe and controlled setting where the risk of injury should be low. Coaches should aim for short, high-intensity practice sessions.

Many school-based sports typically schedule practices for a set time in the afternoon, such as 3:00 to 5:00 p.m., resulting in 8 to 10 hours of practice time per week depending on when games are played. Coaches should replace the question "How will I fill the practice time I'm given" with the more fundamental question "How can I use the least amount of practice time possible in the most efficient way?"

Even at the highest levels of professional sport in which athletes are paid to train, the most successful coaches understand that the best practices are the most efficient practices. Championship coach Tom Coughlin, reflecting on more than 45 years of college and professional football coaching, said, "Contrary to a common belief, long practices are neither desirable nor particularly beneficial."[5 (p. 176)]

Anyone who has coached will tell you that there is never enough time to accomplish all your teaching goals. This reality is another reason why coaches need to familiarize themselves with the long-term athlete development frameworks discussed in chapter 5. A long-term view of athlete development eliminates the need for coaches to feel as if they have to cover everything in a single season of practices.

Many factors need to be considered when determining the optimal length of a practice session, such as athlete age and skill level. Most sport governing bodies provide guidance for coaches on what is considered appropriate in their particular sport. For example, USA Football recommends no more than two or three practices per week of no more than 90 minutes for athletes up to 14 years of age and then no more than 120 minutes for older adolescents.[29] These guidelines are fairly consistent with what is recommended in other sports and coaching research.[30–32]

Based on a review of sport organization guidelines and athlete development literature, recommendations for the optimal number of practice sessions per week and practice length are provided in table 7.3.

Limiting practice sessions to 90 to 120 minutes might seem counterintuitive to popular cultural depictions of what it takes to succeed in sport (e.g., We have to train longer and harder than our opponents!). Regrettably, many coaches early in their careers subscribe to this misguided view, much to the detriment of their athletes. By being mindful of evidence-based guidelines for practice length, coaches can learn this lesson early in their careers instead of painfully coming to this realization later. A perfect example is Bill Cleary, who coached the Harvard men's ice hockey team to their only national championship at the end of his 19-year coaching career:

**Table 7.3 Recommend Number of Weekly Practices and Practice Length**

| Athlete age group | Number of practices | Duration of each practice |
|---|---|---|
| Under 6 years old | 1–2 days per week | 45–60 minutes |
| Under 8 years old | 2 days per week | 60–75 minutes |
| Under 10 years old | 2 days per week | 60–90 minutes |
| Under 12 years old | 2–3 days per week | 75–90 minutes |
| Under 14 years old | 3 days per week | 75–90 minutes |
| Under 16 years old | 3–4 days per week | 90–120 minutes |
| 17 years old and older | 4–5 days per week | 90–120 minutes |

> During the latter half of my coaching career, I came to the conclusion that no student would sit through a two- or three-hour class without nodding off or becoming bored. Why should it be any different for a sports class? It was then that I cut my practice time in half and instituted one fun day of practice each week, which in turn gave my athletes extra time for their schoolwork. You should be able to accomplish all you need to do in a high-tempo 90-minute practice.[33 (p. 4)]

After the ideal number of practice sessions and practice length have been determined, coaches can focus on how to structure a practice to maximize athlete engagement and learning. As a rule, serious coaches should expect to spend almost as much time designing a practice as running the practice.

Former college baseball coach Keith Madison, who coached teams to over 730 wins in his 25-year career, liked to say, "Successful people invest their time, average people spend time, and underachievers waste time."[34 (p. 17)] Showing up to practice without a formal and detailed practice plan is a waste of time because it is a recipe for failure.

The best coaches invest their time by planning every minute of their practice sessions. Each practice has a logical sequence and flow based on the coach's observations of player performance and skill development needs. Coach of the 20th Century John Wooden created eight principles of practice plan design that he used as a guide when planning practices.[35 (p. 75–82)]

- Fundamentals before creativity.
- Use variety.
- Teach new material at the start of practice.
- Quick transitions between activities.
- Increase complexity from practice to practice.
- Conditioning for learning.
- End on a positive note.
- Avoid altering a plan during the lesson.

These principles have stood the test of time and are as valuable today as they were when Coach Wooden created them many decades ago. The principles are described in detail in the following section with supporting examples from other coaches and coaching research.

1. **Fundamentals before creativity.** Basic skills of the sport must be learned before complex skills and strategies can be practiced. Basic skills provide the foundation for athlete creativity.[36] Repeatedly practicing fundamental skills helps athletes build what are referred to as general motor programs—a sort of mental blueprint that contains information about how to perform basic skills.[16] For example, through quality practice athletes develop motor programs for basic skills such as shooting a basketball, catching a football pass, or hitting a pitched ball. Athletes rely on these general motor programs to perform quick and decisive actions that require them to improvise or adjust their movements while

in action. Therefore, developing general motor programs will greatly increase an athlete's ability to perform successfully across various competitive situations. For this reason, regardless of the age or skill level of the athlete, some practice time should always be set aside for learning or reinforcing basic skills. For example, championship football coach Pete Carroll believes that disciplined, repetitive practice of fundamental skills is critical for performing at a championship level not only because it strengthens general motor programs but also because it builds athletes' confidence in their ability.[37]

2. **Use variety.** Practice activities should be regularly changed to keep athletes' engagement and interest high, and new practice activities should be introduced frequently. Variety can also be accomplished by simply rearranging the order in which activities are practiced. Yet another option is to vary the sequence of skill attempts. This method is referred to as random or varied practice.[16] For example, instead of having golf athletes practice blocks of 10 putts from a set distance, they could be required to attempt each of the 10 putts from a different spot on the green. Likewise, instead of hitting a block of shots with one specific club, they could be required to hit the same number of shots with a random sequence of different clubs. This routine promotes what is known as perceptual attunement, which develops the ability to make adjustments based on changes in the performance environment. Although short-term gains in performance may not be evident with this approach, it appears to be more effective than blocked practice for long-term performance improvements.[38, 39 (p. 184)] Another way to add variety to practices is to select a theme for each practice and design activities that all connect to the theme. Successful coaches often add an inspirational quotation to their practice plan, which they share with their athletes at the start of practice as a way to reinforce the practice theme. In addition to books such as *Inspirational Quotes for Sport Coaches*[40] inspiring quotations can easily be found through a quick online search. Two websites that coaches may find particularly helpful are the sport quotations pages of the University of North Texas Center for Sport Psychology and Performance Excellence (https://sportpsych.unt.edu/resources/athletes/31) and Keepinspiring.me (www.keepinspiring.me/100-most-inspirational-sports-quotes-of-all-time/). Coaches who use social media will also find Twitter accounts such as @Sports_Greats (Sports Quotes) and @SportsMotto (Great Sports Quotes) to be valuable sources of inspirational quotations to use at practices.

3. **Teach new material at the start of practice.** Coaches can use the first part of the practice to introduce and teach new skills or strategies. After a proper warm-up that includes light movement and stretching, athletes are most receptive to learning new things because (*a*) they have had a chance to socialize with their teammates for a few minutes and (*b*) they are more physically and mentally ready to learn than later in the practice when they have less energy. An active warm-up that includes some type of aerobic activity such as a game of soccer on a small field, perhaps with multiple balls, primes the brain for learning. Aerobic exercise stimulates the release of chemicals in the brain, referred to as neurotransmitters, that increase focus and strengthen the learning of new concepts.[41]

4. **Quick transitions between activities.** Coaches must also pay careful attention to the flow and sequence of practice activities to ensure that time spent moving from one activity to the next is minimized. Transition time can be minimized by thinking about how equipment will be set up and moved from one activity to the next and by sharing practice plans in advance with assistant coaches. Transition time can also be minimized by arriving early to practice and making sure that the required equipment is in place for each activity before practice starts. Coach Wooden required his athletes to sprint from one activity to the next, but this strategy works only if the next station or activity is set up in advance. A simple way to ensure quick transitions is to send athletes for water breaks individually or in small groups, rather than using the common practice of scheduling full-team water breaks at regular intervals throughout a practice. When large groups of athletes break for water at the same time, off-task behavior is more likely to occur and it takes more time to bring the athletes back on task for the next activity.

5. **Increase complexity from practice to practice.** Early season practices should be designed with an emphasis on fundamental skills, often practiced in repetitive blocks of time. Blocked practice is generally considered more effective when an athlete is first learning a new skill or concept.[16] But after athletes become comfortable performing the skill, the complexity of the practice activities should be increased. For example, after athletes have learned the fundamentals of shooting a basketball, coaches can add complexity to shooting activities by varying the distance of the shots, adding a pass before the shot, or adding defenders. Soccer coach Tony DiCicco believes that this approach to practice design was instrumental in his leading teams to Olympic and World Cup titles. In his words, he layered the design of practices by continually adding small variations to the way they practiced set plays such as free kicks and corner kicks. After winning the 1999 World Cup of soccer, in which his team won many games with corner kicks, the media assumed that his team must have devoted massive blocks of practice time to repeating corner kicks. He explained that although they did practice corner kicks on a regular basis, "It was a continual layering to imprint the basic, subtle nuances of each free-kick opportunity. We imprinted layers rather than attempting to rush perfection." [42 (p. 288)]

6. **Conditioning for learning.** Coaches cannot expect athletes to show up to the first practice in top physical and mental condition. Just as each practice session should have a proper warm-up period, the first few weeks of practice each season should be approached as a time to warm up athletes for increasingly complex and high-intensity practice sessions. Contrary to what people might think, for Coach Wooden this guideline meant scheduling longer practices early in the year. The practice sessions for the first two weeks of the season were 30 minutes longer than normal, but the intensity of the practices was relatively low. Coach Wooden used the extra time to give longer explanations, more detailed demonstrations, and more frequent rest breaks to allow the athletes to get into practice condition. As the season progresses, practices should become shorter and more intense, requiring athletes to be in better mental and physical condition than they were for early season practices. After conditioning has been developed, coaches such as championship wrestling coach Dan Gable also recommend shortening

late-season practices as a way to keep athletes fresh.[43] Shorter practices and extra rest between practices may be required to combat fatigue from a long season. Practice sessions still need to be run at high intensity so that conditioning can be maintained leading into the postseason.

7. **End on a positive note.** Although his former players describe his practices as electric and fast paced, Coach Wooden routinely set aside the last five minutes of practice for a fun or silly activity. Former player Swen Nater recalls one practice in particular when Coach Wooden let the players hold a dunk contest, even though dunking was normally forbidden in practices because it was not allowed in games at that time. Coaches must not lose sight of the fact that fun is one of the primary motives for participating in sport. Quality coaches understand and nurture this basic need, regardless of their athletes' age and competitive level. Training to become a champion requires many thousands of hours of physically and mentally intense practice. Deliberate practice must be counterbalanced with fun and playful activities to sustain athletes' motivation and passion for the sport. One effective strategy for ensuring that athletes finish each practice on a positive note is to allow them to select the final activity at each practice. When given the choice, athletes will always select fun and competitive activities. Coaches should ensure that every athlete gets to select the fun activity at least once during the season. Coaches might also decide to award the selection of the fun activity to an athlete who exemplified a certain characteristic during the practice, such as hardest worker or best teammate. Two-time national high school football Coach of the Year Charles "Chuck" Kyle used a different kind of strategy to ensure that every practice ended on a positive note. He created a 10-second tradition whereby time was set aside at the end of every practice for each player to visualize himself correcting an error he made in practice that day.[44] The goal was for each athlete to leave the practice with a positive image of himself performing successfully.

8. **Avoid altering a plan during the lesson.** Coaches often make changes in the midst of a practice based on things they are noticing. For example, if athletes are struggling with an activity, a coach may want to spend more time on the activity. But veering off the carefully prepared practice plan disrupts the intended flow of the practice and negatively affects remaining activities. For example, if a coach extends one activity by 10 minutes, then either the next activities will have to be shortened or the practice will have to be extended. Neither of these scenarios is desirable or conducive for effective learning and skill development. If subsequent practice activities are shortened or eliminated, then the athletes are losing the opportunity to practice things that the coach believed were critical for individual and team improvement. If the practice is simply extended, athletes may conserve energy or lose focus because they don't know how long they will be practicing. When practices are extended beyond the time initially deemed optimal and athletes tire and begin to lose focus, they become most susceptible to injury.

Elements of Coach John Wooden's practice design principles will be evident in the practices of any successful coach. The principles serve as a timeless guide for helping coaches design quality practices. One of the most comprehensive examples of how a coach applied these design principles to his practices is a study I collaborated on with high school basketball coach Hank Bias.[45]

After several difficult losing seasons, Coach Bias decided to study and apply Coach Wooden's practice design principles. Some of the changes he made included *(a)* never extending a practice beyond the scheduled time, *(b)* never scheduling practices beyond two hours, *(c)* limiting each practice activity to eight minutes, *(d)* integrating water breaks into drills, and *(e)* cutting down transition time between activities by distributing detailed written practice plans to assistant coaches so that everyone would know where and when to place equipment needed for each activity. Coach Bias enjoyed a long and successful coaching career for many years following his discovery and implementation of Wooden's practice design principles. For example, the winning percentage for his teams rose from 29 percent in the three years before implementing the practice design changes to 62 percent in the five years following full implementation, representing the best 5-year winning record for the boys' basketball program in nearly 90 years.

## GIVING ATHLETES A SAY ON PRACTICE DESIGN

Although it should be clear by now that successful coaches meticulously plan every minute of their practices, this does not mean that athletes have no input into the selection of practice activities. Quality coaches understand that athletes will enjoy practice more and show greater commitment to practices when they have some choice and input on practice design.

For example, the system for practice and performance designed by championship football coach Pete Carroll provides athletes with many opportunities to celebrate their individuality and creativity.[46] He believes that this element is particularly important when coaching large teams, such as in football, because athletes need to have space to express their individuality.

The same commitment to finding a balance between coach-imposed structure and athlete freedom was also the foundation for golf coach Paul McGinley, who led the European team to the 2014 Ryder Cup championship. The Ryder Cup, considered one of the world's biggest sporting events, is held every two years. The competition pits America's best golfers against the top golfers from Europe. When asked about his leadership approach, Coach McGinley said, "There has to be structure but space within it for players to be themselves and allow the flair to come out."[47]

Balancing coach-designed structure with athlete choice has been found to be the most effective way to develop athletes' talent. This balanced approach is referred to as an autonomy-supportive approach to coaching.[23, 48–50]

Athlete motivation and coach-athlete relationships are enhanced when coaches create sport environments that help athletes meet three basic needs: (*a*) the need for choice and autonomy, (*b*) the need to learn and feel competent, and (*c*) the need to feel connected to others. Athletes consistently report that playing for coaches who allow and encourage them to share in decision making and give them choices during practices is more enjoyable and fuels athlete initiative and motivation to improve.[48–52]

The opposite of autonomy-supportive coaching is an approach that focuses on controlling and directing athletes as a way to motivate and teach them. Although some short-term performance gains may result from a controlling approach, reliance on this approach dampens athlete motivation, initiative and risk taking, and overall emotional and mental well-being.[53]

USA Football designed a simple self-assessment tool to help coaches distinguish between autonomy-supportive and controlling approaches (see figure 7.1). A coach's use of autonomy-supportive behaviors is referred to as a pull-and-ask approach. The pull-and-ask approach is characterized by frequent questioning, listening, and paraphrasing. At the other end of the spectrum is the push-and-tell approach that emphasizes direct instruction and coach advice. Note that both approaches can be effective at times, but coaches should strive to use a pull-and-ask approach as much as reasonably possible.

One often-cited example of how a coach helped athletes reach their potential by using an autonomy-supportive approach to practice design is the study completed by coaching scientist and former Olympic track and field coach Cliff Mallett.[54] At the time of the study Coach Mallett was coaching the Australian men's

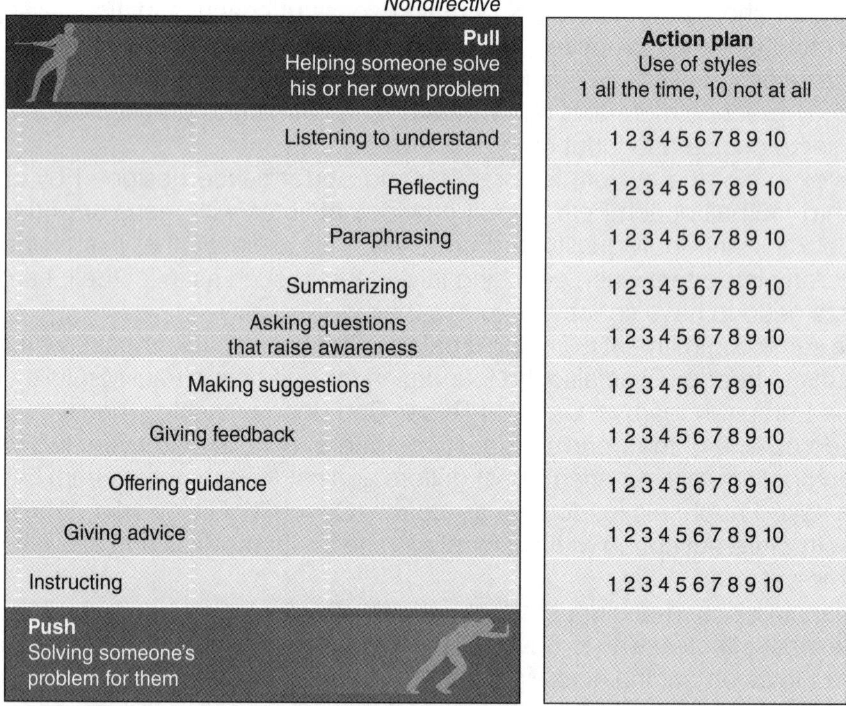


Look at each approach. On a scale of 1 to 10 identify how much you use this approach, with 1 being all the time and 10 being never.

**Figure 7.1** Pull-and-ask approach versus push-and-tell approach to coaching.
Courtesy of USA Football (www.usafootball.com).

sprint relay teams, who were ranked 14th (4 × 100) and 13th (4 × 400) in the world. Coach Mallett decided to experiment with ways to give the athletes more input into practice design and training decisions.

For example, he held formal team meetings with the athletes to ask them for their input into the training and competition approaches that would be used in preparation for the Olympics. Counter to the prevailing approach to relay sprint training at the time, the athletes and the coach jointly decided that focusing solely on relay training would be more valuable and that none of the athletes would enter individual sprint events. Also, during training sessions Coach Mallett moved his coaching to the background[55] and acted more in a facilitative, rather than directive, role. During practices the athletes were always first asked for their perceptions of their training efforts before the coach gave feedback.

These training strategies proved successful; both teams reached the Olympic finals, and the 4 × 400 team won a silver medal. According to Coach Mallett, these strategies were effective primarily because athletes were active participants in designing and evaluating the training activities, thereby helping them meet their basic needs and increase their perceptions of the relevance and value of the practice activities.

An autonomy-supportive approach to practice design has been shown to be effective with adolescent and youth sport athletes as well. For example, in a unique study comparing the behaviors of successful and unsuccessful high school soccer coaches, researchers found that winning coaches offered athletes more choices and accepted athlete input more often during practices.[56]

When they give athletes choice and some freedom to experiment with novel ways of performing skills, coaches are adding functional variability to their practice design. Emerging research shows the value of allowing athletes to experiment with unique and multiple ways to perform a skill.[57]

For example, instead of requiring athletes to perform a skill with the same movement pattern repeatedly, coaches should consider allowing athletes to introduce their own variations into the movement pattern. Athletes should be given opportunities to perform skills in a way that feels right to them. Then the coach and the athlete can jointly determine the most efficient way to perform the skill, or the athlete can be allowed to keep multiple options open for performing the skill.

Table 7.4 provides a summary of sample autonomy-supportive coaching behaviors and the way in which they can be integrated into practice design. For example, setting aside the first 5 or 10 minutes of each practice for athlete free play is recommended because it serves as a mental and physical transition to practice while allowing athletes to reconnect with their teammates.[58]

One of my favorite examples of creating an autonomy-supportive practice design strategy comes from professional rugby coach Gregor Townsend.[59] Drawing from his observations of championship teams, Coach Townsend committed to creating an autonomy-supportive practice environment that includes time for a "great by choice" activity in every practice. Time is scheduled into every practice session for athletes to identify which skills they want to work on and how they want to practice those skills. Athletes are not forced into participating in the "great by

**Table 7.4 Autonomy-Supportive Coaching Behaviors and Application to Practice Design**

| Autonomy-supportive coaching behaviors | Practice design example |
|---|---|
| Provide opportunities for initiative and independent work. | Schedule free time during practice to allow athletes to work on self-determined areas of strength or weakness. |
| Provide choice within boundaries. | Allow athletes to choose a practice activity from a coach-prepared list of activities. |
| Give rationale for tasks. | Explain the advantages of adopting a particular training approach or using a specific practice activity. |
| Acknowledge feelings and perspectives. | Listen openly and nondefensively to athlete feedback during practices and use this feedback to make adjustments to future practices. |
| Solicit athlete input. | Actively seek athlete feedback on practice activities to learn how athletes view practice activities. |
| Avoid controlling behaviors. | Recognize that a skill or practice activity can be executed in several ways; do not use ultimatums or coerce or shame athletes into performing the skill your way. |

choice" training time. Instead, they are given freedom to practice the skills they believe are most important to helping them improve their performance.

One final note must be made about this practice design feature. Some of the most successful coaches in history did not provide athletes with any input into practice design. Legendary basketball coaches John Wooden and Phil Jackson are two such examples. For example, Coach Jackson borrowed a ritual from renowned football coach Vince Lombardi and occasionally required his athletes to line up across the baseline before practice and recite an oath demonstrating their commitment to embracing the coach's structure before being allowed to practice that day.[60]

But closer inspection of these coaching approaches shows that the coaches did in fact provide their athletes with many opportunities to express themselves and contribute to team decisions. For Wooden and Jackson, athlete input and autonomy were typically reserved for the games. Coach Wooden, for example, always looked forward to being surprised by his athletes and their creativity during games, whereas Coach Jackson preferred to let his players work through tough game situations on their own.

Therefore, the principle of balancing athlete choice with coach-implemented structure was still part of their coaching approach, although it wasn't necessarily evident in their practice design. Given the advances in coaching science and athlete talent development, however, it is clear that optimal practice design includes at least some opportunities for athlete input and autonomy.

For example, when the coaching staff of the world's most successful sport team, the New Zealand All Blacks, shifted to allow more athlete input into training decisions, the athlete response was overwhelmingly positive. The change from an all-controlling to an autonomy-supportive coaching climate was cited as a key reason for the team's ability to regain the world championship title, as noted in the following statement from one of the athletes:

> The best thing about the All Blacks at the moment is that players can contribute so much. Beforehand I think it was dictated to us what our days consisted of. [Being able] to contribute . . . makes your work a lot easier than if you are being treated like a schoolkid being dictated to.[61 (p. 66)]

Coaches who take an autonomy-supportive approach to their practice design are perceived by their athletes as more organized, more intense, and more invested in athlete learning.[51] But coaches must be patient when attempting to design practices that are consistent with an autonomy-supportive coaching approach. Changing long-standing coaching habits and the traditional thinking that coaches must always be in control takes time, and coaches may struggle at first with finding the right balance of coach control and athlete independence.[48]

## CREATING COMPETITIVE GAMELIKE PRACTICE ACTIVITIES

Quality practices give athletes opportunities to test and perform skills in competitive gamelike conditions. Being able to execute a skill without pressure or opposition may look great in a practice drill, but it is not indicative of the athlete's ability to perform the skill when it is needed most—in the heat of competition. Coaches and performance psychologists have long recognized that "it is one thing to perform well in a batting cage, but it is another thing altogether to perform well in the ninth inning of a critical game, with game-day intensity and top opponents and noisy crowds and scouts watching."[62 (p. 33)]

The world's best coaches unanimously agree that practice conditions must mimic competition demands as much as possible. For example, seven-time NCAA volleyball championship coach Russ Rose explains, "I create drills that are both physically and emotionally challenging, drills that require teamwork and collective effort. I want to place my players in demanding competitive situations and see how they respond physically and mentally."[7 (p. 47)]

Creating gamelike practice activities is perhaps even more important when coaching young athletes who are much more interested in playing than in mastering perfect technique. As former Olympic coach and sport scientist Alan Launder stresses, coaches should never forget that "good technique, while important to ultimate performance, is only a means to an end, not an end in itself."[63 (p. 301)]

With the conventional drill approach, a coach organizes a series of practice activities that isolate specific techniques or tactics. Athletes then practice the activities in a sequence of repetitive blocks. For example, a baseball coach is using a conventional training approach when athletes move from a catching drill to a hitting drill to a baserunning drill in which the skills are practiced in isolation and without opposition.

AP Photo/Mike Carlson, File

**Penn State head coach Russ Rose prepares his teams for championship performances by designing competitive and gamelike practices.**

The drill approach is sometimes referred to as training form.[64, 65] In these drills coaches reduce the performance demands by isolating technical or fitness-related skills that are then performed without opposition or the normal pressure that would be found in actual competition. The drill approach can indeed be effective in helping athletes learn and refine sport skills, but some have argued that it may come at the expense of helping athletes develop decision-making skills.[66]

The alternative approach that is increasingly advocated is to create practice activities that simulate competitive game conditions, also referred to as playing form.[64, 65] With this approach techniques and tactics are taught primarily through small-sided games that closely replicate competition demands, providing athletes with a more authentic and challenging learning experience.[58] Rules, areas of play, and game focus are typically modified to maximize athlete engagement and skill practice.

For example, in small-sided games in sports such as soccer, lacrosse, and ice hockey, a gamelike practice activity might be won not by the number of goals scored, but instead by the team that records the largest number of passes, or shots, in a five-minute match. In sports such as baseball and softball, instead of using a baserunning drill in which each player takes turns running between bases, the coach might create a small-sided game in which players race against each other to see who can get to the next base fastest after a pitcher throws a strike.

One of the key principles of using a gamelike approach to practice design is ensuring that each athlete is active as much as possible, a concept referred to as maximum individual participation (MIP).[63] Observation studies show that athletes often spend much of their time in practices standing around, either listening to lengthy instructions or waiting in line. My personal observation of thousands of practice sessions tells me that this approach to practice design is still common today.

Alan Launder, together with fellow coach Wendy Piltz, has compiled many strategies for ensuring maximum individual participation for just about any sport imaginable.[63] For example, in striking games such as baseball, softball, and cricket, the use of sector games is encouraged. Instead of the common practice of having one athlete at bat at a time, which severely limits the number of touches that each athlete has either hitting or fielding the ball, the playing field can be divided into any number of sectors.

Using batting tees, the number of potential touches for each athlete can be doubled just by placing a tee on either side of home plate and having each hitter try to score a run by hitting the ball past distance markers inside the designed sector (imaginary line or cones separating home, first base, and second base in one sector from home, second base, and third base in another sector). This simple redesign of a common practice activity can easily keep 10 to 12 athletes (2 hitters and 4 or 5 fielders in each sector) highly engaged and focused for the duration of the activity.

Perhaps the quickest and easiest way for coaches to ensure maximum individual participation is to divide the practice area into multiple activity areas, commonly referred to as a teaching-grid approach to practice design. This practice design approach has been used with great success by USA Hockey. The traditional approach to an ice hockey practice has been for one team to use the entire ice surface and run activities from end to end. At the youth level, two or three teams now share a single ice surface during practice and run activities across the ice (from side board to side board). This simple teaching-grid practice redesign strategy has resulted in dramatic increases in skill attempts during practices: six times more shot attempts, five times more passes received, and two times more touches on the puck (number of times each athlete actually stickhandles with a puck).[67]

An example of how a typical soccer field could be organized as a teaching grid to maximize athlete participation and learning is shown in the teaching grid prepared by Coach Launder (see figure 7.2). Notice how what was once a single practice area is now reconfigured to provide athletes with a variety of training and constant movement, leading to more touches on the ball and improved fitness. Coaches can use this teaching-grid example as a guide to modify their practice area in a way that makes sense and is practical for their particular setting.

Successful coaches use this approach frequently when designing practices. For example, a series of studies with hundreds of experienced and successful collegiate basketball coaches found that nearly 100 percent of the coaches rated creating gamelike pressure situations in practices as a highly effective practice design feature.[68] Furthermore, college athletes cite gamelike practices as a

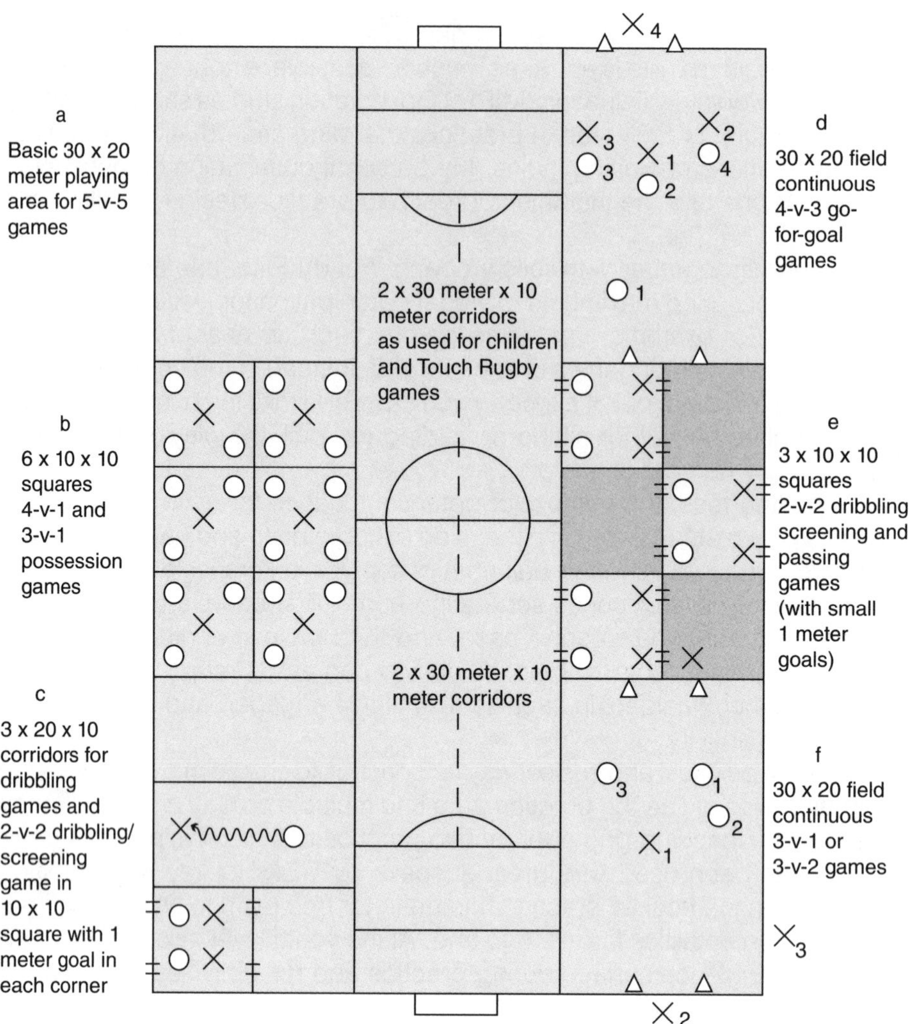


**Figure 7.2** Teaching-grid example for soccer.

Reprinted, by permission, from A.G. Launder and W. Piltz, 2013, *Play practice: Engaging and developing skilled players from beginner to elite* (Champaign, IL: Human Kinetics), 88.

defining quality of great coaches.[69] Championship baseball coach Augie Garrido summed it up well when he stated, "Every major college program today has a teacher-coach at the helm, and they all run practices that are highly organized with competitive segments that mimic game conditions."[1 (p. 241)]

Legendary professional soccer coach Sir Alex Ferguson routinely set aside time in practices for specific game scenarios that his teams might face, such as needing to score a tying goal with only a few minutes left in a match.[28] As a result, his championship teams at Manchester United were renowned for scoring late-game goals. Many argue that the team's late-game success was not the result of superior technical skills, but instead because of the way that Ferguson designed practices with a focus on highly relevant gamelike situations.

Coaches can use three strategies to design gamelike practice activities: shaping play, focusing play, and enhancing play.[63, 70] When coaches change the rules of the game, alter the number of players who participate, or modify the size of the playing area, they are shaping the way the activity is played. For example, requiring everyone to touch the ball before a shot can be taken in a lacrosse game is a way to shape how athletes play the game.

Quality coaches not only shape the play but also provide athletes with direction on how to focus their attention while playing the game. For example, in a 3v3 soccer game a coach can focus the play by reminding athletes to run to open space to create passing lanes for their teammates when they have possession of the ball.

Lastly, a gamelike approach is most effective when coaches also enhance the play by creating a reward system to increase athlete motivation and focus. For example, after players have had some time to practice a shooting game, the coach can set aside time in practice for a shooting tournament in which athletes get to pick team names and compete for a practice reward (such as selecting a game to use in a future practice).

An example of the gamelike approach to practice design in action for a basketball practice is provided in figure 7.3. In this example, Rainer Martens, author of *Successful Coaching*, explains a basketball practice game called Slick Shot.[70] Notice in the example how the coach addresses all three of the competitive gamelike practice activity considerations: shaping play, focusing play, and enhancing play.

Although the competitive gamelike approach might appear most relevant for coaches of team sports, with some creativity coaches of any sport can design gamelike practice activities. For example, U.S. women's national team archery coach Guy Krueger shared with me that he often divides athletes into small teams who are given a series of target challenges split across the practice, or even across multiple practices, with points awarded for each challenge. The challenges can include traditional target practice as well as nonarchery activities that help athletes develop foundational archery skills such as focus, arousal control, physical strength, and flexibility.

Athletes across various sports report a preference for the competitive gamelike approach to practice design, and expert athletes believe that this approach is most relevant to improving performance.[71] The competitive gamelike approach to practice design is effective because it provides athletes with critical opportunities, in a controlled environment, to practice skills while simultaneously having to read and react to changing game conditions, such as opponent pressure.

Practices that are designed with a competitive gamelike approach are information rich and provide athletes with opportunities to couple their practice movements with relevant cues from the environment. This approach is most beneficial for helping athletes increase the speed and efficiency of their decision making skills and actions in actual performance settings.[62, 72, 73]

For example, the Sevilla Football Club, one of the most successful soccer clubs in the world, teaches all their coaches to design competitive gamelike practice sessions because such sessions increase the cognitive load that athletes must learn to process. Every practice activity must include a soccer ball (no mindless

## Figure 7.3 Martens' Slick Shot Practice Activity

### A Games Approach to a Basketball Practice

Here's an example of how to use a games approach in basketball using the processes of shaping, focusing, and enhancing play.

The coach identifies the purpose of the practice as follows:

- To improve passing and develop midrange set-shot execution on offense
- To develop the defensive principles of putting pressure on the ball, providing defensive support by sagging, and recovering one's position

The coach calls the game Slick Shot. (It is useful to name your games to help your players remember them for future practices.) The aim of the game is for the offensive players to pass the ball and locate an unguarded team member who can put up a set shot within the designated area. The two defensive players work as a team to cover the passes and deny the shot. Each team gets five attempts to score on offense.

#### How the Coach Shapes Play

**Playing area:** The area is inside the three-point line of court and bounded by the baseline.

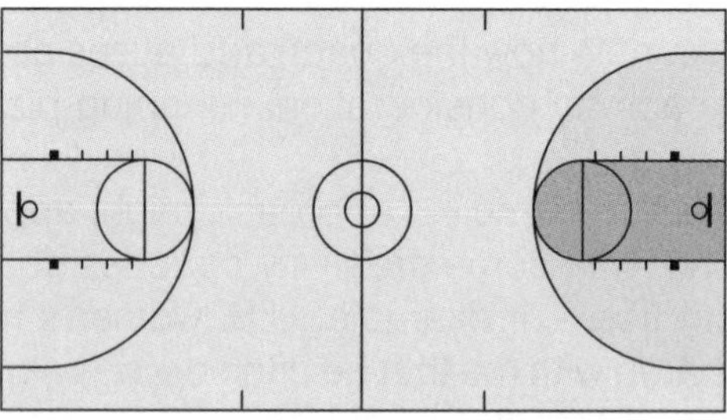

**Numbers:** Teams of three players. The game involves three offensive and two defensive players. The extra defender observes the others and then rotates into the defense. You can have as many of these games going on as your facility allows, with you and your assistant coaches moving from game to game.

**Scoring:** The offensive players score one point for shooting when unguarded (the defender must be at least three feet [about one meter] or more away) as well as for shooting from anywhere in the area outside the key and within the three-point line. An additional two points are scored for sinking the basket. A maximum of three points can be scored with each attempt to score. The defending team scores points for intercepting the ball or for forcing the offensive team to make more than three passes before shooting. Each team keeps a record of the points it scores.

**Rules of the game:** The offensive players may not dribble, and they may only receive the ball in the designated area (outside the key and within the three-point line). If the offensive players break this rule, they cannot score any points on that attempt. Defensive players may only intercept the pass; they cannot take the ball from the offensive players' hands. If they do, the offensive team gets to repeat the attempt to score.

#### How the Coach Focuses Play

The coach focuses the offensive team's attention on the following:

- Scanning the court to identify the open player (by reminding players to look up)
- Moving into position to provide passing and shooting options

- Recognizing when a player is open for a shot, then receiving the pass and squaring up for a well-balanced shot

The coach focuses the defensive team's attention on the following:

- Applying pressure to the ball and then recovering
- Providing defensive support by sagging, and then moving out to pressure the ball. (The additional player in defense can be directed to observe these elements as the others are playing and then provide information to improve this aspect of play.)

The coach can use a variety of methods for focusing the play, including the following:

- Providing direct instruction and then giving feedback as play is observed
- Freezing play and asking questions of the players
- Giving the team time-outs so that players can reflect on and discuss their performances

### How the Coach Enhances Play

Following some initial practice of the game, the coach announces that teams will now have a mini-competition called the Slick Shot State Tournament. The coach determines the number of divisions or levels of competition, and then the teams decide on their team names and in which division of competition they will play (e.g., division one of two). Results are recorded and awards and recognition given. During the competition, the coach focuses on catching players doing good.

Reprinted, by permission, from R. Martens, 2012, *Successful coaching*, 4th ed. (Champaign, IL: Human Kinetics), 158.

conditioning drills), and all tactical drills include both offensive and defensive components (just like the conditions that athletes face during an actual game).[74]

In sum, athletes report enhanced motivation and enjoyment from practices designed with a competitive gamelike approach. The evidence shows that these types of practices are highly effective for teaching athletes to

- search for and use relevant visual cues from the performance environment,
- recognize patterns of play and typical opponent reactions to various tactics,
- identify and predict opponent movements from body-positioning cues,
- anticipate teammates' actions and improve their off-the-ball support movements, and
- make quick and effective decisions under pressure.

Simply asking more experienced and successful coaches is perhaps the most effective strategy for getting ideas about how to create competitive gamelike practice activities. The best coaches in every sport will have designed and tested many competitive gamelike practice activities over their careers. Coaches should also check sport-specific resources for ideas on designing competitive gamelike practice activities, such as the *Soccer Practice Games* book written by Joseph Luxbacher that includes 175 competitive gamelike practice activities.[75]

Many successful coaches prefer to place their gamelike practice activities at the end of the practice as a way to finish with something fun and competitive. Former Duke University baseball coach Sean McNally liked to end almost every practice with an activity he called 27, or Practice to Win.[76] The goal of this gamelike practice activity was for the team as a whole to earn 27 outs, the equivalent of a nine-inning baseball game, without committing any mental or physical errors. If an error occurs, the team starts back at 0 outs.

The coach shapes the play by having a pitcher simulate a pitch. The coach then hits a ball and calls out a game scenario. The players on the field must respond with the correct play to earn the out. Coach McNally believed that this high-tempo, focused game was instrumental in helping players become game ready. Although the players needed an hour to earn the 27 outs when McNally first introduced the activity, as they increased their game readiness they eventually were able to complete the game in 8 to 12 minutes.

Because the competitive gamelike approach to practice design is considered a nontraditional approach to designing practices, coaches normally experience some doubt and discomfort when first attempting to shift from the standard skill and drill practice design mind-set.[72, 77] Furthermore, coaches may feel pressure from others to conform to the traditional way of designing practices.

Although preparing practices with a competitive gamelike approach is advised, in reality each practice will likely include a mix of traditional drills and gamelike activities. What is the optimal split between drill and game approaches when designing practices? The answer is, "It depends." There is no magical practice design ratio.

The key for coaches is to identify the goal for the practice, consider the athletes' age and current skill level and readiness to achieve the practice goal, and then ensure that the practice includes an appropriate mix of both traditional drill and gamelike activities. Generally, athlete enjoyment and engagement will be higher in competitive gamelike activities. In a study on the role of competitive games between teammates in practices one college coach plainly stated, "You want your practices as gamelike as possible. You want to replicate the game environment."[78] This guidance applies with athletes of any age. But the traditional drill approach has a definite place, particularly when coaches determine that athletes need time for isolated skill practice without the added constraints of teammates or opponent pressure.

## Wrap-Up

Efficient, detailed, and high-quality practices are a timeless defining characteristic of quality coaches. As championship golf coaches Lynn Marriott and Pia Nilsson note, "While change is inevitable, growth is optional. Practice is intentional growth."[79 (p. 3)] Learning how to design practices that maximize athletes' focus, motivation, and learning is the surest way to ensure that practices lead to intentional growth in athletes' skill and performance.

A comprehensive review of the literature and practices of great coaches shows that four features are common to effective practices:

- Feature 1: Set challenging and specific practice goals.
- Feature 2: Keep athletes physically and mentally active throughout the practice.

- Feature 3: Give athletes choices and ask them for input on practice design.
- Feature 4: Create competitive gamelike practice activities.

Successful coaches set aside a few minutes after each practice session to reflect on the quality of the practice.[80] Figure 7.4 is a postpractice coach reflection sheet that uses the four practice design features as a guide. The reflection sheet is designed to serve as a quick reminder for the coach of the keys to a quality practice session. A high-quality practice that maximizes athlete learning and motivation is one for which the coach can check off all the worksheet items.

The best coaches invest many years developing and refining practice plans that align with these four design features. Thankfully, many examples of quality practice plans are available in the coaching literature.

## Figure 7.4 Postpractice Coach Reflection Sheet

### Feature 1: Set challenging and specific practice goals.

☐ Were practice goals shared with the athletes at or before the start of practice?

☐ Were practice activities demanding yet attainable for most athletes?

☐ Did I tell the athletes why we were doing each activity before they started it?

☐ Were athletes given feedback on their practice performance today?

Coach comments on feature 1: ______________________________

______________________________

______________________________

______________________________

______________________________

### Feature 2: Keep athletes physically and mentally active throughout practice.

☐ Was practice the right length to sustain athlete focus and energy right to the end?

☐ Did I arrive with a detailed written practice plan for today's session?

☐ Did I teach new material at the start of the practice?

☐ Was transition time between activities kept to a minimum?

☐ Did I end practice with a fun, positive activity?

Coach comments on feature 2: ______________________________

______________________________

______________________________

______________________________

______________________________

### Feature 3: Give athletes choices and ask them for input on practice design.

☐ Were athletes asked for their input when designing the practice?

☐ Were a few minutes set aside for free play or athlete-directed practice?

☐ Were athletes given some choice of activities in today's practice?

☐ Was I open to allowing athletes to perform skills in ways that felt right to them?

Coach comments on feature 3: ______________________________

______________________________

______________________________

______________________________

______________________________

### Feature 4: Create competitive gamelike practice activities.

☐ Were athletes required to perform some activities under competition-like pressure?

☐ Was each athlete physically active and on-task most of the time?

☐ Was there a reward or consequence for athlete performance during the gamelike activity?

☐ Did I recognize athletes who gave maximum effort for the gamelike activity?

Coach comments on feature 4: ______________________________

______________________________

______________________________

______________________________

______________________________

Chapter 8

# Ensure Precompetition Readiness

**Key Concepts**

Sleep guidelines
Food and hydration needs
On-site warm-up
Stretching
Individual zone of optimal functioning
Deep belly breathing
Progressive muscle relaxation
Imagery and pregame music
Pregame speeches
Checklists and routines

Game days are special. Any coach or athlete will tell you that game days feel different. And for good reason. Game days present coaches and their athletes with added pressure and distractions such as performing in front of friends and family and matching up against a particularly challenging opponent.

Game days elicit a wide range of heightened emotions ranging from excitement to fear, particularly when competing against a tough rival, in championship events, or in playoff games, when success depends on absolute physical and mental readiness and peak performance.

Professional basketball coach Steve Kerr, himself a five-time professional championship athlete, understands the pressure of competition days as well as anyone. In his first year as a head coach, while coaching his team to the NBA championship, he described the playoff competitions in particular as a different animal because of the high emotional cost to athletes and coaches: "I felt it as a player, but to feel it as a coach you can tell the difference in preparation from one day to the next."[1]

All the hours of hard practice may be wasted if the coach neglects to prepare a detailed plan of action for competition days. An inability to cope with the increased demands and pressures of game day will hurt performance in many ways. An athlete's ability to focus on important competition cues and coaching signals will drop, and negative emotions such as fear, anger, tension, and frustration are likely to rise.[2] These changes, of course, affect not only the athlete's individual performance but also her or his ability to help teammates perform at their best.

With the right preparation, opportunities to test themselves against their competition will become the most highly anticipated and exhilarating moments for coaches and their athletes. The focus of precompetition activities should be on helping athletes get to a point where they feel physically and mentally ready for peak performance.[3] One of the competition-day strategies that Coach Kerr liked to use to lower precompetition anxiety was to encourage coaches and athletes to read one hour each day. The purpose of the reading time was to "get lost in your thoughts and forget about the game a little bit."[1]

The purpose of this chapter is to share strategies and research on how to coach athletes to peak performance in the days and hours leading up to the competition. The goal is for coaches to learn how to help their athletes consistently be ready when it counts.

With the extensive focus they place on preparing their athletes, coaches can neglect to take care of their own competition readiness needs.[4] Although the information presented in this chapter is focused on how coaches can best help their athletes achieve optimal precompetition readiness, much of the advice applies equally well to coaches themselves.

## PREPARING PHYSICALLY

Precompetition physical preparation depends on the physical demands of the sport, the role and position to be played by the athlete, and competition structure. For example, the precompetition physical warm-up for a sprinter competing in multiple heats throughout the day at a track and field event will be much different from the warm-up that a softball pitcher uses to prepare to play a few innings in a regular-season game. But precompetition physical readiness for athletes and their coaches requires careful attention to at least four issues that can have a big effect on competition performance: final practice walk-through, sleep, energy requirements, and on-site warm-up.

### Final Practice Walk-Through

The last practice session immediately before a competition, often referred to as a walk-through, is an important time for coaches to help ready their athletes for the upcoming event. Typically, the final practice will be shorter than normal, but the intensity should remain high. Before starting the final practice before a game, legendary five-time national championship high school basketball coach Morgan Wooten would tell his team, "We're not going to go long, but we're going to go strong."[5 (p. 238)]

Besides helping athletes stay fresh and release some nervous energy, the final practice walk-through reinforces competition strategy. Football coaches are known for preparing detailed pregame scouting reports to counter opponent tendencies. National championship coach Nick Saban is no exception; he meticulously scouts the habits and tendencies of all players on the opposing team. In his mind, "Proper preparation prevents piss-poor performance."[6 (p. 81)]

Although the level of detail they use varies, successful coaches in every sport always prepare a precompetition plan that positions their athletes for success. For example, in cross country running, successful coaches survey the course to identify challenges and potential attack points such as hills or narrow trails. Championship high school coach Pat Tyson even had his team run the actual course two days in advance of the competition to ensure that his athletes were familiar with the competition site.[7] He referred to this precompetition readiness strategy as a course rehearsal.

Armed with a precompetition scouting report, successful coaches design the final practice before a competition to focus on the skills and strategies that will be most relevant for their athletes in the upcoming event. For example, knowing the tendencies, strengths, and weaknesses of an opponent will help the coach create practice activities that best prepare athletes to capitalize on this awareness.

Views are mixed, however, on whether coaches should tell their athletes that the activities were designed based on scouting the opponent. High-performance athletes in college and professional sport will recognize the intention behind the selection of practice activities, and they will benefit from knowing how and why the activities will counter opponent tendencies. But for younger or less experienced athletes in high school or club settings, withholding a rationale for the design of the final precompetition practice activities may be preferable.

Coach Morgan Wooten, whose teams won nearly 87 percent of their games across his 46-year career, is an example of a highly successful coach who believed it was more beneficial to avoid telling players why they were practicing specific activities in the final precompetition practice. He learned to tell his athletes that the activities were designed to help them become a better basketball team, regardless of when or whom they were playing next.

> Telling the players why you are working on certain phases of the game often leads to mistaken perceptions. In other words, you run the risk of building the opponent up too much or not enough. If I inform the team that we are going to face some tough full-court pressure, I could be intimidating my players into thinking that team is better than it is. They may think, "Well, if the coach says they're good and we need to work on it in practice, they might be tougher than we thought. What if we can't get the ball up the court against them?" Such doubts and negative thoughts can lead to poor performance. The opposite is also true. If I tell the team that our opponent does not handle pressure very well, and that we are going to try to take advantage of that, our players may think they are facing a weak team when that may not be the case.[5 (p. 238)]

Regardless of how the practice design is communicated to the players, every coach should have a precompetition practice that addresses key performance skills and tactics specific to the upcoming competition. The effectiveness of this practice will depend on how well the coach has scouted important competition factors that will affect performance, such as opponent tendencies, playing conditions such as facility characteristics if visiting an opponent, and the weather forecast if competing outside.

Finally, successful coaches use the final practice walk-through to rehearse important organizational and logistical details that can affect competition performance. For example, every Friday before a game, championship college football coach Bo Schembechler had his team practice how to organize themselves on the sidelines to ensure that the team was prepared for every play. Coach Schembechler referred to this walk-through activity as sideline discipline.

> We'd line up all the offensive starters in their positions: linemen in front, backs right behind them, wideouts on the sides. Then we put the second-string player at each position right behind the starters, all up and down the bench. Everyone had a particular place to sit, so we knew immediately if someone was injured or missing. It was the backup's job to watch the game and be ready the second the starter came out, for any reason. And we'd do the same thing with the defense. Everyone knew what they were doing. Do this correctly, and you will never get called for too many men on the field.[8 (p. 174)]

In sum, the purpose of the final practice walk-through is to help athletes feel prepared, confident, and physically ready to compete. The practice should be kept short and should focus on key skills, tactics, and organizational reminders that the coach believes will be most relevant for succeeding in the upcoming competition.

## Sleep and Rest

Lack of quality sleep is considered one of the top reasons for poor performance and risk of injury in sport.[9] This issue is even more important for high school and college athletes, who are at an age that requires deeper and longer sleep for restoration and recovery.

Professional and Olympic teams now regularly hire "sleep doctors" as part of their athlete performance staff. As sleep specialist and consultant to Olympic teams Mark Rosekind has stated, "People need to be as smart about sleep as they are about diet and exercise."[10] The evidence is clear. Athletes perform better when they get more regular and optimal amounts of sleep.[11–13] Most experts recommend that athletes strive for 9 to 10 hours of sleep each night.

Some of the most compelling evidence to show the direct effect of adequate sleep on athletic performance comes from a 2011 study with the Stanford University men's basketball team.[11] Eleven players on the team were given the goal of sleeping as much as they could. They had a goal to sleep a minimum of 10 hours per night for approximately six weeks during the basketball season. Athletes then completed a series of fitness and basketball tests during every practice and answered questions about their mood and well-being each week.

During the course of the study the athletes slept on average around 9 hours each night. The effect on athletic performance and mood was astounding. Average sprint times (baseline to half-court and back to baseline and then to full-court and back to baseline) dropped by nearly one second, free throw shooting percentage increased by 9 percent, three-point field goal shooting percentage improved by 9.2 percent, and athletes reported dramatic increases in overall well-being and energy. These performance improvements are all the more impressive when considering that many sport competitions are decided by just one possession or very small differences in time.

Adequate sleep is an integral part of precompetition preparation for several reasons. First, during sleep the body releases hormones that contribute to muscle repair and growth. Second, failing to sleep enough results in a decline in energy (because less glucose is digested), and stress levels can increase (because cortisol levels rise). Given that athletes, and coaches, are typically more anxious than normal the evening before a competition, getting the right amount of sleep is more important than ever leading up to a competitive event.

Athletes should be advised to prepare for a good night's sleep by avoiding screen time in the hour before bedtime. The use of light-emitting electronic devices (e.g., smart phones or tablets) is common for today's athletes; more than 95 percent of all Americans use a light-emitting electronic device in the hour before bedtime.[9, 14] Light-emitting electronic devices are particularly disturbing to sleep because they give off blue light, a form of enhanced light. Blue light is highly disruptive to sleep because it tricks the brain into thinking that it is still daytime. This type of light also suppresses production of melatonin, sometimes referred to as the body's sleep gate.[15] Melatonin, a hormone normally triggered by darkness, prepares the body for sleep.

Using a light-emitting electronic device in the hour before bedtime negatively affects sleep and performance in many ways. For example, when compared with reading a printed book in a dimly lit room, reading a book on a light-emitting electronic device caused people to need more time to fall asleep, to have lower-quality sleep, and to experience reduced alertness the following morning.[14] In fact, people report that they often need hours longer to wake up fully when they use light-emitting electronic devices for extended periods before bedtime. The same negative sleep trends are reported by youth who sleep with a TV in their room or use handheld electronic devices before bedtime.[16] Clearly, this scenario is the exact opposite of what athletes need for optimal game-day performance, particularly for morning competitions.

Coaches should teach their athletes about the negative effects of using electronic devices before bedtime. The hour leading up to bedtime should be used to listen to music, read printed material in a dimly lit room, talk with a friend, or simply rest and think about the upcoming competition. When athletes do use electronic devices before bedtime, they should dim the light of the device to its lowest level, which may help reduce the detrimental effects on their sleep.

Championship cycling coach Sir Dave Brailsford, who guided athletes to Olympic gold medals and two Tour de France wins, had his athletes bring their own pillows for competitions when staying away from home.[17] This simple strategy might not seem like a big deal, but sleeping with a familiar pillow reduces the likelihood that an athlete will wake up the morning of a competition with a sore neck because of an uncomfortable sleep. Coaches can also help their athletes decrease the chances of having their sleep disrupted by encouraging them to wear an eye mask to keep light out of the eyes. Rooms should be kept as dark as possible, quiet, and at the right temperature (which may vary for each athlete, so coaches should consider this variable when assigning athletes to hotel rooms when traveling for competitions).

Where schedules permit, such as for college, Olympic, or professional athletes who have more flexible schedules than the typical high school athlete does, coaches should encourage a brief daily nap. Because of naturally occurring body rhythms (circadian rhythm), people normally feel sleepy in the early afternoon around 1 or 2 p.m. Even a 10- or 15-minute nap can result in immediate improvements in focus, performance, and energy level.

Short naps seem to result in immediate benefits (1 to 3 hours postnap). Naps of 30 minutes or longer may result in drops in focus and performance at first but will provide gains several hours later and for up to 24 hours postnap.[18] Athletes should not wait until the day of a competition to experiment with nap taking, because it is learned skill. Some athletes may even find it difficult to fall asleep at night the first few times they try an afternoon nap. Lastly, keep in mind that naps aren't just for athletes; coaches should practice taking brief power naps to model and sustain physical and mental alertness.

## Food and Hydration

Although competition-day energy requirements vary widely for athletes depending on factors such as the type and length of activity they will perform, coaches can start by familiarizing themselves with some general precompetition fuel guidelines.[19–21] The following guidelines are appropriate both for female and male athletes. When working with female athletes, however, coaches should take additional steps to learn about their unique energy demands. For example, female athletes often are deficient in important micronutrients such as calcium, vitamin D, iron, and magnesium and therefore may require some additional gender-specific guidance on optimal competition-day fueling.[22]

For starters, athletes ideally should eat and drink things they are familiar with to avoid unexpected digestion issues. Competition day is not the time to experiment with the latest energy bar or sports drink.

In terms of competition-day fluid intake, athletes should drink fluids on a regular basis from the moment they wake up to the start of their event instead of waiting until they feel thirsty. As a general guideline, the optimal amount of fluid intake (in ounces) for an athlete in the 2 to 4 hours before exercise can be estimated by multiplying their body weight in pounds by 0.1.[23] For a typical 150 pound high school athlete this would translate to 15 ounces of fluid. During competition, a fluid intake guide for most athletes is to drink approximately 20 ounces of fluid during each hour of performing.[23] Flavored, cold drinks may be more appealing to athletes and have the added benefit of helping reduce core body temperature.

Athletes can self-check their hydration status by checking the volume and color of their urine throughout competition day. For example, if an athlete releases only a little urine when first using the bathroom after waking, this is a likely sign that he or she is already dehydrated and should pay particular attention to fluid intake leading up to the event.

The urine color chart created by exercise scientist Lawrence Armstrong is a simple and widely used tool that athletes can use to check their hydration status on competition day (see www.hydrationcheck.com/wall_chart.php).[24, 25] Clear or light-colored urine indicates an acceptable level of hydration. Darker colors are signs that the athlete is somewhat dehydrated. The athlete is in a state of dehydration if the urine is tan to brown.

Coaches should post a copy of the hydration status chart in locker rooms and bathrooms at their home competition venue. For away competitions, coaches could provide athletes with a laminated pocket copy they can leave in their equipment bags or perhaps even tape on water bottles as a visual reminder to check their hydration status continually.

As for food intake, small snacks can be eaten one to three hours before competing, and large meals should be eaten at least three to four hours before the event. Half of the last big meal for athletes before competition, either the night before for an early morning event or during the day of the event for a competition that takes place in the afternoon or evening, should include high-carbohydrate items such as rice, pasta, potatoes, and bread. The other half of the meal should be evenly split between vegetables and lean protein such as fish, chicken, or eggs. Sport nutritionists for U.S. Olympic athletes refer to this plan as the athlete's plate for competition days.[26]

When possible, coaches should direct their athletes to locally grown fresh fruit and vegetables. Locally grown food generally has a higher nutritional value than food shipped in from elsewhere or processed food because of the short time between when it is harvested and when it ends up at local grocery stores or restaurants. When traveling to out-of-town competitions, coaches might consider spending a bit of time in advance researching markets and restaurants that provide access to locally grown food. They can do this by searching online or by speaking to other coaches who have competed in the same region.

On competition day, athletes should avoid or limit consumption of foods high in fat, protein, or fiber, which may cause digestion uneasiness while competing.[73] Foods high in protein in particular, such as cheese or hamburgers, are likely to give athletes a quick sugar high followed by a drop in energy. Foods can be rated on how quickly they provide energy by reviewing what is known as the glycemic index. Foods with a high glycemic index are converted into energy quickly. These types of foods are most beneficial to athletes during or after a competition. Foods with a low glycemic index take longer to digest and provide energy over an extended period. Therefore, they are ideal choices for precompetition meals.

Coaches can use the summary provided in figure 8.1 to help athletes make wise choices about which types of foods to include in their precompetition routines and when to include the foods in their routines (e.g., night before, morning of, few minutes before competing, and so on).

## Figure 8.1 Glycemic Index of Common Foods

| HIGH-GLYCEMIC INDEX FOODS (GI > 85) | | | |
|---|---|---|---|
| Angel food cake | Cornflakes | Maltose | Rye flour bread |
| Bagel, white | Cornmeal | Melba toast | Shredded wheat |
| Barley flour bread | Couscous | Millet | Soda crackers |
| Brown rice | Cream of wheat | Molasses | Soft drinks |
| Cake doughnut | Crispix cereal | Müeslix | Sports drinks |
| Carrots | Croissant | Muffins | Sucrose |
| Cheerios | Glucose | Oatmeal | Total cereal |
| Cheese pizza | Grape-Nuts | Potatoes | Waffles |
| Corn bran cereal | Hard candy | Raisins | Watermelon |
| Corn Chex cereal | Honey/syrups | Rice cakes | White bread |
| Corn chips | Ice cream | Rice Krispies | Whole-wheat bread |
| **MODERATE-GLYCEMIC INDEX FOODS (GI = 60-85)** | | | |
| All-Bran cereal | Durum spaghetti | Mixed grain bread | Rye kernel bread |
| Banana | Fruit cocktail | Oat bran bread | Special K cereal |
| Basmati rice | Grapefruit juice | Oat bran cereal | Sponge cake |
| Bran Chex cereal | Grapes | Orange (whole or juice) | Sweet corn |
| Buckwheat | Ice cream, low-fat | Parboiled rice | Sweet potato or yams |
| Bulgur | Kiwi fruit | Pastry | Wheat, cooked |
| Bulgur bread | Linguine | Pita bread, white | White rice, long grain |
| Cracked barley | Mango or papaya | Popcorn | Wild rice |
| **LOW-GLYCEMIC INDEX FOODS (GI < 60)** | | | |
| Apples | Cherries | Milk | Rice bran |
| Apricots (dried) | Dried peas | Peaches (fresh) | Spaghetti |
| Barley | Fructose | Peanuts | Tomato soup |
| Barley kernel bread | Grapefruit | Pears (fresh) | Wheat kernels |
| Beans (all types) | Lentils | Plums | Yogurt (all types) |

Reprinted, by permission, from R. Martens, 2012, *Successful coaching*, 4th ed. (Champaign, IL: Human Kinetics), 308.

With the never-ending introduction of new food trends and products that promise to deliver extra energy, coaches have difficulty making sense of the vast amount of nutrition information and providing simple guidelines for their athletes. Renowned scientist Tudor Bompa, who has personally trained athletes to multiple Olympic and world championship medals, and exercise physiologist Michael Carerra have done coaches a great favor by summarizing their expertise about precompetition energy needs in 10 basic tips.[27 (pp. 235–236)] These proven tips will help coaches provide simple and practical guidelines for ensuring that their athletes' energy needs will be met when needed most on competition days.

- Choose foods rich in carbohydrate, including pasta, whole-grain breads, cereals, and rice.
- Include vegetables that you are accustomed to eating and generally cause little, if any, gas or bloating.
- Avoid spices of any kind, especially hot spices such as curry, turmeric, and cayenne pepper.
- Avoid fried foods of any kind, including fried eggs and meats.
- Avoid soft drinks, fruits juices, and candy of any kind.
- Eat the same amount you are accustomed to eating at everyday meals.
- If possible, avoid eating on the run or in the car. Try to take your time and eat while seated.
- Eat real food (e.g., whole fruits and vegetables) and save the protein bars or snacks for postgame meals.

## On-Site Pregame Warm-Up

The on-site warm-up is an important and long-standing tradition in sport. This brief period before the competition can often make or break an athlete's performance on that day. An effective physical warm-up for athletes should include activities that prepare and activate them for fluid movement, referred to as enhanced movement capacity.[28] The precompetition on-site physical warm-up can generally be divided into three phases: (*a*) light aerobic activities, (*b*) stretching, and (*c*) sport-specific technical skills.[19, 29] For most high school aged athletes each phase should last approximately 5 to 7 minutes, resulting in a 15- to 20-minute physical warm-up.

Coaches are encouraged to refer to the latest physical and skill training recommendations specific to their sport to learn how to design optimal physical warm-ups for their athletes. But given the controversial and potentially harmful role of stretching before competitions, some general guidelines from the scientific literature are provided here.[30–34]

Stretches are often described as either static or dynamic.[30] When athletes hold a stretch for several seconds, they are performing static stretching. This image of stretching is the most common and traditional, evident in many sports when athletes gather in a circle and follow each other through a series of activities requiring them to hold a stretch for 10 to 30 seconds. An example of a static stretch is extending one leg onto a bench, bending forward, and holding the position for 10 to 30 seconds to stretch out the hamstring.

Conversely, when athletes repeat a series of movements in a controllable, smooth, and deliberate fashion, they are performing dynamic stretching. For example, instead of placing a leg on a bench and bending forward, athletes could place their hands on their hips and use walking lunges across the width of a soccer or football field as a form of dynamic stretching for the hamstrings.[31]

Generally, all training programs should include some form of stretching to help athletes improve their flexibility and ability to perform sport skills, sometimes referred to as their functional range of motion.[32] As part of a precompetition routine, stretching can hinder performance because it temporarily decreases an athlete's ability to generate maximal force, referred to as stretch-induced strength loss.[33, 34] This effect can be particularly harmful for athletes competing in sports that require explosive and maximal force, such as short-distance sprinting in track or swimming or playing the lineman position in football.

Coaches can use the following guidelines as a general approach to integrating stretching into an athlete's precompetition readiness routine. Because few findings about stretching and performance are definitive, coaches should view these guidelines as informed suggestions rather than proven laws of stretching.

- For sports or positions that require explosive force and speed, such as short sprint events, receivers in football, and shortstops in baseball, athletes should perform four or five dynamic stretching activities of 60 seconds each. If these athletes also want to include static stretching in their warm-ups as a way to relax and focus mentally, they should hold each stretch for less than 30 seconds to reduce potential drops in strength and power.
- For sports or positions that require a high degree of static flexibility, such as catchers in softball or goalies in ice hockey who must hold a crouching position for extended periods, a series of static stretching activities may be helpful. Each stretch should be performed four or five times for 45 to 60 seconds to pain tolerance.
- Ensure that all stretching activities are performed bilaterally (e.g., both shoulders, both legs).
- Target preparticipation stretches to muscle groups that are most at risk for strains or injury specific to each sport or position (e.g., hip flexor strain in ice hockey, hamstring strain in soccer).
- All athletes, regardless of sport or position, should follow stretching with a light dynamic technical skills warm-up to counter potential stretch-induced strength loss (e.g., passing activities in team sports, layup drill in basketball, starts or turns in running or swimming).

Time set aside for precompetition stretching can also play a critical role in helping athletes mentally prepare for performance. When done in a team or group setting, precompetition stretching can help alleviate some of the normal precompetition jitters by promoting socializing among teammates. As they stretch, athletes can also use the time to visualize their upcoming performance and review competition strategies.

## PREPARING MENTALLY AND EMOTIONALLY

Precompetition physical preparation will be wasted unless the coach also helps the athlete design effective precompetition mental and emotional preparation strategies. Athletes are known for finding creative ways to lower their stress before a competition.[35, 36] Some examples include Olympic medalist and U.S. national champion figure skater Gracie Gold who juggles before stepping out onto the ice; Hall of Fame baseball player Wade Boggs who had to eat chicken before every game; three-time Ironman champion Chrissie Wellington who liked to watch uplifting movies the night before a race; World Cup soccer player Laurent Blanc who had to kiss the shaven head of his goalkeeper before every match during France's run to the world title in 1998; and 11-time NBA champion Bill Russell who said, "The last thing I did before I went out was throw up [before every game]. I can't remember it not happening. Just like taping your ankles."[37]

What should be clear from these contrasting examples is that if left to their own devices, all athletes will find a strategy that seems to work best for them. Therefore, the role of the coach is not to create precompetition mental and emotional coping strategies for their athletes. Rather, the coach should help her or his athletes learn how to monitor their precompetition mental and emotional states and provide guidance for creating personalized and appropriate strategies. Coaches, therefore, need to have a basic understanding of how emotions influence performance and how to harness emotions in the moments leading up to an event.

### The Zone

Decades of research on arousal, emotions, and athletic performance shows that every athlete has unique precompetition mental and emotional needs, commonly referred to as individual zones of optimal functioning, or IZOF.[38, 39] Russian sport psychologist Yuri Hanin first coined the term *IZOF* based on his research with Olympic athletes.

Hanin made three key discoveries about emotions and peak performance. First, optimal precompetition arousal is best thought of as a zone or range of readiness as opposed to a single point in the arousal-performance relationship. Athletes consistently perform better when they report that their emotions are in the zone compared to when their emotions are out of the zone.[40]

Second, there is no one ideal level of precompetition mental and emotional arousal; every athlete has a different ideal state. Notice in figure 8.2 that athlete A is most ready to perform when she is calm and relaxed. In contrast, athlete B is most ready to perform when he is more emotionally activated.

Third, both pleasant (i.e., joy) and unpleasant (i.e., anger) emotions can be either helpful or detrimental to performance depending on the unique perspective of each athlete. This finding is perhaps the most surprising and important for coaches. When studying athlete emotions and peak performance, emotions are divided into four categories.

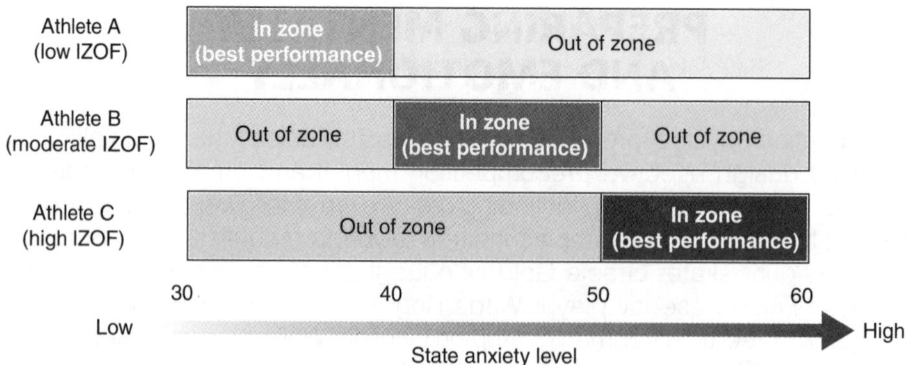


**Figure 8.2** Individualized zones of optimal functioning (IZOF).

Reprinted, by permission, from R.S. Weinberg and D. Gould, 2015, *Foundations of sport and exercise psychology*, 6th ed. (Champaign, IL: Human Kinetics), 87.

- [U−] unpleasant emotions perceived by the athlete as disruptive to peak performance
- [U+] unpleasant emotions perceived by the athlete as helpful to peak performance
- [P+] pleasant emotions perceived by the athlete as helpful to peak performance
- [P−] pleasant emotions perceived by the athlete as disruptive to peak performance

Although each athlete believes that specific emotions, such as joy or anger, either help or hinder performance, a consistent emotion-performance profile is associated with peak performance.[41] With this profile, commonly referred to as the iceberg profile, athletes report low levels of unpleasant and pleasant emotions as ineffective and high levels of unpleasant and pleasant emotions as useful to peak performance. The goal, then, for coaches is to help athletes identify which emotions are most associated with peak performance for them personally.

Coaching scientist and former college coach Robin Vealey has created a simple exercise that coaches can use with their athletes to help them identify their individual zones of optimal functioning.[42] An example of an individual zone of optimal functioning for a golfer, prepared using this type of exercise, is provided in figure 8.3.

- Step 1: Ask athletes to write down three or four pleasant emotions (e.g., confident, energetic, certain) and three or four unpleasant emotions (e.g., tense, nervous, irritated) they believe help them perform at their best.
- Step 2: Ask athletes to write down three or four pleasant and unpleasant emotions they believe hurt their ability to perform at their best.
- Step 3: Ask athletes to rate, on a scale of 0 (not at all) to 10 (most possible), how much they need to feel that emotion during their precompetition routine. For example, athletes may identify confidence as a pleasant emotion that

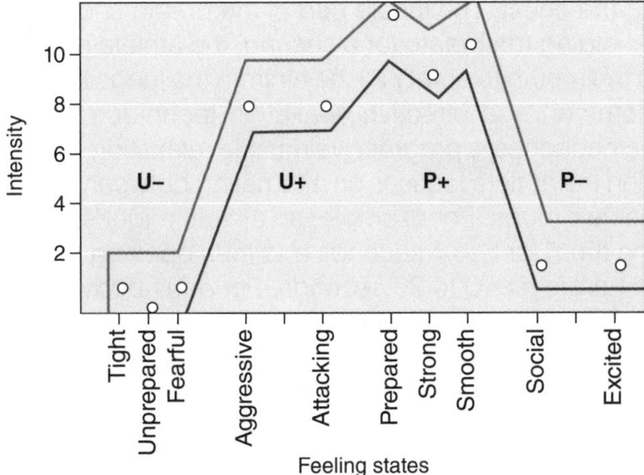


**Figure 8.3** Golfer IZOF profile.

Reprinted, by permission, from R. Vealey, 2005, *Coaching for the inner edge* (Morgantown, WV: Fitness Information Technology), 390. Permission conveyed through the Copyright Clearance Center, Inc.

they believe helps them perform best, and they believe that their confidence needs to be at least an 8 in the moments before a competition.

- Step 4: Have athletes plot the scores for each emotion by placing a small circle or dot on a graph with intensity on the y-axis and feeling states on the x-axis. This point represents the athlete's preferred intensity for each type of emotion identified in steps 1 and 2.
- Step 5: Have athletes then draw their zone of optimal functioning by drawing a line 1 point above and 1 point below each circle on the graph. For example, using the example of wanting to feel an 8 on confidence, the athlete would draw the top line of the zone at 9 and the bottom line of the zone at 7 for confidence.

# Relaxation and Psych Up

After coaches and their athletes have found their optimal emotional and mental performance zones, they need to create strategies for consistently achieving their individual zones of optimal functioning. Common relaxation strategies include deep belly breathing and progressive muscle relaxation. Frequently used strategies for psyching up include imagery and listening to music.

Relaxation strategies are most effective if they help lower muscle tone and keep the athletes focused on the present and the way they are feeling. The simplest, and most effective, relaxation technique that coaches can teach their athletes is deep belly, or diaphragmatic, breathing.[43–45]

When tense or anxious, people commonly take short and shallow breaths, which serves only to activate the body further and create tension in the shoulders and neck. To counter this situation, the athlete can place one hand on the belly and practice breathing in through the nose while focusing on raising the belly and then expanding the chest. The inhale part of the breath should take three to five seconds. After holding the breath for a second, the athlete should then forcefully exhale through the mouth to empty all the air from the lungs by pulling in the belly.

A second common and effective relaxation technique used by successful athletes and their coaches is progressive muscle relaxation.[43–45] With progressive muscle relaxation the athlete focuses on alternating between tightening and relaxing various muscle groups. For example, an athlete might start by clenching the fists and holding them for 5 to 7 seconds and then opening the fists and relaxing the fingers and hands for 20 to 30 seconds. For a full-body progressive muscle relaxation approach, the athlete would repeat this process across other muscle groups and body parts (arms, shoulders, neck, face, abdomen, thighs, calves, and feet). Some athletes, however, may need or want to focus only on specific muscle groups or body parts (such as a baseball or softball pitcher focusing on just the hand, arm, and shoulder). With practice, this relaxation technique helps athletes learn to become more aware of when they may start to feel tense and gives them a simple strategy for releasing some of that tension.

When learning how to practice deep belly breathing and progressive muscle relaxation, athletes may find it helpful to follow an audio script, with eyes either open or closed depending on athlete preference. Many free audio scripts are available online, such as the Diaphragmatic Breathing (9:13), Deep Breathing I (6:43), Deep Breathing II (7:28), and Progressive Muscle Relaxation (8:39) scripts prepared by the Counseling Center at Georgia Southern University (http://studentsupport.georgiasouthern.edu/counseling/resources/self-help/relaxation-and-stress-management/). For athletes and coaches who prefer to create their own audio-recorded progressive muscle relaxation script, the one presented in figure 8.4 can serve as a guide.

Imagery, sometimes referred to as visualization, is perhaps the most common technique that athletes and coaches use to prepare mentally for competition. For example, in one study of 21 successful college and national team coaches, over 90 percent of the coaches set aside time on the day of the competition to visualize how they would respond to situations that could arise in the competition.[4] The coaches used this precompetition mental rehearsal as a way both to control their emotions and to review game strategy.

One basketball coach liked to visualize the inevitable close or controversial calls that would happen during the game so that he "could decide in advance how I was going to react"[4 (p. 133)] to avoid losing emotional control in the midst of the game. Conversely, an ice hockey coach preferred to use precompetition mental rehearsal time to anticipate tactical decisions by trying to "visualize what might happen, different scenarios; if this line is not going well, who would I move into that position."[4 (p. 133)]

When asked, most athletes report that they think or dream about their upcoming performances. Although sport psychology consultants are becoming more common, other than in professional and Olympic sport, coaches and athletes rarely have regular access to a sport psychologist to help them with their imagery. The quality and effectiveness of athlete' precompetition imagery therefore typically depends on how well the coach is able to teach them how to use imagery.

## Figure 8.4 Sample Progressive Muscle Relaxation Script

Progressive muscle relaxation helps you to first tense each of four muscle groups, part by part, in order to tire it out and then relax it deeply. When you tense a muscle group, gradually build up the tension. Like a car gradually accelerating, work up to 100 mph by starting at 10, then increasing to 20, then 30, 40, 50, 60, 70, 80, 90 and finally 100 percent maximum tension. Then you're going to hold that all-out tension for five to seven seconds before letting it all go at once. When you do, relax those muscles as deeply and completely as possible for 20-30 seconds. (Standard protocol is to relax each muscle group twice before moving on, but this should be adjusted up or down to meet individual needs.) To begin, get into a comfortable position, seated or lying down.

To tense the muscles of **muscle group 1,** the **shoulders, arms, and hands**, make a tight fist with both arms and push the elbows down and into your sides. Ready—go! 10, 20, 30, 40, 50, 60, 70, 80, 90, 100. Hold the tension, feel it pull, tighter, tighter, RELAX. Just let it all go now. Let all the tension go from the muscles of your shoulders, arms, and hands, allowing those muscle fibers to loosen up, to smooth out, to unwind, and to relax. Let the tension flow down your arms and out the tips of your fingers. Use your breathing to fuel your relaxation, allowing those muscles to go deeper and deeper into relaxation. With each breath, feel the relaxation deepening and spreading. Concentrate on learning to recognize what relaxation feels like so you can compare and contrast it to the tension you experienced before. Use your deep diaphragmic breathing to allow those muscles to relax as deeply and completely as possible. Feel your muscles getting very loose, limp, heavy, and relaxed. (Repeat cycle for group 1 as needed.)

Keeping the muscles of the shoulders, arms, and hands as relaxed as possible, move to **muscle group 2,** the muscles of the **face and neck.** Tense these muscles by lifting the eyebrows high, wrinkling up your nose, biting down hard, and pulling the corners of your mouth back while doing an isometric contraction with your neck (i.e., use the muscles of the front part of the neck to try to touch your chin to your chest as you use the muscles of the back part of the neck to try to prevent that from happening). Ready—go! 10, 20, 30, 40, 50, 60, 70, 80, 90, 100. Hold the tension, feel it pull, tighter, hold it, hold it, RELAX. Just let all of the tension go and feel it slowly draining out of your face and neck. Feel those muscle fibers loosening up, smoothing out, unwinding, and gradually relaxing. Use your breathing to help that relaxation to deepen and spread. Consciously focus on the feelings of relaxation. Learn what those feelings of relaxation are like and how they differ from the feelings of tension that you sometimes have. Allow your breathing to continue to promote greater relaxation of the face and neck as more and more muscle fibers unwind and relax with each breath. Allow those muscles to get very loose, limp, heavy, and relaxed. Concentrate on letting go the final residual tension from your face and neck, along with your shoulders, arms, and hands. Relax these muscles deeply and completely. (Repeat cycle for group 2 as needed.)

While maintaining the relaxation in your shoulders, arms, and hands and face and neck, move to the **third muscle group**—the **chest, back, and stomach**. Tense these muscles by taking a deep breath and holding it while pulling your shoulders back and together and making your stomach hard. Ready—go! 10, 20, 30, 40, 50, 60, 70, 80, 90, 100. Hold the tension, feel it pull, tighter, hold it, tighter, hold it, RELAX. Just let all the tension flow out of your chest, back, and stomach. Allow those muscles to loosen up, smooth out, unwind, and relax. Use your breathing to promote deeper and more complete relaxation, helping the relaxation deepen and spread with each breath. Be aware of how your relaxation feels and distinguish it from the tension you were experiencing before. Concentrate on the differences as well as the similarities so that you'll be able to diagnose even small levels of tension in your chest, back, or stomach when they occur. Use your breathing to help promote deeper levels of relaxation. Remember that the longer you relax, the more muscle fibers will let go and get loose, limp, heavy, and relaxed. (Repeat cycle for group 3 as needed.)

*(continued)*

**Figure 8.4** *(continued)*

Keeping the muscles in the upper body relaxed, move to the **final muscle group**—the **hips, thighs, calves, and feet.** Tense this muscle group by making your upper legs—both quads and hamstrings—hard using an isometric contraction, pulling your toes back toward you or pointing them away from you—whichever gets the best tension in your calves—and turning your feet slightly inward and curling your toes slightly. Ready—go! 10, 20, 30, 40, 50, 60, 70, 80, 90, 100. Hold the tension, feel it pull, hold it, tighter, hold that tension, tighter, RELAX. Just let it all go now. Feel all of that tension draining down your legs and out your toes. Feel those muscle fibers slowly letting go as they loosen up, smooth out, unwind, and relax. Let your breathing fuel your relaxation, with each slow, deep, regular diaphragmic breath helping your muscle fibers to go deeper and deeper and deeper into relaxation. Feel relaxation slowly consuming these muscles, and feel it deepen and spread. Concentrate on those feelings of deep relaxation and distinguish them from the tension you experienced before. Learn to diagnose even minute levels of tension in your muscles and relax it away. Use your breathing to continue to relax more and more muscle fibers. Feel your relaxation deepening and spreading. Feel those muscles becoming very loose, limp, heavy, and relaxed. Let it all go and allow yourself to experience deep, enjoyable levels of relaxation. (Repeat cycle for muscle group 4 as needed.)

To ensure that you are completely relaxed, go back and scan each muscle group in turn for any remaining tension. If you are already relaxed in a muscle group, continue relaxing. If you have residual tension, do another tension-relaxation cycle to help you relax again as deeply and completely as possible.

Having scanned your body for any residual tension in the four muscle groups and eliminated it, you should feel pretty relaxed throughout your entire body. Shift your attention from specific muscles groups to the relaxation throughout your entire body and how that relates to your deep, regular diaphragmic breathing. Continue breathing deeply and regularly and focusing totally on the feelings of relaxation in every part of your body.

Follow with a conditioned relaxation process. Each time you exhale say your relaxation cue word to yourself while focusing on your breathing and what it feels like to be deeply relaxed. Pairing those feelings of deep relaxation with your cue word each time you exhale strengthens the association between the two, so that you can use your cue word to trigger rapid relaxation in your daily life. If you happen to have any stray thoughts, worries, or concerns, just let them go and allow them to float out of your mind as you continue to focus on your breathing and the feelings of deep relaxation throughout your body. Focus on those feelings of relaxation, and contrast them to the tension you felt before so that you can diagnose and release even minute levels of tension as needed. Continue to take slow, deep, and regular breaths, and each time you exhale say that cue word to yourself.

Once you've counted 15-20 breaths during conditioned relaxation, end the session by counting backward from four to one. At four, begin to move your legs and feet to get the circulation going again. At three, move your arms and hands. At two, roll your head and neck. At one, open your eyes when it feels comfortable. Your body should feel very relaxed as if you've just awoken from a refreshing nap. Your mind should be calm and relaxed but alert and focused on the goals you must accomplish today.

---

Reprinted, by permission, from D. Burton and T.D. Raedeke, 2008, *Sport psychology for coaches* (Champaign, IL: Human Kinetics), 257-258. Adapted from D.A. Bernstein, T.D. Borkovec, and H. Hazlett-Stevens, 2000, *New directions in progressive relaxation training: A guidebook for helping professionals* (New York: Praeger).

A common error that performers make when using imagery is to neglect to use all their senses. Imagery is most effective when it taps into multiple senses—sight, sound, smell, feel, and emotion. The more vivid the imagery is, the better the performer will be able to use the imagery to simulate and practice performing a real experience as opposed to simply pretending to perform.[39] For example, besides seeing themselves walking onto a pool deck before a competition, swimmers should try to feel the texture of the pool deck under their feet or the sun on their face if swimming outdoors, smell the chlorine in the air, hear the sounds of other competitors walking on the deck, and think about how they would like to feel emotionally at that moment.

Athletes and coaches alike will benefit from writing out an imagery script to guide them in their precompetition imagery. Preparing and practicing a written precompetition imagery script will help reinforce and internalize desired behaviors and emotions. The script should be divided into three sections—one for the precompetition phase, one for the performance itself, and one for the moments immediately following the competition. In each section the script should include brief statements about how the athlete wants to feel and reminders to focus on important performance cues.

When using imagery athletes will naturally tend to use one of two perspectives.[46] They may visualize their performance from the perspective they would have when actually competing, referred to as a first-person perspective. For example, when a soccer player visualizes taking a shot and sees the ball coming off the foot and heading toward the net, he or she is using a first-person perspective. Conversely, athletes may visualize their performance as a sort of out-of-body experience in which they are watching their performance from a spectator's perspective, sometimes referred to as a third-person perspective.

Coaches should speak with their athletes to learn which perspective is most helpful and prepare imagery scripts that are written from the desired perspective.[46] Ideally, with practice athletes will learn to switch between both perspectives to strengthen imagery effectiveness.

The imagery guidelines and examples prepared by sport psychologist Kay Porter are good starting points for coaches to help their athletes prepare quality imagery scripts.[43] Porter's 10 steps to writing your own visualization is provided in figure 8.5, and a sample imagery script for a field player in soccer is provided in figure 8.6. Although coaches of other sports can easily adapt the soccer imagery example to the demands of their own sport, Porter also shares scripts specific to many other sports such as tennis, golf, track and field, football, basketball, baseball and softball, and volleyball.

## Music

Playing music during a precompetition warm-up has long been common practice in sport. Athletes and coaches alike believe that listening to music while preparing for competition helps create the right atmosphere for peak performance. For example, in several studies with high school volleyball athletes and coaches, investigators found that playing music during the warm-up increased motivation to play (or coach) well, helped athletes feel less anxious because they were having more fun, and improved feelings of closeness and cohesion on the team.[47, 48]

Imagery also seems to have a stronger influence on performance when combined with music.[49] Athletes report being in the zone and performing better

## Figure 8.5 Ten Steps to Writing Your Own Visualization

1. See, hear, and feel yourself performing your event.
2. Write down and dictate into a recorder every detail you can see, hear, and feel.
3. Begin with arriving at the event, going through your normal preparatory routine, and the few minutes before you perform.
4. Go into vivid detail about the event and your experience of it, including sounds, colors, smells, the crowd, the weather, the positive feelings in your body, and your mental state.
5. Imagine yourself being totally relaxed, confident, powerful, and in complete control of your body and mind. Include your affirmations and key words that will help you during your real performance.
6. Go through your whole event thinking of each significant point or play. Feel yourself moving smoothly and performing with strength and endurance.
7. After writing your visualization, write statements of relaxation, and remind yourself of your confidence, power, and mental toughness.
8. Now write your visualization in script form. Reread it and edit it. Then dictate it yourself or have someone else dictate it into your recorder.
9. Listen to the recorded visualization for flaws and make changes to the script. When you are satisfied with the script, dictate a progressive relaxation section that you feel will relax you most effectively before the visualization. Then dictate your finished script so that it follows the relaxation section.
10. Listen to the finished tape once a day or at least three or four times a week before an event. Pick a quiet time and place where you won't be disturbed. Morning or night is usually a good time. Try to stay awake to get the full effect. Sitting up is helpful. It is best to be relaxed and aware. Please do not listen to it while you are driving a motor vehicle.

Reprinted, by permission, from K. Porter, 2003, *The mental athlete* (Champaign, IL: Human Kinetics), 69.

when their precompetition imagery script is played with background music. For example, after becoming the 2012 all-around Olympic gold medalist, Gabby Douglas said, "I listened to some (music) to pump me up and visualized the floor set I wanted to do. Then I went out and hit the best floor routine of my life."[46]

Finally, music selection should match the emotional needs and musical taste of the athlete. After an athlete and coach have reviewed the athlete's individual zone of optimal functioning profile, the athlete should select personally meaningful music that will elicit the desired emotions. When working with teams of athletes and preparing a precompetition music list, the team may find it helpful to designate the music selection role to one or two members of the team. The playlist should represent the varied musical tastes and emotional needs of the team as a whole.

This strategy was used by the U.S. women's national soccer team during their championship run at the 2015 World Cup. Lauren Holliday assumed the role of musical director for the team and took suggestions from teammates to prepare the following precompetition game-day music list (see table 8.1).[50]

## Figure 8.6 Soccer Visualization Script

Begin to remember the best soccer match you ever played . . . where it was, who was playing with you, all the sights and sounds of it . . . the excitement, the power, the achievement of your peak performance . . . allowing yourself to feel all the feelings from that time . . . of pride, confidence, achievement, excitement, fun . . . see the match . . . hearing all the sounds of your teammates yelling and supporting each other . . . the crowd and its cheering and clapping . . . remember it all . . . and begin to think of a word that represents that state of mind and that state of being . . . to represent all those feelings of confidence, pride, excitement, achievement . . . saying the word over to yourself . . . knowing your word will bring that time back to you whenever you wish . . . that time of peak performance and achievement.

Now begin to think of your next match . . . your goals and what you want to accomplish . . . how you want to play . . . what you want to do . . . knowing about the other team . . . imagining what your strategy will be . . . and what you want to accomplish personally.

Imagine yourself at the soccer field where your next match will be held . . . see yourself and your teammates warming up . . . running, making your moves . . . practicing your shots . . . getting ready for your match . . . feeling the familiar feeling in your stomach . . . excitement . . . anticipation . . . really enjoying the whole process . . . and remembering your word that connects you with your previous peak performances . . . saying it over to yourself . . . bringing up your confidence in yourself and your teammates.

Imagine yourself being as aggressive as you want to be . . . getting the ball . . . looking for a pass . . . breathing deeply, running powerfully, looking, committing yourself to your move . . . being completely relaxed and poised . . . in total control . . . being fast and aggressive . . . confident . . . powerful.

And seeing yourself on the field, focusing on the player you're guarding . . . thinking about what you're going to do next . . . staying alert . . . knowing when to make your move . . being ready . . . remembering your affirmations.

"I'm strong. I'm fast. I have good concentration and focus. I stay with the player I'm guarding. When the time is right, I go for it! I'm mentally tough." Knowing that you are intimidating . . . aggressive, powerful . . . making good shots . . . having great endurance and speed . . . using your body well—shielding . . . heading . . . good at getting it, jumping up and heading . . . having a good shot . . . concentrating really well and focusing on hitting it directly . . . hearing how it sounds when you hit the sweet spot of the ball . . . following through . . . solidly kicked and feeling good . . . seeing your fakes, your moves, your one-on-ones . . . all well done . . . with good intensity and focus . . . anticipating what is coming your way and being ready for it.

Imagine yourself collecting a pass . . . turning the ball away from a defender . . . making good contact with the ball . . . feeling in control and powerful . . . then passing to a teammate . . . seeing who to pass to . . . seeing where the space is . . . staying in close proximity after passing it off.

Know that you have everything you need to play well and at your best . . . you and your teammates play well as a team . . . supporting each other . . . yelling to each other . . . playing together as a well-oiled machine . . . enjoying the team play . . . getting better and better with each game . . . and when you are getting tired . . . reminding yourself that you are strong, powerful, and fast . . . you are as tough as anyone else on the field today . . . believing in yourself and your ability . . . knowing you are a winner.

Slowly allow the images to fade . . . remembering your word . . . your word of power and strength . . . become aware of your body sitting in the chair or lying on the couch . . . on a count of three, you can open your eyes . . . feeling refreshed, relaxed, and ready for the rest of the day or evening . . . one . . . move your hands and feet, taking a deep breath . . . letting it out with a sigh . . . two . . . stretch your neck and shoulders . . . and three . . . open your eyes when you're ready.

Reprinted, by permission, from K. Porter, 2003, *The mental athlete* (Champaign, IL: Human Kinetics), 95-97.

**Table 8.1 Game-Day Music List for 2015 World Cup Champion U.S. Women's National Soccer Team**

| | |
|---|---|
| Shut Up and Dance (Walk the Moon) | Try Me (Jason Derulo featuring Jennifer Lopez & Matoma) |
| Trap Queen (Fetty Wap) | Hands in the Air (Sire Castro) |
| Bad Blood (Taylor Swift featuring Kendrick Lamar) | King Kunta (Kendrick Lamar) |
| Honey, I'm Good. (Andy Grammar) | Got Your Money (ODB) |
| Want to Want Me (Jason Derulo) | Too Close (Next) |
| Worth It (Fifth Harmony featuring Kid Ink) | Thinking Out Loud (Ed Sheeran) |
| Fight Song (Rachel Platten) | FourFiveSeconds (Rihanna and Kanye West and Paul McCartney) |
| Watch Me (Whip/Nae Nae) | Conqueror (Empire Cast featuring Estelle and Jussie Smollett) |
| Photograph (Ed Sheeran) | Best of 2013 Mash-Up (Anthem Lights) |
| Beautiful Like (Nick Fradiani) | Hey Mama (David Guetta featuring Nicki Minaj, Bebe Rexha) |
| My House (Flo Rida) | GDFR (Flo Rida featuring Sage the Gemini & Lookas) |
| Renegades (X Ambassadors) | Don't Tell 'Em (Jeremih featuring YG) |
| Dreams (Life of Dillon) | See You Again (Wiz Khalifa featuring Charlie Puth) |
| I Know There's Gonna Be (Good Times) (Jamie xx) | Love Me Like You Do (Ellie Goulding from *Fifty Shades of Grey*) |

## Pregame Speech

Virtually all sport movies have a pivotal scene in which the coach gives a rousing pregame speech that inspires the athletes to storm out of the locker room and win the championship. One of the most famous examples can be seen in the movie *Miracle* in which U.S. hockey coach Herb Brooks implores his team to believe that their destiny is to beat the heavily favored Russian team. The U.S. team won the game and later won the 1980 Olympic championship, considered one of the greatest American sports accomplishments of all time.

Equally well known is the 1928 "Win One for the Gipper" pregame speech delivered by legendary college football coach Knute Rockne, who reportedly was asked before the game by dying player George Gipp to tell his teammates to "go out there with all they've got and win just one for the Gipper." The team managed to pull out a hard-fought victory in the game that was played at Yankee Stadium.[51]

Although the rousing pregame speech always seems to result in victory in the movies, in reality coaches must carefully tailor their pregame speech to the specific moment and immediate needs of their athletes. For example, according to players who were in the room, the pregame speech that Coach Brooks gave was much shorter and less dramatic than what was portrayed in the movie.[52] As for the potential value of a Coach Rockne speech, Hall of Fame football coach Lou Holtz, the only coach to lead six different teams to postseason championship bowl games, concluded, "The pregame locker room speech is overrated."[50]

The most successful coaches understand that an effective pregame speech requires a more thoughtful approach than the emotionally charged one-size-fits-all pregame speech popularized in the movies. Although some athletes need to be pumped up, others in the same moment will need to be calmed down. Also, the moment itself (type of game, history with the opponent) will need to be considered when preparing a pregame speech.

The famous pregame speeches given by Brooks and Rockne were helpful because they gave their athletes the message they needed to hear at those particular moments. Their speeches were what is referred to as an emotional or inspirational pregame speech, which appears to be most effective when the challenge is greatest.[53, 54] For example, in a study with over 200 college athletes, researchers found that they preferred an emotionally charged pregame speech from their coach when they were playing in a championship competition or when they were considered the underdog.[55]

Research also shows that athletes sometimes prefer pregame speeches in which the coach focuses more on competition tactics, referred to as informational or instructional speeches.[53] This type of speech appears to be most beneficial for athletes who already report feeling prepared before the competition (i.e., don't need to be charged up by the coach) or are competing against an unfamiliar opponent.

Championship ice hockey coach Mike Babcock shares a story about how he decided not to give a pregame speech before the first game of the 2010 Winter Olympics. When meeting with the team the night before their opening game, he observed that the athletes were ready and excited to play. Instead of adding to the emotion and energy the athletes already had, he let the moment serve as the pregame message: "I didn't give an emotional speech that night. . . . There was more than enough emotion in the room. The moment sent the message."[56 (p. 46)] The team won their opening game and eventually won the Olympic gold medal in a dramatic overtime win.

Successful coaches also often use short videos or motivational quotations as part of their pregame message. While speaking at a coaching seminar, national championship soccer coach Anson Dorrance shared his unique approach to using video to create the right amount of pregame emotional arousal.[57] He liked to use an 8- to 10-minute video of the athletes performing well when they were about to play a tough opponent. Conversely, he learned that it was more productive to show a short video of the athletes performing poorly before they were about to play a weak team. The highlight video helped athletes feel confident and ready to meet the challenge of a strong opponent. The lowlight video provoked the athletes to prove that they were better than what was shown on the video. This strategy proved extremely effective for Coach Dorrance, whose teams at one point won 92 games and nine championships in a row.

NHL via Getty Images

Toronto Maple Leafs' head coach Mike Babcock has coached multiple teams to championships by carefully matching his messages to athlete needs in the moment.

Sharing a motivational quotation of the game can also be effective in helping create the right precompetition climate for athletes. The motivational quotation will have a much stronger effect if the coach encourages athletes to discuss what it means for them and their upcoming performance.[58] Besides the motivational quotation websites suggested in chapter 7, numerous books provide thousands of inspirational quotations and messages for coaches to consider using with their athletes before competitions.[59–61]

Inspirational quotations or messages can be strengthened by combining a new one for each competition with one that is used throughout the season. The new quotation along with the recurring message can serve as a powerful tool to keep athletes focused on both the immediate competition goals and the broader mission for the season. For example, before the 2016 men's collegiate ice hockey national championship game won by the University of North Dakota, coaches displayed the team's motto for the season ("Believe it. Earn it. Raise it.") in the locker room along with the following message: "We Will Be Known Forever by the Tracks We Leave Behind!!!!!!!!"[62] Each of the eight exclamation points represented one of the previous eight national championships won by the team.

Although some general trends apply to athlete preferences between emotional and informational pregame speeches, athletes report wide individual differences in how they perceive the pregame speech. For example, in one study with competitive soccer players, one-third of the athletes reported that their coaches' pregame speeches did not affect their game performance at all.[63] Clearly, helping only two-thirds of your athletes is not a recipe for long-term success.

Generally, coaches should keep the pregame instructions simple and clear and consider limiting advice to no more than two or three key points.[64] Because athletes are likely to be a little nervous before the competition, particularly for important events, coaches may want to remind athletes that "games are played, not worked." This simple cue reminds athletes to have fun and savor the opportunity to play and compete, or in other words, to play loose.

The most effective speeches seem to share three characteristics.[65] First, the message is delivered with genuine emotion appropriate to the immediate emotional needs of the athletes. Second, specific reference is made during the speech to the team's core values. Third, the speech is short and meaningful. In sum, the most effective pregame speeches are those in which the message is succinctly delivered with genuine coach emotion and connected to core values of the athlete and team.

Many successful coaches prefer to deliver their precompetition message the night before or even a few days in advance of an important competition.[51] For example, championship collegiate football coach Bobby Bowden believed that the pregame speech would be most effective if it was given the night before the competition so that the athletes would have more time to reflect on the message. Fellow championship football coach Lou Holtz has suggested that the pregame speech message may be even more effective if it is given two or three days before the event, allowing even more time for the message to sink in with the athletes.

To prepare for a pregame speech, coaches should review likely scenarios that will occur in the competition and then mentally rehearse the message. Although a precompetition speech might last only five minutes, coaches may spend several hours preparing the message.

Championship and Hall of Fame ice hockey coach Jacques Lemaire was considered a master of the pregame speech. He reportedly spent hours reflecting on what to say and how his players would react to his comments.[66] Although Coach Lemaire liked to find a quiet place to sit and "give it a good think," other successful coaches report that participating in a light run or a walk, either alone or with a friend or another coach, on the morning of a competition is a valuable way to clear the mind and prepare themselves for delivering an effective precompetition message.[4]

Some of the all-time most successful coaches such as wrestling coach Dan Gable and football coach Bobby Bowden also recommend occasionally selecting athletes to deliver the precompetition message. Along his path to becoming one of the winningest college football coaches ever, Bowden discovered that often the most inspiring and effective pregame speeches were given by the athletes rather than the coaches.[51] As a result, he frequently asked a senior player to address the team in the locker room before the game. The athlete would be asked to share why the particular game was important to him, often resulting in deeply personal stories that inspired the team. Similarly, before a big meet, 15-time national championship wrestling coach Dan Gable often asked an athlete to tell the rest of the team about his action plan for winning the title.[67]

Finally, depending on the athlete, sometimes the precompetition message may be more effectively delivered in writing. A championship tennis coach once shared with me a precompetition strategy he used to help coach an athlete to the world number one ranking. After trying all the typical mental readiness strategies, the coach decided to experiment with placing brief handwritten notes of encouragement in the athlete's locker before matches. The athlete liked the notes and was always eager to see what message awaited him before the next match. Soon after the coach started using this strategy, the athlete broke through his performance barrier and reached the pinnacle of his sport. Besides providing moral support, a personalized precompetition note can be used to remind the athlete about competition strategy or individual responsibilities on a team.[68]

Although pregame speeches have a long-standing tradition in sport, the preparation that happens during the practices leading up to the event ultimately determines the quality of performance on game day. Many coaches, including John Wooden, considered by many the greatest coach of all time, avoided pregame speeches altogether for this very reason.

> I prefer thorough preparation over some device to make us "rise to the occasion." Let others try to rise suddenly to a higher level than they had attained previously. We would have already attained it in our preparation. We would be there to begin with. A speech by me shouldn't be necessary.[69 (p. 124)]

Regardless of the view that a coach takes on pregame speeches, they can be effective if they match the moment and emotional needs of the athletes. Careful observation of how athletes are feeling and acting leading up to the competition will help coaches determine what approach is needed before each competition.

## PERFORMING PRECOMPETITION ROUTINES

Successful coaches are known for their preparation of meticulous precompetition routines. In fact, athletes often cite this characteristic when asked to describe the qualities of a great coach.[70] To ensure that athletes and coaches don't miss or forget parts of their routines, a precompetition checklist should be prepared. A carefully prepared and simple precompetition checklist is the surest way to improve game-day performance.

Checklists are a powerful tool used by the top performers in all fields as a way to simplify complex tasks and focus on things that matter most.[71] For example, a simple five-step checklist for presurgery routines has been credited with saving thousands of lives and hundreds of millions of dollars in medical care costs in the United States. To illustrate how easy it is for people to forget even the most basic parts of a routine when arousal levels rise, the first step in the presurgery checklist for doctors is "Wash your hands with soap."[72]

Surgeons who developed the presurgery checklist attribute its incredible success to two factors. First, checklists help performers remember simple or mundane parts of a routine that they can easily overlook, particularly when emotions are high. Second, a good checklist isolates the minimum steps required to prepare for a complex performance.

A sample generic precompetition checklist, based on the key precompetition readiness topics discussed in this chapter, is presented in figure 8.7. The model can serve as a general guide for preparing a checklist that best matches the unique precompetition readiness needs of each athlete, team, or coach. For example, besides including the major components of a precompetition routine listed in figure 8.7, checklists can be expanded to include reminders about the small but important details such as remembering to charge electronic devices and packing headphones for listening to music during the warm-up or when using imagery.

Equipped with a better understanding of the physical, mental, and emotional needs for both themselves and their athletes, coaches are ready to create an effective precompetition routine. Sean McCann, senior sport psychologist and performance director for U.S. Olympic athletes and their coaches, stresses that precompetition routines are critical to peak performance.[73] Precompetition routines are important because they provide athletes and coaches with a sense of control and confidence by keeping them active and focused on useful behaviors and thoughts.

Precompetition routines are helpful when they are used to guide, not prescribe, athlete and coach behaviors. For example, Olympic gold medal swimmers describe their precompetition routines as flexible guidelines they adapt to ever-changing game-day conditions and disruptions.[3] They believe that athletes who attempt to follow a strict pattern of precompetition behaviors are setting themselves up for increased stress because seldom will they be able to adhere 100 percent to their routines.

Precompetition routines are particularly important when athletes travel to competition sites that are new to them. Although common in high-performance sport, even youth sport and high school athletes compete in away games and have to be prepared to cope with unfamiliar performance environments. These new environments can prove extremely distracting to athletes unless they arrive with a well-rehearsed precompetition routine.

A common way to help athletes prepare an effective precompetition routine is to sit down with them and make a list of all the things they need to do in the few hours or day before an event. This list can include precompetition meals, sleep requirements for the night before, equipment checks, when and where to arrive to ensure they make it to the event, review of competition strategy, and on-site physical and mental warm-up.[4, 74, 75] Ideally, the amount of time required to complete these activities will be identified so that athletes don't have to rush or skip steps near the end of their routines.

The routine serves as a physical and mental preparation plan for peak performance on competition day. The form prepared by sport psychologists Damon Burton and Thomas Raedeke can be used to help athletes identify key steps in their physical and mental preparation (see figure 8.8).[44]

When coaching young or inexperienced athletes, the coach should complete this form for the athletes and then make adjustments to the plan as the athletes experiment with it in competitions. When the coach is working with experienced

## Figure 8.7 Precompetition Checklist

### Physical readiness

#### Sleep

- ☐ Get 9 or 10 hours of nightly sleep.
- ☐ Avoid screen time or bright light 1 hour before bedtime.
- ☐ Keep room as dark as possible.
- ☐ Take a 15- or 20-minute afternoon nap when possible.

#### Energy

- ☐ Do not experiment with new foods or drinks.
- ☐ Check urine color for hydration status (clear rather than dark).
- ☐ Eat last large meal no later than 3 to 4 hours precompetition.
- ☐ Eat small snacks 1 to 3 hours precompetition.
- ☐ Check glycemic index of foods to time energy release to energy needs.
- ☐ Eat locally grown and unprocessed food to maximize nutritional value.

#### On-site warm-up (15- to 20-minute example)

- ☐ Light aerobic activities (5–7 minutes)
- ☐ Stretching (5–7 minutes)
  - ☐ Sports or positions that require explosive force and speed: perform four or five dynamic stretching activities for 60 seconds each.
  - ☐ Sports or positions that require high degree of static flexibility: perform static stretching with each stretch repeated four or five times for 45 to 60 seconds.
  - ☐ Perform all stretching activities on both sides of the body.
  - ☐ Target stretches to muscle groups most at risk for strains or injury specific to each sport or position.
- ☐ Practice of sport-specific technical skills (5–7 minutes)

### Mental and emotional readiness

- ☐ Review of individual zone of optimal functioning (IZOF) profile

#### Relaxation or psyching-up strategies (as needed)

- ☐ Deep belly breathing
- ☐ Progressive muscle relaxation
- ☐ Imagery
- ☐ Listen to music

#### Pregame speech (if delivering)

- ☐ Match message to emotional needs of the moment.
- ☐ Deliver with genuine emotion.
- ☐ Connect to core values.
- ☐ Succinct and focused on keys to victory.

From W. Gilbert, 2017, *Coaching better every season: A year-round system for athlete development and program success* (Champaign, IL: Human Kinetics).

## Figure 8.8 Physical and Mental Preparation Plan Development Form

Identify the sequence of your physical and mental warm-ups, looking for ways to combine physical and mental warm-up activities. Write out each step, noting steps that include both physical and mental warm-up activities. Make sure that your routine allows you to warm up completely, both mentally and physically. Make sure your mental warm-up helps develop high levels of focus and concentration, self-confidence, positive mental attitude and motivation, and gets your arousal to the optimal energy zone.

| Crucial steps in physical warm-up routine | Time required | Concerns | Crucial steps in mental warm-up routine | Time required | Concerns | Combined physical and mental warm-up |
|---|---|---|---|---|---|---|
| 1. | | | | | | |
| 2. | | | | | | |
| 3. | | | | | | |
| 4. | | | | | | |
| 5. | | | | | | |
| 6. | | | | | | |
| 7. | | | | | | |
| 8. | | | | | | |

Reprinted, by permission, from D. Burton and T.D. Raedeke, 2008, *Sport psychology for coaches* (Champaign, IL: Human Kinetics), 215.

adolescent or adult athletes, the athletes should first complete the form on their own because they will know from experience what preparation strategies seem to work best for them. Coaches should then review the preparation plan with the athletes and provide guidance where they believe steps are either missing or incomplete.

Burton and Raedeke share a completed precompetition on-site preparation plan for a 400-meter runner to illustrate the types of steps and strategies that an athlete might include in the preparation plan (see figure 8.9).

## Figure 8.9 On-Site Competition Preparation Plan for a 400-Meter Runner

**Step 1. Initial Race Check-In (80 minutes before competition, for 5 minutes)**

Pick up number, check spike length, and get lane assignment.

Find heat number and check competitors in the race.

Control anxiety level using deep breathing and cue word.

Find a shady spot to put stuff and stretch.

**Step 2. Jog (75 minutes before competition, for 8 minutes)**

Nice and easy to start the blood pumping.

Go over race plan from assigned lane, imagining competitors in their lanes.

Imagine running with perfect form; particularly focus on the feelings.

Go over backup plans and how you want to use them.

Listen to self-talk script to focus only on positive thoughts.

**Step 3. Static Stretching (67 minutes before competition, for 15 minutes)**

Breathe into each stretch, focusing on getting muscles really loose.

Control anxiety and focus on race plan.

Be confident and use positive self-talk as I do quick imagery clips of key portions of my race.

**Step 4. Dynamic Stretching (52 minutes before competition, for 7 minutes)**

Create feeling of strength and power in muscles.

Stay tall, drive legs, and use good form with "pawing" action.

**Step 5. Drills (45 minutes before competition, for 10 minutes)**

Feel light and powerful with a strong push-off.

Look stylish with proper technique.

Toe up, heel up, knee drive, hips up, and stay tall.

Shoulders down, relaxed arm swing, relaxed jaw.

**Step 6. Strides (35 minutes before competition, for 10 minutes)**

Accelerate and drive off the ground with a quick first step.

Push, push, push, while staying low.

Transition into driving taller while remaining relaxed.

Feel fast, confident, and totally positive.

Keep PMA (positive mental attitude) high, increase arousal while developing strong motivation—get psyched.

**Step 7. Race Simulation (25 minutes before competition, for 5 minutes)**

120 meters simulating the first part of the race and the corner.

Imagine competitors beside me as I feed off the energy from the crowd and my competitors.

Focus on my personal goal and the subgoals that will make it happen.

**Step 8. Bathroom Break (20 minutes before competition, for 3 minutes)**

Better safe than sorry.

Use rapid relaxation to deal with race jitters.

### Step 9. Check-In (17 minutes before competition, for 2 minutes)

Place my number on my hip.

Stay positive and confident.

Don't let other competitors sidetrack me—stay focused on my race plan.

### Step 10. Isolation (15 minutes before competition, for 10 minutes)

Lie down in the shade away from the others.

I'm now physically ready to race and in a good flow mind-set.

If needed, do rapid relaxation to stay relaxed.

Feel the electricity running through my body as a sign of readiness.

Go over my overall race plan and key parts again in my mind.

Vividly see running my goal time by hitting each split from the button.

Think positive cue words: "quick feet," "fast turnover," "maintain form when I'm hurting."

Be in the zone to run my own race—I'm totally prepared and ready.

Now compete.

### Step 11. Start Preparation (5 minutes before competition, for 5 minutes)

Set up the blocks and do three starts.

Feel explosive and drive off the blocks.

Get out of warm-ups.

Stay relaxed but drive the ground.

"Be hungry" and "feel fast."

Think only of the gun and react.

---

Reprinted, by permission, from D. Burton and T.D. Raedeke, 2008, *Sport psychology for coaches* (Champaign, IL: Human Kinetics), 212-213.

## Wrap-Up

Coaches and their athletes invest countless hours developing their skills, all so that they can test themselves in competition. Yet what coaches and athletes do in the final hours leading up to the event can have a major effect on the outcome of the competition. Just as they carefully design practice sessions and competition strategies, successful coaches also create precompetition routines with their athletes. Precompetition routines work because they help athletes and coaches feel excited, focused, and ready when it matters most.

At minimum, precompetition routines should address sleep and energy needs, the on-site warm-up, and each athlete's individual zone of optimal functioning and strategies to increase the likelihood of playing in the zone. A simple precompetition checklist combined with a standard precompetition routine checklist will help coaches and athletes stay focused on the things they need to do to increase their chances of success on competition day.

Chapter 9

# Coach Effectively on Game Day

**Key Concepts**

Bench coaching
Examine, encourage, educate
Competition checkpoints
Momentum triggers
Momentum strategies
In-game adjustments
Time-outs and contingency plans
Postcompetition routines
Competition reflection cards
Postcompetition checklists

The clock starts, the ball is kicked, the puck drops, the first pitch is thrown, the starter's gun is shot—game on! Competitions provide the moment of truth because as championship basketball coach Mike Krzyzewski stated, "This is when you find out if you've made the most of your time to achieve your ultimate goal."[1 (p. 180)] The competition is a decisive moment not only for athletes but also for coaches.

Competition often brings a restless sense of nervous energy for coaches. Legendary wrestling coach Dan Gable, who won many championships as an athlete before he became a championship coach, once said, "There's nothing like the heat of battle to get your blood flowing. I get more excited about coaching matches than I used to get when I competed."[2 (p. 177)] Coach Gable channeled this energy into a competition coaching approach that worked for him, but he cautioned other coaches to avoid copying the approach they see their favorite coaches using. Each coach must develop a competition coaching approach that aligns with her or his core values and personality.

When thinking about the best approach to use for coaching during competitions, coaches should ask themselves questions such as the following:

George Tiedemann/Sports Illustrated/Getty Images

Legendary University of Iowa wrestling coach Dan Gable frequently praised and encouraged his athletes during matches.

- How much should I intervene during competitions versus silently observing and allowing athletes to work through challenges on their own?
- What strategies have I prepared for making adjustments, handling setbacks and conflict, and regulating momentum shifts?
- How will I communicate with athletes during breaks such as time-outs, halftime, or between events?
- What routines and rituals will I use after the competition to ensure that my athletes and I pull important lessons from the competition, regain emotional stability after a tough loss or a big win, and optimize physical recovery?

This chapter presents proven strategies and effective actions for coaching during competitions. Keep in mind, however, that all these measures require coaches to keep their wits about them and keep their emotions in check in the heat of battle. Such self-control is essential to fulfill the role as coach and leader during these events.

## BENCH COACHING

A common mistake made by many coaches, from youth all the way to Olympic level, is overcoaching during competitions.[3, 4] Spend enough time around competitive sport and you will undoubtedly encounter the puppet master coach.

You know the coach—the one who is constantly hollering and gesturing at the athletes as they are trying to perform or learn a skill. Overcoaching occurs when coaches give too much instruction or excessive feedback during competitions. This approach ultimately overwhelms athletes because it distracts them from focusing on their performance.

In competitions, coaches should trust their athletes and give them enough freedom to perform what they taught them in practices. As five-time NBA championship coach Gregg Popovich noted late in his career, "I've learned to shut up more. Sometimes being quiet and letting the player play is much more important than trying to be Mr. Coach and teach him this or teach him that."[5]

Research on coach behaviors during competitions supports what Coach Popovich has learned through experience.[6–9] For example, coaches who guided athletes to Olympic or Paralympic medals intervened during major competitions only if they thought doing so was absolutely necessary.[6] Attempts to coach athletes during the competition were rare. Ice hockey coach Ken Hitchcock, who has guided teams to Olympic, world, and professional championships, is a prime example. When working with other coaches he often reminds them, "Games are [the players' time]; practice is my time."[10 (p. 22)]

Although championship coaches generally take a less is more approach to coaching during competitions, they are not passive observers throughout the competition. On the contrary, the best coaches take an active role in guiding and supporting their athletes during competitions. Three components define an effective approach to competition coaching: examine, encourage, and educate (see table 9.1).

## Examine

Legendary baseball manager and athlete Yogi Berra, who won 13 World Series championships, once quipped, "You can observe a lot by watching."[11] Silently observing players in action, sometimes referred to as match analysis, is the necessary foundation for effective coaching during competitions. For example, two-time Olympic championship coach Ric Charlesworth tells coaches, "Be ready to react and willing to use your judgment, but be wary of overreaction.

**Table 9.1 Components of Effective Competition Coaching**

| Component | Description |
|---|---|
| Examine | Silently observe the performance of the athlete and opponent. Look for (*a*) opportunities to make strategic adjustments or exploit opponent tendencies, (*b*) praiseworthy athlete behavior, and (*c*) potential signs of athlete fatigue. |
| Encourage | Regularly give praise and support, both for successful performance outcomes (e.g., goal, score) and quality of performance (i.e., correct skill execution, effort). |
| Educate | Use athlete performances as teachable moments by providing quick feedback and reminders of important technical and tactical actions during natural breaks (time-outs, intermissions, when athletes are on the bench). |

Sometimes it is better to do nothing than overreact. Restraint can be a great virtue in coaching."[12 (p. 79)]

Some coaches set a goal for themselves to remain silent and focus only on observing for the first few minutes of a competition.[13] In a 90-minute soccer game the goal might be just to observe for the first 8 to 10 minutes. Coaches should avoid the common error of intervening too quickly. All competitions typically begin with a period when athletes are feeling out the competition—looking for opponent tendencies, strengths, and potential weaknesses. As much as possible, coaches should let athletes simply play during this period and make notes, mental or written, about possible adjustments.

Coaches normally spend 50 percent or more of their time during competitions simply observing the action.[8, 9] To the untrained eye, the coach may appear to be inactive and not doing his or her job. However, the most successful coaches understand that effective coaching during competitions—what, how, and when to communicate with athletes—rests on their ability to notice important competition cues (athlete performance, opponent performance, time left in the event, score, weather, and so on).

When coaching during competitions, effective coaches understand that they are in essence coaching two teams, or multiple groups of athletes. They must not only watch how their own team or athletes are performing but also look for opponent tendencies and anticipate tactical adjustments that the opposing coach will make. Hall of Fame volleyball coach Mike Hebert refers to this activity as listening to the match.[14]

Former Olympic track and field coach and renowned coaching scientist Dr. Alan Launder provides four tips for coaches to improve their ability to listen to the match.[15 (p. 162)]

- Watch players on both teams in a relatively calm and dispassionate manner, even under intense pressure.
- Discern patterns of play and identify the contributions of individual players on both teams.
- See whether the team is attempting to carry out its game plan—and if not, why?
- Remain composed and decide what changes can be made to improve play.

The ability to refrain from immediately intervening and instead to observe the play patiently appears to be a separator between top coaches and less skilled coaches. Some research shows that top coaches give 50 percent fewer comments to their athletes during competitions than less successful and less experienced coaches.[16]

Eleven-time championship professional basketball coach Phil Jackson was noted for his patience and observation skills during competitions. He gained the trust of his players by showing confidence in their ability to solve problems during a game. He said, "Michael Jordan used to say that what he liked about my coaching style was how patient I remained during the final minutes of a game."[17 (p. 21)] The evidence is clear; coaches should observe more and interrupt less for more effective coaching during competitions.

Successful coaches likely notice different things during competitions compared with less successful coaches.[18, 19] The ability to see the right things during a performance is a defining characteristic of expertise. For example, championship ice hockey coach Dennis "Red" Gendron shares how as a young coach he made many mistakes during competitions, "not because I wasn't paying attention, but because I didn't understand what to look for."[20 (p. 217)]

Coaches cannot possibly attend to everything that is happening in an event. Without a clear focus for what to observe during a competition, they can easily fall victim to scattered thoughts and distractions—what legendary championship baseball coach Augie Garrido refers to as "monkey mind."[21] Coach Garrido uses pregame physical exercises with his players to help them become more deliberate and mindful of their thoughts and actions. Mindfulness has been shown to be highly related to an athlete's ability to achieve an optimal performance zone.[22] Coaches will benefit as well from setting aside some time before competitions to focus their thoughts and quiet their minds.

Coaches need a strategy to identify in advance the things that matter most to achieving performance success and then prepare to focus on those items during the competition.[18] Identifying some key performance indicators to look for in advance will decrease a coach's tendency to try to see everything and in the process miss the things that matter most. For example, expert teachers typically start a lesson with some checkpoints in mind to guide their observation of student classroom learning.[23]

As part of their precompetition routine coaches should create a list of competition checkpoints. The list might include a mix of technical, tactical, physical, and mental performance indicators. For example, Coach Gendron took a game coaching card with him to the bench during every game. The card included notes about anticipated matchups, opponent tendencies, and strategies for various game situations, such as playing with a man advantage or the last few minutes of the game.[20]

Five-time college and three-time Olympic championship coach Mike Krzyzewski also relies heavily on this strategy and believes it is one of the keys to his remarkable coaching success.

> Before every game I have ever coached, I have made handwritten notes for myself. . . . I have found that writing these things down—even things I've already heard my assistants say or have seen in the scouting report—cements them in my mind. . . . Those notes help me to not be distracted and to concentrate on what we have to do to be successful.[1 (p. 198)]

These competition checkpoints can be used as triggers, or thresholds, for making quick and effective coaching decisions in the midst of a competition.[24] The fast pace and time pressures of competitions requires coaches to observe enough information, but not everything, to make quality tactical adjustments. This approach is sometimes referred to as the 80 percent rule for decision making, and it is a key for making strategic decisions in high-pressure situations such as military operations. For example, fighter pilot Carey Lohrenz explains, "Eighty percent is good enough. If you have 80 percent of the information you think you need, that's good enough to take action."[25]

## Figure 9.1 Competition Checkpoints— Ice Hockey Coaching Example

During the competition pay special attention to . . .

| Technical cues | Tactical cues | Physical cues | Mental cues |
|---|---|---|---|
| In the net, Kyler exposing large gap between his pads ("five hole"). Remind him to use short shuffle movements and not drag his back leg. | Players out of alignment when killing a penalty in our own end. Keep reminding players to play the "box." | Martin not recovering quickly enough when back-checking. May be sign of fatigue because of large amount of minutes played in yesterday's game. | Gabe slow to make defensive adjustments in our end. Could be sign of drifting focus because of family issue he shared with me in pregame warm-up. |

The worksheet presented in figure 9.1 is a simple tool that coaches can use to help them create their own competition checkpoints. This strategy will prepare them to notice the most important performance cues before a competition. A sample noticing cue is provided for each of the performance areas, using the sport of ice hockey.

## Encourage

Another major role of the coach during competitions is to recognize and praise athletes. According to world-renowned soccer coach Sir Alex Ferguson, the two best words a coach can say to an athlete are "well done."[26] Praising athletes when they perform well is easy, and deserving. Scoring against an opponent and winning a race are obvious examples of successful performances. Praise given by coaches at these moments serves to build the athlete's confidence even more.

Effective coaches, however, focus more on recognizing athletes for off-the-ball performances, such as giving extra effort when playing defense, using proper technique when executing a skill, or showing mental toughness by closing a gap between themselves and the next competitor late in a race. In addition, when athletes are performing well but results are not coming, they most need their coach's encouragement. For example, in softball an athlete may not earn a hit, but she may be helping the team by forcing the pitcher to throw more pitches by letting bad pitches go by and by fouling off difficult pitches. Coaches must remember to focus on reinforcing and encouraging quality performance (process), not just successful performance (outcome).

Frequent encouragement that is focused more on the process (quality) of the performance as opposed to the result (outcome) of the performance consistently leads to improved athlete performance. When given regular praise for quality performance during competitions, athletes not only perform better but also report higher levels of enjoyment, rate their coaches as more effective, and put greater effort into their performances.[27, 28]

Great coaches such as Ric Charlesworth make regular encouragement a priority during competitions because they understand that "every player, even the greatest champion, responds to positive encouragement and feedback. This can be the fuel of better and greater effort every time."[12 (p. 82)] When coaches encourage their athletes during competition, they are building a culture of trust. This support enhances athletes' confidence and their willingness to risk failure.[29, 30]

Coaches should also make a deliberate effort to praise less prominent athletes during competitions. John Wooden rarely praised his star players because he knew they were receiving frequent praise from teammates, peers, and the media. He focused instead of finding reasons to praise the less visible players on the team. For Coach Wooden then, "Most of the compliments and the praise . . . would be given to those that aren't playing too much."[31 (p. 128)]

These athletes are important to the team even though they may not receive much playing time in competitions or may finish near the back of the race. Coaches should pay particular attention to these athletes and look for praiseworthy aspects of their performance. Although these athletes may not play a prominent role, if they are coached well, noticeable improvements should occur in aspects of their performance during competitions.

One of the most difficult challenges that coaches of team sports face during competitions is keeping bench players engaged during the game, particularly when coaching young athletes. Athletes must be coached to understand that regardless of their position on the team, they could be called on at any moment to enter the game and must be mentally ready to help the team. Augie Garrido preaches to his players that the game is always on. He reminds them that if they are wearing the uniform, they must be mentally engaged in the competition and ready to play.[21] Athletes on the bench can imagine making the same plays that they see their teammates making. In the case of failure, they can visualize themselves making the correct play when they get their chance to get in the game.

One way for coaches to encourage and engage athletes who don't play much is to assign them an important observation task.[13] For example, in soccer a player could be given a tablet or a clipboard and asked to chart the number of successful passes made. Another bench player could be asked to chart the number of times the opponent regains possession by stealing the ball.

A final word on praise during competitions. Make no mistake: Praise must be genuine—"earned and deserved," as Coach Wooden liked to say. Surely, in some competitions athlete performance is not praiseworthy. But coaches should make a deliberate effort to notice even small aspects of athlete performance that are praiseworthy and then recognize the athlete for the performance. Acknowledgment may not always be possible in the moment, which is another reason that coaches should have a strategy for taking notes during competitions. If praising the athlete during the competition is not possible, the coach can praise the athlete either in private later or during the postcompetition debriefing.

## Educate

When coaches do decide to share their performance observations with athletes during competitions, they must be careful not to overload or distract them. Coaches should emphasize only a few simple performance cues. Communication with athletes during competition is most effective when coaches use the athlete's name to get their attention, the message is short and repeated, and, when possible, the athlete acknowledges they received and understand the message.[32]

When a coach notices a performance error in competition, she or he does not need to intervene. In fact, many of the world's most successful coaches have learned through experience that often a more effective approach is to give athletes an opportunity to correct errors on their own.

Giving athletes an opportunity to work through performance struggles on their own, at least for a little while, helps build athlete resilience and initiative. For example, championship basketball coach Gregg Popovich recommends, "You interject here or there. You call a play during the game at some point or make a substitution, that kind of thing that helps the team win. But they basically have to take charge or you never get to the top of the mountain."[33]

The common practice of shouting comments at athletes while they are in the midst of action is not an effective coaching strategy. Athletes either do not hear the information or, if they do, are not able to act on it because of the effort they are expending just to keep pace with performance demands. Pick the best coaches in a sport and watch them in action during a competition. More often than not, these coaches will be observing their athletes and limiting their communication to opportune moments either when breaks occur in the action or when the athlete is removed from the competition.

When coaches do pull athletes aside during competitions to teach, they should use the same words, tone of voice, and body language they use when teaching the skill during practices. John Wooden used this strategy extensively. He then taught it to other coaches, including award-winning high school basketball coach Hank Bias.[34, 35] For example, during a game, if a player was in the wrong rebounding position, Coach Bias would pull him aside and tell him the same thing he said during practices: "Brad, when Jamal gets out of position, remember to fill in as the short rebounder at the free throw line."[35 (p. 46)] When athletes hear the same message in the same way across competitions and practices, the message is familiar and they are more likely to respond positively to the information.

In general, the most successful coaches keep their teaching during competitions concise, simple, and focused on athlete needs at the particular moment. A successful national team coach once used the analogy of curling to describe the teaching approach coaches should use during competitions.[6] The athlete is like the rock that is moving down the ice, and the coach is like the brush that follows alongside and intervenes (sweeps) only when the rock appears to be veering off course. Much as a brush is used to keep the rock on target, successful coaches follow their athletes' lead and teach during competitions only when the athletes clearly need a quick reminder to refocus their efforts on relevant performance cues.

Competitions are not the time to try to teach new concepts to athletes or implement a new strategy on a whim.[2] When deciding whether to try to educate their athletes or change strategy, coaches should ask themselves, "Is this something

I've already taught? Have the athletes had a chance to practice it during training?" If the answer is yes, then a concise reminder or a quick change in strategy can be helpful. If the answer is no, then the coach should make a note to address the performance issue in the following practices.

Providing athletes in the midst of a competition with simple reminders of things that have already been taught during practices reassures them that they are prepared for the performance and helps build trust in the coach. The key to effective teaching during competitions is reinforcement of previously practiced skills and strategies. When athletes have to process new information during a competition, their performance can deteriorate, leading to self-doubt and tentativeness.[6] But because athletes are most alert when the pressure is on during competitions, it is an ideal time to educate through reinforcement.

Championship football coach Bo Schembechler discovered this point over his legendary career. He admonished coaches to take advantage of the teachable moments in competition because "everything you were trying to hammer home during training you can reinforce now, and it'll sink in. I think our guys sometimes improved more during a single game than they did in a week of practice."[36 (p. 242)]

## REGULATING MOMENTUM AND MAKING ADJUSTMENTS

A crucial part of the coach's role during competitions is to help athletes stay focused and recover from inevitable failures and momentum swings. Championship ice hockey coach Mike Babcock describes momentum as "an invisible force that makes luck, good or bad, part of your team."[37 (p. 137)]

Psychological momentum is a real and challenging issue for all coaches. It is generally defined as a feeling that performance is swinging rapidly in either a positive or negative direction.[38–41] Unfortunately, athletes don't detect the signs of and capitalize on positive momentum as early as they notice and succumb to negative momentum.[38] Therefore, learning to teach athletes how to notice signs of momentum shifts is critical to competition success.[39]

Momentum is the result of a series of events, sometimes referred to as a momentum chain. Events that have been shown to contribute to an athlete's ability to trigger a positive momentum swing include a positive attitude, encouragement from others, a mistake or negative body language by the opponent, and performance success (e.g., scoring a goal in soccer, getting a hit in softball, making a shot in golf, catching an opponent in a race).

Conversely, athletes report losing momentum when they play nervously or tentatively, lose concentration, receive negative criticism, feel excessive pressure to succeed, or concede an advantage to their opponent (e.g., allow a goal, give up a hit, miss a shot, get caught by an opponent). If left unchecked, perceptions of momentum can dramatically influence an athlete's confidence and performance. An athlete can experience an unusual and quick drop in performance, commonly referred to as choking, when the pressure is greatest.[42]

Classic examples of choking include professional golfer I.K. Kim's miss of a 1-foot (30 cm) putt on the final hole that would have won the 2012 Kraft

Nabisco Championship and Jean Van De Velde's succession of wildly erratic shots to erase his three-shot lead on the final hole of the 1999 British Open. Both players lost the championship in sudden-death playoffs that followed their choking episodes.

Momentum swings and choking are just as common in team sports, in which one team's choke is another team's great comeback. Every sport has its own version of a comeback that coaches can use to educate their athletes about the potential of losing focus during a competition, regardless of how big a lead they have built.

One of the most prominent examples occurred in a 1993 NFL playoff game between the Buffalo Bills and the Houston Oilers. The Bills trailed 35–3 at halftime but went on to outscore the Oilers 38–3 in the second half and overtime. After halftime, the Bills seemingly could not miss and the Oilers could do no right. In football circles the game is referred to simply as "The comeback," and it is still the largest comeback in NFL history.[43]

One way that coaches can combat momentum swings is to keep athletes focused on the present (next play, next shift, next at-bat, next possession) and the process and aspects of the performance that are within their control (effort, technical proficiency, concentration, attitude).[21, 30] In team sports, coaches can remind players to stay focused on their individual roles or assignments and trust their teammates to do the same.

Coaches may also find it helpful to break a competition down into small chunks of time and remind players to focus on the game within the game. For example, a basketball coach might break a 48-minute game into 12 periods of 4 minutes each. A soccer coach might divide a 90-minute game into six 15-minute segments, each with a specific focus.

Championship baseball coach Augie Garrido taught his players to approach each competition as a series of nine one-inning games as a way to battle what he calls "mother momentum."[21] Coaches will find that their athletes can more easily maintain focus and intensity for short periods at a time, interspersed with competition breaks when possible (time-outs, substitutions, naturally occurring breaks in the competition). This strategy also helps overcome the lack of urgency commonly seen in athletes early in a competition. They mistakenly believe they will be able to turn it on later in the game and make up lost ground taken by their opponent early in the competition.

To help athletes avoid choking in big moments of a competition, coaches can use the ACT strategy prepared by coaching scientist and former coach Robin Vealey.[42] ACT is an acronym for a three-step approach to coping with competition performance swings—accept, center, and trust.

First, athletes should be taught to recognize and accept feelings of pressure and anxiety when they occur during competitions. The goal is not to avoid or disregard feelings that will naturally occur in big moments. Instead, athletes should strive for what has been referred to as clean discomfort. They should not panic or fight the emotions that come with important competitions or mistakes; instead, they should acknowledge them and focus on controlled breathing and images of successful performance.

AP Photo/Phil Coale

Texas Longhorns' head coach Augie Garrido, left, used a wide range of cues to keep his athletes focused during competitions.

A study with elite golfers illustrates the power of acceptance for helping athletes regain control after unsuccessful performances during a competition.[44] Golfers were asked to compare how they responded to bad shots during successful competitions (clutch performances) and unsuccessful competitions (when they choked). One golfer explained a unique strategy for accepting and moving on from a bad shot near the end of a competition to secure a strong finish.

> I actually hit a bad shot going down the 17th. But it was like I had just crashed my car and was given a courtesy car. You just have to accept what you have got, and drive that car until you get your old one back. I went on to finish the round really well, thinking like this.[(p. 531)]

Reconnecting with images and thoughts of strength and resilience, which may be facilitated by reminding the athlete to repeat key words, is the second step in coping with competition pressures. A basketball player who suddenly starts to miss open shots might take a few deep breaths and repeat the shooting cues, "Start small, end tall," "Snap the elbow," and "Middle to middle."[45]

For example, during his 2015 rookie season playing with the New York Mets, professional baseball player Kevin Plawecki explained how he used deep breathing to regain emotional control during pressure-filled moments in a baseball game: "You can get kind of amped up, and breathing, as corny as it sounds, can really slow things down for you. It's helped me out. Whenever I feel things speeding up, I just take a deep breath and refocus."[46]

The third and final step in the approach to managing in-competition feelings that can lead to choking is trust in preparation. Coaches should remind athletes that when they are starting to feel anxiety that is causing a drop in their performance, they should think back to all the hard work they did to prepare for these big moments. If athletes trust their preparation and their coach, they should be able to trust their ability to manage the emotions they will feel in key competition moments.

Coaches may also find it helpful to reconnect players to the joy of competing as a way to reduce the pressure often felt during important competitions. For example, with his team entering their 2016 conference tournament as heavy favorites to win, University of Kansas basketball coach Bill Self reminded his players, "Have the pleasure exceed the pressure."[47] Players believed that this reminder helped them stay loose and play to their potential on their way to capturing the tournament championship.

Athletes' willingness to trust their preparation and use that trust to regain momentum will be increased if the coach models confident and controlled behavior. Athletes who play for championship coaches say that their coach's behavior directly influences their ability to regain focus when struggling during games: "If he gets uptight then we get uptight. So when we know he's calm about it or confident about it that makes you confident."[48 (p. 496)]

Another strategy coaches can use to help athletes regain focus and momentum swings that can occur after performance mistakes is the fudge-fix-focus routine described by championship soccer coach Tony DiCicco and sport psychologist Colleen Hacker.[49]

When athletes experience a failure, the first step is to acknowledge it and the resulting emotional disappointment. This stage is referred to as the fudge step. The second step is to shift the focus to fix mode by reflecting on what caused the failure and what could have been done differently. Because performance failures occur regularly and sometimes frequently during competitions, the third and final step is to focus on the immediate performance requirements. Coaches and their athletes need to balance the need to recognize and learn from competition mistakes with the need to stay focused on the present competition demands.

The time needed to complete a fudge-fix-focus cycle depends on the nature of the sport being coached. In fast-paced sports that allow little or no time for reflection in the moment, such as ice hockey, lacrosse, and boxing, this cycle may last a few seconds or may have to be postponed until a stoppage in play. Many other sports have regularly occurring breaks that provide a natural opportunity to employ this strategy, such as breaks between points in a tennis match or between pitches in baseball.

A summary of common triggers to help coaches notice early warning signs of positive and negative momentum and suggested coaching strategies is provided in figure 9.2. Coaches who learn to identify warning cues of potential momentum swings and make appropriate in-competition adjustments will give their athletes a potentially decisive competitive advantage.

## Figure 9.2 Momentum Triggers and Coaching Strategies

### Triggers of positive momentum

- Confidence in ability and preparation
- Sufficient physical and mental readiness
- Positive attitude and body language
- High concentration and energy level
- Trust in competition plan
- Focus on the process and fundamentals
- Acceptance and letting go of mistakes
- Successful performance (e.g., scoring)
- Opponent mistakes or failures
- Negative body language of opponent
- Encouragement from others (coaches, teammates, spectators)
- Successful tactical adjustments by coach
- Familiarity with competition environment
- Favorable officiating decision

### Triggers of negative momentum

- Lack of confidence
- Negative thinking and body language
- Insufficient physical and mental readiness
- Lack of concentration and intensity
- Lack of a clear performance plan
- Trying too hard, not playing assigned role
- Focused on results and winning
- Performance mistakes or failures
- Opponent success
- Lack of teammate support
- External pressure to succeed (spectators, coaches, media, parents)
- Inappropriate or lack of tactical adjustments by coach
- Unfamiliar with competition environment
- Officiating decision in favor of opponent

### Coaching strategies to build or regain positive momentum

- Create a detailed performance plan for each competition.
- Encourage athletes to visualize successful or positive actions.
- Give clear and concise instructions when speaking to athletes during competition.
- Provide frequent encouragement and positive reinforcement to all athletes.
- Stay alert and make tactical adjustments at right moments throughout the competition.
- Share observations about opponent tendencies and weaknesses with athletes.
- Reiterate focus on performance fundamentals and routines (back to basics).
- Use trigger words to help athletes stay focused and play with intensity.
- Remind athletes about previous successful performance experiences.

# CALLING TIME-OUTS AND USING CONTINGENCY PLANS

In many sports, time-outs are the perfect time to help athletes refocus and control momentum swings. For example, if a basketball team quickly gives up 7 or 8 unanswered points, the coach typically calls a time-out in an effort to stop the positive momentum of the other team.

Basketball coach Brad Stevens, who set numerous coaching records while leading his college team to consecutive national championship games, demonstrated a remarkable ability to use time-outs to make successful in-game adjustments.

Time-outs typically are brief, and coaches want to redirect their athletes' attention away from what just happened to what needs to happen in the next part of the competition. For Coach Stevens, this meant giving his athletes instructions on how best to navigate just the next four minutes of the game.[50]

Sometimes, though, the most valuable use of a time-out or break in the competition is to challenge the athletes to solve the performance issue on their own. Coaches should be careful to avoid training the athletes to become dependent on them for figuring out how to solve all the performance issues in a competition. Certainly, if the coach knows from experience that something can be improved by using a specific strategy, then he or she should quickly relay this information to the athletes. But at many times during competitions, either the coach will be unsure of how to resolve the issue or the athletes themselves will have to take ownership of the situation.

Gregg Popovich, one of the most successful basketball coaches of all time, encourages his players to communicate constantly during the competition so that they can help each other identify issues before they lead to big momentum swings for the opponent. Furthermore, he is not afraid to challenge his players to take responsibility for solving their own performance problems if he believes they have the maturity and character to respond to this approach:

> Sometimes in time-outs I'll say, "I've got nothing for you. What do you want me to do? We just turned it over six times. Everybody's holding the ball. What else do you want me to do here? Figure it out." And I'll get up and walk away. Because it's true. There's nothing else I can do for them. I can give them some bulls—, and act like I'm a coach or something, but it's on them.[33]

Unlike time-outs or other short breaks, halftime or intermission presents a unique opportunity for making adjustments and regulating momentum. The best advice for coaches to keep in mind as they prepare for halftime is to give athletes what they need most at that particular moment. The only way to know what they need is to observe the flow of the game to identify signs of athlete fatigue, common technical or strategic mistakes, and opportunities to counter opponent tendencies and attack weaknesses.

Successful coaches start to rehearse what they will say and do at halftime in the few minutes leading up to the break. They can use this time to check competition notes and debrief with assistant coaches if available. While walking back to the locker room or waiting for athletes to get a drink, the coach might also find it helpful to run the ideas by some of the team leaders.

Successful coaches rarely use halftime for inspirational talks. Instead, they use the time to allow the athletes to recover and give them a few points about game strategy, including any major adjustments that they will make in the second half.[13, 36] In a typical 15-minute half-time break the best coaches typically spend only 2-3 minutes talking to the team as a whole. The rest of the time is set aside for athletes to rest, refuel and rehydrate, reflect on their performance, and then rewarm-up for the second half.[50]

The best coaches meticulously prepare a bank of contingency plans to implement immediately following time-outs and other breaks in the competition as a way to regain momentum. For example, 2015 NBA championship basketball coach Steve Kerr constantly watches video of basketball games for strategies he could use in various scenarios during competitions. When he finds a play he likes, together with another coach he makes a record of the play and adds it to what he refers to as his ATO (after time-outs) file.[52]

Preparing contingencies should not be limited to tactical adjustments. The most successful coaches and athletes also think about how they will respond when faced with adversity during competition.[53] For example, to avoid reacting inappropriately, a football coach may rehearse how he will respond to questionable officiating calls or what he will do when one of his athletes shows signs of frustration with teammates.

Coaches may find it helpful to involve their athletes in the contingency planning process. Coaches might first prepare their own coaching version of a competition contingency plan that emphasizes coaching points. This plan will prepare coaches for helping their athletes prepare an athlete-focused contingency plan.

An athlete contingency plan for basketball is provided in figure 9.3. Notice how the plan, developed by coaching and sport psychology experts Damon Burton and Thomas Raedeke, identifies physical and mental goals along with cue words for critical competition moments or trends.[54] This type of contingency planning form can easily be adapted for any sport. A coach's version of the contingency plan might include many of the same responses and cues as well as reminders about specific athlete tendencies or potential substitutions and strategy changes.

Although all the aforementioned strategies apply whether coaching athletes at a home event or on the road, wise coaches prepare a few more contingency plans for away competitions. Historically, teams playing at home win more often than visiting teams do, ranging from around 54 percent in baseball to over 60 percent in basketball and soccer.[55] A similar trend is evident for individual sports, although mostly for sports in which the outcome is based on subjective judging such as diving, gymnastics, and figure skating.[56]

Therefore, when preparing for an away competition, coaches should spend a little more time devising strategies to help athletes control momentum and combat the home-team advantage. Coaches may want to consider reminding athletes about the home-team advantage and encourage them not to panic, or force the play, if the opponent builds positive momentum.

The three biggest factors that appear to contribute to a home-team advantage are the effect of travel on athlete readiness, venue familiarity, and officiating bias.[55–57] Coaches can combat the athlete readiness issue by reinforcing the precompetition sleep, rest, and nutrition guidelines presented in the previous chapter.

As for venue familiarity, coaches can show athletes videos and images of competitions held at the site, ask senior or former athletes to share with the rest of the team their experiences of playing at the site, and if possible arrange to visit or practice at the site before the competition.

Regarding officiating bias, coaches can prepare by ensuring that their athletes are ready to play shorthanded if needed (in sports in which players must sit out

## Figure 9.3 Sample Basketball Athlete Competition Contingency Planning Form

| Predetermined Critical Situations | SITUATION GOALS | | Cue Words |
|---|---|---|---|
| | Physical | Mental | |
| *Critical Situation 1:* first 3 minutes of the half or game | Emphasize defense and rebounding to take advantage of high arousal level. | Focus on being relaxed but aggressive; try to intimidate opponent physically; keep things simple until in flow of the game. | "be quick but don't hurry," "be aggressive but in control," "let the game come to you," "be unselfish and put the team first." |
| *Critical Situation 2:* last 3 minutes of the half or game | Emphasize getting a spurt before half; turn up the aggressiveness on defense; look for every fast break opportunity; emphasize high percentage shots in half court; good time for pressure. | Approach this period confidently and aggressively; maintain a high PMA; focus on pushing the pace without becoming careless; raise arousal level and motivation to push limits | "turn up the pressure," "look for every opportunity to run," "only want high percentage shots," "jump on them before half," "act confident and aggressive." |
| *Critical Situation 3:* after a timeout we call | Emphasize getting a stop or score on the next possession; turn up the intensity; adjust either offense or defense to create a positive mismatch; increase aggressiveness | Regain confidence; enhance PMA; focus on one possession at a time and how to exploit our strengths or minimize our weaknesses; raise arousal and motivation to create a burst. | "critical time for a stop or score," "turn it up," "be positive and find the mismatch," "play to our strengths," "jump on them." |

| Reactions to Good and Bad Performance Trends | SITUATION GOALS | | Cue Words |
|---|---|---|---|
| | Physical | Mental | |
| *Performance Reaction 1:* opponent reels off 10 straight points | Play under control to reduce turnovers; be more patient to get better shots on offense; increase defensive intensity and put more pressure on guards to keep them from getting into their offense. | Focus on increasing energization and motivation; restore confidence and PMA; focus on more physical defense and more patient offense. | "poise and composure under pressure," "make the extra pass to get a good shot," "pressure them into hurrying," "ball pressure and shoot down the passing lanes." |
| *Performance Reaction 2:* make lots of turnovers against the press | Understand where defense is vulnerable; play under control and understand multiple options on where to pass; once break pressure, look to score. | Focus on relaxation and positive self-talk to regain confidence and combat negative thoughts; stay under control; be aggressive when pressure broken. | "poise and composure under pressure," "be quick but don't hurry," "always an outlet pass," "once press broken, look to score." |

| Reactions to Good and Bad Performance Trends | SITUATION GOALS | | |
|---|---|---|---|
| | Physical | Mental | Cue Words |
| *Performance Reaction 3:* officials' calls consistently going against us | Recognize that the aggressive player/team usually gets the calls; be more aggressive; concentrate on moving feet rather than reaching; penetrate and pass rather than try to score. | Focus on energizing and raising motivation; regain confidence and PMA; counter negative thoughts, emphasize that we can't control officials' decisions; play our game and don't worry about officials. | "champions keep their composure in the face of adversity," "don't worry about things we can't control," "aggressive teams make their own breaks and calls," "just do your best." |

Reprinted, by permission, from D. Burton and T.D. Raedeke, 2008, *Sport psychology for coaches* (Champaign, IL: Human Kinetics), 222.

when penalized) and by practicing emotional control strategies (to minimize the tendency of athletes and coaches to overreact and lose focus when officials make questionable calls).

Finally, no contingency plan can account for the countless unanticipated situations that can derail athlete performance during a competition. Successful coaches take the extra step of arming their athletes with simple competition strategies they can use to regain focus. One such example is the strategy used by legendary college football coach Tom Osborne, one of the most successful football coaches of all time. Coach Osborne, along with renowned sport psychologist Ken Ravizza, taught his athletes a routine to use while on the field between plays, referred to as the three Rs—ready, respond, refocus.[52]

When players enter the huddle, the quarterback is responsible for checking to make sure that all his teammates are attentive and ready for the next play. If the quarterback notices a player who appears to be off-task or dwelling on the last play, he yells loudly or taps the player on the helmet as a signal to focus on the current play.

After the players break from the huddle and line up for the next play, they are taught simply to respond to the play. At this point the athletes must trust their preparation and act intuitively based on what they have learned in practice. Finally, when the play is over, the players can take a quick moment to reflect on the play and recognize their emotions—joy for a successful play, anger or disappointment for a failed play. The refocus part of the routine is a bridge between the last play and the next play, and it helps the athletes make in-game adjustments quickly and take responsibility for their play.

Although developed specifically for the competition structure of a football game, the three Rs (ready, respond, refocus) strategy can be adapted to any sport. For example, in sports such as volleyball, tennis, and golf, the same routine could be used between shots. In sports such as soccer, field hockey, and basketball in which fewer natural breaks occur in game play, the three Rs routine can be used quickly during game pauses such as when the ball goes out of bounds or when the referee stops play. Even in events such as distance running or swimming in which no stoppages occur at all during the race, athletes can still use the three Rs routine to ready themselves for a change in pace or move to counter an opponent.

## PERFORMING POSTCOMPETITION ACTIVITIES

Coaches and their athletes are normally in a heightened sense of emotional arousal following competitions. Following a big win, people naturally want to celebrate; a tough loss often leads to frustration and anger. Effective coaches understand that the few moments immediately following a competition are the most emotionally charged and therefore require special consideration when preparing postcompetition rituals.

Quality coaches always remember that one athlete's big win is another athlete's tough loss. Coaches should strive to temper immediate and public postcompetition celebrations as a way to show respect for their opponent. Although the winning athletes and coaches are certainly expected to be enthusiastic and want to celebrate, they may want to return to the locker room or move away from the competition site before they let loose and fully embrace the emotions that naturally come from succeeding in competition.

Championship basketball coach Brad Stevens was once asked how he was able to stay emotionless following a last-second shot made by his team to knock another team out of the championship tournament. He explained that he respected the other coach and that although he was excited to have secured the win and advanced in the tournament, "The last thing I needed to be doing was doing cartwheels with him [the other coach] over there in a game where both teams played great."[50] The real postcompetition celebrations can wait until the coach and athletes return to their private meeting place.

Unfortunately, coaches and athletes often make poor decisions about how to handle victory or defeat in the moments immediately following a competition. In one notorious incident, a youth ice hockey coach assaulted a 13-year old athlete in the postgame handshake, resulting in a broken wrist for the player and a 15-day jail sentence for the coach.[58] Such incidents happen at the highest levels as well; professional football coaches Jim Harbaugh and Jim Schwartz had to be physically restrained while scuffling on the field after a game.[59]

Coaches must be proactive and teach their athletes appropriate postgame strategies for celebrating victory and handling defeat with class. The strategies will mean nothing, however, if the coach behaves inappropriately after the competition. Modeling the desired behaviors is the most powerful way to teach athletes how to behave after a competition.

One strategy that championship wrestling coach Dan Gable liked to use with one of his more fiery athletes was the 10-second-count ritual.[2] The athlete was taught to step back from the center of the wrestling mat and count to 10 before he engaged in the customary postmatch handshake, win or lose. This pause allowed the athlete to check his emotions and calm down before stepping forward to shake hands with his opponent, reducing the likelihood of a heated exchange following the match. This strategy can easily be adapted to any athlete and any sport.

World Cup and Olympic champion women's soccer coach Tony DiCicco extended the cooling-off period to 24 hours following a competition. He referred to this strategy as his 24-hour continuous improvement rule.[49] Coach DiCicco realized that coaches and athletes, who are competitive and self-critical by nature, naturally become highly emotional and disappointed when they fail. So he allowed himself and his athletes to take 24 hours immediately following a failure, such as a tough loss, to process emotions without any concern for trying to regroup or address weaknesses. But 24 hours and 1 minute after the loss, coaches and athletes were required to switch to improvement mode, taking what they could from the experience and using it as fertilizer for growth.

This 24-hour rule is also recommended by successful coaches for dealing with parents after a loss.[60] At the start of the season, parents can be informed that coaches will gladly discuss competition decisions but only after 24 hours have passed since the end of the competition. This policy shows parents that the coach is open and willing to listen to concerns but wants everyone to have time to calm down and carefully think through the situation.

For athletes, some postcompetition physical activity is a valuable way to work out frustrations.[2] Coaches might consider securing exercise space in advance for their athletes to use following a competition and offer to remain on-site with athletes when practical.

Although some athletes will respond well to an opportunity to exercise after a tough loss, others will benefit more from resting or quietly thinking about what happened in the event and how to prepare for the next competition. Some professional sport teams now provide their athletes with relaxation stations they can use following a competition to calm their minds and prepare for a more restful night's sleep. The work of renowned sport psychologist Len Zaichkowsky with the Vancouver Canucks of the National Hockey League has been identified as a key factor in helping the team achieve unprecedented levels of success.[61]

Although at the professional sport level a relaxation station might include the use of sophisticated biofeedback systems that help athletes self-monitor breathing rate and brainwave activity, a coach at any level can at least provide athletes with some additional free time following a competition to transition emotionally from the performance. Championship volleyball coach Terry Pettit encourages coaches to let athletes simply sit and breathe silently for a few minutes as a way to help them let go after a tough loss.[62]

Immediately following a loss is not the time to force athletes to listen to an extensive competition debriefing. That activity should wait until the next day. Some coaches like to prepare a competition summary and individualized feedback for each athlete that they distribute to the team the following day. An example of this type of postcompetition evaluation sheet prepared by championship cross country running coach Pat Tyson is illustrated in figure 9.4.[63]

Any attempt to correct performance weaknesses immediately after the competition will not be received well by the athletes because their emotions will surely cloud their ability to absorb the message. Waiting until the next day gives everyone clarity and perspective. Championship ice hockey coach Mike Babcock credits his mentor, all-time winningest professional ice hockey coach Scotty Bowman,

## Figure 9.4 Postcompetition Evaluation Sheet

### Greater Spokane Dual Competition

#### University High School's Home Course, Liberty Lake

As the headlines said in this morning's *Spokesman-Review*: Panthers serve notice. "The hunter has become the hunted, thanks in part to Mead sophomore Jesse Fayant, who was part of a gritty four-runner effort. In a season-opening Greater Spokane League cross country meet befitting the state's top three teams, Fayant's sprint to third place helped the Panthers to a 27-29 victory over the defending champion and top-rated University Titans. Caught in the crossfire was Mt. Spokane, which lost 27-29 to the Titans and 22-33 to Mead."*

What great stuff, guys! Note feedback:

**Chris Fayant (15:51) 2nd place.** Only 6 seconds off winning! Nice effort for the team. You gave University's No. 1 runner, Max Schmidt, (15:45) all he could handle on his tough home course. I know you are on fire, Chris!

**Jesse Fayant (16:10) 3rd place.** You edged the No. 2 University runner, Brandon Stum, in a same-time photo finish! Just think, Jesse, if you get beat, our team gets beat with a reverse score. You ran incredibly tough on the second hill, and you really were brave coming up that last 40-meter hill to the finish chute. Nice job. Some day you will be a state champion. You are only a sophomore.

**Kelly Compogno (16:24) 5th place.** You beat University's No. 3 runner by 28 seconds! Great pacing and focus. You told me you were going to have no mental lapses during the run. It was evident that you didn't.

**Nate Boyer (16:40) 6th place.** You ran like a veteran over this tough three-mile (1.5 × 2 loops) Liberty Lake course! Finishing 12 seconds ahead of University's No. 3 runner was huge. You showed the value of depth up front.

**Patrick Chessar (17:09) 11th place.** You are our No. 5 runner and thus count in our team score. You were only 17 seconds behind University's No. 3 runner, 13 seconds behind their No. 4, and 12 seconds behind their No. 5! We'll need you closer as the season progresses. You can run with Bo yer. Pack up and feed off of him. You help Nate, and Nate helps you, and this helps the team. Keep believing.

**Tim Schuermer (17:15) 12th place.** You are our No. 6 runner. You ran really well for a young sophomore. You will get stronger. Don't be afraid to go out a bit harder with Nate Boyer. We need to pack up more. It will come. Nice closure over the last 400 meters!

**Bryan Becherini (17:16) 13th place.** You beat University's no. 7 runner by 25 seconds and were running in a nice pack with your buddies Schuermer and Chessar. You, too, are only a sophomore. I am excited to see how you progress throughout the season. Keep believing and knowing you will help our team shock people like we did today!

*Mike Vlahovich. September 23, 1999. "Panthers Serve Notice." *Spokesman Review.*



with teaching him this valuable lesson, "I leave them [athletes] alone when we lose. Talking to players after a loss usually isn't the right time. Things are said in the heat of the moment that are counter-productive or wrong."[37 (p. 57)] On those rare occasions when a coach believes that it is imperative to share something with the athletes immediately following a competition, the information should be brief.

In sum, coaches should resist the temptation to teach or scold athletes immediately following a loss. As championship football coach Bo Schembechler explained, "After a loss—which our guys took as hard as the coaches did—they were already down enough, so piling on just risked demoralizing them."[36 (p. 209)] The most effective postcompetition strategy is to support and encourage the athletes with opportunities to process their emotions in appropriate and personally relevant ways.

Following a win, however, may be an opportune time to work on fixing performance weaknesses. Instead of only celebrating the victory, successful coaches use the moment to teach their athletes humility and a continuous improvement mind-set by showing them areas of their performance that can be improved. Augie Garrido is one of many coaches who advocate using winning as an opportunity to teach: "When you are winning, you can look to get better. When you are in the flow and doing well, work on your weaknesses."[21 (p. 94)]

Because of the many emotions that coaches experience immediately following a competition, they should prepare a postcompetition checklist. As emotional arousal increases, focus narrows, so the moments right after a competition are when coaches are most likely to overlook important parts of their postcompetition rituals.

A postcompetition checklist should include cues for coach-athlete communication as well as coach administrative or organizational responsibilities.[64] In a typical high school setting, this list might include ensuring that the score is reported to the athletics director, meeting with local sports reporters, and thanking volunteers and event staff. In youth sport settings, the list might include having a brief meeting with parents to remind them about upcoming events and helping athletes clean the playing area and put away equipment.

A postcompetition checklist should also include a reminder to reinforce positive and successful athlete behaviors. For example, if a theme of the day is shared with the athletes before the competition, such as teamwork or a specific skill emphasized in practices leading up to the competition, then immediately following the competition is the ideal time to recognize athletes who modeled the behaviors.

When coaching youth baseball I would select two or three athletes who exemplified the theme during the game and let them select a pack of baseball cards from a hat as part of our postgame team ritual. This ritual soon became the highlight of the game for the young athletes, and it was an effective way to reinforce and reward positive athlete behaviors in front of the entire team.

Postcompetition checklists should also include reminders about steps that should be taken to ensure quality recovery and injury prevention. For example, athletes should be encouraged to begin rehydrating and refueling as soon as possible after a competition. Intake of water, sodium, and carbohydrates at a modest rate for four to six hours post-competition will replace sodium loss from sweating and help repair damaged muscle tissue.[65]

The world's greatest athletes go to great lengths to design state-of-the-art recovery protocols. For example, NBA star LeBron James follows a 24-hour recovery program that includes a wide range of sophisticated minute-by-minute treatments.[63] Coaches and athletes should make the best use of the treatments available in their particular settings and keep in mind that quality recovery will require the same attention to detail given to preparing practice plans or competition strategies.

Although many coaches and athletes include stretching in their postcompetition routines, stretching after or between performances does not appear to reduce muscle soreness.[67, 68] But a brief 10-minute physical cool-down after an event can prove extremely valuable in helping athletes process emotions and disconnect from the event. This routine is particularly important when athletes have multiple competitions on the same day or on consecutive days as is common in tournaments.

Finally, the postcompetition checklist should include a few minutes for coaches to reflect on athlete performance. Coaches need to record their observations while the performance is still fresh in their mind and think about the specific performance weaknesses they should address in upcoming practices. Long-term success requires a continuous commitment to closing high-impact performance gaps, something stressed by successful coaches such as two-time Olympic championship coach Ric Charlesworth:

> The coach must be willing to look behind the result every time the team plays to analyze what actually happened and how well the team performed regardless of the sometimes fickle pattern of goal scoring that is the sole focus of the media, other pundits and often, unfortunately, the players.[12 (p. 119)]

If coaches wait until the following day to reflect formally on the performance, recollection of events can become distorted or overlooked. In my work with a wide range of coaches, I have found that coaches find great value in completing a brief one-page competition reflection card. The idea for the competition reflection card came from reviewing research on coach reflection and performance analysis.[69, 70] A sample competition reflection card, based on one created in collaboration with an award-winning high school football coach, is provided in figure 9.5.

The first part of the reflection card provides a space for the coach to report competition information (outcome, location, opponent, and so on). The second part of the card is where the coach rates the quality of the performance by reflecting on competitiveness indicators. The competitiveness indicators are identified by the coach, in this case through consultation with the athletics director in a preseason meeting. The coach is asked to think about the keys to competitive success.

Based on this coach's extensive experience, he believed that if his team achieved these performance outcomes, they would put themselves in the best position to win. Immediately after each competition, the coach took a few minutes to reflect on how well the athletes performed on each of the competitiveness indicators, rating their performance on a scale of 1 (did not meet target) to 5 (exceeded target).

On the third part of the card the coach is asked to reflect on the most important performance weaknesses. This activity helps the coach prepare for designing follow-up practices that will help the athletes close high-impact performance gaps and increase their chance of success in the next competition. Although not

## Figure 9.5 Example of a Postcompetition Reflection Card for Football

### Football

League Nonleague

Playoff Tournament

Return card to athletics director within 24 hours of game or on Monday following a weekend game.

**Opponent:** ________ **Location:** Home/Away ________ **Date:** ________

**Result:** Win/Loss/Tie **Score:** FHS ________ Opponent ________

### Competitive Indicators

| | Did not meet target | | | | Exceeded target |
|---|---|---|---|---|---|
| <2 turnovers | 1 | 2 | 3 | 4 | 5 |
| Rush for >175 yards | 1 | 2 | 3 | 4 | 5 |
| Pass for > 150 yards | 1 | 2 | 3 | 4 | 5 |
| <3 offensive penalties | 1 | 2 | 3 | 4 | 5 |
| No PAT/FG's/Punts blocked | 1 | 2 | 3 | 4 | 5 |
| All punts +35 yard field position | 1 | 2 | 3 | 4 | 5 |
| No returns for touchdowns | 1 | 2 | 3 | 4 | 5 |
| >2 takeaways | 1 | 2 | 3 | 4 | 5 |
| Hold opponent to <150 yards rushing | 1 | 2 | 3 | 4 | 5 |
| Hold opponent to <70 yards passing | 1 | 2 | 3 | 4 | 5 |
| <4 defensive penalties | 1 | 2 | 3 | 4 | 5 |

### Competition Reflections

What weakness did you notice that *should be addressed* in the next practices?

### Athlete of the Game Nomination

Name: ________ ID#: ________

Gender: ______ Male ______ Female ________ Grade

Reason for nomination: ________

Anything else the AD should be aware of?

From W. Gilbert, 2017, *Coaching better every season: A year-round system for athlete development and program success* (Champaign, IL: Human Kinetics).

listed on the reflection card example provided here, coaches may find it helpful to include space on their reflection card for special notes about how to succeed the next time they compete against this opponent.[71]

The fourth and final part of the competition reflection card is used in this particular example for the coach to nominate an athlete of the game, which is a tradition at this particular high school. This part of the card also provides the coach with a place to report any competition issues that should be brought to the attention of the athletics director.

In my applied research we have adapted this reflection card for use with over 20 different sports. The key is to have the coach carefully think about the aspects of performance that are the best indicators of competitiveness and then set reasonable targets for that particular group of athletes. For example, although a high school football coach may know from experience that teams that pass for more than 175 yards have a good chance of success, if the profile of his team now is more suited to a running game, then the performance target will be adjusted accordingly.

Postcompetition reflection cards are valuable for athletes too. Coaches who have learned about this strategy from me have since created athlete versions in sports such as basketball, lacrosse, softball, and canoe and kayak. All the coaches who have used athlete postcompetition reflection cards believe that the strategy has contributed directly to improving performance. Since implementing the postcompetition reflection card strategy, athletes on these teams have achieved breakthrough performances at major international competitions, such as the Canada women's softball team, who won their first gold medal in over three decades at the 2015 Pan American Games.

One of best examples of an athlete postcompetition reflection card I have seen was developed for use with athletes on the Canada canoe and kayak national team (see figure 9.6). The card was developed by team director Peter Niedre along with Penny Werthner, the team's sport psychologist. Notice on the card that the athletes are asked to reflect on both prerace readiness and their focus during the race. Athletes are also asked to reflect on their performance in critical tactical segments of the race (start, middle, and end of the race). Competitions for these athletes comprise multiple races over one to two days, much like many track and field and swimming competitions. Athletes complete these brief reflection cards between races and then complete a more detailed version of the card following the competition.

The competition reflection cards for coaches and athletes are the final piece of an effective postcompetition routine. The components of the postcompetition routine most commonly recommended by successful coaches are identified in the postcompetition coaching checklist provided in figure 9.7. Coaches should experiment with and customize the checklist to fit the unique characteristics of their competition settings.

One of the most dominant coaches of all time, professional soccer coach Sir Alex Ferguson, provides an insightful summary and example of competition management in action. Coach Ferguson believed that meticulous attention to competition coaching was instrumental to his ability to achieve and sustain an unmatched level of competitive success.

## Figure 9.6 Athlete Postcompetition Reflection Card—Canoe and Kayak Example

### Postrace debrief: Athlete

Name: ____________________

Date: __________ Event: ______________ Result: ______________

**Psychological**

Rate on a scale of 0–6 (0 = not at all and 6 = very much)

**Prerace**

| | | | | | | | |
|---|---|---|---|---|---|---|---|
| 1. Physically warmed up | 0 | 1 | 2 | 3 | 4 | 5 | 6 |
| 2. Healthy | 0 | 1 | 2 | 3 | 4 | 5 | 6 |
| 3. Mentally prepared | 0 | 1 | 2 | 3 | 4 | 5 | 6 |
| 4. Eager to race | 0 | 1 | 2 | 3 | 4 | 5 | 6 |
| 5. Confident | 0 | 1 | 2 | 3 | 4 | 5 | 6 |
| 6. Feelings of anxiety | 0 | 1 | 2 | 3 | 4 | 5 | 6 |
| 7. Worried about performance | 0 | 1 | 2 | 3 | 4 | 5 | 6 |
| 8. Distracted | 0 | 1 | 2 | 3 | 4 | 5 | 6 |
| 9. Focused | 0 | 1 | 2 | 3 | 4 | 5 | 6 |
| 10. Technically prepared | 0 | 1 | 2 | 3 | 4 | 5 | 6 |

**During the race**

| | | | | | | | |
|---|---|---|---|---|---|---|---|
| 1. I found myself thinking of unrelated things. | 0 | 1 | 2 | 3 | 4 | 5 | 6 |
| 2. I was able to focus on my race plan. | 0 | 1 | 2 | 3 | 4 | 5 | 6 |
| 3. I was able to use emotions to my advantage. | 0 | 1 | 2 | 3 | 4 | 5 | 6 |
| 4. I felt overwhelmed and not confident. | 0 | 1 | 2 | 3 | 4 | 5 | 6 |
| 5. I let my focus drift to others around me. | 0 | 1 | 2 | 3 | 4 | 5 | 6 |

**Comments**

**Tactical**

| | | | | | | | |
|---|---|---|---|---|---|---|---|
| 1. Start/transition/first 5th of the race | 0 | 1 | 2 | 3 | 4 | 5 | 6 |
| 2. Middle (400-100, 800-200, 150-50) | 0 | 1 | 2 | 3 | 4 | 5 | 6 |
| 3. Last 100 m/200 m/ 50 m/finish | 0 | 1 | 2 | 3 | 4 | 5 | 6 |

**Comments**

Adapted from original version created by Penny Werthner. Used courtesy of Canoe Kayak Canada (www.canoekayak.ca).

## Figure 9.7 Postcompetition Coaching Checklist

- ☐ Quick pause for athletes and coaches to calm down (e.g., Dan Gable's 10-second count).
- ☐ Remind athletes about appropriate postcompetition behavior.
  - ☐ Congratulate opponents on effort (and victory if applicable).
  - ☐ Thank and recognize officials.
  - ☐ Ensure that competition area is clean (bench, sideline, warm-up area, and so on).
- ☐ Quickly debrief with assistant coaches to ensure that the staff give a consistent postcompetition message.
- ☐ Share brief message with athletes.
  - ☐ Recognize model behavior and effort.
  - ☐ Identify strengths if a loss.
  - ☐ Identify weaknesses if a win.
- ☐ Give athletes opportunity to address teammates.
- ☐ Complete postcompetition ritual (team cheer or song, prayer, and so on).
- ☐ Remind athletes about logistics (schedules, travel arrangements, and so on).
- ☐ Remind athletes about guidelines for quality sleep and rest (e.g., avoid screen time 1 hour before sleep, practice breathing or progressive muscle relaxation exercises if restless, aim for 9 to 10 hours of sleep).
- ☐ Allow time and space for athletes to cool down physically and mentally.
  - ☐ Have athletes complete postcompetition reflection cards.
- ☐ Perform quick walk-around to check postcompetition needs of athletes (e.g., anyone in need of special attention regarding physical or emotional distress).
- ☐ Attend to administrative responsibilities.
  - ☐ Complete postcompetition reflection card.
  - ☐ Complete postcompetition reporting as needed (e.g., report score or injuries to athletics director or league commissioner).
  - ☐ Meet with media (if applicable).
- ☐ Do final check-in with coaching staff and athletes for any remaining items that require immediate attention.
- ☐ Perform personal cool-down (e.g., light physical activity, social time with coaches, family, or friends).

From W. Gilbert, 2017, *Coaching better every season: A year-round system for athlete development and program success* (Champaign, IL: Human Kinetics).

A summary of his game management approach in action is shown in figure 9.8.[26, 72] His approach is divided into the three common phases of a competition for which coaches must prepare—precompetition, in competition, and postcompetition. Although the timing and profile of the moments vary depending on the sport and level of competition, the approach used by Coach Ferguson provides a general template to help any coach prepare a competition management plan.

## Figure 9.8 Approach to Competition Management by Championship Coach Sir Alex Ferguson

| Competition phase | Coach Sir Alex Ferguson approach |
|---|---|
| Precompetition readiness | • For weekly Sunday game, select lineup by Wednesday but do not share with players or media.<br>• Prepare game strategy specific to opponent strengths, tactics, and tendencies.<br>• Share in-depth video analysis of opponent with team two days in advance of competition.<br>• Quickly recap opponent strengths and weaknesses and game strategy the day before competition.<br>• Eat team meal three hours before competition.<br>• After team meal, speak with players who will not be in the lineup for the game. "I might be making a mistake here, but I think this is the best team for today."<br>• Talk to the whole team in the locker room immediately before the game; theme-based talk is different for each game but always focuses on own expectations, belief in themselves, and team trust; draw inspiration from wide range of sources—music, politics, history, business, sport. |
| In-competition behaviors | • Prefers to make mental, as opposed to written notes, on game observations (so can focus on the play).<br>• Start preparing halftime talk in last few minutes of first half of game.<br>  ◦ If winning, emphasize concentration on small details to sustain success and avoid getting complacent.<br>  ◦ If losing, emotional talk to make an impact.<br>  ◦ Always recognize quality effort regardless of outcome.<br>• If losing late in game, switch to "Fergie time" strategy: "A bombardment in the box, bodies everywhere, players putting up a real fight. Of course, you can lose on the counterattack, but the joy of winning when you thought you were beaten is fantastic." |
| Postcompetition rituals | • Identify and discuss mistakes with athletes right away so they can move on and focus on next competition.<br>• General team talk followed by media interviews.<br>• Use media interviews to start playing the "second game" (to motivate athletes for the next game before it starts).<br>• For home games, finish game day with postgame social time in office with opposing coach to "get the game out of your system." |

Keep in mind that this approach is the result of decades of trial and error and personal reflection by Coach Ferguson. As was clearly shown in this chapter, the best coaches don't simply copy the approach and strategies used by other coaches. Coach Ferguson's approach is presented as an example that coaches will need to reflect on to create a competition management approach that aligns with their core values, coaching strengths, and athlete needs.

## Wrap-Up

Effective game coaching requires a carefully prepared plan for helping athletes and coaches stay focused on the moment and on aspects of their performance within their control. Coaches should direct their energy during competitions to three important coaching tasks: silently examining player performance, encouraging athletes for their successful performance and quality behaviors (attitude, effort, intensity), and educating athletes by providing clear and concise performance reminders.

Coaches can enhance the quality of their observations during competitions by preparing a list of competition checkpoints. Careful attention to the checkpoints will help coaches notice momentum triggers and make timely and appropriate tactical adjustments that can prevent dramatic negative momentum swings.

During natural breaks during the competition, such as time-outs, coaches should allow and encourage athlete input and keep instructions brief. Simple refocusing strategies used by successful coaches such as ACT (accept-center-trust), fudge-fix-focus, and ready-respond-refocus can be used to help athletes quickly recover from performance mistakes.

A postcompetition checklist is the surest way for coaches to ensure that they attend to important postcompetition responsibilities and rituals and help athletes effectively process and recover from competition. Coaches should always remind themselves that their big win is someone else's disappointing loss. They can use the postcompetition checklist to manage emotions, show respect for the opponent, and model quality coaching behaviors.

Coaches should avoid conducting lengthy postcompetition performance debriefings and instead record observations on a competition reflection card. They can refer back to the card when designing follow-up practice sessions to ensure that they address the most important performance gaps.

Coaches will find that the more prepared they are for competitions, the more they will enjoy the competition, a sentiment summed up by Hall of Fame volleyball coach Mike Hebert:

> The most practical thing I can tell you about coaching the match is that there really shouldn't be that much for you to do. If you have prepared yourself and your team properly, you should be able to sit back and listen to the match as it unfolds, free to respond with an occasional corrective or congratulatory comment when you feel the need.[14, p. 203]

# Part III

# END OF SEASON

## Evaluate

Chapter 10

# Design and Implement an Evaluation System

**Key Concepts**

Program evaluation considerations
Identifying what to evaluate
Sources of evaluation data
Evaluation tools
Formative versus summative evaluation
Reporting evaluation results
Program evaluation in action
Program evaluation scorecard

Regardless of the sport or level of competition, all great coaches do the same thing after the season ends—they get busy conducting a systematic evaluation of their season. As legendary high school basketball coach Morgan Wooten learned over his career, "A coach's job is not over when the season ends; it just changes."[1 (p. 273)] For the most successful coaches the end of the season signals the time to collect as much information as possible to make informed decisions both about what needs improvement and what works.

Championship coaches such as John Wooden and Tom Coughlin are prime examples of successful coaches who placed a premium on end-of-season program evaluations. Coach Wooden liked to set aside time at the end of each season, whether it ended in a loss or in one of his 10 national championships, to review all aspects of his basketball program, including athlete, team, and coach performance.[2]

Super Bowl championship coach Tom Coughlin built cultures of excellence at every stop in his decades-long career by meticulously reviewing all aspects of his program at the end of each season. For Coach Coughlin, the end of each season was the time to "immediately begin preparing for the next season by evaluating our players and our coaching staff. That includes a rigorous self-appraisal, a thorough look at what we did right, and more important, where we can make improvements."[3 (p. 22)]

Although coaches normally pause and reflect at the end of a season, systematic and comprehensive coach and program evaluations appear to be the exception rather than the norm.[4–6] Coach and program evaluations are typically overlooked, leaving coaches isolated, confused, and fearful for how their effectiveness will be measured. National Athletics Director of the Year and nine-time championship college coach Keith Hansen says, "In talking with colleagues over the years I believe coaching evaluation is frequently omitted altogether, or it is completed haphazardly at best."[4 (p. 194)] Three-time Olympic coach and 12-time National Coach of the Year Jeff Huber vividly captured the woeful state of coaching evaluation:

> Coach evaluation? What's that? In 37 years of collegiate coaching I recall being formally evaluated once. The evaluation was conducted by a sport administrator who was never an athlete or coach, knew nothing about my sport, never observed one of my practices, never sat in on a team meeting, and never dropped by my office to see what I actually did when I wasn't coaching.[5 (p. 201)]

AP Photo/James A. Finley

Just like championship coaches such as Jeff Huber routinely evaluate athlete performance, coaches must design formal evaluation systems to improve their performance too.

Quality program evaluation requires consideration of at least four factors: (1) identifying what should be evaluated; (2) collecting evidence from multiple sources such as athletes, coaches, and administrators; (3) ensuring that the evaluation system and tools are practical; and (4) deciding how to communicate and use evaluation results. The primary purpose of end-of-season evaluation procedures should be to help coaches improve. As championship and award-winning soccer college soccer coach Connor Brady noted, "The more systematic and thorough a coaching evaluation is, the more well received it will be by the coach."[4 (p. 196)] When evaluations are done haphazardly or perceived to be an administrative tool focused solely on judging a coach, the evaluation process will not be well received and at worst will become a source of stress and frustration for everyone involved.

Creating a customized program evaluation system based on these considerations is critical for building programs of excellence and continuous improvement because it moves beyond evaluating a season solely on win-loss records.[7–10] The purpose of this chapter is to share examples of approaches and tools used to design and implement quality coach and program evaluation.

## DETERMINING WHAT TO EVALUATE

The first consideration in creating an effective evaluation plan is to identify the right things to evaluate. At minimum all program evaluation systems should include tools for measuring athlete development. As highly respected and Super Bowl champion football coach Tony Dungy once remarked, "The true measure of a coach, or anyone in a leadership role for that matter, is how they help those around them grow."[11 (p. ix)]

Besides athlete development, other evaluation priorities will be dictated by the setting in which a coach works. For example, when coaching in a school-based setting, athlete academic performance and student-athlete eligibility will be important to include in the program evaluation system. Useful, high-quality evaluation requires time and effort, so setting aside some time in the preseason to decide what will be evaluated at the end of the season is a wise investment that will pay valuable dividends.

National and conference college ice hockey Coach of the Year Guy Gadowsky has prepared a list of evaluation categories he uses to assess the quality of his program at the end of each season (see figure 10.1).[12] Notice that his list includes not only the usual team and individual performance statistics that make up most evaluations but also program philosophy, personnel, practices, team environment, and academic performance.

The second consideration when designing an effective program evaluation system is to ensure that evaluation information is collected from all key program stakeholders.[10] At minimum, coach self-evaluations should always be supplemented with feedback from members of the coaching staff and athletes. This method is the only way to ensure a balanced and comprehensive approach to making evaluation decisions. Program feedback from athletes who make up leadership councils and senior or departing athletes in particular can provide helpful insights on how to improve a program.

## Figure 10.1 Evaluation Categories

Systems

Philosophies

Statistics

- Team (goals against, goals scored, power-play and penalty-kill percentages, and so on)
- Individual

Personnel

- Attitude
- Performance
- Leaders
- Followers

Practices

- Times
- Length
- Positives
- Negatives

Road trips

Fund-raising

Alumni relations

Locker room environment

Academic commitment

Academic performance

Reprinted, by permission, from G. Gadowsky, 2016, Communicating a team mission. In *The hockey coaching bible*, edited by J. Bertagna (Champaign, IL: Human Kinetics), 16.

Program evaluation can be further enhanced by collecting feedback from others who have experience with the program or coach. Just as professionals in fields such as business are encouraged to ask a wide range of people for feedback when conducting an evaluation, commonly referred to as a 360-degree evaluation, coaches will benefit from adopting this approach.[13] People who can offer useful feedback might include athletic administrators, opposing coaches, game officials, formal or informal coach mentors, alumni, and trusted coaching colleagues (see figure 10.2). The best coaches understand that building successful programs and cultures of excellence requires honest feedback from everyone, particularly those who are not afraid to tell the truth, regardless of how painful the feedback might be. Head coach of the world champion New Zealand All Blacks men's rugby team Steve Hansen refers to this as "confronting the uncomfortable facts."[14, 15]

The third consideration when designing a quality program evaluation relates to implementation. Program evaluation is limited only by the amount of time and resources a coach is willing to invest. Good evaluation requires valid tools and meaningful data. An endless amount of evaluation information can be collected,

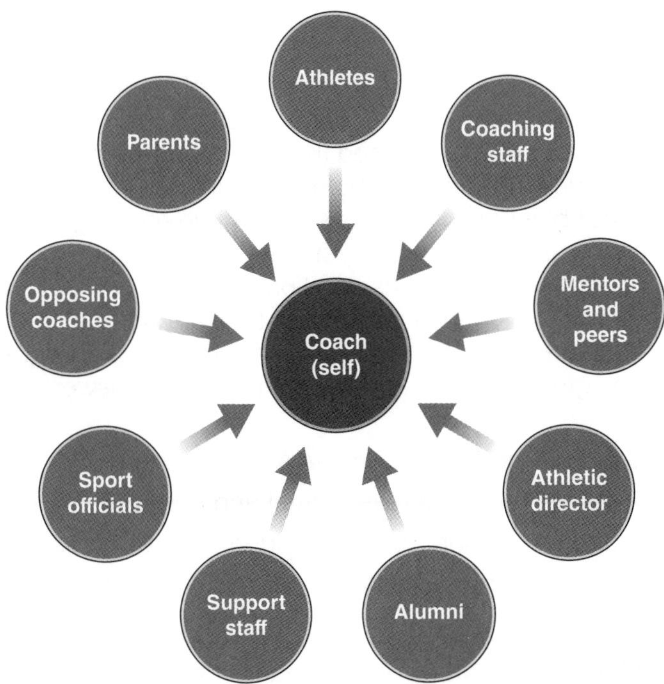


**Figure 10.2** Potential sources of coach and program evaluation feedback.

all of which will have to be analyzed and processed. A quality program evaluation must be practical, so coaches should collect only what is most relevant and can be efficiently gathered and summarized. The goal of end-of-season program evaluation is to collect enough information in a short time to make an informed decision about how to allocate off-season energy to improve coaching ability and enhance the program.

The fourth and final consideration for designing quality program evaluation is determining how the evaluation results will be used. Evaluations are used for two common purposes.[16] The first purpose should be to help coaches improve. This kind of analysis is referred to as formative evaluation; results are used to shed light on strengths and gaps while providing guidance for how the coach can work toward closing the gaps. The second, and often sole, purpose of evaluation is to judge the quality of the coach or program. This sort of assessment is referred to as summative evaluation; results are used to determine whether a coach (or member of the staff) should be retained.

An effective program evaluation system will be both formative and summative. The results should be used to help coaches improve while also providing evidence of coach and program growth. A formal method for reporting evaluation results should be used, such as writing an evaluation narrative or preparing a report that includes end-of-season statistics along with summary observations from those who provided evaluation feedback (e.g., coaches, athletes, administrators, and so on).

Annual evaluation reports should be kept on file so that season-by-season trends can be identified. Evaluation reports should be formally debriefed. This activity would most often be in the form of an end-of-season evaluation meeting among coaches or with program administrators. Distinguished high school athletics director Dr. David Hoch has learned through decades of experience that this type of evaluation meeting "has a lot riding on it; it is during this session that the coach receives her blueprint for improvement. If the meeting is successful and the coach is receptive, this is a good first step for the future."[17 (p. 68)]

The four program evaluation considerations—what to evaluate, what sources of information to use, which evaluation tools to use, and how to use evaluation results—must be balanced with a focus on asking the right program evaluation questions. Meaningful program evaluations will provide answers to the following four questions:

1. How well did we model our purpose and core values?
2. How well did we build a culture of trust and cohesion?
3. How well did we develop athletes through quality training sessions?
4. How well did we prepare athletes to perform at their peak in competitions?

These four overarching evaluation questions provide a guiding framework for designing and implementing a program evaluation system that aligns with the blueprint for success presented in this book.

Careful and systematic attention to both the aforementioned program evaluation considerations and the program evaluation questions will result in a fair and balanced program evaluation system (see figure 10.3). This approach to program evaluation will help create a climate of open and candid communication aimed at both helping coaches improve the quality of their coaching (formative evaluation) and providing an appraisal of coach effectiveness (summative evaluation).

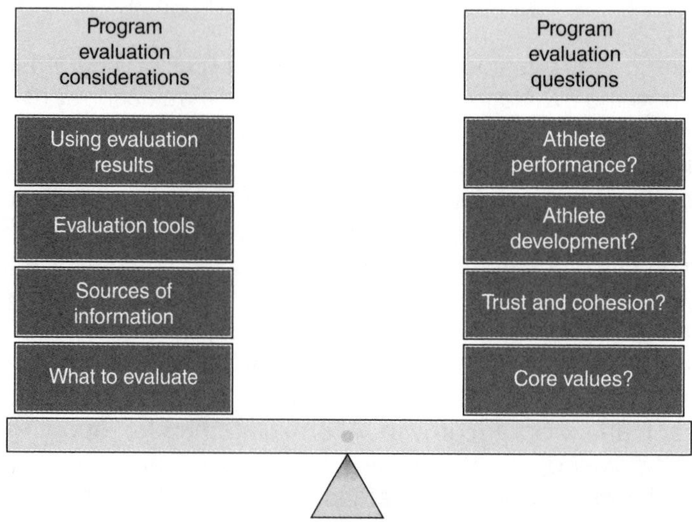


**Figure 10.3** Balancing program evaluation considerations and questions.

Coaches value this type of evaluation approach because, as championship coach Jeff Huber has observed, it "provides accurate and honest feedback that promotes coach insight and development."[5 (p. 201)]

The remainder of this chapter is divided into two sections. The first section provides examples of suggested evaluation tools—some adapted from the literature and others that I have created through my work with coaches and athletics directors. The second section describes an example of a systematic and effective program evaluation system in action. This program evaluation system has proved instrumental in building a record-setting culture of sporting excellence across an entire high school athletics department.

# USING EVALUATION TOOLS

When it comes to program evaluation tools, coaches or athletics directors do not need to re-create the wheel. Although they should experiment with creating their own evaluation tools, many useful examples of evaluation tools are available in the coaching and sport science literature. Drawing on my extensive experience teaching university courses on measurement and evaluation together with decades of testing a wide range of evaluation tools with coaches in the field, I have prepared a list of 15 suggested evaluation tools (see table 10.1).

This list is not meant to be an exhaustive compilation of existing evaluation tools; it is presented simply as a starting point. For example, some of the most sophisticated and powerful coach evaluation tools, such as ones created through rigorous lines of research like the Coaching Success Questionnaire-2[18] and the Coaching Behavior Scale for Sport,[19] are available only by purchase from the creators. Research has shown that athletes who play for coaches who score high on these types of evaluations report greater levels of confidence and enjoyment along with lower levels of exhaustion or burnout than athletes who play for coaches who score low on these evaluations.[18] I encourage you to consider using these evaluation tools in your practice. The list of evaluation tools I have prepared includes only tools that are publicly available and do not require any special scoring instructions, so you can start using them right away.

The list provided here is best viewed as a guide for creating the program evaluation system that best fits your own evaluation needs and resources. Pull the tools out of the evaluation toolbox that align best with your program philosophy and evaluation needs. Also, don't hesitate to experiment with revising the tools to create new ones that might work better in your setting.

## Program and Team Assessments

The element that has the most influence on the probability of having a successful season is the program climate.[20] The importance of program climate was reinforced to me while I was collaborating on a study of championship college ice hockey coaches.[21] When asked to reflect on how his team battled through challenges to

**Table 10.1 Suggested Program Evaluation Tools**

| Evaluation tool | What it measures | Source |
|---|---|---|
| Program evaluation questionnaire[20] (figure 10.4) | Experiences as an athlete, individual strengths and weaknesses, and role on the team | All athletes and coaches |
| Seniors' evaluation form[21] (figure 10.5) | Overall program quality, experience as an athlete, and suggestions for program improvements | Departing senior athletes |
| Program climate rating scale[22] (figure 10.6) | Coaches' ability to inspire and nurture athlete engagement | All coaches and program support staff |
| Social cohesion evaluation[22] (figure 10.7) | Quality of athlete and team relationships, team trust and togetherness | All coaches and athletes |
| Emotional intelligence evaluation[23] (figure 10.8) | Ability to control emotions and build quality connections with others | All coaches and athletes |
| Readiness to repeat success evaluation[22] (figure 10.9) | Readiness to repeat a winning or championship season | All coaches |
| Athlete skill evaluation[7] (figure 10.10) | Athlete technical, physical, mental, and sportsmanship skills | All athletes and coaches |
| Athlete general performance evaluation[24] (figure 10.11) | 14 performance dimensions (motivation, discipline, coachability, leadership, etc.) | All athletes |
| Championship performance template—volleyball[25] (figure 10.12) | Team-level meaningful competition performance indicators | All coaches |
| Fundamental performance skills checklist—swimming[26] (figure 10.13) | Fundamental skills required by individual athletes | All coaches |
| Fundamental performance skills checklist—baseball infielders[27] (figure 10.14) | Fundamental skills required by individual athletes for specific positions on a team | All coaches |
| Competition performance chart—baseball pitcher[27] (figure 10.15) | Individual athlete competition performance | All coaches |
| Coach global self-evaluation[7] (figure 10.16) | Coaches' strengths and weaknesses | All coaches |
| Practice coaching evaluation checklist (figure 10.17) | Quality of coaching during practice sessions | All coaches or athletics director |
| Competition coaching evaluation checklist (figure 10.18) | Quality of coaching during competitions | All coaches or athletics director |

**Table 10.2 Triggers of Optimal Performance Experiences**

| Trigger | Description |
|---|---|
| Serious concentration | Focused and sustained efforts on improving performance. |
| Shared, clear goals | Program and season goals are agreed on by all members of the team. |
| Good communication | Regular and honest feedback. |
| Equal participation | Everyone feels like a valued contributor to program success. |
| Element of risk | High standards with clear and measurable consequences. |
| Familiarity | Shared understanding of what the group is trying to accomplish and what it takes to achieve the common goals. |
| Blending egos | Humility and commitment to serving others. |
| Sense of control | Everyone feels supported and encouraged to share opinions and suggestions for how to improve performance. |
| Close listening | Mindfulness and empathy for concerns and needs of others. |
| Always say yes | Openness to novel ideas and suggestions from others. |

win the national championship, one of the coaches revealed that ultimately it was "our culture that helped us win the game."

Creating a culture of excellence requires diligent work to ensure that athletes and coaches are constantly being challenged to improve in a supportive atmosphere. The likelihood of achieving a successful season will be greatly increased by paying attention to behaviors and practices that are known to trigger optimal performance experiences. In his review of the science behind ultimate human performance, Steven Kotler identified 10 triggers of optimal performance experiences (see table 10.2).[22]

The remainder of this section describes evaluation tools that can be used to assess the presence of these types of optimal performance triggers.

## *Program Evaluation Questionnaire*

As a rule, any amount of end-of-season evaluation is better than none at all. Highly sophisticated and complex program evaluation systems will not be helpful if they take too long to complete and result in mounds of information that are difficult to analyze. A simple program evaluation questionnaire such as the one created by award-winning athletics director Sheri Stice will provide a quick check on athlete and coaching staff perceptions of individual and team performance (see figure 10.4).[23]

Another informal evaluation strategy for measuring the overall quality of the season is to meet as a coaching staff and review key aspects of the program. Successful high school cross country running coach Pat Tyson, who coached his teams to 12 state championships and helped dozens of athletes gain college entrance, recommends taking the coaching staff out for an end-of-season dinner.[24] At the outing coach Tyson would pose a series of questions

## Figure 10.4 Sample Program Evaluation Questionnaire

Name ______________________ Position ______________________

Desired change ______________________

**Personal**

1. What is one thing you like best about the program?
2. What is one thing you liked least about the program?
3. How can we improve team chemistry? Did you feel like a part of the team?
4. What is one relationship you are having a tough time with?

**Sport Related**

1. Provide two of your strongest points.
2. Provide two areas where you need to improve.
3. What role do you see yourself playing on this team next year?

**Staff Feedback (completed by coach)**

1. This is your best attribute as a team member.
2. This is an area I think you need improvement in as a team member.
3. Here is what you need to do to fulfill your role.
4. How I see you right now as a player and why.

**Rank yourself in each of the following three areas:**

1. Academics
2. Physical habits and conditioning
3. Team member

Reprinted, by permission, from S. Stice, 2013, Student-athlete development. In *NIAA's guide to interscholastic athletic administration*, edited by M.L. Blackburn, E. Forsyth, J.R. Olson, and B. Whitehead for the National Interscholastic Athletic Administrators Association (Champaign, IL: Human Kinetics), 91.

to his coaching staff aimed at getting their thoughts on the season, such as the following:(p. 146)

- What went right?
- Did the team buy into the vision we laid out before them in August?
- Did the team peak at the end of the year and perform up to expectations?
- Did a bad attitude corrupt the unity of the team?
- Was the season plagued by injuries or illness?
- Did we choose the right hotel to stay in on our overnight trip to a midseason invitational?
- Was our schedule too ambitious? Was it too easy?

### *Seniors' End-of-Season Evaluation Form*

Departing senior athletes are an extremely valuable source of evaluation information. Because of the amount of time spent in the program and with the coaches, these athletes have the best vantage point for providing feedback on the overall quality of the program experience. Furthermore, they may give the most honest and open evaluation because they no longer have any concern for how their feedback might affect their position on the team. The list of evaluation questions for departing seniors in high school or college sport settings created by Michael and Ralph Sabock[25] provides a good template for creating your own athlete feedback form (see figure 10.5).

### *Athlete-Centered Program Climate Evaluation*

Creating an athlete-centered motivational climate is an effective way to build trust and quality coach-athlete relationships. Beswick[26] has created a two-point rating scale that coaches can use to self-evaluate how well they believe they were able to create an inspiring and engaging athlete-centered environment (see figure 10.6). Although designed for use by coaches, assistant coaches and perhaps other members of a program support staff such as equipment and facilities managers or administrators could complete the self-evaluation. Collectively, this feedback will provide a vivid portrait of how well the program staff is able to create and nurture the right type of learning and performance environment for the athletes.

### *Team Cohesion Evaluation*

Another way to measure the quality of the program climate is by assessing how well athletes and coaches support each other. Often referred to as social cohesion, this ingredient is important for building programs of excellence. Athletes and teams will never reach their performance potential if they feel unsupported or, even worse, feel as if they can't trust teammates or coaches. The social cohesion checklist created by Beswick[26] is a practical tool for self-assessing the quality of athlete and team relationships, team trust, and overall togetherness (see figure 10.7).

### *Emotional Intelligence Evaluation*

The ability to recognize and control emotions and respond effectively to the emotions of others is an important skill for both coaches and athletes. Widely referred to as emotional intelligence, this ability can be improved with practice and has been shown to have a positive effect on performance across a wide range of settings including sport.[27] For example, a study with Olympic-level athletes showed that an athlete's ability to read and use emotions had a direct connection to his or her performance at the Olympic Games.[28]

Numerous tools have been created for measuring emotional intelligence, but the most popular ones can take 40 minutes to complete and are expensive to purchase. A practical alternative for coaches is a quick 16-question emotional intelligence tool (see figure 10.8). This evaluation tool was adapted from the Wong and Law Emotional Intelligence Scale (WLEIS).[29, 30]

A five-point response scale is used, and a higher score suggests a higher level of emotional intelligence. The purpose of this tool is to provide coaches with a general sense of how well their athletes or members of their coaching or support staff, including themselves, are able to control emotions and connect with other

## Figure 10.5 Seniors' End-of-Season Evaluation Form

### Seniors' Evaluation

In order to improve our program, it is important to take stock of our accomplishments, shortcomings, and objectives. We, as a coaching staff, will do this, but another valuable source of information is the seniors on the squad, whom we are now asking to help us. Will you please take the time to give us your frank and honest views and ideas? We'd really appreciate it. You need not sign this form.

Thank you,
Coach

1. Did anything happen during the season to make you upset with your coaches, teammates, opponents, teachers, administration, or student body?
2. Did you feel that you were ever called upon to do something for which you were not properly prepared?
3. List any personal criticisms that you think will be helpful to our team for the future.
4. Did you really enjoy the season? Why?
5. Did you hear any comments by parents, fans, or others about the games or players that you feel would be helpful to the team or coaches?
6. How can we, as coaches, help our players perform better?
7. What was your opinion about our scouting reports? [If appropriate to your sport]
8. How did you feel about squad morale?
9. How can we improve our total program?
10. What do you think of our video sessions?
11. Are there any ways you feel we could better use our facilities?
12. Do you have any ideas regarding our total organization?
13. What do you think of our promotional ideas and activities? Do you have any other ideas along these lines?
14. What are your feelings about our training room procedures?
15. What do you think about the way we planned and organized practices?
16. Regarding our younger team members: Who do you feel will be our best players next year?
17. Were there any players on the squad who you feel were playing out of position, or who should have played more? Was there any player who you feel should have played ahead of someone else?
18. What is your opinion for or against special awards?
19. Do you feel you were given a fair chance to show your ability?
20. What do you think about the scout team?
21. Do you think you were well prepared to compete?
22. What are your views on electing captains for the season?
23. List any other points or ideas you feel would be helpful.

Thanks a lot for taking the time to help us evaluate our program. It has been a pleasure having you on the team.

## Figure 10.6 Program Climate Rating Scale

| | We do this well | We need to do better |
|---|---|---|
| Our players feel secure and are looked after. | | |
| Our team is a community with togetherness. | | |
| We share winning and losing together. | | |
| We deal with setbacks well. | | |
| The atmosphere is usually calm and informal. | | |
| Players enjoy coming to practice. | | |
| Everything is planned and prepared. | | |
| There is purpose in everything we do. | | |
| Our players are offered the best teaching. | | |
| We treat mistakes as part of learning. | | |
| Coaches listen as well as speak. | | |
| Players' feelings are important to us. | | |
| We balance praise and criticism well. | | |
| We know when to work and when to rest. | | |
| We praise in public and criticize in private. | | |
| We focus on excellence, not just results. | | |
| Communication is everything to us. | | |
| Our players accept their responsibilities. | | |
| Our players understand their jobs on the field. | | |
| Our players understand others' roles. | | |
| Everyone is clear on our targets. | | |
| Practice is varied, challenging, and fun. | | |
| The head coach is inspirational. | | |
| Our players can get all the help they want. | | |
| Bad news is dealt with honesty, face to face. | | |
| Achievements are celebrated and rewarded. | | |

Reprinted, by permission, from B. Beswick, 2016, *One goal: The mindset of winning soccer teams* (Champaign, IL: Human Kinetics), 14.

## Figure 10.7 Social Cohesion Evaluation

Assess, as a coaching staff, how well your team scores on the following situations.

| Situation | True | Some truth | False |
|---|---|---|---|
| Players enjoy playing for our team. | | | |
| Very few players willingly leave our team. | | | |
| We have a high level of communication. | | | |
| It's hard work, but fun to be on our team. | | | |
| Our team is never bored. | | | |
| Players on our team grow as people. | | | |
| Ethnic and cultural differences are respected on our team. | | | |
| Players respect, appreciate, and encourage each other. | | | |
| We have stars but no isolates. | | | |
| We have a good record of developing player leadership. | | | |
| Honesty and trust are key words for us. | | | |
| We deal quickly with players who disrupt team harmony. | | | |
| Setbacks and defeats do not undermine morale. | | | |
| We surround our players with good, positive adults. | | | |
| Parents are part of the solution, not the problem. | | | |
| Togetherness is a key theme in our meetings. | | | |
| Relationships between coaches are positive and respectful. | | | |

The higher the number of true scores is, the more the team can be considered socially cohesive. A significant number of false answers gives the coach a signal that action is needed.

## Figure 10.8 Emotional Intelligence Questionnaire for Coaches and Athletes

*Directions:* Think about how you normally feel during practices and competitions and respond to the following statements.

| Question | Strongly disagree | | | | Strongly agree |
|---|---|---|---|---|---|
| 1. I am always aware of the emotions I am feeling. | 1 | 2 | 3 | 4 | 5 |
| 2. I understand why I am feeling these emotions when they occur. | 1 | 2 | 3 | 4 | 5 |
| 3. I can sense what other people around me are feeling. | 1 | 2 | 3 | 4 | 5 |
| 4. I understand why other people around me are feeling certain emotions. | 1 | 2 | 3 | 4 | 5 |
| 5. I know how to respond effectively to other people's emotions. | 1 | 2 | 3 | 4 | 5 |
| 6. I am confident in my ability to use my own emotions to reach my goals. | 1 | 2 | 3 | 4 | 5 |
| 7. I always encourage myself to try my best. | 1 | 2 | 3 | 4 | 5 |
| 8. I am capable of controlling my emotions to handle difficult situations. | 1 | 2 | 3 | 4 | 5 |
| 9. I can calm down quickly when I'm angry. | 1 | 2 | 3 | 4 | 5 |

Adapted from C.S. Wong and K.S. Law, 2002, "The effects of leader and follower emotional intelligence on performance and attitude: An exploratory study," *The Leadership Quarterly* 13(3): 243-274.

people in the sport program. Self-awareness and control of emotions are important skills for building an environment of open communication and trust.

### *Readiness to Repeat Success Evaluation*

By following the coaching principles described in this book and having some good fortune, coaches and athletes will put themselves in a position to experience those magical seasons that end with a championship or a near miss. On those occasions, coaches must be ready to evaluate their readiness to repeat the success. End-of-season evaluation is just as important following a championship season as it is after a losing season. Dan Gable, one of the most successful college coaches of all time, learned this lesson the hard way when midway through his coaching career "with a string of nine NCAA titles under my belt, I said, 'If it's not broken, why fix it?' The answer became evident when that string of championships was broken."[31 (p. 193)]

Beswick[26] has created a 15-question checklist for coaches to rate their readiness to repeat in the following season (see figure 10.9). Notice that many of the questions address the coach's and team's ability to raise the bar, not just maintain

**Figure 10.9 Readiness to Repeat Success Evaluation**

| | Yes | Somewhat | No |
|---|---|---|---|
| 1. Have we improved our work ethic? | | | |
| 2. Is the team as fit as they can be? | | | |
| 3. Have we increased intensity and raised the level of internal competition? | | | |
| 4. Have we raised quality by challenging players to be better? | | | |
| 5. Have we given good enough feedback? | | | |
| 6. Have we toughened responsibility and accountability? | | | |
| 7. Have we set more complex training problems to make the team smarter? | | | |
| 8. Do all the players understand the game plan? | | | |
| 9. Do all the players understand their jobs? | | | |
| 10. Can we be one of the best at set pieces? | | | |
| 11. Have we identified players to be on or off the bus? | | | |
| 12. Have we recruited well? | | | |
| 13. Have we managed injury prevention well? | | | |
| 14. Have we balanced stress and recovery? | | | |
| 15. Are we ready to win again? | | | |



the current level of performance. Although created specifically for soccer (see question 10), the questions are general enough to be applicable to almost any sport.

## Practice and Performance Assessments

The most obvious indicator of athlete and program success is observable performance statistics. Coaches typically record a wide array of competition statistics such as runs scored (baseball, softball), race times (swimming, cross country running), or completion percentages (passing in football or shooting in basketball).

In professional sport most teams now employ full-time staff who focus solely on collecting and analyzing performance statistics.[32] This increased emphasis on what is known as data analytics received immense attention after the release of *Moneyball*, the story of coach Billy Beane's innovative approach to using performance statistics to build a winning professional baseball team.[33]

Outside professional sport settings, however, coaches rarely have the resources, or the need, to use high-powered data analytic techniques to measure athlete competition performance. Also, athlete performance in practices must be assessed to provide a more comprehensive evaluation of athlete progress. The following is a list of practical tools and examples for evaluating athlete performance across both competitions and practices.

## *Athlete Skill Evaluation*

The surest way to get an accurate evaluation of an athlete's skill level is to test her or his ability to perform a skill. Ideally, coaches measure athlete skill level in the preseason to establish a baseline against which they can compare results of the same skill tests administered at the end of the season. Many proven tests are available for measuring athlete fitness and sport-related skills such as agility, balance, coordination, speed, flexibility, endurance, and strength. A complete presentation of these tests is beyond the purpose and scope of this chapter. Coaches can refer to free online resources such as Topend Sports[34] or review common measurement and evaluation texts[16] that provide thorough descriptions of hundreds of athlete skill tests.

Although recommended, physical skill testing may not be practical in some sport settings because of time and equipment limitations. Furthermore, unlike physical skills, important soft skills such as attitude, character, and work ethic cannot be objectively measured by any test. A quick and practical alternative to evaluating athletes' skills is simply to rate them on their skill level.

The athlete skill evaluation tool prepared by Hammermeister[7] is one such example. This tool is used to rate athletes using a 1 to 5 scale (poor to excellent) for their general technical, mental, physical, and sportsmanship skills (see figure 10.10). Depending on the age and maturity of the athletes, besides completing their own rating of each athlete's ability, coaches may find it valuable to have athletes self-evaluate their ability using this evaluation tool. Coach and athlete results can then be compared, revealing potential areas of miscommunication or misunderstanding. For example, I have found that athletes often overrate their ability based on inflated views of their competence. Other athletes underrate their ability, which could be the result of low self-confidence.

## *Athlete General Performance Evaluation*

Successful coaches know that peer feedback is a valuable source of information that can serve as a powerful motivational force for improvement. Ideally, the end-of-season evaluation toolkit will include some type of peer evaluation tool. For example, Hall of Fame college soccer coach Anson Dorrance has each of his players grade their teammates on how well they model the team's core values (see chapter 1 of this book for examples of his team's core values). Coach Dorrance then presents a summary of the grades to each athlete during individual meetings. When discussing this evaluation strategy with me, coach Dorrance shared that "it is the BEST thing we have ever done for character development".

The most comprehensive self and peer end-of-season evaluation tool I have seen is the one created by Dr. Robert Brill and his colleagues while working with

## Figure 10.10 Athlete Skill Evaluation Tool

A coach's skill evaluation tool should include all the technical, tactical, physical, and psychological aspects of performance they consider to be vital to learning and performances. Coaches may also use this tool to evaluate their athletes on other behaviors that represent core values of the program such as sportsmanship.

Scale: 1 = Poor, 3 = Average; 5 = Excellent

| TECHNICAL | | | | | |
|---|---|---|---|---|---|
| Technical skills important to the sport and/or position | 1 | 2 | 3 | 4 | 5 |
| Tactical | 1 | 2 | 3 | 4 | 5 |
| Decision making | 1 | 2 | 3 | 4 | 5 |
| Understanding strategy | 1 | 2 | 3 | 4 | 5 |
| Self-evaluation of strengths and limitations | 1 | 2 | 3 | 4 | 5 |
| Recognition of opponents' strengths and limitations | 1 | 2 | 3 | 4 | 5 |
| **MENTAL** | | | | | |
| Motivation | 1 | 2 | 3 | 4 | 5 |
| Self-confidence | 1 | 2 | 3 | 4 | 5 |
| Concentration | 1 | 2 | 3 | 4 | 5 |
| Emotional control | 1 | 2 | 3 | 4 | 5 |
| Communication | 1 | 2 | 3 | 4 | 5 |
| Coachability | 1 | 2 | 3 | 4 | 5 |
| Leadership | 1 | 2 | 3 | 4 | 5 |
| **PHYSICAL** | | | | | |
| Speed | 1 | 2 | 3 | 4 | 5 |
| Strength | 1 | 2 | 3 | 4 | 5 |
| Flexibility | 1 | 2 | 3 | 4 | 5 |
| Endurance | 1 | 2 | 3 | 4 | 5 |
| Power | 1 | 2 | 3 | 4 | 5 |
| Balance | 1 | 2 | 3 | 4 | 5 |
| **SPORTSMANSHIP—RESPECT AND CONCERN FOR** | | | | | |
| Rules | 1 | 2 | 3 | 4 | 5 |
| Officials | 1 | 2 | 3 | 4 | 5 |
| Opponents | 1 | 2 | 3 | 4 | 5 |
| Teammates | 1 | 2 | 3 | 4 | 5 |
| Coaching staff | 1 | 2 | 3 | 4 | 5 |

Reprinted, by permission, from J.J. Hammermeister, 2010, *Cornerstones of coaching: The building blocks for sport coaches and teams* (Traverse City, MI: Cooper Publishing), 201.

a men's college soccer team.[24] Athletes rate themselves and their teammates on 14 performance dimensions. One of the unique strengths of this evaluation tool is that each of the 14 performance dimensions includes a detailed description of athlete behaviors (see table 10.3). This ensures the ratings are based on observable actions. Furthermore, the dimensions and behaviors were generated by the athletes themselves with guidance from coaches and the researchers.

Once all the questionnaires are scored, coaches show each athlete how perceptions of their own behavior compare to how their teammates perceive their performance. It was found that using the tool this way provided a reality check for athletes while also increasing their motivation to perform better. Examples of how athlete behaviors are scored for three of the dimensions are provided as a guide for creating an evaluation tool that is meaningful with your own team (see figure 10.11*a-c*).

## Practice and Competition Statistics

The key to meaningful and efficient evaluation of athlete performance across practices and competitions is first to identify the most important performance indicators. Of course, these markers will vary widely across sport and levels of competition, requiring coaches to reflect carefully on the skills and behaviors that most directly contribute to successful performance in their sport. When working with coaches I always encourage them to spend time in the preseason to create a list of 5 to 10 key performance indicators that can be evaluated. Some examples of performance indicators identified by successful coaches, and the way in which they are used as part of a quality program evaluation system, are shared in this section. Coaches can use these examples to create their own sport-specific evaluation tools.

Renowned volleyball coach Mike Hebert, a former national Coach of the Year and recipient of USA Volleyball's All-Time Great Volleyball Coaches award, identified meaningful performance indicators by comparing his team with the championship finalists from the previous season. Using key volleyball performance indicators such as kills, attack errors, and kill efficiency, each season he created a championship template for evaluating team performance (see figure 10.12).[36]

The championship template gave coach Hebert and his athletes the right evaluation data for identifying high-impact performance gaps. For example, using the 2009 championship template, they determined that the team would have to improve their offensive efficiency substantially to contend for a national championship. Practices in the following season were then designed to close those performance gaps. Coach Hebert believed that the championship template evaluation strategy was one of the key reasons that his teams reached the national championship semifinals (Final Four) five times.

Besides evaluating overall team performance statistics, successful coaches create evaluation tools that can be used to assess individual athlete performance during practices and competitions. The first step in creating a meaningful performance evaluation for individual athletes is to generate a list of fundamental performance skills needed to succeed in the sport.

Stephan Widmer, who has coached swimmers to multiple Olympic and world championship gold medals as well as nearly two dozen world records, is an

**Table 10.3 General Performance Dimensions Used for Athlete Self and Teammate Evaluation**

| Dimension | Description |
|---|---|
| Discipline | Ability to properly control one's impulses, emotions, desires, and behavior; ability to avoid giving in to instant gratification or past success, and therefore not continuing to work and get better. |
| Mental Toughness | Degree to which a player can cope with the many demands such as competition, training, lifestyle, placed on them as an athlete; remaining determined, focused, confident, resilient, and in control under pressure throughout the year on and off the field. |
| Intrinsic Standards | The degree to which a player sets their own high standards; rather than having to have the coach, captain or someone else set standards. |
| Coachability | The ability to transfer positive attitude, skill enhancement, and sense of team chemistry demonstrated in practice to actual game situations. |
| Positive Practice Transfer | The ability to transfer positive attitude, skill enhancement, and sense of team chemistry demonstrated in practice to actual game situations. |
| Motivation | General desire, passion or willingness to contribute an important piece to the team in order to optimize positive thinking and performance. |
| Selflessness | A player never expects anything in return for the deed, act, or accomplishment made; putting others ahead of himself. |
| Consistency | A player whose attitude, effort and performance remain at the same high level with little variation no matter the day/circumstance. Performance and effort does not vary greatly in quality over time. |
| Dependability | The degree that a person is very reliable and will put all time and efforts to help others and complete tasks they are asked to do. Be there for your teammate both on and off the field. Treat it like a family where mutual trust and respect are givens and important values. |
| Leadership | Ability to inspire/motivate others, and hold themselves and others accountable in a constructive manner; not afraid to speak out when it is needed and many times takes the initiative for change. |
| Fear of Failure | Excessively self-conscious about making a mistake or not achieving top performance; a player who is very negatively affected when there is no positive outcome. The player lacks composure under pressure. |
| Task Persistence | Ability to stick with something and persevere despite distractions, physical or emotional discomfort, or lack of immediate success. |
| Personality | The combination of emotional, attitudinal, and behavioral response patterns of an individual. Personalities tend to be positive or negative. |
| Team Chemistry | Fully committed and vested to the team's goals, rules and all it has to offer. This dimension includes many of the other dimensions, but accentuates contributing to the creation of team cohesion and morale. |

General Performance Dimensions used for Athlete Self and Teammate Evaluation

**Positive Practice Transfer**

The ability of a player to transfer positive attitude, skill enhancement, and sense of team chemistry demonstrated in practice to actual game situations.

**(1 or 2) A player at this level may:**

- Rationalize that practice does not matter since it is just practice. Then struggle on game day because of their bad habits.
- Allow status on the team and other outside forces to divert their attention from practice so that they do not have a sense of what to do in the game.

**(5) A player at this level may:**

- Get caught up in the intensity of the game and often forget how to execute set plays.
- For the most part, not adjust based on competition.
- Be lax in prep leading up to game just because the next game is a weak competitor.

**(8 or 9) A player at this level may:**

- Practice hard even if they are not a starter, practice harder with the idea that they can earn a starting spot.
- Approach practice with understanding that it is a critical requirement for game day success.
- Be able to consistently carry over what is learned (e.g, set plays or formations) and apply it in game situations.
- Tend to approach practice with the intensity of real game situations and does all they can to ensure that intensity carries over (and tries to exceed it) to the game day situation.

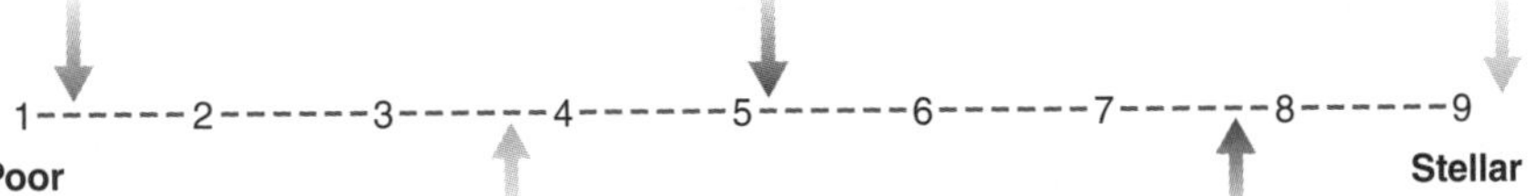


**(3 or 4) A player at this level may:**

- Approach practice with mediocre intensity, but struggles in games.
- Tend to dog it or slack off during practice; and then tries with limited success to get up their best in game sitautions.
- Modify drills to be fun and what they want it to be, rather than what the drill needs to be for game prep.

**(6 or 7) A player at this level may:**

- At practice before a game, does not let the fact that it is a physically easier practice bring down the intensity he will need tomorrow.
- Consistently approach practice and drills as if it is a real game situation.
- Focus and use information from scouting reports.

**Figure 10.11a** Sample behavior-based evaluation scales for athlete general performance: Positive practice transfer.

Reprinted by permission of Robert Brill, Fernando Cifuentes, and Logan Stano of Moravian College.

**Intrinsic Standards**

The degree to which a player sets their own high standards: rather than having the coach, captain, or someone else set their standards for them.

**(1 or 2) A player at this level may:**

- Set low goals and exhibits laziness and unwillingness to put forth effort.
- Behave in a way to suggest that they have virtually no standards or care about their manner of play.
- Be motivated solely as if playing was a required chore.
- Get easily discouraged when trying to reach goals; instead of working harder to acheive it, they adjust the goal downward.

**(5) A player at this level may:**

- Recognize their level of play, but need the coach or captain to set goals for them.
- Attempt to set goals, but the coach or captain must step in and help them set better more concrete and appropriate goals.

**(8 or 9) A player at this level may:**

- Not accept average or mediocre standards, and therefore set them higher, which makes them work hard for it. "Goals are a push."
- Show a hardworking, devoted work ethic toward getting things done the way they need to get done.
- Set a goal standard and encourage the team to embrace it as well.
- Consistently set an expectation for himself above current performance and holds himself accountable to that.

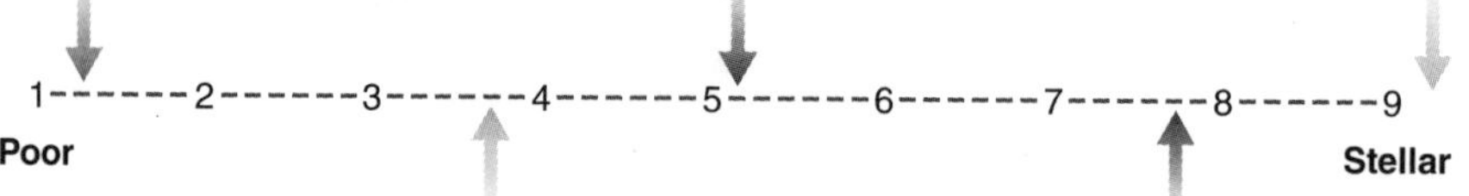


**(3 or 4) A player at this level may:**

- Tend to totally rely on the coach for information about their level of play.
- Be unable to embrace the passion to want to achieve a higher standard.
- Have the desire to win, but does not do what is needed to reach that level.
- Be committed to doing the bare minimum; motivated just enough to stay on the team and please the coach.
- Not push themselves beyond team goals.

**(6 or 7) A player at this level may:**

- Generate goals and be sure they align with team goals.
- Try to get better and set improvement goals that are directed by and aligned with the big game plan and what the team needs from them.

**Figure 10.11b** Sample behavior-based evaluation scales for athlete general performance: Intrinsic standards.

Reprinted by permission of Robert Brill, Fernando Cifuentes, and Logan Stano of Moravian College.

**Coachability**

The degree to which a player realizes and accepts that there are things he cannot do on his own: willingness to listen, learn, and accept constructive feedback with maturity from the coach: a player's trust that the coach is providing valuable information for his betterment as a player.

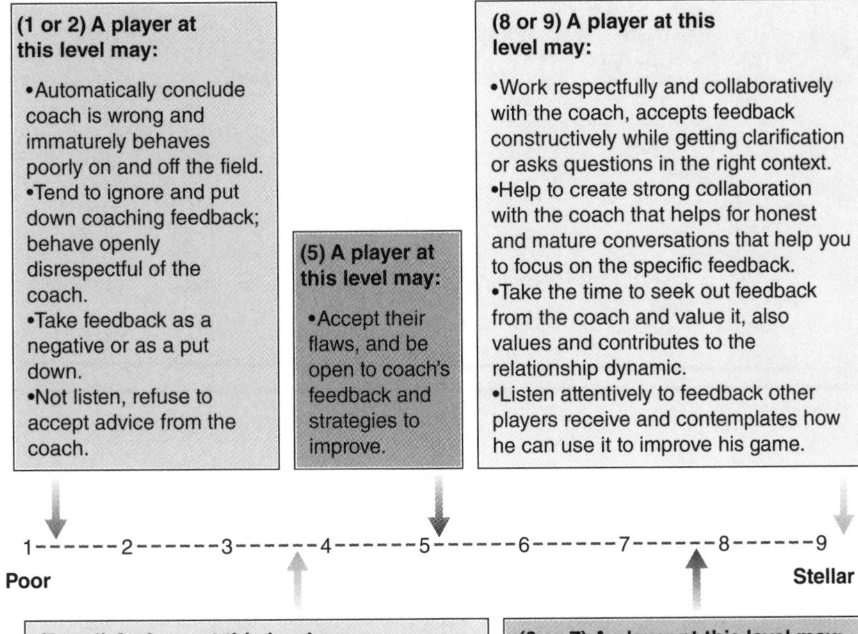


**(3 or 4) A player at this level may:**

- Tend to blame the coach more and take less responsibility when something goes wrong.
- Act as if they know more than the coach.
- Tend to listen to the coach (humor him) but does not take it seriously or apply advice.
- Tend to hold a grudge towards the coach and dwell on a conflict refusing to move on.
- Perform a minimum out of resentment—does just enough to get the coach off of their back.

**(6 or 7) A player at this level may:**

- Play any position and perform how the coach needs you to with commitment and best effort.
- Flexible based on the coach's needs.
- Take what the coach says and diligently apply it on the field.

**Figure 10.11c** Sample behavior-based evaluation scales for athlete general performance: Coachability.

Reprinted by permission of Robert Brill, Fernando Cifuentes, and Logan Stano of Moravian College.

## Figure 10.12 Championship Performance Template—College Volleyball

| School | Kills (K) | Attack errors (E) | Total attack attempts (TA) | Kill efficiency (K – E/TA = KEff) | E% (E/TA) | K% (K/TA) | Kills per set (K/S) |
|---|---|---|---|---|---|---|---|
| PSU | 1734 | 428 | 3352 | .390 | .128 | .517 | 14.9 |
| Stanford | 1731 | 454 | 4069 | .314 | .112 | .425 | 14.7 |
| Nebraska | 1714 | 590 | 4166 | .270 | .142 | .411 | 14.5 |
| Texas | 1719 | 447 | 3795 | .335 | .118 | .453 | 14.6 |
| Average | 1725 | 480 | 3846 | .324 | .125 | .449 | 14.7 |
| Minnesota | 1680 | 626 | 4512 | .234 | .139 | .372 | 10.6 |

Reprinted, by permission, from M. Hebert, 2014, *Thinking volleyball* (Champaign, IL: Human Kinetics), 43.

example of a highly successful coach who has built a program around a clear awareness of fundamental performance skills. Through careful examination of the demands of a typical swimming race, he identified 32 fundamental performance skills (see figure 10.13).[37] Notice that Coach Widmer took the added step of separating the fundamental performance skills into six race-specific parts, allowing for an even more focused approach to performance evaluation.

In sports that have multiple athlete positions, coaches will need to create position-specific fundamental performance skills checklists. For example, championship baseball coaches Pete Dunn and Bob Bennett created separate fundamental performance checklists for catchers, pitchers, infielders, first basemen, second basemen, third basemen, shortstops, outfielders, batters, baserunners, and bunters.[28] A summary of their checklist for infielders is provided as an example of the level of detail that successful coaches use to prepare fundamental performance skills checklists (see figure 10.14). After the required fundamental skills are identified, coaches can create evaluation tools that measure how well an athlete is able to perform the fundamental skills in competitions (either in practice scrimmages or live game situations). A sample performance chart created by Coaches Dunn and Bennett for pitchers is illustrated in figure 10.15.

## Coach Assessments

No end-of-season evaluation system would be complete without tools to assess the coach's own performance. Although a wide range of athlete performance variables are typically scrutinized, quality coaches understand that they too must systematically evaluate how well they executed their season plan.

Nick Saban, one of the most successful college football coaches of all time, cautions coaches on the pitfalls of missed opportunities to improve that come

## Figure 10.13 Fundamental Performance Skills Checklist—Swimming

| RACE PARTS AND COMPONENTS | |
|---|---|
| Start | State of readiness<br>Connected and well-balanced position<br>Hip action<br>Push-off angle<br>Entry in the water<br>Start and turn times |
| Underwater | Streamlined position<br>Underwater speed (start)<br>Breakout timing (first stroke)<br>Break surfacing skill and angle<br>Maintaining streamlined position |
| Surface swimming | Racing analysis and model<br>Specific distance per stroke<br>Specific stroke count<br>Specific stroke rate<br>Race pace (sprint to distance)<br>Front and back end speed |
| Turn | Approach and maintenance of velocity<br>Rotation skill (technique and position)<br>Anticipation of push-off<br>Push-off and streamline posture<br>Underwater speed (turn)<br>Breaking surfacing skill and angle |
| Finish | Approach to wall<br>Speed maintenance<br>Anticipation to wall<br>Timing of last stroke<br>Maintaining streamlined position |
| Self-management | Recovery skills<br>Mentally entering the race zone<br>Race resilience<br>Learning from past performances |

## Figure 10.14 Fundamental Performance Skills Checklist—Baseball Infielders

- ☐ Stance (feet and hand positions)
- ☐ Readiness
- ☐ Position for fielding ground ball (head down, eyes on ball, knees bent, low body, low glove)
- ☐ Footwork (coming in, fielding high hopper)
- ☐ Throwing (grip, rotation, receiving position of hands, throwing from different positions, relays)
- ☐ Tag plays
- ☐ Double plays (footwork, throws, when not to complete double play by way of first base)
- ☐ Infield procedures
- ☐ Signals from catcher (relay to outfielders)
- ☐ Pop flies (communication, leadership, elements, situations)
- ☐ Taking charge of plays
- ☐ Attitude on receiving throws
- ☐ Attitude toward ground balls
- ☐ Watching man tag base
- ☐ Talking to pitcher



from regular evaluation of their own performance:[39] "Remember that success is never final and failure is never fatal"[(p. 69)] and "Learning never ends. Knowledge is power."[(p. 176)] Formal end-of-season coach evaluation provides coaches with the foundation for building knowledge and learning how to coach better every season.

### *Coaching Global Self-Evaluation*

Tools used to evaluate coach effectiveness should be based on clearly outlined behavioral and performance expectations set forth in the preseason. Some coach expectations will likely be unique to each setting, such as dress code or administrative duties, and these should be included in the coach evaluation tool. A good place to start when developing a coach evaluation tool is to refer to national[10] and international standards[40] for sport coaches. These resources, prepared by the world's leading coaching scientists and coach educators, outline expectations against which a coach's performance can be measured.

An example of a coach self-evaluation tool structured around the national standards for coaches in the United States is illustrated in figure 10.16.[7] The tool is used for the coach to self-rate how well they modeled behaviors related to the national standards, such as ensuring athlete safety and communicating effectively with athletes. When applicable, each member of a coaching staff should complete this type of self-evaluation. With some minor revisions in how the statements are worded (change "I" to "The coach"), this type of coach evaluation could be completed by an athletics director. Much as when both coach and athlete complete

## Figure 10.15 Competition Performance Chart—Baseball Pitchers

### Pitcher Performance Chart

Pitcher ______________________ Date ____________

| PITCH COUNT | | | | | | | | |
|---|---|---|---|---|---|---|---|---|
| | Fastballs | | Curveballs | | Changeups | | | |
| Total pitches | Number | Strikes | Number | Strikes | Number | Strikes | Strikes | Balls |
| 50 | 30 | 20 | 10 | 6 | 10 | 6 | 32 | 18 |
| Percentages | 65% | | 60% | | 60% | | 64% | 36% |

| FIRST-PITCH STRIKE | |
|---|---|
| Batters faced | First-pitch strike |
| 10 | 6 |

| HITS, WALKS, AND STRIKEOUTS | | |
|---|---|---|
| Hits | Base-on-balls | Strikes |
| 3 | 1 | 3 |

| PITCH VELOCITY | | | |
|---|---|---|---|
| Best fastball velocity | Average fastball velocity | Curveball velocity | Changeup velocity |
| 90 mph | 88 mph | 78 mph | 80 mph |

| ERRORS | |
|---|---|
| Physical errors | Mental errors |
| Threw wide to second base on start of 1-6-3 double play | Failed to back up third base on base hit to right field with runner on first |

Reprinted, by permission, from P. Dunn and B. Bennett, 2010, Evaluating practice sessions. In *Practice perfect baseball*, edited by B. Bennett (Champaign, IL: Human Kinetics), 225.

the same evaluation, the two evaluations can then be compared to illuminate any misperceptions about coaching ability or responsibilities.

### *Practice and Competition Coaching Evaluation*

Two of the primary functions of a coach are to design and run quality practices and manage competitions. Although measuring and assigning a score to these aspects of coaching is difficult, the most valuable way to assess these functions of a coach is to observe coaches during practices and competitions. For example, championship high school basketball coach Morgan Wooten recommends at the

## Figure 10.16 Coach Self-Evaluation

The purpose of this tool is to assist you in identifying the areas of coaching that you need to improve upon. Give yourself an honest rating under each category. Once you have completed the evaluation, total your score and see how you rate.

(1) Strongly Disagree (2) Disagree (3) Agree (4) Strongly Agree

| PHILOSOPHY AND ETHICS | | | | |
|---|---|---|---|---|
| I have an athlete centered philosophy | 1 | 2 | 3 | 4 |
| I emphasize improvement over winning | 1 | 2 | 3 | 4 |
| I teach responsible behavior and positive values of sport | 1 | 2 | 3 | 4 |
| I demonstrate and model ethical conduct | 1 | 2 | 3 | 4 |
| **SAFETY AND INJURY PREVENTION** | | | | |
| I show concern for the health and safety of all my athletes during practice and competition | 1 | 2 | 3 | 4 |
| I ensure my athletes only perform on safe facilities | 1 | 2 | 3 | 4 |
| I have the ability to treat minor injuries and exhibit prudent conduct when handling accidents or emergencies | 1 | 2 | 3 | 4 |
| I am aware of unsafe environmental conditions and do not allow my athletes to participate if conditions are too dangerous (e.g., hot, cold, lightning, etc.) | 1 | 2 | 3 | 4 |
| **ORGANIZATIONAL SKILLS** | | | | |
| I arrive on time | 1 | 2 | 3 | 4 |
| I dress appropriately | 1 | 2 | 3 | 4 |
| I always prepare a practice/training session plan with logical progressions | 1 | 2 | 3 | 4 |
| I keep good team records | 1 | 2 | 3 | 4 |
| **PHYSICAL CONDITIONING** | | | | |
| I base my athletes conditioning program on sound exercise physiology and biomechanical principles | 1 | 2 | 3 | 4 |
| I teach proper nutrition | 1 | 2 | 3 | 4 |
| I am an advocate for drug free sport | 1 | 2 | 3 | 4 |
| I do not allow my athletes to return to play following injury until they are fully ready and able | 1 | 2 | 3 | 4 |
| **INSTRUCTIONAL SKILLS** | | | | |
| I introduce skills clearly and accurately | 1 | 2 | 3 | 4 |
| I demonstrate skills properly and use correct techniques | 1 | 2 | 3 | 4 |
| I ensure that the activity is suitable for the age, experience, ability, and fitness level of each athlete | 1 | 2 | 3 | 4 |
| I encourage questions and create a non-threatening practice environment | 1 | 2 | 3 | 4 |

| MENTAL SKILLS | | | | |
|---|---|---|---|---|
| I know how to build confidence | 1 | 2 | 3 | 4 |
| I assist in the development of short and long term goals, for each athlete and for the team | 1 | 2 | 3 | 4 |
| I positively motivate my athletes | 1 | 2 | 3 | 4 |
| I help my athlete use positive self-talk | 1 | 2 | 3 | 4 |
| **COMMUNICATION SKILLS** | | | | |
| I am enthusiastic and positive | 1 | 2 | 3 | 4 |
| I am patient and tolerant | 1 | 2 | 3 | 4 |
| I am a good role model and set a positive example at all times | 1 | 2 | 3 | 4 |
| I use appropriate verbal and non-verbal communication | 1 | 2 | 3 | 4 |

Reprinted, by permission, from J.J. Hammermeister, 2010, *Cornerstones of coaching: The building blocks for sport coaches and teams* (Traverse City, MI: Cooper Publishing), 207.

end of the season watching film from at least 10 games with two questions in mind: "Is my team exhibiting the style of play that I want? Are they taking care of the three or four most important points I emphasized throughout the season?"[1 (p. 274)] Honest answers to these questions will help coaches identify potential communication or teaching gaps that need to be addressed in the following season.

Using the four features of quality practice design presented in chapter 7, together with practice observation recommendations from experienced athletics directors,[17] I have prepared a practice coaching evaluation checklist (see figure 10.17). Similarly, using competition coaching guidelines outlined in chapters 8 and 9, I have prepared a competition coaching evaluation checklist (see figure 10.18).

To get an accurate global assessment of coaching ability during practices and competitions, multiple observations should be made, spaced out across the season (early season, midseason, late season). Coaches can ask someone else, such as an athletics director or a mentor, to observe a few practice sessions, or they can videotape some practices and self-assess later. An increasingly common way for coaches to videotape themselves in action is to use a GoPro camera with a chest harness. Super Bowl champion coach Jon Gruden has prepared a coach's field guide to using the GoPro camera, including a short video example of how he used one while coaching a high school football practice.[41]

I have used this strategy multiple times with high school and college coaches to record their behaviors during practice sessions. Although the GoPro method could also be used during competition, the coach may think it is too obtrusive. Generally, when recording coaches during competitions, I have set up a video camera out of the way of the coach and athletes, and the coach has worn a wireless microphone. I encourage coaches to experiment with both videotaping options to determine which strategy is most practical for their particular setting.

## Figure 10.17 Practice Coaching Evaluation Checklist

### Set challenging and specific practice goals.

☐ Were practice goals shared with the athletes at or before the start of practice?

☐ Were practice activities demanding yet attainable for most athletes?

☐ Were athletes told why they were doing each activity before they started it?

☐ Were athletes given feedback on their practice performance and effort?

Observer comments: ____________________________________________

### Keep athletes physically and mentally active throughout practice.

☐ Was practice the right length to sustain athlete focus and energy (no more than two hours)?

☐ Did the coach arrive with a detailed written practice plan for the session?

☐ Was practice space being used to the best advantage?

☐ Was transition time between activities kept to a minimum?

☐ Did the coach end practice with a fun, positive activity?

Observer comments: ____________________________________________

### Give athletes choices and ask them for input on practice design.

☐ Were a few minutes set aside for free play or athlete-directed practice?

☐ Were athletes given some choice of activities in the practice?

☐ Was the coach open to allowing athletes to perform skills in ways that felt right to them?

Observer comments: ____________________________________________

### Create competitive game-like practice activities.

☐ Were athletes required to perform some activities under competition-like pressure?

☐ Were all athletes physically active and on task most of the time?

☐ Did the coach provide sufficient and clear teaching cues?

Observer comments: ____________________________________________

## Figure 10.18 Competition Coaching Evaluation Checklist

### Precompetition readiness

- ☐ Was sufficient time set aside for on-site warm-up (aerobic, stretches, technical skills)?
- ☐ Did the pregame message match emotional needs of athletes and connect to core values?

Observer comments: ______________________________

______________________________

______________________________

______________________________

______________________________

### Competition management

- ☐ Did the coach prepare a list of checkpoints (technical, tactical, physical, and mental cues)?
- ☐ Did the coach make tactical adjustments at appropriate times to control momentum?
- ☐ Did the coach give clear and concise instructions when speaking to athletes?
- ☐ Did the coach provide frequent encouragement and positive reinforcement to all athletes?
- ☐ Did the coach demonstrate emotional control at all times during the competition?

Observer comments: ______________________________

______________________________

______________________________

______________________________

______________________________

### Postcompetition debriefing and closure

- ☐ Did the coach and athletes congratulate opponents and thank officials?
- ☐ Was the competition area left clean (bench, sideline, warm-up area, and so on)?
- ☐ Was model behavior and effort recognized in the coach's postcompetition message?
- ☐ Were athletes given an opportunity to address their teammates and share their competition reflections?
- ☐ Were athletes reminded about the upcoming practice or competition schedule?
- ☐ Did the coach check on individual athlete's postcompetition needs?
- ☐ Did the coach attend to required administrative duties?

Observer comments: ______________________________

______________________________

______________________________

______________________________

______________________________

From W. Gilbert, 2017, *Coaching better every season: A year-round system for athlete development and program success* (Champaign, IL: Human Kinetics).

The completed practice coaching and competition coaching evaluation checklists can be reviewed at the end of the season to identify areas of strength as well as areas in need of improvement. Because of the messiness of coaching, the evaluation checklists are not designed to produce a score or grade. We all know that a coach may have a thoroughly prepared practice or competition plan and then have to adjust because of unforeseen circumstances in the midst of action. Furthermore, the practice or competition context will greatly influence how a coach approaches a practice or competition (time of season, events that occurred just before the practice or competition, team dynamics, and so on). Therefore, practice and competition coaching evaluation checklists should be used as a way to collect direct observations that will facilitate an evidence-based and meaningful end-of-season discussion.

## APPLYING A QUALITY PROGRAM EVALUATION SYSTEM

Armed with a toolkit of potential end-of-season evaluation strategies, you are ready to create a program evaluation system that is most meaningful and practical for you and your athletes. In the remainder of this chapter, I share an example of a comprehensive end-of-season program evaluation system that an award-winning high school athletics director and I tested over a period of five years with 23 different sports.

The program evaluation system is built around the core values that underpin the school's sport programs. As shared earlier in chapter 1, four core values guide coaching and the sport programs at this high school:

- Participate: We create sport programs that are accessible and inclusive to all.
- Retain: We create sport programs that inspire participants to continue their sport participation.
- Engage: We create sport programs that athletes enjoy and that result in skill development.
- Compete: We develop consistently competitive sport programs and student-athletes.

Using a combination of enrollment and performance statistics along with student-athlete feedback questionnaires, we are able to obtain an evidence-based overview of how well each sport program is performing in relation to the four core values. The school's football program is used to illustrate how the end-of-season evaluation system works.

Points are earned specific to each of the core values, and an overall grade is reported on an end-of-season scorecard for each sport (see figure 10.19). Each sport program can earn up to two potential points toward their grade for each of the core values. The points are calculated based on the data collected to evaluate each of the core values. Note that the football program earned more than two points on one of the core value indicators for 2015 (participation) because they exceeded their program targets in that area.

## Figure 10.19 End-of-Season Program Scorecard for Football

| Core Values | 2014 | 2015 |
|---|---|---|
| *Participation:* Are we meeting our roster targets for all teams? | 1.47 | 2.12 |
| *Retention:* Are we inspiring athletes to return the following season? | 1.92 | 1.79 |
| *Engagement:* Do athletes enjoy the experience and feel they are improving? | 1.67 | 1.74 |
| *Competitiveness:* Is the team competitive in their league? | 1.73 | 1.87 |
| | 6.79 | 7.52 |
| | Advanced | Exceptional |

| Point Scale | |
|---|---|
| 7.2-8.0 | Exceptional |
| 6.4-7.1 | Advanced |
| 5.6-6.3 | Proficient |
| 4.8-5.5 | Underperforming |
| 0.0-4.7 | Unsatisfactory |

An eight-point rating scale is used, ranging from unsatisfactory to exceptional, to describe the health of each sport program. This eight-point scale was selected because it aligns with how other curriculum areas and teachers are evaluated in this school. Each of the core values is weighted equally in the evaluation (25 percent or two points on the eight-point scale).

In the football example, end-of-season evaluation results are shown for the past two seasons to illustrate how we use the system to identify trends related to program strengths and gaps. Each year the evaluation results are added to the program scorecard to allow analysis of long-term trends.

When comparing 2015 with 2014, the football program overall improved from "advanced" to "exceptional." The evaluation data show that the coach and the program made great strides in increasing participation (more student-athletes participating in football), showed improvements in the quality of the student-athlete experience (engagement), and were more competitive on the field. On the other hand, fewer student-athletes returned to football in 2015. Although still a good result (1.79 / 2.0), this area should be reviewed by the athletics director and the coach to determine why the score dropped.

A quick look at how the score is calculated for each of the core values illustrates how the evaluation data are collected and how we have approached the evaluation process. The end-of-season participation score is a combination of the total number of athletes in the program plus the number of freshman (first-year) athletes in the program (see figure 10.20).

## Figure 10.20 End-of-Season Participation Data for High School Football Program

| Year | TOTAL PARTICIPANTS | | | | FRESHMAN PARTICIPANTS | | | | Scorecard points |
|---|---|---|---|---|---|---|---|---|---|
| | Ideal | Actual | PR | Points | Ideal | Actual | PR | Points | |
| 2014 | 120 | 101 | 84% | 0.84 | 40 | 25 | 63% | 0.63 | 1.47 |
| 2015 | 120 | 119 | 99% | 0.99 | 40 | 34 | 85% | 0.85 | 2.12 |

PR (participation rate) = (Actual participants / Ideal participants) × 100

An ideal participation target is set in the preseason for total and freshman participants, in this case 120 and 40. A participation rate (PR) is then calculated as a ratio of the actual number of athletes who participated in football that season compared with the target. The PR is used to calculate scorecard points—up to one point for total participants plus up to one point for freshman participants (for a total of two scorecard points for participation).

When creating the program evaluation system, we determined that in this high school sport setting both total participation and freshman participation should be evaluated. Freshman participation serves as a valuable indicator of the health of each sport program because it clearly shows how successful we are at recruiting student-athletes into each of our programs, which is critical for sustaining long-term program success.

The number of athletes who return to our program each year is referred to as our retention rate, which is calculated by dividing the actual number of returning athletes by the potential number of returning athletes. In 2015, for example, 76 football athletes from the previous season were still attending the school (see figure 10.21). Every one of these athletes could potentially return to the football team.

After reviewing several years of data, we observed that the best sport programs in this setting (large inner-city school) typically retain around 75 percent of their potential returners. Therefore, we set an optimal retention rate of 75 percent. Of course, we encourage and work with each coach to strive to retain 100 percent of

## Figure 10.21 End-of-Season Retention Data for High School Football Program

| Year | Potential returners | Actual returners | Retention rate | Scorecard points |
|---|---|---|---|---|
| 2014 | 57 | 41 | 96% | 1.92 |
| 2015 | 76 | 51 | 89% | 1.79 |

Retention rate = (Actual returners / Potential returners) / 0.75

the potential returning athletes each season, but we also understand the importance of setting realistic targets that are practical in each setting. Over time, as the sport program culture continues to grow, the optimal retention rate will be raised.

Looking at the 2015 data again, notice that of the 76 potential returning football athletes, 51 returned that season. Using 75 percent as the target benchmark, the formula for calculating the retention rate is [(51 / 76) / .75], yielding a retention rate of 89 percent for 2015. Two scorecard points are allocated for retention rate. In 2015 the football program achieved 1.79 retention rate points (89 percent × 2 points), a slight decrease from the 2014 season.

To measure the quality of the sport experience for the athletes, we created an athlete feedback questionnaire. The questionnaire has undergone many revisions over the course of five years of testing. We started by testing a series of athlete questionnaires based on a comprehensive review of the literature for valid tools to measure the four Cs of athlete development (competence, confidence, connection, and character) described in the definition of effective coaching.[42–44] We supplemented these questionnaires with questions about coach behavior standards outlined by the school district and the coach's effectiveness in creating a quality sport environment (motivational climate).[45, 46]

The first few versions of the athlete feedback questionnaire included seven questionnaires, each with different rating scales, for a total of 75 questions. We quickly learned that although individually each questionnaire had been validated in research settings, the toolkit was not practical for efficiently collecting the evaluation information we needed. Based on feedback from athletes and coaches and repeated testing of different versions of the toolkit over several years, we were able to create a simplified version of the questionnaire that athletes can now complete in less than 10 minutes. This revised questionnaire still addresses each of the four Cs (competence, confidence, connection, character), coach behavior, and coaching climate, and it now uses a standardized rating scale of 1 to 7 for all questions (see figure 10.22).

Questions 1 through 3 address athletes' perceptions of competence, specifically how well they believe their coach helped them improve their physical, technical, and tactical sport competence the past season. Questions 4 through 6 ask the athletes to evaluate how well they demonstrated good character during the season. Athletes' perceptions of their self-confidence are covered in questions 7 and 8. Questions 9 through 11 require athletes to reflect on the strength of their relationship with their coach (athlete-coach connection), whereas questions 12 through 14 shed light on team connectedness (e.g., cohesion and group trust). General coaching behaviors and the coach's ability to create a positive and productive environment for athlete development are addressed in questions 15 through 22.

The final five to seven questions relate to sport-specific athlete skill development (competence). In the preseason each coach is asked to identify the main five to seven sport skills critical to athlete and team success that should be emphasized in practices throughout the season. Examples of these types of sport-specific skills include hitting (baseball and softball), blocking (football), passing (water polo), serving (tennis), putting (golf), dribbling (basketball), pacing (cross country), and shooting (soccer).

## Figure 10.22 End-of-Season Athlete Engagement Questionnaire

*Sport:* ______________________________

*Level:* (please circle one) Freshman JV Varsity

You are being asked to answer some questions about your sport experience this past season at Fresno High School. These questionnaires will be used to help us learn more about your development as a student-athlete at Fresno High School.

There are no right or wrong answers. Please respond truthfully about how you feel about each of the questions specific to this season of sport participation and your head coach. Circle the number that best corresponds to your perceptions.

For the first three questions, rate how well you think your coach prepared you to meet the demands of your sport this past season.

| | **Not prepared at all** | | **Somewhat prepared** | | | **Very well prepared** | |
|---|---|---|---|---|---|---|---|
| 1. How well do you think your coach prepared you to meet the physical demands of your sport? | 1 | 2 | 3 | 4 | 5 | 6 | 7 |
| 2. How well do you think your coach prepared you to meet the technical skill demands of your sport? | 1 | 2 | 3 | 4 | 5 | 6 | 7 |
| 3. How well do you think your coach prepared you to use the correct strategy in different games or competitive situations? | 1 | 2 | 3 | 4 | 5 | 6 | 7 |

Below is a list of behaviors likely to happen during competitions. Please think about your experiences while playing your sport. Circle the number that best represents your behavior this past season in this sport.

| | **Never** | | | **Sometimes** | | | **Always** |
|---|---|---|---|---|---|---|---|
| 4. I encouraged a teammate. | 1 | 2 | 3 | 4 | 5 | 6 | 7 |
| 5. I responded appropriately after receiving a penalty. | 1 | 2 | 3 | 4 | 5 | 6 | 7 |
| 6. I treated opponent with respect. | 1 | 2 | 3 | 4 | 5 | 6 | 7 |

Read each statement and then circle the appropriate number to indicate how you generally feel while participating in your sport.

| | | | | | | | |
|---|---|---|---|---|---|---|---|
| 7. I am confident about performing well. | 1 | 2 | 3 | 4 | 5 | 6 | 7 |
| 8. I am confident of coming through under pressure. | 1 | 2 | 3 | 4 | 5 | 6 | 7 |
| 9. I feel committed to my coach. | 1 | 2 | 3 | 4 | 5 | 6 | 7 |
| 10. I trust my coach. | 1 | 2 | 3 | 4 | 5 | 6 | 7 |

| | Strongly disagree | | Neither agree or disagree | | | | Strongly agree |
|---|---|---|---|---|---|---|---|
| 11. I respect my coach. | 1 | 2 | 3 | 4 | 5 | 6 | 7 |
| 12. As a team, we all share the same commitment to our goals. | 1 | 2 | 3 | 4 | 5 | 6 | 7 |
| 13. As a team, we are united. | 1 | 2 | 3 | 4 | 5 | 6 | 7 |
| 14. My teammates support my efforts to improve my own performance. | 1 | 2 | 3 | 4 | 5 | 6 | 7 |
| 15. My coach made sure I really understood the goals of the team for the season. | 1 | 2 | 3 | 4 | 5 | 6 | 7 |
| 16. I feel good about the way my coach talked to me. | 1 | 2 | 3 | 4 | 5 | 6 | 7 |
| 17. I think that my coach cares about me as a person. | 1 | 2 | 3 | 4 | 5 | 6 | 7 |
| 18. My coach was fair and consistent with all athletes. | 1 | 2 | 3 | 4 | 5 | 6 | 7 |
| 19. My coach treated all players, parents, officials, fans, and fellow coaches with respect. | 1 | 2 | 3 | 4 | 5 | 6 | 7 |
| 20. My coach used appropriate language. | 1 | 2 | 3 | 4 | 5 | 6 | 7 |
| 21. My coach was willing and available to meet outside practices and games. | 1 | 2 | 3 | 4 | 5 | 6 | 7 |
| 22. My coach stressed academics and monitored grades and attendance. | 1 | 2 | 3 | 4 | 5 | 6 | 7 |

For the following questions rate how well you think your coach taught you to perform these specific skills this past season.

| | Strongly disagree | | Neither agree or disagree | | | | Strongly agree |
|---|---|---|---|---|---|---|---|
| **FUNDAMENTAL SKILL #1** | | | | | | | |
| 23. My coach taught me or helped improve my performance on this skill. | 1 | 2 | 3 | 4 | 5 | 6 | 7 |
| **FUNDAMENTAL SKILL #2** | | | | | | | |
| 24. My coach taught me or helped improve my performance on this skill. | 1 | 2 | 3 | 4 | 5 | 6 | 7 |
| **FUNDAMENTAL SKILL #3** | | | | | | | |
| 25. My coach taught me or helped improve my performance on this skill. | 1 | 2 | 3 | 4 | 5 | 6 | 7 |

*(continued)*

**Figure 10.22** *(continued)*

| | Strongly disagree | | Neither agree or disagree | | | | Strongly agree |
|---|---|---|---|---|---|---|---|
| **FUNDAMENTAL SKILL #4** | | | | | | | |
| 26. My coach taught me or helped improve my performance on this skill. | 1 | 2 | 3 | 4 | 5 | 6 | 7 |
| **FUNDAMENTAL SKILL #5** | | | | | | | |
| 27. My coach taught me or helped improve my performance on this skill. | 1 | 2 | 3 | 4 | 5 | 6 | 7 |
| **FUNDAMENTAL SKILL #6** | | | | | | | |
| 28. My coach taught me or helped improve my performance on this skill. | 1 | 2 | 3 | 4 | 5 | 6 | 7 |
| **FUNDAMENTAL SKILL #7** | | | | | | | |
| 29. My coach taught me or helped improve my performance on this skill. | 1 | 2 | 3 | 4 | 5 | 6 | 7 |

From W. Gilbert, 2017, *Coaching better every season: A year-round system for athlete development and program success* (Champaign, IL: Human Kinetics).

Immediately following the season, all athletes on a team complete the questionnaires, which are administered by the athletics director when the coach is not present. To encourage candid feedback, athletes do not write their names on the questionnaires. The questionnaire responses are then tabulated using a custom-designed spreadsheet (Microsoft Excel) we created that includes formulas that summarize the responses.

Borrowing from the standardized fitness testing (Fitnessgram)[47] that is mandated in many American schools, we use the concept of healthy target zones for measuring success with the athlete questionnaire scores. Every question on the questionnaire uses the same seven-point rating scale (1 being a very low or negative score, 4 being a neutral score, and 7 being a high or very positive score). As an athletics department we set our healthy target zone as 5 to 7 for each of the questions. A score of 5 to 7 indicates that the athlete had a positive experience in the sport during the past season. A composite engagement rate is then calculated based on the percentage of athlete responses that fall in the 5 to 7 range.

Two scorecard points are allocated for engagement rate. In 2015 the football program achieved 1.74 engagement rate points (87 percent × 2 points), a slight improvement from the 2014 season (see figure 10.23).

The final 25 percent of the end-of-season evaluation score for each sport program is based on how well the athletes and teams perform in competitions, referred to as their competitiveness rate. After much trial and error, we settled on a nine-item competitiveness evaluation tool that fits any type of interscholastic sport program (see figure 10.24). In other words, the same competitiveness indicators apply to every sport program, whether it is an individual-oriented

## Figure 10.23 End-of-Season Engagement Data for High School Football Program

| | | 2014 | 2015 |
|---|---|---|---|
| | Engagement rate (% of responses in the positive zone) | 83% | 87% |
| | Scorecard Points | 1.67 | 1.74 |

| Question # | Questions | % in Zone | % in Zone |
|---|---|---|---|
| 1. | How well do you think your coach prepared you to meet the physical demands of your sport? | 93% | 96% |
| 2. | How well do you think your coach prepared you to meet the technical skill demands of your sport? | 95% | 96% |
| 3. | How well do you think your coach prepared you to use the correct strategy in different game or competitive situations? | 96% | 94% |
| 4. | I encouraged a teammate. | 83% | 88% |
| 5. | I responded appropriately after receiving a penalty. | 66% | 69% |
| 6. | I treated an opponent with respect. | 51% | 75% |
| 7. | I am confident about performing well. | 90% | 92% |
| 8. | I am confident of coming through under pressure. | 88% | 92% |
| 9. | I feel committed to my coach. | 98% | 90% |
| 10. | I trust my coach. | 100% | 88% |
| 11. | I respect my coach. | 100% | 96% |
| 12. | As a team, we all share the same commitment to our goals. | 83% | 85% |
| 13. | As a team, we are united. | 88% | 88% |
| 14. | My teammates support my efforts to improve my own performance | 83% | 88% |
| 15. | My coach made sure I really understood the goals of the team for the season. | 95% | 98% |
| 16. | I feel good about the way my coach talked to me. | 93% | 94% |
| 17. | I feel that my coach cares about me as a person. | 90% | 94% |
| 18. | My coach was fair and consistent with all athletes. | 83% | 85% |
| 19. | My coach treated all players, parents, officials, fans, and fellow coaches with respect. | 90% | 98% |
| 20. | My coach used appropriate language. | 73% | 94% |
| 21. | My coach was willing and available to meet outside of practices and games | 78% | 88% |

*(continued)*

**Figure 10.23** *(continued)*

| Question # | Questions | % in Zone | % in Zone |
|---|---|---|---|
| 22. | My coach stressed academics and monitored grades and attendance. | 90% | 98% |
| 23. | My coach taught me how to perform this skill. [O-Line Skills: Stay low, engage opponent, maintain contact with opponent] | 61% | 79% |
| 24. | My coach taught me how to perform this skill. [D-Line: Stay low, extend arms on blocker, gap control] | 61% | 79% |
| 25. | My coach taught me how to perform this skill. [Running backs: Running, ball security, pass reviewing, blocking skills] | 66% | 79% |
| 26. | My coach taught me how to perform this skill. [Wide out: Route running, blocking, ball catching/securing] | 66% | 79% |
| 27. | My coach taught me how to perform this skill. [Quarterbacks: Huddle command, leadership, ball handling, passing] | 93% | 63% |
| 28. | My coach taught me how to perform this skill. [Linebackers: Alignment, key reading, tackling, coverage skills] | 81% | 82% |
| 29. | My coach taught me how to perform this skill. [DB's: Alignment, key reading, coverage execution, cover and tackling skills] | 82% | 82% |

sport like cross country running or swimming or a team sport like basketball or football. This standardization greatly simplifies the evaluation process by measuring the competitiveness of each sport program against the same meaningful evaluation standards.

The first six competitiveness indicators relate to overall program performance, starting with simply fielding a team. Although this indicator may not seem like a measure of competitiveness, the first step toward building a culture of sustained competitive excellence is ensuring that a team is fielded for each level of competition in the sport, something that has not always happened in this high school.

Points are then earned for accomplishments such as winning important competitions, like beating their league rival, and end-of-season placement in the league standings. Up to three competitiveness bonus points can be earned for special distinctions that are further evidence of the program's competitiveness, such as winning an individual or team championship.

Two scorecard points are allocated for competitiveness rate. The competitiveness rate is calculated as a percentage of points earned out of 15 (potential points earned for competitiveness indicators excluding the bonus points).

This end-of-season evaluation process is completed with the head varsity coach for all 23 teams each year. Administrators and coaches alike report that this evaluation system is the driving force behind the remarkable culture change in the school's athletics department (record athlete participation, multiple league titles across sports, and regional and state distinctions of excellence for the athletics director).

## Figure 10.24 End-of-Season Competitiveness Data for High School Football Program

| Indicators | 2014 | 2015 | Potential points |
|---|---|---|---|
| Team fielded on all levels required within sport (fresh/jv, varsity) | 2 | 2 | 2 |
| Beat league rival (at least once) | 2 | 2 | 2 |
| Number of teams tied or placed above in final standings | 2 | 2 | 2 max (1 for each school) |
| Top 3 finish in league | 3 | 3 | 3 |
| Won the league | 0 | 3 | 3 |
| Playoff win or qualification for section | 3 | 0 | 3 |
| **BONUS POINTS: TEAM OF INDIVIDUAL CHAMPIONSHIP** | | | |
| Team or individual section championship | 0 | 0 | 1 |
| Athlete distinction (school record, section qualification, scholar-athlete, All-star, scholarship) | 1 | 1 | 1 |
| Coach individual award or honor | 0 | 1 | 1 |
| Total | 13 | 14 | 15 |
| Competitiveness rate | 86.7% | 93.3% | Total score divided by 15 |
| Scorecard points | 1.73 | 1.87 | 2 points toward scorecard |

Coaches overwhelmingly agree that the evaluation system directly contributes to an improvement in their sport programs and the quality of their coaching. Typical responses from coaches include the following:

- Very helpful. It gave me a true insight as to what I needed to improve on and what I was doing well.
- Feedback from the athlete survey was definitely helpful. It tells me how well I am doing as a coach.
- The process is great. It works really well for me.

Coaches now have a clear understanding of what matters and how their program will be evaluated. Furthermore, coaches now look forward to their end-of-season meeting because the evaluation system gives them a clear and evidenced-based picture of program strengths and gaps. Perhaps the greatest value in this type of evaluation system is that it clearly shows coaches where to focus their energy and resources to improve their coaching and their program as they head into the off-season.

## Wrap-Up

This chapter described strategies used by successful coaches and athletics directors to conduct meaningful and practical end-of-season evaluations. Successful coaches recognize the fundamental importance of quality evaluation systems. Two of the winningest college baseball coaches of all-time—Pete Dunn and Bob Bennett, each of whom coached their teams to over 1,000 wins—summed it up well: "An efficient and consistent evaluation system is a key component of any winning program."[38 (p. 210)]

A quality end-of-season evaluation system should shed light on the coach's ability to (*a*) model and teach the program core values, (*b*) build trust and cohesion across the program, (*c*) develop athlete competencies, and (*d*) help athletes perform at their peak in competitions. Measuring a coach's ability in these four areas must be balanced with practical considerations such as identifying what is most important to measure, which sources of data might be used, how the information will be collected, and how the evaluation data will be used.

The best coaches create customized evaluation systems that help them clearly and quickly identify things that are working, as well as important program gaps. Mike Smith, award-winning championship professional football coach, attributed much of his success to the systematic and formal end-of-season evaluations he conducted with all his teams:

> At the end of each year, you must go through an extensive evaluation of the entire organization to identify what you did well and where you fell short of your expectations. The most important aspect of this exercise is to identify how you are going to make sure that you are going to innovate and improve in the future.[48 (p. 44)]

The many tools and strategies shared in this chapter are intended to serve as a guide for creating your own evaluation toolkit. Your program core values and coaching context will determine what evaluation toolkit will work best for you and your athletes. I encourage you, as I have encouraged many coaches and athletics directors in my work, to take a long-term view to creating your end-of-season evaluation system. Experiment with existing evaluation tools until you find the strategy that best fits your coaching situation. You will likely need several years of testing until you find the strategy that is most efficient and valuable for your program.

Chapter 11

# Recognize and Build on Strengths

**Key Concepts**

Award banquets
End-of-season rituals
Athlete recognition strategies
Recognizing program contributors
Strengths-based coaching
Spotting signature coaching strengths
4-D cycle of coaching strengths
Building coaching resilience
Coaching efficacy
Storing and applying lessons learned

The final step before transitioning into the off-season is to make sure you recognize the good things that are happening in your program. Although the formal evaluations described in the previous chapter shed light on important performance gaps that need to be addressed in the off-season, equally important is recognizing the things that are working. The end of season presents a natural opportunity to reflect on what works and take steps to ensure that effective coaching strategies are detected and retained.

University of Alabama football coach Nick Saban, whose teams have won multiple national championships, appreciates the need to identify those individuals and elements of the program that contribute significantly to its success. He encourages coaches to ask themselves, "What are your strengths? What do you bring to the table? Make it a point to emphasize those features and use them for success."[1 (p. 85)] When coaches acknowledge and formally recognize the strengths of their players, programs, and themselves, they are building a culture of confidence and preparing to win every season.

Besides reflecting on their own strengths, effective coaches also formally recognize and reward athlete and team strengths. End-of-season banquets and

Championship coaches such as Nick Saban emphasize and build on strengths to put their athletes in a strong position to realize their goals.

ceremonies are vital opportunities to reward and reinforce team core values and expectations. For example, in addition to the traditional awards for most valuable player, effective coaches use a wide range of creative strategies to celebrate and honor athletes who model desired team values such as work ethic and character. Winning matters and should be recognized and celebrated. Equally important for building a culture of excellence is recognizing and celebrating the values that lay the foundation for success.

Identifying and augmenting strengths is also important in boosting athletes' and coaches' confidence. And as their self-efficacy increases, so too does their mental toughness, focus, and optimism. This chapter presents many positive, confidence-enhancing ways to recognize athletes' strengths and program achievements, as well as means by which to recognize and build on strengths as a coach.

# AWARD BANQUETS AND END-OF-SEASON RITUALS

A quality and meaningful end-of-season recognition ceremony is an important bridge from the past to the future. End-of-season closure and celebration is critical for building durable cultures of excellence, and it requires the same level of planning that goes into preparing for a big competition. The most common end-of-season recognition ceremony is the team awards banquet.

The team awards banquet is a unique opportunity with a captive audience of key program stakeholders—perhaps the only time all these important people will be in the same room at the same time all year—to emphasize the core values. Typically, a printed outline is distributed at the team banquet. Besides listing team members, award recipients, and key supporters, the outline should include an overview of the program's core values.

I have worked with several high school and college coaches who have printed their program core values and a brief description of each one on either the front or back of the banquet pamphlet. One coach liked to leave a small printed card, similar to a business card, with each of the team's three core values printed in the team's colors on the table in front of each seat. One side of the card listed the team's core values, and the other side listed coach and program contact information.

All team banquets require some amount of public speaking by the head coach. Although the coach may decide to designate some of the speaking to other members of the coaching staff or administration, athletes and program supporters will expect to hear from the head coach. Public speaking is a performance, and like any type of performance, thorough preparation and practice are the keys to success. Fortunately, by following some general rules, coaches can enhance the quality of their speaking at end-of-season recognition events.[2]

- **Personalize comments:** Show that you genuinely care and value the recipient by preparing comments that highlights unique aspects of the athlete's personality and an example of a specific contribution she or he has made to the program.
- **Practice your timing:** A common frustration with team banquets is that they are too long, often because speakers are ill prepared. When preparing comments be mindful of the amount of time that people will be expected to sit and listen to speeches. Set a time goal for each recognition and stick to it.
- **Don't force humor:** Although everyone enjoys a humorous speaker, coaches should be careful about trying to insert humor into their comments if they are not experienced public speakers. If they use humor, coaches should avoid telling inside jokes that only a few people in the audience will appreciate.
- **Keep it positive:** Above all else, the end-of-season banquet should be a celebration of all that is good with the program. Although banquets often include good-natured roasts, any sarcastic or negative comments that belittle others—such as presenting young athletes with "crybaby awards"[3, 4]—have no place at the banquet.
- **Write comments out in advance:** Off-the-cuff or spontaneous comments rarely succeed and often give the impression that the coach places little value on the recipient or the recognition. Finding positive things to say after an unsuccessful or losing season may be particularly difficult for coaches. Dr. Ralph Pim, a long-time coach and athletics administrator at West Point Military Academy, has prepared a thoughtful script that coaches can use as a guide for preparing a team banquet speech to highlight the positives after a tough season (see figure 11.1).[2]

## Figure 11.1 Script for a Coach's Speech After a Losing Season

This dinner tonight stands as a testimony to how everyone feels about this special group of athletes. It provides an opportunity to look back at our successes over the past season.

At first, you may question my use of the word *successes* to describe the events of the past year. If a team's record is nothing more than a number indicating the games won and lost, then I suppose we would have to agree that this season was not the best in our school's history. But I believe that a team's record stands for a lot more than what is indicated in the win-loss column.

When I look at the team record, I ask myself the following questions:

- Did the team become the best that it could be?
- Did the players stay united throughout the entire season?
- Did the team compete every minute on the playing field and refuse to ever quit?
- Did the players demonstrate respect, responsibility, integrity, sportsmanship, fair play, and unselfishness?

If the answer to all of these questions is yes, I would call that team successful. And that is definitely the case with the team we are about to honor.

- Our team was committed and dedicated the entire season.
- They refused to be outworked, no matter what the situation.
- Our players were united and never stopped believing in each other.
- Our players never backed down from a challenge or quit.
- They demonstrated the strength and courage to pick themselves up after many heartbreaking losses.
- They allowed nothing to defeat their winning spirit.
- Our team's optimism never faltered.

This group of athletes should be a source of pride for everyone associated with our school. They demonstrated to all of us what commitment really looks like. Our seniors learned valuable lessons that will help them be successful throughout their lives. Our returning players established a strong foundation that will pay dividends next year. The experiences of this season have prepared us to take the next step.

To our fans, we thank you for your unwavering support. You lifted our spirits and strengthened our desire to succeed. You never stopped believing in us.

We are all very proud of these players and excited to honor them this evening.



End-of-season team banquets can also be used to promote leaders for the following season. For example, the outgoing captains or team leaders can speak for a few minutes about the season and then pass the leadership baton over to the next group of team leaders.[5, 6] This activity could be something as simple as naming the next captain or leadership group or as formal as physically handing over some symbol of leadership such as an armband, jersey, or team leadership handbook.

Although holding an end-of-season team awards banquet is a traditional and proven strategy for recognizing achievements and building tradition, successful coaches often supplement the team banquet with other formal rituals. Prominent high school football coach Joe Erhmann has created a comprehensive and powerful series of end-of-season ceremonies that includes rituals for the last practice, the last day, and the banquet.[7]

After the final practice, athletes exit the locker room in pairs holding hands, seniors first, and are led on a guided walk through significant parts of the school. At important monuments or locations, coaches or alumni who are present have the team pause and then share the significance and meaning of the tribute. One such spot is a tree planted on the school's grounds to commemorate those who lost their lives trying to save others during the 9/11 terrorist attack on America.

The walk concludes at the practice field, where the returning athletes circle the field and silently observe while the departing senior athletes are given time to "make peace with the field on which they battled, were tested, succeeded, and failed."[7 (p. 241)] Some athletes sprint or jog up and down the field, some kneel and feel the grass, others simply stand and reflect. Finally, the seniors come together and hold their last huddle.

On the final day before the athletes begin the season for other sports or leave the football program for good, the team meets and the senior athletes read their own obituaries they have written. The purpose of this end-of-season ceremony is to encourage departing athletes to reflect on the type of person they want to become and the way in which they can live a life aligned with the core values promoted in the football program: empathy, integrity, responsibility, and service to others. Here is an example of one such self-written obituary:

> Today we are gathered to celebrate the life of my father, Bryan Kowalski. He was truly a great man who was not the wealthiest, strongest, or most powerful man, but he was the man who cared for everyone no matter what their situation was. . . . What set him apart was the fact that he did not succumb to the false sense of masculinity. He treated everyone the same no matter how many houses they owned, the type of car they drove, or the size of their wallets.[8 (p. 243)]

At the final team awards banquet, the senior athletes are again asked to read their obituaries but now in front of a much larger audience of family and program supporters. Time is then set aside for an open mic session when anyone in attendance can share his or her feelings about the athletes, the team, the program, or the season. A separate ceremony was also sometimes held to present each departing athlete with a plaque engraved with the statement "A Man Built for Others" along with his name.

## END-OF-SEASON TEAM BANQUET RECOGNITION STRATEGIES

Successful coaches use a wide range of strategies to recognize athletes and program contributors at their end-of-season team awards banquet. A standard procedure at all team banquets is the presentation of athlete achievement awards.

Identifying and recognizing athlete achievements will be easy after the end-of-season evaluation described in chapter 10 has been completed. To promote overall team culture and recognize individual and team progress toward goals as well as competitive achievements (wins, titles, and so on), coaches should create growth recognitions that can be awarded to all deserving athletes.

Much as students earn distinction for academic achievement at the end of the school year, athletes can earn distinction for goal achievement at the end of the season. For example, coaches could create a wall of champions or team plaque that would include names of athletes who achieved their season goals, or at least some percentage of their goals (e.g., 80 percent). Athletes could also be awarded badges or certificates recognizing various levels of goal achievement, such as gold (100 percent), silver (more than 90 percent), and bronze (80 percent). Coaches can get creative to adapt the badges and recognitions to their program, such as by using program colors and sport-relevant symbols.

Besides honoring athletes who have achieved personal goals and high-performance standards (e.g., most outstanding offensive player, most outstanding defensive player, individual titles or championships, program records, and so on), the best coaches also formally honor athletes who were exemplary models of team core values and standards.[9–13] When coaches formally recognize a range of athlete behaviors that extends beyond the obvious performance achievements, they are helping to build athlete confidence and motivation that will carry over into the following season.[14]

Legendary Hall of Fame high school basketball coach Morgan Wooten is a prime example of a coach who knew the value of formally recognizing athletes who modeled program core values. Based on his experience one season with an athlete who demonstrated great selflessness and constantly infused the team with enthusiasm and positive energy, despite rarely getting to play in games, he created a special honor in the athlete's name.[12] The Tilden Brill award was subsequently given to the top team leaders at the end-of-season team banquet each year both as a way to recognize current athletes for their special contributions and as a way to sustain a culture of excellence and program tradition.

A potent example of how one team recognizes one athlete at the end of each season for modeling the program's core values is the hard hat strategy used by a college lacrosse team. Author Jon Gordon, himself a former member of the team, shares how the team selects one first-year player each year who best demonstrates the values of selflessness, work ethic, and commitment to be the keeper of the hard hat.[10] A red construction hat is awarded to the player, who is then entrusted with carrying the hat to every team practice and competition. The hard hat is an important team symbol that not only represents the program core values but also recognizes a former highly respected teammate and former hard hat winner who died while playing lacrosse. The former player's jersey number, 21, is permanently displayed on the hard hat as a vivid and constant reminder of the core values.

A comparable strategy has been used by championship swim coach Bob Steele, but instead of a hard hat, the symbol is a yellow jersey (similar to the one awarded to the leading cyclist in the Tour de France).[5] Throughout the season the coach selects one athlete at the end of each practice as the recipient of the yellow jersey, representing the athlete who had the best practice. That athlete is then formally awarded the jersey in an informal podium presentation on the pool deck, and she or he is responsible for wearing the jersey when walking in to the following practice session. Each athlete who is awarded the jersey throughout the season has her or his name placed on the jersey. At the end-of-season team banquet a special recognition is given to all athletes who won the yellow jersey throughout the season.

Jeff Janssen, consultant to many championship teams, has helped many coaches create these types of player recognitions. Two such examples he shares are the Nails Award and the Glue Award.[8] Although designed originally to be awarded through the season after practices and competitions, the values that underpin the awards can be reinforced by presenting an end-of-season cumulative recognition to one or several athletes.

The Nails Award is given to the athlete who demonstrates the most mental toughness ("tough as nails"). The Glue Award is presented to the athlete who shows the most concern and sacrifice for teammates ("the glue that holds the team together"). These types of recognition strategies will be most valued by the athletes if they are allowed to have input into creating the award, which may vary each season depending on the team's personality and profile, and selecting the award recipient.

Although special distinctions are the norm at team banquets, ideally, each athlete on the team will receive some form of recognition for his or her efforts and contribution to the program. Distinguished high school and college cross country running coach Pat Tyson, who has led his high school teams to 12 state championships, believes that rule number one in putting on a quality end-of-season team banquet is to ensure that no athlete is left out.[11] One way that Coach Tyson recognizes every athlete on his teams is to provide each runner with a team booklet commemorating the season. Coach Tyson keeps a binder of materials all season long—meet results, press clippings, workout schedules, and so on—and then puts all the materials together into a season booklet that is photocopied and awarded to each athlete at the banquet. Each booklet is personalized with a photo of the athlete on the cover of the booklet.

A baseball coach I know presented each athlete with a personalized baseball at the end of the season. On the baseball was written the athlete's jersey number and a statement recognizing that athlete's unique strengths or contribution to the team. Some examples from the 2016 end-of-season celebration include "The Iceman" (the athlete who modeled emotional control throughout the season), "The Hit" (the athlete who had a big hit in an important competition that resulted in the winning run), and "Stretch" (the athlete who consistently pushed himself to the limit to make big defensive plays).

Many coaches also like to add special recognitions for athletes who are graduating from the team. For example, record-setting high school football coach Bob Ladouceur liked to present departing athletes with a letter of gratitude.[15] A sample letter from Coach Ladouceur to his graduating seniors is reprinted in figure 11.2. The statement about remaining forever young at the end of the letter is in reference to the music that Coach Ladouceur selected that year to play at the final team service.

## Figure 11.2 End-of-Season Letter to Departing Athletes

I want to thank you for the opportunity to coach you through your varsity football days at De La Salle. My association with you has been a positive experience for me that will stay with me for the rest of my life. You have provided me with some wonderful memories that I know I will look back on with pride—and smile.

I know you have all improved as football players because I have witnessed the growth. However, this is not what is most important to me. What is my hope and dream is that you have all improved and grown as human beings through your experiences at De La Salle. I believe that you have, but only "the man in the glass" knows for sure.

You all know and lived the "secrets" to De La Salle's success—love, brotherhood, sacrifice, discipline, heart, courage, passion, honesty. These are not just catch words we throw around to impress others or justify our existence. We know what these mean because we created it and lived it. Understand that with that knowledge there is no turning back for us—ignorance is not an option. It is your future duty, no matter where you end up, to create the environment you have created here by bringing your best selves to the table.

It is my hope and prayer that your future significant others (friends, wives, children, coworkers) will have the good fortune to experience you as I have. Remember to always take the difficult look at yourselves and have the courage to change, evolve, and grow.

Go out tomorrow and play like you are—dare to be you—Spartans. And as for me, you will remain "Forever Young."

With respect,
Coach Lad



Regardless of what type of end-of-season recognition strategies they use, coaches should also create strategies for recognizing the achievements and contributions of important program support staff and contributors. Team success depends on all those associated with the team doing their jobs, and the best coaches understand the importance of recognizing everyone's contributions. For example, after a national championship season, college softball coach Mike Candrea made sure that everyone who contributed to the program's success received a championship ring, including administrative staff, equipment managers, and groundskeepers.[8]

Of course, not every season will end with a championship ring, but every season should end with the coach providing sincere recognition of the efforts and contributions of others. One of the simplest and most powerful recognition strategies is a handwritten note or card. The note should include recognition of a specific behavior that added value to the program the past season. Some suggested prompts for writing recognition notes are "I love how you . . ." or "You did an amazing job at . . ."[16]

End-of-season recognition—for both athletes and other key contributors to your program—is critical for building tradition and a culture of excellence. Coaches often rush through this coaching phase because of the normal exhaustion that comes from completing a season and the desire to start working on ways to improve the program for the next season. But the coach who invests thoughtfully in recognizing and honoring the achievements and progress from the previous season is building a legacy of pride and distinction that will produce valuable rewards for many seasons to come.

The remainder of this chapter is focused on helping coaches learn about end-of-season strategies for identifying and building on their strengths. This phase is critically important because coaches need positive reinforcement to sustain their own motivation and commitment to excellence. In addition, identifying and building on coaching strengths is a surefire way to achieve steady improvement in coaching effectiveness.

## IDENTIFYING AND COACHING TO YOUR STRENGTHS

The traditional approach to coaching is sometimes referred to as a deficits-based approach because coaches focus their energy on identifying and fixing weaknesses, or deficits, in their athletes, programs, and coaching practices.[17] Although coaches should certainly work toward closing performance gaps (the focus of chapter 12 of this book), the most successful people focus more on knowing and growing the things they are good at, referred to as a strengths-based approach to coaching. World and Olympic championship soccer coach Tony DiCicco knew the value of this approach and advised coaches to "Know your limitations, but coach to your strengths."[18 (p. 287)]

Coaching strengths are those instinctive coaching characteristics—such as behaviors, feelings, or ways of thinking—that are authentic and energize optimal performance.[19] Coaching strengths are authentic because coaches feel like the "real me" when they are using their strengths. By focusing on their strengths, coaches act in ways that are aligned with their purpose and core values; they are acting with authenticity. When people use their strengths, they are more engaged with their work and report a surge in energy and performance, greater happiness, and more optimism.[19, 20]

The strengths-based approach is founded on five core principles:[21 (p. 5)]

1. The strengths approach focuses on what is right, what is working, and what is strong.
2. Strengths are part of our basic human nature; therefore, every person in the world has strengths and deserves respect for those strengths.
3. Our areas of greatest potential are in the areas of our greatest strengths.
4. We succeed by fixing our weaknesses only when we are also making the most of our strengths.
5. Using our strengths is the smallest thing we can do to make the biggest difference.

Five-time national championship and all-time winningest American college baseball coach Augie Garrido is another example of a coach who has built a successful career around the principles of strength-based coaching. He advises coaches to build around their natural strengths: "Why not focus on strengths instead of weaknesses? My contention is that we should use the best weapons available to us. Build momentum by building on whatever comes naturally to you."[22 (p. 138)]

Although knowing and growing coaching strengths has many benefits, including counterbalancing the inherent tendency to focus on the negative, the most effective coaches develop a keen awareness of how and when they can best use their strengths.[21, 23] If coaches understate or minimize their strengths, they will miss prime opportunities to maximize performance. On the other hand, if coaches overstate or blindly emphasize their strengths regardless of the situation, they risk missing opportunities for identifying and growing other strengths.

Coaches should always use their strengths but in varying degrees depending on the particular situation, much as we adjust the volume control on our electronic devices.[21] For example, a coach may determine that one of her strengths is listening to others. She should always use this strength, but the situation will dictate whether she needs to dial up her listening (listen more before acting) or dial down her listening (listen less and move quickly to action). This ability to control the use of strengths is a defining characteristic of wise strengths application.

The process of identifying strengths is commonly referred to as strengths spotting.[21] Although perhaps not self-evident when starting a coaching career, the best coaches learn over time what aspects of coaching suit them best. Successful coaches like legendary American college basketball coaches Pat Summitt and John Wooden were keenly aware of their strengths. For Coach Summitt it was teaching and building young people: "If I were not coaching I'd be in a classroom. I'd be somewhere spending my time with young people. They give me energy. I just love it. It's in my system."[23 (p. 162)] For Coach Wooden it was observation and analysis skills: "I have always considered myself average in many areas. However, my strength is in analyzing players and statistics. I loved digging deep into information to see what I could find."[24 (p. 48)]

Unfortunately, coaches often go many years, sometimes decades, into a coaching career before they become fully aware of their strengths. Many strengths-spotting tools are available, but typically these have a fee and none of them appears to be created specifically for sport coaches. The following section contains suggestions for accessing and in some cases adapting some common tools for spotting strengths. These tools will help coaches and those who work with coaches, such as athletics directors and coach educators, to identify and build on coaching strengths.

Dr. Alex Linley describes three strengths-spotting strategies that can easily be adapted for sport coaching: (*a*) day-to-day strengths spotting, (*b*) listening for strengths, and (*c*) strengths-based interviewing.[21] Day-to-day strengths spotting requires coaches either to have someone else observe them or to observe themselves on videotape in their regularly coaching activities such as during a practice, competition, or meetings. The goal of this strengths-spotting exercise is simply to watch the coach in action and be open to noticing moments of strength.

Moments of strength are revealed when coaches display one or more of the telltale signs of a coaching strength:

- Visible sense of heightened energy and engagement
- Positive and desired response from athletes or other coaches
- Successful and timely completion of a task

The key to the day-to-day strengths-spotting exercise is to look for repeated moments that demonstrate patterns that indicate a coaching strength. Athletes should definitely be considered prime candidates for serving as strength spotters because they are the ones who have the most direct view of the coach in action across various situations. For example, coaches might consider asking their athletes to complete anonymous strengths-spotting cards at the end of the season. Athletes could be asked to complete the following prompt: "You were at your best as a coach this season when you . . ." Clear patterns will emerge across athlete responses to reveal coaching strengths that should be used often.

Strengths can also be revealed by listening carefully to the way that coaches speak about their work. People sound noticeably different when they are asked to speak about a weakness compared with talking about a strength.[21] A list of the differences between the sounds of weaknesses and strengths that has been adapted for sport coaches is presented in table 11.1.

Listening for strengths can be accomplished by asking coaches to describe typical coaching situations. The responses should be audiotaped so that the coach, or coach mentor, can listen for the sounds listed in table 11.1 to learn whether the coach was displaying a strength in handling the coaching situation. For example, coaches may set aside a few minutes after practices and competitions to record themselves speaking freely about two or three situations that occurred that day (e.g., interactions with athletes or officials, planning decisions, or strategy adjustments). This exercise will help coaches increase their self-awareness of coaching strengths and the types of situations in which they can use those strengths more effectively.

**Table 11.1 Difference Between Sounds of Coaching Strengths and Coaching Weaknesses**

| Sounds of a coaching strength | Sounds of a coaching weakness |
|---|---|
| More immediate and graphic description | More hesitant and less expressive |
| Passionate, clear, and focused voice | Dejected or deflated voice |
| Confident and authentic tone | Self-critical and heavy tone |
| Broad focus on diverse examples | Narrow focus on problems |
| Relaxed and energized | Express annoyance and impatience |
| Optimistic and forward looking | Retrospective and backward looking |
| Rhythmic, natural-paced dialogue | Disjointed, halting dialogue |

A third strengths-spotting strategy for coaches is strengths-based interviewing. With this strategy, coaches write responses to three items:

1. What was your best day of coaching this past season, and why was this the best day?
2. Describe a specific coaching situation when you were at your best as a coach this past season.
3. What aspects of coaching most energize you?

The coach, or a coach mentor, then looks across the written responses for patterns that reveal coaching strengths. For example, my responses to these three questions based on a recent season of coaching youth soccer follow. This example can be used as a practice activity for identifying a coach's strengths. What strengths can you identify in these responses?

- What was your best day of coaching this past season, and why was this the best day? *The day the girls overcame a two-goal deficit at halftime against a strong team during a cold and rainy game. It gave me great pride and joy to see the girls exert full effort in tough conditions right up to the final play of the game, and for that effort to be rewarded with a hard-fought 3–2 win.*
- Describe a specific coaching situation when you were at your best as a coach this past season. *A game situation in which our opponent was awarded a questionable penalty shot, which resulted in the tying goal on the final play of the game. Despite the frustration and charged emotion of the situation, I remained overtly positive and ensured that our coaches and athletes honored the game and their opponent by congratulating the opposing team and the officials on a well-played game. I also used the situation as a teachable moment to remind the girls to focus on things they can control such as their attitude, effort, and response to adversity.*
- What aspects of coaching most energize you? *Observing the girls play with expressions of focus, joy, and no fear for failure. These are the moments that ignite and sustain their passion and commitment to sport and physical activity long after they leave my team.*

For coaches who want more comprehensive and formal guidance on identifying their strengths, several fee-based strengths spotting assessment are commercially available. Two of the more common ones are the Clifton StrengthsFinder (www.strengthsfinder.com) and Realise2 (www.cappeu.com/R2StrengthsProfiler). Based on decades of research, the Clifton StrengthsFinder questionnaire includes 177 statements related to 34 potential strengths, such as discipline, empathy, and focus, and it produces a report describing the respondent's top five strengths.[25] An access code is required to take this questionnaire, which is provided with the purchase of the book *StrengthsFinder 2.0* by Tom Rath.[26]

Realise2, developed by Dr. Alex Linley and the team at the Center for Applied Positive Psychology, is another common questionnaire used to spot strengths. Realise2 provides information on both strengths and weaknesses, and assesses 60 different strengths according to energy, performance, and use.[20, 21] At the end of the 180-question survey, respondents are provided with a personalized report that identifies their top seven realized and top seven unrealized strengths, top four learned behaviors and top three weaknesses, as well as guidance on how to realize strengths while minimizing weaknesses (www.cappeu.com/R2StrengthsProfiler).

## BUILDING ON SIGNATURE COACHING STRENGTHS

Another popular approach to spotting strengths comes from the positive psychology movement.[17, 19, 21] Dr. Martin Seligman is considered a pioneer in positive psychology. A review of his work provides valuable insights and tools to help coaches identify and build on what are referred to as signature strengths.

Seligman and his colleagues organize positive character traits into 6 overarching virtues and 24 character strengths (see table 11.2) that are most associated with leading a meaningful, engaged, and happy life. Research shows that people who recognize and regularly use their strengths experience a greater sense of well-being, self-esteem, and vitality while also reporting lower levels of stress.[27] Clearly, strengths-based coaching can help coaches sustain a positive outlook and the high energy levels needed to lead athletes and teams.

Although not created for sport coaching, the virtues and strengths align extremely well with the character traits modeled by effective coaches. For example, the virtues of temperance, wisdom, and knowledge are consistent with how intrapersonal coaching knowledge is defined in the integrated definition of coaching effectiveness, and the virtues of humanity and justice match well with how interpersonal knowledge is defined.[28] The remaining virtues of courage and transcendence are consistent with many of the character traits identified in the Pyramid of Teaching Success in Sport.[29]

Among the many strategies and exercises designed by Seligman and his colleagues to help people recognize and build strengths, three have proved to be most effective: Gratitude Visit, Three Good Things in Life, and Using Signature Strengths in a New Way.[19, 30] The following description of these exercises have been adapted for use with sport coaches.

**Table 11.2 Seligman's Virtues and Character Strengths**

| Virtue | Sample strengths |
|---|---|
| Wisdom and knowledge | Creativity, curiosity, open-mindedness |
| Courage | Authenticity, bravery, persistence |
| Humanity | Kindness, love, social intelligence (empathy) |
| Justice | Fairness, leadership, teamwork |
| Temperance | Forgiveness, modesty, prudence |
| Transcendence | Gratitude, hope, humor |

Adapted from M.E.P. Seligman, T.A. Steen, N. Park, and C. Peterson, 2005, "Positive psychology progress: Empirical validation of interventions," *American Psychologist* 60(5): 410-421, by permission of the American Psychological Association.

The Gratitude Visit exercise requires coaches to write and deliver a letter of gratitude to a coach who has been particularly kind and influential in their development but has never been properly thanked. Although this exercise requires coaches to recognize strengths in another coach, the exercise will raise their own awareness of strengths considered particularly valuable in effective coaching.

The Three Good Things in Life exercise was originally designed to have people write down three things that went well each day and what they think were the causes of the three good things, over the course of one week. This activity can be adapted for coaches to use at the end of the season by having them write three good things that happened with each athlete they coached in the previous season, along with an explanation for why each good thing occurred (see figure 11.3). For example, a coach may write that an athlete achieved a personal best in some area of performance or that an athlete demonstrated a positive change in attitude.

Having coaches reflect on the causal explanation for the good things provides an opportunity to connect the good things to coaching behaviors—actions taken by coaches that, in their view, directly contributed to the occurrence of the good things. After the coach completes this exercise for each athlete, a review of the worksheet will reveal patterns of coaching behaviors that are connected to athlete growth and development. These coaching behaviors should be recognized as coaching strengths, and coaches should make a conscious effort to continue these behaviors.

Using Signature Strengths in a New Way is the third strategy for effectively identifying coaching strengths. Coaches must first complete the VIA Survey of Character Strengths that is available free of charge on the Authentic Happiness website maintained by the University of Pennsylvania (www.authentichappiness.sas.upenn.edu/testcenter). After coaches have registered and completed the survey, they will receive individualized feedback about their top five, or signature, strengths. For example, after completing the survey a coach may learn that her or his five signature strengths are perspective wisdom; capacity to love and be loved; self-control and self-regulation; creativity, ingenuity, and originality; and industry, diligence, and perseverance.

The challenge, then, for the coach is to think about how to use these five strengths in new ways for the following season. If the coach learns that one of his or her signature strengths is perspective wisdom, which is described as being viewed by others as someone whose advice and wisdom is valued because the person has a unique way of looking at the world that helps others make sense of their own situations, the coach might decide to share his or her views more frequently on challenging life situations encountered by athletes. The goal with using signature strengths in new ways is for coaches to recognize and capitalize on their unique personal assets that will help them improve their overall coaching effectiveness.

## 4-D CYCLE OF COACHING STRENGTHS

Whereas the field of psychology has provided sport coaching with a valuable source of information and tools for identifying and building signature strengths, a parallel movement has occurred in business and organizational development.

## Figure 11.3 Three Good Things Worksheet

| Athlete | Good things | Causal coaching behaviors |
|---|---|---|
| Randy | 1. Personal best in the 800 meters<br>2. Positive attitude toward feedback<br>3. Initiative to train on his own | Reduced his training load, increased rest and recovery between training sessions, shared examples and biographies of world-class performers across sports |
| | 1.<br>2.<br>3. | |
| | 1.<br>2.<br>3. | |
| | 1.<br>2.<br>3. | |
| | 1.<br>2.<br>3. | |
| | 1.<br>2.<br>3. | |
| | 1.<br>2.<br>3. | |
| | 1.<br>2.<br>3. | |
| | 1.<br>2.<br>3. | |
| | 1.<br>2.<br>3. | |

From W. Gilbert, 2017, *Coaching better every season: A year-round system for athlete development and program success* (Champaign, IL: Human Kinetics).

Referred to as appreciative inquiry (AI), or the strengths revolution,[31] this movement is viewed as a shift from the traditional focus on problem solving to identifying and enhancing what we already do well.

The underlying assumption of appreciative inquiry is that all people and organizations have something that works well that, when used repeatedly, becomes a source of increased energy and joy. Successful coaches understand that building programs of excellence is a long grind filled with many setbacks that can easily demoralize a coach. Championship coaches such as Mike Babcock, who has led teams to college, professional, Olympic, and world championships, take an appreciative inquiry approach to their work: "You have to embrace and celebrate each day for the progress you make. If you don't feel like you've made progress, celebrate the effort. Success is a marathon, not a sprint. And endurance needs joy.[32 (p. 49)]

Appreciative inquiry, as a form of strengths-based coaching, includes four phases referred to as the 4-D cycle: discovery, dream, design, and destiny.[31] The 4-D cycle can be applied to coaching as follows.[33, 34] The first step, discovery, requires that coaches reflect on positive moments and successes in their coaching. The process of discovery can be enhanced by asking others such as athletes, coaches, athletics directors, and perhaps parents, depending on the sport context, to join the dialogue. The goal is to identify the best of what the coach already does. This step is also sometimes referred to as the appreciating phase because the focus is on identifying those things that are most appreciated.

The dream phase is used to build on the strengths identified in the discovery phase by taking the best of what a coach already does and envisioning how those strengths can be even further developed. In the dream phase the goal is to imagine possibilities for even greater use of existing strengths.

Although inspirational, dreaming about how to build on strengths is insufficient unless it is followed with a plan of action. In the design phase, the coach, along with trusted advisors when possible, constructs a strategic plan for moving the dream to reality. The design phase can be considered the push phase, whereas the destiny phase can be thought of as the pull phase. In the design phase, coaches push their strengths into action, and in the destiny phase, coaches make adjustments and improvisations that are pulled forward by a sense of what the future will look like if they sustain their strength-building efforts.

The promise of appreciative inquiry as a form of recognizing and building on coaching strengths is only beginning to be realized. One such example is an appreciative inquiry project completed by Dr. Sandy Gordon and Dr. Daniel Gucciardi to help athletes build mental toughness.[17] Using their work with athletes, together with what I have learned from collaborating on many strengths-based coaching projects,[33, 34] an outline of how the 4-D cycle of appreciative inquiry can help coaches improve their strengths is provided in table 11.3.

## USING STRENGTHS TO DEVELOP COACHING RESILIENCE

When coaches recognize their strengths, they build coaching confidence and mental toughness. The ability to overcome performance failures and emotionally

**Table 11.3 4-D Cycle for Building on Coaching Strengths**

| Four Ds | Strength-based coaching effectiveness questions |
|---|---|
| Discovery | Think about a moment this past season when you were really engaged in and excited about your coaching. What was happening? What were you feeling? What made it a great moment? What were others doing that contributed to this being a great moment? What did you contribute to creating this moment? |
| Dream | Imagine coaching in a sport program where these moments of full engagement and excitement are normal and occur all the time. What would this envisioned coaching future look like for you? |
| Design | When you return from the off-season, how will you act differently to make this coaching dream a reality? How best can you develop and sustain your coaching strengths? What role can your athletes, fellow coaches, and administrators play in developing your coaching strengths and bringing the dream to life? |
| Destiny | How can you improve your coaching environment to promote collaborative and ongoing appreciation of your efforts to realize your coaching dream? What types of changes are needed to shift the focus from evaluation to valuation of your coaching efforts, so that you can discover new coaching strengths? |

difficult situations is a key characteristic of resilient coaches. For example, legendary soccer coach Sir Alex Ferguson attributed his long and decorated career to his resilience as a coach, something he developed first as an athlete: "The adversity gave me a sense of determination that has shaped my life. I made up my mind that I would never give in."[35 (p .6)]

With ever-growing public scrutiny of coaches, the pressures that come with coaching will continue to mount. For coaches of high-performance teams in college and professional ranks, and increasingly in the high school and club sport levels, coaching tenures are highly unstable. For example, the normal tenure for professional sport coaches in the four major North American sport leagues ranges from a low of 2.5 years for the National Hockey League to a high of just 4.1 years for the National Football League.[36] Many college coaches in high-profile sports such as American football fare even worse; one study showed that the average coaching tenure in one conference was only 2.3 years.[37]

Recognizing coaching strengths is a valuable exercise because it gives coaches confidence to enhance other areas of their coaching, something noted by championship coaches such as Augie Garrido: "Mastery in one area tends to help you focus on others, which is another reason to focus on developing strengths."[22 (p. 134)] Becoming a resilient coach requires self-confidence, sometimes referred to as coaching efficacy.[38, 39] Coaching efficacy can be separated into five dimensions, or areas, of coaching confidence: game strategy, motivation, technique, character building, and physical conditioning.

Coaches' confidence in their decision making and ability to lead athletes and teams during competitive events is referred to as game strategy efficacy. When coaches believe they can help their athletes control their emotions, focus, and attitude, they are said to have high motivation coaching efficacy. The heart of coaching is teaching, and coaches who consider themselves good teachers of their sport exhibit technique coaching efficacy. The character-building aspect of coaching efficacy refers to coaches' belief in their ability to teach values, integrity, morals, and respect to their athletes. Finally, coaches must show confidence in their ability to structure appropriate strength and conditioning programs for their athletes, described as physical conditioning efficacy.

Recently, some have called for the addition of a sixth type of coaching efficacy, labeled academic efficacy,[40] for coaches who coach in school-based settings. Given that the mission of school-based athletics is to develop student-athletes who excel not only in their sport but also in the classroom, it makes sense that effective coaches would have confidence in their ability to help their athletes maintain academic eligibility and graduate.

Several questionnaires have been created for coaches to identify their strengths by self-assessing their coaching efficacy.[39] A simplified and adapted version of a coaching efficacy scale is provided in figure 11.4 as an example of a self-assessment tool to identify coaching strengths.[41] Items on which the coach scores high (3s and 4s on the questionnaire) may be considered personal coaching strengths, and the coach should try to increase the use of those coaching behaviors.

Coaches who have high coaching efficacy scores have been shown to have more effective teaching styles, more satisfied athletes, and better win-loss records than coaches who have low coaching efficacy scores.[38] Furthermore, coaching efficacy appears to predict overall team efficacy, meaning that when coaches are confident in their abilities and maximize their strengths, their athletes also feel more confident in their abilities.

## Figure 11.4 Coach Efficacy Self-Assessment

| In relation to the team that you coached this past season, how confident were you in your ability to . . . | Low confidence | | | Full confidence |
|---|---|---|---|---|
| 1. teach athletes sport-specific technical and tactical skills? | 1 | 2 | 3 | 4 |
| 2. prepare appropriate physical conditioning plans for athletes? | 1 | 2 | 3 | 4 |
| 3. positively influence athletes' character development? | 1 | 2 | 3 | 4 |
| 4. create strategies to maximize athletes' strengths during competition? | 1 | 2 | 3 | 4 |
| 5. help athletes stay motivated and confident when performing poorly? | 1 | 2 | 3 | 4 |
| 6. support athletes' efforts to succeed in the classroom and maintain good academic standing? | 1 | 2 | 3 | 4 |

Adapted from N.D. Myers, D.L. Feltz, M.A. Chase, M.D. Reckase, and G.R. Hancock, 2008, "The Coaching Efficacy Scale II—High School Teams," *Educational and Psychological Measurement* 68(6): 1059-1076.

Not surprisingly, more experienced coaches typically report greater coaching efficacy than less experienced coaches do, but even coaches early in their careers have many potential untapped sources of coaching confidence. Most coaches have some experience as athletes, typically in the sport they now coach.[42, 43] This experience as coach watchers is a rich potential source of coaching confidence.

Coaches can take a moment to think back to their favorite coaches and ask themselves questions such as the following: Why did I enjoy playing so much for this coach? What were some of the most effective or fun strategies employed by this coach? What were this coach's strongest personal characteristics or attributes? Coaches can then challenge themselves to integrate the strengths of their favorite coaches into their own coaching style. Chances are they will find that they already embody many of these strengths, which in turn will further increase their coaching efficacy.

Recognizing and building on strengths also helps coaches build their mental toughness, another key component of coaching resilience. Although coaches certainly require mental toughness, rarely is this topic addressed in the coaching literature. On the other hand, much has been written about strategies for helping athletes build mental toughness.[44, 45] A review of that literature provides a useful foundation for creating strategies to help coaches build their own mental toughness.

One model of mental toughness is referred to as the four Cs model, which includes four components of mental toughness: control, challenge, commitment, and confidence.[45] Control is described as the ability to remain focused and disciplined while juggling multiple and sometimes competing demands. Mentally tough coaches demonstrate control by developing strong organizational skills that allow them to prioritize their many tasks and to delegate responsibilities to other members of their staff and to their athletes when possible. The most effective coaches also show control by setting aside dedicated and protected time in their daily schedules to prepare practice and competition plans.

The challenge component of mental toughness refers to the ability to perceive the constant challenges and changes that occur in our lives as opportunities for development. In this sense, mentally tough coaches are growth mind-set coaches who embrace obstacles and setbacks as valuable moments for improvement. Mentally tough coaches don't shy away from adversity; they tackle it head on and display deliberate and timely decision making. Coaching is complicated, and seldom is time available to create or implement the best solution to a challenge. Mental toughness increases each time a coach acts with purpose and conviction.

The third C of mental toughness, commitment, is described as the intense and constant pursuit of goals, despite difficulties that are encountered. Mentally tough coaches embrace the goal-setting philosophy of plan backward and execute forward. Mental toughness is exhibited when coaches help their athletes set realistic and challenging goals and then work diligently to help athletes incrementally close gaps between their current levels of performance and the target goal. Staying focused on long-term goals that may take years to achieve requires great coaching commitment.

Confidence, the fourth and final C of the mental toughness model, is self-belief in spite of setbacks. Besides undertaking the coaching efficacy activities already suggested in this chapter, coaches can build the confidence part of their mental toughness by practicing mental skills such as imagery and positive self-talk. For example, coaches can imagine themselves leading an efficient and productive practice session or coaching with composure and integrity during tough competition situations.

Several mental toughness questionnaires have been created for use with athletes, including the Mental Toughness Scale (MTS).[46] A simplified version of the Mental Toughness Scale adapted for coaches to self-assess their mental toughness is provided in figure 11.5. Questions on which the coach scores high (4 or 5) should be recognized as a mental toughness strength for the coach. Questions on which the coach scores low (1 or 2) present opportunities for improving the coach's mental toughness.

## Figure 11.5 Coach Mental Toughness Questionnaire

| | Strongly disagree | | | | Strongly agree |
|---|---|---|---|---|---|
| 1. I believe I can help my athletes achieve anything we set our minds to. | 1 | 2 | 3 | 4 | 5 |
| 2. I know what needs to be done to achieve the level of performance we desire. | 1 | 2 | 3 | 4 | 5 |
| 3. I have total commitment to our performance goals until every possible opportunity of success has passed. | 1 | 2 | 3 | 4 | 5 |
| 4. I know when to celebrate and recognize our successes but also when to stop and focus on the next challenge. | 1 | 2 | 3 | 4 | 5 |
| 5. I model the patience and discipline needed to stay focused on our target goals. | 1 | 2 | 3 | 4 | 5 |
| 6. Even though I am tired, I continue to model the intensity we need to achieve our goals. | 1 | 2 | 3 | 4 | 5 |
| 7. When an obstacle is in our way I find a way to help my athletes overcome it. | 1 | 2 | 3 | 4 | 5 |

Adapted, by permission, from L. Madrigal, S. Hamill, and D.L. Gill, 2013, "Mind over matter: The development of the Mental Toughness Scale (MTS)," *The Sport Psychologist* 27(1): 62-77.

## STORING AND APPLYING LESSONS LEARNED FOR ADDITIONAL STRENGTH

To build continually on strengths, coaches need strategies for storing what they learn about their strengths so that they can easily retrieve and review lessons learned when needed. All coaches will have their own preferences and ways of storing what they learn about their strengths, but several examples can help coaches think about novel and effective ways to archive lessons learned.

The first example comes from the United States Army, which has created the Center for Army Lessons Learned (CALL). CALL is an extreme example of the tremendous potential of identifying strengths and storing lessons learned. Military leaders, much like coaches, must continually adapt to ever-changing and complex situations, albeit with much greater consequences hinging on their actions. Many years ago the U.S. Army leadership recognized the urgent need to capture and share lessons learned from their operations around the world. With the creation of CALL, the U.S. Army now has a formal structure in place to share their strengths and train leaders on how to build on what works across a wide variety of mission settings (http://usacac.army.mil/organizations/mccoe/call).

Lessons learned about strengths are regularly shared in updated handbooks, such as handbooks for disaster response and guides for supporting refugee and displaced persons operations. CALL also shares what works with military personnel through five-day lessons-learned courses. Although most coaches won't have access to the same level of infrastructure and support as the U.S. Army does, coaches can create their own versions of lessons-learned handbooks. Furthermore, those responsible for helping coaches realize their strengths, such as athletics directors, should consider creating regular opportunities for coaches to share and discuss lessons learned.

I have found that recording coaches speaking about lessons learned from using their coaching strengths is a relatively simple and valuable way of storing and sharing local best practices. Coaches enjoy and are energized by speaking about their coaching strengths. In my applied research with high school coaches, we hold formal end-of-season meetings with each head coach to review strengths. After the meeting coaches are sometimes invited to share, in a three- to five-minute video, a lesson learned about using one of their coaching strengths. Coaches are then videotaped sharing their insights. The video is uploaded to a "coaching strengths coaching channel" using the free version of the *Vimeo* video-sharing platform (http://vimeo.com/fresnohscoachingchannel).

Similar lessons-learned and coaching strengths video libraries have been created by a wide range of sport coaching associations. Some, such as the American Football Coaches Association, provide open access to master coaches sharing their wisdom (www.afca.com/article/article.php?id=42) and shorter two-minute lessons learned (www.afca.com/article/article.php?id=954). Others have created an extensive fee-based online video library of coaches sharing how they build successful programs. For example, the American Swimming Coaches Association has created a "sound coaching library" that offers access to presentations from their annual convention available for as low as $1.99 per audio podcast (https://swimmingcoach.org/product-category/audio/), and the American Baseball Coaches Association sells videos on demand at a higher rate covering a wide range of coaching topics delivered by baseball coaching experts (http://abcavideos.org/). Finally, the *What Drives Winning* website is a valuable source for free videos of championship coaches across sports sharing some of the most valuable lessons learned over their distinguished careers (http://whatdriveswinning.com/#video-link).

## Wrap-Up

Effective coaches understand the importance of setting aside time at the end of the season to recognize and build on strengths, not only athlete and program strengths but also their own emerging strengths as a coach. Formal team banquets and end-of-season rituals are important opportunities for recognizing and reinforcing program core values while celebrating individual and team accomplishments. Effective end-of-season recognition strategies help build a culture and tradition of excellence. These activities will help to sustain (after a successful season) or rekindle (after a tough season) the motivation and commitment needed to have a successful off-season.

Regardless of the final performance outcome each season, with disciplined review coaches will be able to identify moments of success that occurred as a direct result of using their strengths. Coaches should reinforce these strengths and reflect on how they can use their strengths more often. Although knowing and growing strengths will position coaches to maximize their coaching potential, coaches need to remember to use the right strength in the right way at the right time. Ultimately, building on strengths contributes to coaching resilience and coaching efficacy, helping to counterbalance setbacks and negative emotions that naturally occur across a coaching career.

# Part IV

# OFF-SEASON

## Enhance

# Chapter 12

# Close Performance Gaps

**Key Concepts**

Personal mastery
Industriousness
Curiosity
Resourcefulness
Self-examination
Self-monitoring
Growth mind-set
Continuous improvement
Systematic reflection
Reflective practice
Problem setting
Critical reflection
Systems thinking
High-impact performance gaps

Just as it is essential to recognize and build on strengths (chapter 11), so too is it critical to identify weaknesses or areas for growth and then chart a course to address them. Successful coaches are humble enough to recognize that even in championship seasons, they make mistakes that need to be corrected in the off-season. True to form, legendary baseball coach Yogi Berra playfully captured the importance of recognizing and closing performance gaps when he stated, "We made too many wrong mistakes."[1]

The most effective coaches are lifelong learners who are on a constant quest to identify and close performance gaps.[2, 3] Roger Kingdom, a coach of the Arizona Cardinals professional football team and former Olympic champion, provides a vivid example of how successful coaches approach failure. After the team was badly beaten one game short of reaching the 2016 Super Bowl—what many would consider a demoralizing defeat—he stated, "You win or you learn. We can learn a lot from that game. If we can figure out what we need to work on and improve, then we will be playing in the Super Bowl next year."[4]

Once end-of-season business is done (see part III of this book), serious coaches get busy building up their coaching knowledge. Just as many athletes use the off-season to rest briefly and refocus on physical training, in the off-season the best coaches devote the same type of energy and effort into learning more about effective coaching. The off-season is prime time for coach development, a sentiment shared by all the best coaches, like World Cup championship soccer coach Tony DiCicco: "The season is over. But the work isn't over yet. In many ways, it's just begun because off-season preparation is critically important in determining how your team will perform next season."[5 (p. 208)]

The purpose of this chapter is to share examples of the deliberate, targeted activities that successful coaches use to optimize coaching improvement in high-impact performance gaps. The primary method used to close performance gaps in the off-season is personal reflection.

A commitment to off-season training for coaches requires a high degree of initiative and eagerness to keep learning, regardless of how many years a coach has been coaching. This commitment is associated with personal mastery and a growth mind-set, both of which provide the foundation for continuous improvement aimed at closing performance gaps.

## EMPHASIZING PERSONAL MASTERY

Legendary physicist Albert Einstein reportedly stated, "I have no special talent. I am only passionately curious."[6] The same can be said of successful coaches. Having a deep-rooted passion for learning and an inherent curiosity about the whys and hows of life is referred to as personal mastery. Influential leadership and learning expert Peter Senge[7] defines personal mastery as a process:

> **People with a high level of personal mastery live in a continual learning mode. They never "arrive." Personal mastery is not something you possess. It is a process. It is a lifelong discipline. People with a high level of personal mastery are acutely aware of their ignorance, their incompetence, their growth areas.**[(pp. 132–133)]

Coaches who exhibit personal mastery are self-driven to figure out why performance gaps exist and how they can close those gaps. These types of coaches don't wait for someone else to mandate that they attend a clinic, read a new book, or visit another coach to learn about their strategies. Coaches with a personal mastery orientation view ongoing learning as a beloved and essential part of coaching.

Grant Teaff, member of the College Football Hall of Fame and former executive director of the American Football Coaches Association (AFCA), shares a vivid example of a successful coach who modeled personal mastery across his life. In his book *A Coach's Influence: Beyond the Game*,[8] he describes an encounter with fellow Hall of Fame football coach Don Faurot, considered one of the most innovative offensive minds ever to have coached the game.

> A few years ago, at age 92, Don was attending the AFCA Convention and I was lecturing on short-yardage offense. I noticed Don was sitting in the front row and scribbling in a small book. After the session, Coach Faurot sought me out, asking for details of my lecture. After answering his questions, I asked, "Coach, you have been retired for 25 years, so why do you still attend lectures and keep extensive notes?" Coach Faurot said without hesitation, "Never stop learning."[(p. 114)]

Recall from chapter 2 ("Connect Values to Philosophy") that the core values and philosophy of effective coaches always includes a commitment to ongoing learning. The Pyramid of Teaching Success in Sport (PoTSS)[9] was introduced as an example of a coaching philosophy that embodies personal mastery. At this point in the book, a more thorough description of the personal mastery elements of the PoTSS will provide coaches with a sharper image of specific coaching qualities associated with personal mastery.

The four characteristics of a personal mastery approach to learning for coaches as described in the PoTSS are industriousness, curiosity, resourcefulness, and self-examination (see figure 12.1).

Industriousness is the term used to describe coaches who are constantly working to improve. Industrious coaches are energetic and proactive instead of reactive—they never stop working at getting better. College swim coach Brian Reynolds, who has coached his men's and women's teams to a combined 33 national team championships, highlights the importance of constantly trying to improve as a coach:

> Anyone who tries to do something for a long time really, really well, understands that you have to be constantly feeling like a sense of urgency a little bit in that process, because if you don't have that, then I think you're probably on cruise control, and you want to stay off that.[10]

Industriousness, however, also requires focus. Five-time Super Bowl–winning coach Bill Belichick identified focus as the most important characteristic for

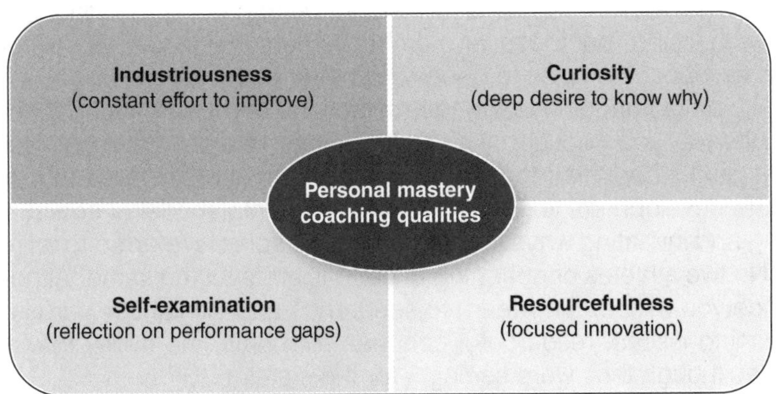


**Figure 12.1** Personal mastery coaching qualities.

becoming a successful coach. For example, he described friend and college football championship coach Nick Saban as a master of self-improvement who

> "is all about focus—on one thing. Whether it is the next opponent, the next practice, or the next recruit, he has the ability—at any given time—to devote his absolute attention and energy to solving the problem or challenge at hand before moving on to the next one."[11 (p. xii)]

Industrious coaches are careful to focus their energy and learning efforts on meaningful performance gaps. For example, although learning more about your favorite offense or coach may be enjoyable and personally relevant, if it does not directly relate to closing an important gap in your knowledge or athlete performance, then you are not truly demonstrating industriousness and personal mastery.

The next characteristic, curiosity, is defined as the deep desire to know why, not just how. Returning to the example of wanting to learn more about your favorite offense or coach, if the learning is directed at gaining a deeper appreciation for the underlying principles that explain why the offense is designed as it is or more fully understanding why your favorite coach uses a certain strategy, then the learning effort is consistent with the curiosity element of personal mastery.

Coach Sean Foley, who has coached champion golfers around the world including Tiger Woods and Justin Rose, is a perfect example of a curious coach. When talking about his development as a coach, he shared that he has always had a deep-rooted curiosity about the technical aspects of his sport, something that he believes helped him become one of the world's top golf coaches:

> I was a "why" person even as a kid. I questioned everything, and with the golf swing there's an awful lot of "why." When my dad took me to the Canadian Open at Glen Abbey when I was 14, he went onto the course to watch the players, and I went to the range to watch teachers work with players. I sat on a hillside watching David Leadbetter work with Nick Faldo for as long as they were there. The instruction articles in the golf magazines fascinated me. . . . I've always had a need to figure out what made a good swing work.[12]

Curious coaches view failure as fertilizer for deeper learning. Coaches typically struggle with losing, but those who embrace personal mastery use defeat and setbacks as launching pads to becoming better coaches.

Curiosity-driven ongoing learning provides the necessary foundation for reorganizing the way you think about coaching and athlete development. Recall from chapter 1 of this book that the way you organize your thinking about coaching and athlete development is referred to as your mental model of coaching.

Finding and inventing ways to get around obstacles is referred to as resourcefulness. No two athletes or coaching dilemmas are ever the same. Although with experience you will certainly learn to see trends and similarities across athletes and coaching issues, resourceful coaches also have the ability to view every situation as though they were seeing it for the first time.

One of the great paradoxes of coaching and ongoing learning is the ability to see patterns while simultaneously suspending judgment and a rush to action by taking a fresh look at the situation. Furthermore, the most challenging coaching issues will not be easily resolved and will require creative solutions. When facing these types of issues, coaches can easily become frustrated and leave the issue unresolved. The resourceful coach is relentless and will not rest until the issue has been satisfactorily resolved.

The final component of personal mastery for coaches as described in the PoTSS is self-examination, sometimes also referred to as self-monitoring.[2, 3] Self-monitoring requires a desire to improve continuously, which leads to constant renewal as a coach. Recall that the essence of great coaching is quality teaching. Not surprisingly then, successful coaches share this desire for constant improvement with the world's best teachers: "Teaching better implies a perpetual pursuit of improvement. It suggests that we never 'arrive' at a point of complete mastery but are continuously and relentlessly in search of enhancing our craft."[13 (p. 7)]

The off-season presents coaches with a natural break from everyday coaching activities. For that reason, the off-season is the ideal time of the year for coaches to reflect on what works (strengths) and what needs adjustment (gaps). Successful coaches set aside time in the off-season to review all aspects of their program and then select a few gaps to study in depth.

Self-examination was one of the keys to Coach John Wooden's unprecedented success. Following every season he wrote out a list of things to consider for the following season. A copy of Coach Wooden's handwritten to-consider list that he prepared at the end of the 1973–74 season is shown in figure 12.2.

His list that off-season included 14 areas that he believed were critical for improvement for the following season. Some of the items related to athlete discipline and leadership (be patient with players on the floor, but be firm in discipline both on and off the floor), but others focused more on technical and tactical issues (work on the zone offense a little more). Coach Wooden believed that improvement in these areas would result in the team's regaining the national championship, which they lost in the 1973–74 season. His team did in fact win the 1975 national championship, his final season of coaching.

History has shown that embracing all four personal mastery characteristics for coaches identified in the PoTSS—industriousness, curiosity, resourcefulness, and self-examination—will lead to improved coaching. Championship baseball coach Joe Torre, who led the New York Yankees to four championships and was himself a nine-time all-star athlete in Major League Baseball, epitomizes a personal mastery approach to learning. Each of the personal mastery characteristics is evident in the following quotation from Coach Torre:[14]

> To get the most out of yourself, you must know yourself—your strengths, your limits, your potential. Stay within yourself, but recognize that within those bounds there is no telling what you can accomplish. Don't be reckless in your pursuit of individual and team goals, but don't be afraid to make mistakes, either. Accept these paradoxes—you can acknowledge your limits and yet exceed all expectations; you can be disciplined and careful in your work habits, but fearless as you strive to realize your highest potential. Self-knowledge plus maximum effort is a valid formula for success.

## Figure 12.2 Coach Wooden's Off-Season Self-Examination Notes Following the 1973–74 Season

**Consider for 1974–75 season—UCLA**
**(Compiled at the close of the 1973–74 season)**

1. Build confidence in Drollinger and Trgovich.
2. Get McCarter under control with the basketball.
3. Be patient in determining the proper pressing defense.
4. Use 3 on 2 continuity drill at least three times a week.
5. Defense the passing game a little more.
6. Work on our offense against zone defense a little more.
7. Use weak side post drill without shooting more frequently and possibly in our pre-game warm-up.
8. Organize our time-outs better.
9. Try out the "4 corner" as a lead protector.
10. Make Dave Meyers "captain".
11. Be very cautious with Marques Johnson—hepatitis.
12. Forget the past and concentrate on each day of practice—analyze, prepare, evaluate, etc.
13. Prepare Richard Washington for both high and low post as well as forward.
14. Be patient with players on floor, but be firm in discipline both on and off floor.
15. Do not take anything for granted just because we have done so well in the past.



The journey from good coach to great coach is riddled with setbacks, countless hours of focused self-study, and constant tinkering with coaching strategies. Moments of self-doubt will surely surface, and challenges will arise from those who don't share the same level of personal mastery. Your desire, patience, persistence, and confidence will ultimately determine your ability to close performance gaps and become a coach who models personal mastery.[15]

Hearing the stories of other coaches who model personal mastery is a simple strategy that coaches can use to stay motivated and energized while practicing personal mastery. The coaching autobiographies cited throughout this book are good places to start. Don't limit yourself to reading only about successful coaches in your sport. You will find that coaching autobiographies are a great source of inspiration because they reveal the struggles and self-doubt that successful coaches overcome when they strive for personal mastery.

Finally, coaches can accelerate their path to personal mastery and coaching success by learning the stories of successful people outside coaching, particularly from books or documentaries that profile multiple success stories. One such example is the book *Mastery* by Robert Greene.[15] Recommended to me by several coaches, the book details dozens of personal mastery stories of both historical and contemporary masters across a wide range of professions.

## ADOPTING A GROWTH MIND-SET

On October 12, 2014, the USA women's national volleyball team accomplished something never before achieved in volleyball history. They won their first major championship, beating China in the finals of the world volleyball championships. Although the women's team had claimed multiple silver medals at world championships and Olympic Games, Karch Kiraly became the first coach in the program's long history to lead the team to a championship. The core of Coach Kiraly's approach to coach and athlete development is a commitment to personal mastery and continuous improvement.

One week after the team's historic achievement, I had an opportunity to speak with Coach Kiraly about his coaching approach. He explained that he expects his athletes, among the best in the world at their sport, to be improving constantly if they want to maintain their spot on the team. He also shared that this relentless drive to improve must be modeled first by the coaching staff. A commitment to personal mastery is the first pillar of Kiraly's coaching approach, which he describes as a growth mind-set.[16]

The term *growth mind-set* is often attributed to pioneering American psychologist Carol Dweck, who conducted decades of research on personal mastery and its effect on teaching, learning, and performance.[17] Recall from chapter 7 of this book that *mind-set* is the term used to describe how people view learning and

AP Photo/Chris Carlson

Karch Kiraly coached the U.S. women's volleyball team to their first world championship by creating a practice environment focused on personal mastery and continuous improvement.

ability. People generally lean toward one of two mind-sets: a fixed mind-set or a growth mind-set.

The idea of a growth mind-set is based on implicit theories of human ability. We can separate assumptions about ability into two distinct ways of thinking—one referred to as the entity view and the other referred to as the incremental view.[18] Coaches who have the entity view believe that ability is innate and somewhat stable. When people refer to an athlete as a natural talent, they are assuming an entity view of ability. This view is what we consider a fixed mind-set. Unfortunately, much of the athlete recruiting that occurs in sport is falsely grounded in a fixed mind-set, assuming that an athlete's talent at a young age is predictive of her or his ability at higher levels of competition.

On the other hand, coaches who have an incremental view of ability believe that ability is unstable and flexible. Ability is primarily the result of focused deliberate practice and resilience. When a coach praises an athlete for his or her work ethic and attributes the athlete's success to effortful and focused practice, the coach is modeling an incremental view of ability, what we commonly refer to as a growth mind-set.

A valuable way to think about the differences between a fixed mind-set (entity view) of talent and a growth mind-set (incremental view) of ability is that those who hold a fixed mind-set direct their focus and efforts on proving their ability, whereas those who hold a growth mind-set direct their focus and efforts on improving their ability (see figure 12.3).

People who adopt a growth mindset report higher levels of motivation, persistence, and effort, and a greater preference for and willingness to accept challenges.[17] In other words, coaches with a growth mind-set are more resilient and seek opportunities to improve despite encountering failures and setbacks.

Some evidence suggests that novice coaches are less oriented to a growth mind-set compared with experienced coaches.[19] A growth mind-set is particularly important for novice coaches who will surely experience many setbacks early in their careers. Their careers may be cut short, and they will not reach their true coaching potential if they view the inevitable setbacks as the result of fixed coaching ability (e.g., either you have what it takes to coach, or you don't). The lesson here is to stay focused on learning and continuously improving; all else is somewhat beyond your control.

A quick online test is available to assess which type of mind-set best describes you.[20] Using this test and other examples of mind-set questions,[21] I created a coaching mind-set self-assessment tool (see figure 12.4). After reading each pair of statements, place an X on the line that best represents your view on the two statements. For example, if you strongly agree with one statement, place your X directly under that statement. Conversely, you may decide to place your X near the middle of the line if you think that both statements are somewhat true for you as a coach.

Successful people across professions have a growth mind-set because they define success in terms of continuous learning and improvement. A phrase from Carol Dweck that captures the essence of growth mind-set coaching is "becoming is better than being." Effective coaches understand that true success comes

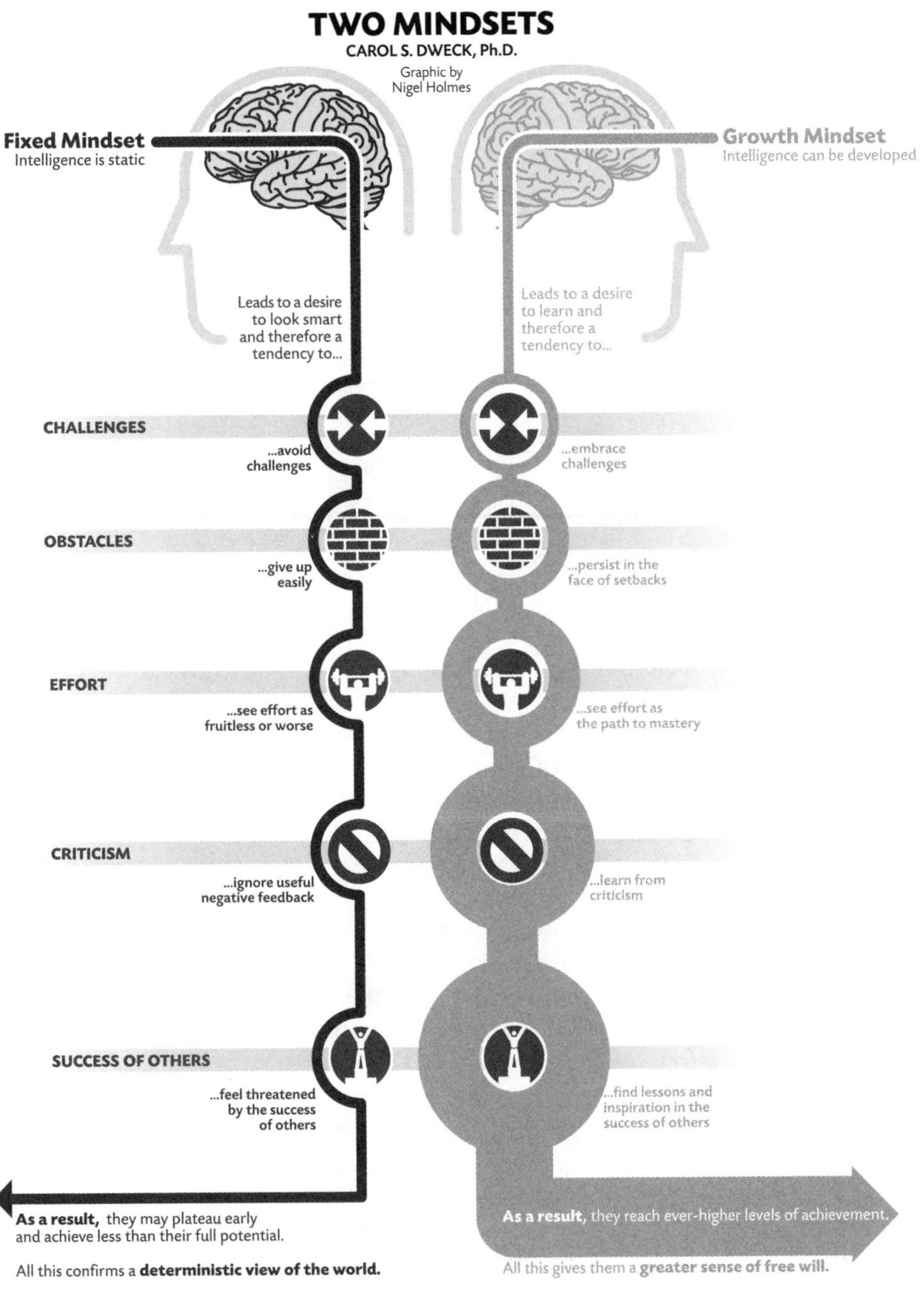


**Figure 12.3** Fixed mind-set versus growth mind-set.

## Figure 12.4 Coaching Mind-Set Self-Assessment

| Growth mind-set coach | Fixed mind-set coach |
|---|---|
| I can learn and improve any aspect of my coaching that I want to. | Great coaches are natural-born leaders. |
| When I'm frustrated as a coach, I persevere. | When I'm frustrated as a coach, I give up easily. |
| I constantly challenge myself to get better as a coach. | I am comfortable with my current ability as a coach. |
| When I fail as a coach, I look for the lessons from the failure. | When I fail as a coach, I wonder if I'm just not cut out for coaching. |
| Seeing other coaches succeed inspires me to get better. | Seeing other coaches succeed makes me feel threatened. |
| My effort and attitude determine my success as a coach. | My natural abilities as a coach determine my success. |

from an unrelenting focus on becoming; they focus on the process of getting better every day.

Returning to the example of championship volleyball coach Karch Kiraly, he uses the term *training ugly* to help his athletes focus on using mistakes as learning opportunities for becoming better. Training sessions are designed deliberately to stretch players out of their comfort zones, which will lead to many mistakes and the appearance of an ugly practice. With a growth mind-set, mistakes are a necessary part of the ongoing learning process.

Coaching legend Dan Gable, who coached college wrestling teams to 16 national titles, is another prime example of a growth mind-set coach. Coach Gable once explained that constantly changing for the better was his life philosophy. He said that he was always updating and revising his coaching strategies.[22]

A review of virtually any literature on the world's most successful coaches will reveal growth mind-set qualities, although seldom will coaches specifically mention the term *growth mind-set*.

For example, American college baseball coach Augie Garrido exposes his growth mind-set when he describes the never-ending process of "sharpening the saw." Setbacks and failures are viewed as normal and temporary bumps in the road if action is taken immediately to learn from the failure. Coach Garrido has created a six-part formula for dealing with failure that is firmly grounded in a growth mind-set approach to coaching.[23]

1. Acknowledge the failure.
2. Analyze what went wrong.
3. Consider your successful recoveries from past failures and setbacks.
4. Make the adjustments you need to make based on what you learned.
5. Keep adjusting until it works.
6. Focus on doing your best in each and every moment.

Clearly, successful coaches across sports and levels of competition operate with a growth mind-set. A growth mind-set is needed to learn from setbacks and build a bank of coaching strategies that will lead to durable sporting success.

## SEEKING CONTINUOUS IMPROVEMENT

Successful coaches have an inner drive to change and evolve. This approach sustains their passion for coaching and keeps them fresh and excited for what is next. The best coaches are never content with resting on prior accomplishments; they are always trying to create a higher standard for the future. National football championship coach Nick Saban refers to continuous improvement as a standard of excellence, and, he says, "The standard of excellence is always under construction, it's never complete."[24]

Across their careers coaches have to counterbalance the natural preference to stick with what works with efforts to adjust to the ever-changing demands of their sport and needs of their athletes. Some coaches, such as two-time NBA championship coach Erik Spoelstra, describe this as a willingness to reinvent themselves as coaches. Coach Spoelstra guided LeBron James and the Miami Heat to four straight championship finals, but he was quick to acknowledge that it required a never-ending commitment to finding new ways to improve:

> How many times have you reinvented yourself to become somebody new, somebody better? But in order to do that you have to be uncomfortable. You can't stay who you are. . . . Things change and you have to be able to adapt.[25 (p. 59)]

The combination of personal mastery and a growth mind-set for coaches provides the foundation for long-term, incremental, continuous improvement. Continuous improvement comes from a steady focus on deliberately closing performance gaps. Championship college and professional football coach Pete Carroll is a prime example of an effective coach who is committed to continuous improvement. He stated that all he tries to do is "just get a little better every day."[26] The dramatic outcomes that can result from focusing on steady incremental progress toward shortening performance gaps was on full display in 2013–2014 when Coach Carroll lead the Seattle Seahawks to one of the most dominating championship victories in Super Bowl history.

Many coaches have a tendency to try to fix too much at one time. As a result they can find themselves endlessly chasing, but never closing, performance gaps. Leadership guru Harvey MacKay frequently uses examples from sport coaches to illustrate principles of continuous improvement. He once referenced an ancient parable that states, "The hunter who chases two rabbits catches neither one" to reinforce the importance of focusing on one performance gap at a time. In Harvey MacKay's words, "Trying to get everything will get you nothing."[27] The key, then, to a long and successful coaching career is to address performance gaps steadily, one at a time.

Continuous improvement has been formally defined as "moving toward a desired state through an unclear territory by being sensitive to and responding to actual conditions on the ground."[28 (p. 43)] The keys to this definition and the way that it guides the continuous improvement efforts of successful leaders in all fields including coaching are (*a*) engaging in focused efforts to close performance gaps while (*b*) realizing that there is no clear or predictable path between your current performance and the target performance level.[28–31]

Continuous improvement requires a keen awareness of both your current situation and your desired performance level, as well as a commitment to staying focused on the next best step. Successful coaches approach their continuous improvement efforts thinking evolution, not revolution, an attitude captured well in statements from world championship and Olympic gold medal–winning swim coach Stephan Widmer:

> Don't expect to change instantly or with rapid progression. Everything worthwhile takes time! Make sure you recognize little steps forward and celebrate them accordingly. The journey ahead of a coach is exciting. Any small change should encourage you, your swimmers, and your team. The accumulation of 100 little steps forward will lead you to the improvement you are looking for on your new chosen path.[32 (p. 121)]

Regardless of how much experience a coach has or how carefully thought out improvement strategies are, the effectiveness of continuous improvement strategies is impossible to predict. Simultaneous attention to studying the current situation and the intended target, while accepting the messiness and complexity of the path between present performance and desired performance, is the defining characteristic of all continuous improvement models.

In a continuous improvement model, the target condition serves as the guiding light for the next best step. The world's most successful companies, such as Toyota, use the following five questions to guide their continuous improvement efforts.[28 (p. 155)] Answering these questions allows them to close the gap systematically and incrementally between where they are and where they want to be.

1. What is the target condition?
2. What is the actual condition right now?
3. What obstacles are preventing us from reaching the target condition?
4. What is our next best step?
5. When can we go to see what we have learned from taking that step?

Disciplined attention to answering these five questions on a regular basis is the key to continuous improvement and the creation of a culture of sustained excellence for a sport program. Figure 12.5, inspired by the continuous improvement models created by Mike Rother in the business world, was created to provide an overview of the principles of continuous improvement and the way on which they can be applied to sport coaching.

In sum, successful coaches and leaders in other fields share the realization that constant change is mandatory. In the words of two-time national high school football Coach of the Year Chuck Kyle, "A leader must always be on the cutting edge of techniques and new strategy"[33 (p. 96)] Coaches gain the trust and respect

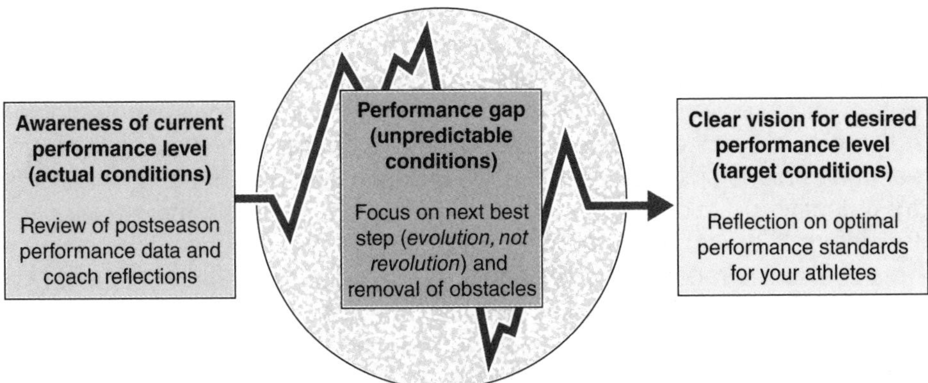


**Figure 12.5** Continuous improvement model for coaches.

of their athletes when they show they are willing to evolve and grow with them, instead of sticking to old ways even when change is clearly needed.

Successful coaches acknowledge that change is difficult. Early in her career, legendary eight-time championship college basketball coach Pat Summitt admitted to not feeling secure enough as a coach to show the vulnerability that change requires. As she gained experience and wisdom, however, she became more open to change, realizing that it was the only way to stay fresh as a coach and help her athletes reach their potential: "They demanded that I be flexible enough and secure enough to change. They challenged me every day to coach up to their talents, to be more creative, and to explore their seemingly open-ended capacity for winning."[34 (pp. 280–281)]

# ENGAGING IN SYSTEMATIC REFLECTION

The ability to close performance gaps consistently requires disciplined and focused introspection. The term used most often to describe this process is *self-reflection.* The most effective coaches are reflective practitioners.[35, 36] Successful coaches, like 12-time national Coach of the Year and three-time U.S. Olympic diving coach Jeffrey Huber, come to realize over their careers that "in many ways, coaching is a reflective activity.[37 (p. 8)]

Coach reflection can be defined as the process of thinking about your coaching. But simply thinking about coaching without a clear focus on a specific performance gap or your general approach to coaching will not result in durable improvements. Focused thinking about performance gaps or your coaching philosophy is referred to as systematic reflection. Coaches must learn to harness this type of reflection to make the most of their off-season continuous improvement efforts. Systematic reflection can be divided into reflective practice and critical reflection.

## Reflective Practice

Reflective practice is the type of reflection that coaches engage in when they are focused on solving a specific coaching problem (i.e., closing a performance gap). The result of reflective practice is revised, or new, coaching strategies. Reflective practice is characterized by working through problem-solving cycles, often referred to as the plan-do-check-act, or PDCA, cycle.[28]

For example, college rowing coach Jan Harville credits a five-step reflective practice process for helping her lead rowers to 11 national championships (and 3 team championships) across her 16-year career. The five steps in Coach Harville's reflective practice process are: (*a*) define and evaluate the situation, (*b*) gather information, (*c*) develop and analyze options, (*d*) choose the best course of action, and (*e*) implement and review the decision.[38] Although this reflective practice model served her well, she acknowledges that coaches should be open to learning about a variety of reflective practice models and adapt what they learn to create the model that works best for them.

While conducting one of the first studies to examine how coaches learn through reflective practice, we discovered that effective coaches consistently cycled through four steps when reflecting on how to close performance gaps (figure 12.6).[39] The four steps in reflective practice are collectively referred to as a reflective conversation and include problem setting, strategy generation, experimentation, and evaluation.

Problems, or performance gaps, don't simply present themselves to coaches. Coaches interpret their observations differently depending on their mental model of coaching, unique knowledge of their athletes, and desired target outcomes. The unique perspective that each coach holds determines which situations are worthy of pursuing as relevant performance gaps.

This process of interpretation and decision making is referred to as problem setting. In this sense, problems must be properly set before they can be effectively solved. When reflecting on their observations, coaches should pause to ponder why they consider a situation problematic in the first place and how the issue influences athlete and team performance.

For example, a coach may notice that athletes are periodically off-task during practice. Depending on the context and the coach's philosophy, the matter may not be an issue if athletes sometimes engage in playful and off-task behavior

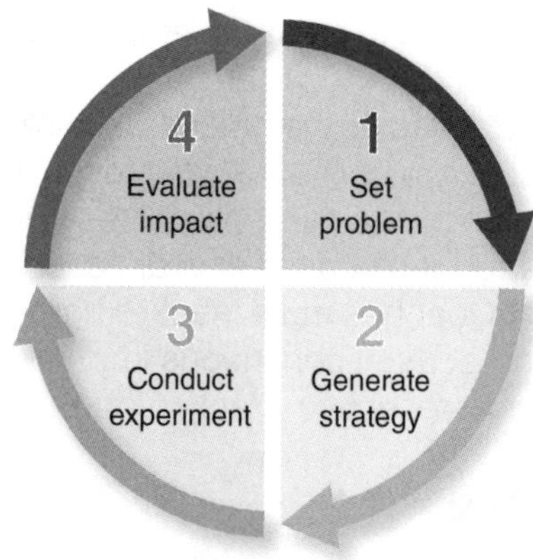


**Figure 12.6** Steps in coach reflective practice cycle.

during a training session. Similar to the common fire safety cue taught to children ("Stop, drop, and roll"), the reflective practice cue "Stop, think, and set" may be helpful for coaches to remember.

- Stop before taking action.
- Think about potential causes of what you are noticing.
- Set the situation as a problem if it is significant performance obstacle or ignore it and focus on more important issues.

If a situation is set as a problem or a significant performance gap, then coaches should proceed to the next step in the reflective conversation, which is strategy generation. Coaches can use many potential sources of information to develop coaching strategies, such as discussions with coaching peers, books, videos, websites, and live observations of other coaches. After they have formulated a potential strategy, effective coaches test it to get a sense of how effective the strategy will be at closing the performance gap.

Coaches don't need to test their strategies on a full scale to obtain feedback. Effective coaches often conduct virtual experiments to test their strategies before trying them with their athletes. For example, a coach may first test a potential new defensive strategy by asking a trusted coaching peer for another opinion on the strategy. The feedback will either confirm that the strategy is ready to test in a real experiment with the athletes or show that the strategy is not quite ready and needs to be revised. This method is similar to the way that professionals in fields such as architecture, business, engineering, and medicine test potential solutions using computer modeling and simulations.[40]

One way to review the outcome of new coaching strategies is to examine how well they worked for other coaches. Although this groundwork will delay the testing of coaching strategies with your athletes, it may keep you from repeating mistakes made by other coaches.

Graham Henry and Wayne Smith, coaches of the New Zealand All Blacks rugby team, used this strategy to close high-impact performance gaps that allowed them to regain the title of world champions. After losing in the 2007 World Championships, they made time to consult with a wide range of other coaches whose teams were unsuccessful. The purpose of this activity was to look for clues and strategies that would help them avoid errors made by others: "We . . . looked at their campaigns, and came up with what we thought were the reasons why they'd failed. We then planned strategically to put things in place to try and combat past errors."[41 (p. 64)]

Legendary coach John Wooden's off-season self-study strategy is likely the most well-known documented example of a coach who systematically engaged in reflective practice to close performance gaps across a coaching career. Coach Wooden was renowned for conducting detailed off-season analyses on how to close performance gaps.

Each off-season Coach Wooden would carefully sift through all the potential topics identified as performance gaps and select what he considered the question most worthy of studying at that particular time. With his off-season research

AP Photo/Tom Hevezi

**Strategic planning based on careful observations and learning from past mistakes is a hallmark of championship coaches such as former All Blacks coach Graham Henry.**

question in hand, he would then carefully select a sample of other coaches and experts who were renowned, through either reputation or statistical evidence, for their knowledge of how to address the research question effectively.

Coach Wooden would then create a tool, such as a survey, to collect information from the sample of coaches and experts and systematically map out a plan for collecting and analyzing the data.

Unlike Coach Wooden, coaches today have access to a virtually unlimited source of coaching wisdom in the form of coaching books, websites, videos, and coaching journals. Besides speaking with other coaches and reviewing sport-specific coaching materials, coaches seeking to gain a competitive edge also look to coaching and sport science journals.

Numerous articles can provide insights into any imaginable performance gap that a coach will face. But coaching-related articles are published across hundreds of professional journals, so coaches cannot quickly find relevant information.[42, 43] To help coaches find high-quality coaching-related articles, I have created a top 10 list of professional journals for coaches:

*Coaching Edge*

*Coaches Plan*

*International Journal of Sports Science & Coaching*

*International Sport Coaching Journal*
*Journal of Physical Education, Recreation & Dance*
*Journal of Sport Psychology in Action*
*Olympic Coach E-Magazine*
*Physical Education and Sport Pedagogy*
*Strategies: A Journal for Physical and Sport Educators*
*The Sport Psychologist*

I regularly share articles from these journals with coaches because these journals publish science-based articles that include practical implications for coaches in the field.

Some of these journals are free, and even the ones that require a paid subscription often provide open access to the most popular articles. Besides subscribing to some of these journals, coaches should check with local university libraries for journal access. University libraries often subscribe to many of these journals and may offer opportunities to access journal articles as a guest.

Like any good researcher, Coach Wooden would close his continuous improvement study by writing a summary of his conclusions that could then be tested in the upcoming season and added to his ever-growing library of personal coaching research. A worksheet for helping coaches conduct their own off-season research, just like the one that Coach Wooden used while building a championship dynasty in college basketball, is presented in figure 12.7.

A detailed illustration of how Coach Wooden used this continuous improvement research process during the off-season to learn how to close his team's free-throw shooting performance gap is provided in chapter 3 of *You Haven't Taught Until They Have Learned*, written by Swen Nater and Ronald Gallimore.[44] Coach Wooden provides a vivid example of industriousness in action and the way in which commitment to making small improvements each year can eventually lead to big breakthroughs in performance.

By adding a new tool to his coaching toolbox each off-season, Coach Wooden steadily closed important performance gaps, edging closer and closer to the target condition—a national championship—every year. After 14 years of adhering to this focused process of continuous improvement, Coach Wooden finally led a team to a national championship, which was promptly followed by nine more championships in the next 11 years. A summary of Coach Wooden's conclusions from his off-season free-throw shooting study is reproduced in figure 12.8.

## Critical Reflection

Unlike reflective practice, critical reflection is not focused on solving a specific problem. Critical reflection is used more sparingly, but still regularly, to update evolving views on coaching. The off-season, when coaches typically have fewer demands on their time, is the ideal time for coaches to reflect on their coaching purpose, core values, and general approach to coaching. Critical reflection is the type of reflection coaches engage in when they think about their feelings or general coaching philosophy.

## Figure 12.7 Worksheet for Conducting Off-Season Continuous Improvement Research

**Define research question.**
Select a high-impact performance gap that will be studied.

**Select sources of evidence.**
Identify potential resources (coaches, books, articles, videos, and so on) that will be used to learn more about how to close the performance gap.

**Create data collection tool.**
Describe how you will record what you learn while collecting information (coaching journal, audio or video recordings, computer software, and so on).

**List data collection steps.**
Indicate the timeline and procedures for collecting information.

**Describe how data will be summarized.**
Explain the format of the report you will create and how you will make sense of the information.

From W. Gilbert, 2017, *Coaching better every season: A year-round system for athlete development and program success* (Champaign, IL: Human Kinetics).

The result of critical reflection is the reorganization of the coach's mental model of coaching and better coaching. For example, a study with 35 soccer coaches found that regularly setting aside time for critical reflection was considered a transformative coaching experience.[45, 46] Through critical reflection on performance issues and their own coaching behaviors, coaches increased their confidence and built more positive relationships with their athletes.

Reflective practice and critical reflection can be portrayed as two separate, but interconnected, wheels of learning. Reflective practice is sometimes referred to as single-loop learning (one wheel), whereas critical reflection is sometimes described as double-loop learning (both wheels).[7]

## Figure 12.8 Conclusions of Coach Wooden's Off-Season Free-Throw Continuous Improvement Research

### Individual Fundamentals

1. Style—such as where to stand—routine, and elbow position are taught, if the player is not a good shooter. If he is already a good free-throw shooter, don't tamper with success.
2. For those who need help:
   a. Feet a little wider than the shoulders.
   b. Balance.
   c. Right-handers shoot slightly to the left corner and left-handers shoot slightly to the right.
   d. Shoulders should be squared to the backboard.
   e. Elbow should start above the knee, never stop moving, and end up above the ear on the follow through.
   f. Arc should be medium, not too high and not too low.
   g. Player should follow through as if he has an extended arm that can reach into the basket. However, balance must be maintained.
   h. Player should keep his eye on the front of the rim.
   i. Head should follow the shot but no leaning.
   j. Player should take three dribbles, look up at the basket, and shoot. No staring at the basket too long, or shooting too quickly.
   k. After follow through, the arm should retreat in the same path as when the shot was executed.

### Team Fundamentals

1. Free-throw shooting should be integrated into the practice session and should be as game-like as possible.
2. We must place pressure on the player when he shoots free throws in practice.
3. We must have players shoot free throws when they are in various states of physical and mental fatigue.
4. A significant number of free throws must be taken toward the end of the practice session, in game-like conditions.



Reflective practice involves cycling through the four steps in a reflective conversation (problem setting, strategy generation, experimentation, and evaluation). Coach thinking is focused on addressing and ultimately resolving a specific performance gap, hence the single-loop analogy.

With critical reflection, coaches will naturally still reflect on performance gaps (single loop) but will also pause to think about their coaching philosophy and coaching approaches (double loop). The value of critical reflection is that it provides coaches with a more vivid awareness of their general coaching philosophy, potential areas for targeting future continuous improvement efforts, and a more authentic and humble view of what it takes to succeed as a coach, referred to as practical wisdom.[47] Leadership expert Peter Economy[48] provides examples of critical reflection, or double-loop learning, questions that leaders should ponder on a regular basis. The questions, adapted for coaches, follow:

- What did I do well this past season?
- What coaching tasks could I have done better?
- Why were these tasks challenging?
- What are two things I really enjoyed about coaching this past season?
- What was my biggest waste of time?
- What made me feel most fulfilled as a coach this past season?

## USING A SYSTEMS APPROACH TO CLOSING GAPS

Armed with an understanding of the principles and examples of how to close performance gaps, coaches are well positioned to make regular improvements from season to season. Efforts to close performance gaps can be enhanced even further by considering one last piece of the continuous improvement puzzle, known as systems thinking.[7, 49]

Systems thinking refers to an ability to view performance, and performance gaps, as interconnected pieces of a larger puzzle, or a system. Systems thinking requires a shift from viewing performance gaps as isolated problems to recognizing that all performance gaps are the result of underlying patterns and processes that affect all aspects of a sport program.

Coaches naturally approach performance gaps with a narrow focus on the isolated performance issue. Coaches, like teachers, are typically trained to learn how to break down performances into small pieces. This narrow focus, however, can result in venturing down the wrong path in search of a solution to a specific problem. This process is similar to trying to complete a puzzle by taking one piece at a time out of the box without being able to see the full image and the way in which the individual pieces relate to one another.

Coaches who approach continuous improvement from a systems thinking approach not only identify isolated performance gaps but also consider how these gaps are interconnected to and influenced by the larger performance system and associated demands.[48]

For example, during the off-season an ice hockey coach may decide to address a team's lack of scoring as a performance gap. If the coach focuses only on learning more about technical aspects of shooting (e.g., hand position on the stick, different types of shots) without also learning more about the tactical aspects of shooting (e.g., how players must position themselves in relation to their teammates and opponents to put themselves in an optimal position to shoot and score), she or he will be less likely to close the performance gap.

After a performance gap is identified and selected for off-season study, coaches must step back and situate the issue within the larger system of athletic performance unique to their sport and level of competition.

Coaches can use the performance gap worksheet to identify potential areas for off-season continuous improvement efforts (see figure 12.9). This performance gap worksheet integrates all the continuous improvement principles and lessons from successful coaches shared in this chapter. This worksheet should be completed at the start of the off-season to reflect on unfulfilled potential and areas most in need of improvement.

The first step in using the worksheet is to list all the important performance gaps noticed during the previous season. Coaches should not limit themselves here by trying to identify only the most important or biggest performance issues. Step 1 is simply to list all performance issues.

In step 2, coaches review the list and select three performance gaps they believe are central to helping them improve their coaching effectiveness. The goal here is to target the performance gaps that will have the greatest effect on enhanced athlete and team performance if successfully addressed.

A helpful approach at this step is for coaches to distinguish between important and high-impact performance gaps. Important performance issues are those listed in step 1 that the coach believes are holding the athletes or team back from reaching their full potential. Coaches will likely be able to identify dozens of important performance gaps every season.

On the other hand, high-impact performance issues (those listed in step 2) are those select few performance gaps that are game changers—the fundamental issues that directly affect many other performance aspects of the system. Another way to think about how to identify high-impact performance gaps is for coaches to ask themselves which performance gaps provide the greatest points of leverage for improved performance. In other words, even a small improvement in these performance gaps will potentially produce big results. Systematically addressing high-impact performance gaps will provide coaches with the greatest return on their off-season continuous improvement investment.

In sports such as field hockey or soccer, shooting may be listed as an important performance issue, but poor fitness may be an underlying high-impact performance gap. Regardless of how skilled an athlete is at shooting, if she or he is not fit enough to gain the strategic advantage needed to reach an optimal position to shoot, then the shooting performance issue will never be adequately resolved. Instead of fitness, maybe the larger or higher impact performance issue is team trust. If teammates don't trust each other enough to sacrifice personal glory for team success, then they will be unlikely to do the work needed, such as pressuring a defender, to put teammates in optimal scoring situations.

Coaches should complete step 2 on their own first and then discuss their list with members of their coaching staff (if available) and one or more trusted coaching peers. After agreement is reached on three high-impact performance gaps, the coach should identify other aspects of the performance system that will directly influence the athlete's or team's ability to close the performance gap (step 3).

## Figure 12.9 Off-Season Performance Gap Worksheet

**Step 1:** List the performance gaps you noticed from the last season.

**Step 2:** Identify three high-impact performance gaps.

**Step 3:** Identify factors limiting your ability to close the performance gap.

**Step 4:** List goals for next season

By start of season:

By end of season:

By start of season:

By end of season:

By start of season:

By end of season:

From W. Gilbert, 2017, *Coaching better every season: A year-round system for athlete development and program success* (Champaign, IL: Human Kinetics).

These aspects are sometimes referred to as growth-limiting factors.[7] For example, if team trust is identified as a high-impact performance gap, then growth-limiting factors might be team core values, athlete role clarification, and coach and athlete communication skills. All these related components of the performance system are interconnected with team trust. Unless these issues are also addressed, closing the high-impact performance gap of team trust will be difficult or impossible. True systems thinking requires coaches to develop the ability to see both the forest and the trees when striving to optimize continuous improvement efforts.

The fourth and final step in completing the off-season performance gap worksheet is to set some short-term and long-term goals specific to closing each gap. Coaches should set a target for how the gap will be closed by the start of the season (short term) and by the end of the season (long term).

Returning to the example of team trust as a high-impact performance gap, a short-term goal could be to arrive in the preseason ready to try two or three team-building strategies identified through off-season self-study. The long-term goal for closing the gap by the end of the following season could be for all athletes to score above 5.0 on the peer connections and coach-athlete relationships questionnaires (see the questionnaires described in part III of this book).

## Wrap-Up

Continuous improvement efforts should be a regular and constant part of coaches' everyday work. As Olympic and collegiate championship basketball coach Mike Krzyzewski correctly notes, self-assessment and learning how to enhance performance is something that should be happening all the time.[50]

But the off-season provides a unique opportunity for coaches to pause and conduct comprehensive and systematic reviews of performance gaps. Continuous improvement requires industriousness, curiosity, resourcefulness, and honest self-examination—characteristics associated with personal mastery and a growth mind-set.

Time should be allocated in the off-season not only for thinking about how to resolve high-impact performance gaps, referred to as reflective practice, but also for critically reflecting on core values, coaching philosophy, and general coaching effectiveness. A steady and deliberate focus on incrementally closing high-impact performance gaps through off-season coach research projects keeps the focus on the next best step in the career-long quest to becoming a more effective coach.

# Chapter 13

# Collaborate and Learn

**Key Concepts**

Networking strategies
Mentoring
Identifying mentors
Mentoring phases
Learning networks
Coach learning groups
Learning group guidelines
Team science
Technology for learning groups
Measuring learning group impact

To keep improving as a coach, you must look for ways to connect with other coaches regularly so that you can exchange and test coaching ideas. Coaches such as John Cook do this to ensure they are constantly evolving. Coach Cook has coached the University of Nebraska women's volleyball team to three national championships. Over his career he has learned to surround himself with a strong and trusted network that gives him regular and honest feedback about how he can improve as a coach: "I bounce things off of them and I ask about situations—how I could've done it better."[1]

Just as important, Coach Cook welcomes coaches of opposing teams who ask to visit and observe him, even though these meetings sometimes result in Cook's team later getting beat by a colleague's team.[2] Successful coaches are happy to share their wisdom with other coaches who demonstrate the same zest for continued learning, because as American novelist Robert Heinlein famously observed, "When one teaches, two learn."

The previous chapter included an example from championship football coach Nick Saban, who talked about the constant drive to improve. Coach Saban certainly has an inner drive and work ethic that has helped him acquire a wealth of knowledge on his own. But he also realizes how this learning can be enhanced with the help of informed and willing mentors, as well as respected colleagues who readily share their expertise and insights when available.

During his more than 40 years of coaching, Coach Saban has built a deep and diverse learning network. Although he has coached alongside other highly successful coaches, including five-time Super Bowl champion coach Bill Belichick, Saban is quick to point out that you can learn something from anyone.[3]

Connecting with other coaches helps coaches improve their coaching skills, alleviates some of the isolation they experience, and helps them learn to cope with the pressures of coaching.

On their way to winning the 2015 World Cup, the U.S. women's national soccer team experienced many moments of adversity. But throughout the tournament, head coach Jill Ellis was a stable and calming presence, helping the athletes build and maintain their confidence. Coach Ellis attributes her ability to handle pressure situations to coaching tips she received from legendary basketball coach John Wooden. Recalling advice given by Coach Wooden, Ellis said, "Pressure is a great thing because one, it means you are there and in the mix and two, he said, 'Embrace it.' "[4] These simple words of wisdom greatly influenced her approach to coaching and clearly illustrate the power of seeking others to collaborate and learn.

Unfortunately, though, coaching can be a lonely job. Even when coaches work in high school or college settings alongside dozens of other coaches in the same athletics department, rarely is time set aside for regular or formal sharing of ideas.

AP Photo/Elaine Thompson

Jill Ellis, right, coached Carli Lloyd and her teammates to the Women's World Cup championship by modeling poise under pressure.

This shortage of interaction is even more evident during the season when coaches can easily become so immersed in their own work that they barely interact with coaches outside their immediate staff.

Successful coaches—whether seasoned like John Cook, Nick Saban, and Jill Ellis or those early in their coaching careers like first-year coach Steve Kerr of the 2015 NBA champion Golden State Warriors—acknowledge that their winning approaches have been greatly influenced by those in their learning networks.[5] This chapter describes strategies that successful coaches use to boost their learning by collaborating with others and building strong learning networks.

## NETWORKING STRATEGIES

For championship coaches such as college basketball coach Amy Ruley, "At its core, networking means developing meaningful relationships in our professional lives.[6 (p. 246)] Networking has also been described as the process of developing a list of people who can bring value to your coaching.[7] The purpose of networking is to create direct access to a team of trusted colleagues.

Coaches can benefit from thinking of networking as trail building. Much as explorers regularly review maps and identify target destinations, effective coaches regularly scan the coaching landscape to identify other coaches they would like to visit as part of their coaching journey. The most effective coaches build a comprehensive network of trails across their map of the coaching landscape.

Eddie Robinson, one of the most influential American college football coaches of all time, was proactive in gaining access to the college football coaching community when he was a young coach. The first time he attended a national football coaching convention, he waited in line simply to shake the hand of Amos Alonzo Stagg, considered by many the greatest football coach ever. Coach Stagg, who attended the convention long after he retired, reportedly attended his final convention at the age of 102. Coach Robinson recalled:

> Meeting Coach [Alonzo] Stagg was surely the highlight of my first convention. I'd always go looking for him at future conventions to chat with him. Each time I tried to learn something new. Sometimes it was about football. More often, it was about life.[8 (p. 95)]

Coach Robinson's story illustrates the importance of seeking ways to gain increasingly deeper access to coaches who are leaders in their sport. People who share a common mission—coaching college football in the case of Coach Robinson and Coach Stagg—are potential members of a coach's learning network.

Coaches cite many benefits of networking, including learning about effective coaching practices, enhancing their career mobility, and receiving much-needed social support. The first step, then, in building a strong coaching network is to identify existing and potential members of your coaching network.

As coaches, we spend a tremendous amount of time building networks for our athletes. For example, a typical high school or college athlete's network includes other athletes, coaches, sport science and medical professionals, teachers, and friends (see figure 13.1). Coaches must invest similar time and energy in

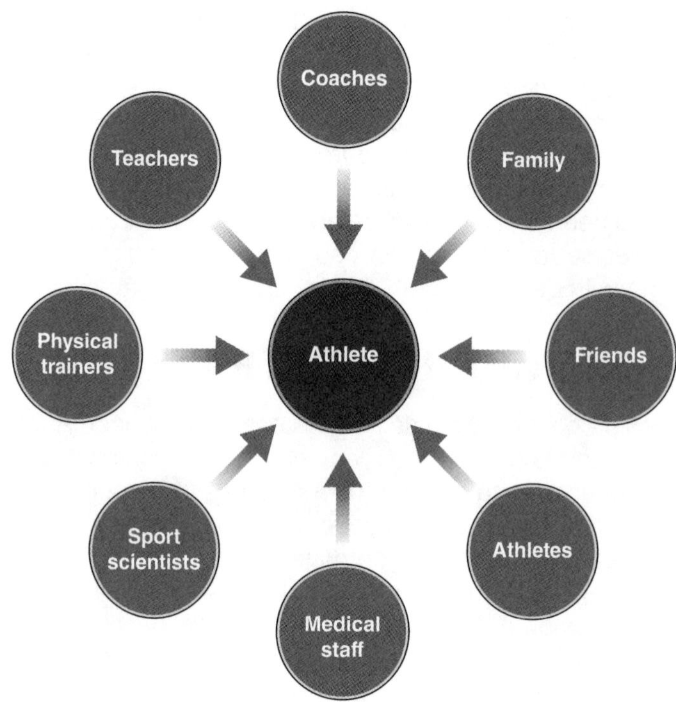


**Figure 13.1** Members of a typical athlete network.

building their own networks. Just as athletes need a strong team around them to maximize their development, coaches need their own team to optimize their learning.

An activity that I like to do when working with groups of coaches is to have them spend a few minutes thinking about who they have, or would like to have, in their coaching networks. Coaches list names of people they connect with regularly in their networks. The intent is not to list all the coaches they know or have met. Instead, the goal is to identify a small group of trusted people whom they regularly connect with to enhance their learning as coaches.

I then push the coaches to add people to their networks who aren't coaches, such as medical professionals, sport scientists, teachers, athletics directors, and program stakeholders. Coaches may find it useful to create two versions of the network worksheet—one just with other coaches and one with noncoaches. Coaches will find that some of their richest learning experiences will come from collaborating with people outside coaching who bring a fresh perspective to typical coaching issues.

After identifying potential members of a coaching network, a coach's next step is to build the network. After deciding that he wanted to be a full-time coach, Cameron McCormick, long-time coach of world number one ranked golfer Jordan Spieth, built his coaching network by creating a list of the top 75 golf coaches in the United States. He then wrote a letter to each of them with one simple question, "Would you mind if I came and watched you work?"[9] Of the 75 coaches, fewer than half responded and fewer than 15 invited him to visit, but one of them who eagerly accepted his request was Butch Harmon, former coach of Tiger Woods and considered one of the top golf instructors in the world.

The quality of the learning that occurs from these types of experiences is more important than the number of people you add to your coaching network. When building a coaching network you should expect setbacks, but the persistent coach will eventually make the connections needed to build a strong and valuable coaching network.

Championship college basketball coach Amy Ruley provides a range of off-season strategies that coaches can use to build their coaching networks.[6] Her first suggestion is to volunteer in sport and coaching professional organizations. For Coach Ruley this task meant serving on various committees for the Women's Basketball Coaches Association and the National Collegiate Athletics Association. Every sport has various levels of governing bodies across local, regional, national, and international levels, providing ample opportunities to serve.

Although service to the profession is time consuming, the activity contributes to growth of the sport and is a valuable investment in a coach's development. While serving on sport committees, coaches gain critical access and exposure to other coach leaders in their sport. The relationships built during time served on coaching committees often lead to lifetime coaching friendships. Serving on coaching committees also provides another opportunity for coaches to demonstrate their strengths and gain the trust of their peers, who subsequently will become more likely to share their coaching knowledge.

A second networking suggestion shared by Coach Ruley is to coach in the off-season at coaching clinics and sport camps. When approached with an open mind, coaching alongside other coaches in these events can serve as a form of coaching boot camp. Off-season clinics and camps typically last only a few days or weeks, so coaches need to collaborate and make adjustments under time pressures. Learning to work with coaching peers in these coaching conditions can provide meaningful shared experiences that set a foundation for long-term professional relationships.

Coach Ruley also reminds coaches not to overlook their own internal networking opportunities in the off-season. Typically, networking is thought of as building relationships outside your immediate setting. Ruley has found much success by creating strategies to strengthen and expand relationships with alumni and other sport program stakeholders such as booster clubs and administrative support groups. For example, Coach Ruley shares the example of holding an annual off-season weekend retreat at her home with former players. Internal networking experiences renew and strengthen existing bonds, leading to continued opportunities for sharing insights about the program, life lessons, and potential leads for adding new members to the coaching network.

Successful coaches also understand that they must continually work to maintain and enhance their coaching networks. Just as trails must be regularly maintained to preserve access to destinations, relationships within coaching networks also require constant maintenance.

Sending brief notes of recognition and support is one of the most effective strategies that successful coaches use to maintain their coaching networks. Legendary Coach of the 20th Century John Wooden was notorious for his random and unsolicited acts of kindness, regularly surprising coaches and athletes with handwritten notes of recognition and support.[10]

A renowned high school football coach I worked with sent letters to college and professional football coaches as a way to show support and empathy, even though he had not met them before. He understood the loneliness that coaches can often feel, particularly when struggling with performance issues. He made time to write short notes of encouragement and support to coaches he followed when they were experiencing low points in their careers. Although networking was not the express purpose of this exercise, his note writing invariably led to the creation of new trails in his coaching network. He often received personalized thank-you notes in return, along with words of wisdom and coaching insights.

Sometimes when I share this note-writing strategy with coaches, they lament that they don't have time for this extra work. I can tell you from direct experience that successful coaches make time for this type of network-building activity. They view it as crucial to their development, not as extra work. Long-time college and high school basketball coach Jerry Wainwright is legendary for his routine of hand writing inspirational notes to other coaches.[11]

For the past 30 years he has been writing 300 to 500 notes of inspiration each week, affecting thousands of coaches and building an incredibly rich coaching network in the process. He pulls ideas and quotations from books and personal experiences and personalizes them before sending them to a coach. For example, if he learns that a fellow coach has lost a key player to injury, he might send a quick note with a quotation about overcoming adversity such as "The only easy day was yesterday."

When coaches openly share their knowledge and show a genuine concern for their coaching colleagues, they develop a reputation as a valued coach. They become known as value-added members of the coaching network, which results in more invitations to join the networks of other coaches. Coaches will find they profit most from their networking efforts when they think of giving first and gaining second.[12]

Leadership coach and business consultant Tim Sanders uses the term *lovecat* to describe people who succeed in business and life by adopting this approach.[13] Lovecat coaches are highly sought out by other coaches because they become known for their ability and willingness to share coaching insights. Coaches can greatly expand their coaching networks by regularly sharing resources with at least one fellow coach.

Social media advances make it easy for coaches to act like lovecats. Regardless of the method used to share coaching insights, all coaches should make time to share coaching insights and resources regularly as a means for building their personal coaching networks.

Former athletics director Dr. David Hoch, drawing on his more than 20 years as a high school athletics director and his 20 years of coaching experience, has created a valuable summary of networking tips for coaches that aligns with the networking recommendations found across the literature.[7] Using his summary as a foundation, an updated list of networking strategies is provided in table 13.1.

**Table 13.1 Networking Strategies for Coaches**

| Strategy | Description |
|---|---|
| Create contact profile | Whenever you meet someone you believe can become a valued member of your coaching network, immediately make notes about the interaction, such as when and where the interaction occurred and what was shared or discussed. For example, if you exchange business cards at a coaching clinic, write the date and name of the clinic and the topic of the conversation on the back of the business card. |
| Initial contact follow-up | After meeting or connecting with someone for the first time, send the person a short note of gratitude with an invitation to continue sharing: "I am glad we had the opportunity to meet. . . . looking forward to seeing you at [insert next coaching event]." or "Thank you for making time to chat. . . . Looking forward to more opportunities to share coaching insights." |
| Offer assistance | Regularly scan social media and coaching networks to stay aware of potential opportunities to support other coaches. Send a quick note to the coach offering assistance or send coaching resources you believe can be valuable in addressing the coaching issue. Share some of your own experience, when possible, in dealing with similar coaching issues: "I'm sorry to hear about the challenges you are experiencing with [insert coaching issue]. I too faced this challenge at one point in my coaching. Thought you might find [insert coaching resource information or insight] valuable as you work through this situation." |
| Acknowledge contributions | Thank coaches or other people who have provided you with valuable sources of information. For example, send a note to a presenter following a coaching clinic: "I really enjoyed your recent presentation at the [insert name and location of clinic]. The information will help me very much in dealing with [provide specific example of how the information will be useful to you]. Do you have other related material that I can access?" |
| Recognize achievements | Regularly scan media reports to learn about the accomplishments of coaches you follow and admire. If the coach is an existing contact, send a quick note to let the person know you are proud of her or his success. If the coach is a new contact, introduce yourself and recognize the coaching success, "My name is [insert name], and I am a [insert coaching position]. Congratulations on your recent [insert coaching achievement]. Your coaching success is inspiring. Well done!" |

# MENTORING

Networking helps coaches build a support system for regular and ongoing coach learning. Effective networking can lead to opportunities to connect with a coach who is willing to spend more time to serve as a mentor. At its core, mentoring is simply the process of helping someone else get better. Mentors help other coaches get better by teaching, inspiring, prodding, leading, molding, encouraging, or praising.[14, 15] Often, the most important role that a quality mentor plays is serving as a sounding board—just being available to listen.

Effective mentoring results not only in improved coaching but also in increased coaching confidence. This aspect is particularly important for coaches just starting their careers, who often have the needed skills but lack confidence because of limited coaching experience.

For example, NBA coach Steve Kerr, who guided his team to the championship in his first year as a coach, attributes his quick rise to coaching success to the guidance he received from his many mentors. He claims that the best piece of mentoring advice he received was a simple reminder to be himself: "That's what all my mentors have told me: 'Just be yourself, be true to yourself, stick to your principles, and it'll work.' "[5] This basic suggestion helped him gain confidence in his own unique coaching style, instead of trying to emulate a style that worked for someone else.

When seeking potential mentors, coaches should look for other coaches who are passionate about learning, trustworthy, knowledgeable, up to date on coaching trends, and willing to share their coaching insights.[16] World and Olympic championship coach Debbie Muir, recognized as among the best coaches ever in the sport of synchronized swimming, exemplifies the sentiments of successful coaches who eagerly accept opportunities to mentor other coaches:

> I enjoy the opportunity to pass on the lessons I've learned. It is exciting to spend time with coaches who are so passionate about what they are doing and so excellent and to be a small part of helping them to reach even higher levels.[17]

Building a mentoring relationship can be as easy as asking another coach if he or she has a few minutes to chat. But to gain the full benefits of a quality mentoring experience, coaches should follow a six-step strategy for building a mentoring relationship.

- **Step 1—Identify a potential mentor.** Ask yourself questions such as these: Who do I look up to as a coach in my community? Who would I like to spend more time with as a coach? Who uses tactics and team strategies that I would like to learn more about?
- **Step 2—Be specific with mentoring needs.** Before contacting your potential mentor, make a list of specific areas of coaching that you believe the person could most help you improve. Identify things that the potential mentor does or knows as a coach that you find particularly intriguing and want to learn about. This list will show that you are serious about getting better and alleviate some potential mentor concerns about her or his ability to help you improve by providing clarity of purpose.
- **Step 3—Make contact with the potential mentor.** Reach out to the person, ideally face-to-face or over the phone when the coach is in the off-season, and share how much you admire how he or she coaches. Ask whether you could spend some time together to learn from the person and improve your ability as a coach. Mention the areas of coaching you identified in step 2 that you specifically want to learn about from the coach.
- **Step 4—Discuss the "rules of engagement."** Be clear with the potential mentor about what you need and want from the mentoring experience. Discussing this point in the first meeting is important so that the potential mentor can get

a clear understanding of the type of guidance you are expecting and the likely time commitment. For example, discuss potential meeting schedules (how often, where, when, duration of meetings, acceptable forms of communication). If you are expecting to watch the coach in action, ask whether observation is acceptable and how you can do that without being too intrusive or disrupting practice and competition routines. Also, discuss up front what information can be shared with others. This item is critical for building trust.

- **Step 5—Schedule meetings or ask for suggestions for another mentor.** If the potential mentor agrees, the next step is to schedule some times to meet. If the potential mentor is not willing or available to help at the moment, ask whether she or he knows other coaches who might be a good fit to serve as a mentor. By clearly describing your mentoring needs at the outset, the other coach can more readily steer you in the direction of others who can help you learn what you want to learn.
- **Step 6—Formally thank mentor.** Regardless of the length or quality of the mentoring relationship, a handwritten note or other simple gesture of appreciation should be given to the mentor. I have found that coaches who have mentored me greatly appreciate it when I thank them by giving them a copy of one of my favorite coaching books with a handwritten note on the inside cover. This show of gratitude not only further strengthens the relationship but also gives the mentee a chance to play the role of mentor and helps the other coach learn.

Sometimes mentoring for coaches is a more formal arrangement whereby one coach is assigned a mentor. For example, an athletics director might implement a formal buddy system in which a new coach is paired with an experienced coach in the same school.[14, 18]

Formal mentoring arrangements like this are most effective when the relationship follows well-defined sequential phases. For example, the four phases of a mentoring relationship in coaching have been described as the introductory, participatory, developmental, and self-regulatory phases.[19]

In the introductory phase the emphasis is on creating a foundation for a trusting relationship and identifying potential learning needs of the mentored coach. At this time the coaches should openly share their coaching philosophies, ambitions, perceived strengths and weaknesses, and professional development goals.

The focus of the participatory phase is on observation of the mentee's coaching. Sufficient time should be provided for the mentor simply to watch the coach in action across training and competition. An experienced coach asked to assume the role of a mentor often finds it difficult not to intervene, particularly when he or she identifies areas of potential growth when observing the mentee coach.

When speaking about characteristics of effective mentor coaches, world and Olympic championship women's soccer coach Tony DiCicco places being a good listener at the top of his list.[20] Good listeners show empathy and patience.

With the advent of inexpensive and varied tools for video sharing, mentor coaches can observe mentees easier than ever, regardless of physical location. Ideally, mentee coaches should provide the mentor with two or three examples of training sessions and at least one competition event. Sharing of written plans for the training sessions and competitions is also recommended.

Effective mentors will resist the temptation to intervene too quickly as they recognize the complexity and situation-specific nature of coaching. A genuine portrait of a coach requires multiple observations across various coaching situations.

In the developmental phase mentors shift their focus from observation to facilitation. Mentors play many roles, not the least of which is a facilitator who can accelerate coach learning by shining a light on specific areas of coaching that can be enhanced.[21, 22]

The primary role of mentors in the developmental phase is not to provide answers, although they certainly will be expected to share insights and experiences. The most effective mentors are skilled at posing challenging questions that lead to healthy debate and increased coach self-awareness. Effective mentors will pose questions such as the following: What did you do well during pressure situations? Can you explain why you approach coaching the way you do? How did you positively or negatively influence the performance of your athletes? What areas of your coaching can you improve?[21, 22]

Effective mentors also understand the importance of the timing of their questions. Emotions can, and often do, run high in coaching. Good mentors have a keen sense of how others are feeling, sometimes referred to as emotional intelligence.[20] Feedback from a mentor will be best received when the mentee coach is most open to receiving it. The confidence to be brutally honest in responding to challenging questions depends on the level of trust that is established in the first two phases of the mentoring relationship.

Effective mentoring relationships reach the fourth and final phase, referred to as the self-regulatory phase of mentoring. At this point effective mentors gradually phase themselves out of their formal role as observers and facilitators and shift to being trusted members of a coaching network who are available when needed. Ideally, mentors will continue to check in intermittingly with the mentee coach, both to nurture the relationship and to inspire the mentee coach to continue her or his efforts to enhance coaching knowledge.

Formal mentoring programs based on these four phases are increasingly part of the coach education programs developed for high-performance coaches around the world. Coaches of national and Olympic teams are often partnered with senior coaches as part of a mentoring relationship that lasts hundreds of hours across several years.[23] Formal mentoring for coaches in youth sport, high school, and college settings, however, still appears to be relatively rare.

A cautionary note about formal mentoring concerns situations in which coaches do not get to choose their mentors, such as when the mentoring is arranged as a formal part of coach education program. When mentor coaches approach their role from a position of authority and power, attempting to impose their style and strategies on a mentee coach, the results can be demoralizing and lead to coach burnout instead of coach development.[24] Mentoring is most effective when the mentoring relationship is built on trust and empathy.

Whether the relationship is informal or formal, all successful coaches rely on mentors to enhance their learning through collaboration. Although the mentoring process may seem daunting at first, many experienced coaches out there find great satisfaction in serving as mentors. The best coaches have a deep-rooted love for their sport and willingly embrace opportunities to give back to the sport through mentoring. As noted by Hall of Fame college football coach Grant Teaff, "The impact of giving back to the sport we coach cannot be overestimated. We have all been influenced positively by other coaches who took the extra time to add to our own knowledge base."[21 (p. vi)]

You will find that your coaching experience is much richer and more enjoyable when you collaborate with mentors and when you in turn mentor other coaches. When coaches speak about their mentoring experiences, they routinely acknowledge that both the mentor and the mentee enhance their coaching knowledge through the shared experience.[19, 22, 25]

## BUILD AND RUN A COACH LEARNING GROUP

By developing and using networking skills and participating in mentoring experiences, coaches are actively building a coach learning group. The goal of making formal connections with others, with coaches and noncoaches alike, is to build capacity for ongoing collaborative learning, that is, to build more trails to more destinations.

Although networking is about making connections, and mentoring is about building deep one-on-one relationships, a coach learning group is like a special operations task force. When coaches select a high-impact performance gap to tackle in the off-season, their learning will be accelerated by assembling a small group of people who can create coaching strategies for closing the performance gap. These work teams are referred to as coach learning groups.

Regular participation in a coach learning group is valuable for coaches in many ways. Besides making noticeable improvements in their coaching practice, those who participate in a coach learning group gain greater coaching confidence, a deeper understanding of coaching issues and philosophies, and enriched social connections with other coaches.[26]

Collaborative learning guidelines can be drawn from carefully evaluating what is known about how the world's most effective teachers learn through collaboration. For example, just as the coaches in the USA Hockey model take a team approach to coaching athletes, teachers in high-performing schools take a team approach to learning how to resolve common teacher dilemmas. The most well-documented examples of this teacher collaborative learning approach is referred to as lesson study and is often traced back to schools in Japan.[27, 28]

With lesson study, teachers who teach the same subject and work in the same school have collaborative learning time set aside in their weekly teaching schedules. Teachers start by identifying common teaching issues. In the next step they jointly prepare lesson plans aimed at closing the student learning gap. Lesson study teachers then watch each other teaching the lesson plan and redesign the lesson plan based on their collective observations. This cycle is repeated until a noticeable improvement in student learning occurs.

Teacher lesson study is an effective, time-tested example of a collaborative learning strategy that can be adapted for coaches.[29] The process starts by clearly identifying and describing the most important and repetitive issues experienced by a coach. In any given week, coaches will notice countless performance issues that they could address. Together with members of their coach learning group, effective coaches carefully pick the most important, or high-impact, issues to address, one at a time. These issues are the ones that repeatedly bubble to the surface.

After identifying and clearly defining the performance issue, effective coaches set about preparing and testing meticulous plans of action. These plans of action might be in the form of a practice plan, just a few specific activities in a practice, or perhaps a strategic plan to be tested in competition. Another defining feature of collaborative learning for coaches is the reliance on evidence, not opinion, to drive collaborative learning. Coaches need to devise formal strategies to measure the effectiveness of new coaching strategies.

There are five keys to developing and sustaining an effective coach learning group.[30–33]

1. **Dedicated time is set aside to improve coaching.** Regular time is set aside for learning group exchanges, ideally 45 to 60 minutes every 2 to 3 weeks.
2. **Group consists of coaches with similar concerns.** Learning teams are composed of three to seven coaches who coach in the same setting; they do not have to coach the same sport, but they should experience common issues with similar types of athletes.
3. **Protocol guides but does not prescribe.** Rules of engagement should be in place to ensure that meetings stay focused on knowledge sharing and coach learning. For example, a standard agenda could include 15 to 20 minutes for sharing ideas from a group assigned reading (such as a coaching biography or a coaching article that is agreed on or assigned before the meeting), followed by 20 to 30 minutes for discussing current coaching issues.
4. **Peer facilitates learning group engagements.** Each learning group requires a leader, one of the participating coaches who coordinates the exchanges and encourages and inspires other coaches to participate actively in the learning group. This role can be rotated periodically to distribute the workload and build leadership capacity across coaches.
5. **Work continues until there is evidence of improvement.** The group should ensure that time is set aside in every meeting to follow up on previously discussed or unresolved coaching issues or topics. Simply discussing issues or topics is not enough—coaches must push each other to find practical applications based on their exchanges.

An example of the coach learning group in action is the "power hours" strategy created by the Alliance of Women's Coaches. Power hours are described as informal ways for coaches—in this case, female coaches—to stay in the loop, build their coaching networks, and deepen their coaching knowledge.[34] Power hours can take multiple forms:

- On-campus meetings with other coaches, staff, and administrators in the coach's athletics department
- In-town meetings or get-togethers with coaches and administrators at nearby schools
- Teleconferences for coaches with specific interests

Finally, because group membership will normally change over time, the group may find it useful to create a repository for coaching insights or particularly valuable lessons learned. This collection could take many forms, ranging from a blog to short video summaries. This item is particularly valuable for early career coaches who can quickly learn from experienced coaches about what works in a particular setting. One such example is the free coaching channel mentioned in chapter 11 of this book (https://vimeo.com/fresnohscoachingchannel).

Another simple way to capture and share lessons learned from participating in a coach learning group is to distribute follow-up notes (see figure 13.2).

A coach gains credibility among peers by building a reputation as a coach of character who consistently develops successful athletes and teams. Attaining this goal, of course, can take many years. Coaches should begin by building a local coach learning group within their own league, club, or school. The approach implemented by USA Hockey provides an example of how coaches can actively build the idea of coach learning groups into their everyday practices.[35]

Recognizing that coach learning groups will not occur without formal support from the local sport organization, USA Hockey asks local hockey organizations to add a coach learning group coordinator for teams competing in the same age group. In the typical coaching scenario, each coach in a league works in isolation and is solely responsible for coaching his or her team. On the contrary, with the USA Hockey example, the coach coordinator helps prepare joint practice sessions in which two or three teams practice together at the same time. Coaches then spend part of the practice session coaching a particular skill or strategy at their coaching station, allowing all the athletes to benefit from the collective wisdom of all coaches in the league.

With a coach learning group coordinator guiding the experience, coaches collaborate and learn from each other while coaching. This approach also teaches coaches to adopt an "our athletes" approach as opposed to the "my athletes" approach prevalent in typical sport settings. This method is sometimes also referred to as the whole-club approach to coaching. Whole-club coaching is common in the club sport system long practiced by successful coaches and sport programs in many European countries, particularly in soccer.[36]

The USA Hockey approach is effective because it is aligned with evidence-based guidelines for creating high-impact coach learning groups. The coaching coordinator serves as the trained facilitator, time is scheduled in each hockey practice for coaches to co-coach, and coaches are grouped into teams of three or four who coach the same age group and level of competition.[37, 38]

When coaches don't have the benefit of coaching in a setting that is ready to adopt or support a coaching community of practice, they can still take steps to create their own coach learning group. For example, coaches should reach

## Figure 13.2 Fresno High School's Coach Academy Follow-Up Notes

### Session 3 (4-22-16)

#### Key Discussion Points [chapters 8–11]

- Strategies for building competitive toughness
- Athlete rewards for practice and competition performance
  - Wrestling—athlete receives a "pin" for each pin
- Can we create Warrior badges for all athletes (like helmet stickers in football)?
- Role of competition in training
  - Track and field—competition Fridays (fun games, e.g., wheelbarrow races)

#### Featured Coaching Tools and Tips from Book Reading (*One Goal* by Bill Beswick, 2016)

- Player Code of Conduct (p. 107)
- 8 Keys to Creating a Winning Mood on Your Team (p. 115)
- Task Cohesion Checklist (p. 140)
- Social Cohesion Checklist (p. 142)
- Momentum Triggers (p. 152)
- Strategies for Shaping Team Momentum (p. 158)

#### Online Bonus Resources

- Three keys to championship coaching (www.asep.com/news/ShowArticle.cfm?ID=262)
- Commentary on lessons learned from 22-time national champion soccer coach Anson Dorrance (University of North Carolina)
- How to design practice sessions that teach competitive toughness (www.youtube.com/watch?v=hyr2whgIj0A)
- 5-minute video of practice session and commentary from soccer coach Anson Dorrance

#### Preparation for Next Session

- Friday, May 20, 12:30–1:30
- Book chapters 12–15

out to other coaches who they believe have important coaching strengths that they themselves may be missing. This strategy, also common among championship athletes, is sometimes referred to as finding a complementary partner.[39]

After a partner coach has been identified, time should be scheduled to watch the partner coach in action, ideally in both training and competition settings. The goal of this activity is not to copy and mirror the behaviors of the complementary coach, but instead to learn vicariously from watching how coaching strengths are enacted in actual coaching situations.

Coach development is richest when a coach participates in a learning group that stimulates new ways of looking at common coaching issues. You should select others to join your coach learning group who will challenge you and not be afraid to share dissenting views.

Olympic and world championship soccer coach Tony DiCicco is a successful coach who built this type of coach learning group by hiring assistant coaches who would stimulate his ongoing learning and development. As Coach DiCicco acknowledges, this approach requires the courage to expose your weaknesses as a coach, which provide the foundation for further learning.

> I see many coaches hire assistants who are clearly less knowledgeable than they are. They don't want to be overshadowed or upstaged, so they cheat their teams by hiring assistants who are less than the best. This doesn't make much sense, does it? At times I left myself vulnerable, but my guiding principle was always to try to help the team get to the next level, not hold them back because of my own insecurities.[20 (p. 287)]

This idea of building a coaching team aligns well with what is referred to as team science. A popular, long-held view is that major breakthroughs and successes are the result of the lone scientist toiling away in isolation. Albert Einstein epitomizes this image. He is often characterized as an eccentric genius who worked alone for extended periods.[40] Yet advances in most fields are the result of collaborative efforts.

For example, a review of nearly 20 million scientific papers and 2.1 million patents spanning five decades shows that team science dominates all fields from medicine to engineering to psychology.[41] The evidence is compelling; the lone scientist doesn't stand a chance in today's world dominated by team science. The same holds true for coaches.

The most successful coaches have always practiced team science. For example, legendary American college football coach Eddie Robinson, considered one of the greatest football coaches of all time, describes many examples of observing and learning from other football coaches across his 57-year coaching career.[8] True team science, however, is different from the typical cross-coach collaboration described by Coach Robinson. A defining feature of team science is that it is cross-disciplinary, meaning that coaches will improve most when they add people to their coaching learning groups who bring insights and expertise from outside coaching.[42]

Legendary professional soccer coach Sir Alex Ferguson is renowned as a pioneer in building high-impact coach learning groups. During his long and successful tenure as coach of Manchester United in England, he created a diverse coaching team that included health professionals to support player development, culminating with the building of an on-site medical facility.[43]

How can typical coaches, who don't have the same resources and access to specialists as Coach Ferguson did, build a cross-disciplinary coach learning group to maximize coach knowledge enhancement?

One strategy comes from an exercise that an athletics director and I used with high school coaches. We asked coaches to identify their performance gaps and their level of confidence in addressing the gaps, related to common coaching topics such as teaching technical and tactical skills, mental skills, and physical conditioning for athletes. The goal of the activity was to use the worksheets to match up coaches based on their needs and strengths as a way to stimulate high-impact coach learning groups within one athletics program.

For example, if a soccer coach indicated that athlete focus was an important performance gap but that she was not confident in teaching that mental skill, she would be partnered up with other coaches in the school who expressed confidence in teaching athletes how to improve their focus.

The first column of the worksheet lists key components of coaching (see figure 13.3). The list is based on suggested roles and responsibilities of coaches found in national and international coaching frameworks and common performance issues that coaches address on a regular basis.[44–46] Coaches then rate how confident they are in addressing each coaching component; a score of 1 represents low confidence, and a score of 5 indicates high confidence.

## Figure 13.3 Learning Group Worksheet for Coaches

| Coaching components | How confident am I in this component of my coaching? (1 = low, 3 = average, 5 = high) | Is there someone in my coaching network who is strong in this area? | Who should I ask to join my coaching network to strengthen this area? |
|---|---|---|---|
| Vision and long-term planning | 1 2 3 4 5 | | |
| Athlete selection | 1 2 3 4 5 | | |
| Communication skills | 1 2 3 4 5 | | |
| Designing quality practices | 1 2 3 4 5 | | |
| Teaching tactics and strategies | 1 2 3 4 5 | | |
| Team dynamics | 1 2 3 4 5 | | |
| Physical conditioning | 1 2 3 4 5 | | |
| Nutrition | 1 2 3 4 5 | | |
| Injury prevention and recovery | 1 2 3 4 5 | | |
| Assessment | 1 2 3 4 5 | | |
| Organizational skills | 1 2 3 4 5 | | |
| Fiscal management | 1 2 3 4 5 | | |
| Use of new technologies | 1 2 3 4 5 | | |
| Work-life balance | 1 2 3 4 5 | | |

From W. Gilbert, 2017, *Coaching better every season: A year-round system for athlete development and program success* (Champaign, IL: Human Kinetics).

In the third column of the worksheet, coaches list the top one or two people in their existing coaching network who they believe would score a 5 in this area of coaching. These people, who are not necessarily coaches, are their go-to sources when they need advice on how to address specific performance gaps. Coaches can include the same person from their coaching team for more than one performance gap or multiple people for a particular performance gap. Conversely, coaches might leave the space blank if they currently do not have anyone in their coaching network who is skilled in that area.

In the fourth column, coaches should identify, as needed, at least one person who they would like to add to their coaching network to help them enhance their learning specific to that particular area of coaching. The off-season presents an ideal time for coaches to use this type of coach learning group worksheet to review the strengths and weaknesses of their learning group and enhance their ability to practice collaborative learning.

Regardless of the approach that coaches take to creating and operating a coach learning group, the experience will be enhanced by using tools for regular sharing of information and ideas.[47] Given the availability of a wide range of digital collaborative learning tools now available, many of them free, coaches should not limit membership in their coach learning groups to people who live close to them. Some common digital collaborative learnings tools that I frequently use when participating in coach learning groups are Skype (free web-chat audio and video chat software) and Google Docs (free online document sharing and editing).

Long-time successful high school coach and athletics director Roy Turner has compiled a list of useful technology tools that can help coaches build and sustain their coach learning team, regardless of where team members reside.[48] An abbreviated version of his list is included in figure 13.4. Given the constant and rapid changes in technology, coaches should use a list such as this as a starting point for creating their own list of personal favorites. They should be sure to keep an eye out for new tools to add to the list (or replace tools that no longer meet their needs).

## MEASURING THE EFFECT OF COLLABORATIVE LEARNING

How will you know whether all the time and effort invested in working with a coach learning group results in strategies that close high-impact performance gaps? The only way to know whether the strategies are effective is to collect and review data. As Hall of Fame championship rowing coach Jan Harville states, "You will make better decisions if you follow a systematic process."[49 (pp. 84–85)]

The best approach for evaluating the effect of collaborative learning efforts is one that gives the coach meaningful and sufficient data on which to make an informed decision. The choice of a method will depend on the coach's resources and the amount of time available for testing and evaluating coaching strategies.

A coach might decide to try comprehensive data collection and analysis strategies like the competitive cauldron[50, 51] approach described in chapter 7 of this

## Figure 13.4 Popular Technology Tools for Building and Sustaining a Coach Learning Group

| Technology tool | Description | Cost |
|---|---|---|
| Athleon | Share video, statistics, and announcements | Fee based |
| Bracken Learning Mobile | Share and edit video, insert comments, and build a running dialogue on video content | Fee based |
| Coach's Eye | Online video recording and sharing | Fee based |
| DigitalTown | Share video, photos, and livestreaming | Fee based |
| Dropbox | Document, video, and photo sharing; synced collaborative file editing | Free and fee based |
| Evernote | Shared online workspace for text and illustrations | Free and fee based |
| Fitstats Technologies | Record, report, analyze, and share athlete and program statistics | Fee based |
| FreeConference | Audio and video conference calls, screen sharing, audio recording | Free and fee based |
| Google+ | Text, photo, and video sharing | Free |
| Google Docs | Write, edit, and collaborate on shared documents | Free |
| GoToMeeting | Video conferencing, screen sharing, personal meeting rooms, audio recording | Fee based |
| Groupme | Group messaging | Free |
| Hudl | Video analysis and video sharing | Fee based |
| Mindmeister | Collaborative brainstorming, create presentations, link any type of file | Free (up to three projects) and fee based |
| Pinterest | Visual bookmarking and chatting | Free |
| SharePoint | Share documents, social feeds, project groups, and online searching | Fee based (per user) |
| Skype | Audio and video conferencing, messaging | Free |
| Tumblr | Blogging service, create text and post any type of media or file | Free |
| TweetDeck | Customized individual and group Twitter accounts | Free |
| Vimeo | Video presentation sharing | Free |
| WebEx | Online videoconferencing and screen sharing | Free (up to three people) and fee based |
| WordPress | Blogging and website creation | Free and fee based |
| XMind | Create and share brainstorming graphical displays and notes | Free and fee based |
| XOS Digital | Video editing and online video sharing | Fee based |

book. On the other hand, simply recording personal observations in a notepad and then debriefing them with members of the coach learning group may be sufficient.

The ability to conduct and analyze coaching strategies developed through collaborative learning hinges on persistence. Successful coaches have the mental and physical conditioning to weather the frequent setbacks and dead-ends that occur while testing coaching strategies. The collaborative learning effort must continue until the high-impact performance gap is satisfactorily resolved; otherwise, the issue will continue to detract from athlete, team, and coach performance. How long are successful coaches willing to engage in a collaborative learning effort? The simple answer is, as long as it takes.

For example, successful high school basketball coach Hank Bias spent eight years systematically testing coaching strategies designed to close high-impact performance gaps. Through his own initiative, he was fortunate to have none other than Coach John Wooden as a member of his coach learning group.

The study that I coauthored on his multiyear collaborative learning efforts shows the power of collaborative learning groups when the group has the will to persist until evidence of improvement is measurable.[52] Recall from the discussion in chapter 7 of this book that Coach Bias' teams steadily improved their winning percentage over his 8-year collaborative learning process from 29 percent to 62 percent. His persistence in performing systematic testing of coaching strategies developed through the coach learning group resulted in the best 5-year winning record for the boys' basketball program in over 80 years.

Near the end of the study Coach Bias shared three specific strategies he used throughout the collaborative learning process to track evidence of progress:[52 (p.15)]

1. Made notes on the back of my file cards if a drill was inappropriate for the intended goal; made a tally as to how many repetitions of each offensive or defensive set to try to add up to 100; Wooden's rep rule he told me about.

2. Asked questions of players, staff, and guest observers. Reviewed each practice mentally afterwards to see how it could improve. I was super conscious of all the things that came out of my mouth that were not instruction or information related or took too long.

3. Monitor. I allowed the clock to monitor how on-task I was becoming during practices. I had a checklist of overall drills, etc. for the season and the day that I would check off as I made a lesson for the day.

## Wrap-Up

Coach learning is elevated when coaches take initiative to build and maintain a wide range of learning support systems. Gaining access to coaching networks, mentors, and coach learning groups is critical for optimizing coach development. Regularly collaborating with fellow coaches, as well as specialists in other fields, affords coaches the best opportunity to create innovative new strategies for addressing high-impact coaching issues.

Mentoring, an increasingly popular collaborative learning strategy for coaches, provides many benefits for both mentor and mentee. Although not all coaches will be formally recognized as mentors, every coach is a mentor through her or his daily coaching actions. The most effective coaches understand that all of life is a performance, viewed not only by other coaches but also by their athletes. Today's athletes are the future members of the coaching community.

Collaborative learning efforts are enhanced when coaches follow established guidelines for operating collaborative learning groups. The steps in collaborative learning are examples of deliberate practice for coaches, and the process is evident in the learning histories of the world's most successful coaches. A wide range of technology tools, many of them free, is now available for coaches to build and sustain their collaborative learning groups. These tools provide coaches with limitless possibilities for expanding membership in their coaching networks and learning groups.

The path to enhanced coaching through collaborative learning requires persistence, but the path to excellence is hiding in plain sight for coaches willing to immerse themselves in the collaborative learning process. Although quality coaches are constantly learning through collaboration, the off-season is an opportune time for maximizing collaborative learning efforts.

# Chapter 14

# Recharge and Ignite

**Key Concepts**

Stress and burnout
Coaching wellness
Expectancies
Early morning routines
Mindfulness
Positive self-talk
Athlete selection guidelines
Emotional support network
Work-life balance
Family and personal time
Self-care
Personal creed

Coaching is more than a job; it is an all-consuming lifestyle. Although coaching can be extremely rewarding because of the potential for having a lifelong positive effect on athletes, the effort can also easily wear down even the most accomplished and resilient coach. The long coaching journey from preseason team building to end-of-season reviews and recognitions is a grind.

Even the most successful and battle-hardened coaches will admit that by the time the off-season arrives they are emotionally and physically spent.[1] Professional baseball manager Don Mattingly described it as, "You feel like you just hit the ground."[2] Coach Mattingly acknowledged that he feels this state of exhaustion at the end of every season. Unfortunately, this type of coach burnout is common, often causing quality coaches to leave the profession.

There is no denying that quality coaching comes at a high personal cost to coaches. Legendary high school football coach Bob Ladouceur knows as well as anyone what it takes to build winning programs while developing athletes at the same time. While coaching his record-setting De La Salle High School teams, he acknowledged how stressful it can be to show up every day during the season ready to lead and teach.

> Pushing kids to accomplish what they don't consider achievable is a long, painful process, as much for the coach as the player. I'm relieved when it's all over. It's not that I don't enjoy it. But right now I'm looking at it and thinking, "Damn, it's a long haul." [3 (p. 9)]

Without a strong emotional support network and personal strategies for counterbalancing the emotional and physical toll of coaching, coaches will never reach their full potential or, worse, will suffer debilitating breakdowns. In his autobiography 10-time national college basketball championship and 6-time national Coach of the Year Geno Auriemma shared one such defining moment in his career.

Midway through his coaching career at the University of Connecticut, several years after his team had won their first national championship, Auriemma walked away in the middle of a frustrating practice and collapsed under the bleachers. That day could have easily been his final day of coaching. His description of the moment illustrates in vivid detail the toll that coaching can take on a coach's physical and emotional health.

> That day really drove home for me how stressful coaching is. I don't realize the toll it takes on me sometimes. It's so much work, and your whole job is dependent on these young college kids who are having trouble with their boyfriends, or at home, or with school, or in their dorm. . . . that day under the bleachers, I'm not sure it is worth it.[4 (p. 74)]

Luckily for the rest of us, Coach Auriemma recovered from that potential career-ending moment and went on to lead his teams to 10 more national championships and the USA women's basketball team to multiple world championships and Olympic gold medals.

Because of the increasing demands and professionalization of sport coaching, the off-season presents coaches with a rare opportunity to recharge—emotionally, physically, and socially. Fortunately, many lessons can be learned from examining how successful people in all walks of life create work-life balance and stay energized across their careers. The purpose of this final chapter is to share strategies for preventing burnout and show coaches how they can use these strategies to reignite their passion for the upcoming season.

## WATCHING FOR AND AVOIDING BURNOUT

Coaches sometimes joke that there are only two times when they feel stressed—day and night.[5] Although that story represents the extreme case, certainly all coaches experience moments where they question their decision to coach. Perceived or real pressures to win, along with ever-present scrutiny, often public, of coaching decisions, can easily cause coaches to feel isolated and worn out.

Add to this the prevailing win-now goal of many administrators and program stakeholders and low or nonexistent job security for most coaching positions and you have a perfect recipe for potential burnout. People have said that there are three kinds of coaches today—those who resign before they get fired, those who have been fired, and those who will be fired.[6]

Burnout has long been recognized as an occupational hazard for coaches. Burnout is generally defined as withdrawal from an activity because of physical and emotional exhaustion.[7] Famous coaches from Ara Parseghian, who led Notre Dame to national championships in 1966 and 1973, to more recent championship coaches such as Steve Spurrier, who resigned midseason in 2015, have had their careers cut short because of emotional fatigue and frustration.[8, 9]

Surely, an untold number of lesser-known coaches, at every level of sport, have left coaching prematurely because of stress and burnout. Signs of burnout include loss of interest, depression, and increased anxiety. Coaches experience burnout when they become unable to cope with the stress of coaching.

Coaches by nature are competitive people who strive to win. But the constant pressure, both self-induced and brought by others who follow the coach, will lead to burnout and serious health issues for coaches who don't learn how to cope effectively with the stresses of coaching.

A coach who does not cope well with stress has a negative effect on her or his athletes. When a coach shows up with low energy or depressed, athletes notice. Their ability to learn and perform declines, and team culture diminishes.[10, 11] For example, high school and college athletes who play for coaches who suffer from emotional exhaustion have higher levels of anxiety and burnout than athletes who play for spirited coaches. Moreover, because they are not able to give 100 percent to their coaching, emotionally exhausted coaches are perceived by their athletes to be less effective teachers and to give less praise.[10, 11]

To combat coaching stress and prevent burnout, coaches need to be aware of the common stressors that can plague them. Five major sources of stress and burnout can affect coaches: (1) communication and conflict, (2) pressure and expectations, (3) athlete discipline and team dynamics, (4) program support and isolation, and (5) sacrificing personal time.[10–17] A description of each stressor is provided in table 14.1.

The off-season is the ideal time for coaches to pause and reflect on how well they are handling these common sources of stress and burnout. Coaches should take a few minutes at the start of the off-season to complete a coaching wellness checkup (see figure 14.1). Questions listed in the wellness checkup are based on tools that have been tested through extensive research with coaches and athletes.[16–21] The higher the score is on the wellness checkup, the greater the risk is that a coach will succumb to stress and burnout.

By honestly answering these nine simple questions, you can select the right off-season coach wellness activities to ensure that you return to the next season energized and ready to lead your athletes.

Your motivation and confidence as a coach is strongly linked to how well you handle coaching stress. Coaches who believe that they are meant to coach and who coach because they love having the opportunity to lead and develop athletes are said to be intrinsically motived. Coaches with high intrinsic motivation and confidence in their ability as coaches are more resilient.[22]

**Table 14.1 Five Major Sources of Stress and Burnout for Coaches**

| Stressor | Description |
|---|---|
| Communication and conflict | Mismatch between coach and administrator philosophies, interference from parents, miscommunication and lack of trust among coaching staff, communication with officials |
| Pressure and expectations | Pressure from self and others to meet unrealistic performance targets, being evaluated as a coach based solely on athlete results, lack of job security |
| Athlete discipline and team dynamics | Lack of commitment, focus, effort, and character by athletes; team cohesion issues related to role acceptance and playing time; recruiting, selecting, or dropping athletes from the team |
| Program support and isolation | Inadequate support for the program (recognition, funding, facilities, equipment) or personal development as a coach (no formal opportunities to learn with and from other coaches) |
| Sacrificing personal time | Conflicting demands with family, strain on relationships, keeping pace with multiple roles and workload, health issues because of lack of sleep or regular physical activity |

## Figure 14.1 Coach Wellness Checkup

*Instructions:* Circle the answer that best represents how you feel right now about coaching.

| Question | Not at all how I feel | Somewhat how I feel | Exactly how I feel |
|---|---|---|---|
| 1. I don't look forward to coaching as much as I used to. | 1 | 2 | 3 |
| 2. I feel physically and emotionally worn out from coaching. | 1 | 2 | 3 |
| 3. I don't feel that I can cope very well with the demands of coaching. | 1 | 2 | 3 |
| 4. I don't feel like I'm accomplishing many worthwhile things as a coach. | 1 | 2 | 3 |
| 5. Athletes and others I work with don't show the same level of commitment that I do. | 1 | 2 | 3 |
| 6. I don't feel supported in my coaching. | 1 | 2 | 3 |
| 7. There is a lack of communication and trust where I coach. | 1 | 2 | 3 |
| 8. I don't feel secure in my current coaching position. | 1 | 2 | 3 |
| 9. I question if the amount of time and energy I spend on coaching is worth it. | 1 | 2 | 3 |

From W. Gilbert, 2017, *Coaching better every season: A year-round system for athlete development and program success* (Champaign, IL: Human Kinetics).

Resilient coaches have what is known as a hardy personality. Coaches who demonstrate hardiness are more committed to their work, feel confident and in control, and view unexpected setbacks as challenges rather than threats.[17]

When coaches succumb to stress, their passion for coaching drains away and their hardiness weakens. Although coaches need strategies for recharging and coping with stress at all times throughout the year, the off-season presents a unique time for coaches to recover and recharge. For example, coaches can replenish their motivation for coaching by attending clinics, watching videos, or reading books.

In the remainder of this chapter the focus is on sharing proven strategies for recharging in the off-season that will help coaches develop the hardiness needed to handle common sources of stress and burnout.

## MANAGING PRESSURE AND EXPECTATIONS

Only one thing is guaranteed when you start coaching. You will lose. All coaches face this reality, and they normally head into the off-season coming off a loss. In most sports, for all but one athlete or team, the season will end with a loss. The most successful American collegiate basketball coach of all time, former University of Tennessee women's basketball coach Pat Summitt, once shared how hard she took losing at the end of a season.

> When I lose, I've been known to take to my bed. In 1994, the Lady Vols lost to Louisana Tech in the first round of the regionals. Afterward, I went to bed. Literally. I crawled underneath the covers and didn't raise my head for two days. I might have brushed my teeth. I don't remember.[23 (p. 290)]

Even if you built a winning program, as coach Summitt did, your athletes and teams will have off-days or come up short in a competition. Learning how to bounce back from losing, particularly a losing season, is critical for improving and persevering as a coach.

Often, the most driven and successful coaches take losing the hardest. Three-time college football championship coach Urban Meyer once shared that he resorted to pills and alcohol to cope with the stress of losing even one game:

> The toll on my body, the toll on my mind . . . I would just get sick, I mean like physically ill—what could I have done better, it's my fault we lost this game. I'm taking two Ambiens, I would drink a beer on top of that just to get some sleep.[24]

Regardless of how much you win or lose, as a coach you will have moments of high stress. Mistakes, frustrations, pressure—these all come with the territory when you coach. And unlike many other types of jobs, a coach's work is never over. As renowned University of Texas swim coach Jill Sterkel astutely observed, "A coach's responsibilities are never done. It is a 24-hour-a-day, 7-day-a-week job."[25 (p. 116)]

Coach Sterkel, like many other coaches, learned the hard way that trying to control everything and living in constant fear of getting it wrong is a surefire route

AP Photo/Mark Humphrey

Coaching athletes to peak performance requires strategies for coping with pressure and expectations, something legendary basketball coach Pat Summitt learned over her career.

to burnout and health issues that can cut a coaching career short. After just five years as a head coach, she had to take a four-month leave to recover.

One of the greatest sources of pressure experienced by coaches is self-induced. The following statement by an experienced college coach is representative of how all serious coaches approach their work: "I put more stress on myself than anybody else does. My expectations of myself are higher than anybody else's."[11 (p. 45)]

Furthermore, coaches by nature are helpers; they have a genuine concern for others and cherish the opportunity to serve as trusted advisors. However, coaches can easily lose sight of the need to take care of themselves first. This approach may sound selfish, but coaches won't be able to help and lead others if their personal life is in disarray. As one college coach put it, coaches are "supposed to be problem solvers, not people with problems."[11 (p. 38)] Of course, coaches have problems just as anyone else does, and they can benefit from the same stress and coping strategies they teach their athletes.

Coaches improve their ability to cope with pressure and stress by using the off-season to practice viewing setbacks as normal and opportunities for growth. The title of a bestselling book on how to lead a successful life says it all: "Don't sweat the small stuff . . . and it's all small stuff."[26]

In his book, Richard Carlson shares 100 hundred strategies for thriving in life, all of which apply equally well to coaching. One of my favorite suggestions, and one that I have seen many successful coaches use, is to set aside some quiet time every day.

Waking up a few minutes earlier in the morning is a simple time-tested way to gather yourself and reflect on your goals for the day.[27] Successful coaches are notorious early risers. Some, such as renowned basketball coach Jerry Wainwright, rise as early as 3:30 a.m. every day. Coach Wainwright uses the early morning quiet time to prepare handwritten notes of inspiration for coaches he has met over his many years of coaching.[28] He, like many other coaches I have met, finds that making time to recharge the batteries of others is an effective way to recharge his own enthusiasm for coaching.

The off-season is also a time when many coaches do some form of physical activity, whether it is stretching, yoga, going for a walk, running, or riding a bike. Coaches will soon find that their early morning routine becomes an indispensable part of preparing to coach at their best. Besides the obvious physical health benefits of doing regular exercise, this strategy is helpful when used as a mental break from the stress of coaching.[11] Successful coaches recommend using physical activity time to unplug and think about anything other than coaching. For example, renowned swim coach Jill Sterkel found that walking her dog several mornings each week was an ideal way to recharge.

> Several mornings a week I take my golden retriever, Jake, for long walks. During those walks with the dog, I let my head go and enjoy the solitude. This is my personal time to unplug and relax and also enjoy my dog and the outdoors.[25 (p. 118)]

Because schedules vary widely among coaches, there is no optimal wake up time. Instead, the key is to carve out some amount of dedicated uninterrupted personal time each day. Early morning works well for several reasons. First, an early start allows you to build confidence and begin the day on a positive note. Start the day with things that are most important to you—your morning run or walk, 30 minutes of reading that book you still haven't finished, or watching an interview with a well-known coach. Second, early morning provides you with a distraction-free zone. The daily bombardment from others has yet to start. Practice not checking your phone or e-mail for at least the first 30 minutes of this personal quiet time. Charging your own battery first, referred to as starting your day on offense, before you start helping others meet their needs is a proven strategy for increasing productivity.[29]

Whereas what you do when you first wake up sets the stage for a productive day, how you end your day lays the foundation for a healthy and fulfilling personal life outside coaching. Although coaches by nature are almost constantly thinking about coaching, they need a mental and emotional cool-down before they connect with family and friends each night.

One way to transition from coach to the other roles we play in life (father, mother, spouse, partner, friend, and so on) is to pull over physically before walking into your home.[26] For those who commute by car, this process would mean pulling off the road at a scenic or calming spot close to home, turning off the car, and taking a few uninterrupted minutes to recalibrate. Focus on relaxing, enjoying the scenery, and putting aside coaching concerns for the moment.

The common theme across all these stress and coping strategies is learning how to become more present minded and less self-critical. When coaches set aside a few minutes each day to reflect on their thoughts and emotions, they are practicing mindfulness. Successful coaches have long recognized the power of mindfulness, including renowned high school football coach Joe Ehrmann who concluded that the "development of mindfulness, the ability to perceive ourselves and others accurately, is the most profound journey a coach can take."[30 (p. 129)] As a way to enhance mindfulness, Coach Ehrmann recommends that coaches ask themselves four "mindsight" questions: Why do I coach? Why do I coach the way I do? What does it feel like to be coached by me? How do I define success?[30 (p. 131)]

The key to mindfulness is to suspend judgment and simply observe the thoughts and emotions that you are experiencing at the moment. Coaches can easily get bogged down in negative thinking about situations that are beyond their control or by wishing things were different. The goal with learning how to accept your thoughts is to become more aware of negative thoughts and less emotionally reactive.

Coaches of the world champion New Zealand All Blacks rugby team describe mindfulness as having a "blue head"—staying loose, in the moment, calm and focused on the immediate task. This state is contrasted with having a "red head"—tight, anxious, unfocused, and desperate. Mindfulness leads to greater emotional stability, a defining characteristic of great coaches and their athletes.

Championship coaches and athletes are increasingly recognizing the value of mindfulness for achieving success.[31–33] For example, Super Bowl and college championship football coach Pete Carroll has made mindfulness training, in the form of meditation, a regular part of his team's training schedule. As one of his football players said, "Meditation is as important as lifting weights and being out here on the field for practice."[31] By practicing meditation, Coach Carroll has created a team culture that emphasizes awareness and positivity that in turn frees up athletes to put themselves into a mind-set of greatness.

The results speak for themselves. After integrating meditation fully into regular training, Coach Carroll's team reached two consecutive Super Bowls and won the franchise's first-ever league championship. Here are the basic steps to follow when learning how to practice meditation:[5, 34]

- Find a quiet place free of distraction and set a timer for at least 10 minutes. Settle into a comfortable seated position with eyes closed or fixed on a spot in front of you.
- Relax by taking five deep breaths, focusing on raising your belly when you inhale and pulling your belly in when you exhale.
- Bring your attention to the process of thinking, seeing thoughts as events in your mind.
- Simply allow any thoughts to arise without pushing them away or analyzing them.
- Practice noticing the thoughts and letting them pass like clouds in the sky or cars on a highway.
- When ready, end the exercise and practice taking this mindfulness approach to your interactions with others throughout the day.

Before you say, "I don't have time for thinking about my thinking," consider the results of a groundbreaking study that tested mindfulness training with college coaches.[35] Some coaches completed a self-guided, daily 20-minute mindfulness training program for six weeks, while other coaches acted as a comparison group (no mindfulness training). At the end of the six weeks, the coaches who practiced the daily meditation exercises had lower anxiety, had more positive moods, and were more patient and better able to control their emotions. Adding a few minutes of meditation to their daily routine increased their emotional stability and improved their ability to connect with others. In other words, regular meditation helped them become better coaches. As one coach stated, "I'm able to see the big picture. . . . I could be a little bit calmer or a little bit more mindful of what is coming out of my mouth."[35 (p. 129)]

Any coach can follow the program used in the mindfulness training study by using the meditation resources prepared by renowned mindfulness teacher Dr. Jon Kabat-Zinn. A series of self-guided meditation exercises are available, either as CDs or as MP3 files that can be instantly downloaded, at the Guided Mindfulness Meditation website (www.mindfulnesscds.com). The self-guided six-week program that proved valuable for the college coaches is reproduced in figure 14.2.[35 (p. 137)]

## Figure 14.2 Self-Guided Mindfulness Training Program for Coaches

| Week | Mindfulness activities (Kabat-Zinn CD Series 3) |
|---|---|
| 1 | Day 1 to day 4: CD 1 (Activity 1 Breathscape—20 minutes)<br>Day 5 and Day 6: CD 1 (Activity 2 Bodyscape—20 minutes)<br>Day 7: CD 3 (Activity 2 Walking Meditation—10 minutes + 10 minute walking practice) |
| 2 | Repeat Week 1 schedule |
| 3 | Day 1 to Day 3: CD 1 (Activity 3 Breathscape and Bodyscape—20 minutes)<br>Day 4: CD 3 (Activity 2 Walking Meditation—10 minutes + 10 minute walking practice)<br>Day 5 to Day 7: CD 2 (Activity 2 Mindscape—20 minutes) |
| 4 | Repeat Week 3 schedule |
| 5 | Day 1: CD 3 (Activity 2 Walking Meditation—10 minutes + 10 minute walking practice)<br>Day 2 and Day 5: Coach-selected activities from the CDs<br>Day 3 and Day 6: CD 1 (Activity 3 Breathscape and Bodyscape—20 minutes)<br>Day 4: CD 3 (Activity 1 Nowscape—20 minutes)<br>Day 7: CD 4 (Activity 1 Heartscape—20 minutes) |
| 6 | Day 1: CD 3 (Activity 2 Walking Meditation—10 minutes + 10 minute walking practice)<br>Day 2 and Day 5: CD 3 (Activity 1 Nowscape or coach's choice—20 minutes)<br>Day 3 and Day 6: CD 1 (Activity 3 Breathscape and Bodyscape—20 minutes)<br>Day 4: CD 4 (Activity 1 Heartscape or coach's choice—20 minutes)<br>Day 7: CD 4 (Activity 1 Heartscape—20 minutes) |

Reprinted, by permission, from K. Longshore and M. Sachs, 2015, "Mindfulness training for coaches: A mixed-method exploratory study," *Journal of Clinical Sport Psychology* 9(2): 116-137.

Besides learning how to become more mindful, coaches who have long productive careers also learn how to overturn self-doubt and negative self-talk. Coaches who are serious about success typically question themselves after conflicts with athletes or tough losses. How many coaches can honestly say they slept well after a frustrating practice or disappointing loss? Much of the stress from these normal setbacks is self-induced through second guessing our coaching decisions. In many cases we are our most vocal critic.

Successful coaches combat this self-doubt and overly critical questioning by learning how to use positive self-talk, a time-tested strategy used by champion athletes and performers of all types.[36–38] Positive self-talk, sometimes also called affirmations, helps boost confidence and motivation and builds optimism and hardiness.

Positive self-talk is used to reframe negative thinking. For example, after a tough season, coaches are particularly vulnerable to negative self-talk. Instead of dwelling on all the things that went wrong, such as injuries or conflict in the locker room, coaches could think about how fortunate they are to have a job that allows them to lead and shape the lives of others. They might also remind themselves, "Other coaches have to put up with this and they still succeed."[37 (p. 247)]

Positive self-talk is a valuable strategy to counterbalance the tendency to dwell on mistakes and question decisions. Championship college football coach Bobby Bowden included positive self-talk as one of his six keys to leading a successful coaching life.[39 (pp. 257–258)]

1. Make time for yourself and your family.
2. Surround yourself with the best possible people.
3. Be open to new ideas and better ways to do things. Keep all lines of communication open with your staff.
4. Like what you do.
5. Don't dwell on your mistakes or setbacks—learn and grow from them, and then move on. Never let your mistakes defeat or discourage you. Never take criticism personally.

The list of self-talk do's and don'ts is illustrated in figure 14.3. Although the list was prepared for athletes, it applies equally well to coaches. In the off-season coaches can use this list to write positive self-talk statements that align with the do's instead of the don'ts. For example, before a competition, instead of dwelling on how much more preparation you could have done, remind yourself of all the game planning you were able to complete and the moments of quality practice that occurred leading up to the event.

## IMPROVING COMMUNICATION

Miscommunication is repeatedly cited as the number one source of stress for coaches. Effective communication is a learned skill, and like any physical skill, it must be practiced to achieve improvement. The off-season is a perfect time for coaches to reflect on and enhance their communication and interpersonal skills.

## Figure 14.3 Self-Talk Do's and Don'ts

| Do's | Don'ts |
|---|---|
| **BEFORE PRACTICE OR COMPETITION** | |
| Focus on positive self-perceptions and strengths. | Don't focus on negative self-perceptions and weaknesses. |
| Focus on your effective preparation. | Don't focus on inadequacy of or problems with preparation. |
| Remind yourself of previous successes. | Avoid thinking about previous failures. |
| Focus on positive expectations and goals. | Avoid unrealistic expectations and negative goals. |
| Reframe any irrational beliefs using effective counterarguments. | Don't allow irrational beliefs to go unchallenged. |
| **DURING PRACTICE OR COMPETITION** | |
| Limit thinking and rely on automated skills. | Don't think too much, overanalyze, or try to make it happen. |
| Focus on the present, not the past or future. | Don't dwell on past mistakes or potential future problems. |
| Focus on process, not product, using effective cue words. | Avoid thinking about the product too much. |
| Appraise the situation as a challenge and maintain positive expectations and goals. | Don't appraise the situation as a threat. |
| Reframe negative thoughts and use effective problem-solving strategies. | Avoid haphazard reframing or unsystematic problem-solving. |
| **FOLLOWING PRACTICE OR COMPETITION** | |
| Attribute success to internal, controllable factors such as effort and mental prep that will increase perceived competence. | Don't attribute success to external factors or failure to stable, internal ones that will reduce perceived competence. |
| Develop positive future expectations and goals, complete with action plans for how to achieve them, and minimize oversights. | Avoid negative expectations and goals. |

Reprinted, by permission, from D. Burton and T.D. Raedeke, 2008, *Sport psychology for coaches* (Champaign, IL: Human Kinetics), 117.

A major source of miscommunication is the preconceived notions we hold of the people with whom we are trying to communicate. Whenever we are about to communicate with someone—an athlete, another coach, friend, or family member—we create an image of how we believe that the other person behaves, thinks, and will respond to our message. These expectancies we hold of others has been shown to have an extremely strong influence on how we approach these people.[22]

For example, if you believe that an athlete is lazy or isn't fully committed to the program, then you are less likely to approach that athlete with a positive attitude or enthusiasm. Furthermore, you will hold lower expectations of this athlete and offer less feedback and instruction.[22] In other words, based on how you perceive a person, you may not expect much of him or her, and in turn the person will feel as if you don't expect much of him or her. A lack of mutual trust develops, and the athlete will continue to reinforce the negative image you have of him or her, which only strengthens the preconceived notions you hold. This mechanism is called an expectancy cycle, also known as a self-fulfilling prophecy.[22]

Fortunately, coaches can overcome the expectancy cycle and improve coach-athlete communication by following some simple guidelines based on recommendations from leading coaching scientists.[22]

- Be mindful of the assumptions and views you hold of your athletes and regularly test and update these views.
- Set appropriate and realistic performance targets based on regular assessment of athlete ability.
- Ensure that athletes are not always paired with the same partner or group during practice activities, to develop a more comprehensive and accurate portrait of each athlete's maturity and skill level.
- Communicate high expectations for all your athletes, not just the most talented or physically gifted ones.

Coaches can also use a four-step exercise to help improve their communication by approaching each person, and each interaction, with a fresh set of eyes. This exercise, adapted from mindfulness training guidelines for coaches,[5] will help improve your ability to leave preconceived notions behind when communicating with others. The exercise is designed to cultivate and strengthen what has been referred to as a beginner's mind. Practice completing the following four steps when greeting someone:

1. Note any thoughts or emotions that arise when you encounter this person.
2. Ask yourself whether you are seeing the person based on your preconceived notions or simply as the person is at the moment.
3. Remember that each person is unique and that you should avoid prejudging others.
4. Before making assumptions, ask clarifying questions and consider alternative explanations for the person's behavior or reaction to your message.

During the off-season, coaches could also create an expectancy profile for each of their athletes. Using the athlete expectancy worksheet provided in figure 14.4, coaches should note any assumptions or beliefs they hold about each of their athletes (e.g., "Larissa doesn't respect me as a coach."). After you identify assumptions, the next step is to ask yourself what evidence you have to support these beliefs (e.g., "Larissa rarely looks me in the eyes when I speak to her."). The third step is then to challenge yourself to think of other plausible explanations for

## Figure 14.4 Expectancy Profile Worksheet

Name: ______________________________________________

Assumptions (expectancies) I hold about this athlete.

Reasons why I hold this expectancy (evidence to support the assumption).

Other plausible explanations for why the athlete behaves this way (am I basing my expectancy on accurate and reliable information?)

Ways I could approach this athlete with a fresh perspective next season.

From W. Gilbert, 2017, *Coaching better every season: A year-round system for athlete development and program success* (Champaign, IL: Human Kinetics).

the athlete behavior (e.g., "Is it possible that Larissa is intimidated by me or the way I communicate?"). Finally, the last step is used to think of ways you could approach the athlete with a fresh (unbiased) perspective when you start the next season (e.g., "In my preseason individual meeting with Larissa, I will share with her some information about different communication styles and ask her to identify which style best describes her."). The same worksheet could be used for thinking about how you communicate and interact with administrators and other coaches.

A final off-season strategy that addresses both communication and expectancies while simultaneously recharging your emotional tank as a coach is a gratitude note. Practice writing a short note, or even a short letter, for each athlete about something you are thankful for that happened the previous season. The note could be related to how the athlete influenced your life in a positive way or how you influenced the athlete's life. For example, perhaps an athlete helped you cope with a stressful season by making you laugh and bringing positive energy to practices. Or perhaps you helped an athlete improve study habits, pass a class, or learn how to cope with a difficult family or friendship situation. These experiences are an important source of enjoyment that feeds coach motivation and buffers against burnout.[11] A good example of this viewpoint comes from a successful college coach who participated in a study on coach burnout:

> I love seeing a freshman come in and as a senior she's a young woman. Here, we take some kids that, they could have a pretty bad life, and all of a sudden they get their degree here and they turn it around a little bit, and I feel good about that. [The enjoyment] is the kids and how much you can affect their lives in a positive manner.[11 (p. 49)]

Recognize and be thankful for the multitude of ways you win with each athlete. This strategy builds resolve and confidence, and prepares you to approach the next season with a positive outlook.

## CREATING POSITIVE TEAM ENVIRONMENTS

Athlete attitude and team discipline are routinely cited as the major sources of stress for coaches. One way to eliminate this source of stress is simply to remove the offending athlete from the team. This approach is used by the world's most successful team, the New Zealand All Blacks rugby team, who became the first team to win consecutive rugby world championships in 2015.

One of their core principles for building healthy and productive team environments is their "no dickheads" rule. The rule, which has long guided team selection as well as decisions to eliminate bad apples and enemies in the tent, is summarized as follows:

> "No one is bigger than the team and individual brilliance does not automatically lead to outstanding results. One selfish mindset will infect a collective culture."[33 (p. 81)]

The easiest way to eliminate or reduce athlete and team dysfunction is to have clear guidelines for team selection and written expectations for athlete behavior. After making time in the off-season to work on your mindfulness skills, you are now ready to create, or enhance, your team selection protocols and athlete behavior standards. Having a clear sense of how to select your athletes and how you expect them to behave as productive members of a team will build your enthusiasm for starting the next season. These protocols and guidelines will also help buffer coaching stress during the season.

Although in some sports such as cross country running and track and field, where having a no-cut policy may be practical, most coaches will likely have to cut athletes from their team. Even if coaches are able to accommodate any athlete who has a desire to play on their team, team membership must be earned and treated as a privilege. An effective athlete selection process requires that coaches have a clear sense of how they will screen athletes for inclusion on their team and how they will communicate nonselection when needed.

In the off-season, coaches should review the criteria they will use for selecting athletes. Before tryouts, coaches will need a list of not only the sport and physical skills they are looking for in prospective athletes but also the personal characteristics that athletes should have to limit the discipline issues and team conflicts that might arise during the season. Coaches should ask themselves one simple question that will go a long way to preventing stress during the season: What kind of person am I looking for to join my team?

Coaches might start by looking for athletes who show desire. A checklist for identifying athlete desire might include the following items:[40 (p. 248)]

- The desire to play
- The desire to win
- The desire to work hard
- The desire to learn
- The desire to get better
- The desire to compete

This type of list is a good starting point, but to be of real value for a coach the list must include examples of observable behaviors that exemplify the attribute as well as names of athletes familiar to your players who are models of the attribute. The sample behaviors and athlete models should be shared with prospective athletes during tryouts as a way to communicate the type of athlete you are seeking. For example, coaches might define the desire to compete as embracing the challenge, never giving up, and playing to the final whistle.

A powerful example of an athlete modeling the desire to compete that I routinely use in my classes and when working with coaches is college runner Heather Dorniden. With only one lap remaining in an indoor race she tripped. What appeared to be an insurmountable gap opened between her and the other runners. Undeterred, she jumped back up and unbelievably caught up and edged the final runner at the finish line to win the race. The video of this incredible feat of athlete desire in action has been viewed over 14 million times.[41]

Coaches will find it helpful to have a clear description of sough-after athlete characteristics and a bank of examples they can show to athletes. Using the example of athlete desire as an athlete selection criteria, coaches could prepare a collection of athlete desire examples in the off-season using the worksheet provided in figure 14.5.

Simply telling athletes you are looking for players who show desire is not as powerful as being able to offer a clear description of what desire means and then showing them real examples of athlete desire in action. I have provided an example of desire to compete, but coaches should create definitions and use examples that are meaningful to them and their athletes. Investing time in the off-season to find vivid examples of athlete desire and other coveted athlete characteristics will pay big dividends during the season and reduce coaching stress by helping you select the right types of athletes.

Understanding what type of athlete you are looking for to build a healthy and productive team environment will allow you to enter the next season feeling prepared to select the right athletes. Perhaps the most stressful moment that coaches will face when building their teams is communicating nonselection decisions. Renowned high school football coach Joe Erhmann calls this the single most difficult day of the season.

## Figure 14.5 Examples of Athlete Desire Worksheet

| Type of desire | Description | Example |
|---|---|---|
| Desire to compete | Embracing the challenge, never giving up, playing to the final whistle | Heather Dorniden www.youtube.com/watch?v=xjejTQdK5OI |
| Desire to play | | |
| Desire to win | | |
| Desire to work hard | | |
| Desire to learn | | |
| Desire to get better | | |

From W. Gilbert, 2017, *Coaching better every season: A year-round system for athlete development and program success* (Champaign, IL: Human Kinetics).

> I appreciate how difficult it is for coaches when they have to make final cuts. Most sports are not conducive to carrying large rosters and many coaches say this is the single most difficult day of the season. My problem is with the way too many coaches cut players. To publicly post a list of players who did and didn't make the team on a wall outside the locker room adds insult to injury. Players who are cut deserve a constructive conversation and affirmation of their value and worth. That is how a caring community treats every member.[30 (p. 149)]

Communicating nonselection to athletes, and their parents as needed, will be much less stressful if coaches take some time in the off-season to reflect on how they plan to address this difficult coaching task. Coaches should consider asking themselves questions like the ones that follow, reproduced from an insightful article about dealing with athlete nonselection.[42 (pp. 18–20)]

- How do I feel about the ways in which I have experienced being eliminated or observed others being eliminated when I participated in sport?

- What can I learn from the examples of other coaches regarding the manner in which they announced tryout decisions?
- Should I consider using a combination of communication methods? (For example, lists with follow-up meetings, lists with letters, letters with follow-up phone calls, and so on.)
- To what extent does the way that I plan to inform athletes of their elimination match the amount of time I can spend, or am willing to spend, with this process?
- What can I do to clarify how tryout results will be communicated?
- To what extent does the way I plan to inform athletes of their elimination answer their questions of why they didn't make the team. . .
    - In a way that is personal and relevant?
    - In a way that is sensitive to their age?
    - In a way that considers their investment and future goals in this sport?
- To what extent does the way I plan to inform athletes of their elimination . . .
    - Let me inform them of their strengths?
    - Provide me with the opportunity to discuss with them the alternative programs, leagues, camps, or instructional programs in our sport?
    - Invite them to ask questions about their evaluation and follow-up questions about feedback I provided?
    - Consider the environment (surroundings, other people) in which they will react to being eliminated?
- To what extent does the way I plan to inform athletes of their elimination encourage or discourage confrontations with parents?

A final step to take when building a team that will help minimize stress from potential miscommunication is to have athletes, and parents if the athletes are younger than 18, sign a team membership contract. The contract should clearly outline, in one page, expectations for athlete conduct. The expectations you hold for your athletes must be clearly communicated before team selection to avoid misunderstandings that can lead to conflict later in the season.

Many examples of player contracts are available, but I particularly like the one shared by Michael and Ralph Sabock.[37] Their sample contract includes an athlete pledge, behavior standards and expectations, and a parental acknowledgement (see figure 14.6). The fact that the contract is referred to as an application reinforces that participation on the team is an earned privilege that comes with a shared understanding of how players and coaches will act as a team.

Many of the strategies used to select the right athletes for your team can be adapted to ensure you select the right people to join your coaching staff. Making time to reflect on the desirable characteristics of assistants you want to bring into your coaching team will minimize stress that can result from conflict and disagreements among coaches. Pat Summitt, who holds the record for most wins of all time in college basketball, summed it up well: "Hire good people and your headaches will be greatly reduced."[43 (p. 138)]

## Figure 14.6 Application for Team Membership Athlete Contract

### Pledge and Declaration

1. I, ______________________________, promise to abide by all the rules and regulations set up by the school district, the school, and the coaches. I will attend practice faithfully and work as hard as I possibly can to learn the fundamentals and to develop the skills necessary for becoming a championship player. I will always conduct myself in a manner that will be a credit to my family, my school, my community, and myself. I will try to maximize the interest of others in sports, to help players younger than myself, to encourage fair play at all times, and to respect the judgement and advice of all personnel associated with the school and the team.
2. I am proud to be an American and a participant in the school's athletic program. In appreciation of these privileges, I will serve to prove myself as a worthy citizen and athlete. My goal will be to assist the team in being one of which everyone can be proud—a team of *Champions* and a *Championship Team*.

### Standards and Understandings

1. I hereby agree to:
   - Be neat and clean and have my hair above my ears and collar.
   - Not have evening dates prior to practice or game days.
   - Be home by 10:00 PM and in bed early before school days.
   - Never miss a practice, unless sick. If sick, I will notify one of the coaches.
   - Not to be tardy for practice.
   - Be modest in attire. (Good appearance is important since athletes are always on parade.)
   - Not curse.
   - Display good sportsmanship at all times.
   - Be courteous to officials.
   - Never fake an injury.
   - Not smoke or use tobacco products.
   - Not drink alcoholic beverages or use any type of illegal drug.
   - Keep in top physical condition (eating properly, working out in weight room, and so on).
2. I understand that:
   - If I fail to keep my pledge, if I exhibit behavior inconsistent with my above declaration, or if I do not observe all of the foregoing standards, I will be disciplined or dropped from the team (at the discretion of the coach and the athletic director).
   - Neither the school district (including the school) nor any of its employees (including coaches) can be held liable for any injury I may sustain or be held responsible for the payment of any medical costs I may incur (including hospital, doctor, or pharmacy charges).

______________________ ______________________________________

Date Candidate's signature

### Parental Request, Acknowledgment, and Certification

1. I, the undersigned, hereby request that my son/daughter, ______________________________,

   be permitted to participate in the sport of ______________________________.
2. I acknowledge my recognition and acceptance of the condition of team membership that neither the school district nor any of its employees can be held liable for any injury my son/daughter may sustain or be responsible for any medical costs that may be incurred by them.
3. I certify that I hold insurance that will pay any medical costs that may be associated with

   ______________________________'s participation in the sport of ______________________________.

______________________ ______________________________________

Date Parent's signature

Courtesy of Coach John McKissick, Summerville High School, SC (retired). Reprinted, by permission, from M.D. Sabock and R.J. Sabock, 2011, *Coaching: A realistic perspective*, 10th ed. (Plymouth, UK: Rowman & Littlefield), 235. Permission conveyed through the Copyright Clearance Center, Inc.

You want to make sure you enlist assistants you can trust and who share your general philosophy and approach to coaching and athlete development. The off-season is a good time to revisit the expectations you have for members of your coaching staff. Put in writing the specific roles and responsibilities you envision for each member of the coaching staff. This process will help avoid potential problems stemming from misunderstandings that can arise during the season. Coach Summitt recommends preparing coaching staff guidelines for items such as dress code, punctuality, relationships with players, appropriate language, and office hours.[43]

Surrounding yourself with the right assistants will help keep you motivated and energized throughout the season, as opposed to becoming another source of coaching stress. Bringing in people who share your general coaching philosophy and clearly stating expectations will reduce stress and conflict during the season. Successful coaches learn to trust those they hire and delegate program duties to prevent burnout and build healthy and productive team environments.[43, 44]

## BUILDING SUPPORT SYSTEMS

Many coaches feel lonely and isolated, even when they work alongside dozens of other coaches and administrators in a large athletics department. All coaches, at some point in their career, will relate to the following statements shared by an experienced coach who was asked to reflect on the amount of support she received from her sport organization: "I've noticed people are quite isolated. . . .

NBAE via Getty Images

While understanding the importance of supporting their athletes, championship coaches like Coach Krzyzewski also build their own support systems to keep themselves fresh.

You are so on your own. . . . I have absolutely nobody to talk to. . . . The isolation is unbelievable really."[45 (p. 12)] Conversely, coaches who work in environments where ongoing professional development opportunities are encouraged and provided tend to score higher on measures of well-being.[21]

Just as championship athletes require a strong support team, so to do coaches. Successful coaches like championship basketball coach Mike Krzyzewski recognize the importance of building a strong emotional support team to help them coach at their best.

> To perform at their best, every individual on a team also needs the relationships that comprise their own individual support systems. The leader, in particular, needs this system of support because he needs to be fully invested all the time. Having a strong personal system of support behind you makes it easier to immerse yourself in your team and its mission.[46 (p. 58)]

The ability to persist despite setbacks and new challenges that constantly arise requires great focus and energy. Coaches should pay careful attention to fellow coaches who are models of coaching vitality—always full of energy and ready to lead. These types of coaches can nourish your coaching soul, and you should target them as potential members of your coaching network.

One of the primary benefits of building a strong coaching network is the emotional support that is gained.[25, 36, 47] Spending time with other high-energy, positive, and action-oriented people is emotionally rewarding. Jon Gordon, author of the popular book *The Energy Bus*, shares 10 rules for creating the right type of support team for professional growth and life satisfaction.[48] I have found that coaches enjoy this book enormously and often read it with their athletes.

Using the fictional story of a man who rides a bus to work, Gordon shares how we have control over the choices we make about who we let on our bus, or in other words, who we chose to spend time with on a daily basis. He distinguishes between two types of people we can let on our bus—energy givers and energy vampires.

Energy givers are people who bring value to our lives and help fill our emotional tanks. Energy vampires, on the other hand, are people who drain our energy and distract us from realizing our full potential. Coaches need to surround themselves with energy givers as they consider who to add to their support system.

Ice hockey coach Mike Babcock, who has coached teams to college, professional, world, and Olympic championships, suggests that coaches regularly ask themselves the following question: "Do you surround yourself with people who make you better?"[49 (p. 116)] Energy givers make you better; energy vampires make you worse.

How can coaches spot fellow energy givers? Energy givers are easy to identify because they exude positive energy and enthusiasm, they work with an uncommon drive and sense of purpose, and they genuinely enjoy what they do. Energy givers also model a service ethic. They produce energy for both others and themselves.

Lastly, energy givers are not afraid to hold others accountable, or what Gordon refers to as being able to love tough. Trusting relationships are essential for creating a support system in which coaches are comfortable with challenging each other and are receptive to being challenged.

## Figure 14.7 Checklist for Identifying Candidates for a Coach Emotional Support Network

- ☐ Exude positive energy and enthusiasm
- ☐ Display uncommon drive
- ☐ Work with a clear sense of purpose
- ☐ Are service and other-oriented
- ☐ Hold others accountable
- ☐ Are trustworthy
- ☐ Known for their relationship skills
- ☐ Offer frequent and genuine praise
- ☐ Show humility and gratitude
- ☐ Are good listeners
- ☐ Open to learning from others
- ☐ Show positive body language

From W. Gilbert, 2017, *Coaching better every season: A year-round system for athlete development and program success* (Champaign, IL: Human Kinetics).

Much as Jon Gordon provides strategies for building a support system composed of energy givers, Jim Thompson, founder of the Positive Coaching Alliance, has created a list of suggestions to help coaches act like energy givers for their athletes.[50] I have adapted these collective ideas to create a checklist of energy-giver characteristics that coaches can use to identify and add people to their emotional support networks (see figure 14.7). The off-season is the ideal time to reflect on your emotional support network and add, or replace, members of your network.

Coaches should look for people who offer frequent and genuine praise. The key is that the praise must be authentic, or truthful. Coaches of the world's most successful team, the New Zealand All Blacks, use the phrase *in the belly, not the back* to reinforce the fundamental importance of honest and genuine feedback.[33] Coaches will not benefit from surrounding themselves with people who ignore their weaknesses and blindly offer undeserved praise.

Coaches should also seek people who regularly express appreciation and demonstrate strong listening skills. The ability to express appreciation demonstrates humility and a willingness to learn from others. Building a support system of effective listeners is also crucial for ensuring that a coach's needs and concerns will be recognized.

Finally, coaches can quickly identify potential energy givers by observing someone's nonverbal, or body, language. Coaches typically spend many hours observing other coaches as part of their preparation for competitions. Coaches should notice the nonverbal responses that other coaches exhibit when they face adversity during competitive situations. Coaches who demonstrate a steady and positive demeanor during these situations are examples of energy givers. They are good candidates to reach out to when building an emotional support network. Remember that moments of adversity don't build character; they reveal it.

As a coach you should strive to embody these energy-giver characteristics yourself. Doing this will increase the frequency with which other coaches invite you to join their support networks, further enhancing your ability to stay emotionally charged as a coach.

Other effective ways to combat isolation and build your support network include attending off-season coaching clinics and increasing your coaching knowledge through reading about and listening to inspiring stories from successful people. Clinics and workshops are obvious places to connect with other energy givers. Reading and listening to inspirational stories provide similar energy-recharging benefits because they help to fill your emotional tank and build your leadership and coaching capacity.

Asking other coaches to recommend books they have found helpful is a great starting point for finding valuable off-season reading material. I have included references in this book to many of the most popular books recommended to me by the coaches I have connected with over the years.

Another source where coaches can find guidance on recommended reading materials is in the Resource Review and Digest sections of the *International Sport Coaching Journal*. These free online sections of the journal include brief summaries of recommended books, articles, talks, and apps that fellow coaches and those who work with coaches have found particularly helpful. Finally, the Coach Doc section of the Human Kinetics Coach Education website also provides regularly updated free coaching materials and recommended readings.

The popular TED Talk series of brief, free online lectures on a wide range of topics is also a popular source of inspiration for coaches. Among the thousands of TED Talks,

## Figure 14.8 "How to be a Great Leader" TED Talk Playlist

| Title | Speaker | Length of talk |
|---|---|---|
| How Great Leaders Inspire Action | Simon Sinek | 18:04 |
| Learning From Leadership's Missing Manual | Fields Wicker-Miurin | 16:35 |
| Lead Like the Great Conductors | Itay Talgam | 20:51 |
| Everyday Leadership | Drew Dudley | 6:14 |
| What It Takes to Be a Great Leader | Roselinde Torres | 9:19 |
| Trial, Error, and the God Complex | Tim Harford | 18:07 |
| Tribal Leadership | David Logan | 16:39 |
| Listen, Learn . . . Then Lead | Stanley McChrystal | 15:38 |
| Inspiring a Life of Immersion | Jacqueline Novogratz | 17:48 |
| How to Start a Movement | Derek Sivers | 3:09 |
| Why We Have Too Few Women Leaders | Sheryl Sandberg | 14:58 |
| The Difference Between Winning and Succeeding | John Wooden | 17:36 |

some of the most inspiring and relevant to sport coaches have been organized into a "How to Be a Great Leader" playlist.[51] The playlist includes 12 of the most popular leadership talks from a diverse range of speakers including legendary coach John Wooden. A summary of these 12 leadership talks is provided in figure 14.8.

Watching or reading some new information is not the same as learning something new. To realize the full benefit of the time you invest in reading books, watching videos, and listening to podcasts, coaches should consider developing a strategy for capturing the lessons learned from the experience. For example, a successful strategy for retaining bits of wisdom from books is to use the inside cover of the book as a place to jot down page references for quotations or ideas you find particularly interesting. Without such a strategy you will find it increasingly difficult to find the quotations and stories that you will want to revisit during stressful situations that arise during the season.

A free resource that coaches can use to make and retrieve notes when watching online videos is VideoNot.es. Coaches will need a Google Chrome account (free) to access this easy-to-use program. After you open VideoNot.es, you simply paste the link to the desired video into the viewing area. The video can then be viewed while you simultaneously type notes in a space beside the video.

The real value of this tool is that each note is automatically linked back to the exact spot in the video where you took the note. An added benefit is that you can share the video and the notes with others. This tool not only provides coaches with a quick and effective way to make notes on videos but also can accelerate shared learning across a coaching staff, coach learning network, or team of athletes.

## ESTABLISHING WORK-LIFE BALANCE

The long and late hours kept by many coaches often causes great strain on personal relationships. Unfortunately, many coaches realize too late that they have neglected to spend sufficient time with family and friends while pursuing their coaching goals. Even when coaches are physically present with family and friends, their minds are frequently on coaching because they are so emotionally invested in their work. Coaching isn't something you can easily turn off.

Coaches with children often feel particularly guilty because of the amount of time they spend away from their families. One such example is former professional football coach Mike Smith. Although he experienced much success coaching the Atlanta Falcons, he regretted not doing a better job at home. Like many professional sport coaches, he was eventually fired, but he came to view it as a blessing because it forced him to reevaluate his work-life balance.

> It's a lesson I want to share with all coaches out there. It doesn't matter how much success you have in your career; if you fail at home you are a failure. We only get one shot to be a parent and spouse, and we must give it everything we've got and commit to our "team" at home. When I return to coaching, I will be just as committed to the football team, but I will do a better job of committing to my home team. It's possible to do both. You just have to make it a priority.[52 (p. 91)]

Coaches commonly set aside one to two weeks of family vacation time during the off-season as a way to refresh and counter-balance the stress of a competitive season. However, research shows that the recovery benefits of a few weeks away from coaching are short lived.[53] A more effective strategy for long-term well-being is to schedule additional regular small doses of dedicated family and friend time. Setting aside more time for family and friends may not be realistic for some coaches, but they can use some simple evidence-based strategies to increase the quality of time spent with family and friends. For example, making it a priority to eat together as a family a few times per week will reap many rewards for busy coaches and their families.

Eating a regular meal together as a family is associated with a whole host of benefits for kids: higher academic achievement, lower stress, more positive outlook on life, better relationships with parents, better ability to cope with challenges, and fewer misbehaviors at home and at school.[54, 55] But these benefits of eating together as a family will not be realized if the family is preoccupied during the meal with watching television or checking their smartphones. The value of eating meals together comes from dedicated time, however brief, for sharing stories and listening to each other with full focus and attention.

Coaches often use the off-season to attend coaching clinics and refresher courses or to coach at camps or special events, which means more time away from family and friends. This kind of schedule can add even more tension to already strained relationships. When possible, coaches should consider combining these important career opportunities with family vacation time.

For example, successful coaches such as ice hockey coach Mike Babcock and basketball coach Mike Krzyzewski learned to balance special off-season coaching opportunities, such as coaching at the Olympic Games or world championships, with family time by bringing their families with them to some of these events. Coach Mike Babcock believes that being able to share the Olympic experience with his family was key to helping him, his coaching staff, and his athletes stay emotionally balanced and perform at their peak.

> Sharing the Olympic experience with family enriched it beyond belief. Being with our families helped keep us fresh and loose. I think being able to share the bigger Olympic experience with our families, changing up our focus, helped us win the gold. A distraction? No way. A different focus, a change of pace? Yes. Moments to remember? For sure.[49 (p. 99)]

A typical high school or college coach might be able to bring family or friends along to a coaching clinic and set aside a few extra days either before or after the clinic to focus on enjoying the trip. This strategy can work if coaches clearly communicate the responsibilities and commitments they will have during the coaching event before the trip happens. Also, taking family or friends along on off-season coaching trips works best when it supplements, rather than replaces, dedicated family vacation time.

To create work-life balance, coaches must first take care of themselves. Being selfish for at least a few moments each day is OK. In fact, being a little selfish is required if you want to sustain your energy as a coach and nurture meaningful

## Figure 14.9 "The Importance of Self-Care" TED Talk Playlist

| Title | Speaker | Length of talk |
|---|---|---|
| Why We All Need to Practice Emotional First Aid | Guy Winch | 17:24 |
| The Power of Vulnerability | Brené Brown | 20:19 |
| All It Takes Is 10 Mindful Minutes | Andy Puddicombe | 9:24 |
| Want to Be Happy? Be Grateful | David Steindl-Rast | 14:30 |
| How to Make Stress Your Friend | Kelly McGonigal | 14:28 |
| In Praise of Slowness | Carl Honore | 19:15 |
| Got a Meeting? Take a Walk | Nilofer Merchant | 3:28 |
| Own Your Body's Data | Talithia Williams | 17:03 |
| Why Dieting Doesn't Usually Work | Sandra Aamodt | 12:42 |

relationships with others. If you aren't centered and healthy as a coach, then this will show and your ability to connect and lead others will be severely diminished.

The off-season is an ideal time to take steps toward creating a better balance in your life and practicing self-care strategies. A good place to start is to watch the short videos on the "Importance of Self-Care" TED Talk playlist (see figure 14.9).[56] These talks cover a wide range of important topics—such as using stress to your advantage, the power of slowing down, and ways of practicing emotional first aid—that can help coaches recharge and find healthy ways to achieve work-life balance.

An important step in creating work-life balance is gaining a broader perspective on the challenges you face. Reading stories about how others overcame adversity in their life is inspiring and helps us view our own stressors from a healthier viewpoint. Many coaches I have worked with find great value in reading these types of personal redemption stories, and they often use the stories to teach important life lessons to their athletes. Some examples of books that championship coaches and I have found particularly inspiring include the following:

- *The Road to Character* (David Brooks, 2015)
- *Endurance: Shackleton's Incredible Voyage* (Alfred Lansing, 2015)
- *Unbroken: A World War II Story of Survival, Resilience, and Redemption* (Laura Hillenbrand, 2014)
- *Lone Survivor: The Eyewitness Account of Operation Redwing and the Lost Heroes of SEAL Team 10* (Marcus Luttrell, 2013)
- *Enzo Calzaghe: A Fighting Life* (Enzo Calzaghe with Michael Pearlman, 2012).
- *Perseverance: Life Lessons on Leadership and Teamwork* (Marc Trestman with Ross Bernstein, 2010)
- *Team of Rivals: The Political Genius of Abraham Lincoln* (Doris Goodwin, 2006)

- *Long Walk to Freedom: The Autobiography of Nelson Mandela* (Nelson Mandela, 1995)
- *The Boys in the Boat: Nine Americans and Their Epic Quest for Gold at the 1936 Berlin Olympics* (Daniel James Brown, 2013)

Other proven strategies for improving work-life balance include making priority lists, delegating some responsibilities to others, working on tasks you've been avoiding, and writing a personal creed.[5, 25, 43, 57, 58]

Coaches have a tendency to want to control everything, but that approach is a recipe for burnout and frustration. Successful coaches follow the widely cited advice of leadership guru Steven Covey and prioritize by putting first things first. Everything that you need and want to do, in both your work life and your personal life, is not equally important and urgent. A simple matrix has been created to organize tasks into one of four categories:[57]

1. Critical and urgent—things that are important and that we must do now.
2. Critical but not urgent—things that are important but that we can do later without jeopardizing our ability to complete the task effectively.
3. Not critical but urgent—things that are not that important but that need to be done soon (coaches should try to delegate these things when possible).
4. Not critical and not urgent—things that we often do, or think we need to do, that add little or no value to our work or life (we should try to eliminate or discontinue these things as much as possible).

Many tools are available, including free apps such as Priority Matrix (www.appfluence.com), to help coaches prioritize their time and create work-life balance based on this putting-first-things-first matrix.

Delegating some of the less urgent, or less critical, coaching responsibilities is an effective way for coaches to improve their ability to find work-life balance. The possibility of using this strategy reinforces the importance of surrounding yourself with trusted assistants and supportive colleagues and friends.

Coaches may have a tendency to avoid tackling some of the less urgent or less critical items on their to-do lists. A good strategy for making progress on these activities is to set aside a few minutes each day, even just 10 to 15 minutes, to work on a task you have been avoiding. While working on the task, practice your mindfulness skills, and you will notice that the time passes more quickly. Making small, incremental progress on these tasks will give coaches a sense of personal satisfaction while helping them learn to tolerate some of the mundane but necessary coaching and personal life responsibilities.[5]

Finally, successful coaches have long recognized the value of writing a personal creed to help them stay grounded and ensure that they invest time daily in the things that will sustain their well-being. A personal creed provides a blueprint for daily work-life balance. But as legendary coach John Wooden noted, a personal creed is more an ideal we can strive for than something we can expect to accomplish every single day. Coach Wooden used the following aphorism, adapted from the writings of John Newton (1725-1807), as a reminder of this important lesson:[58 (p. 14)]

I am not what I ought to be,
Not what I want to be,
Not what I am going to be,
But I am thankful that
I am better than I used to be.

Over many years of reflecting on coaching, teaching, and life, and the lessons he learned from his father, Coach Wooden created his own seven-point creed for finding work-life balance (see figure 14.10).[59] A creed must have personal meaning, so although coach Wooden's creed worked for him, coaches should use his creed as a starting point for reflecting on what they want to include in their own creed.

**Figure 14.10 Coach John Wooden's "The Creed I Live By"**

Be true to yourself.
Make each day your masterpiece.
Help others.
Drink deeply from good books, especially the Bible.
Make friendship a fine art.
Build a shelter against a rainy day.
Pray for guidance and give thanks for your blessings every day.

## Wrap-Up

Coaching can be extremely stressful and can often lead to career-ending burnout. Some of the common stressors that coaches face include miscommunication and interpersonal conflict, pressure from self and others, team conflict and athlete discipline, isolation, and work-life imbalance.

Fortunately, coaches can use many time-tested strategies to counter these common sources of burnout. Common strategies include mindfulness training, physical activity, building an emotional support network, and prioritizing how they spend their time to ensure better work-life balance.

The off-season is the ideal time to invest in learning or refining strategies that allow you to recharge as a coach. There is no better way to start the next preseason than with renewed optimism and energy. The peace of mind that comes with greater emotional stability, focus, and overall well-being will have a powerful effect on your athletes and other coaches, setting the stage for an enjoyable and successful season.

# Closing: Repeating Success

*Coaching Better Every Season*—a lofty standard indeed, yet a very attainable one. The time-tested principles and strategies of quality coaching presented in the preceding chapters will undoubtedly help you achieve that goal.

Sure, you will encounter setbacks and challenges as a coach. Conflicts and errors will still occur; tough losses will still come your way. But by consistently and diligently applying the principles, strategies, and practices provided in this book, you will enjoy coaching more and find success through most of your coaching career.

The key is to use what you've learned here and steadily work on improving your skills as a coach and building the right team culture. Continuous improvement and creation of standards, rituals, and routines that build a winning team culture provide a stable foundation for durable success. Jon Gordon, author of several bestselling coaching books and advisor to many coaches summarized it well when he stated, "If you want to win, you don't focus on winning. You focus on the culture, people, and process that produce wins."[1 (p. 108)]

If nothing else, I hope this book has given you a greater appreciation of the four seasons of the annual coaching cycle and provided you with insights and tools that will help you be a more effective coach during each of those phases of the year. Whether you remember them as the four Es—envision (preseason), enact (in-season), evaluate (postseason), and enhance (off-season)—or label them something entirely different isn't important. What is essential to success is how you lead and manage your athletes through each period.

Sustainable success comes from evolution, not revolution, a process that both championship coaches and great leaders throughout history have recognized.[2, 3] Franklin D. Roosevelt, considered one of the most influential leaders of the 20th century, realized many significant achievements because "he took a step and adjusted, a step and adjusted. Gradually a big change would emerge."[3 (p. 41)] The evidence-supported practices and useful tools provided in this book will help you take a step and adjust, and successfully navigate each of the four coaching seasons.

Initial success, however, will be short lived unless you approach the four seasons each year with the same vigor. What worked one year may not work the next. Just ask Stanford football coach David Shaw, who in 2015 became the first head coach in 80 years to lead his school's football team to three conference championships. He recommends that coaches approach each year with a clean slate—refreshed and ready to observe, learn, and grow through each of the four seasons.

Sustaining excellence is within reach for every coach.[4, 5] Even if you never lift a championship trophy in your career, by embracing the timeless principles of success presented in this book you will be *Coaching Better Every Season*. Moreover, you will coach with more confidence and enthusiasm, which in turn will energize and inspire your athletes.

Coaching is messy and complicated. Certainly, there will be times during each of the four seasons when you feel overwhelmed and unprepared for coping with unexpected challenges. It is during those times that you will most benefit from reviewing the *Coaching Better Every Season* principles that have helped many coaches successfully navigate the obstacles and upsets that all coaches periodically experience. A concise summary of the *Coaching Better Every Season* principles is provided in figure C.1. Keep this list handy and review it regularly.

## Figure C.1 *Coaching Better Every Season* Principles

### Preseason: Envision

- I have a clear awareness of why and how I coach (coaching Golden Circle).
- All athletes and coaches understand core values and shared team standards.
- Rituals, routines, and protocols are in place for nourishing the right team culture.
- I have an athlete-centered coaching philosophy.
- We regularly check progress toward shared goals and realizing our team vision.
- All athletes understand their roles and regularly contribute to the team's trust bank.
- I build trusting relationships with athletes by modeling transformational leadership.

### In-Season: Enact

- Athletes' individual learning needs and prior knowledge influence how I coach.
- I create detailed practice plans that maximize athlete participation.
- Practices are the right length to sustain athlete focus and energy right to the end.
- Practice activities are gamelike and demanding (challenge-skill balance).
- I teach athletes how to achieve optimal precompetition readiness.
- Precompetition messages are tailored to meet athlete needs in the moment.
- My focus during competitions is on examining, encouraging, and educating.
- I understand momentum triggers and make effective in-competition adjustments.
- Routines are established for postcompetition recovery and learning.

### End of Season: Evaluate

- We have clearly identified what is most important to evaluate in our program.
- Evaluation information is collected from multiple sources (athletes, coaches, and so on).
- We have created procedures for reporting and debriefing evaluation results.
- Athletes are recognized through end-of-season rituals and ceremonies.
- Coaching strengths are identified and used to build coaching confidence.

### Off-Season: Enhance

- High-impact performance gaps are closed through systematic and critical reflection.
- I actively seek opportunities to grow and network as a coach.
- I set aside regular time to nourish relationships, personal health, and wellness.
- I eagerly approach each new season with renewed energy and purpose.
- I encourage sport sampling because it enhances long-term athlete development.

Think of it as your coaching compass—a tool for keeping you on the right path, the same path the most successful predecessors and colleagues in the coaching profession have navigated each year.

Samuel Johnson, one of the most distinguished writers in history, once said: "The greatest part of a writer's time is spent in reading, in order to write; a man [sic] will turn over half a library to make one book." I have endeavored to bring to you the best of what I have learned about successful coaching through my decades of working with coaches and "turning over half a library" of coaching science and practice. I am hopeful that this book has given you new insights to enhance your effectiveness as a coach.

As you know, the imprint you leave with your athletes and programs will be felt long after you stop coaching. This certainty has been referred to as the 20-year rule, summarized well by a former national champion and Olympic athlete who went on to have a successful career and family life. While reflecting many years later on the influence his renowned high school water polo coach had on his life, he encouraged coaches to "Coach as though your athletes will evaluate you not at the end of the season, nor upon graduation, but 20 years later."[6] And that alone is sufficient inspiration to ensure that we're *Coaching Better Every Season*.

# References

## Introduction


1. Haworth, R., & Whitaker, T. (2010). *What great coaches do differently: 11 elements of effective coaching.* Larchmont, NY: Eye on Education.
2. Potrac, P., Gilbert, W., & Denison, J. (eds.). (2013). *The Routledge handbook of sports coaching.* London: Routledge.
3. Rangeon, S., Gilbert, W., & Bruner, M. (2012). Mapping the world of coaching science: A citation network analysis. *Journal of Coaching Education, 5*(1), 83–108.
4. Côté, J., & Gilbert, W.D. (2009). An integrative definition of coaching effectiveness and expertise. *International Journal of Sports Science & Coaching, 4,* 307–323.
5. Gilbert, W.D., & Trudel, P. (2004). Analysis of coaching science research published from 1970–2001. *Research Quarterly for Exercise and Sport, 75,* 388–399.
6. Gilbert, W. (2010). The passing of a legend: Coach John Wooden. *International Journal of Sports Science & Coaching, 5,* 339–342.
7. Fellowship of Christian Athletes. (2010). *The greatest coach ever: Timeless wisdom and insights of John Wooden.* Ventura, CA: Regal.
8. Gilbert, W., Nater, S., Siwik, M., & Gallimore, R. (2010). The pyramid of teaching success in sport: Lessons learned from applied science and effective coaches. *Journal of Sport Psychology in Action, 1,* 86–94.
9. Coughlin, T., & Fisher, D. (2013). *Earn the right to win: How success in any field starts with superior preparation.* New York: Penguin.
10. Clark, M. (2015, October 10). Legendary York cross country coach Joe Newton still going strong at 86. *Chicago Tribune.* www.chicagotribune.com/sports/highschool/ct-spt-1011-prep-xc-york-joe-newton-20151003-story.html


## Chapter 1


1. Ladouceur, B., & Hayes, N. (2015). *Chasing perfection: The principles behind winning football the De La Salle way.* Chicago: Triumph.
2. Yukelson, D., & Rose, R. (2014). The psychology of ongoing excellence: An NCAA coach's perspective on winning consecutive multiple national championships. *Journal of Sport Psychology in Action, 5,* 44–58.
3. Meyer, U., with Coffey, W. (2015). *Above the line: Lessons in leadership and life from a championship season.* New York: Penguin.
4. Erhmann, J., with Ehrmann, P., & Jordan, G. (2011). *InSideOut coaching: How sports can transform lives.* New York: Simon & Schuster.
5. Pim, R. (2010). *Perfect phrases for coaches: Hundreds of ready-to-use winning phrases for any sport—on and off the field.* New York: McGraw-Hill.
6. Hanzus, D. (2015, September 9). "Do Your Job" offers inside access to Patriot way. *NFL Enterprises.* www.nfl.com/news/story/0ap3000000524860/article/do-your-job-offers-inside-access-to-patriot-way
7. Kerr, J. (2015, January 26). How Bill Belichick's "Do Your Job" mantra applies to leadership. *Inc.* www.inc.com/james-kerr/how-do-your-job-can-be-a-difference-maker-for-your-company.html
8. Garrido, A., & Smith, W. (2011). *Life is yours to win: Lessons forged from the purpose, passion, and magic of baseball.* New York: Touchstone.
9. Jackson, P., & Delehanty, H. (2013). *Eleven rings: The soul of success* (p. 16, 94). New York: Penguin.
10. Collins, J.C., & Porras, J.I. (1994). *Built to last: Successful habits of visionary companies.* New York: HarperCollins.
11. Collins, J.C., & Porras, J.I. (1996, September–October). Building your company's vision. *Harvard Business Review,* 65–78.
12. Sinek, S. (2009). *Start with why: How great leaders inspire everyone to take action.* New York: Portfolio/Penguin.
13. Sinek, S. (2009). *How great leaders inspire action.* www.ted.com/talks/simon_sinek_how_great_leaders_inspire_action?language=en
14. Hayes, N. (2005). *When the game stands tall: The story of the De La Salle Spartans and football's longest winning streak.* Berkeley, CA: Frog.

15. Kyle, C., & Hodermarsky, M. (1997). *The object of the game*. Dubuque, IA: Kendall/Hunt.
16. Silva, J.M. (2006). Psychological aspects of competition: An interview with Anson Dorrance, head women's soccer coach at the University of North Carolina. *Journal of Excellence, 11*, 88–102.
17. Robbins, S. (2012, February 17). *University of North Carolina women's soccer team's core values—Anson Dorrance (2006)*. www.studentleaderseminar.com/university-of-north-carolina-womens-soccer-teams-core-values-anson-dorrance-2006/
18. Gilbert, W. (2016, April 20). *After 22 NCAA titles and a World Cup championship: Winning lessons from Anson Dorrance*. www.asep.com/news/ShowArticle.cfm?ID=262
19. Johnson, T., Martin, A.J., Palmer, F.R., Watson, G., & Ramsey, P.L. (2013). A core value of pride in winning: The All Blacks' team culture and legacy. *International Journal of Sport & Society, 4*(1), 1–14.
20. Johnson, T., Martin, A.J., Palmer, F.R., Watson, G., & Ramsey, P.L. (2013). Artefacts and the All Blacks. Rites, rituals, symbols and stories. *Sport Traditions, 30*(1), 43–59.
21. Hodge, K., Henry, G., & Smith, W. (2014). A case study of excellence in elite sport: Motivational climate in a world champion team. *The Sport Psychologist, 28*, 60–74.
22. Gilbert, W. (2015, December 16). What I learned from the All Blacks coaches. *Human Kinetics Coach Education Center*. www.asep.com/news/ShowArticle.cfm?ID=257
23. Valleé, C.N., & Bloom, G.A. (2016). Four keys to building a championship culture. *International Sport Coaching Journal, 3*(2), 170–177.
24. Gilbert, W., & Trudel, P. (2001). Learning to coach through experience: Reflection in model youth sport coaches. *Journal of Teaching in Physical Education, 21*, 16–34.
25. Schön, D.A. (1987). *Educating the reflective practitioner*. San Francisco: Jossey-Bass.
26. Batista, E. (2014, August 20). The most productive people know who to ignore. *Harvard Business Review*. http://blogs.hbr.org/2014/08/the-most-productive-people-know-who-to-ignore/
27. Gilbert, W. (2015, July 8). Recharge and become a better coach through writing. *Human Kinetics Coach Education Center*. www.asep.com/news/ShowArticle.cfm?ID=248
28. Zadra, D. (2009). *5: Where will you be five years from today?* Seattle, WA: Compendium.
29. Collins, J. (2001). *Vision framework*. www.jimcollins.com/tools.html
30. Van Gaal reveals his four key principles. (2014, July 17). *ESPN*. www.espn.co.uk/football/sport/story/324789.html
31. Beswick, B. (2016). *One goal: The mindset of winning soccer teams*. Champaign, IL: Human Kinetics.
32. Gordon, J., & Smith, M. (2015). *You win in the locker room first: The 7 C's to build a winning team in business, sports, and life*. Hoboken, NJ: Wiley.
33. Reilly, R. (2012, December 21). Paint like a champion. *ESPN.com*. http://espn.go.com/espn/story/_/id/8765862/notre-dame-play-champion-today-sign
34. Kidman, L. (2005). *Athlete-centred coaching: Developing inspired and inspiring people*. Christchurch, NZ: Innovative.
35. Krzyzewski, M., & Spatola, J.K. (2009). *The gold standard: Building a world-class team*. New York: Business Plus.
36. Denyer, D. (2013, Autumn). 15 steps to peak performance: The transformation of British cycling from near bankruptcy to a dominant global force offers insights for any business looking to improve their performance. *Management Focus*, 10–13. www.daviddenyer.com/15-steps-to-peak-performance/
37. Newell, K. (2008, May 1). Man on a mission. *Coach & Athletic Director, 77*(10), 52–60.
38. Kimiciek, J., & Gould, D. (1987). Coaching psychology: The case of James "Doc" Counsilman. *The Sport Psychologist, 1*, 350–358.
39. Schroeder, P.J. (2010). Changing team culture: The perspectives of ten successful head coaches. *Journal of Sport Behavior, 33*(1), 63–88.
40. Kovacs, M. (2014, January 8). The peculiar side of sports: College football helmet stickers. *Last Word on Sports*. http://lastwordonsports.com/2014/01/08/the-peculiar-side-of-sports-college-football-helmet-stickers/
41. Valleé, C.N., & Bloom, G.A. (2005). Building a successful university program: Key and common elements of expert coaches. *Journal of Applied Sport Psychology, 17*(3), 179–186.
42. Martin, J. (2015). Ohio Wesleyan soccer. In P. Otte (ed.), *We leadership* (pp. 57–84). Ross Leadership Institute.

43. Staley, D. (2015, June 15). The secret. *The Players' Tribune*. www.theplayerstribune.com/dawn-staley-south-carolina-coach/
44. SFGS. (2014, May 18). The Don Meyer interview revisited. *Sports Feel Good Stories*. www.sportsfeelgoodstories.com/the-don-meyer-interview-revisited/


## Chapter 2


1. Wacker, B. (2014, December 10). Q&A: Foley talks Tiger, instruction, philosophy & more. *PGA Tour*. www.pgatour.com/instruction/foley-qanda-wacker.print.html
2. Coughlin, T., & Fisher, D. (2013). *Earn the right to win: How success in any field starts with superior preparation*. New York: Penguin.
3. Hammermeister, J.J. (2010*). Cornerstones of coaching: The building blocks for sport coaches and teams*. Traverse City, MI: Cooper.
4. Huber, J.J. (2013). *Applying educational psychology in coaching athletes*. Champaign, IL: Human Kinetics.
5. Côté, J., & Gilbert, W.D. (2009). An integrative definition of coaching effectiveness and expertise. *International Journal of Sports Science & Coaching*, *4*, 307–323.
6. Gilbert, W.D., & Côté, J. (2013). Defining coaching effectiveness: A focus on coaches' knowledge. In P. Potrac, W. Gilbert, & J. Denison (eds.), *Routledge handbook of sports coaching* (pp. 147–159). London: Routledge.
7. International Council for Coaching Excellence, Association of Summer Olympic International Federations, & Leeds Metropolitan University. (2013). *International sport coaching framework* (version 1.2). Champaign, IL: Human Kinetics.
8. Mayer, J.D., & Salovey, P. (1997). What is emotional intelligence? In P. Salovey & D. Sluyter (eds.), *Emotional development and emotional intelligence: Implications for educators* (pp. 3–31). New York: Basic Books.
9. Schempp, P.G., & McCullick, B. (2010). Coaches' expertise. In J. Lyle & C. Cushion (eds.), *Sports coaching: Professionalisation and practice* (pp. 221–231). Edinburgh, UK: Churchill Livingstone Elsevier.
10. Gavazzi, S. (2015). Turning boys into men: The incentive-based system in Urban Meyer's plan to win. *International Sport Coaching Journal*, *2*, 298–304.
11. Miller, G.A., Lutz, R., & Fredenburg, K. (2012). Outstanding high school coaches: Philosophies, views, and practices. *Journal of Physical Education, Recreation & Dance*, *83*(2), 24–29.
12. Camiré, M., Trudel, P., & Forneris, T. (2012). Coaching and transferring life skills: Philosophies and strategies used by model high school coaches. *The Sport Psychologist*, *26*, 243–260.
13. McRae, A.E. (2015). *The keys to success: Coaching styles of professional championship team sport coaches*. Saarbrucken, Germany: LAP Lambert Academic.
14. Gilbert, W. (2015, July 20). Championship coaching starts with relationship building. *Human Kinetics Coach Education Center*. www.asep.com/news/ShowArticle.cfm?ID=249
15. Jones, R., Armour, K., & Potrac, P. (2004). *Sports coaching cultures: From practice to theory*. London: Routledge.
16. Voight, M., & Carroll, P. (2006). Applying sport psychology philosophies, principles, and practices onto the gridiron: An interview with USC football coach Pete Carroll. *International Journal of Sports Science & Coaching*, *1*(4), 321–342.
17. Barron, D. (2016, July 17). Aimee Boorman redefines coaching relationship with Simone Biles. *Houston Chronicle*. Retrieved from www.houstonchronicle.com/olympics/article/Aimee-Boorman-redefines-coaching-relationship-8382626.php#photo-10560277
18. National Association for Sport and Physical Activity. (2006). *National standards for sport coaches: Quality coaches, quality sports* (2nd ed.). Reston, VA: Author.
19. Gilbert, W., Nater, S., Siwik, M., & Gallimore, R. (2010). The Pyramid of Teaching Success in Sport: Lessons learned from applied science and effective coaches. *Journal of Sport Psychology in Action*, *1*, 86–94.
20. Gilbert, W. (2010). The passing of a legend: Coach John Wooden. *International Journal of Sports Science & Coaching*, *5*(3), 339–342.
21. Wooden, J. (2015). *Pyramid of Success*. www.coachwooden.com/pyramid-of-success
22. Nater, S. & Gallimore, R. (2010). *You haven't taught until they have learned: John Wooden's teaching principles and practices*. Morgantown, WV: Fitness International Technology.
23. Collins, K., Gould, D., Lauer, L., & Chung, Y. (2009). Coaching life skills through football: Philosophical beliefs of outstanding

high school football coaches. *International Journal of Coaching Science, 3*(1), 29–54.

24. Positive Coaching Alliance. (2016). Positively chart your players' success. *PCA development zone*. http://devzone.positivecoach.org/resource/worksheet/positively-chart-your-players-success
25. Trestman, M., & Bernstein, R. (2010). *Perseverance: Life lessons on leadership and teamwork*. Eagan, MN: Bernstein Books.
26. Anders, B. (2005). Coaching philosophy. In C. Reynaud (ed.), *She can coach!* (pp. 3–11). Champaign, IL: Human Kinetics.
27. Stuntz, C. (2016). Cross-domain relationships with assistant and head coaches: Comparing levels and correlates. *International Sport Coaching Journal, 3*(1), 17–30.
28. NCAA. (n.d.). *DiSC behavioral assessment*. Retrieved from www.ncaa.org/disc-behavioral-assessments
29. People Academy. (2015). *Surging out of the blocks: Coaching an Olympic coach*. www.people.academy/blog/coaching-an-olympic-coach
30. Staley, D. (2015, June 15). The secret. *The Players' Tribune*. www.theplayerstribune.com/dawn-staley-south-carolina-coach/
31. Pew Research Center. (2010, February 24). *Millennials: Confident. Connected. Open to change: Executive summary*. www.pewsocialtrends.org/2010/02/24/millennials-confident-connected-open-to-change/
32. Elmore, T. (2010). *Generation iY: Our last chance to save their future*. Atlanta, GA: Poet Gardener.
33. Williams, A. (2015, September 18). Move over, Millennials, here comes Generation Z. *New York Times*. www.nytimes.com/2015/09/20/fashion/move-over-millennials-here-comes-generation-z.html
34. Clark, K. (2015, June 16). The NFL team that is solving Millennials: The 49ers are changing how they operate to cater to the iPhone generation. *Wall Street Journal*. www.wsj.com/articles/the-nfl-team-that-is-solving-millennials-1434484144
35. Elmore, T. (2015, July 14). A model for coaches to connect with Millennials. *Growing leaders: Tim Elmore on leading the next generation*. http://growingleaders.com/blog/a-model-for-coaches-to-connect-with-millennials/
36. Jenkins, S. (2010). Coaching philosophy. In J. Lyle & C. Cushion (eds.), *Sports coaching: Professionalisation and practice* (pp. 233–242). Edinburgh, UK: Elsevier.
37. Gallimore, R., & Tharp, R. (2004). What a coach can teach a teacher, 1975–2004: Reflections and reanalysis of John Wooden's teaching practices. *The Sport Psychologist, 18*, 119–137.
38. American Sport Education Program. (2012). *Coaching principles: Workbook* (4th ed.). Champaign, IL: Human Kinetics.
39. Baghurst, T.M., & Parish, A. (2010). *Case studies in coaching: Dilemmas and ethics in competitive school sports*. Scottsdale, AZ: Holcomb Hathaway.
40. Gardner, H., & Laskin, E. (1995). *Leading minds: An anatomy of leadership*. New York: Basic.
41. Bishop, G. (2016, July 29). In order to reconnect with players, Pete Carroll altered off-season approach. *Sports Illustrated*. Retrieved from www.si.com/nfl/2016/07/pete-carroll-seahawks-offseason-doug-baldwin
42. Jackson, P., & Delehanty, H. (2013). *Eleven rings: The soul of success*. New York: Penguin.
43. Pfluger, S. (2005). Team cohesion. In C. Reynaud (ed.), *She can coach!* (pp. 203–215). Champaign, IL: Human Kinetics.
44. Carless, D., & Douglas, K. (2011). Stories as personal coaching philosophy. *International Journal of Sports Science & Coaching, 6*(1), 1–12.
45. Martens, R. (2012). *Successful coaching* (4th ed.). Champaign, IL: Human Kinetics.
46. Sabock, M.D., & Sabock, R.J. (2011). *Coaching: A realistic perspective* (10th ed.). Plymouth, UK: Rowman & Littlefield.
47. Smith, R.E., & Smoll, F.L. (2002). *Way to go coach! A scientifically-proven approach to youth sports coaching effectiveness*. Portola Valley, CA: Warde.

## Chapter 3

1. Berra, Y., & Kaplan, D. (2001). *When you come to a fork in the road, take it! Inspiration and wisdom from one of baseball's greatest heroes*. New York: Hyperion.
2. Kimiciek, J., & Gould, D. (1987). Coaching psychology: The case of James "Doc" Counsilman. *The Sport Psychologist, 1*, 350–358.
3. Rother, M. (2010). *Toyota Kata: Managing people for improvement, adaptiveness, and superior results*. New York: McGraw-Hill.
4. Janssen, J. (1999). *Championship team building: What every coach needs to*

know to build a motivated, committed and cohesive team. Tucson, AZ: Winning the Mental Game.

5. Voight, M., & Carroll, P. (2006). Applying sport psychology philosophies, principles, and practices onto the gridiron: An interview with USC football coach Pete Carroll. *International Journal of Sports Science & Coaching*, *1*(4), 321–342.
6. Burton, D., & Raedeke, T.D. (2008). *Sport psychology for coaches*. Champaign, IL: Human Kinetics.
7. Weinberg, R. (2010). Making goals effective: A primer for coaches. *Journal of Sport Psychology in Action*, *1*(2), 57–65.
8. Burton, D., & Weiss, C. (2008). The fundamental goal concept: The path to process and performance success. In T. Horn (ed.), *Advances in sport psychology* (3rd ed.), pp. 340–375. Champaign, IL: Human Kinetics.
9. Zimmerman, B.J. (2008). Goal setting: A key proactive source of academic self-regulation. In D.H. Schunk & B.J. Zimmerman (eds.), *Motivation and self-regulated learning: Theory, research, and applications* (pp. 267–295). New York: Lawrence Erlbaum.
10. Doran, G.T. (1981). There's a SMART way to write management's goals and objectives. *Management Review*, *70*(11), 35–36.
11. Day, T. & Tosey, P. (2011). Beyond SMART? A new framework for goal setting. *Curriculum Journal*, *22*(4), 515–534.
12. Senécal, J., Loughead, T., & Bloom, G. (2008). A season-long team-building intervention: Examining the effect of team goal setting on cohesion. *Journal of Sport & Exercise Psychology*, *30*(2), 186–199.
13. Weinberg, R.S., & Burke, K.L. (1997). Coaches' and players' perceptions of goal setting in junior tennis: An exploratory investigation. *The Sport Psychologist*, *11*(4), 426–439.
14. Weinberg, R., Butt, J., & Knight, B. (2001). High school coaches' perceptions of the process of goal setting. *The Sport Psychologist*, *15*(1), 20–47.
15. Weinberg, R., Butt, J., Knight, B., & Perritt, N. (2001). College coaches' perceptions of their goal-setting practices: A qualitative investigation. *Journal of Applied Sport Psychology*, *13*(4), 374–398.
16. Maitland, A., & Gervis, M. (2010). Goal-setting in youth football. Are coaches missing an opportunity? *Physical Education and Sport Pedagogy*, *15*(4), 323–343.
17. Collins, J.C., & Porras, J.I. (1996, September–October). Building your company's vision. *Harvard Business Review*, 65–78.
18. Yukelson, D. (1997). Principles of effective team building interventions in sport: A direct services approach at Penn State University. *Journal of Applied Sport Psychology*, *9*, 73–96.
19. Barnson, S.C. (2014). The authentic coaching model: A grounded theory of coaching. *International Sport Coaching Journal*, *1*, 61–74.
20. Kidman, L., & Hanrahan, S.J. (2011). *The coaching process: A practical guide to becoming an effective sports coach* (3rd ed.). London: Routledge.
21. Garrido, A., & Smith, W. (2011). *Life is yours to win: Lessons forged from the purpose, passion, and magic of baseball*. New York: Simon & Schuster.
22. Osborne, T. (2002). Leading your team. In American Football Coaches Association, *The football coaching bible* (pp. 69–77). Champaign, IL: Human Kinetics.
23. Hebert, M. (2014). *Thinking volleyball: Inside the game with a coaching legend*. Champaign, IL: Human Kinetics.
24. Shoop, R.J., & Scott, S.M. (1999). *Leadership lessons from Bill Snyder*. Manhattan, KS: AG Press.
25. Gendron, D.R. (2003). *Coaching hockey successfully* (pp. 20–22). Champaign, IL: Human Kinetics.
26. Schembechler, B., & Bacon, J.U. (2007). *Bo's lasting lessons: The legendary coach teaches the timeless fundamentals of leadership*. New York: Business Plus.
27. Valleé, C.N., & Bloom, G.A. (2005). Building a successful university program: Key and common elements of expert coaches. *Journal of Applied Sport Psychology*, *17*(3), 179–186.
28. Auriemma, G., & MacMullan, J. (2006). *Geno: In pursuit of perfection*. New York: Warner.
29. Vierimaa, M., Erickson, K., Côté, J., & Gilbert, W. (2012). Positive youth development: A measurement framework for sport. *International Journal of Sports Science & Coaching*, *7*, 603–616.
30. Côté, J., & Gilbert, W.D. (2009). An integrative definition of coaching effectiveness and expertise. *International Journal of Sports Science & Coaching*, *4*, 307–323.
31. Ordóñez, L.D., Schweitzer, M.E., Galinsky, A.D., & Bazerman, M.H. (2009, February 11).

Goals gone wild: The systematic side effects of over-prescribing goal setting. *Harvard Business School Working Knowledge*. Retrieved from http://hbswk.hbs.edu/item/goals-gone-wild-the-systematic-side-effects-of-over-prescribing-goal-setting.

32. Stulberg, B. (2016, August 3). Big goals can backfire. Olympians show us what to focus on instead. *The Science of Us*. Retrieved from http://nymag.com/scienceofus/2016/08/why-having-big-goals-can-backfire.html.

## Chapter 4

1. Jackson, P., & Delehanty, H. (2013). *Eleven rings: The soul of success*. New York: Penguin.
2. Garrido, A., & Smith, W. (2011). *Life is yours to win: Lessons forged from the purpose, passion, and magic of baseball*. New York: Simon & Schuster.
3. Longman, J. (2015, July 4). Women's World Cup final: Jill Ellis, a serene and innovative tactician, leads the U.S. *New York Times*. www.nytimes.com/2015/07/05/sports/soccer/jill-ellis-a-serene-and-innovative-tactician-leads-the-us-team.html
4. Kawakami, S. (2014, December 11). Warriors' Kerr found a mentor in Seahawks' Carroll. *San Jose Mercury News*. www.mercurynews.com/tim-kawakami/ci_27118329/kawakami-warriors-kerr-found-mentor-seahawks-carroll
5. Hebert, M. (2014). *Thinking volleyball: Inside the game with a coaching legend*. Champaign, IL: Human Kinetics.
6. Brown, B. (2010). *The power of vulnerability* [Online video]. www.ted.com/talks/brene_brown_on_vulnerability?language=en
7. Brown, B. (2015). *Daring greatly: How the courage to be vulnerable transforms the way we live, love, parent, and lead*. New York: Penguin.
8. Gilbert, W., Nater, S., Siwik, M., & Gallimore, R. (2010). The Pyramid of Teaching Success in Sport: Lessons learned from applied science and effective coaches. *Journal of Sport Psychology in Action, 1*, 86–94.
9. Dirks, K.T. (2002). Trust in leadership and team performance: Evidence from NCAA basketball. *Journal of Applied Psychology, 85*(6), 1004–1012.
10. Purdy, L., Potrac, P., & Nelson, L. (2013). Exploring trust and distrust in coaching. In P. Potrac, W. Gilbert, & J. Denison (eds.), *Routledge handbook of sports coaching* (pp. 309–320). London: Routledge.
11. Meyer, U., & Coffey, W. (2015). *Above the line: Lessons in leadership and life from a championship season*. New York: Penguin.
12. Miller, G.A., Lutz, R., & Fredenburg, K. (2012). Outstanding high school coaches: Philosophies, views, and practices. *Journal of Physical Education, Recreation & Dance, 83*(2), 24–29.
13. Balduck, A-L., Buelens, M., & Philippaerts, R. (2010). Short-term effects of midseason coach turnover on team performance in soccer. *Research Quarterly for Exercise and Sport, 81*(3), 379–383.
14. Bennett, G., Phillips, J., Drane, D., & Sagas, M. (2003). The coaching carousel: Turnover effects on winning in professional sport. *International Journal of Sport Management, 4*(3), 192–204.
15. Lago-Peñas, C. (2011). Coach mid-season replacement and team performance in professional soccer. *Journal of Human Kinetics, 28*, 115–122.
16. White, P., Persad, S., & Gee, C.J. (2007). The effect of mid-season coach turnover on team performance: The case of the National Hockey League (1989–2003). *International Journal of Sports Science & Coaching, 2*(2), 143–152.
17. Robinson, E., & Lapchick, R. (1999). *Never before, never again: The stirring autobiography of Eddie Robinson, the winningest coach in the history of college football*. New York: St. Martin's.
18. Prisbell, E. (2015, July 14). How the only coach he's had built Jordan Spieth into a champion. *USA Today Sports*. www.usatoday.com/story/sports/golf/2015/07/14/jordan-spieth-british-open-grand-slam-coach-cameron-mccormick/30147837/
19. Jowett, S., & Felton, L. (2014). Coach-athlete relationships and attachment styles within sport teams. In M.R. Beauchamp & M.A. Eys (eds.), *Group dynamics in exercise and sport psychology* (pp. 73–90). London: Routledge.
20. Kraus, M.W., Huang, C., & Keltner, D. (2010). Tactile communication, cooperation, and performance: An ethological study of the NBA. *Emotion, 10*(5), 745–749.
21. Milius, I. (2014). *Profile and meaning of p-touch in collegiate women's basketball: A case study*. Unpublished master's thesis. California State University, Fresno.
22. Lorimer, R., & Jowett, S. (2013). Empathic understanding and accuracy in the coach-

athlete relationship. In Potrac, P., Gilbert, W., & Denison, J. (eds.), *Routledge handbook of sports coaching* (pp. 321–332). London: Routledge.

23. Côté, J., & Gilbert, W.D. (2009). An integrative definition of coaching effectiveness and expertise. *International Journal of Sports Science & Coaching, 4*, 307–323.
24. Nuwer, R. (2016, August 5). Coaching can make or break an Olympic athlete: Competitors at the most elite level require more than technical support. *Scientific American.* Retrieved from www.scientificamerican.com/article/coaching-can-make-or-break-an-olympic-athlete/
25. Cacciola, S. (2016, January 25). Billy Donovan's one-on-one game plan to connect with Thunder players. *New York Times.* www.nytimes.com/2016/01/26/sports/basketball/oklahoma-city-thunders-billy-donovan-goes-one-on-one-to-foster-team-unity.html?smid=tw-nytsports&smtyp=cur&_r=1
26. Camiré, M. (2015). Examining high school teacher-coaches' perspective on relationship building with student-athletes. *International Sport Coaching Journal, 2*, 125–136.
27. Gordon, J. (2015). *The hard hat: 21 ways to be a great teammate.* Hoboken, NJ: Wiley.
28. Gordon, J., & Smith, M. (2015). *You win in the locker room first: The 7 C's to build a winning team in business, sports, and life.* Hoboken, NJ: Wiley.
29. Vealey, R. (2005). *Coaching for the inner edge.* Morgantown, WV: Fitness Information Technology.
30. Burton, D., & Raedeke, T.D. (2008). *Sport psychology for coaches.* Champaign, IL: Human Kinetics.
31. Fitzgerald, S. (September 15, 2014). *Montreal Canadiens to play 2014–2015 season without a captain.* http://sports.nationalpost.com/2014/09/15/montreal-canadiens-to-play-2014-15-season-without-a-captain/
32. Gould, D., & Voelker, D.K. (2010). Youth sport leadership development: Leveraging the sports captaincy experience. *Journal of Sport Psychology in Action, 1*, 1–14.
33. Gould, D. (2009). *Becoming an effective team captain: Student-athlete guide.* Lansing, MI: Institute for the Study of Youth Sports, Michigan State University.
34. Beauchamp, M.R. (2007). Efficacy beliefs within relational and group contexts in sport. In S. Jowett, & D. Lavallee (eds.), *Social psychology in sport* (pp. 181–193). Champaign, IL: Human Kinetics.
35. Carron, A.V., & Brawley, L.R. (2008). Group dynamics in sport and physical activity. In T.S. Horn (ed.), *Advances in sport psychology* (3rd ed., pp. 213–237). Champaign, IL: Human Kinetics.
36. Tuckman, B. (1965). Developmental sequence in small groups. *Psychological Bulletin, 63*(6), 384–399.
37. Janssen, J. (1999). *Championship team building: What every coach needs to know to build a motivated, committed and cohesive team.* Tucson, AZ: Winning the Mental Game.
38. Martin, L.J., Evans, M.B., & Spink, K.S. (2016). Coach perspectives of "groups within the group": An analysis of subgroups and cliques in sport. *Sport, Exercise, and Performance Psychology, 5*(1), 52–66.
39. Senge, P.M. (2006). *The fifth discipline: The art & practice of the learning organization.* New York: Doubleday.
40. Muzio, E. (2011, January 26). *The ladder of inference creates bad judgment* [Video file]. www.youtube.com/watch?v=K9nFhs5W8o8
41. Yukelson, D. (1997). Principles of effective team building interventions in sport: A direct services approach at Penn State University. *Journal of Applied Sport Psychology, 9*, 73–96.
42. DiCicco, T., & Hacker, C., with Salzberg, C. (2002). *Catch them being good: Everything you need to know to successfully coach girls.* New York: Viking.
43. Eys, M.A., Schinke, R.J., Surya, M., & Benson, A.J. (2014). Role perceptions in sport groups. In M.R. Beauchamp & M.A. Eys (eds.), *Group dynamics in exercise and sport psychology* (2nd ed., pp. 132–146). New York: Routledge.
44. Berra, Y., & Kaplan, D. (2008). *You can observe a lot by watching.* Hoboken, NJ: Wiley.
45. Senécal, J., Loughead, T., & Bloom G. (2008). A season-long team-building intervention: Examining the effect of team goal setting on cohesion. *Journal of Sport & Exercise Psychology, 30*(2), 186–199.
46. Hammermeister, J.J. (2010). *Cornerstones of coaching: The building blocks for sport coaches and teams.* Traverse City, MI: Cooper.
47. Loughead, T.M., & Bloom, G.A. (2013). Team cohesion in sport: Critical overview and implications for team building. In Potrac, P., Gilbert, W., & Denison, J. (eds.),

*Routledge handbook of sports coaching* (pp. 345–356). London: Routledge.

48. Carron, A.V., Colman, M.M., Wheeler, J., & Stevens, D. (2002). Cohesion and performance in sport: A meta-analysis. *Journal of Sport and Exercise Psychology, 24,* 168–188.
49. Martin, L.C., Paradis, K.F., Eys, M.A., & Evans, B. (2013). Cohesion in sport: New directions for practitioners. *Journal of Sport Psychology in Action, 4,* 14–25.
50. Turman, P.D. (2003). Coaches and cohesion: The impact of coaching techniques on team cohesion in the small group sport setting. *Journal of Sport Behavior, 26*(1), 86–104.
51. Schembechler, B., & Bacon, J.U. (2007). *Bo's lasting lessons: The legendary coach teaches the timeless fundamentals of leadership.* New York: Business Plus.
52. Wooden, J., with Jamison, S. (1997). *Wooden: A lifetime of observations and reflections on and off the court.* Chicago, IL: Contemporary.
53. Hayes, N. (2005). *When the game stands tall: The story of the De La Salle Spartans and football's longest winning streak.* Berkeley, CA: Frog.
54. Gould, D., Collins, K., Lauer, L., & Chung, Y. (2007). Coaching life skills through football: A study of award winning high school coaches. *Journal of Applied Sport Psychology, 19,* 16–37.
55. Falcão, W.R., Bloom, G.A., & Gilbert, W.D. (2012). Coaches' perceptions of a coach training program designed to promote youth developmental outcomes. *Journal of Applied Sport Psychology, 24,* 429–444.
56. Bowden, B., & Schlabach, M. (2010). *Called to coach: Reflections on life, faith, and football.* New York: Howard.
57. Beauchamp, M.R. (2007). Efficacy beliefs within relational and group contexts in sport. In S. Jowett, & D. Lavallee (eds.), *Social psychology in sport* (pp. 181–193). Champaign, IL: Human Kinetics.
58. Chow, G., & Chase, M. (2014). Collective efficacy beliefs and sport. In M.R. Beauchamp & M.A. Eys (eds.), *Group dynamics in exercise and sport psychology* (pp. 298–315). London: Routledge.
59. Armstrong, S. (2001). Are you a "transformational" coach? *Journal of Physical Education, Recreation and Dance, 72*(3), 44–47.
60. Lynch, J. (2001). *Creative coaching: New ways to maximize athlete and team potential in all sports.* Champaign, IL: Human Kinetics.
61. Bass, B.M., & Riggio, R.E. (2006). *Transformational leadership* (2nd ed.). Mahwah, NJ: Erlbaum.
62. Valleé, C.N., & Bloom, G.A. (2005). Building a successful university program: Key and common elements of expert coaches. *Journal of Applied Sport Psychology, 17*(3), 179–186.
63. Otte, P. (2015). *We leadership.* Westerville, OH: Ross Leadership Institute.
64. Price, M.S., & Weiss, M.R. (2013). Relationship among coach leadership, peer leadership, and adolescent athletes' psychosocial and team outcomes: A test of transformational leadership theory. *Journal of Applied Sport Psychology, 25,* 265–279.
65. Hoption, C., Phelan, J., & Barling, J. (2014). Transformational leadership in sport. In M.R. Beauchamp & M.A. Eys (eds.), *Group dynamics in exercise and sport psychology* (2nd ed., pp. 55–72). New York: Routledge.
66. Coach Meyer. (2013). *Coach Meyer.* http://coachmeyer.com/
67. Hammermeister, J. Chase, M., Burton, D., Westre, K, Pickering, M., & Baldwin, N. (2008). Servant leadership in sport: A concept whose time has arrived. *Journal of Servant Leadership, 4,* 185–215.
68. Rieke, M., Hammermeister, J., & Chase, M. (2008). Servant leadership in sport: A new paradigm for effective coach behavior. *International Journal of Sports Science & Coaching,* 3(2), 227–239.
69. Fry, M.D., & Gano-Overway, L.A. (2010). Exploring the contribution of the caring climate to the youth sport experience. *Journal of Applied Sport Psychology, 22,* 294–304.
70. Gillham, A., Gillham, E., & Hansen, K. (2015). Relationships among coaching success, servant leadership, cohesion, resilience and social behaviors. *International Sport Coaching Journal, 2,* 233–247.
71. Miller, L.M., & Carpenter, C.L. (2009). Altruistic leadership strategies in coaching: A case study of Jim Tressel of the Ohio State University. *Strategies, 22*(4), 9–12.
72. Gogol, S. (2002). *Hard fought victories: Women coaches making a difference.* Terre Haute, IN: Wish.
73. Sachson, S. (2013, March 26). Decisions, drive push Lori Dauphiny to continued coaching brilliance. *Princeton Athletic Communications.* www.goprincetontigers.

com/ViewArticle.dbml?ATCLID=206932762

74. Pelissero, T. (2015, August 2). Jack Del Rio says Raiders' turnaround starts now with positive thinking. *USA Today Sports*. www.usatoday.com/story/sports/nfl/raiders/2015/08/02/jack-del-rio-changing-culture-positive-thinking-raiders-training-camp/31034467/
75. Positive Coaching Alliance. (2016). Hugh McCutcheon on positive feedback, expectations, and accountability. *PCA Development Zone*. Retrieved from http://devzone.positivecoach.org/resource/video/hugh-mccutcheon-positive-feedback-expectations-and-accountability?utm_source=h5m&utm_medium=e&utm_campaign=devzone
76. Jenkins, S. (2014). John R. Wooden, Stephen R. Covey, and servant leadership. *International Journal of Sports Science & Coaching, 9*(1), 1–23.
77. Hammermeister, J. (2014). John R. Wooden, Stephen R. Covey, and servant leadership: A commentary. *International Journal of Sports Science and Coaching, 9*(1), 65–67.

## Chapter 5

1. Associated Press. (2015, January 12). Roger Federer notches 1,000th win. *ESPN*. http://espn.go.com/tennis/story/_/id/12149924/roger-federer-records-1000th-career-match-win-claims-brisbane-international-title
2. Schatz, H. (2002). *Athlete*. New York: HarperCollins.
3. My Modern Met. (2013, November 9). *Comparing vastly different body types of Olympic athletes*. www.mymodernmet.com/profiles/blogs/howard-schatz-beverly-ornstein-athlete
4. Valerie S. (2014, April 25). Michael Phelps: The man who was built to be a swimmer. *Telegraph*. www.telegraph.co.uk/sport/olympics/swimming/10768083/Michael-Phelps-The-man-who-was-built-to-be-a-swimmer.html
5. Epstein, D. (2013). *The sports gene: Inside the science of extraordinary athletic performance*. New York: Penguin.
6. Baker, J. (2012). Do genes predict potential? Genetic factors and athletic success. In J. Baker, S. Cobley, & J. Schorer (eds.), *Talent identification and development in sport: International perspectives* (pp. 13–24). London: Routledge.
7. Thompson, W. (2001, February 16). Basketball; Stiles practices a jumper, and another, for her sister. *New York Times*. www.nytimes.com/2001/02/26/sports/basketball-stiles-practices-a-jumper-and-another-for-her-sister.html
8. Hines, C. (2008). *Whitewater wanderings* (p. 202). Bloomington, IN: AuthorHouse.
9. Kelley, S. (1992, July 8). Racewalker gains respect. *Seattle Times*. http://community.seattletimes.nwsource.com/archive/?date=19920708&slug=1501049
10. Ericsson, K.A., Krampe, R.T., & Tesch-Römer, C. (1993). The role of deliberate practice in the acquisition of expert performance. *Psychological Review, 100*, 363–406.
11. Gladwell, M. (2008). *Outliers: The story of success*. New York: Little, Brown and Company.
12. Coyle, D. (2009). *The talent code: Greatness isn't born. It's grown. Here's how*. New York: Random House.
13. Baker, J., & Young, B. (2014). 20 years later: Deliberate practice and the development of expertise in sport. *International Review of Sport and Exercise Psychology, 7*(1), 135–157.
14. Ericsson, A., & Pool, R. (2016). *Peak: Secrets from the new science of expertise*. Boston: Houghton Mifflin Harcourt.
15. Ward, P., Hodges, N.J., Williams, A.M., & Starkes, J.L. (2004). Deliberate practice and expert performance: Defining the path to excellence. In A.M. Williams & N.J. Hodges (eds.), *Skill acquisition in sport: Research, theory and practice* (pp. 231–258). London: Routledge.
16. Coughlan, E.K., Williams, A.M., McRobert, A.P., & Ford, P.R. (2013). How experts practice: A novel test of deliberate practice theory. *Journal of Experimental Psychology: Learning, Memory & Cognition, 40*, 449–458.
17. McLaughlin, D. (2016). *The Dan Plan*. http://thedanplan.com/
18. Ward, V., & Hough, A. (2012, August 1). London 2012 Olympics: Helen Glover only began rowing four years ago. *Telegraph*. www.telegraph.co.uk/sport/olympics/news/9444529/London-2012-Olympics-Helen-Glover-only-began-rowing-four-years-ago.html
19. Gilbert, W. (2016, August 12). Coaching mental toughness: From Red Bull to Bob Bowman. *Human Kinetics Coach Educa-*

*tion Center.* Retrieved from www.asep.com/news/ShowArticle.cfm?ID=265

20. Bowman, B., & Butler, C. (2016). *The golden rule: 10 steps to world class excellence in your life and work.* New York: St. Martin's.
21. Nash, C., Sproule, J., & Horton, P. (2011). Excellence in coaching: The art and skill of elite practitioners. *Research Quarterly for Sport and Exercise, 82*(2), 229–238.
22. Balyi, I., Way, R., & Higgs, C. (2013). *Long-term athlete development.* Champaign, IL: Human Kinetics.
23. Afonso, J. (2014, August 27). *Long-term athlete development model—A critique* [Video]. www.youtube.com/watch?v=VVwPXcCWr8o&feature=youtu.be
24. Ford, P., De Ste Croix, M., Lloyd, R., Meyers, R., Moosavi, M., Oliver, J., Till, K., & Williams, C. (2011). The long-term athlete development model: Physiological evidence and application. *Journal of Sports Sciences, 29*(4), 389–402.
25. Lloyd, R.S., Cronin, J.B., Faigenbaum, A.D., Haff, G.G., Howard, R., Kraemer, W.J., Micheli, L.J., Myer, G.D., & Oliver, J.L. (2016). National Strength and Conditioning Association position statement on long-term athletic development. *Journal of Strength & Conditioning Research, 30*(6), 1491–1509.
26. Borms, J. (1986). The child and exercise: An overview. *Journal of Sports Sciences, 4,* 3–20.
27. sports coach UK. (2015). *Research summary no 1: More than just physical maturity. How coaches, parents and children all influence the relative age effect.* www.sportscoachuk.org/resource/research-summary-no1-more-just-physical-maturity-how-coaches-parents-and-children-all-influ
28. Cobley, S., Baker, J., & Wattie, N., & McKenna, J. (2009). Annual age-grouping and athlete development: A meta-analytical review of relative age effects in sport. *Sports Medicine, 39*(3), 235–56.
29. Barreiros, A., Côté, J., & Fonseca, A. (2012). From early to adult sport success: Analysing athletes' progression in national squads, *European Journal of Sport Science, 14,* S178–S182.
30. Güllich, A. (2014). Many roads lead to Rome: developmental paths to Olympic gold in men's field hockey. *European Journal of Sport Science, 14*(8), 763–771.
31. Rees, T. Hardy, L., Gullich, A., Abernathy, B., Côté, J., Woodman, T., Montgomery, H., Laing, S., & Warr, C. (2016). The Great British Medalists Project: A review of current knowledge on the development of the world's best sporting talent. *Sports Medicine, 46,* 1041–1058.
32. Dweck, C. (2006). *Mindset: The new psychology of success.* New York: Ballantine.
33. Côté, J., & Vierimaa, M. (2014). The developmental model of sport participation: 15 years after its first conceptualization. *Science & Sports, 29,* S63–S69.
34. Vierimaa, M., Erickson, K., & Côté, J. (2016). The elements of talent development in youth sport. In K. Green & A. Smith (eds.), *Routledge handbook of youth sport* (pp. 464–475). London: Routledge
35. Côté, J., Murphy-Mills, J., & Abernethy, B. (2012). The development of skill in sport. In N.J. Hodges & A.M. Williams (eds.), *Skill acquisition in sport: Research, theory and practice* (pp. 269–286). New York: Routledge.
36. Côté, J., Erickson, K., & Abernethy, B. (2013). Play and practice during childhood. In J. Côté & R. Lidor (eds.), *Conditions of children's talent development in sport* (pp. 9–20). Morgantown, WV: Fitness Information Technology.
37. Hornig, M., Aust, F., & Güllich, A. (2016). Practice and play in the development of German top-level professional football players. *European Journal of Sport Science, 16*(1), 95–105.
38. Hargrove, T. (2011, January 8). *The importance of play for motor learning.* www.bettermovement.org/2011/the-importance-of-play-for-motor-learning/
39. Bowers, M.T., Green, C.B., Hemme, F., & Chalip, L. (2014). Assessing the relationship between youth sport settings and creativity in adulthood. *Creativity Research Journal, 26*(3), 314–327.
40. Memmert, D., Baker, J., & Bertsch, C. (2010). Play and practice in the development of sport-specific creativity in team ball sports. *High Ability Studies, 21*(1), 3–18.
41. Gulbin, J.P., Oldenziel, K.E., Weissensteiner, J.R., & Gagne, F. (2010). A look through the rear view mirror: Developmental experiences and insights of high performance athletes. *Talent Development & Excellence, 2*(2), 149–164.
42. USA Football (2016, April 28). *90% of first round draft picks in this year's NFL Draft played multiple sports in high school* [Tweet]. https://twitter.com/usafootball/status/725905634047053824

43. Frollo, J. (2015, May 4). Nearly 90 percent of NFL Draft selections played multiple sports in high school. *USA Football.* http://usafootball.com/blogs/americas-game/post/10194/nearly-90-percent-of-nfl-draft-selections-played-multiple-sports-in-high-school
44. Samuels, D. (2015, April 27). 85% of NFL draft picks from the last two years were multi-sport athletes in HS. *Footballscoop.* http://footballscoop.com/news/85-of-the-510-nfl-draft-picks-of-the-last-two-years-were-multi-sport-athletes-in-hs/
45. Sports and Society Program: The Aspen Institute Project Play. (2015). *Sport for all play for life: A playbook to get every kid in the game.* http://youthreport.projectplay.us/
46. O'Sullivan, J. (2015, January 25). The perils of single-sport participation. *Changing the Game Project.* http://changingthegameproject.com/the-perils-of-single-sport-participation/
47. Ellison, M. (2014, September 3). Changing the world: Vanderbilt baseball coach Tim Corbin. *Mickey Ellison Show* [Podcast]. www.voiceamerica.com/episode/79964/changing-the-world-vanderbilt-baseball-coach-tim-corbin
48. Saban, N., & Curtis, B. (2007). *How good do you want to be? A champion's tips on how to lead and succeed* (p. 65). New York: Ballantine.
49. Rogers, M. (2015, July 3). U.S. women were multi-sport athletes before focusing on soccer. *USA Today Sports.* www.usatoday.com/story/sports/soccer/2015/07/03/abby-wambach-morgan-brian-lauren-holiday/29665797/
50. Farrey, T. (2008). *Game on: The All-American race to make champions of our children.* New York: ESPN books.
51. Bompa, T., & Carrera, M. (2015). *Conditioning for young athletes.* Champaign, IL: Human Kinetics.
52. Bridge, M.W., & Toms, M.R. (2013). The specializing or sampling debate: A retrospective analysis of adolescent sports participation in the UK. *Journal of Sports Sciences, 31*(1), 87–96.
53. Solana-Sánchez, A., Lara-Bercial, S., & Solana-Sánchez, D. (2016). Athlete and coach development in the Sevilla Club de Fútbol youth academy: A values-based proposition. *International Sport Coaching Journal, 3*(1), 46–53.
54. Bergeron, M.F., Mountjoy, M., Armstrong, N., et al. (2015). International Olympic Committee consensus statement on youth athletic development. *British Journal of Sports Medicine, 49*, 843–851.
55. United States Olympic Committee. (2015). *American development model.* www.teamusa.org/About-the-USOC/Athlete-Development/American-Development-Model
56. Young, B.W., Callary, B., & Niedre, P.C. (2014). Exploring novel considerations for the coaching of masters athletes. *International Sport Coaching Journal, 1*, 86–93.
57. Martel, K. (2015). USA Hockey's American Development Model: Transforming coaching and coach education. *International Sport Coaching Journal, 2*, 39–49.
58. Snow, S. (2012). *US Youth Soccer player development model: A player-centered curriculum for US youth soccer clubs.* www.usyouthsoccer.org/us_youth_soccer_debuts_player_development_model/
59. Bloom, B.S. (ed.) (1985). *Developing talent in young people.* New York: Ballantine.
60. USA Hockey. (2014, February 26). *From child's view, parents find full-ice hockey no fun* [Video]. www.youtube.com/watch?v=cXhxNq59pWg
61. Sussex County FA. (2013, January 30). *Let's see how the adults like it* [Video]. https://www.youtube.com/watch?v=X9Pc1vf_tlg
62. Baseball Canada LTAD Workgroup. (2007). *Baseball Canada: Long term athlete development.* Ottawa, Canada: Baseball Canada.


## Chapter 6


1. Claire, F. (2008, October 12). Kissell taught Cards right way to play: Longtime St. Louis coach remembered for fundamentals. *Cardinals.com.* http://stlouis.cardinals.mlb.com/news/print.jsp?ymd=20081012&content_id=3614341&vkey=news_stl&fext=.jsp&c_id=stl
2. Nater, S., & Gallimore, R. (2010). *You haven't taught until they have learned. John Wooden's teaching principles and practices.* Morgantown, WV: Fitness Information Technology.
3. Launder, A., & Piltz, W. (2013). *Play practice. Engaging and developing skilled players from beginner to elite* (2nd ed.). Champaign, IL: Human Kinetics.
4. Ambrose, S.A., Bridges, M.W., DiPietro, M., Lovett, M.C., & Norman, M.K. (2010). *How*

*learning works: 7 research-based principles for smart teaching.* San Francisco: Jossey-Bass.

5. Becker, A.J. (2013). Quality coaching behaviors. In P. Potrac, W. Gilbert, & J. Denison (eds.), *Routledge handbook of sports coaching* (pp. 184–195). London: Routledge.
6. Voight, M., & Carroll, P. (2006). Applying sport psychology philosophies, principles, and practices onto the gridiron: An interview with USC football coach Pete Carroll. *International Journal of Sports Science & Coaching, 1*(4), 321–342.
7. Huber, J.J. (2013). *Applying educational psychology in coaching athletes.* Champaign, IL: Human Kinetics.
8. Wrisberg, C.A. (2007). *Sport skill instruction for coaches.* Champaign, IL: Human Kinetics.
9. Hannula, D., & Thornton, N. (eds.). (2001). *The swim coaching bible.* Champaign, IL: Human Kinetics.
10. American Football Coaches Association (ed.). (2002). *The football coaching bible.* Champaign, IL: Human Kinetics.
11. Adams, D., Ashford, K.J., & Jackson, R.C. (2014). Priming to promote fluent motor skill execution: Exploring attentional demands. *Journal of Sport & Exercise Psychology, 36*, 366–374.
12. Vella, S.A., & Perlman, D.J. (2014). Mastery, autonomy and transformational approaches to coaching: Common features and applications. *International Sport Coaching Journal, 1*, 173–179.
13. Reyes, L. (2015, January 8). Bill Belichick takes same approach no matter the game. *USA Today.* www.usatoday.com/story/sports/nfl/patriots/2015/01/08/bill-belichick-tom-brady-divisional-playoff/21476239/
14. Deci, E.L., & Ryan, R.M. (2000). The 'what' and 'why' of goal pursuits: Human needs and the self-determination of behavior. *Psychological Inquiry, 11*(4), 227–268.
15. Jackson, S., & Csiksentmihalyi, M. (1999). *Flow in sports: The keys to optimal experiences and performances.* Champaign, IL: Human Kinetics.
16. Kotler, S. (2014). *The rise of Superman: Decoding the science of ultimate human performance.* New York: Houghton, Mifflon, Harcourt.
17. Winkelman, N. (2014, May 15). Coaching cues that actually work. *STACK.* www.stack.com/2014/05/15/best-coaching-cues/
18. Weinberg, R.S., & Gould, D. (2015). *Foundations of sport and exercise psychology* (6th ed.) (p. 123). Champaign, IL: Human Kinetics.
19. Fortner, N. (2005). Motivation. In C. Reynaud (ed.), *She can coach! Tools for success from 20 top women coaches* (pp. 63–72). Champaign, IL: Human Kinetics.
20. Gordon, J. (2015). *The hard hat: 21 ways to be a great teammate.* Hoboken, NJ: Wiley.
21. Compton, R.A. (2006, December 7). Hard hat reflects blue collar attitude. *Harvard Crimson.* www.thecrimson.com/article/2006/12/7/hard-hat-reflects-blue-collar-attitude-after/
22. Human Kinetics. (2011). *E-products: Apps* [Mobile application software]. www.humankinetics.com/search#&sSearchWord=&sTopics=,13
23. Gilbert, W.D., Côté, J., & Mallett, C. (2006). Developmental paths and activities of successful sport coaches. *International Journal of Sports Sciences & Coaching, 1*(1), 69–76.
24. Gilbert, W.D., Lichktenwaldt, L., Gilbert, J.N., Zelezny, L., & Côté, J. (2009). Developmental profiles of successful high school coaches. *International Journal of Sports Science & Coaching, 4*, 415–431.
25. Young, B.W. (2013). Coaching expertise and the quantitative examination of developmental experiences. In P. Potrac, W. Gilbert, & J. Denison (eds.), *Routledge handbook of sports coaching* (pp. 437–450). London: Routledge.
26. Nathan, M.J., & Petrosino, A. (2003). Expert blind spot among preservice teachers. *American Educational Research Journal, 40*(4), 905–928.
27. Fitts, P.M., & Posner, M.I. (1967). *Human performance.* Belmont, CA: Brooks Cole.
28. Martens, R. (2012). *Successful coaching* (4th ed.). Champaign, IL: Human Kinetics.
29. Flegal, K.E., & Anderson, M.C. (2008). Overthinking skilled motor performance: Or why those who teach can't do. *Psychonomic Bulletin & Review, 15*, 927–932.
30. Emmett, M. (2015). Review: Man on a mission: Born to run—the secret of Kenyan Athletics. *International Sport Coaching Journal,* 2(2), 223–225
31. GoPro Tutorials. (2015, November 3). *Jon Gruden's football field guide—the coach's POV (Ep 4)* [Video]. https://community.gopro.com/t5/Video-Tutorials/Jon-Gruden-s-Football-Field-Guide-The-Coach-s-POV-Ep-4/td-p/3145

32. Magill, R.A., & Anderson, D.I. (2012). The roles and uses of augmented feedback in motor skill acquisition. In N.J. Hodges & A.M. Williams (eds.), *Skill acquisition in sport: Research, theory and practice* (pp. 3–21). New York: Routledge.
33. Carpentier, J., & Mageau, G.A. (2013). When change-oriented feedback enhances motivation, well-being and performance: A look at autonomy-supportive feedback in sport. *Psychology of Sport and Exercise, 14*, 423–435.
34. Cutton, D.M., & Hearon, C.M. (2013). Applied attention-related strategies for coaches. *Journal of Sport Psychology in Action, 4*, 5–13.
35. Bennett, S., Button, C., Kingsbury, D., & Davids, K. (1999). Manipulating visual information constraints during practice enhances the acquisition of catching skill in children. *Research Quarterly for Exercise and Sport, 70*, 220–232.
36. Christian Ronaldo tested to the limit [Video file]. www.youtube.com/watch?v=BeNLd68TTsM
37. Eccles, D., & Tran, K. (2012). Getting them on the same page: Strategies for enhancing coordination and communication in sports teams. *Journal of Sports Psychology in Action, 3*, 30–40.
38. Dartfish. (2015). *Unleash the power of your videos.* www.dartfish.com/
39. Coach Logic. (2015). *Develop smarter players: A set of online sport tools to empower players to learn.* www.coach-logic.com/
40. Prozone Sports. (2015). *Sports performance analysis.* www.prozonesports.com/
41. Nelson, L.J., Potrac, P., & Groom, R. (2014). Receiving video-based feedback in elite ice-hockey: A player's perspective. *Sport, Education and Society, 19*(1), 19–40.
42. Groom, R., Cushion, C., & Nelson, L. (2011). The delivery of video-based performance analysis by England youth soccer coaches: Towards a grounded theory. *Journal of Applied Sport Psychology, 23*, 16–32.
43. Liu, J., & Wrisberg, C.A. (1997). The effect of knowledge of results delay and the subjective estimation of movement form on the acquisition and retention of a motor skill. *Research Quarterly for Exercise and Sport, 68*(2), 145–151.
44. Wulf, G., Shea, C.H., & Matschiner, S. (1998). *Journal of Motor Behavior, 30*(2), 180–192.
45. Badami, R., VaezMousavi, M., Wulf, G., & Namazizadeh, M. (2011). Feedback after good versus poor trials affects intrinsic motivation. *Research Quarterly for Exercise and Sport, 82*(2), 360–364.
46. Smith, R.E., & Smoll, F.L. (2002). *Way to go coach!* (2nd ed.). Portola Valley, CA: Warde.


## Chapter 7


1. Garrido, A., & Smith, W. (2011). *Life is yours to win: Lessons forged from the purpose, passion, and magic of baseball.* New York: Simon & Schuster.
2. BBC. (2012, January 17). Muhammed Ali—In his own words. *BBC Sport.* www.bbc.com/sport/0/boxing/16146367
3. ESPN. (2012, May 7). *Original Allen Iverson practice rant* [Video file]. www.youtube.com/watch?v=eGDBR2L5kzI
4. ESPN.com. (2015, June 4). New book says former 76ers star Allen Iverson drunk during "practice" rant. *ESPN.* http://espn.go.com/nba/story/_/id/13011685/new-book-says-former-philadelphia-76ers-star-allen-iverson-was-drunk-practice-rant
5. Coughlin, T., & Fisher, D. (2013). *Earn the right to win: How success in any field starts with superior preparation.* New York: Penguin.
6. Starkes, J. (2000). The road to expertise: Is practice the only determinant? *International Journal of Sport Psychology, 31*, 431–451.
7. Yukelson, D., & Rose, R. (2014). The psychology of ongoing excellence: An NCAA coach's perspective on winning consecutive multiple national championships. *Journal of Sport Psychology in Action, 5*, 44–58.
8. Coyle, D. (2012). *The little book of talent: 52 tips for improving your skills.* New York: Bantam.
9. Smith, R.E., & Smoll, F.L. (2002). *Way to go coach!* (2nd ed.). Portola Valley, CA: Warde.
10. Vella, S., & Gilbert, W. (2014). Coaching young athletes to positive development: Implications for coach training. In R. Gomes, R. Resende, & A. Albuquerque (eds.), *Positive human functioning from a multidimensional perspective: Promoting high performance* (vol. 3) (pp. 83–105). Hauppauge, NY: Nova.
11. Miller, G.A., Lutz, R., & Fredenburg, K. (2012). Outstanding high school coaches: Philosophies, views, and practices. *Journal of Physical Education, Recreation & Dance, 83*(2), 24–29.
12. Vella, S.A., & Perlman, D.J. (2014). Mastery, autonomy and transformational approaches

to coaching: Common features and applications. *International Sport Coaching Journal, 1*, 173–179.

13. Smoll, F.L., Smith, R.E., & Cumming, S.P. (2007). Effects of a motivational climate intervention for coaches on changes in young athletes' achievement goal orientations. *Journal of Clinical Sports Psychology, 1*, 23–46.
14. Youth Enrichment in Sports. (n.d.). *The science behind the mastery approach programs.* www.y-e-sports.com/Research.html
15. Dweck, C.S., & Leggett, E.L. (1988). A social-cognitive approach to motivation and personality. *Psychological Review, 95*, 256–273.
16. Wrisberg, C.A. (2007). *Sport skill instruction for coaches.* Champaign, IL: Human Kinetics.
17. Bulger, S.M., Mohr, D.J., Rairigh, R.M., & Townsend, J.S. (2007). *Sport education seasons: Featuring basketball, soccer and fitness education.* Champaign, IL: Human Kinetics.
18. Dweck, C. (2006). *Mindset: The new psychology of success.* New York: Ballantine.
19. Goodreads, Inc. (2016). *A.P.J. Abdul Kalam quotes.* Retrieved from www.goodreads.com/quotes/1015959---if-you-fail-never-give-up-because-f-a-i-l-means
20. Dweck, C. (2015, September 22). Carol Dweck revisits the "growth mindset." *Education Week: Commentary.* www.edweek.org/ew/articles/2015/09/23/carol-dweck-revisits-the-growth-mindset.html
21. Associated Press. (2012, June 7). *Novak Djokovic outlasts Rafael Nadal.* http://espn.go.com/tennis/aus12/story/_/id/7515950/2012-australian-open-novak-djokovic-outlasts-rafael-nadal-longest-grand-slam-final
22. Mageau, G.A., & Vallerand, R.J. (2003). The coach-athlete relationship: A motivational model. *Journal of Sports Sciences, 21*, 883–904.
23. Gilbert, W. (2016). *After 22 NCAA titles and a World Cup championship: Winning lessons from Anson Dorrance.* www.asep.com/news/ShowArticle.cfm?ID=262
24. Crothers, T. (2006). *The man watching: A biography of Anson Dorrance, the unlikely architect of the greatest college sports dynasty ever.* Ann Arbor, MI: Sports Media Group.
25. Dorrance, A., & Nash, T. (1996). *Training soccer champions.* Chapel Hill, NC: JTC Sports.
26. Hebert, M. (2014). *Thinking volleyball: Inside the game with a coaching legend.* Champaign, IL: Human Kinetics.
27. Elberse, A., & Ferguson, A. (2013, October). Ferguson's formula. *Harvard Business Review*, 2–11.
28. Comstock, R.D., Currie, D.W., & Pierpoint, L.A. (2016). *Summary report: National high school sports-related injury surveillance study: 2014–2015 school year.* www.ucdenver.edu/academics/colleges/PublicHealth/research/ResearchProjects/piper/projects/RIO/Pages/Study-Reports.aspx
29. USA Football. (2010). *Player progression development model: The right age. The right stage.* http://usafootball.com/programs/ppdm
30. Ford, P.R., .Yates, I., & Williams, A.M. (2010). An analysis of practice activities and instructional behaviors used by youth soccer coaches during practice: Exploring the link between science and application. *Journal of Sports Sciences, 28*(5), 483–495.
31. Snow, S. (2012). *US Youth Soccer player development model: A player-centered curriculum for US youth soccer clubs.* www.usyouthsoccer.org/us_youth_soccer_debuts_player_development_model/
32. USA Hockey. (2013). *American development model: Practice plans.* www.admkids.com/page/show/915460-practice-plans
33. Cleary, B. (2016). Keeping a balance. In J. Bertagna (ed.), *The hockey coaching bible* (pp. 1–5). Champaign, IL: Human Kinetics.
34. Jamieson, T. (2010). Perfecting positional play. In American Baseball Coaches Association & B. Bennett (ed.), *Practice perfect baseball* (pp. 85–105). Champaign, IL: Human Kinetics.
35. Nater, S. & Gallimore, R. (2010). *You haven't taught until they have learned: John Wooden's teaching principles and practices.* Morgantown, WV: Fitness International Technology.
36. Ambrose, S.A., Bridges, M.W., DiPietro, M., Lovett, M.C., & Norman, M.K. (2010). *How learning works: 7 research-based principles for smart teaching.* San Francisco: Jossey-Bass.
37. Carroll, P. (1997). Foreword. In W.T. Gallwey, *The inner game of tennis: The classic guide to the mental side of peak performance* (rev. ed., p. xii). New York: Random House.
38. Fajen, B.R., Riley, M.A., & Turvey, M.T. (2009). Information, affordances and the control of action in sport. *International*

*Journal of Sport Psychology*, *40*, 79–107.

39. Huber, J.J. (2013). *Applying educational psychology in coaching athletes*. Champaign, IL: Human Kinetics.
40. Wilson, C.H. Jr. (2013) (Ed.). Inspirational quotes for sports coaches (18th ed.). *Back to Basics Sports*. Retrieved from www.coachingbasketballwisely.com/quotes/
41. Ratey, J.J., & Hagerman, E. (2013). *SPARK: The revolutionary new science of exercise and the brain*. New York: Little, Brown and Company.
42. DiCicco, T. (2004). Mentoring the next generation of coaches (pp. 283–293). In National Soccer Coaches Association of America (ed.), *The soccer coaching bible*. Champaign, IL: Human Kinetics.
43. Gable, D. (1999). *Coaching wrestling successfully*. Champaign, IL: Human Kinetics.
44. Kyle, C., & Hodermarsky, M. (1997). *The object of the game*. Dubuque, IA: Kendall/Hunt.
45. Gallimore, R., Gilbert, W., & Nater, S. (2014). Reflective practice and ongoing learning: A coach's ten year journey. *Reflective Practice*, *15*(2), 268–288.
46. Jenkins, S. (2015). Winning formula, man management and the Inner Game: Commonalities of success in the Ryder Cup and Super Bowl. *International Journal of Sports Science and Coaching*, *10*(2–3), 171–283
47. Garside, K. (2014, December 11). Interview: Paul McGinley rewrites art of captaincy. *Independent*. www.independent.co.uk/sport/golf/interview-paul-mcginley-rewrites-art-of-captaincy-9919252.html
48. Occhino, J.L., Mallett, C.J., Rynne, S.B., & Carlisle, K.N. (2014). Autonomy-supportive pedagogical approach to sports coaching: Research, challenges and opportunities. *International Journal of Sport Science and Coaching*, *9*(2), 401–415.
49. Carpentier, J., & Mageau, G.A. (2013). When change-oriented feedback enhances motivation, well-being and performance: A look at autonomy-supportive feedback in sport. *Psychology of Sport and Exercise*, *14*, 423–435.
50. Langdon, J., Harris, B.S., Burdette, G.P., & Rothberger, S. (2015). Development and implementation of an autonomy supportive training program among youth sport coaches. *International Sport Coaching Journal*, 2, 169–177.
51. Sheldon, K.M., & Watson, A. (2011). Coach's autonomy support is especially important for varsity compared to club and recreational athletes. *International Journal of Sports Science and Coaching*, *6*(1), 109–123.
52. Cronin, L.D., & Allen, J.B. (2015). Developmental experiences and well-being in sport: The importance of the coaching climate. *Sport Psychologist*, *29*, 62–71.
53. Bartholomew, K.J., Ntoumanis, N., & Thøgersen-Ntoumani, C. (2009). A review of controlling motivational strategies from a self-determination theory perspective: Implications for sports coaches. *International Review of Sport & Exercise Psychology*, *2*(2), 215–233.
54. Mallett, C.J. (2005). Self-determination theory: A case study of evidence-based coaching. *Sport Psychologist*, *19*, 417–429.
55. Gilbert, W. (2015, January 15). Coaching the background. *Human Kinetics Coach Education Center* [Podcast]. www.asep.com/news/ShowArticle.cfm?ID=240
56. Webster, C.A., Hunt, K., & LaFleche, M. (2013). Are winning coaches more autonomy-supportive? Examining the context of varsity boys' soccer. *Journal of Sport Behavior*, *36*(2), 209–232.
57. Barris, S., Farrow, D., & Davids, K. (2014). Increasing functional variability in the preparatory phase of the takeoff improves elite springboard diving performance. *Research Quarterly for Exercise and Sport*, *85*, 97–106.
58. Nash, C., Sproule, J., & Horton, P. (2011). Excellence in coaching: The art and skill of elite practitioners. *Research Quarterly for Sport and Exercise*, *82*(2), 229–238.
59. Winning Scotland Foundation. (2014, September 7). *Gregor Townsend: Coaching and growth mindset*. www.youtube.com/watch?v=t4-3Zb6cyes&utm_content=bufferc3c5d&utm_medium=social&utm_source=twitter.com&ut
60. Jackson, P., & Delehanty, H. (2013). *Eleven rings: The soul of success* (p. 16, p. 94). New York: Penguin.
61. Hodge, K., Henry, G., & Smith, W. (2014). A case study of excellence in elite sport: Motivational climate in a world champion team. *Sport Psychologist*, *28*, 60–74.
62. Driskell, T., Sclafani, S., & Driskell, J.E. (2014). Reducing the effects of game day pressures through stress exposure training. *Journal of Sport Psychology in Action*, *5*, 28–43.
63. Launder, A., & Piltz, W. (2013). *Play practice. Engaging and developing skilled*

*players from beginner to elite* (2nd ed.). Champaign, IL: Human Kinetics.

64. Ford, P.R., Yates, I., & Williams, A.M. (2010). An analysis of practice activities and instructional behaviors used by youth soccer coaches during practice: Exploring the link between science and application. *Journal of Sports Sciences, 28*(5), 483–495.
65. Partington, M., & Cushion, C.J. (2011). An investigation of the practice activities and coaching behaviours of professional top-level youth soccer coaches. *Scandinavian Journal of Medicine and Science in Sport, 23*, 374–382.
66. Cushion, C., Ford, P., & Williams, A.M. (2012). Coach behaviours and practice structures in youth soccer: Implications for talent development. *Journal of Sport Sciences, 30*(15), 1631–1641.
67. USA Hockey. (2015, September 4). *Did you know: 8U players receive 5x more passes in cross-ice hockey? Check out all seven key measurable* [Tweet]. https://twitter.com/usahockey/status/639881397520441344
68. Stier, W.F., Jr., & Schneider, R.C. (2008). Effectiveness of basketball coaching methods and player qualities—a national survey of coaches. *Applied Research in Coaching and Athletics Annual, 23*, 43–67.
69. Becker, A.J. (2009). It's not what they do, it's how they do it: Athlete experiences of great coaching. *International Journal of Sports Science & Coaching, 4*, 93–118.
70. Martens, R. (2012). *Successful coaching* (4th ed.). Champaign, IL: Human Kinetics.
71. Singer, R.N., & Janelle, C.M. (1999). Determining sport expertise: From genes to supremes. *International Journal of Sport Psychology, 30*, 117–150.
72. Beek, P.J., Jacobs, D.M., Daffertshofer, A., & Huys, R. (2003). Expert performance in sport: Views from joint perspectives of ecological psychology and dynamical systems theory. In J.L. Starkes & K.A. Ericsson (eds.), *Expert performance in sport: Advances in research on sport expertise* (pp. 321–344). Champaign, IL: Human Kinetics.
73. Harvey, S., & Jarrett, K. (2014). A review of the game-centred approaches to teaching and coaching literature since 2006. *Physical Education & Sport Pedagogy, 19*(3), 1–23.
74. Solana-Sánchez, A., Lara-Bercial, S., & Solana-Sánchez, D. (2016). Athlete and coach development in the Sevilla Club de Fútbol youth academy: A values-based proposition. *International Sport Coaching Journal, 3*, 46–53.
75. Luxbacheer, J.A. (2010). *Soccer practice games: 175 games for technique, training, and tactics* (3rd ed.). Champaign, IL: Human Kinetics.
76. McNally, S. (2010). Incorporating competitive drills and games. In B. Bennett (ed.), *Practice perfect baseball* (pp. 193–208). Champaign, IL: American Baseball Coaches Association and Human Kinetics.
77. Harvey, S., Cushion, C.J., & Massa-Gonzalez, A.N. (2010). Learning a new method: Teaching Games for Understanding in the coaches' eyes. *Physical Education & Sport Pedagogy, 15*(4), 361–382.
78. Harenberg, S., Riemer, H.A., Karreman, E., & Dorsch, K.D. (2016). Coaches' perspectives of intrateam competition in high performance sport teams. *International Sport Coaching Journal, 3*, 156–169.
79. Marriott, L., Nilsson, P., & Sirak, R. (2007). *The game before the game*. New York: Gotham.
80. Carr, T. (2005). *How to coach a soccer team: Professional advice on training plans, skill drills, and tactical analysis*. New York: Sterling.

## Chapter 8

1. Gonzalez, A. (2015, May 17). Warriors' coach Steve Kerr coming through in playoffs again. *Associated Press*. www.nba.com/2015/news/05/17/warriors-steve-kerr.ap/
2. Driskell, T., Sclafani, S., & Driskell, J.E. (2014). Reducing the effects of game day pressures through stress exposure training. *Journal of Sport Psychology in Action, 5*, 28–43.
3. Grant, M.A., & Schempp, P. (2014). Elements of success: Olympic swimming gold medalists' understanding of their competition-day routines. *International Journal of Sports Science & Coaching, 9*(2), 287–305.
4. Bloom, G.A., Durand-Bush, N., & Salmela, J.H. (1997). Pre- and postcompetition routines of expert coaches of team sports. *Sport Psychologist, 11*, 127–141.
5. Wooten, M., & Wooten, J. (2013). *Coaching basketball successfully* (3rd ed.). Champaign, IL: Human Kinetics.
6. Saban, N., & Curtis, B. (2007). *How good do you want to be? A champion's tips on how to lead and succeed*. New York: Ballantine.

7. Tyson, P., & Binder, D. (2014). *Coaching cross country successfully.* Champaign, IL: Human Kinetics.
8. Schembechler, B., & Bacon, J.U. (2007). *Bo's lasting lessons: The legendary coach teaches the timeless fundamentals of leadership.* New York: Business Plus.
9. Randle, J. (2015, July 8). Hurt locker rooms: The four injury risks today's young players face. *ESPN.* http://espn.go.com/nba/story/_/id/13217004/the-four-injury-risks-today-young-nba-players-face
10. Keating, P. (2012, April 5). Sleeping giants. *ESPN.* http://espn.go.com/espn/commentary/story/_/id/7765998/for-athletes-sleep-new-magic-pill
11. Mah, C.D., Mah, K.E., Kezirian, E.J., & Dement, W.C. (2011). The effects of sleep extension on the athletic performance of collegiate basketball players. *SLEEP, 34*(7), 943–950.
12. Sekeres, M. (2011, June 6). Sleep doctor has Canucks peaking at right time. *Globe and Mail.* www.theglobeandmail.com/sports/hockey/sleep-doctor-has-canucks-peaking-at-right-time/article582351/
13. Thornton, L. (2016, Winter). Elite athletes and sleep: How much are they getting? What happens when they don't get enough? Why short term sleep extension might be a performance enhancement strategy. *Olympic Coach Magazine, 27*(1), 4-11. Retrieved from http://www.teamusa.org/About-the-USOC/Athlete-Development/Coaching-Education/Coach-E-Magazine
14. Changa, A., Aeschbacha, D., Duffya, J., & Czeislera, C. (2015). Evening use of light-emitting eReaders negatively affects sleep, circadian timing, and next-morning alertness. *PNAS, 112,* 1232–1237.
15. Khullar, A. (2012, July 9). The role of melatonin in the circadian rhythm sleep-wake cycle. *Psychiatric Times.* www.psychiatrictimes.com/sleep-disorders/role-melatonin-circadian-rhythm-sleep-wake-cycle
16. Falbe, J., Davison, K., Franckle, R., Ganter, C., Gortmaker, S., Smith, L., Land, T., & Elsie M. Taveras, E. (2015). Sleep duration, restfulness, and screens in the sleep environment. *Pediatrics, 135*(2), e367–e375.
17. Denyer, D. (2013, Autumn). 15 steps to peak performance: The transformation of British cycling from near bankruptcy to a dominant global force offers insights for any business looking to improve their performance. *Management Focus,* 10–13. www.daviddenyer.com/15-steps-to-peak-performance/
18. Lovato, N., & Lack, L. (2010). The effects of napping on cognitive functioning. In G.A. Kerkhof & H.P.A. Van Dongen (eds.), *Progress in brain research: Human sleep and cognition,* volume 185 (pp. 155–166). Oxford, UK: Elsevier Science.
19. Martens, R. (2012). *Successful coaching* (4th ed.). Champaign, IL: Human Kinetics.
20. Meyer, N.L. (2014). Fueling the winter sport athlete on the road to Sochi. *Olympic Coach Magazine, 25*(1), 17–21.
21. American College of Sports Medicine & Academy of Nutrition and Dietetics, and Dieticians of Canada. (2016). Nutrition and athletic performance: Joint position statement. *Medicine & Science in Sports & Exercise, 48*(3), 543–568.
22. Hueglin, S. (2014). Nutrition and the female athlete. *Olympic Coach Magazine, 25*(4), 29–32. www.teamusa.org/About-the-USOC/Athlete-Development/Coaching-Education/Coach-E-Magazine.aspx
23. American College of Sports Medicine & Academy of Nutrition and Dietetics, Dietitians of Canada. (2016). Nutrition and athletic performance. *Medicine & Science in Sports & Exercise, 48*(3), 543–568.
24. Armstrong, L.E. (2000). *Performing in extreme environments.* Champaign, IL: Human Kinetics.
25. Human Hydration, LLC. (2011). *Hydration check: Wall chart.* www.hydrationcheck.com/wall_chart.php
26. United States Olympic Committee. (2015). *Resources and fact sheets: General nutrition guidelines.* www.teamusa.org/About-the-USOC/Athlete-Development/Sport-Performance/Nutrition/Resources-and-Fact-Sheets
27. Bompa, T., & Carrera, M. (2015). *Conditioning young athletes.* Champaign, IL: Human Kinetics.
28. Nolan, E. (2015, January 21). Warm-ups: A simple framework. *Propelperform.com.* http://propelperform.com/warm-ups-simple-framework/
29. Behm, D.G., & Chaouachi, A. (2011). A review of the acute effects of static and dynamic stretching on performance. *European Journal of Applied Physiology, 111,* 2633–2651.
30. Blahnik, J. (2011). *Full-body flexibility* (2nd ed.). Champaign, IL: Human Kinetics.
31. Plack, L.A. (2011, April 20). *Stretching tips for athletes: Dynamic and static stretching.*

www.hss.edu/conditions_stretching-tips-athletes-dynamic-static.asp#.VVD-wraOA6So

32. McHugh, M.P., & Cosgrave, C.H. (2010). To stretch or not to stretch: The role of stretching in injury prevention and performance. *Scandinavian Journal of Medicine & Science in Sports*, *20*, 169–181.
33. Stojanovic, M.D., & Ostojic, S.M. (2011). Stretching and injury prevention in football: Current perspectives. *Research in Sports Medicine*, *19*, 73–91.
34. Kay, A.D., & Blazevich, A.J. (2012). Effect of acute static stretch on maximal muscle performance: A systematic review. *Medicine & Science in Sports & Exercise*, *44*(1), 154–164.
35. Nunez, A. (2014, February 19). Gracie Gold's weird pre-competition ritual. *SHAPE*. www.shape.com/blogs/fit-famous/gracie-golds-weird-pre-competition-ritual
36. Yeager, S. (2011, August 15). Pregame rituals of the pros. *ESPNW*. espn.go.com/espnw/training/article/6857252/pregame-rituals-pros
37. Begun, B. (2001, December 6). Questions and answers: Bill Russell. *Newsweek*. www.newsweek.com/questions-amp-answers-bill-russell-153217
38. Hanin, Y.L. (2000). *Emotions in sport*. Champaign, IL: Human Kinetics.
39. Weinberg, R.S., & Gould, D. (2015). *Foundations of sport and exercise psychology* (6th ed.). Champaign, IL: Human Kinetics.
40. Jokela, M., & Hanin, Y.L. (1999). Does the individual zones of optimal functioning model discriminate between successful and less successful athletes? A meta-analysis. *Journal of Sports Sciences*, *17*, 873–887.
41. Hagtvet, K.A., & Hanin, Y.L. (2007). Consistency of performance-related emotions in elite athletes: Generalizability theory applied to the IZOF model. *Psychology of Sport and Exercise*, *8*, 47–72.
42. Vealey, R. (2005). *Coaching for the inner edge*. Morgantown, WV: Fitness Information Technology.
43. Porter, K. (2003). *The mental athlete: Inner training for peak performance in all sports*. Champaign, IL: Human Kinetics.
44. Burton, D., & Raedeke, T.D. (2008). *Sport psychology for coaches*. Champaign, IL: Human Kinetics.
45. Vealey, R.S., Low, W., Pierce, S., & Quinones-Paredes, D. (2014). Choking in sport: ACT on it! *Journal of Sport Psychology in Action*, *5*, 156–169.
46. Williams, S.E., Colley, S.J., Newell, E., Weibull, F., & Cumming, J. (2013). Seeing the difference: Developing effective imagery scripts for athletes. *Journal of Sport Psychology in Action*, *4*, 109–212.
47. Yeats, J.T., Rhoads, M.C., Smith, M.A., & White, L. (2014). High school volleyball athletes' perceptions of creating and using pre-competition warm-up music. *Sport Science Review*, *23(3/4)*, 127–150.
48. Yeats, J.T., & Smith, M.A. (2011). High school volleyball coaches' instructional approaches and perceptions to using athlete created pre-competition warm-up music. *Sport Science Review*, *20(5/6)*, 25–56.
49. Pain, M.A., Harwood, C., & Anderson, R. (2011). Pre-competition imagery and music: The impact on flow and performance in competitive soccer. *Sport Psychologist*, *25*, 212–232.
50. U.S. Soccer. (2015, June 22). *#USWNT reveals its gameday playlist*. www.ussoccer.com/stories/2015/06/22/10/22/150622-wnt-reveals-their-gameday-playlist
51. Landman, B. (2006, September 3). Gipper-type hype speech? Only in Hollywood. *Tampa Bay Times*. www.sptimes.com/2006/09/03/Sports/Gipper_type_hype_spee.shtml
52. Brown, J. (2014, February 7). "Miracle" players recall Herb Brooks as gruff, great. *NHL.com*. www.nhl.com/ice/news.htm?id=704235
53. Vargas, T.M., & Short, S.E. (2011). Athletes' perceptions of the psychological, emotional, and performance effects of coaches' pre-game speeches. *International Journal of Coaching Science*, *5*, 27–43.
54. Vargas-Tonsing, T.M., & Bartholomew, J.B. (2006). An exploratory study of the effects of pregame speeches on team efficacy beliefs. *Journal of Applied Social Psychology*, *36*, 918–933.
55. Vargas-Tonsing, T.M., & Guan, J. (2007). Athletes' preferences for informational and emotional pre-game speech content. *International Journal of Sports Science & Coaching*, *2*, 171–180.
56. Babcock, M., & Larsen, R. (2012). *Leave no doubt: A credo for chasing your dreams*. Montreal & Kingston: McGill-Queen's University Press.
57. Gilbert, W. (2016, April 4). After 22 NCAA titles and a World Cup championship: Win-

ning lessons from Anson Dorrance. *Human Kinetics Coach Education.* Retrieved from http://www.asep.com/news/ShowArticle.cfm?ID=262

58. Gadowsky, G. (2016). Communicating a team mission. In J. Bertagna (ed.), *The hockey coaching bible: Insights and strategies from 16 of the sport's top coaches* (pp. 13–23). Champaign, IL: Human Kinetics.
59. Roseberg, S. (2015). *Inspiration for the graduate: Thoughts & quotes from the world of athletics to enhance the next stage of your life.* Livingston, MT: Author.
60. Brown, B. (2003). *Another 1001 motivational messages and quotes.* Monterey, CA: Coaches Choice.
61. Orshoshki, P. (2015). *To any athlete: A collection of motivational quotes, slogans, and poems for athletes and coaches!* Author.
62. Schlossman, B.E. (2016, May 2). On eve of national championship, a dream keeps UND players wide awake. *INFORUM.* www.inforum.com/sports/4022829-eve-national-championship-dream-keeps-und-players-wide-awake
63. Vargas-Tonsing, T.M. (2009). An exploratory examination of the effects of coaches' pregame speeches on athletes' perceptions of self-efficacy and emotion. *Journal of Sport Behavior, 32,* 92–111.
64. McCarry, P. (2007). Game day coaching: The weekend contest should be viewed as an extension of the weekday training sessions. *Soccer Journal, September/October,* 8–9.
65. Breakey, C., Jones, M., Cunningham, C.T, & Holt, N. (2009). Female athletes' perceptions of a coach's speeches. *International Journal of Sports Science & Coaching, 4,* 489–504.
66. Gendron, D. (2003). *Coaching hockey successfully.* Champaign, IL: Human Kinetics.
67. Gable, D. (1999). *Coaching wrestling successfully.* Champaign, IL: Human Kinetics.
68. Eberhardt, D. (2014, April 3). Preparation never ends: What NBA coaches do before games. *SB Nation.* www.sbnation.com/nba/2014/4/3/5578296/nba-coach-pregame-workout-gregg-popovich
69. Wooden, J., & Jamison, S. (1997). *Wooden: A lifetime of observations and reflections on and off the court.* Chicago: Contemporary Books.
70. Becker, A.J. (2009). It's not what they do, it's how they do it: Athlete experiences of great coaching. *International Journal of Sports Science & Coaching, 4,* 93–118.
71. Gawande, A. (2009). *The checklist manifesto: How to get things right.* New York: Metropolitan.
72. Gawande, A. (2007, December 10). The checklist: If something so simple can transform intensive care, what else can it do? *New Yorker.* www.newyorker.com/magazine/2007/12/10/the-checklist
73. McCann, S. (2008). Routines, rituals, and performing under pressure. *Olympic Coach Magazine, 20*(2), 14–15. www.teamusa.org/About-the-USOC/Athlete-Development/Coaching-Education/Coach-E-Magazine.aspx
74. Taylor, J. (2012, July 16). Sports: Why the world's best athletes use routines: Consistent routines lead to consistently high sports performance. *Psychology Today.* www.psychologytoday.com/blog/the-power-prime/201207/sports-why-the-worlds-best-athletes-use-routines
75. SIRC Sport Research. (2014, June 13). *The effectiveness of a pre-competition routine.* http://sirc.ca/blog/effectiveness-pre-competition-routine

## Chapter 9

1. Krzyzewski, M., & Spatola, J.K. (2009). *The gold standard: Building a world-class team.* New York: Business Plus.
2. Gable, D. (1999). *Coaching wrestling successfully.* Champaign, IL: Human Kinetics.
3. Gilbert, W. (2015, January 12). Coaching in the background. *Human Kinetics Coach Education Center.* www.asep.com/news/ShowArticle.cfm?ID=240
4. Gould, D., & Maynard, I. (2009). Psychological preparation for the Olympic Games. *Journal of Sports Sciences, 27*(13), 1393–1408.
5. Blinebury, F. (2014, June 12). Pop's lesson: Learning to shut up. *Sekou Smith's Hang Time Blog.* http://hangtime.blogs.nba.com/2014/06/12/pops-lesson-learning-to-shut-up/
6. Allen, J., & Ritchie, D. (2015). "Let them get on with it": Coaches' perceptions of their roles and coaching practices during Olympic and Paralympic Games. *International Sport Coaching Journal, 2,* 108–124.
7. Becker, A. (2013). Quality coaching behaviors. In P. Potrac, W. Gilbert, & J. Denison (eds.), *Routledge handbook of sports coaching* (pp. 184–195). London: Routledge.

8. Cushion, C. (2010). Coach behavior. In J. Lyle & C. Cushion (eds.), *Sports coaching: Professionalization and practice* (pp. 43–61). Edinburgh, UK: Churchill Livingstone Elsevier.
9. Erickson, K., & Gilbert, W. (2013). Coach-athlete interactions in children's sport. In J. Côté & R. Lidor (eds.), *Conditions of children's talent development in sport* (pp. 139–156). Morgantown, WV: Fitness Information Technology.
10. Gadowsky, G. (2016). Communicating a team mission. In J. Bertagna (ed.), *The hockey coaching bible: Insights and strategies from 16 of the sport's top coaches* (pp. 13–23). Champaign, IL: Human Kinetics.
11. Berra, Y., & Kaplan, D. (2008). *You can observe a lot by watching: What I've learned about teamwork from the Yankees and life.* Hoboken, NJ: Wiley.
12. Charlesworth, R. (2001). *The coach: Managing for success.* Sydney: Macmillan.
13. McCarry, P. (2007). Game day coaching: The weekend contest should be viewed as an extension of the weekday training sessions. *Soccer Journal, September–October*, 8–9.
14. Hebert, M. (2014). *Thinking volleyball: Inside the game with a coaching legend.* Champaign, IL: Human Kinetics.
15. Launder, A.G. (2001). *Play practice. The games approach to teaching and coaching sports.* Champaign, IL: Human Kinetics.
16. Hagemann, N., Strauss, B., & Büsch, D. (2008). The complex problem solving competence of team coaches. *Psychology of Sport and Exercise, 9*, 301–317.
17. Jackson, P., & Delehanty, H. (2013). *Eleven rings: The soul of success* (p. 16, p. 94). New York: Penguin.
18. Jones, R.L., Bailey, J., & Thompson, A. (2013). Ambiguity, noticing and orchestration: Further thoughts on managing the complex coaching context. In P. Potrac, W. Gilbert, & J. Denison (eds.), *Routledge handbook of sports coaching* (pp. 271–283). London: Routledge.
19. Ericsson, K A., ed. (1996). *The road to excellence: The acquisition of expert performance in the arts and sciences, sports, and games.* Mahweh, NJ: Lawrence Erlbaum.
20. Gendron, D. (2003). *Coaching hockey successfully.* Champaign, IL: Human Kinetics.
21. Garrido, A., & Smith, W. (2011). *Life is yours to win: Lessons forged from the purpose, passion, and magic of baseball.* New York: Simon & Schuster.
22. Cathcart, S., McGregor, M., & Groundwater, E. (2014). Mindfulness and flow in elite athletes. *Journal of Clinical Sport Psychology, 8*, 119–141.
23. van Es, E.A., & Sherin, M.G. (2002). Learning to notice: Scaffolding new teachers' interpretations of classroom interactions. *Journal of Technology and Teacher Education, 10*(4), 571–596.
24. Harvey, S., Lyle, J.W.B., & Muir, B. (2015). Naturalistic decision making in high performance team sport coaching. *International Sport Coaching Journal, 2*, 152–168.
25. Weisul, K. (2015, October 23). What a fighter pilot can teach you about teamwork and focus. *Inc.* www.inc.com/kimberly-weisul/how-to-do-business-like-a-fighter-pilot.html
26. Elberse, A., & Ferguson, A. (2013, October). Ferguson's formula. *Harvard Business Review*, 2–11.
27. Vella, S.A., & Perlman, D.J. (2014). Mastery, autonomy and transformational approaches to coaching: Common features and applications. *International Sport Coaching Journal, 1*, 173–179.
28. Vella, S., & Gilbert, W. (2014). Coaching young athletes to positive development: Implications for coach training. In R. Gomes, R. Resende, & A. Albuquerque (eds.), *Positive human functioning from a multidimensional perspective: Promoting high performance* (vol. 3) (pp. 83–105). Hauppauge, NY: Nova.
29. Dreher, D. (2012, February 29). Do you live in a culture of courage or fear? *Psychology Today.* www.psychologytoday.com/blog/your-personal-renaissance/201202/do-you-live-in-culture-courage-or-fear
30. Lynch, J. (2001). *Creative coaching: New ways to maximize athlete and team potential in all sports.* Champaign, IL: Human Kinetics.
31. What a coach can teach a teacher, 1975–2004: Reflections and reanalysis of John Wooden's teaching practices. *Sport Psychologist, 18*, 119–137.
32. Eccles, D. W., & Tran, K. B. (2012). Getting them on the same page: Strategies for enhancing coordination and communication in sports teams. *Journal of Sport Psychology in Action, 3*, 30–40.
33. Freeman, E. (2014, March 6). Spurs coach Gregg Popovich explains how he gets players to buy into his system. *Yahoo!*

*Sports*. http://sports.yahoo.com/blogs/nba-ball-dont-lie/spurs-coach-gregg-popovich-explains-how-he-gets-players-to-buy-into-his-offensive-system-224429957.html

34. Gallimore, R., Gilbert, W., & Nater, S. (2014). Reflective practice and ongoing learning: A coach's ten year journey. *Reflective Practice, 15*(2), 268–288.
35. Gallimore, R., Ermeling, B., & Nater, S. (2012). Timeless lessons: Encouraging your coaches to take a page from the Wizard of Westwood can turn them into teachers, and have a profound effect. *Athletic Management, Feb/Mar*, 43–47.
36. Schembechler, B., & Bacon, J.U. (2007). *Bo's lasting lessons: The legendary coach teaches the timeless fundamentals of leadership*. New York: Business Plus.
37. Babcock, M., & Larsen, R. (2012). *Leave no doubt: A credo for chasing your dreams*. Montreal & Kingston, Canada: McGill-Queen's University.
38. Jones, M.I., & Harwood, C. (2008). Psychological momentum within competitive soccer: Players' perspectives. *Journal of Applied Sport Psychology, 20*, 57–72.
39. Larsen, C.H., & Henriksen, K. (2015). Psychological momentum in team sport: An intervention program in professional soccer. *Sport Science Review, 24*(1–2), 27–40.
40. Moesch, K., & Apitzsch, E. (2012). How do coaches experience psychological momentum? A qualitative study of female elite handball teams. *Sport Psychologist, 26*, 435–453.
41. Briki, W., Hartigh, R.J.R.D, Markman, K.D., Micallef, J-P., & Gernigon, C. (2013). How psychological momentum changes in athletes during a sport competition. *Psychology of Sport and Exercise, 14*, 389–396.
42. Vealey, R.S., Low, W., Pierce, S., & Quinones-Paredes, D. (2014). Choking in sport: ACT on it! *Journal of Sport Psychology in Action, 5*, 156–169.
43. Foss, M. (2013, September 25). The 10 greatest comebacks in sports history. *USA Today Sports*. http://ftw.usatoday.com/2013/09/the-10-greatest-comebacks-in-all-of-sports
44. Hill, D.M., & Hemmings, B. (2015). A phenomenological exploration of coping responses associated with choking in sport. *Qualitative Research in Sport, Exercise and Health, 7*(4), 521–538.
45. Allan, T.J. (2014, October 23). 3 cues for better basketball shooting. *USA Basketball*. www.usab.com/youth/news/2012/08/3cues-for-better-basketball-shooting.aspx
46. Lemire, J. (2015, June 2). With psychologists, MLB teams try to win "six inches between the ears." *USA Today Sports*. www.usatoday.com/story/sports/mlb/2015/06/02/major-league-baseball-sports-psychology/28366403/
47. Bedore, G. (2016, March 10). K-State awaits Kansas in tourney opener. *KU Sports.com*. www2.kusports.com/news/2016/mar/10/k-state-awaits-ku-tourney-opener/
48. Breakey, C., Jones, M., Cunningham, C.T, & Holt, N. (2009). Female athletes' perceptions of a coach's speeches. *International Journal of Sports Science & Coaching, 4*, 489–504.
49. DiCicco, T., & Hacker, C., with Salzberg, C. (2002). *Catch them being good: Everything you need to know to successfully coach girls* (p. 151). New York: Viking.
50. Positive Coaching Alliance. (2015). Brad Stevens: Be great at things that take no talent. *PCA Development Zone* [Audio podcast]. http://devzone.positivecoach.org/resource/audio/brad-stevens-be-great-things-take-no-talent
51. Russell, M., West, D. J., Harper, L. D., Cook, C. J., & Kilduff, L. P. (2015). Half-time strategies to enhance second-half performance in team-sports players: A review and recommendations. *Sports Medicine, 45*, 353–364.
52. Ballard, C. (2015, February 20). Warriors: From one-dimensional and one-and-done to NBA title favorites. *Sports Illustrated*. www.si.com/nba/2015/02/20/golden-state-warriors-steve-kerr-stephen-curry-klay-thompson-joe-lacob
53. Ravizza, K., & Osborne, T. (1991). Nebraska's 3 R's: One-play-at-a-time preperformance routine for collegiate football. *Sport Psychologist, 5*, 256–265.
54. Burton, D., & Raedeke, T.D. (2008). *Sport psychology for coaches*. Champaign, IL: Human Kinetics.
55. Pollard, R., & Pollard, G. (2005). Long-term trends in home advantage in professional team sports in North America and England (1876–2003). *Journal of Sports Sciences, 23*, 337–350.
56. Jones, M.B. (2013). The home advantage in individual sports: An augmented review. *Psychology of Sport and Exercise, 14*, 397–404.

57. Pinger, N. (2014, March 4). Home field advantage: The facts and the fiction. *Capital Ideas*. www.chicagobooth.edu/capideas/magazine/spring-2014/home-field-advantage-the-facts-and-the-fiction
58. Burgmann, T. (2013, February 27). B.C. hockey coach jailed for 15 days for tripping 13-year-old during post-game handshake. *National Post*. http://news.nationalpost.com/news/canada/b-c-hockey-coach-jailed-for-15-days-for-tripping-13-year-old-during-post-game-handshake
59. Hanzus, D. (2011, October 16). Bad blood: Schwartz, Harbaugh have words after 49ers' win. *NFL.com*. www.nfl.com/news/story/09000d5d8232bfe9/article/bad-blood-schwartz-harbaugh-have-words-after-49ers-win
60. Gilbert, W.D., Gilbert, J.N., & Trudel, P. (2001). Coaching strategies for youth sports. Part 2: Personal characteristics, parental influence, and team organization. *Journal of Physical Education, Recreation and Dance*, *72*(5), 41–46.
61. Benjamin, A. (2011, June 2). Ex-BU professor has them psyched up. *Boston Globe*. www.boston.com/sports/hockey/bruins/articles/2011/06/02/ex_bu_professor_has_them_psyched_up/
62. Pettit, T. (2008). *Talent and the secret life of teams* (see poem "After the Loss" on p. 55). Marceline, MO: Walsworth.
63. Tyson, P., & Binder, D. (2014). *Coaching cross country successfully*. Champaign, IL: Human Kinetics.
64. Miller, G.A., Lutz, R., & Fredenburg, K. (2012). Outstanding high school coaches: Philosophies, views, and practices. *Journal of Physical Education, Recreation & Dance*, *83*(2), 24–29.
65. American College of Sports Medicine & Academy of Nutrition and Dietetics, and Dietitians of Canada. (2016). Nutrition and athletic performance. *Medicine & Science in Sports & Exercise*, *48*(3), 543–568.
66. Haberstroh, T. (2015, June 14). LeBron James' unfathomable workload. *ESPN*. http://espn.go.com/nba/playoffs/2015/story/_/id/13071387/lebron-james-unfathomable-workload
67. McHugh, M.P., & Cosgrave, C.H. (2010). To stretch or not to stretch: The role of stretching in injury prevention and performance. *Scandinavian Journal of Medicine & Science in Sports*, *20*, 169–181.
68. Kay, A.D., & Blazevich, A.J. (2012). Effect of acute static stretch on maximal muscle performance: A systematic review. *Medicine & Science in Sports & Exercise*, *44*(1), 154–164.
69. Gilbert, W., & Trudel, P. (2013). The role of deliberate practice in becoming an expert coach: Part 2—reflection. *Olympic Coach Magazine*, *24*(1), 35–44.
70. Hughes, C., Lee, S., & Chesterfield, G. (2009). Innovation in sports coaching: The implementation of reflective cards. *Reflective Practice*, *10*(3), 367–384.
71. Hoch, D. (2011). *Blueprint for better coaching*. Ithaca, NY: MomentumMedia.
72. Elberse, A., & Dye, T. (2012, September 20). *Sir Alex Ferguson: Managing Manchester United* [Report number 9-513-051]. Boston: Harvard Business School.

## Chapter 10

1. Wooten, M., & Wooten, J. (2013). *Coaching basketball successfully* (3rd ed.). Champaign, IL: Human Kinetics.
2. Nater, S., & Gallimore, R. (2010). *You haven't taught until they have learned: John Wooden's teaching principles and practice*. Morgantown, WV: Fitness Information Technology.
3. Coughlin, T. (2013). *Earn the right to win: How success in any field starts with superior preparation*. New York: Portfolio/Penguin.
4. Gillham, A., Hansen, K., & Brady, C. (2015). Coach evaluation from three perspectives: An athletic director, a coach and a consultant. *International Sport Coaching Journal*, *2*, 192–200.
5. Huber, J. (2015). Coach evaluation from three perspectives: An athletic director, a coach and a consultant: A commentary. *International Sport Coaching Journal*, *2*, 201–202.
6. Snyder, C. (2015). Coach evaluation from three perspectives: An athletic director, a coach and a consultant: A commentary. *International Sport Coaching Journal*, *2*, 206–207.
7. Hammermeister, J.J. (2010). *Cornerstones of coaching: The building blocks of success for sport coaches and teams*. Traverse City, MI: Cooper.
8. Hoch, D. (2008, Winter). The key to a better evaluation process is helping your coaches understand it. *Interscholastic Athletic Administration*, 18–19.
9. Sheridan, M.P. (2013, Spring/Summer). Using evidence (not simply win/loss

records) to evaluate coaching effectiveness. *FutureFocus*, 8–12.

10. National Association for Sport and Physical Activity. (2006). *National standards for sport coaches: Quality coaches, quality sports* (2nd ed.). Reston, VA: Author.
11. Bowden, B., with Schlabach, M. (2010). *Called to coach: Reflections on life, faith, and football.* New York: Simon & Schuster.
12. Gadowsky, G. (2016). Communicating a team mission. In J. Bertagna (ed.), *The hockey coaching bible: Insights and strategies from 16 of the sport's top coaches* (pp. 13–23). Champaign, IL: Human Kinetics.
13. O'Boyle, I. (2014). Determining best practice in performance monitoring and evaluation of sport coaches: Lessons from the traditional business environment. *International Journal of Sports Science & Coaching, 9*(1), 233–246.
14. Hansen, S. (2015, December 4). *The All Blacks story.* Presentation at the 2015 New Zealand Connecting Coaches Conference [Video]. http://connectingcoaches.org.nz/resources/
15. Gilbert, W. (2015, December 15). What I learned from the All Blacks coaches. *Human Kinetics Coach Education Center.* www.asep.com/news/ShowArticle.cfm?ID=257
16. Lacy, A.C. (2015). *Measurement and evaluation in physical education and exercise science* (7th ed.). San Francisco: Pearson/Benjamin Cummings.
17. Hoch, D. (2013). Personnel management. In M.L. Blackburn, E. Forsyth, J.R. Olson, & B. Whitehead (eds.), *NIAA's guide to interscholastic athletic administration* (pp. 55–73). Champaign, IL: Human Kinetics.
18. Gillham, A., Burton, D., & Gillham, E. (2013). Going beyond won-loss record to identify successful coaches: Development and preliminary validation of the Coaching Success Questionnaire-2. *International Journal of Sports Science & Coaching, 8*(1), 115–138. (To obtain a copy of the Coaching Success Questionnaire-2, contact Dr. Andrew Gillham at drgillham@gmail.com or visit www.ludusconsulting.biz.)
19. Mallett, C., & Côté, J. (2006). Beyond winning and losing: Guidelines for evaluating high performance coaches. *Sport Psychologist, 20,* 213–221. (To obtain a copy of the Coaching Behavior Scale for Sport, contact Dr. Côté , jc46@queensu.ca.)
20. Gilbert, W. (2016, January 11). Keys to creating a winning environment. *Human Kinetics Coach Education Center.* www.asep.com/news/ShowArticle.cfm?ID=258
21. Allain, J., Bloom, G.A., & Gilbert, W. (Forthcoming). *Knowledge and routines of NCAA hockey coaches during intermissions.* Manuscript in preparation.
22. Kotler, S. (2014). *The rise of superman: Decoding the science of ultimate human performance.* Boston: Houghton, Mifflin, Harcourt.
23. Stice, S. (2013). Student-athlete development. In M.L. Blackburn, E. Forsyth, J.R. Olson, & B. Whitehead (Eds.), *NIAA's guide to interscholastic athletic administration* (pp. 75–94). Champaign, IL: Human Kinetics. [p. 91]
24. Tyson, P., & Binder, D. (2014). *Coaching cross country successfully.* Champaign, IL: Human Kinetics.
25. Sabock, M.D., & Sabock, R.J. (2011). *Coaching: A realistic perspective* (10th ed.). Lanham, MD: Rowman & Littlefield.
26. Beswick, B. (2016). *One goal: The mindset of winning soccer teams.* Champaign, IL: Human Kinetics.
27. Juravich, M., & Babiak, K. (2015). Examining positive affect and job performance in sport organizations: A conceptual model using an emotional intelligence lens. *Journal of Applied Sport Psychology, 27*(4), 477–491.
28. Pensgaard, A.M., and Duda, J.L. (2003). Sydney 2000: The interplay between emotions, coping, and the performance of Olympic-level athletes. *Sport Psychologist, 17,* 253–267.
29. Wong, C.S., & Law, K.S. (2002). The effects of leader and follower emotional intelligence on performance and attitude: An exploratory study. *Leadership Quarterly, 13*(3), 243–274.
30. Law, K.S., Wong, C-S., & Song, L.J. (2004). The construct and criterion validity of emotional intelligence and its potential utility for management studies. *Journal of Applied Psychology, 89*(3), 483–496.
31. Gable, D. (1999). *Coaching wrestling successfully.* Champaign, IL: Human Kinetics.
32. Medeiros, J. (2014, January 23). The winning formula: Data analytics has become the latest tool keeping football teams one step ahead. *Wired.* www.wired.co.uk/magazine/archive/2014/01/features/the-winning-formula
33. Lewis, M. (2004). *Moneyball: The art of winning an unfair game.* New York: Norton.

34. Topend Sports Network. (2016). *Rob's home of fitness testing.* www.topendsports.com/testing/index.htm

35. Dorrance, A., & Nash, T. (1996). *Training soccer champions.* Chapel Hill, NC: JTC Sports.

36. Hebert, M. (2014). *Thinking volleyball: Inside the game with a coaching legend.* Champaign, IL: Human Kinetics.

37. Widmer, S. (2012). Planning for success. In D. Hannula & N. Thornton (eds.), *The swim coaching bible: Volume II* (pp. 85–121). Champaign, IL: Human Kinetics.

38. Dunn, P., & Bennett, B. (2010). Evaluating practice session. In B. Bennett (ed.), *Practice perfect baseball* (pp. 209–230). Champaign, IL: Human Kinetics.

39. Saban, N., & Curtis, B. (2007). *How good do you want to be? A champion's tips on how to lead and succeed* (p. 85). New York: Ballantine.

40. International Council for Coaching Excellence, Association of Summer Olympic International Federations, & Leeds Metropolitan University. (2013). *International sport coaching framework* (version 1.2). Champaign, IL: Human Kinetics.

41. GoPro. (2015). *GoPro presents Jon Gruden's field guide.* https://gopro.com/news/gopro-presents-jon-grudens-field-guide

42. Côté, J., & Gilbert, W.D. (2009). An integrative definition of coaching effectiveness and expertise. *International Journal of Sports Science & Coaching, 4,* 307–323.

43. Vierimaa, M., Erickson, K., Côté, J., & Gilbert, W. (2012). Positive youth development: A measurement framework for sport. *International Journal of Sports Science & Coaching, 7,* 603–616.

44. Gilbert, W., Dubina, N., & Emmett, M. (2012). Exploring the potential of assessment efficacy in sports coaching: A commentary. *International Journal of Sports Science & Coaching,* 7, 211–214.

45. Newton, M., Duda, J.L., & Zenong, Y. (2000). Examination of the psychometric properties of the Perceived Motivational Climate in Sport Questionnaire-2 in a sample of female athletes. *Journal of Sports Sciences, 18,* 275–290.

46. Appleton, P.R., Ntoumanis, N., Quested, E., Viladrich, C., & Duda, J.L. (2016). Initial validation of the coach-created Empowering and Disempowering Motivational Climate Questionnaire (EDMCQ-C). *Psychology of Sport and Exercise, 22,* 53–65.

47. Cooper Institute. (2015). *Fitnessgram.* www.fitnessgram.net/

48. Gordon, J., & Smith, M. (2015). *You win in the locker room first: The 7 C's to build a winning team in business, sports, and life.* Hoboken, NJ: Wiley.

## Chapter 11

1. Saban, N., & Curtis, B. (2007). *How good do you want to be? A champion's tips on how to lead and succeed* (p. 85). New York: Ballantine.

2. Pim, R. (2010). *Perfect phrases for coaches.* New York. McGraw-Hill.

3. USA Today. (May 5, 2004). Middle school coach could lose job over Crybaby Award. http://usatoday30.usatoday.com/sports/preps/basketball/2004-05-05-crybaby-award_x.htm

4. CBC News. (2015, March 29). *Winnipeg youth centre criticized after "cry baby" award given to boy.* www.cbc.ca/news/canada/manitoba/winnipeg-youth-centre-criticized-after-cry-baby-award-given-to-boy-1.3014358

5. Steele, B. (2012). Making your program fun for swimmers. In D. Hannula, & N. Thornton, N. (eds.). *The swim coaching bible* (vol. II). Champaign, IL: Human Kinetics.

6. Sabock, M.D., & Sabock, R.J. (2011). *Coaching: A realistic perspective* (10th ed.). Lanham, MD: Rowman & Littlefield.

7. Ehrmann, J., with Ehrmann, P., & Jordan, G. (2011). *Inside out coaching: How sports can transform lives.* New York: Simon & Schuster.

8. Janssen, J. (1999). *Championship team building.* Tucson, AZ: Winning the Mental Game.

9. Gable, D. (1999). *Coaching wrestling successfully.* Champaign, IL: Human Kinetics.

10. Gordon, J. (2015). *The hard hat: A true story about how to be a great teammate.* Hoboken, NJ: John Wiley & Sons.

11. Tyson, P., & Binder, D. (2014). *Coaching cross country successfully.* Champaign, IL: Human Kinetics.

12. Wooten, M., & Wooten, J. (2013). *Coaching basketball successfully* (3rd ed.). Champaign, IL: Human Kinetics.

13. Young, J. Getting the competitive mental edge. In American Football Coaches Association, *The football coaching bible* (pp. 301–313). Champaign, IL: Human Kinetics.

14. Huber, J.J. (2013). *Applying educational psychology in coaching athletes.* Champaign, IL: Human Kinetics.
15. Hayes, N. (2005). *When the game stands tall: The story of the De La Salle Spartans and football's longest winning streak.* Berkeley, CA: Frog.
16. Haldorsen, D. (2015, May 6). 36 great employee recognition ideas your team will love! *LinkedIn: Pulse.* www.linkedin.com/pulse/36-great-employee-recognition-ideas-your-team-love-haldorsen-m-a-
17. Gordon, S., & Gucciardi, D.F. (2011). A strengths-based approach to coaching mental toughness. *Journal of Sport Psychology in Action, 2,* 143–155.
18. DiCicco, T. (2004). Mentoring the next generation of coaches. In National Soccer Coaches Association of America (ed.), *The soccer coaching bible* (pp. 283–293). Champaign, IL: Human Kinetics.
19. Seligman, M.E.P., Steen, T.A., Park, N., & Peterson, C. (2005). Positive psychology progress: Empirical validation of interventions. *American Psychologist, 60*(5), 410–421.
20. Linley, P.A., Woolston, L., & Biswas-Diener, R. (2009). Strengths coaching with leaders. *International Coaching Psychology Review, 4*(1), 37–48.
21. Linley, P.A. (2008). *Average to A+: Realising strengths in yourself and others.* Coventry, UK: CAPP Press.
22. Garrido, A., & Smith, W. (2011). *Life is yours to win: Lessons forged from the purpose, passion, and magic of baseball* (p. 101). New York: Simon & Schuster.
23. Packer, B., & Lazenby, R. (1998). *Why we win: Great American coaches offer their strategies for success in sports and life.* New York: McGraw-Hill.
24. Nater, S., & Gallimore, R. (2010). *You haven't taught until they have learned: John Wooden's teaching principles and practices.* Morgantown, WV: Fitness International Technology.
25. Asplund, J., Lopez, S.J., Hodges, T., & Hartner, J. (2007). *The Clifton StrengthsFinder 2.0 technical report: Development and validation.* http://strengths.gallup.com/private/Resources/CSFTechnicalReport031005.pdf
26. Rath, T. (2007). *StrengthsFinder 2.0.* New York: Gallup.
27. Wood, A.M., Linley, P.A., Maltby, J., Kashdan, T.B., & Hurling, R. (2011). Using personal and psychological strengths leads to increases in well-being over time: A longitudinal study and the development of the strengths use questionnaire. *Personality and Individual Differences, 50,* 15–19.
28. Côté, J., & Gilbert, W.D. (2009). An integrative definition of coaching effectiveness and expertise. *International Journal of Sports Science & Coaching, 4,* 307–323.
29. Gilbert, W., Nater, S., Siwik, M., & Gallimore, R. (2010). The Pyramid of Teaching Success in Sport: Lessons learned from applied science and effective coaches. *Journal of Sport Psychology in Action, 1,* 86–94.
30. Seligman, M.E. (2011). *Flourish: A visionary new understanding of happiness and well-being.* New York: Free Press.
31. Cooperrider, D.L., Whitney, D., & Stavros, J.M. (eds.). (2008). *Appreciate inquiry: For leaders of change* (2nd ed.). Brunswick, OH: Crown Custom.
32. Babcock, M., & Larsen, R. (2012). *Leave no doubt: A credo for chasing your dreams.* Montreal, CA: McGill University Press.
33. Bertram, R., Culver, D., & Gilbert, W. (2016). Using appreciative inquiry to create high-impact coach learning: Insights from a decade of applied research. *AI Practitioner: International Journal of Appreciative Inquiry, 18*(2), 58–64.
34. Trudel, P., Rodrigue, F., & Gilbert, W. (2016). The journey from competent to innovator: Using appreciative inquiry to enhance high performance coaching. *AI Practitioner: International Journal of Appreciative Inquiry, 18*(2), 39–45.
35. Elberse, A., & Ferguson, A. (2013, October). Ferguson's formula. *Harvard Business Review,* 2–11.
36. Dodd, M. (2012, March 6). Which city has the hottest seats for its pro coaches? *USA Today.* http://usatoday30.usatoday.com/sports/story/2012-02-29/managers-coaches-tenure/53376918/1
37. Bachman, R. (2012, September 17). The conferences where coaches rent. *Wall Street Journal.* http://online.wsj.com/news/articles/SB10000872396390443816804578000344106107644?mod=_newsreel_3
38. Chase, M.A., & Martin, E. (2012). Coaching efficacy beliefs. In P. Potrac, W. Gilbert, & J. Denison (eds.), *Routledge handbook of sports coaching* (pp. 68–80). London: Routledge.
39. Feltz, D.L., Chase, M.A., Moritz, S.E., & Sullivan, P.J. (1999). A conceptual model of coaching efficacy: Preliminary investigation

and instrument development. *Journal of Educational Psychology, 91*(4), 765–776.

40. Dahlin, S., & Pastore, D.L. (2016). The academic dimension: Its impact on the model of coaching efficacy. *Applied Research in Coaching and Athletics Annual*, 31, 19–44.
41. Myers, N.D., Feltz, D.L., Chase, M.A., Reckase, M.D., & Hancock, G.R. (2008). The Coaching Efficacy Scale II—High School Teams. *Educational and Psychological Measurement, 68*(6), 1059–1076.
42. Gilbert, W.D., Côté, J., & Mallett, C. (2006). Developmental paths and activities of successful sport coaches. *International Journal of Sports Sciences & Coaching, 1*(1), 69–76.
43. Gilbert, W.D., Lichktenwaldt, L., Gilbert, J.N., Zelezny, L., & Côté, J. (2009). Developmental profiles of successful high school coaches. *International Journal of Sports Science & Coaching, 4*, 415–431.
44. Crust, L., & Clough, P.J. (2011). Developing mental toughness: From research to practice. *Journal of Sport Psychology in Action, 2*, 21–32.
45. Connaughton, D., Hanton, S., & Jones, G. (2010). The development and maintenance of mental toughness in the world's best performers. *The Sport Psychologist, 24*, 168–193.
46. Madrigal, L., Hamill, S., & Gill, D. (2013). Mind over matter: The development of the Mental Toughness Scale (MTS). *The Sport Psychologist, 27*, 62–77.

## Chapter 12

1. Berra, Y., & Kaplan, D. (2001). *When you come to a fork in the road, take it! Inspiration and wisdom from one of baseball's greatest heroes.* New York: Hyperion.
2. Webster, C.A., & Schempp, P.G. (2008). Self-monitoring: Demystifying the wonder of expert teaching. *Journal of Physical Education, Recreation & Dance, 79*(1), 23–29.
3. Schempp, P.G., Webster, C., McCulick, B.A., Busch, C., & Sannen Mason, I. (2006). The self-monitoring strategies of expert sport instructors. *International Journal of Sports Science & Coaching, 1*(1), 25–35.
4. Schempp, P.G. (2016, February 3). One game short of the Super Bowl: "You win or you learn." *Performance Matters.* www.performancemattersinc.com/posts/one-game-short-of-the-super-bowl-you-win-or-you-learn/
5. DiCicco, T., & Hacker, C., with Salzberg, C. (2002). *Catch them being good: Everything you need to know to successfully coach girls.* New York: Viking.
6. Michel, J. (2014, August 22). Great leadership isn't about you. *Harvard Business Review.* http://blogs.hbr.org/2014/08/great-leadership-isnt-about-you/
7. Senge, P.M. (2006). *The fifth discipline: The art & practice of the learning organization.* New York: Doubleday.
8. Teaff, G. (2012). *A coach's influence: Beyond the game.* Lewiston, NY: IBP.
9. Gilbert, W., Nater, S., Siwik, M., & Gallimore, R. (2010). The Pyramid of Teaching Success in Sport: Lessons learned from applied science and effective coaches. *Journal of Sport Psychology in Action, 1*, 86–94.
10. Connell, J. (2015, February 21). Prestige in the pool: Drury swimming success. *Springfield News-Leader.* www.news-leader.com/story/sports/college/2015/02/21/family-atmosphere-breeds-unmatched-success-drury-swimming/23786233/
11. Saban, N., & Curtis, B. (2007). *How good do you want to be? A champion's tips on how to lead and succeed.* New York: Ballantine.
12. Yocum, G. (2011, September). My shot: Sean Foley. *Golf Digest*, September, www.golfdigest.com/story/sean-foley-one-shot?currentPage=1
13. Emerling, B.A., & Graff-Ermeling, G. (2016). *Teaching better: Igniting and sustaining instructional improvement.* Thousand Oaks, CA: Corwin.
14. Torre, J., & Dreher, H. (1999). *Joe Torre's ground rules for winners.* New York: Hyperion.
15. Greene, R. (2012). *Mastery.* New York: Penguin.
16. Arizona Sidelines Coaching Blog. (2014, March 8). California adventures—riding the wave [web log post]. http://arizonasidelines.blogspot.com/2014_03_01_archive.html
17. Dweck, C. (2006). *Mindset: The new psychology of success.* New York: Ballantine.
18. Dweck, C.S., & Leggett, E.L. (1998). A social-cognitive approach to motivation and personality. *Psychological Review, 95*(2), 256–273.
19. Chase, M.A. (2010). Should coaches believe in innate ability? The importance of leadership mindset. *Quest, 62*(3), 296–307.
20. Dweck, C. (2006). *Test your mindset.* http://mindsetonline.com/testyourmindset/step4.php

21. Wilson, R. (2014, December 2). *Growth vs. fixed mindset for elementary students: What kind of mindset do you have?* www.coetail.com/wayfaringpath/2014/12/02/growth-vs-fixed-mindset-for-elementary-students/
22. Packer, B., & Lazenby, R. (1998). *Why we win: Great American coaches offer their strategies for success in sports and life.* New York: McGraw-Hill.
23. Garrido, A., & Smith, W. (2011). *Life is yours to win: Lessons forged from the purpose, passion, and magic of baseball* (p. 101). New York: Simon & Schuster.
24. Schwab, D. (Producer). (2015, September 3). *The Seth Davis Show: Nick Saban* [video podcast]. *Campus Insiders.* http://campusinsiders.com/shows/sethdavisshow#/episode/w1NmVjdzpHivdF34UP9HttIw-WfrHuaBO
25. Jenkins, L. (2014, September 29). Heat and light. *Sports Illustrated, 121*(12), 56–63.
26. Voight, M., & Carroll, P. (2006). Applying sport psychology philosophies, principles, and practices onto the gridiron: An interview with USC football coach Pete Carroll. *International Journal of Sports Science & Coaching, 1*(4), 321–342.
27. MacKay, H. (2014, October 12). A successful person is an average person, focused. *Des Moines Register.* www.desmoinesregister.com/story/money/business/2014/10/12/harvey-mackay-focus-succeed/17173785/
28. Rother, M. (2010). *Toyota kata: Managing people for improvement, adaptiveness, and superior results.* New York: McGraw-Hill.
29. Gawande, A. (2007). *Better: A surgeon's notes on performance.* New York: Picador.
30. Stigler, J.W., & Hiebert, J. (1999). *The teaching gap: Best ideas from the world's teachers for improving education in the classroom.* New York: The Free Press.
31. Senge, P., Cambron-McCabe, N., Lucas, T., Smith, B., Dutton, J., & Kleiner, A. (2000). *Schools that learn: A fifth discipline fieldbook for educators, parents, and everyone who cares about education.* New York: Doubleday.
32. Widmer, S. (2012). Planning for success. In D. Hannula & N. Thornton (ed.), *The swim coaching bible: Volume II* (pp. 85–121). Champaign, IL: Human Kinetics.
33. Kyle, C., & Hodermarsky, M. (1997). *The object of the game.* Dubuque, IA: Kendall/Hunt.
34. Summitt, P., & Jenkins, S. (1998). *Raise the roof: The inspiring inside story of the Tennessee Lady Vols' groundbreaking season in women's college basketball.* New York: Broadway.
35. Gilbert, W.D., & Côté, J. (2013). Defining coaching effectiveness: A focus on coaches' knowledge. In P. Potrac, W. Gilbert, & J. Denison (eds.), *Routledge handbook of sports coaching* (pp. 147–159). London: Routledge.
36. Trudel, P., Rodrigue, F., & Gilbert, W. (2016). The journey from competent to innovator: Using appreciative inquiry to enhance high performance coaching. *AI Practitioner: International Journal of Appreciative Inquiry, 18*(2), 39–45.
37. Huber, J.J. (2013). *Applying educational psychology in coaching athletes* (p. 8). Champaign, IL: Human Kinetics.
38. Harville, J. (2005). Decision making. In C. Reynaud (ed.), *She can coach: Tools for success from 20 top women coaches* (pp. 73–85). Champaign, IL: Human Kinetics.
39. Gilbert, W., & Trudel, P. (2001). Learning to coach through experience: Reflection in model youth sport coaches. *Journal of Teaching in Physical Education, 21*, 16–34.
40. Schön, D.A. (1983). *The reflective practitioner. How professionals think in action.* New York: Basic Books.
41. Hodge, K., Henry, G., & Smith, W. (2014). A case study of excellence in elite sport: Motivational climate in a world champion team. *The Sport Psychologist, 28*, 60–74.
42. Gilbert, W.D., & Trudel, P. (2004). Analysis of coaching science research published from 1970–2001. *Research Quarterly for Exercise and Sport, 75*, 388–399.
43. Gilbert , W. (2014, December 3). *Coaching smart: Using quality research and best practices to excel in sport* [webinar]. ww.humankinetics.com/human-kinetics-coach-education-webinars/human-kinetics-coach-education-webinars/coaching-smart-using-quality-research-and-best-practices-to-excel-in-sport
44. Nater, S., & Gallimore, R. (2010). *You haven't taught until they have learned.* Morgantown, WV: Fitness Information Technology.
45. Jacobs, F., Claringbould, I., & Knoppers, A. (2014). Becoming a "good coach." *Sport, Education and Society, 19*(8), 1–20.
46. sports coach UK. (2014). Using critical reflection to become a "good coach."

*Sports Coach UK Research Summary 11*. www.sportscoachuk.org/resource/research-summary-no11-using-critical-reflection-become-%E2%80%98good-coach%E2%80%99

47. Brendel, D. (2014, September 19). How philosophy makes you a better leader. *Harvard Business Review*. http://blogs.hbr.org/2014/09/how-philosophy-makes-you-a-better-leader/
48. Economy, P. (2016, March 10). These 7 questions will change your life. *Inc.* www.inc.com/peter-economy/these-7-questions-will-change-your-life.html?cid=sf01001&sr_share=twitter
49. Soltanzadeh, S., & Mooney, M. (2016). Systems thinking and team performance analysis. *International Sport Coaching Journal*, *3*(2), 184–191.
50. Krzyzewski, M., & Spatola, J.K. (2009). *The gold standard: Building a world-class team*. New York: Business Plus.

## Chapter 13

1. Sipple, S.M. (2015, December 17). Cook's evolution puts Huskers on brink of crown. *Lincoln Journal Star*. http://journalstar.com/sports/huskers/sipple/steven-m-sipple-cook-s-evolution-helps-put-huskers-on/article_4211e189-f6e4-5634-9744-ddc94d58bb09.html
2. Sipple, S.M. (2015, December 8). BYU coach appreciates Cook's open-door policy. *Lincoln Journal Star*. http://journalstar.com/sports/huskers/sipple/steven-m-sipple-byu-coach-appreciates-cook-s-open-door/article_42b50b05-9100-58ac-af5d-89ddf0905a5b.html
3. Schwab, D. (producer). (2015, September 3). *The Seth Davis Show: Nick Saban* [video podcast]. *Campus Insiders*. http://campusinsiders.com/shows/sethdavisshow#/episode/w1NmVjdzpHivdF34UP9HttlwWfrHuaBO
4. Narducci, M. (2015, June 7). U.S. coach Jill Ellis learned from UCLA legend John Wooden. *Philly.com*. http://articles.philly.com/2015-06-07/sports/63120322_1_u-s-soccer-lauren-holiday-u-s-women
5. Keh, A. (2014, November 13). This teacher spends life being taught: Warriors coach Steve Kerr's style is molded by many mentors. *New York Times*. www.nytimes.com/2014/11/14/sports/basketball/warriors-coach-steve-kerrs-style-is-molded-by-many-mentors.html?_r=0
6. Ruley, A. (2005). Networking. In C. Reynaud (ed.), *She can coach: Tools for success from 20 top women coaches*, (pp. 245–252). Champaign, IL: Human Kinetics.
7. Hoch, D. (2002, December). Expand your horizon with networking. *Coach and Athletic Director*, *72*(5), 6–7.
8. Robinson, E., & Lapchick, R. (1999). *Never before, never again: The stirring autobiography of Eddie Robinson, the winningest coach in the history of college football*. New York: St. Martin's.
9. VanSickle, G. (2015, June 23). A Q&A with Jordan Spieth swing coach Cameron McCormick. *Golf.com*. www.golf.com/tour-and-news/interview-cameron-mccormick-swing-coach-jordan-spieth
10. Fellowship of Christian Athletes. (2010). *The greatest coach ever: Tony Dungy, David Robinson, Tom Osborne and others pay tribute to the timeless wisdom and insights of John Wooden*. Ventura, CA: Regal.
11. Ansberry, C. (2015, October 14). Inspiring messages from a coach: Why longtime coach Jerry Wainwright sends hundreds of notes every week to former players, colleagues. *Wall Street Journal*. www.wsj.com/articles/inspiring-messages-from-a-coach-1444850689
12. Gerdes, D. (2014, November 21). *Using your network in leadership positions to build relationships*. www.nfhs.org/articles/using-your-network-in-leadership-positions-to-build-relationships/
13. Sanders, T. (2003). *Love is the killer app: How to win business and influence friends*. New York: Three Rivers.
14. Hoch, D. (2010, Fall). An integrated mentoring program for your coaches. *Interscholastic Athletic Administration*, 18–19.
15. Stefanac, R. (2015). Guiding lights: Having a coach mentor can be essential in your sport development. *Coaches Plan*, *22*(3), 13–15. www.coachesplan-digital.com/coachesplan/fall_2015?pg=2#pg2
16. Bloom, G.A. (2013). Mentoring for sport coaches. In P. Potrac, W. Gilbert, & J. Denison (eds.), *Routledge handbook of sports coaching* (pp. 476–485). London: Routledge.
17. Robertson, S. (2014). *Groundbreaker: Debbie Muir accorded her sport's highest international honour*. www.coach.ca/groundbreaker-debbie-muir-accorded-her-sport-s-highest-international-honour-p154743

18. Hoch, D. (2013). Personnel management. In M.L. Blackburn, E. Forsyth, J.R. Olson, & B. Whitehead (eds.), *NIAA's guide to interscholastic athletic administration* (pp. 55–73). Champaign, IL: Human Kinetics.
19. Robertson, S., & Hubball, H. (2005). Coach-to-coach mentoring: Raising the bar. *Strategies, 18*(5), 6–10.
20. DiCicco, T. (2004). Mentoring the next generation of coaches. In National Soccer Coaches Association of America (ed.), *The soccer coaching bible*, (pp. 283–293). Champaign, IL: Human Kinetics.
21. American Football Coaches Association. (2002). *The football coaching bible*. Champaign, IL: Human Kinetics.
22. Muir, D. (2009). The value of mentoring. *Coaches Plan, 16*(3), 45.
23. Callary, B., Culver, D., Werthner, P., & Bales, J. (2014). An overview of seven national high performance coach education programs. *International Sport Coaching Journal, 1*, 152–164.
24. Zehntner, C., & McMahon, J.A. (2014). Mentoring in coaching: The means of correct training? An autoethnographic exploration of one Australian swimming coach's experiences. *Qualitative Research in Sport, Exercise and Health, 6*(4), 596–616.
25. Koh, K.T., Bloom, G.A., Fairhurst, K., Paiement, D.M., & Kee, Y.H. (2014). An investigation of a formalized mentoring program for novice basketball coaches. *International Journal of Sport Psychology, 45*, 11–32.
26. Bertram, R., Culver, D.M., & Gilbert, W. (2016). Creating value in a sport coach community of practice: A collaborative inquiry. *International Sport Coaching Journal, 3*, 2–16.
27. Stigler, J.W., & Hiebert, J. (1999). *The teaching gap: Best ideas from the world's teachers for improving education in the classroom*. New York: The Free Press.
28. Ermeling, B.A., & Ermeling, G. (2014). Learning to learn from teaching: A first-hand account of lesson study in Japan. *International Journal for Lesson and Learning Studies, 3*(2), 170–191.
29. Ermeling, B.A. (2012). Improving teaching through continuous learning: The inquiry process John Wooden used to become Coach of the Century. *Quest, 64*(3), 197–208.
30. Bertram, R., & Gilbert, W. (2011). Learning communities as continuing professional development for sport coaches. *Journal of Coaching Education*, 4, 40–61.
31. Gilbert, W., Gallimore, R., & Trudel, P. (2009). A learning community approach to coach development in youth sport. *Journal of Coaching Education, 2*(2), 1–21.
32. Krzyzewski, M., & Spatola, J.K. (2009). *The gold standard: Building a world-class team* (p. 58). New York: Business Plus.
33. Wegner, E., McDermott, R., & Snyder, W.M. (2002). *Cultivating communities of practice: A guide to managing knowledge*. Boston: Harvard Business School.
34. Alliance of Women's Coaches. (2016). *Power hours*. http://gocoaches.org/programs-events/power-hours/
35. Martel, K. (2015). USA Hockey's American Development Model: Changing the coaching and player development paradigm. *International Sport Coaching Journal, 2*, 39–49.
36. Diment, G.M. (2014). Mental skills training in soccer: A drill-based approach. *Journal of Sport Psychology in Action, 5*, 14–27.
37. Gilbert, W., Gallimore, R., & Trudel, P. (2009). A learning community approach to coach development in youth sport. *Journal of Coaching Education, 2*(2), 1–21.
38. Culver, D.M., Trudel, P., & Werthner, P. (2009). A sport leader's attempt to foster a coaches' community of practice. *International Journal of Sports Science & Coaching, 4*(3), 365–383.
39. Gordon, S., & Gucciardi, D.F. (2011). A strengths-based approach to coaching mental toughness. *Journal of Sport Psychology in Action, 2*, 143–155.
40. Halpern, P. (2014, December 8). Einstein knew when to turn off the phone. *Fresno Bee*. www.fresnobee.com/opinion/article19528128.html
41. Wuchty, S., Jones, B.F., & Uzzi, B. (2007). The increasing dominance of teams in production of knowledge. *Science, 316*, 1036–1039.
42. Stokols, D., Hall, K.L., Taylor, B.K., and Moser, R.P. (2008). The science of team science: Overview of the field and introduction to the supplement. *American Journal of Preventive Medicine, 35*, S77–S89.
43. Elberse, A., & Ferguson, A. (2013, October). Ferguson's formula. *Harvard Business Review*, 2–11.
44. Baghurst, T.M., & Parish, A. (2010). *Case studies in coaching: Dilemmas and ethics in competitive school sports*. Scottsdale, AZ: Holcomb Hathaway.
45. International Council for Coaching Excellence, Association of Summer Olympic

International Federations, & Leeds Metropolitan University. (2013). *International sport coaching framework* (version 1.2). Champaign, IL: Human Kinetics.

46. National Association for Sport and Physical Education. (2006). *National standards for sport coaches: Quality coaches, quality sports* (2nd ed.). Reston, VA: Author.
47. Culver, D.M., & Trudel, P. (2006). Cultivating coaches' communities of practice: Developing the potential for learning through interactions. In R.L. Jones (ed.), *The sports coach as educator: Re-conceptualising sports coaching* (pp. 97–112). London: Routledge.
48. Turner, R. (2013). Technology. In M.L. Blackburn, E. Forsyth, J.R. Olson, & B. Whitehead (eds.), *NIAA's guide to interscholastic athletic administration* (pp. 189–219). Champaign, IL: Human Kinetics.
49. Harville, J. (2005). Decision making. In C. Reynaud (ed.), *She can coach: Tools for success from 20 top women coaches* (pp. 73–85). Champaign, IL: Human Kinetics.
50. Dorrance, A., & Nash, T. (1996). *Training soccer champions*. Brattleboro, VT: Echo Point Books & Media.
51. Wang, J., & Straub, W.F. (2012). An investigation into the coaching approach of a successful world class soccer coach: Anson Dorrance. *International Journal of Sports Science & Coaching, 7*(3), 431–447.
52. Gallimore, R., Gilbert, W., & Nater, S. (2013). Reflective practice and ongoing learning: A coach's ten year journey. *Reflective Practice, 15*(2), 268–288.

## Chapter 14

1. Short, S.E., Short, M.W., & Haugen, C.R. (2015). The relationship between efficacy and burnout in coaches. *International Journal of Coaching Science, 9*(1), 37–49.
2. Saxon, M. (2015, October 23). Don Mattingly's Dodgers exit sincerely mutual, comes with "lot of emotions." *ESPN*. http://espn.go.com/losangeles/mlb/story/_/id/13949956/don-mattingly-says-decision-leave-losangeles-dodgers-came-days-meetings
3. Hayes, N. (2005). *When the game stands tall: The story of the De La Salle Spartans and football's longest winning streak*. Berkeley, CA: Frog.
4. Auriemma, G., & MacMullan, J. (2006). *Geno: In pursuit of perfection*. New York: Warner.
5. Etzel, E., McAlarnen, M., Gross, M., & Dieffenbach, K. (2015). Mindfulness for the elite coach. *Olympic Coach Magazine, 26*(3), 32–38.
6. Kroner, F. (2015, June 11). Is coaching worth the trouble? *News-Gazette*. www.news-gazette.com/sports/prep-sports/baseball/2015-06-11/kroner-coaching-worth-trouble.html
7. Weinberg, R.S., & Gould, D. (2015). *Foundations of sport and exercise psychology* (6th ed.). Champaign, IL: Human Kinetics.
8. Kolbenschlag, M. (1976). Tranquilizers, towel chewing, tantrums: All are part of coach stress. *Physician and Sportsmedicine, 4*(1), 97–101.
9. Schlabach, M. (2015, October 13). Steve Spurrier announces resignation. *ESPN*. http://espn.go.com/college-football/story/_/id/13879057/steve-spurrier-south-carolina-gamecocks-announces-resignation
10. Olusoga, P., Butt, J., Maynard, I., & Hays, K. (2010). Stress and coping: A study of world class coaches. *Journal of Applied Sport Pedagogy, 22*, 274–293.
11. Frey, M. (2007). College coaches' experiences with stress—"problem solvers" have problems too. *The Sport Psychologist, 21*, 38–57.
12. Olusoga, P., Butt, J., Hays, K., & Maynard, I.W. (2009). Stress in elite sports coaching: Identifying stressors. *Journal of Applied Sport Pedagogy, 21*, 442–459.
13. Price, M.S., & Weiss, M.R. (2000). Relationships among coach burnout, coach behaviors, and athletes' psychological responses. *The Sport Psychologist, 14*, 391–409.
14. Wang, J., & Ramsey, J. (1998). The relationship of school type, coaching experience, gender and age to new coaches' challenges and barriers at the collegiate level. *Annual for Research in Coaching and Athletics, 13*, 1–22.
15. Thelwell, R.C., Weston, N.J.V., Greenlees, I.A., & Hutchings, N. (2008). Stressors in elite sport: A coach perspective. *Journal of Sports Sciences, 26*, 905–918.
16. Raedeke, T.D., & Kenttä, G. (2013). Coach burnout. In P. Potrac, W. Gilbert, & J. Denison (eds.), *Routledge handbook of sports coaching* (pp. 424). London: Routledge.
17. Fletcher, D., & Scott, M. (2010). Psychological stress in sports coaches: A review of concepts, research, and practice. *Journal of Sports Sciences, 28*(2), 127–137.

18. Lonsdale, C., Hodge, K., & Rose, E.A. (2008). The behavioral regulation in sport questionnaire (BRSQ). Instrument development and initial validity evidence. *Journal of Sport and Exercise Psychology, 30*, 323–355.
19. Cohen, S. (n.d.). Perceived Stress Scale (PSS). *Measurement instrument database for the social sciences*. www.midss.org/content/perceived-stress-scale-pss
20. Lundkvist, E, Stenling, A., Gustafsson, H., & Hassmén, P. (2014). How to measure coach burnout: An evaluation of three burnout measures. *Measurement in Physical Education & Exercise Science, 18*, 209–226.
21. Alcaraz, S., Viladrich, C., Torregrosa, M., & Ramis, Y. (2015). Club and players' pressures on the motivation, vitality and stress of development coaches. *International Journal of Sport Science & Coaching, 10*(2–3), 365–378.
22. Solomon, G.B., & Buscombe, R.M. (2013). Expectancy effects in sports coaching. In P. Potrac, W. Gilbert, & J. Denison (eds.), *Routledge handbook of sports coaching* (pp. 247–258). London: Routledge.
23. Summitt, P., & Jenkins, S. (1998). *Raise the roof: The inspiring inside story of the Tennessee Lady Vols' groundbreaking season in women's college basketball*. New York: Broadway.
24. Mandell, N. (2015, January 12). Urban Meyer: "I was addicted to winning at Florida." *USA Today*. http://ftw.usatoday.com/2015/01/urban-meyer-florida
25. Sterkel, J. (2005). Stress management. In C. Reynaud (ed.), *She can coach! Tools for success from 20 top women coaches* (pp. 113–121). Champaign, IL: Human Kinetics.
26. Carlson, R. (1997). *Don't sweat the small stuff . . . and it's all small stuff: Simple ways to keep the little things from taking over your life*. New York: Hyperion.
27. Misra, S. (2015, October 15). Are good habits the secret to success? *Refinery29*. www.refinery29.com/best-productive-work-habits?utm_source=inc&utm_medium=syndication&cid=sf01001#.zru1xm:g9pM
28. Ansberry, C. (2015, October 14). Inspiring messages from a coach: Why longtime coach Jerry Wainwright sends hundreds of notes every week to former players, colleagues. *Wall Street Journal*. www.wsj.com/articles/inspiring-messages-from-a-coach-1444850689
29. Friedman, R. (2015, December 31). 9 productivity tips from people who write about productivity. *Harvard Business Review*. https://hbr.org/2015/12/9-productivity-tips-from-people-who-write-about-productivity?utm_campaign=harvardbiz&utm_source=twitter&utm_medium=social
30. Ehrmann, J., with Ehrmann, P., & Jordan, G. (2011). *Inside out coaching: How sports can transform lives*. New York: Simon & Schuster.
31. Roenigk, A. (2013, August 23). Lotus pose on two. *ESPN*. http://espn.go.com/nfl/story/_/id/9581925/seattle-seahawks-use-unusual-techniques-practice-espn-magazine
32. Rush, I.R. (2014, March 17). Athletes using meditation to improve performance. *Philly.com*. http://articles.philly.com/2014-03-17/news/48269271_1_meditation-jon-kabat-zinn-strength-coach
33. Kerr, J. (2013). *Legacy: 15 lessons in leadership. What the All Blacks can teach us about the business of life*. London: Constable.
34. Scott, E. (2014, December 4). Learn how to meditate: Simple and effective strategies. *About.com*. http://stress.about.com/od/meditation/tp/Learn-How-To-Meditate.htm
35. Longshore, K., & Sachs, M. (2015). Mindfulness training for coaches: A mixed-method exploratory study. *Journal of Clinical Sport Psychology, 9(2)*, 116–137.
36. Levy, A., Nicholls, Marchant, D., & Polman, R. (2009). Organizational stressors, coping, and coping effectiveness: A longitudinal study with an elite coach. *International Journal of Sports Science & Coaching, 4*, 31–45.
37. Sabock, M.D., & Sabock, R.J. (2011). *Coaching: A realistic perspective* (10th ed.). Lanham, MD: Rowman & Littlefield.
38. Thelwell, R.C., Weston, N.J.V., & Greenlees, I.A. (2010). Coping with stressors in elite sport: A coach perspective. *European Journal of Sports Sciences, 10*(4), 243–253.
39. Bowden, B., & Schlabach, M. (2010). *Called to coach: Reflections on life, faith, and football*. New York: Howard.
40. Burton, D., & Raedeke, T.D. (2008). *Sport psychology for coaches*. Champaign, IL: Human Kinetics.
41. Mosbergen, D. (2014, May 27). This inspiring runner took a nasty fall, but she didn't stay down for long [video]. *Huffington Post*. www.huffingtonpost.com/2014/05/27/runner-falls-wins-race-heather-dorniden_n_5395232.html

42. Capstick, A.L., & Trudel, P. (2010). Reflection about the communication of nonselection: A shared responsibility. *Journal of Sport Psychology in Action, 1*, 15–24.
43. Summitt, P. (2010). Staff management and mentoring. In C. Reynaud (ed.), *She can coach!* (pp. 137–153). Champaign, IL: Human Kinetics.
44. Rosemond, L.D. (2014). Stress and burnout in coaching: Dr. Coach Rose's seven answers to, "What can I do to change the things I cannot change?" *Olympic Coach Magazine, 25*(2), 18–24.
45. Allen, J.B., & Shaw, S. (2013). An interdisciplinary approach to examining the working conditions of women coaches. *International Journal of Sports Science & Coaching, 8*(1), 1–17.
46. Krzyzewski, M., & Spatola, J.K. (2009). *The gold standard: Building a world-class team.* New York: Business Plus.
47. Rosemond, L.D. (2014). It's called being intentional coach: Prioritizing family and life in coaching. *Olympic Coach Magazine, 25*(4), 4–10.
48. Gordon, J. (2007). *The energy bus: 10 rules to fuel your life, work, and team with positive energy.* Hoboken, NJ: Wiley.
49. Babcock, M., & Larsen, R. (2012). *Leave no doubt: A credo for chasing your dreams.* Montreal & Kingston: McGill-Queen's University Press.
50. Thompson, P. (2003). *The double-goal coach: Positive coaching tools for honoring the game and developing winners in sports and life.* New York: Quill.
51. TED Conferences. (n.d.). How to be a great leader. *Playlist (12 talks).* www.ted.com/playlists/140/how_leaders_inspire
52. Gordon, J., & Smith, M. (2015). *You win in the locker room first: The 7 C's to build a winning team in business, sports, and life.* Hoboken, NJ: Wiley.
53. Kellmann, M., Altfeld, S. & Mallett, C.J. (2016). Recovery–stress imbalance in Australian Football League coaches: A pilot longitudinal study. *International Journal of Sport and Exercise Psychology, 14*(3), 240–249.
54. Schwab, D. (producer). (2015, September 3). The Seth Davis Show: Nick Saban [video podcast]. *Campus Insiders.* http://campusinsiders.com/shows/sethdavisshow#/episode/w1NmVjdzpHivdF34UP9HttIw-WfrHuaBO
55. Fulkerson, J.A., Story, M., Mellin, A., Leffert, N., Neumark-Sztainer, & French, S.A. (2006). Family dinner meal frequency and adolescent development: Relationships with developmental assets and high-risk behavior. *Journal of Adolescent Health, 39*, 337–345.
56. TED Conferences. (n.d.). *Playlist (9 talks): The importance of self-care.* www.ted.com/playlists/299/the_importance_of_self_care
57. Covey, S. (2013). *The 7 habits of highly effective people. Powerful lessons in personal change.* New York: Simon & Schuster.
58. Wooden, J., with Jamison, S. (1997). *Wooden: A lifetime of observations and reflections on and off the court.* Chicago: Contemporary.
59. Office of Media Relations. (2010, June 4). Coach John Wooden's 7-point creed. *UCLA Newsroom.* http://newsroom.ucla.edu/releases/xx-wooden-seven-point-creed-84181

## Closing

1. Gordon, J., & Smith, M. (2015). *You win in the locker room first: The 7 C's to build a winning team in business, sports, and life.* Hoboken, NJ: Wiley.
2. Brooks, D. (2015). *The road to character.* New York: Random House.
3. Fellowship of Christian Athletes. (2010). *The greatest coach ever: Timeless wisdom and insights of John Wooden.* Ventura, CA: Regal.
4. Beswick, B. (2016). *One goal: The mindset of winning soccer teams.* Champaign, IL: Human Kinetics.
5. Gilbert, W. (2015, June 2). Coaching for sustainable excellence. *Human Kinetics Coach Education Center.* www.asep.com/news/ShowArticle.cfm?ID=246
6. Bowen, J. (2016, March 10). *Coaches: 20 years from now they'll know, so now you know.* http://law.scu.edu/sports-law/coaches-twenty-years-from-now-theyll-know-so-now-you-know-2/

# Index

Note: Page references followed by an italicized *f* or *t* indicate information contained in figures and tables, respectively.

# About the Author

**Wade Gilbert, PhD,** is an award-winning professor in the department of kinesiology at California State University at Fresno.

Dr. Gilbert holds degrees in physical education, human kinetics, and education and has taught and studied coaching at the University of Ottawa (Canada), UCLA, and Fresno State. He has more than 20 years of experience in conducting applied research with coaches around the world spanning all competitive levels, from youth leagues to the FIFA World Cup and the Olympic Games. He is widely published and is frequently invited to speak at national and international events. Gilbert is a coach education advisor to USA Football and a regular contributor to coaching seminars for Olympic and national team coaches in the United States and Canada.

In addition, Gilbert is editor in chief of the *International Sport Coaching Journal*, published by Human Kinetics in conjunction with SHAPE America and the International Council for Coaching Excellence (ICCE). As Human Kinetics' coach education advisor, "The Coach Doc" writes articles and conducts webinars on a variety of coaching issues.

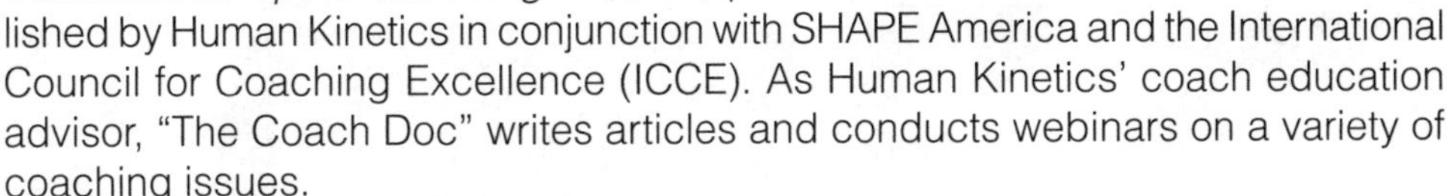

Gilbert lives in Clovis, California.